ON THE EVE

On the
EVE

THE JEWS OF EUROPE
BEFORE THE
SECOND WORLD WAR

Bernard Wasserstein

P

PROFILE BOOKS

First published in Great Britain in 2012 by
PROFILE BOOKS LTD
3a Exmouth House
Pine Street
London EC1R 0JH
www.profilebooks.com

First published in the United States of America in 2012 by
Simon & Schuster, Inc.

10 9 8 7 6 5 4 3 2 1

**305.
892**

Designed by Akasha Archer
Maps by Paul J. Pugliese

Printed and bound in Great Britain by
Clays, Bungay, Suffolk

A CIP catalogue record for this book is available from the British Library.

ISBN 978 1 84668 180 6
eISBN 978 1 84765 345 1

The paper this book is printed on is certified by the © 1996 Forest Stewardship
Council A.C. (FSC). It is ancient-forest friendly. The printer holds FSC chain of
custody SGS-COC-2061

FSC
Mixed Sources
Product group from well-managed
forests and other controlled sources

Cert no. SGS-COC-2061
www.fsc.org
© 1996 Forest Stewardship Council

To Shirley

The historian's essential creative act is the resurrection of the dead.
—Simon Dubnow

CONTENTS

LIST OF MAPS

Note on Transliterations and Place-names

In general, I have used the standard *Encyclopaedia Judaica* and YIVO systems for transliterations from Hebrew and Yiddish respectively. But I have not hesitated to diverge from these where it seemed sensible. Believing with T. E. Lawrence that scientific systems of transliteration are helpful mainly to those "people who know enough . . . not to need helping, but a washout for the world," I have tried in this sphere to do what will be most helpful to the English-speaking reader without worrying unduly about the hobgoblin of consistency.

GLOSSARY

badkhn (Yid.)/**badkhan** (Heb.) jester and master of entertainments at weddings

badkhones the repertoire and performance of the *badkhn*

besmedresh (Yid.)/**bet hamidrash** (Heb.) study hall

bris (Yid.)/**brit** (Heb.) circumcision

dybbuk an evil spirit

Evsektsiia Jewish sections of the Soviet Communist Party

get religious bill of divorce

gymnasium academic high school

hachsharah (pl. **hachsharot**) (lit. "preparation"), training farm

halachah Jewish law

halutz (pl. **halutzim**) (Zionist) pioneer (in the Land of Israel)

Hasidism popular religious movement, founded in the eighteenth century, with a large following in eastern Europe (hence Hasid, Hasidim)

haskalah Jewish Enlightenment

hazan cantor

heder (pl. **hadorim**) religious elementary school

humash Pentateuch

kaddish prayer for the dead

kapote long black, generally gaberdine coat

kehillah (pl. **kehillot**) community

korenizatsiia nativization/indigenization (policy in USSR in 1920s)

luftmensh (Yid.)/**Luftmensch** (Ger.) lit. "man of air," impractical person with no definite occupation or visible source of income

magid wandering preacher

matzah (pl. **matzot**) unleavened bread (eaten at Passover)

melamed (pl. **melamdim**) teacher

mezuzah (pl. **mezuzot**) door amulet, encased parchment containing holy writ

mikveh (pl. **mikvaot**) ritual bath

minyan quorum of ten adult males required for Jewish prayer

misnagdim opponents (of Hasidism)

mitzvah (pl. **mitzvot**) commandment, good deed

mohel (pl. **mohalim**) ritual circumciser

nigun tune

rebbe leader of a Hasidic sect

seder festive Passover dinner

Sejm lower house of Polish parliament

semikhah rabbinic ordination

shames (Yid.)/**shamash** (Heb.) sexton of a synagogue

shechitah kosher meat slaughter

shochet kosher slaughterer

shtetl (pl. **shtetlakh**) small town

shtibl (pl. **shtiblakh**) Hasidic conventicle

shund trash (esp. literary or theatrical)

soyfer (Yid.)/**sofer** (Heb.) scribe

talmud torah religious school

tefillin phylacteries

tish table (esp. at the court of a Hasidic *rebbe*)

Torah Pentateuch, the Hebrew Bible, the body of Jewish law

tsedoko (Yid.) charity/**tsedakah** (Heb.)

yeshiva (pl. **yeshivot**) talmudical college

yeshiva bokher *yeshiva* student

INTRODUCTION

A spectre haunted Europe in the 1930s—the spectre of the Jew. Simultaneously feared and despised as a Christ-killer, a devil with horns, subversive revolutionary and capitalist exploiter, obdurate upholder of an outmoded religion and devious exponent of cultural modernism, the Jew was widely regarded as an alien presence. Increasingly excluded from normal society and extruded from common human fellowship, the Jew was transmogrified from fellow citizen into bogey, a subhuman, at best an inconvenience, eventually almost everywhere a hunted beast. Even before the outbreak of the Second World War, this was true not just in those areas of Europe already directly ruled by the Nazis but over the greater part of the continent.

In the 1920s the European Jews had presented the appearance of a vibrant, dynamic, and flourishing people. For the first time in their history they were recognized as citizens in every country in which they lived. Especially in western Europe and the Soviet Union, an ambitious, meritocratic middle class was rapidly climbing the social ladder. The best-educated ethnic group in Europe, Jews shone in all fields of science, dazzled in the theater and literature, and constituted the beating heart of musical life. But this book does not rehearse what are often called the "contributions" of Jews to European culture and society in this period. That is a familiar story.

Within the short space of two decades a dramatic change transformed the Jewish position. By 1939, two years before the Nazi decision to commit genocide, European Jewry was close to terminal collapse. In much of the continent Jews had been deprived of civil rights and were in the process of being turned into outcasts. The demographic outlook was bleak, heading in a downward spiral toward what some contemporaries forecast would be "race suicide."

The great mass of Jews in east-central Europe were sunk in dire poverty—and sinking further into total immiseration. A nation of shopkeepers, the Jews found themselves superfluous men, both in a Soviet Union that had abolished the marketplace and in militantly nationalistic states that complained of Jewish dominance of it. The USSR at least allowed the Jew to change from *homo economicus* to the new Stalinist model worker; Germany, Poland, and Romania regarded the Jews as unregenerate and demanded that they leave.

A large part of the explanation was anti-Semitism. The roots of the antipathy toward Jews have been endlessly explored. No discussion of the Jews in this period is feasible without reference to this antagonism, deeply entrenched in the consciousness of European civilization. But that is not the primary focus of this book, which is squarely on the Jews themselves, not their persecutors.

Nor is anti-Semitism by itself a satisfactory explanation of the Jews' predicament. In large measure the Jews were victims of their own success. Whether in the USSR, Poland, Germany, or France, Jews sincerely protested their loyalty to states of which they were citizens. Yet the more they took advantage of their newfound legal equality and embraced the national life of their countries of residence, the more they evoked a jealous, exclusionist hostility. Many responded by trying even harder to throw off their distinctive traits, hoping to blend in so as to be unnoticed. Confronted by violent enmity, they embarked on a road toward collective oblivion that appeared to be the price of individual survival.

As a result, Jewish culture was in retreat. Religious practice was decreasing and the orthodox, in particular, felt embattled and threatened. Secular alternatives that sought to replace religion as the core of Jewish identity found themselves increasingly overwhelmed by apparently invincible forces of acculturation to the non-Jewish world. The cultural glue that had long bound Jews together was losing its cohesive power. A telling index of this process was the fading away of Jewish languages such as Yiddish and Judeo-Espagnol, the tongues, respectively, of the Jews of northeastern and southeastern Europe.

Yet in a continent that in the 1930s was overwhelmed by economic depression and racist resentment, the Jews found that assimilation and acculturation, rather than easing their path to acceptance, aroused still more hatred against them. This book therefore examines the position of a people confronted with an impossible dilemma.

Who was the European Jew in the 1930s? Or rather, since the notion of a single national, ethnic, or religious type, so commonly held in that period, is now indefensible, who were the European Jews, in the plural? Were they atomized individuals or did they, or some among them, share ideals, outlooks, assumptions, memories, expectations, fears—in short, can we identify collective Jewish mentalities? What values did they hold in common? Was theirs a distinctive culture or set of subcultures? Can we locate Jewish milieux, whether as geographical sites, as social clusters, or as dwelling places of the imagination? What meaning should we attach to such terms as Jewish literature, music, or art? How cohesive were Jewish communities? How effective were Jews in building social capital—the networks of connectedness in the form of institutions (political parties, representative organizations, charitable bodies, hospitals, schools, newspapers, and so on) that might shape their lives? Was the Jew merely a passive object, acted upon by a hostile, circumambient society, or could the individual, whether alone or in concert with others, try to attain at least some degree of control over the threatening vagaries of fate?

My answer to the last question, at least, may be stated at the outset in the affirmative, even if the results were often tragically out of proportion to the efforts invested. The European Jews in the 1930s were actors in their own history, though they have too often been depicted otherwise. They struggled by every available means to confront what was already perceptible to many as a challenge to their very survival.

They faced a common threat but they were far from a unified monolith. Economically they ranged from a tiny elite of gilded plutocrats to a horde of impoverished pedlars, hawkers, and beggars. A large minority, mainly in east-central Europe, remained strictly orthodox; others, particularly in western Europe and the Soviet Union, were thoroughly securalized; a broad, middling majority of the semi-traditional were comfortably selective in their degree of

religious practice. Politically the Jews were deeply divided but none
of the ideologies in which they reposed confidence, whether liberalism, socialism, or Zionism, offered any immediate solution to their
predicament. As for utopian schemes for settlement in exotic locations around the world, these too failed to alleviate their deepening
plight.

By 1939 more and more Jews in Europe were being reduced to
wandering refugees. They were being ground down into a camp people, without the right to a home anywhere and consequently with
rights almost nowhere. Growing numbers were confined in concentration or internment camps—not just in Germany but all over the
continent, even in democracies such as France and the Netherlands.
Indeed, in the summer of 1939, more Jews were being held in camps
outside the Third Reich than within it.

From there to mass murder was not an inevitable step. I have
tried, as far as possible or reasonable, to avoid the wisdom of hindsight and to bear in mind that the nature and scale of the impending
genocide was unforeseeable to those I am writing about—though, as
we shall see, there were surprisingly frequent and anguished intima-
tions of doom.

While the word *Europe* appears in the title and although the book
is in some ways a forerunner to my history of postwar European
Jewry, *Vanishing Diaspora* (1996), the spotlight here is on those
parts of the continent that were occupied by the Nazis or their allies
between 1939 and 1945. Countries such as Britain and Turkey consequently lie outside my purview.

As in *Vanishing Diaspora*, the Jew is defined inclusively as that
person who considered him- or herself or was considered by others
as a Jew. In this period, when racial, religious, and secular conceptions of Jewishness battled in the ideological arena and within the
souls of individuals, such a broad framework of consideration is essential for understanding what was known at the time, by Jews and
non-Jews alike, as the "Jewish question." Indeed, it is precisely in
the frontier area of the "non-Jewish Jew" that we may glean valuable
insights into the aspirations, the achievements, and the agony of the
European Jews.

My account ends with the outbreak of the Second World War

in Europe in September 1939. But the reader will very likely have a natural human desire to know what later became of many of the individuals who appear here. The epilogue therefore gives brief details, so far as these have been possible to establish, of their subsequent destinies.

There exists a huge literature on the genocide of the Jews under Nazi rule. We know in precise detail almost every stage of the process by which the Nazis annihilated the Jews in every country of occupied Europe. By contrast, much less attention has been paid to the worlds that were destroyed: the private worlds of individuals and families and the public ones of communities and institutions. What has been written about all this has too often been distorted by special pleading or sentimentality.

This book, therefore, seeks to capture the realities of life in Europe in the years leading up to 1939, when the Jews stood, as we now know, at the edge of an abyss. It discusses their hopes and beliefs, anxieties and ambitions, family ties, internal and external relations, their cultural creativity, amusements, songs, fads and fancies, dress, diet, and, insofar as they can be grasped, the things that made existence meaningful and bearable for them. The fundamental objective has been to try to restore forgotten men, women, and children to the historical record, to breathe renewed life momentarily into those who were soon to be dry bones.

THE MELTING GLACIER

Four Zones

Ten million Jews lived in Europe in the late 1930s. They were distributed among four zones, each with a different history, divergent conditions of life, and, on the face of things, varying prospects for the future. In the democracies of western Europe, Jews had been emancipated for several generations and enjoyed a civic equality that, in spite of the rising tide of anti-Semitism, protected them, for the time being, against any threat to their security. By contrast, in Germany and those parts of central Europe that had already been absorbed into the Third Reich, Jews were in the process of being stripped of citizenship, subjected to discriminatory laws, driven out of the professions, and deprived of the bulk of their possessions, and were under intense pressure to emigrate. In a third zone, comprising all the states of east-central Europe, anti-Semitism, often drawing on deep popular roots, formed a significant element in political discourse and in most countries had been integrated into public policy in the shape of explicitly or implicitly anti-Jewish laws. Finally, in the Soviet Union, where the Jews had been emancipated in 1917, later than anywhere else in Europe (save only Romania), they enjoyed dramatic upward social mobility in the interwar period. But collective Jewish life, whether religious, political, or cultural, was, like other aspects of existence under Stalin, subject to severe restrictions.

In German, the word *Judentum* means simultaneously "Judaism" and "Jewry." But in the heart of the European Jew since the Enlightenment a schism had arisen between the conceptions of

Judaism as a religion and as a *Volksgemeinde*, a community based on common ethnicity. In France, since their emancipation during the revolution, many Jews had come to regard it as a cardinal principle that Jewishness was a purely religious category and that in every respect they were as French as other Frenchmen. In Germany, where emancipation had come later and where social relations between Jews and gentiles, even in the liberal Weimar period between 1918 and 1933, were more fragile, matters were slightly different. There, writes George Mosse, a scion of the German-Jewish elite, "there was no either/or—either German or Jew. . . . Jewishness was not merely a religion but was primarily linked to pride of family, from which it could not be divorced."[1] In eastern Europe, where boundaries of state and nation rarely ran together, and where most Jews still spoke Yiddish, lived in dense concentrations, and held more closely to their own cultural patterns, Jewishness tended to be seen by Jews themselves as well as by their neighbors as primarily an ethnic category. This was true also in the USSR, where "Jewish" was a legally recognized national distinction.

Like God in France

The democratic zone of interwar Europe was the most comfortable for Jews. But it held the smallest share of the continent's Jewish population, under a million, or less than 10 percent of the total.

In western Europe, however, the security that Jews enjoyed was no longer quite so automatic or unquestioned as in the past. True, a Jew had been elected prime minister of France in 1936. But the socialist Léon Blum's victory as head of the left-wing Popular Front was regarded as a mixed blessing by many French Jews. The government's enemies on the right focused on Blum's Jewishness and used it, to some effect, as a propaganda bludgeon against the left. Even in the Netherlands, with its long history of Christian-Jewish amity, stretching back to the friendly reception of "New Christians" (Marranos) from the Iberian peninsula in the sixteenth and seventeenth centuries, a certain unease entered into the relationship in the 1930s following the arrival of large numbers of refugees from Nazi Germany.

The phrase *heureux comme un juif en France* ("happy like a Jew in France") had come to have the proverbial meaning of *very* happy. But over the previous generation it had often been tinged with irony. At the turn of the century, the Dreyfus Affair had suggested that there were limits to the recognition of Jews as French. Since 1919, with the return by Germany of Alsace and Lorraine to France, French Jews, a majority of whom traced their origins to the two regained provinces, might again feel content to be fully part of the national patrimony. But their enemies now turned the phrase against them, suggesting that the Jews were *too* happy in France, in other words that they were doing too well, at the expense of others.

Mendelssohn's Heirs

In its origin, the phrase was a play on the German/Yiddish *leben wie Gott in Frankreich*, which meant to live *very* well. Under the Weimar Republic in Germany, Jews looked forward to the consolidation of more than a century of progress toward legal equality and social acceptance in a country and culture in which they felt no less at home than French Jews did in France.

That sense of ease was manifested all over Germany in September 1929, when Jews and Christians alike celebrated the two hundredth anniversary of the birth of Moses Mendelssohn, father of the Jewish enlightenment and progenitor of a dynasty of bankers, musicians, and scholars who remained a significant force in the culture, economy, and politics of the country. The minister of the interior, Carl Severing, and the leading Liberal rabbi in Berlin, Leo Baeck, were among those who delivered encomia to mark the occasion. At a Sunday matinée concert in Mendelssohn's birthplace, Dessau, works by Bach and Beethoven were performed in his honor. A representative of the city of Berlin laid a wreath at the philosopher's grave in memory of a "great fellow-citizen." His descendants, all now Christians, reserved an entire luxury hotel for three days for a gathering of the clan. The series of events was a symbolic high point of the modern German-Jewish symbiosis.[2]

One month later, the Wall Street crash marked the start of the

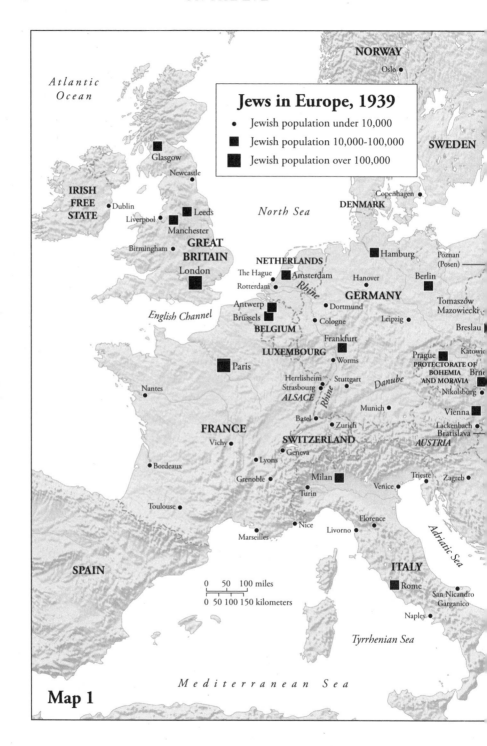

Map 1

Jews in Europe, 1939

- Jewish population under 10,000
- Jewish population 10,000–100,000
- Jewish population over 100,000

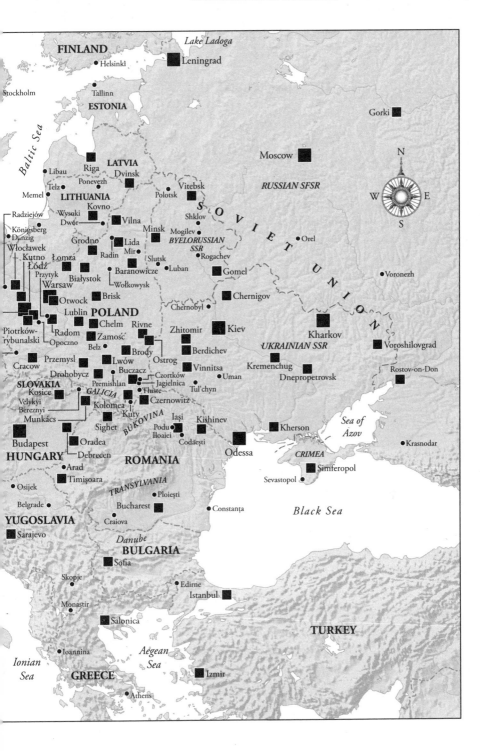

FINLAND
Lake Ladoga
Helsinki
Leningrad
Stockholm
Tallinn
ESTONIA
Gorki
Baltic Sea
Libau Riga LATVIA
Dvinsk
Moscow
RUSSIAN SFSR
Ponevezh
Telz
Memel Polotsk Vitebsk
LITHUANIA
Radziejów Wysoki Kovno Shklov
Königsberg Dwór Vilna
Danzig Minsk Mogilev Orel
Włocławek Grodno Lida BYELORUSSIAN
Kutno Łomża Radin Mir SSR
Łódź Baranowicze Slutsk Rogachev
Przytyk Białystok Luban Gomel Voronezh
Warsaw Wołkowysk
Otwock Brisk Chernigov
Lublin POLAND Chernobyl
Piotrków- Chelm Rivne Zhitomir Kiev
rybunalski Radom Zamość Kharkov Voroshilovgrad
Opoczno Belz Brody UKRAINIAN SSR
Przemysl Lwów Ostrog Berdichev Rostov-on-Don
Cracow Buczacz Vinnitsa Kremenchug
Drohobycz Czortków Uman Dnepropetrovsk
SLOVAKIA Premishlan Jagielnica Tul'chyn
Kosice GALICIA Huste
Velykyi Kolomea Czernowitz
Bereznyi Kury Iaşi Kishinev Sea of
Munkács BUKOVINA Podu Azov
Sighet Iloaiei Kherson Krasnodar
Budapest Oradea Codăeşti
HUNGARY Debrecen Odessa CRIMEA
Arad ROMANIA Simferopol
Timişoara Sevastopol
Osijek TRANSYLVANIA Black Sea
Belgrade Ploieşti
YUGOSLAVIA Bucharest Constanţa
Sarajevo Craiova
Danube
BULGARIA
Sofia
Skopje
Edirne
Monastir Istanbul
Salonica
TURKEY
Ioannina Aegean
Ionian Sea
Sea GREECE Izmir
Athens

world's descent into depression and war—and the toppling of German Jewry from its pedestal as the most proud, wealthy, creative, and forward-looking Jewish community in Europe.

Immediately upon attaining power in January 1933, the Nazis launched a campaign of terror and violence against Jews and leftists. Synagogue and shop windows were smashed. Jews were killed or beaten up in random street attacks. A nationwide boycott of Jewish businesses on April 1, 1933, met with mixed success. It was followed, however, by the dismissal of almost all Jewish civil servants, including teachers and university professors. Jewish doctors and lawyers were restricted in their professions. State welfare support for Jews was limited. Quotas were introduced for Jewish university students. Such early anti-Jewish measures resulted in at least three hundred suicides.

As early as April 1933, just three months after Hitler's capture of power, Baeck, who emerged as German Jewry's leader and spokesman in its final decade, declared, "The thousand-year history of German Jewry has come to an end."[3] Of the half million "Jews by religion" in Germany, about forty thousand fled the country within a year.

The Reichsvertretung der Deutschen Juden (Reich Representation of German Jews), with Baeck at its head, secured de facto recognition from the Nazi regime in September 1933 as the representative body of German Jews. For the next six years the Reichsvertretung formed a kind of internal self-government of German Jewry. On the one hand, Baeck and his colleagues sought to shield German Jews from the savage onslaught to which they were subjected. On the other, they found themselves compelled to act in compliance with Nazi orders and to facilitate the orderly execution of Nazi policies. These were, of course, ultimately incompatible functions; but for a time the Reichsvertretung succeeded to some extent in harmonizing them, through its efforts to organize social welfare, education, and cultural activities. While seeking to preserve desperately needed working relationships with the authorities, the Reichsvertretung did not, in the early years, shrink from remonstrance: in May 1934, for example, in response to scurrilous anti-Semitic statements, it dispatched a telegram to Hitler: "Before God and men, we raise our voices in protest against this unparalleled calumny against our faith."[4]

"Content and Sap"

Eastern Europe had been the heartland of Jewish settlement since the early modern period and remained so until 1939. More than half the Jews of Europe lived in this third zone, comprising the states between Germany and the Soviet Union. While Romania and Hungary also boasted large Jewish populations, one country in this region held an undisputed preeminence in the Jewish world.

Numbering 3.2 million in 1939, Poland's Jews formed the largest Jewish community on the continent. Although deeply attached to the country, which most of them regarded unquestioningly as their home, Polish Jews were to a considerable degree isolated from the rest of the population, religiously, socioeconomically, and politically. They had their own residential areas, political parties, newspapers, theaters, labor unions, and professional organizations, often operating in their own language, Yiddish. Together these formed the scaffolding of a largely self-contained world within which it was possible, if one chose, to live almost without venturing into broader society.

The Polish Jews formed, in a legal sense, a community, and were so regarded by the rest of society. But they were deeply divided among themselves. Ben-Zion Gold, who grew up in a strictly orthodox family in Poland in the 1930s, recollects that "religious Jews looked on assimilationists with a mixture of pity and contempt."[5] Theodore Hamerow, a child of professional actors on the Yiddish stage, records how, as a child in the small town of Otwock, near Warsaw, in the 1920s, he would peep through a chink in the fence on Friday night at the Sabbath celebration of neighboring Hasidim: "They appeared to me almost as strange, almost as exotic as the whirling dervishes of Turkey I had read about or the frenzied worshippers of Jagannath in India. I felt an invisible but insurmountable barrier separated me from them. They and I seemed to belong to two totally different social and cultural worlds."[6]

The differences were as much matters of class as of ideology. The lawyer, parliamentarian, and Zionist leader Apolinary Hartglas confessed in his postwar memoirs the contempt with which he regarded many of his fellow Polish Jews: "I was offended by their lack of European culture, lack of social graces. . . . A sheet of glass separated me from them."[7]

Poland was the main arena in which the conflicting ideological and cultural forces in European Jewry contended for supremacy. Warsaw, with its 381,000 Jews in 1939, the most in any city on the continent, came closest to the status of capital of the European diaspora. Here were the headquarters of the major Jewish political parties, charities, school systems, newspapers, and cultural organs. "Polish Jewry," according to one of its best-informed contemporary observers, "gave content and sap to all our national, political, and cultural movements. Least affected by assimilation, it remained nationally the most conscious, politically the most militant, individually the proudest of the Jewish communities."[8]

Advancing Toward Disappearance

The three million Jews in the Soviet Union in 1939 constituted the fourth zone of European Jewry. In the late Tsarist period, opposition to the persecution of Russian Jews had been a humanitarian cause that engaged gentiles as well as Jews throughout the civilized world. Emancipation of the Jews had been one of the first acts of the Russian Revolution—of the February rather than the October revolution, a distinction that was often glossed over by Jewish Communists in the 1930s. At the same time Jews had been granted freedom to settle beyond the Pale of Settlement, the western regions of the Russian Empire to which they had been restricted in the late Tsarist period.

The Bolsheviks reaffirmed the principles of equality and liberty of conscience but, in the case of Jews, quickly emptied them of much meaning by their antireligious campaign and by creation of the category of *lishentsy* (literally "deprived"). These were members of the "exploiting classes," that is, nonproletarians and nonpeasants, especially merchants and ex-bourgeois, who, together with their families, were disenfranchised under the new regime and turned into social outcasts, deprived of civil rights, discriminated against in higher education, employment, medical care, and food rations, and required to pay higher taxes and rents. They might reclaim civil rights only after five years of productive labor. Jews were heavily represented among the *lishentsy* because of their disproportionate membership of the prerevolutionary, "exploiting" commercial class, which made a partial reappearance during the period of the New Economic Policy in the 1920s. In 1928–31, the number of Jewish *lishentsy* was estimated to be as high as 1,875,000 (a million small traders and 875,000 artisans), two-thirds of the entire Jewish population of the USSR.[9]

Soviet Jewry, although almost as large as Polish, lacked the collective dynamism, institutional structures, or cultural vitality of its western neighbor. Indeed, whether it might be called a community at all was doubtful, since it had no organizational unity, nor much in the way of collective cohesion. In 1918 the Bolshevik Party had established *Evsektsii*, Jewish sections, whose main role was to combat Zionism, "clericalism," and the Jewish socialist Bund. By 1930, however, having achieved their purpose of eradicating this triple-headed monster on Soviet territory, the *Evsektsii* were summarily abolished.

In the late 1920s Soviet Jews were subdivided into five *narodnosti* (national groups), based on geographical location, but by the time of the 1939 census all Jews in the Soviet Union were consolidated in one nationality.[10] The Soviet state in the interwar period not only recognized Jewish ethnicity but encouraged its expression within circumscribed limits. Yiddish schools flourished until the late 1930s. Yiddish newspapers and books appeared. Yiddish theaters were subsidized. Far more than those in Poland, however, such institutions were closely controlled by the state and the ruling party.

The prudent Jew in Stalinist Russia, no less than elsewhere, did not advertise his Jewishness and, where possible, often sought to discard it. Yet there lingered among Soviet as among other Jews on the continent an intuitive mutual recognition that might be instantly sparked by a Yiddish phrase, a shrug, a gesture, or something left unsaid—and with that an implicit, defensive solidarity.

In the 1930s Soviet Jews were caught in the swirling eddies of political debate between Communist sympathizers and their enemies. In France, for example, the Jewish sociologist Georges Friedmann, who studied the Soviet Union and spent several long periods there between 1932 and 1936, stressed the rapid upward social mobility of Jews under Soviet rule. He contrasted the "physical and moral degeneration" of the Polish ghettos with what he regarded as the social achievements of Soviet Jews: "It is hard to understand, if one has not seen it oneself, the difference in the physical and moral standing of Jews on either side of the Polish-Soviet frontier." Soviet Jews, he reported, "rarely present the old marks of servility and fear that one may observe in the ghettos of Poland and Galicia—and for such a long time even among those who have been able to escape to the great cities of the West."[11] Friedmann reported that young Jews in the USSR, buoyed up by their progress under the Soviet regime, were absorbing its values and merging into general society.

In a fierce riposte, Léon Baratz, a French lawyer of Russian-Jewish origin, protested that antireligious pressures in the USSR were leading to the "integral dejudaization" of young Jews. Zionism, he pointed out, was persecuted more than under either the tsars or Hitler. Jewish scholarship, especially history, was suppressed. Hebrew was a forbidden tongue. Actually, the difference between Baratz and Friedmann was less in their conclusions than in their evaluations. Both could agree with the historian Simon Dubnow that Jews in the USSR, as a distinct entity, were "advancing rapidly towards complete disappearance."[12]

European Jews in the 1930s thus lived in four zones of varying degrees of heat. Yet though divided by geography, politics, and much else, they shared some basic characteristics.

Demographic Decline

Prophecies of Jewish extinction were not limited to the Soviet Union. In 1927 the Polish-born Jewish historian Lewis Namier wrote that "dissolution and ultimate disappearance seem the inevitable future of the Jewries of Western and Central Europe." Given their low birthrates and high rates of outmarriage, he predicted, they would vanish. Only further immigration from the slowly melting glacier of mainly orthodox East European Jewry, he suggested, might sustain these communities.[13] Across the four zones of Jewish Europe, local observers reached similar conclusions.

JEWISH POPULATIONS IN EUROPE, SEPTEMBER 1939	
Belgium	110,000
Bulgaria	50,000
Denmark	7,000
Estonia	5,000
Finland	2,000
France	320,000
Germany*	345,000
Gibraltar	1,000
Greece	75,000
Hungary†	625,000
Ireland	5,000
Italy	47,000
Latvia	95,000
Lithuania	155,000
Luxembourg	4,000
Netherlands	140,000
Norway	2,000
Poland	3,225,000
Portugal	1,000
Romania	850,000
Slovakia	58,000
Spain	500
Sweden	10,000
Switzerland	19,000
Turkey**	80,000
United Kingdom	380,000
USSR**	3,025,000
Yugoslavia	75,000
TOTAL	9,711,500

* Including Austria and Protectorate of Bohemia and Moravia.
† Including annexed areas of Slovakia and Subcarpathian Ruthenia.
** Including Asiatic regions.

In Holland, a report in 1936 noted that the Jewish birthrate was much lower than that of the non-Jewish population, a difference attributed by the report's author to "the great influence of birth control among the Jews."[14] They were also on average older than the rest of the population. In February 1939 an expert on Jewish population maintained, in an address to the Amsterdam Anthropological Society, that Dutch Jewry was in danger of disappearing altogether as a result of intermarriage and the decrease in the birthrate.[15] A commentator in Strasbourg in 1938 despaired of the prospects for Judaism in that province. Evidence of declining birthrates, late marriage, and nonmarriage, he concluded, could be summed up in one sentence: "Alsatian Jewry is dying."[16]

In Germany, the Jewish population had been declining before the Nazis came to power. Between 1925 and 1933 it shrank from 564,000 to 503,000, that is, by 11 percent in just eight years. Since religion, in Germany as in other central European countries, was a matter of public registration, these figures give a reliable picture of the number of self-professing Jews and indicate a precipitous decline. There were many contributory causes, including conversions, exogamy, and resignations from the religious community, though resigners did not necessarily intend thereby to deny altogether their Jewishness. But the chief explanation, and the one most fraught with long-term implications, was the collapse of the Jewish birthrate. As a result, German Jewry by 1933 was said to be "for the most part in a state of senilization."[17] Just 21 percent of Jews were below twenty years of age, compared with 31 percent of the general population.

The German-Jewish philosopher Hannah Arendt later wrote:

When Hitler came to power . . . German Jewry as a whole, after a long period of steady growth in social status and numbers, was declining so rapidly that statisticians predicted its disappearance in a few decades. Statistics, it is true, do not necessarily point to real historical processes; yet it is noteworthy that to a statistician Nazi persecution and extermination would look like a senseless acceleration of a process which would probably have come about in any case.[18]

Arendt took the underlying idea for this passage from writers like Felix Theilhaber, whose book *The Downfall of the German Jews*, published in 1911, had set out a grim prognosis of demographic collapse of the Jews in Germany and, by extension, of European Jewry in general.[19]

After the Nazis' ascent to power, the Jewish birthrate in Germany declined further, as young Jews emigrated or chose to be childless. Most German-Jewish families had no more than one or two children. In 1936 the total number of Jewish births (that is, births where at least one of the parents was Jewish) was 1,714; the equivalent number for 1925 had been 5,785.

Trends elsewhere in central Europe were similar. "Vienna Jewry is moving towards extinction," wrote the sociologist Arthur Ruppin in 1936.[20] A sober sociologist, not given to hyperbole, he referred to the extraordinarily low birthrate of Jews in Vienna, which was replicated in nearly all the major Jewish communities of central Europe. Ruppin noted other "disruptive forces in Jewry": assimilation, decline of Jewish religion, "weakening of the links of common descent and fate," "loosening of family ties," and "economic adaptation of the Jews to their surroundings." By 1939 Ruppin had reached an ominous conclusion: "Much as primitive peoples lose their traditional ways of living and their enjoyment of life under the impact of alien influences, and voluntarily die out, the Jews in these countries are tending to 'race suicide.' "[21]

The demographic outlook was similarly depressing in eastern Europe. The Jewish birthrate in the region as a whole is estimated to have halved between 1900 and the late 1930s.[22] In Hungary, a declining birthrate, conversions, mixed marriages, and emigration contributed to a fall in Jewish population, from 473,000 in 1920 to 400,000 by 1939.[23] In Lithuania in 1937, an analyst noted that the number of Jewish births was "horribly low and declining from year to year." In 1934 the rate of Jewish natural increase there was only 2.6 per thousand, compared with 10.2 for the country as a whole.[24]

In the USSR the Jewish birthrate had been in decline since before the revolution. Although it rose slightly in the late 1930s, possibly as a result of official natalist policies, it remained low, particularly in Moscow and Leningrad. This was in spite of the relative youth of the Jewish population in those cities by comparison with Jews in the former Pale. In the USSR, as elsewhere, Jews, on average, were older than the rest of the population and produced fewer children. The age of Jewish marriage, already higher than that of the rest of the population, rose further in this period. Between 1926 and 1939, the average fertility of Soviet Jewish women declined by a third. There was also a significant imbalance of the sexes: more than eleven women for every ten men. That may help to explain the "conspicuous decline" in marriages by Jews (whether with other Jews or at all) in the USSR in the 1930s.[25]

Intercontinental migration added a further negative weight to the European Jewish population balance. The closure of the United States to large-scale immigration from 1924, the political difficulties attending emigration from the Soviet Union after the early 1920s, and the limits set by British mandatory authorities to Jewish entry to Palestine after 1936 all constrained Jewish movement out of Europe. Nevertheless, more than a million Jews left the continent in the interwar period. Between 1933 and 1938 Nazi anti-Jewish measures led an estimated 169,000 Jews to flee Germany. And at least 400,000 left the second Polish republic during the two decades of its existence. This was 13 percent of all the Jews in the country but for Polish anti-Semites it was not enough. They insisted that Poland was overpopulated with Jews and demanded their total removal.

The sum of all these elements was that Jewish population increase was rapidly slowing and in several countries had turned into absolute decrease.

Jewish demographic decline was clearly linked to urbanization, social mobility, and what may loosely be termed modernization. Yet what is often called Jewish assimilation has a perverse or inverse significance when viewed through a demographic lens in the early twentieth century: the more European Jews became like their neighbors in other ways, the less they resembled them in their demographic patterns. Jewish fertility, infant mortality, and death rates all declined faster than non-Jewish, the average age of marriage climbed higher, and the average size of family became smaller than those of non-Jews. Almost invariably such trends were visible earlier and on a greater scale among the less traditional, more secularized strata of

Jewish society. In the sphere of population, indeed, the Jews were much less assimilators to existing social patterns than pioneers of the demographic transition that, over the next two generations, was to transform European society as a whole.

High Life Expectancy

As a collectivity, then, European Jews might appear to have been heading toward extinction. Yet individually they could expect to live longer than ever before and longer than their neighbors. Their high life expectancy arose from their relatively favorable levels of health. Alcoholism, a major contributor to early death in many countries, was almost unknown among Jews: in 1925 the number of arrests for drunkenness in Warsaw, where Jews were one-third of the population, was 87 for Jews and 11,994 for non-Jews.[26] Deaths from cirrhosis of the liver, reflecting alcoholism, were less common among Jews than in the general population. The incidence of syphilis and other venereal diseases was lower among Jews. They also exhibited greater resistance than others to contagious diseases such as tuberculosis (even when comparing Jews and non-Jews of the same social class).[27]

In the 1930s, however, a change of direction in relative Jewish health was detected. Overall, the general Jewish medical condition in eastern Europe, though still more robust than that of the general population, was reported by knowledgeable observers to be deteriorating. Jews were particularly susceptible to digestive and vascular troubles. They died disproportionately from diabetes, heart disease, and, in the slums of Warsaw, respiratory illnesses.[28] Moreover, certain less serious ailments were endemic among poor Jews in eastern Europe, notably scabies. In the wretched Jewish working-class areas of Łódź the prevalence of typhoid fever was above average and an investigator in 1930 reported that "the sick-rate curve for Jews has grown in recent years, while that for Christians has kept on falling."[29]

A doctor in Kovno (Kaunas), Lithuania, in 1937 lamented the squalor in which the greater part of the Jewish working class of the city lived:

> Ritual requirements notwithstanding, people don't wash much.
> Hands are dirty, nails are black, people are afraid of soap, don't
> change underwear often enough, and as for toothbrushing, that's
> already a sign of a bourgeois situation. Parasites still play a consider-
> able part in Jewish life. . . . Lice, fleas, and bugs are, in effect, family
> members in far too many Jewish households. Worms are constant
> companions among children and very widespread among adults.[30]

Venereal diseases, including syphilis, were said to be spreading
among Jews, although they were still far less prevalent among Jews
than non-Jews.

The Jewish diet, according to the Kovno report, was unhealthy:
unvaried, poor in vitamins, too fatty and spicy. The very poorest
would subsist on little more than black bread, potatoes, cabbage,
borscht, and tea. Challah (braided white bread) would be eaten only
on the Sabbath. Cheaply available herring was consumed a great
deal. But "the Jew exhibits an aversion to all green vegetables."[31]
Moreover, complained the same doctor in Kovno, food was gobbled
down rather than chewed.

Marrying Out

Most European Jews in the nineteenth century married other Jews.
By the early twentieth century, however, a significant growth in
exogamy was registered across the continent. At first the trend was
strongest in western and central Europe, but by the 1930s it was no-
ticeable elsewhere, particularly in the Soviet Union.

In Denmark and Italy, where relations between the small Jewish
communities and general society were generally harmonious, more
than half of all marriages by Jews in the mid-1930s were with non-
Jews. In Bohemia and Moravia, where the intermarriage rate before
the First World War had been under 5 percent, it reached 30 percent
by the 1930s.

In Hungary and Germany, the graph of Jewish intermarriage
showed an inverted V. In Hungary the rate was 25 percent in
the early and mid-1930s. Thereafter it declined as anti-Semitism

poisoned the social atmosphere and Jewish partners became less attractive marital propositions.[32] In Germany the change was drastic. In the early 1930s a majority of German-Jewish marriages were with non-Jews. After the enactment of the Nuremberg Laws in 1935, however, the rate plummeted to zero, as marriages of Jews with "Aryans" became illegal, though existing mixed marriages generally remained intact.

More men married outside the faith than women: in central Europe in 1929 about three men did so for every two women. As a result, the children of mixed marriages were, in their great majority, not regarded as Jewish according to religious law (which recognized only the child of a Jewish mother as Jewish). Mixed marriages tended to produce even fewer children, on average, than all-Jewish marriages: in Germany the average was just 0.5 per couple. The reasons, in the sociopolitical atmosphere of the 1930s, were not far to seek. One demographic expert suggested: "Birth control is even more intensive in mixed marriages, because the sore points are more numerous and the desire is dominant to avoid the possibilities of conflict, which may arise because of the children."[33] Moreover, the children of mixed marriages in Germany and Hungary were much more likely to be brought up in the Christian (or in no) faith than as Jews. According to an estimate in Germany in 1928–29, a mere 2 percent of children of such unions were raised in the Jewish faith.[34] Intermarriage, on the scale and in the form that it took in central Europe in the interwar period, thus portended the rapid disappearance of the Jewish community.

In the Russian Empire mixed marriages were not permitted before 1917 (the legal ban remained in force in the former Russian provinces of Poland in the interwar period). After the revolution, however, marriage between Jews and non-Jews in the USSR increased rapidly. By 1939 out of every thousand marriages in which one partner was a Jew, 368 were mixed marriages. In Moscow and Leningrad around half of all Jewish marriages were mixed. In the Soviet Union too, far more men than women married non-Jews, with the result that, by 1939, there were much larger numbers of unmarried Jewish women than men in the USSR, with a consequent further negative effect on the Jewish birthrate.

A Nation of Shopkeepers

The Jewish social pyramid was like no other in Europe. Very small proportions of Jews worked in the occupations that constituted the largest categories of labor almost everywhere: agriculture, domestic service, mining, or public employment. Peasants, an absolute majority of the population throughout eastern Europe, were to be found in significant numbers among Jews only in a few backward regions, such as Bessarabia (in Romania between the wars) and Subcarpathian Ruthenia, the easternmost province of Czechoslovakia. In Europe as a whole no more than 5 percent of Jews engaged in agriculture.

Jews were heavily underrepresented in the civil service and in the armed forces. In 1931, fewer than 2 percent of civil servants in Poland were Jews. In the whole of the country there were just seven Jewish university professors out of a total of 596 (all university teachers were public employees), this in spite of the high level of education among Jews. Not a single Jew in Poland was principal of a government secondary school. In Germany, hardly any Jews, even under the Weimar Republic's ostensibly meritocratic order, were employed as civil servants (less than 0.1 percent, as compared with 4.8 percent of the general population in 1933).

Almost everywhere Jews were heavily concentrated in commerce. In 1933 more than 60 percent of German Jews in the labor force were engaged in trade, generally as small shopkeepers. In some branches of the economy, such as clothing manufacture and the grain trade, the Jewish presence was so dominant that these were regarded as characteristically Jewish occupations.

In general, Jews showed a tendency to prefer self-employment over wage labor. Most worked on their own or in small units with members of their families. In Lithuania 60 percent of Jewish artisans in 1937 worked at home—among them 90 percent of tailors, 81 percent of shoemakers, and 77 percent of bakers. The Jewish urban working class, therefore, was only to a limited degree proletarianized.

In the interwar period Jews continued to move rapidly into the professions. Although only a minority of Jews belonged to this class, they dominated certain professions, especially law and medicine, in central and eastern Europe.

Formally there was no Jewish aristocracy, save in Hungary (where, in any case, most of its Jewish-origin members were converts to Christianity). Great wealth had lifted certain families out of the bourgeoisie into a social stratosphere far beyond the rest of Jewish society. At its apex were plutocratic families such as the Warburgs in Hamburg, the Hatvanys in Budapest, the Gunzburgs (exiled from Russia) in Paris, and the Rothschilds almost everywhere. These patricians attracted disproportionate attention and hostility from anti-Semites but they were completely unrepresentative of Jews in general.

With the virtual elimination of private commerce in the USSR, the occupational distribution of Soviet Jews in the Stalinist period differed from the pattern elsewhere. The commercial class had constituted 40 percent of the Jewish working population in the Russian Empire in 1897. By 1926 in the Soviet Union it had shrunk to 12 percent—Jews were even then disproportionately represented among "NEP-men," the traders permitted to operate during the period of the New Economic Policy. By 1939, however, this class had virtually disappeared. As in other countries, Jews moved strongly into the professions. In the Slavic republics of the USSR in 1939, a quarter of all doctors, dentists, and pharmacists and a fifth of all lawyers were Jews. But the Soviet Union was unlike most other countries in its readiness to admit Jews to state employment, a much larger and more significant segment of the labor force in a socialized economy than elsewhere. Ten percent of all those employed in the "upper echelons of the intermediate stratum" of economic management in 1939 were Jews (who comprised only 1.8 percent of the total population). More than half of all Jewish workers were in white-collar occupations, a higher percentage by far than for any other nationality in the USSR.

Jews were eager to integrate into Soviet society and successful in doing so. In the process, many internalized the prevalent ideology. But in spite of that thought system's glorification of the urban working class and notwithstanding an official policy aimed at their

productivization, Jews were not absorbed into the proletariat as they
sovietized. Compelled to abandon their classic roles as petty traders
and middlemen, most of them did not head for factories, mines, or
steel mills. Instead, with an ability to see through official sloganeer-
ing and with a perception of the real locations of power and privilege
in the workers' and peasants' state, Jews proceeded in large numbers, via high schools and universities, toward bureaucratic posts,
scientific laboratories, judicial chambers, medical consulting rooms,
university lecture theaters, newsrooms, and managerial offices. The
USSR became the country in Europe in which Jews were most
disproportionately represented in the power elite. This, however,
availed them nothing if they came under attack, either as individuals
or as a collectivity: in the years of Stalinist terror they were no less
endangered than any other section of Soviet society.

Institutional Ramparts

The European Jews were great institution builders. They created
political parties, youth movements, trade unions, fraternal lodges,
burial societies, charitable bodies, and every other type of associational form imaginable. In the absence of a unified political
framework for their existence, they invested heavily in what a later
generation has come to term social capital.

In Cracow, for example, the sixty thousand Jews in the interwar
period operated more than three hundred institutions: not only
synagogues, *chevra kadisha* burial societies, and *yeshivot*, but twenty-
nine charitable bodies, seven women's organizations, political parties, labor unions, hospitals, orphanages, old-age homes, bathhouses,
several primary and secondary schools (including the orthodox boys'
Takhkemoni, the orthodox girls' Beys Yankev and its related teachers' college, a coeducational Hebrew high school, and a secular girls'
Nasza Szkoła), sports clubs (Maccabi, the leading one, with fifteen
sections, among others for rowing, fencing, riding, and chess), the
Association of Jewish Artists, the Jewish Music Society, Szir (a
choral club), a theater society, the Union of Hebrew Journalists,
the Radio Social Club, Tarbut (a Hebrew cultural club), a Yiddish

theater society, and Toynbe [*sic*] Hala (primarily a cultural association but inspired by Toynbee Hall in the East End of London)—all this not counting more strictly commercial enterprises such as newspapers (especially the influential Polish-language daily *Nowy Dziennik*), Hebrew printers, kosher butchers, and delicatessens.[35]

The basic Jewish institution was the *kehillah* (community). In most countries of central and eastern Europe, with the notable exception of the Soviet Union, Jewish communities had a recognized legal status and the right to tax their members. While operating under government supervision, the *kehillot* enjoyed a limited degree of autonomy that enabled them to spend some money also on educational, social, and cultural activities, such as hospitals, old-age homes, orphanages, and beggars' shelters. The *kehillot* were generally democratic institutions, at least in the sense that all males had the vote. In Poland, in particular, where there were an estimated nine hundred *kehillot*, elections were often fiercely contested, sometimes on a party-political basis.

Polish Jews still lived with the historic memory of the quasi-autonomous federation of *kehillot*, the "Council of Four Lands," which had represented them in the Polish-Lithuanian Commonwealth between 1580 and 1764. The Polish Republic after 1918 curtailed the powers of the *kehillot*, restricting them to strictly religious functions. They were permitted to levy taxes that supported the salaries of the rabbinate, as well as kosher meat slaughter and maintenance of synagogues, ritual baths, and cemeteries. (A new law in 1928 allowed them also to spend on some social needs.) Taxation was graduated and the very poorest members did not have to pay at all. In the largest community, Warsaw, half of all Jews fell into the exempt category, an index of the dire impoverishment of much of the population. The government made a small contribution, amounting to less than 1 percent of the operating costs of the *kehillot* (on a per capita basis, this was one-twelfth the size of the contribution made to Christian institutions).[36]

The synagogue was less an institution than a building, the outer shell of the *kehillah* in its religious dimension. Houses of worship came in all shapes and sizes. Poland was famous for its wooden and fortress synagogues, Italy for the ornate decoration of synagogues such as those of Venice, Florence, and Livorno. The oldest in Europe was the medieval synagogue of Worms, the origins of which dated back to the eleventh century, followed by the Altneushul in Prague, built in the late fourteenth century. The largest on the continent had for a long time been the great Portuguese Jews' Esnoga in Amsterdam. It was overtaken in 1859 by the resplendent three-thousand-seat Dohány Street temple in Budapest. The smallest synagogues were the Hasidic *shtiblakh*, small prayer rooms in which a *minyan* (quorum of ten men) would gather to recite the morning, afternoon, and evening services.

In many synagogues, particularly in central and southern Europe, the biblical prohibition against "graven images" had somehow been reconciled with lavish decoration, stained-glass windows, and representative art. Substantial amounts might be spent on ornamenting and beautifying the building and such expenditures were rarely grudged in spite of the burning pressure of other demands on funding, particularly for *tsedakah* (charitable help for the poor). The little synagogue of Lackenbach in Burgenland, the easternmost province of Austria, bore wall paintings of the exodus from Egypt and other biblical scenes. In the Great Synagogue of the Romanian *shtetl* (small town) Podu Iloaiei, allegorical figures of griffons, lions, deer, and double-headed eagles were carved on the ark and *bimah* (reading platform), and the building was adorned with representations of the Western Wall, Rachel's Tomb, and the "waters of Babylon."

Compared with western Europe, where social service organizations to help the Jewish poor were highly developed, eastern Europe, notwithstanding its masses of Jewish paupers, had much more primitive provision of this kind. A large part of such activity was generated by organizations based elsewhere, notably the American Jewish Joint Distribution Committee (the "Joint"), the wealthiest Jewish charitable body in the world, and ORT.

The Organization for Rehabilitation of Jews through Training traced its origins in Russia back to 1880. After 1917 Russian-Jewish émigrés reestablished it in Berlin and Paris. Almost alone among Russian émigré organizations, it succeeded in establishing a working relationship with the Soviet regime, with which, as with other east European governments, it undertook social welfare activities through most of the interwar period. ORT tried to find practical means of "productivizing" the Jewish population. It founded trade schools, artisanal courses, and evening classes, supplied craftsmen with modern equipment, and sponsored producers' cooperatives.

But in the 1930s the financial capacities of both the Joint and ORT were squeezed by the effects of the Great Depression and the demand for aid to victims of Nazi persecution. German Jewry, through the Hilfsverein der deutschen Juden, had once been an exporter of charitable assistance. Overnight, in 1933, German Jews became supplicants rather than benefactors. As a result, the Joint, in particular, was compelled to divert resources that had formerly gone to eastern Europe toward German-Jewish relief.

In the absence of large-scale government action in the sphere of public health, and with a great part of the Jewish population unable to afford medical insurance, much of the burden of health care in east-central Europe was carried by voluntary organizations. About fifty Jewish hospitals operated in Poland, with 3,500 beds (about 5 percent of the total number in the country). They were funded by *landsmanshaftn* (groups, especially in the United States, of emigrants from a particular locality), *kehillot*, small grants from municipalities, and general philanthropy.

The Society for Safeguarding the Health of Jews, TOZ, founded in 1921, sought to raise standards of hygiene and public health among Jews in Poland. An outgrowth from the prerevolutionary organization OZE, established in St. Petersburg in 1912, TOZ built four hundred hospitals and clinics in seventy-two towns by 1939, as well as sanatoria and bathhouses. TOZ devoted special efforts to children and mothers, providing tuberculosis and other vaccines, dental services, school medical stations, and nutritional advice. It undertook preventive measures against venereal diseases, trachoma, and ringworm and sought to alleviate malnutrition.

TOZ's parent organization, OZE (later OSE, Oeuvre de Secours aux Enfants), with headquarters from 1933 in Paris, remained active in Soviet Russia in the 1920s. It also ran a children's home in Kovno and clinics in Romania. It conducted propaganda in favor of breast-feeding and educated mothers in hygienic methods of preparation of bottled milk. Much of the funding for OSE and TOZ, which spent

over $2 million annually, a considerable sum in the 1930s, was sup-
plied by sympathizers abroad, particularly the Joint, but a large part
of its budget was raised in Poland by means of membership campaigns, balls, concerts, and lotteries.

By these and other means, voluntary institutions furnished, in
greater measure than for most population groups, the basic elements
of social welfare provision. Beyond all this, they provided a framework that might serve as some sort of bulwark for Jews in the face
of not only the minimal state but the hostile state. They were often
weakened, however, by the internal disunity of the Jews.

Brotherhoods of Contempt

Jews often preached unity but no less often they meant different
things by it. Though the European Jews shared many social and cultural characteristics, they were riven by deep divisions. Historically,
the most fundamental was between Ashkenazim (Jews of German
origin) and Sephardim (descendants of Jews expelled from Spain
and Portugal at the end of the fifteenth century). "We lived together
with the Spanish Jews on the same continent as close neighbours
for several hundred years until the expulsion from Spain in close
spiritual and everyday contact and yet how estranged we have become!" exclaimed the social commentator Jacob Lestchinsky, an
Ashkenazi.[37]

In west European cities such as Amsterdam, London, and Bor-
deaux, the long-established Sephardim regarded themselves as an
aristocracy and a cut above the Ashkenazim. But Sephardim were
by this time a minority among Jews in these places. Emigration from
the Balkans and other parts of the Ottoman Empire in the late nineteenth and early twentieth centuries also produced a large Sephardi
community in Paris, said by the 1930s to number fifty thousand.
Smaller Sephardi communities existed in Altona (near Hamburg),
Vienna, and Romania. A few Sephardim lived in Budapest but their
congregation there was dissolved in 1938 "for lack of members."[38]
The Jews of Italy included many descendants of emigrants from
Spain but nevertheless regarded themselves as a distinct group,

since, at any rate in Rome, they could trace their origins back to the second century of the Christian era, long before either Ashkenazim or Sephardim existed as Jewish categories.

Most European Sephardim were concentrated in the Balkans, where they were a majority of Jews in Turkey, Greece, and Bulgaria. In the larger Sephardi centers, such as Salonica and Istanbul, Judeo-Espagnol was still widely spoken and Jews took great pride in their Hispanic heritage. In Yugoslavia, Sephardim lived mainly in Belgrade, Sarajevo, and Skopje, and amounted to about a third of the seventy-thousand-strong community. They were in general poorer than their Ashkenazi neighbors and their straitened economic condition in the 1930s led the local branch of the Zionist fund-raising organization, Keren Hayesod, to allocate 20 percent of its receipts to charitable purposes in Yugoslavia rather than in Palestine. In Sarajevo a small group of intellectuals formed a Sephardic Circle with the object of preserving their distinctive culture against gathering Ashkenazi dominance.

The Union Universelle des Juifs Sépharadim, formed (under a different name) in 1925, with headquarters in Paris, aspired to represent the Sephardim of the world. It published a magazine and held meetings of Sephardim from most of the major communities of Europe as well as of the Levant and North Africa. But internal disputes and rivalries weakened the organization. When its first international conference convened in London in 1935, the Greek, Turkish, and Bulgarian communities did not send representatives. In spite of speechifying about "Séphardisme" and a "Sephardi renaissance," and notwithstanding some sparks of local cultural dynamism, the Sephardim never developed into a unified or significant political force in the Jewish world.

Ashkenazim, who constituted at least 90 percent of the Jews of Europe, were themselves deeply divided: between *Litvaks* and *Galitsyaner*, between Hasidim and *misnagdim*, between western (particularly German) Jews and *Ostjuden* (emigrants from eastern Europe), as well as among orthodox, liberal/reform, and secularized Jews, not to mention crosscutting political differences.

The *Litvak* and *Galitsyaner* were both types of *Ostjude* but each had its own stereotype, which was applied to inhabitants of the areas in question as well as to emigrants from them and even to their descendants. The *Litvak* originated in Lite, an area broader than interwar Lithuania, stretching as far east as Vitebsk and as far south as Minsk and Białystok. The *Litvak* was "smart, analytical, learned, worldly, skeptical, proud, stubborn, dynamic, and energetic."[39] He was also dry, rational, and unemotional. By contrast, the *Galitsyaner*, a Jew from the southern Polish province of Galicia, was warmhearted, sly, witty, sharp, stingy, *ibergeshpitst* (crafty), and something of a trickster. He had a "peculiar mix of shrewdness and heartiness."[40] "To be called a . . . Galitzianer was for long not much of a compliment. . . . It denoted folksy backwardness and at times also a petty mercantile mentality and moral shiftiness."[41] The two types spoke different kinds of Yiddish: the Lithuanian version was regarded as more cultivated; Polish/Galician Yiddish was homespun and earthy. The split was also partly culinary. The *Litvaks* prepared their *gefilte fish* savory rather than sweet and their *farfl* (egg noodle dough cooked in broth) as small pellets rather than rolled into flat sheets that were then sliced, as was the custom among *Galitsyaners*.[42]

The division between *Litvak* and *Galitsyaner* followed, in large measure, the lines of division between Hasidism and its enemies, the *misnagdim*. The greatest opponent of Hasidism in its early phase had been Eliyahu ben Shlomo-Zalman (1720–97), the gaon (a high rabbinic title) of Vilna. But Hasidism had some adherents in Lite, in particular the followers of Shneur Zalman of Lyady (1745–1813), founder of the Chabad movement, better known, from the small-town location of the rabbinical court of the second *rebbe* of the dynasty, as Lubavitcher Hasidim. Even in Galicia, however, the overenthusiastic, dancing, singing Hasidim were often viewed with a raised eyebrow. The writer S. Y. Agnon recalled that in his home *shtetl* of Buczacz the Hasidic prayer house was called the *laytsim shlikhel* (the little synagogue of clowns).[43]

Litvak and *Galitsyaner*, Hasid and *misnaged* were all types of Ostjude. One in five Jews in Germany in the 1920s was an *Ostjude* (many more fell into this category in terms of their ancestry). Immigrants from eastern Europe were also a significant element in the Jewish populations of France, Austria, and other countries, notably the United States, to which over two million Jews from eastern

Europe had emigrated between 1881 and 1914. The *Ostjuden*, by their clothing, their retention of Yiddish, their kosher food shops and restaurants, the hyperreligiosity of some and the revolutionary politics of others, impressed their mark on the central immigrant areas of cities, such as the Marais in Paris, known in Yiddish as the Pletzl, and Leopoldstadt, the poorest district of Vienna. Situated between the River Danube and the Danube Canal, it was dubbed "*matzah* island" on account of its dense concentration of Jews, more than a third of the population of the area.

Ever since the Enlightenment, German, Austrian, Hungarian, and French Jews had learned to look down on the *Ostjuden*, even though many were themselves immigrants or descendants of immigrants from eastern Europe. The writer Joseph Roth observed with some justice: "The more western the origin of a Jew, the more Jews there are for him to look down on. The Frankfurt Jew despises the Berlin Jew, the Berlin Jew despises the Viennese Jew, the Viennese Jew despises the Warsaw Jew. Then there are Jews from all the way back in Galicia, upon whom they all look down, and that's where I come from, the lowest of all Jews."[44]

Franz Kafka was a significant exception: "I would like to run to these poor Jews of the ghetto," he wrote, "kiss the hems of their garments and say nothing, absolutely nothing. I would be perfectly happy if, in silence, they would endure my presence."[45] Few west European Jews shared Kafka's engaging humility. Robert de Rothschild, head of the Consistoire de Paris, the main Jewish religious body in the city, expressed the common disdain toward recent arrivals from eastern Europe with unusual bluntness in a speech to the organization's general assembly in 1935: "If they are not happy here, let them leave. They are guests whom we have warmly received but they should not go about rocking the boat."[46]

In Germany in the early twentieth century, however, such attitudes began to change. The encounter during the First World War between Jews in German-occupied Poland and German-Jewish soldiers and army chaplains led to a new respect on the part of some German Jews for what they regarded as the more authentic traditionalism of the *Ostjuden*. German Jewry consequently experienced what came to be called a *Bewusstseinswandel*, a shift of consciousness

that involved also attitudes to *Ostjuden*. The redaction and popular-
ization by Martin Buber of tales of the Hasidic masters accentuated
this new tendency toward sympathetic respect. But stigmas, once
implanted, are difficult to remove and the old arrogance lingered.

The *Ostjuden*, for their part, often had their own chip-on-the-
shoulder scorn for *yekes* (the nickname for German Jews), as in the
line of doggerel:

> *Yeke iz a nar*
>> The *yeke* is a fool
> *un fun a nar hot men tsar*
>> and a fool just gives you trouble;
> *un ven dem nar vilt zikh zayn a har*
>> when a *yeke* wants to become a gentleman
> *vert er a gefar.*[47]
>> he becomes dangerous.

All Jews might have been brothers but, in this as in other ways,
theirs was often a fraternity of mutual contempt.

Such internal fissures hobbled the Jews' resistance in the 1930s
to the pandemic of anti-Semitism.

2

THE CHRISTIAN PROBLEM

"We Are All Semites"

Jews and Christians alike spoke of the "Jewish problem" but this was a misnomer for what should more properly have been called the Christian problem. In its essence, after all, anti-Semitism was a phenomenon that arose out of the failure of European Christendom to live up to the most fundamental teaching of its Jewish founder: "love thy neighbor as thyself."

In assessing the role and responsibility of the Christian churches in the prevalence of anti-Semitism in Europe in the 1930s, it is instructive to dwell not on the worst but on the best. A few leading Christian thinkers in the 1930s, such as the neo-Thomist theologian Jacques Maritain in France and the Protestant bishop of Debrecen, Dezső Baltazár, in Hungary, were outspoken in their condemnation of anti-Semitism.

Yet even in such a figure as Maritain, genuinely and passionately opposed to anti-Semitism, we may notice a mote in his eye. In a powerful essay (originally a lecture delivered at the Théâtre des Ambassadeurs in Paris) in February 1938, Maritain attacked all forms of anti-Semitism: racial, political, cultural, social—all, that is, except one, Christian anti-Semitism, which, according to him, was a contradiction in terms.

Maritain, whose sincerity and fervor in opposing racial hatred cannot be doubted, could nevertheless suggest that the Nazis, "in seeking to reject Israel," had "embraced the very worst of Israel." He detected in the Nazis "that sentiment of racial pride which is, in some carnal Jews, the naturalistic corruption of the supernatural idea of divine election." "The racists," he argued, were "indebted to the Old Testament as the Communists are to the New."[1] In both cases, as he understood it, the message of the sacred text had been corrupted. Whom he meant to impugn by the designation "carnal Jews" is unclear. It seems, however, that even a brave and undoubted opponent of anti-Semitism could not quite shake off a common trope of anti-Jewish discourse down the ages, the notion of overweening Jewish pride arising from the chosenness of the people of Israel.

In trying to identify the purpose or "vocation" of Jewish existence, Maritain suggested that "while the Church is assigned the labor of the supernatural and supratemporal redemption of the world,"

> Israel, we believe, is assigned, on the plane and within the limits of secular history, a task of *earthly activization* of the mass of the world. Israel, which is not of the world, is to be found at the very heart of the world's structure, stimulating it, exasperating it, moving it. Like an alien body, like an activating ferment injected into the mass, it gives the world no peace, it bars slumber, it teaches the world to be discontented and restless as long as the world has not God, it stimulates the movement of history.[2]

For Maritain the Jews would "always be outsiders in a supernatural sense." "To be hated by the world is their glory, as it is also the glory of Christians who live by the faith."[3] Here again Maritain was undoubtedly moved by a benevolent spirit. But the critic might observe that whereas the Christian could choose for himself the sublimity of the suffering servant, the Jew, according to Maritain's scheme, had the role thrust upon him whether he liked it or not.

Maritain did not deny that, in the world as it was, some Christians were anti-Semites. How could he, when the evidence in every day's newspaper in the late 1930s testified to the fact? But he argued that anti-Semitism on the part of Christians was an aberration that could occur "only when they obey the spirit of the world rather than the spirit of Christianity." The problem with such an interpretation from the sociological point of view, however, was that if, as Maritain implied, anti-Semites were not true Christians, then the number of Christians in Europe at the time must have been much smaller than was commonly perceived.

Maritain's treatment of Catholic and non-Catholic Christian utterances on the Jewish issue was not altogether evenhanded. He quoted disapprovingly a recent pronouncement by the patriarch of the Romanian Orthodox Church that Jews had "bled white" the Romanian people but he passed over similar comments by Catholic prelates, for example in Poland. The closest he came to this delicate area was in his assurance that the Polish primate, Cardinal Hlond, had repudiated "systematic and unconditional hostility towards Jews"—a generous reading of Hlond's public statements on the subject. In 1936 Hlond had issued a pastoral letter in which he castigated Jews as fraudsters, pornographers, and white slavers. Hlond conceded that "not all Jews are like this" and opposed the use of violence against them while supporting the boycott of Jewish businesses.[4] True, Maritain gently and by implication reproved the Polish Catholic bishops when he expressed the hope that they would "understand that it is not enough to abstain from hating Jews as such in the heaven of spiritual feeling, while conceding to their enemies all the legends, the prejudices, the heated arguments in whose name they are persecuted on the earth of temporal realities."[5] Yet while admitting that in Poland "anti-Semitism has taken a Catholic form" and acknowledging that the Catholic press "has all too often been an accomplice," he suggested that such behavior arose not from a religious source but rather "from the fact that, sociologically, it is natural, all too natural, that passions, however misleading, which claim to defend a country's national interests, should claim also support from its traditional religion."[6]

Maritain went further, defending the Roman Catholic Church against any accusation of complicity in anti-Semitism, even historically, as at the time of the Spanish Inquisition: "The Church itself and as such was not responsible for the excesses, even if some of its ministers were" (an old and rather pallid apologetic line). Skating lightly over the historical record, Maritain maintained that "the Popes repeatedly defended the Jews, notably against the absurd charge of ritual murder, and . . . all in all the Jews were generally less unhappy and less badly treated in the Papal States than elsewhere."[7]

Of course, in dwelling on those instances and elements in Catholic doctrine and history that rejected anti-Semitism, Maritain (whose wife had been born Jewish) had a polemical purpose, directed primarily toward redeeming his fellow Christians from the sin of racism. In the process he lost sight of the *fons et origo* of anti-Jewish ideology in Europe, namely the Christian concept of the Jews as a deicide nation and all that flowed from that in the teaching, including the contemporary teaching, of the Church. Perhaps, as a believing Christian, he could do no other.

For all his blind spots, backslidings, and mitigations, let us remember again that Maritain's was one of the rare pro-Jewish voices among churchmen in Europe in the 1930s. More representative of the general ruck of Catholic thought on the issue were Maritain's former associates in Action Française, the conservative movement with which he had been associated until its interdiction, for reasons unconnected with the Jewish issue, by Pope Pius XI in 1926. Many Catholics continued, even after the pope's condemnation of the movement, to be attracted to its reactionary, antidemocratic ideology, in which anti-Semitism was an important element. At the time of the papal ban, eleven of France's seventeen cardinals and archbishops were reliably reported to be favorable to Action Française.[8]

The Roman Catholic Church in Poland, to which the overwhelming majority of Poles still looked for guidance on all moral issues, was still more deeply imbued with anti-Jewish doctrines and anti-Semitic prejudices. In 1934, responding to an appeal by a group of rabbis, Cardinal Kakowski, archbishop of Warsaw, condemned anti-Jewish violence. But he undercut the effectiveness of his statement by accusing Jews of offending Christian feelings, of propagating atheism, of publishing pornography, and of financing Communism.[9]

Pope Pius XI, in a meeting with pilgrims in September 1938, termed anti-Semitism "inadmissible," adding, with tears in his eyes, "We are all spiritually Semites."[10] Perhaps he wept out of remorse for having written, when papal nuncio in Poland in 1919 (a time of widespread pogroms there): "One of the most evil and strongest influences that is felt here, perhaps the strongest and most evil, is that of the Jews."[11]

In 1938 the pope ordered the preparation of an encyclical condemning all forms of racism. The draft text of *Humani Generis Unitas* was submitted to the pontiff in February 1939. But he died a few days later and his successor, Cardinal Pacelli, who reigned as Pius XII, chose not to proceed with it. The draft, while condemning racism, retained several expressions of religious hostility to the Jews for rejecting Christ. The decisions to delay submission of the text to Pius XI and to shelve it altogether after his death have been attributed to the influence of the Polish head of the Jesuit order, Father-General Włodzimierz Ledóchowski, but it is impossible to gauge the extent of his responsibility since the file on the subject in the Vatican archives remains closed.[12]

Was anti-Semitism, in fact, as Maritain and others maintained, antithetical to the Christian message? Or is the disinterested historical observer, able to draw on an arsenal of evidence comprising the record of actual behavior of Christian churches and churchmen in Europe in the early twentieth century, bound to conclude the opposite: that hostility to Jews was intrinsic to Christian doctrine, as it was then generally understood and taught, especially by the Roman Catholic Church? This, after all, was a time when the Church prayed every Good Friday "pro perfidis Judaeis" (without kneeling and without saying "Amen" at the end). The churches for the most part repudiated explicitly racist forms of anti-Semitism, particularly as applied to Jewish converts to Christianity. But that kind of anti-Semitism was comparatively new, a phenomenon of the late nineteenth century and after. Much older and more deeply ingrained in Christian culture was the image of the nation of Christ-killers, with the mark of Cain on its forehead.

The blood libel, the accusation that Christian boys were murdered by Jews so that their blood might be used in the preparation of Passover *matzot*, a recurrent feature of anti-Jewish propaganda since its origin in twelfth-century England, resurfaced in interwar Europe. In Bitolj (Monastir) in Yugoslavia, for example, the charge was revived in 1921, 1922, and 1926. In 1930 a ritual murder charge in the town of Velykyi Bereznyi in Subcarpathian Ruthenia resulted

in a legal case that dragged on for two years. Throughout the period
Nazi propaganda devoted extensive attention to such allegations.
These incidents drew on the inventory of Christian anti-Judaism
but compounded religious antagonism with new, no less poisonous
ingredients.

Bagatelles for a Massacre

Since the late nineteenth century, a new form of Jew-hatred had
come into being: political anti-Semitism (the word was coined at
that time). This ideology, or social psychopathology, developed
mainly in France, Germany, and Austria, was sustained by collective
paranoias and conspiracy theories that flourished in the age of mass
politics. The Jews were now seen not merely as a decaying vestige
of the past but as a worldwide agency of evil, bent on destroying all
societies, whether through capitalist exploitation or revolutionary
subversion.

All new ideologies require authoritative texts. Anti-Semitism
found its theoretical construction in the works of German writers such as Wilhelm Marr and Houston Stewart Chamberlain.
More popular and widely disseminated were two others. Edouard
Drumont's *La France juive* (1886) exalted the "Aryan race," here
given a Gallic complexion, and denounced the deicide, ritual murder, pornography, materialism, social climbing, ugliness, foul smell,
treachery, criminality, and contagious diseases of the Jews, who,
with the Protestants, Freemasons, and anticlericals, had been drag-
ging France into the gutter since the revolution. The original version of the book, 1,200 pages long, was published in two volumes;
abridged editions appeared later. Lavishly praised by the Catholic
press, it became an enormous bestseller in France. Over the next two
decades, the book furnished useful material for anti-Dreyfusards
and anti-anticlericals and it provided a matrix for the next generation of anti-Semitic propagandists.

More international in its appeal was *The Protocols of the Elders of
Zion*, the supposed minutes of a secret conclave of Jews who plot-
ted world domination. The *Protocols* were concocted in the early

years of the twentieth century, probably by officers in Paris of the Okhrana, the Russian secret police, who plagiarized an earlier French work that had nothing to do with the Jews. Translated into many languages, the *Protocols* were the most widely disseminated anti-Semitic text of the interwar period, second only to *Mein Kampf*, and in the late 1920s were reported to be circulating even in the Soviet Union.[13]

In France there was a clear line connecting the anti-Semitism of the Dreyfus period with that of the 1930s, when the same texts, themes, and images reappeared in contemporary guise. Louis-Ferdinand Céline's *Bagatelles pour un massacre* (1937), which echoed both Drumont and the Protocols, was a merry, modernist, scatological eruption of loathing for Jews, accusing them, among much else, of leading France toward war. Received as an incitement to murder, the book was actually something different—though not necessarily more excusable. In the perverse, slippery, purposefully devious conception of the author, the "bagatelles" (literally "trifles") of the title were to be understood in two specialized senses: light musical compositions, deliberately intended to contrast grotesquely with the deadly seriousness of the subject matter; and the patter of a fairground barker (the Jew) summoning the French people to a massacre, that is, war.[14] Céline's book, with a first print run of twenty thousand copies soon exhausted, was merely the outer edge of a much broader phenomenon of literary anti-Semitism that was detectable in more subtle forms in such civilized writers as André Gide, Georges Duhamel, and François Mauriac. Anti-Semitism in France, particularly among Catholics, was part of the perfume of the age. By contrast, "anti-anti-semitism," as Eugen Weber observed, "simply did not sell."[15]

A Declaration of War

In east-central Europe, the very establishment of the nation-state successors to the defeated empires after the First World War, it has been argued, "implied a declaration of war against the Jews."[16] In these relatively backward regions of the continent, Jews had hitherto fulfilled many of the economic and cultural functions of a middle class. The acquisition of state sovereignty was seen by the greater part of public opinion, not merely by rabid nationalists, as necessarily implying the removal of the Jews, an alien element, from positions of undue power and their replacement by nationals of the country. Throughout east-central Europe, and particularly in Poland, Romania, and Hungary, the most virulent enemies of the Jews were to be found among the nationalist intelligentsia.

Why, they asked, should aliens control industry, commerce, the theater, journalism, and other key institutions of the national economy and culture in these nation-states? The Jews, it is true, were not the sole targets for such xenophobia. Millions of nationals of former imperial powers—Hungarians in Romania, Turks in Bulgaria and Greece, and Germans everywhere—also encountered hostility. But there was at least one important difference. All these ethnic minorities had a nation-state to which, even if they were not citizens, they might look for political support and redress of their grievances. The Jews' only potential recourse was to international legal instruments.

At the Paris Peace Conference in 1919 the victorious allies had required east European states to sign treaties guaranteeing the rights of minority populations, including Jews. These states, particularly Poland and Romania, fiercely resisted the imposition on them of what they regarded as unjust requirements that the great powers did not, after all, impose on themselves. The representatives of these states complained that the treaties were the product of undue influence exercised by an American-Jewish lobby at the conference. The Polish prime minister, Ignacy Paderewski, protested that his country was being treated as if it were "a nation of inferior standards of civilization."[17] If states were recognized as fully sovereign, why should others have any right of interference in their internal affairs? Negotiations on the treaties, conducted to the far-off drumbeat of pogroms in the Russo-Polish borderlands, generated resentment and distrust.

The treaties called for religious freedom and civil equality for all, as well as the right of minorities, within certain limits, to use their own languages. Primary schools functioning in those languages were to be funded by the state. Jewish Sabbath observance was to be protected (in the case of Poland, but not in Greece or Romania).

Minorities were granted the right of petition to the League of Nations in cases of alleged transgression.

Rather than assuaging ethnic resentments, the treaties exacerbated them. Lithuania, which initially granted Jews far-reaching rights of autonomy, soon withdrew them. Poland and Romania, in particular, honored their obligations for the most part in the breach. The League of Nations Minorities Section, charged with monitoring observance, proved to be a weak reed. Jews were generally fearful of submitting complaints against their own governments: nearly all petitions on Jewish issues were therefore lodged by external Jewish bodies such as the Joint Foreign Committee of the Anglo-Jewish Association and the Board of Deputies of British Jews. Of the 883 petitions the League received between 1920 and 1939, only four resulted in condemnation of the accused state. The League of Nations Council, which bore ultimate responsibility for enforcing the treaties, failed utterly in what the former British foreign secretary Lord Balfour called its "hard and thankless task."[18]

"Yes, but Without Violence"

Anti-Semitism was a European-wide phenomenon in the interwar period. Few countries, even those with small Jewish populations, were unaffected. The causes were manifold. Christian indoctrination fused with inflamed nationalism, rural-urban antagonism, traditional superstition, and populist propaganda. Restraining bonds of social control snapped as a result of the horrors of war, revolution, and depression. In the ramshackle polities of east-central Europe, strong intermediate institutions between state and citizen were generally lacking. The only exceptions were church and army, both usually hostile to Jews. Political participation in these states often took the form of follow-my-leader conformism, and politicians fell over one another in copycat efforts to adopt racist policies that appealed to the self-regard of declining social groups and the self-interest of ascending ones.

A few countries seemed, for a time, immune from infection. The small, long-established Jewish communities of Italy and Bulgaria were comfortably integrated into society and Jews rarely encountered hostility. In Czechoslovakia, Jews were to some extent shielded by the liberal-democratic ethos imprinted on the new state by Tomáš Masaryk.

In the USSR, anti-Semitism appeared, on the face of things, to have been eliminated. Deeply embedded as it was in Russian and Ukrainian social attitudes, it did not, of course, disappear overnight after 1917. But the extent of its subterranean prevalence is difficult to judge, given the controls on free expression in the USSR. There is evidence that, especially among the peasantry, anti-Jewish attitudes lingered in the popular consciousness. In Byelorussia, the blood libel accusation was heard in 1928 and again in 1933. In the acute town-country antipathies aroused by the collectivization campaign in the early 1930s, the Jew, regarded as the prototypical urbanite, attracted continued hostility. Still, at least at the official level, the Soviet state sternly disapproved of such "chauvinist attitudes."[19]

Even in these four countries, however, the Jews were granted only a temporary respite.

An early indication of what Jews might expect on the continent as a whole was the reappearance of the *numerus clausus*. This quota system, limiting Jewish admissions to high schools and universities, had first been imposed in the Russian Empire in 1887. It was abolished in Russia after the revolution of February 1917 but reappeared shortly afterward elsewhere and was first enacted into law in Hungary in November 1920. Taking as its basis the proportion of Jews to the population as a whole, this legislation provided that no more than 6 percent of admissions to universities were to be Jewish. Protests at the League (not by Hungarian Jews themselves, since they feared retribution) failed to secure the law's withdrawal, although enforcement was initially lax. The measure was significant as the first anti-Semitic law in interwar Europe.

Its passage was a serious blow to Hungarian Jews, who for the most part had hitherto felt at home in Hungarian society and culture. For many of them, the period between 1867 and 1914 had seemed like a golden age. Freed from legal restrictions, some had prospered greatly, moved into the professions and into the nobility. In spite of occasional disturbing throwbacks, notably a ritual murder trial at Tiszaeszlár in 1882, anti-Semitism seemed to belong to a less civilized past.

The revolution of 1918–19 and its aftermath changed all that. The short-lived Soviet regime of Béla Kun, a Communist of Jewish origin, was followed by a white terror in which hundreds of Jews were slaughtered by nationalist militias. Admiral Miklós Horthy, who proclaimed himself regent of Hungary in March 1920, presided thereafter over a reactionary, fiercely anti-Communist regime. The radical-right government of Gyula Gömbös between 1932 and 1936 courted Hitler and Mussolini and brought anti-Semitism into the center of public discourse. A fascist movement, the Arrow Cross, advocated discrimination against Jews and the removal of Jews from positions of economic and cultural power.

In Romania, independence in 1878 had been recognized by the powers at the Congress of Berlin only on condition that Jews would be granted citizenship and equality. That conditionality, seen as an impairment of the state's sovereignty, heightened long-standing enmity toward Jews. In the event, fewer than three thousand were permitted to become citizens by 1914. Under renewed pressure from the powers at the Paris Peace Conference, Romania recognized Jewish residents as citizens in 1919. But what was given with one hand was soon half taken away with the other. A large part of the political class, reflecting public opinion, would not reconcile themselves to Jewish emancipation. A new law in 1924 limited the rights of two-thirds of the Jewish population of the country who lived in territories newly acquired as a result of the First World War (Bessarabia, Transylvania, and Bukovina). In formerly Hungarian Transylvania, the identification of Jews with the culture of the former ruling power exacerbated Romanian hostility. In 1934 a "Law for the Employment of Romanian Workers in Factories" made it difficult for Jews to find or retain jobs. The radical-right Legion of the Archangel Michael, founded in 1927 and led by the theatrical Corneliu Zelea Codreanu, won support from many sectors of society, including much of the intelligentsia.

In Poland too Jews encountered difficulty in securing implementation of the minority treaty. In spite of numerous declarations of intent, remaining discriminatory legal provisions against Jews in

territories inherited from the Russian and Austrian empires were
not finally abolished until 1931. Meanwhile, the treaty's opponents
undertook a number of measures designed to empty it of effectiveness. A Sabbath observance law, restricting the ability of shopkeepers to trade on Sundays, had serious effects on orthodox Jews, now
compelled to close their businesses on both Saturday and Sunday.
In 1934 the Polish government, to general public applause at home,
unilaterally repudiated the minority treaty.

Political attitudes toward Jews in Poland in the 1930s ranged
from guarded cooperation on the left to outright hostility on the
right. The Socialist Party, while condemning attacks on Jews, was
not immune to anti-Jewish influences and in the late 1930s some
socialists were among those calling for Jewish emigration. The Peasant Party, which had opposed anti-Semitism in the early 1920s,
declared the Jews an "alien nation" in 1935 and endorsed a policy of
encouraging Jewish emigration. The strongest opposition party, the
right-wing National Democrats (Endeks), saw the Jews as no more
than "sub-tenants" on Polish soil and favored their complete elimination from Polish society. They should be deprived of the vote,
denied access to all public offices, and removed from the professions,
industry, and commerce. Pending the emigration of the entire Jewish population, Jews who lived in Poland should be confined to ghettos. Such views were shared by other, smaller, right-wing parties.
The leader of the Conservative Party, Prince Janusz Radziwiłł, for
example, called in 1937 for the "forcible emigration of the Jews."[20]
Most important, OZON, the "Camp of National Unity," which
became the dominant political force in the late 1930s, was outspo-
kenly anti-Semitic, refusing even to admit Jews to membership, calling for discriminatory legislation, and demanding large-scale Jewish
emigration.

Anti-Jewish disturbances in fifty Polish towns and villages in
1935–36 resulted in at least ten deaths. Passengers on trains on the
Warsaw-Otwock line were attacked. Shops and homes were looted.
Jews complained that the authorities stood idly by. "Polish Jewry,"
wrote an observer, was "surrounded by an atmosphere of incitement
and hostility." Jews were living "in a state of panic" and they all felt
"a sense of outrage."[21]

In March 1936 a pogrom in Przytyk, a *shtetl* near Radom in central Poland, left two Jews and one gentile dead and many others injured, as well as property damage. The riot erupted when peasants attacked Jewish-owned market stalls. A hundred Jewish homes were plundered and destroyed. In subsequent trials of those involved in the fighting, the Jewish defenders received much heavier sentences than the Polish rioters. Thousands of Jews participated in a protest march in Radom. Similar demonstrations took place throughout the country but, in the atmosphere of heightened Polish-Jewish tension, the pogroms spread.

The violence erupted in a climate of fierce political rhetoric and activity directed against Jews. In 1936 the Polish parliament approved a law, ostensibly based on humanitarian considerations, banning *shechitah* (kosher slaughter of meat). Although complete prohibition was postponed until 1942, limitations on kosher slaughter took effect in January 1937. Emil Sommerstein, a Zionist deputy in the Sejm (lower house of parliament), expressed the general Jewish view when he complained: "The slogan of humanitarianism appears with the goal of making the Jewish religion repugnant. [It serves as] support for barbarian superstitions and humiliation of the Jewish people as savage barbarians in the eyes of the Polish community."[22] The phrase echoed Paderewski's 1919 statement, quoted earlier: it is worth noting how often both Jews and Poles, in their troubled, chip-on-shoulder relationship with each other, chanted the refrain "*we* are not barbarians." An economic boycott of Jews in the late 1930s gained widespread support and was approved by the Church and members of the government. The prime minister, Felicjan Sławoj-Składkowski, endorsed it, though he added the qualifier "yes, but without violence."[23]

"A Tolerable Relationship"

The anti-Semitism of the Nazis differed from that of the rest of the continent in its radical brutality and bureaucratic systematization not, for the most part, in its origins. Hitler's obsessional preoccupation with the Jews was different in degree but not in kind from the racist thinking of other far-right demagogues, both German and non-German. His writings and speeches justified, broadcast, and amplified but did not in themselves create hatred of Jews in Germany. Anti-Semitism there shared many of the same causes as elsewhere, drew on similar, traditional imagery and exploited collective experiences of defeat, famine, inflation, and, after 1929, unemployment. The prominent role played by leftists of Jewish birth in the revolutions on German soil in 1918–19 helped feed the "stab-in-the-back" theory of Germany's defeat in the First World War. The assassination by a right-wing fanatic of the foreign minister, Walther Rathenau, a Jew, in 1922 was an early indication that the enemies of Weimar democracy would stop at nothing.

Between 1918 and 1933 anti-Semitism was prominent in the rhetoric not only of the Nazis but of respectable conservative parties. In Germany, as elsewhere, Jews often noticed a strange disconnection between the personal friendliness of some non-Jews and their readiness to avow far-reaching anti-Jewish attitudes. In a memoir of his time as a young hospital doctor in Germany in the late Weimar years, Martin Andermann relates how one of his colleagues, a convinced Nazi, used to debate with him. Andermann had the impression that his interlocutor "did not harbour any personal hatred towards me. . . . He fought not individual Jews but what he called 'the Jew.' 'The Jew' was for him exactly what 'Satan' had been for a medieval Christian. In fact, he said to me once at the end of a long discussion and with total seriousness: 'You are for me the incarnation of Satan.'" The man added that he had nothing against Andermann as an individual and "in fact, he felt he could be quite fond of me." Yet he would not shy away from killing him if necessary, albeit with "personal regrets."[24]

Burke's dictum that "all that is necessary for the triumph of evil is that good men do nothing" has a special resonance in relation to the victory of Nazism. The success of the Nazi onslaught on the Jews required not only the active participation of a minority of fanatics but the passive acquiescence of a cowardly or indifferent majority. The Hamburg banker Max Warburg found that the eagerness of former business associates to cultivate him had given way since 1933 to a tendency to avoid or even snub him: "On my way to the bank I met not a single acquaintance, while in former times I was continually doffing my hat in greeting."[25] The young lawyer Sebastian Haffner was shocked at his own reaction when Nazi brownshirts invaded the library of the Berlin court building where he was working and barked, "Non-Aryans must leave the premises immediately." One of the brownshirts came up and asked whether he was an "Aryan."

> A moment too late I felt the shame, the defeat. I had said "Yes!" Well, in God's name, I was indeed an "Aryan." I had not lied, I had allowed something much worse to happen. What a humiliation, to answer the unjustified question . . . so easily, even if the fact was of no importance to me! What a disgrace to buy with a reply, the right to stay with my documents in peace![26]

Haffner eventually left Germany to work as an anti-Nazi journalist in Britain. Most of his fellow readers in the library remained behind—save the "non-Aryans."

Before 1933, Germany, concerned for the fate of German minorities in eastern Europe, had been a vocal champion of minority rights in that region. After 1933 she was suddenly called upon to answer for her own treatment of a minority. The general issue of German persecution of the Jews was brought before the League of Nations Assembly's Sixth Committee (dealing with the protection of minorities) in the autumn of 1933. The German delegate denied that the committee had any jurisdiction, maintaining that "the Jewish problem in Germany is a special problem *sui generis* and cannot possibly be treated here simply like an ordinary minority question."[27] It was indeed true that German Jews had, in general, not thought of themselves hitherto as a "minority." Like French Jews they preferred to insist on their rights as individual citizens rather than on any collective right to special treatment. But as the French delegate in the committee's discussion put it, "The Jewish minority as such may not have existed in Germany. It is created when discriminatory treatment is accorded to the German Jews."[28] Shortly afterward, the exchange was rendered academic by the withdrawal of Germany from the League and all its affiliated organizations.

The only productive intervention of the League on a Jewish claim against Germany came as a result of the "Bernheim Petition" in May 1933. This case concerned a Jewish resident of German Upper Silesia who had been dismissed from his job because he was a Jew. The petition was seen as a test case of the League's ability to assert its role as a treaty guarantor. The League Council compelled Germany to suspend anti-Jewish legislation in the region, on the ground that it violated the German-Polish Convention of 1922. The respite was short-lived: when the convention expired in 1937, the full force of Nazi anti-Jewish laws was applied in the region.

The League, reduced to little more than an Anglo-French debating club, had in the meantime decided to appoint a "High Commissioner for Refugees (Jewish and other) coming from Germany." This new organ was designed to deal with the problems arising from the flight of thousands of Jews from Germany after Hitler's accession to power. But the high commissioner was not given an adequate budget to fulfill its task. In fact, he was not granted League funding at all. Article 12 of the High Commission's Statute, adopted in December 1933, declared: "The resources of the High Commission are constituted by funds contributed voluntarily from private or other sources."[29]

The magnitude of the challenge facing the High Commission became clear in 1935, when a new surge of refugees fled Germany as a result of the hardening of Nazi policy toward Jews. The decree laws announced by Hitler at Nuremberg in September that year reduced "non-Aryans" from the status of citizens to subjects. The laws prohibited Jews from employing as servants "Aryan" women younger than forty-five, forbade Jews to display the German flag, and provided a basis for further regulations restricting Jewish employment.

Subsequent announcements set forth a detailed racial classification of Aryan and non-Aryan. A Jew was a person with three or four grandparents who had been Jewish by religion. Persons with a smaller proportion of Jewish ancestors were categorized as "half-Jews" or "quarter-Jews." These categories too were refined, depending on other factors such as marital status. The laws barred marriage or sexual relations between non-Aryans and Aryans (existing marriages were tolerated, although Aryan spouses were encouraged to sue for divorce). The laws led to a wave of suicides, particularly by non-Aryans accused of "race defilement."[30]

Some Jews consoled themselves that the Nuremberg Laws, however objectionable, at any rate clarified their status and, after two years of threats, boycotts, exclusion, and uncertainty, provided them with a fixed basis for what Hitler termed "a tolerable relationship with the Jewish people."[31]

"A Force of Nature"

As the menace of anti-Semitism grew, Jews adopted a variety of explanations for it. Many, especially Zionists, saw Jew-hatred as endemic in all European societies. In eastern Europe, Jews commonly regarded anti-Semitism not so much as something that required explanation but rather, as Abraham Ascher, describing the outlook of his Polish-Jewish parents in the then-German city of Breslau, put it, "almost as a force of nature, about which little could be done except escape."[32] For some, anti-Semitism was not only ineradicable but natural in a world ordered mainly on the basis of ethnic polities. For optimistic liberals, anti-Semitism was a "medieval" relic that would disappear with greater education and enlightenment. Marxists, on the other hand, often argued that, like nationalism, anti-Semitism was a form of false consciousness, a device employed by the possessing classes to divide the working class and divert to another target proletarian hostility to the bourgeoisie. Since Jews were merely being used as scapegoats, anti-Semitism would automatically evaporate once a classless society was achieved.

Some assigned blame to Jews themselves or, to be more precise, to *other* Jews. The French philosopher Henri Bergson, the first Jew to be elected to the Académie Française, for example, attributed the rise of anti-Semitism "in great part, alas" to "a certain number of Jews entirely deprived of moral sense."[33] Bernard Kahn, the Swedish-born European director of the American Jewish Joint Distribution Committee, laid responsibility in part at the door of the *Ostjuden*. In a telephone conference call with leaders of the Joint in November 1936, he said: "There is especially a growing, serious anti-Semitic movement in that part of Holland called Maastricht. This is a Catholic section and a mining district where Eastern Jews who came in during the last four or five years have caused anti-Jewish feeling. This is because they peddle around in these mining districts, furnishing all sorts of goods to the miners on credit at higher prices than normal, and in these critical, harsh times demand payment of their money."[34]

The Frankfurt sociologist Max Horkheimer, a Marxist of Jewish origin, wrote provocatively and succinctly in an essay on "The Jews and Europe," completed on September 1, 1939: "He who does not wish to speak of capitalism should also be silent about fascism." He sneered at the "good Europeans" who still held to liberal shibboleths. The "century-long interlude of Liberalism," he declared, was over. It had served the Jews well. But "the fact that they were better off under Liberalism does not guarantee its fairness." ("Dass es ihnen im Liberalismus besser ging verbürgt nicht seine Gerechtigkeit.")[35]

Horkheimer's fierce hostility to Nazism did not prevent his sharing some elements of their analysis of the Jewish role in society, in particular their stress on the role of Jewish "finance-capitalism." This he saw as the chief pretext for the Nazi deployment of anti-Semitism as a propaganda weapon. He was not alone in such appropriation of Nazi concepts. The political theorist Hannah Arendt, like Horkheimer in exile from Germany after 1933, considered herself a Zionist in the 1930s. She absorbed from Nazi historians an interpretation of anti-Semitism that owed much to their contention that it was the conduct of the Jews themselves that was the chief cause of it.[36]

"I Would Love Her Even More"

Jewish responses to anti-Semitism ranged along a spectrum from sighing resignation through belief in the power of reasoned argument to advocacy of combative resistance. Strictly orthodox Jews were the most passive in their reactions, liberals more hopeful that political and diplomatic action could yield results, leftists and Zionists the most militant in calling for measures such as economic boycott of Nazi Germany, protest strikes in Poland, or even physical resistance to anti-Jewish violence.

Orthodox Jewish leaders in Germany initially adopted an

emollient attitude toward Hitler. In interviews with the press in 1933, Rabbi Jehiel Jacob Weinberg, rector of the orthodox seminary in Berlin, minimized Nazi anti-Semitism and expressed gratitude to Hitler for combating Communism and atheism. In October that year, leading orthodox figures including Rabbi Esra Munk of the Adass Jisroel, a secessionist orthodox group, and Jacob Rosenheim, leader of the ultra-orthodox Agudas Yisroel movement, wrote a long joint letter to Hitler. They denounced "Marxist materialism and Communist atheism" and pledged their opposition to the economic boycott of Germany being organized by anti-Nazis in other countries. At the same time they complained that Nazi measures against the Jews condemned them "to a slow but certain death from starvation." The writers declared their conviction "that the German government does not seek the destruction of German Jewry," adding: "But if we are wrong, if you Herr Reich Chancellor and the National Government you lead . . . should indeed have made it their objective to eradicate German Jewry from the German body politic, then we would rather cease nurturing illusions and learn the bitter truth."[37] The letter was not favored with so much as an acknowledgment of receipt.

The economic boycott of Nazi Germany by Jews in the United States and elsewhere, championed by the prominent American-Jewish leader Rabbi Stephen Wise, was controversial in the Jewish world. The Reichsvertretung publicly opposed the boycott. In Czernowitz (capital of the province of Bukovina in Romania) Jewish merchants continued to trade with Germany surreptitiously, using assumed names.[38] The German government cunningly succeeded in undercutting the boycott by negotiating the *ha'avara* (transfer) agreement with the Zionist Organization. Under this, Jewish emigrants from Germany were permitted to export a limited part of their capital by depositing Reichsmarks in Germany in return for German goods that would be exported to Palestine and exchanged there for pounds.

In response to anti-Semitic attacks, many Jews who had hitherto been on the fringe of involvement in the community felt driven to adopt a more assertively Jewish posture. As they were excluded from fellowship with their neighbors and deprived of citizenship,

Jews, often for the first time, made common cause with one another across boundaries of class, ideology, or religious affiliation. In Germany, the early Nazi years saw an enthusiastic rediscovery of Jewish religion and culture and growth in support for Zionism.

Some Jews believed that reason was the best answer to unreason. The head of the Romanian Jewish community, Wilhelm Filderman, a Liberal member of parliament, rejected the proposition that the mass of the population was inherently anti-Semitic. Hatred of Jews, he maintained, was disseminated from above and could best be countered by rational discussion. Thus when, in response to an essay by Filderman in 1937, the prominent intellectual and former prime minister Nicolae Iorga published a viciously anti-Semitic tract, *Iudaica*, Filderman responded with further apologetic articles. As Jean Ancel has written, "Filderman loved Romania and could not understand why Romania did not love him and his coreligionists."[39] Mutatis mutandis, the same might have been said of many Jewish leaders and thinkers throughout Europe.

While Communists stressed their faith in internationalist ideals, bourgeois Jews sought to emphasize their patriotism, hoping thereby to undercut anti-Semites' accusations of disloyalty. Sometimes their affirmations took surprising forms. In Paris between 1933 and 1936, ceremonies honoring war dead at the Notre Dame de Nazareth synagogue included a parade down the aisles by hundreds of members of the right-wing, antiparliamentary Croix de Feu. This annual affirmation of the *union sacrée* terminated only in 1936 with the dissolution of the Croix de Feu, together with other right-wing "leagues," by Léon Blum's Popular Front government.

Some of the most spontaneous responses to anti-Semitism, illustrating how readily it could inspire fear or be internalized by its victims, came from the young. Hans Floersheim, a boy in the small town of Rotenburg in Hessen in western Germany, rarely encountered anti-Semitism in daily life. Occasionally schoolmates would call Jewish children "Judenstinker," whereupon they would respond "Christenstinker."[40] That, at any rate, was before 1933. A few months after the Nazi takeover, however, his father, a textile merchant and Social Democrat, was driven out of the town. The family settled in Leipzig, hoping, like many Jews from small towns, to find easier acceptance in the relative anonymity of a big city. In Leipzig Hans experienced little direct anti-Semitism. But he later recalled one telling episode. Like most German children, he was expected to wear a distinctive cap to and from school, with a badge denoting his school and class. But he felt uncomfortable wearing a cap that showed he was a pupil at the Carlebach Realschule, a Jewish school. He therefore persuaded his parents to search out a shop that would sell them a generic cap without the distinctive badge. Or perhaps this was his parents' precautionary idea—later he could not quite recall.[41]

Another example from further east: the Polish-Jewish poet Aleksander Wat records the occasion in the late 1930s when his seven-year-old son came home from school and reported that a Jewish woman shopkeeper's window had been smashed "because the Jews are terrible, they're ugly and they're dirty." His mother revealed to the child that she herself was a Jew. "And so, do you love your mother?" To which he responded: "I would love her even more if she weren't a Jew."[42]

On the printed page, the platform, the stage, and the painted canvas, in song, in private letters and conversations, and, where they could prudently do so, in public statements, Jews gave voice to a broad range of emotions in response to their vilification and persecution. Some of the most anguished expressions of pain were in verse. These followed an age-old Jewish literary tradition that in its modern form had transmuted lamentation into protest and defiance. After the Kishinev pogrom of 1903, Haim Nahman Bialik had written a searing Hebrew poem, "City of Slaughter," in which he denounced not only the perpetrators but also the passivity of the Jewish victims and onlookers. In 1938, Mordkhe Gebirtig, a popular composer of Yiddish songs who was close to the consciousness of the Jewish masses in Poland, ran into trouble with the Polish censor when he wrote "Unzer shtetl brent" (Our town is burning):

> *S'brent! briderlekh, s'brent!*
> It's on fire, brothers, it's on fire!
> *oy, unzer orem shtetl, nebekh, brent!*
> Our poor town, alas, is burning!

Beyze vintn mit yirgozn
   Angry gusts in a rage
raysn, brekhn un tseblozn
   Rip and smash and fan
shtarker nokh di vilde flamen
   The wild flames ever stronger
alts arum shoyn brent!
   Everything around is on fire!
un ir shteyt un kukt azoy zikh
   And you stand and stare
mit farleygte hent
   with folded arms,
un ir shteyt un kukt azoy zikh.
   and you stand and stare.
Unzer shtetl brent![43]
   Our town is on fire!

The text ran into trouble with the Polish censor. Such spasms of outrage were, alas, more common among Jews than the difficult task of devising a coherent, let alone a unified, political strategy for defense against their tormentors.

3

GRANDEES AND GRANDSTANDERS

Jewish Politics

Disunity was the hallmark of Jewish politics between the wars. Divided by frontiers, by ideologies, and by class, Jewish politics was highly factionalized, raucous, and uncompromising. Without a state apparatus and with little in the way of potential rewards, however, it was generally free of corruption. In the 1920s it mirrored to some degree the politics of the states and peoples among whom Jews lived. But as the condition of European Jews became more precarious in the 1930s, their politics turned into an existential struggle, waged with increasing desperation and, in some cases, a zeal that slipped over into fanaticism.

Pre-democratic political modes had not completely disappeared. The traditions of the *gvir* (local bigwig) and the *shtadlan* (grandee intercessor with governments) had not altogether died out. Figures like Wilhelm Filderman in Romania performed this function in a somewhat updated form. Even in democratic France, the Rothschilds still held sway over many communal institutions, though restive plebeians, mainly immigrants and leftists, challenged patrician dominance.

Jewish politics was conducted in three arenas: communal, national, and international. Internal community political life dealt not only with the narrowly religious business of the *kehillot*, maintenance of synagogues and ritual baths, appointment of rabbis, control of kosher slaughter, and so forth, but with the administration of schools, hospitals, old people's homes, and other institutions, as well as representation of the community to surrounding society.

In international diplomacy, having no nation-state apparatus at their disposal, Jews could defend themselves only through nongovernmental organizations such as the Paris-based Alliance Israélite Universelle, in spite of its name, really a French-Jewish organization, or the Comité des Délégations Juives, a body of unofficial diplomats from a dozen countries who had played a role at the Paris Peace Conference, or through the good offices of the decreasing number of friendly national governments. The Comité gave way in 1936 to the World Jewish Congress, founded under the leadership of Stephen Wise and largely organized by Nahum Goldmann. The WJC aspired to be the "permanent address of the Jewish people."[1] Its first plenary assembly in Geneva gathered 280 representatives from Jewish communities in thirty-two countries—by far the largest delegation came from the United States. The organization set up its headquarters in Paris and an office in Geneva. With affiliates and branches in most countries where Jewish communities lived, with the exception of the Soviet Union, the WJC played a role in Jewish international politics. Its representative pretensions, however, were hollow: many Jewish organizations were suspicious of it as a Zionist front organization and refused to affiliate.

At the national level, the character of Jewish politics differed radically across the four zones of European Jewry. In the Soviet Union, its scope, like that of politics in general, steadily narrowed. In the early 1920s nearly all traces of non-Communist politics were eliminated. In 1930 the closure of the *Evsektsiia* rendered any specifically Jewish political activity, other than in the Jewish autonomous region of Birobidzhan, open to suspicion of "nationalist deviation." In the late 1930s purges, show trials, and terror cut a swathe through the Old Bolsheviks, among whose leading personalities Jews had been disproportionately prominent. By the end of the decade, any vestige of Jewish politics in the USSR had been effectively snuffed out.

In the Third Reich the creation of the one-party state and the exclusion of Jews from citizenship abruptly ended their participation in what remained of national politics. The Nazis nevertheless permitted some limited political activity to continue within the

Jewish community, allowing, in particular, Zionists to continue to propagandize, recruit, and train potential emigrants to Palestine. Within its sphere, the Reichsvertretung was granted a certain autonomy in administering Jewish institutions. At any rate, until 1938 it could negotiate with the government or, more precisely, supplicate on behalf of the Jewish community.

In the democracies, given the small electoral weight of the Jewish communities, Jewish political participation in national politics was generally individual rather than collective. Jews overwhelmingly supported the liberal center or the left. In France most backed the Popular Front. In Weimar Germany they voted mainly for the liberal German Democratic Party (DDP) or for the Social Democrats, in the case of the former so much so that it became damagingly identified in the public eye as a Jewish party. Many Jews rose to prominent positions in these parties. The DDP mayor of Frankfurt from 1924 to 1933, for example, was a Jew, Ludwig Landmann. In Austria, where the Liberals had faded almost out of existence by the mid-1920s, the bulk even of middle-class Jewish votes went to the Social Democrats.

In east-central Europe, Jews were almost by definition excluded from three of the most important political groupings: peasant parties, since Jews were overwhelmingly urban; clerical parties, since they were not Christians; and nationalist ones, since they were not regarded as members of the dominant ethnic or national group.

During the years of turmoil after 1917, Jews had briefly won recognition as an ethnopolitical entity in parts of the region. But experiments in Jewish autonomy in independent Ukraine, before its partition between Poland and Soviet Russia in 1921, and in Lithuania in the early 1920s were short-lived and were not repeated elsewhere.

In Romania, where Jews formed 4 percent of the population in the 1930s, a Jewish Party enjoyed success for a short time. In 1932 it won a majority of Jewish votes and five seats in parliament. But its support was mainly concentrated in the former Hungarian province of Transylvania. It did not have much of a following elsewhere and in subsequent elections failed to cross the minimum threshold to regain entry into parliament.

In Czechoslovakia, until the country's dissolution in 1938–39, a Jewish Party, composed mainly of Zionist elements, secured representation in parliament between 1929 and 1938 (after 1935 in electoral cooperation with the Czech Social Democrats). But Czechoslovak Jews were deeply divided in their cultural outlooks, religious views, and ideological sympathies. Zionism was opposed by Marxist internationalists in Prague, by Hungarian assimilationists in Slovakia, and by the dominant orthodox elements in Subcarpathian Ruthenia. Given the small size of the Jewish community, the party could not exercise effective leverage in national politics.

In Poland there was no significant liberal party like that of Weimar Germany that might have attracted middle-class Jewish votes. And the Polish Socialist Party, although not anti-Semitic, tended to view its Jewish members as something of an embarrassment in its efforts to win support in the broader working-class.

Herman Liebermann, a lawyer from Drohobycz in Galicia, who had fought in the Polish Legion in the First World War, became the Socialist Party's most prominent Jewish politician, representing it in the Sejm from 1919 to 1933. A brilliant orator of great force and pathos, he considered himself a Pole first and a Jew second. His deepest commitment was to the Polish working class. He once told his mistress that in his fantasies he saw himself as Christ taking on the cross of mankind's suffering.[2] After the coup d'état of Marshal Piłsudski in 1926, which introduced a semi-authoritarian regime to the country, Liebermann became a leader of the Centrolew (Center-Left) democratic opposition. Sentenced to a prison term in 1933, he escaped to Czechoslovakia and later to France, where he joined the large community of political exiles active in the democratic socialist Second International.

Such figures, however, were unusual in Polish political life. Most Jewish politicians in Poland, except for Communists, operated through specifically Jewish parties, which won 34 seats (out of 444) in the Sejm in 1922 and 12 (out of 111) in the senate. These numbers were never again attained but the Jewish vote and Jewish parties remained bit players on the Polish political stage until 1939.

During the interwar period, therefore, Poland became the focal point of Jewish politics. Although divided among many parties, each of which in turn was subdivided into contending factions, Jewish politics in Poland, reflected to some degree in other countries, was organized around three major blocs: orthodox, Zionist, and leftist, each vying for the allegiance of a highly mobilized, articulate, and fractious constituency.

"We Do Not Get Involved"

Orthodox Jews in Europe traditionally sought to cultivate good relations with governing authority, of whatever hue, and shunned oppositional political activity. In fact their predisposition was to shun political activity altogether. Modern realities, however, compelled them to organize to defend their sectoral interests.

Founded in 1912, the Agudas Yisroel claimed not to be a political party at all but rather a movement, guided by rabbinical authorities, representing orthodox Jewry. It sought to unite all orthodox Jews, Hasidim and *misnagdim*, ultra- and modern orthodox, in common opposition to Reform Judaism, secularism, and assimilation, all despised as works of the devil. Its following was strongest in formerly Russian-ruled "Congress Poland," particularly among Gerer Hasidim, followers of Rabbi Abraham Mordechai Alter of Gur (or Góra Kalwaria).

While purporting to be non- (or super-) political, the Aguda played the political game with consummate skill. In Poland it achieved considerable success in elections to the Sejm and the senate. In other countries its followers compensated for their smaller numbers by zealous devotion to the cause.

Although they trumpeted their hostility to Jewish nationalism, the Agudists treasured the small enclave of ultra-orthodox Jewish residents in Palestine, whom they regarded as their protégés and peculiar preserve, and they sought immigration certificates to the Jewish National Home with no less eagerness than the Zionists whom they vilified.

The Agudists found Piłsudski's paternalistic regime after 1926 relatively palatable. The government showed some readiness to accommodate orthodox Jewish demands and institutions as against those of secular Jewish parties. In return the Agudists backed the government in the elections of 1928 and 1930. Hasidic rabbis issued preelection fliers with instructions to their followers on how to vote. The Bobover *rebbe*, Ben-Zion Halberstam, for example, issued such decrees in 1930 and 1938.[3]

Not all orthodox Jews supported the Agudah. The most conservative rabbinical leaders, led by the Munkácser *rebbe* Hayim Eleazar Shapira, vehemently opposed the Aguda. Shapira excoriated the Agudists for admitting "admixtures of secular learning" in their schools. They were "defiling the children's minds and hearts with foolishness that leads to levity and heresy."[4] Shapira's anti-Agudist, as also his anti-Zionist, ideas were shared by the Satmarer *rebbe*, Yoel Teitelbaum, though the two men fell out in a territorial dispute.

The Belzer *rebbe*, Aharon Rokeach, one of the foremost Hasidic leaders in Poland, stood somewhat aloof from the Agudists. In 1928, however, handbills issued in the *rebbe*'s name called on all Jews to vote for the "Non-Partisan Bloc for Cooperation with the Government," headed by Piłsudski. This, the *rebbe* proclaimed, was their "holy duty" from which they should not be seduced by unbelievers and liars who advised differently. But shortly before the election he issued a new announcement, repudiating the earlier one and insisting that "we do not get involved in these matters."[5] What prompted the change of position (if change there was) is unknown. Whether both were authentic or not, the fliers were an indication of the importance attached to the *rebbe*'s endorsement.

The death of Piłsudski in 1935 ended the cozy arrangement between the government and orthodox Jews and removed a bulwark against overt discrimination against Jews. The outbreak of the Great Depression had meanwhile enhanced the appeal to the Polish electorate of the anti-Semitic right. Under the "regime of the colonels" between 1935 and 1939, the far right acquired an increasing voice in government. Jews, including the orthodox, became increasingly targets for attack. In these circumstances, support grew among Jews for the more assertive positions of the Zionists and the left.

Here-and-Now Work

Zionism, like all modernizing forces in Jewry, founded its ideology on a critique not just of the surrounding world but of existing Jewish society. Often the condemnation was harsh and unsparing, bordering on collective self-disgust that was sometimes a hairsbreadth removed from anti-Semitism. The life of the Jewish masses in eastern Europe, wrote the Yiddish literary critic (and Zionist) Bal-Makhshoves (Isidor Eliashev), "repels every healthy man. . . . They live like a worm reared in the gutter of a roof which then falls off the roof into a street-drain, but perforce then acclimatizes itself to its new environment."[6]

Zionists viewed the diaspora in negative terms and argued that it was hopeless to seek its regeneration anywhere other than in the ancestral homeland. At the same time, they found themselves obliged, willy-nilly, to conduct most of their political activity in the diaspora in the form of what was called *Gegenwartsarbeit* (here-and-now work).

Zionism aspired to become an international force but in reality its geography was severely circumscribed. Its primary focus was on the state-building enterprise in Palestine; yet only a small fraction of Jewry (around 2 percent of the total) had made their homes there by the late 1930s. The World Zionist Organization's headquarters were in London and it was heavily dependent on financial support from American Jewry; yet in the Americas or western Europe it could count on active support from only a small minority of Jews. In the Soviet Union Zionism was proscribed altogether and emigration to Palestine was impossible.

Among German-speaking Jews, where Zionism had hitherto been the enthusiasm of a small clique, it began to attract interest in the 1920s and won victories in communal elections in Berlin in 1926 and Vienna in 1932. After 1933 it gained further support among Jews in the Third Reich, less on intrinsic ideological grounds than as offering an escape route in extremis.

With these exceptions, the movement's popular base in the 1930s was therefore largely restricted to east-central Europe and the

Balkans. Its greatest center was in Poland. Out of 976,000 shekel payers (members of the Zionist Organization paying the small, minimum membership subscription) in the world in 1935, 406,000 were in Poland. Zionism there, moreover, was a significant force not only in the Jewish community but in national politics. Zionists, however, were far from united. Within the movement a spectrum of parties from right to left battled for dominance.

The General Zionists represented the broad mainstream. They were led internationally by the towering figure of Chaim Weizmann. Born in Russia but a British citizen, he had enormous prestige as the leader whose diplomacy had won for the Zionists the Balfour Declaration of 1917, promising British support for a Jewish National Home in Palestine. A world statesman, a skillful organizer, and wily political maneuverer, he was an assured negotiator, well-known in the chancelleries of power. A powerful speaker in several languages, he dominated the movement. His mastery was recognized even between 1931 and 1935, when he temporarily yielded presidency of the Zionist Organization to the journalist Nahum Sokolow.

Yitzhak Gruenbaum was the foremost Zionist leader in Poland. A newspaper editor, he led the Jewish parliamentary caucus. An outspoken advocate of Jewish rights, he managed, by force of personality, to compensate for the General Zionists' comparative lack of ideological coherence. His departure for Palestine in 1933, however, left a void at the head of the movement in Poland.

In the early 1920s, Jewish parliamentarians, led by Gruenbaum, had tried by a variety of means to secure governmental compliance with the minority treaty. Both conciliation, in the form of negotiations with the government, and concerted opposition in a Minorities Bloc together with Ukrainians and Germans failed to achieve anything. The alternative policy of the Ugoda (compromise agreement), negotiated in 1925 between some Zionists and government ministers, collapsed in mutual recriminations within a few months.

The General Zionists' paramountcy within the movement eroded in the 1930s as Zionism tended to polarize, with the socialist Poalei Zion and the right-wing Revisionists gaining ground.

Socialist Zionism, which emerged, thanks largely to its preeminent position in Palestine, as the leading force in the world Zionist movement in the 1930s, was inspired by the ideas of the

Russian-Jewish thinker Ber Borokhov (1881–1917). His ideology synthesized Zionism with Marxism, arguing that there was a "stychic" (elemental) connection binding the Jewish people to Palestine. Within the Poalei Zion, founded in 1906, strains developed between rigid Marxists and those who stressed the national element in the doctrine. In 1920, at a congress in Vienna, the party split. The Left Poalei Zion joined the Third International (the Comintern), withdrawing from participation in Zionist congresses. This decision enabled it to survive as a legal organization in the Soviet Union until 1928, when it was dissolved there. It remained active in Poland and elsewhere, walking a narrow line between diaspora and Zion, between Hebrew and Yiddish, and between Communism and democratic socialism. The party's support peaked in the late 1920s; thereafter it lost ground to other socialist Zionist parties and to the Bund and in 1937 it rejoined the World Zionist Organization.

The Revisionist Zionists constituted the right wing of the movement. Vladimir Jabotinsky, a journalist from a Russian-speaking family in Odessa, who founded and led Revisionist Zionism until his death in 1940, attracted an ardent following particularly among young Zionists in Poland. A spellbinding orator, with a pocketful of rhetorical effects, Jabotinsky could muster pathos and sarcasm, as well as grandeur of vision and logic (albeit sometimes chop-logic). He lacked only physical stature: at five feet seven inches, he was five inches shorter than his great rival, Weizmann. Even an eight-year-old boy who encountered him for the first time in 1938 found him

> small; he was dressed in a gray suit with a pale stripe; he seemed calm and self-assured, and more interested in us than I had expected him to be. But what struck me most of all about him was that he had some powder on his face. It was, I suppose, some kind of talcum powder which he had put on after shaving and which he had not bothered to wipe off; but then it seemed quite mysterious to me and not a little embarrassing.[7]

A grandstander rather than a statesman, Jabotinsky never quite succeeded in translating rhetorical triumphs into real political achievements.

In Palestine the Revisionist movement called for the early

establishment, under British auspices, of a Jewish state on both banks of the Jordan. In the diaspora Jabotinsky urged the adoption of a ten-year program of organized mass emigration of 1.5 million European Jews to Palestine.

The great stronghold of Revisionism was in Poland but it also commanded support elsewhere. In Vienna, its local leader in the early 1930s, Robert Stricker, was one of the most colorful and controversial figures in Austrian politics. In 1919 he had won a seat in the Constituent National Assembly as a candidate for the Jewish Nationalist Party in a heavily Jewish area of Vienna. A populist who said bluntly what was in his and other people's minds, Stricker was a formidable public speaker and commanded a loyal following among Viennese Jews.

In 1935 Jabotinsky split away from the mainstream Zionists and founded the New Zionist Organization, which did not, however, succeed in supplanting the parent body. Freed of their anchor in the broader movement, the Revisionists moved away from democracy toward the ideals, methods, and symbols of the European radical right. His youthful embrace of rationalism had been an error, Jabotinsky confessed in 1939.[8] His critics condemned his readiness to engage in friendly negotiations with anti-Semites, Ukrainian nationalists in the early 1920s, and the right-wing Polish "government of colonels" of the late 1930s. Often accused by their opponents of fascist tendencies, the Revisionists did not wholly jettison democratic forms but they shared fascism's solipsistic nationalism, hatred of socialism, focus on a single leader, and fascination with uniforms, militarism, and violence.

Operating in a different dimension from other Zionist parties was Mizrachi, the religious Zionist movement. Mizrachi appealed to the profound yearning, deeply embedded in Jewish tradition, for a return to Zion. Its founder, Rabbi Yitzhak Yaakov Reines, who died in 1915, had established a *yeshiva* (Talmudic college) at Lida that, shockingly in the eyes of traditionalists, had included some secular studies in its curriculum. Condemned by the most authoritative orthodox authorities of the day, Mizrachi mobilized only a small fraction of religious Jewry. In Poland about 10 percent of rabbis, mostly the more modernized and less influential, supported it.

Adherence to the Zionist movement was not generally understood as entailing personal commitment to settle in Palestine, any more than adherence to socialism entailed a promise to share one's wealth. The Yiddish writer Melech Ravitch recalled that when he first met the young historian Emanuel Ringelblum, a member of the Left Poalei Zion, at the Jewish writers' club in Warsaw in 1928, he advised him to leave Poland. "In general, I advised young people to leave Poland, especially Zionists such as Ringelblum." But Ringelblum insisted that he would remain where he was and "defended his enthusiasm and faith in the future of Poland Jewry."[9]

Beauty of a Thousand Stars

The European left was in large measure a Jewish creation. In Germany in the mid-nineteenth century Marx, Hess, and Lassalle, all three of Jewish origin, had founded and shaped the socialist movement. In Russia at the end of the century Jews had been prominent among the early leaders of the Social Democratic Party, particularly its Menshevik wing, and had founded the Bund as a distinct, Yiddish-language party within the broader movement. Jews were less attracted to Bolshevism but nevertheless were prominent among its leaders too: a quarter of the members of the Bolshevik central committee in 1917 were Jews.

After the October revolution many Russian Jews rallied to the Soviet cause. Throughout Europe, Jews in the interwar period played a disproportionate role in the socialist and Communist movements. They were strongly represented among left-wing intellectuals and also among so-called salon-Marxists, such as Felix Weil, the millionaire's son who became chief benefactor of Max Horkheimer's Frankfurt Institute for Social Research.

Jews, even more than most of socialism's working-class supporters, found specially attractive the left's internationalism, secularism, and commitment to enlightenment values. Unlike the nationalist and clericalist right, which excluded Jews, the left offered Jews a path toward integration, acceptance, and involvement in shaping the destinies of the societies in which they lived. Jews were particularly drawn to socialism's millenarian vision of a future "clothed with the beauty of a thousand stars," as the Austrian Jewish socialist Julius Braunthal romantically described it.[10] Jews often rose to leadership positions in left-wing parties. Yet by the late 1930s the relationship between Jews and the left was in profound crisis.

In truth, the alliance between Jews and the left was not quite as natural as it might appear. In their majority, after all, Jews, although highly urbanized, were not proletarians. Most belonged to the petty bourgeoisie of small traders and craftsmen, self-employed shopkeepers or artisans in small, often family-owned, workshops. Even where a Jewish proletariat was in the process of formation, as, for example, in the textile industry in ex-Russian Poland, Jews were often cut off from their fellow workers by barriers of language and custom that broke down only slowly. Hence the special attraction of particularist Jewish parties such as the Bund or the socialist Zionists. Moreover, the natural affinity that European Jews felt toward the heirs of the French Revolution, to which they owed their first liberation, was often cruelly tested by confrontation with the harsh reality of left-wing anti-Semitism, as in France at the time of the Dreyfus Affair.

Many Jewish socialists took care to avoid appearing explicitly as defenders of Jews against anti-Semitism. In Austria, for example, the mainly Jewish leaders of the Social Democratic Party avoided, as far as possible, involvement in Jewish issues, fearful lest such identification might rebound electorally to the disadvantage of the party. Such defensiveness was not universal. In the Netherlands, where the Jewish proletariat of Amsterdam was more happily integrated into the working class, Henri Polak, the Dutch socialist leader, was, at any rate in the 1930s, outspoken in his condemnation of anti-Semitism. And Léon Blum, the French socialist leader, did not hesitate from his early days as a defender of Dreyfus to declare his Jewishness or his support for Zionism. While his party did not appear to suffer electorally on that account, his enemies on the right had no compunction about drawing attention to (and sinister consequences from) his Jewishness. In the feverish political climate of the 1930s, they attacked him mercilessly: "Voilà un homme à fusiller, mais dans le dos!" wrote Charles Maurras, the leading intellectual spokesman of the far right.[11]

Although most leftists abandoned religion, they were not necessarily all assimilationists, nor, as their enemies sometimes asserted, "self-hating." Many were drawn from the Yiddish-speaking working class and held on to much of the cultural baggage of their background. In general they followed Lenin in rejecting the idea of a separate Jewish nation. But some displayed ambiguous or conflicting attitudes toward their Jewish heritage.

David Wijnkoop, founder and leader of the Dutch Communist Party, son of a rabbi, while rejecting religious belief and practice, kept the traditional *mezuzah* (amulet) on the doorpost of his house.[12] Marcel Pauker, a Romanian Communist leader, in an autobiographical statement he wrote for his interrogators when under arrest in Moscow in 1937, declared: "I reproached my father with the fact that he was ashamed of his Jewish origin, something that could be attributed only to the influence of the prevailing anti-Semitism."[13] And the young Polish Trotskyist Isaac Deutscher, who in later years popularized the concept of the "non-Jewish Jew," wrote: "I spent my best years, my politically active years, among Jewish workers. I was writing in Polish and in Yiddish and I felt my identity was merged with the labour movement of Eastern Europe in general, and of Poland in particular." And he added, "as Marxists we tried theoretically to deny that the Jewish labour movement had an identity of its own, but it had it all the same."[14]

Links in the Golden Chain

Most Jews were not Communists and most Communists were not Jews. Yet the Communist movement almost everywhere was, much to its annoyance, frequently tarred by its enemies with the Jewish brush. The association was given a tincture of verisimilitude by the fact that Jews were indeed disproportionately represented in the membership of the Communist Party throughout east-central Europe. The party was illegal in most east European countries and the size of its Jewish component is hard to estimate. Scattered figures are available. In Poland Jewish membership fluctuated between 22 and 35 percent of the total. Jews were even more heavily represented in the party leadership: in 1935 they are said to have constituted 54 percent of the "field leadership" and 75 percent of the *technika* (responsible for propaganda).[15]

This large Jewish participation led to internal strains. Moshe Zalcman, a Jewish Communist who was imprisoned for a time in Poland, records that non-Jewish Communist prisoners refused to share their food parcels with their Jewish comrades. He notes that the party, obviously anxious about the outsize membership of Jews, operated an affirmative action system, promoting non-Jews to responsible positions without subjecting them to a testing period. This offered, according to Zalcman, an opening for the police to infiltrate agents provocateurs.[16]

In the Soviet Union after the revolution, the Bolsheviks succeeded in winning over to their standard a significant number of members of other socialist parties. A Bund congress in 1920 led to a split in that party, with a group of "left-Bundists" or "Com-Bund" going over to the Bolsheviks. In the late 1920s, however, many of these were removed in anti-Bundist purges. After 1926, Stalin's anti-Trotsky campaign carried with it a distinct whiff of anti-Semitism. During the terror of the late 1930s many of the remaining Jews in the highest ranks of the party leadership, notably Grigory Zinoviev and Lev Kamenev, were arrested and shot. Middle-level functionaries who had earlier been members of the Bund or of left-Zionist parties fell under special suspicion and large numbers of them too were arrested. Of the twenty-four senior figures in *Evsektsiia* at the time of its closure in 1930, eighteen were arrested in the purges.

Jews, qua Jews, were not a primary target of the Great Terror. They appeared prominently among the persecutors as well as the victims. Some were first one then the other, as in the case of Genrikh Yagoda, head of the secret police from 1934 until 1936, who was arrested in 1937 and shot as a traitor a year later.

Although the proportion of Jews in leadership positions declined in the late 1930s, they were not automatically excluded by virtue of their origin. Mikhail Koltsov, a Jewish journalist who had been outspoken in his criticism of anti-Semitism, was appointed joint editor in chief of *Pravda* in December 1938 (though he too was arrested shortly afterward). In 1939, 10 percent of the membership of the central committee of the Communist Party of the Soviet Union was still Jewish. According to Sheila Fitzpatrick, who has examined the log of official visitors to Stalin's office in the 1930s, between 75 and 90 percent of these callers had Jewish names.

On the other hand, Jews suffered heavily by virtue of their disproportionate representation in the intellectual elite who were among the chief casualties of the Terror. Jews also figured largely among Stalin's foreign victims, if only because of their prominence in European Communist parties.

In France, few Jews were formal members of the Communist Party. A secret party report in 1934 estimated a total of just 700 Jewish party members in the whole of France, of whom only 250 were members of the Jewish *sous-section*.[17] A partial explanation for these unimpressive statistics is that noncitizens, among whom the Communists propagandized heavily, were legally prohibited from joining political parties. East European immigrants nevertheless enrolled in large numbers in the party's various front organizations. And the Communists were the only French political party with a specifically Jewish *sous-section*, more properly a Yiddish section, since it was not based on ethnicity but was one of a number of foreign-language sections.

A few Jews were to be found among the leadership of the French party. Charles Rappoport, born in a *shtetl* near Kovno, had grown up in a traditional Jewish environment. In his youth he wrote articles for the nascent Hebrew press. After university study in Switzerland, he moved to France, where he became a founding member of the Communist Party in 1920. He played an important part in its relations with the Comintern and in mobilizing support among Yiddish-speaking Jews in Paris. Moshe Zalcman, who met him there in the early 1930s, admired his vivacity and humor. For the young Zalcman, Rappoport, who had known Engels, Plekhanov, and Jaurès, was a grand old man of the movement and a model Communist. But in 1938 Rappoport resigned from the party in protest against the Moscow trials. His daughter, who remained faithful to Communism, repudiated him. Rappoport stuck to his decision.

The writer Jean-Richard Bloch took a different road through

Communism. Born in Paris in 1884 to an assimilated Jewish family from Alsace, he was a nephew of the distinguished Orientalist Sylvain Lévi and brother-in-law of the writer André Maurois. For Bloch, as for many others of his generation, the Dreyfus Affair was a trigger for political engagement. By 1911 his route forward was clear: "Judaism? No, Socialism!"[18] But he remained engaged with Jewish issues and his early novels grappled with themes of Jewish assimilation and alienation. Bloch joined the Communist Party in 1921 but then veered off toward a leftist, non-Communist stance. At the same time he encountered Zionism. In 1925, visiting Palestine for the founding ceremony of the Hebrew University of Jerusalem, he experienced an emotional shock: "I saw a people constitute itself—my own people," he wrote.[19] But after the anti-Jewish riots in Palestine in 1929 he shifted away from Zionism.

In 1934 he visited the Soviet Union for the first Soviet Writers' Congress. With help from his friend the writer Ilya Ehrenburg, who acted as interpreter, he addressed the gathering of Communist and fellow-traveling writers from around the world, offering a heterodox plea for pluralism and warning against "vulgar mass conceptions."[20] He was favorably impressed by what he saw of the Soviet Union. Meanwhile, the rise of the fascist "leagues" in France and the civil war in Spain, on which he reported from Madrid, cemented his adhesion to the Communist Party. With Louis Aragon he founded the Paris Communist evening paper Ce Soir in 1937. Soon after the Munich pact, he rejoined the Communist Party. Thereafter his paper's columns followed the twists and turns of policy dictated from Moscow, including the Ribbentrop-Molotov pact, until Ce Soir was banned by the government on August 25, 1939.

Perhaps the most important figure in determining French Communist Party policy in the 1930s was a foreigner, almost unknown to the public—Eugen Fried (or "Camarade Clément," one of his several "party names"). Born in Slovakia to Jewish parents, he arrived in Paris in 1931 as the Comintern's representative there. He became "Moscow's eye" in the French Communist Party in the 1930s.[21] Ana Pauker, wife of Marcel Pauker, daughter of a cantor, a former Hebrew teacher and Romanian Comintern official (in 1947 to become foreign minister of Romania), gave birth to a daughter by Fried in

1932. Fried's influence, powerful even though invisible, helped ensure that party policy conformed to the requirements of Moscow.

In 1934 the Communists, together with the Bund and the Left Poalei Zion, called for the formation in France of a Jewish Popular Front. But it rapidly deteriorated into a front for the Communist Party, since the two other parties commanded support only among little groups of east European immigrants in France. By the spring of 1936 the Jewish Popular Front had disintegrated and a year later the Jewish section of the Communist Party was quietly dismantled. About the same time, for reasons that are still debated, Stalin ordered the Polish Communist Party to disband.

Communism nonetheless retained its attraction to some Jews on grounds of its alleged internationalism (when, in fact, all Communist parties were thoroughly subservient to Moscow) and on grounds of its alleged antifascism (even when, in 1939, Stalin moved toward alignment with Hitler).

Jewish leftists were prominent among the "premature antifascists" who participated in the Spanish Civil War. Volunteers from Paris rushed to join in the defense of the endangered republic from the very outset of the conflict in July 1936. Many French, German, and Polish Jews were among the early recruits to the International Brigades a few months later. Most were Communists, for example Szaja Kinderman ("Jorge"), a Jewish tailor from Cracow, who had spent several years in prison for Communist activity in Poland and fled to Spain in 1933. He was reported to be the only subscriber in Spain to the Yiddish *Literarishe bleter*, published in Warsaw.

In December 1937 the Naftali Botwin Company was formed in Spain as part of the Polish Dombrowski brigade. Named after a Polish-Jewish Communist hero from Lwów who was executed in 1925 for killing a secret police agent, the company was said to be "the first, last, and only military unit that performed its exercises in Yiddish."[22] It published a Yiddish newssheet and one of its members broadcast a speech in Yiddish on the radio station of the republic. Not all its members, however, were Jewish and it incorporated a small minority of the Jewish volunteers in the Republican army. In 1938 it performed a ceremonial march past the Catalan government headquarters in Barcelona and the president of the Generalidad,

Luis Companys, addressed them: "This company, on whose flag
Hebrew letters are embroidered, forges a link in the golden chain
from the embattled Spanish Republic to the glorious Jewish chapter
in our history that was so brutally cut short by the Catholic Inquisition."[23] Its political commissar, Eugeniusz Szyr, had enrolled at the
age of sixteen, falsifying his passport. The company, later a battalion, saw action on several fronts but within nine months was wiped
out on the battlefield.

Jews were prominent among the foreign casualties of the war.
The last member of the International Brigades to die in the defense
of the republic was Chaskel Honigstein from Lublin. The "último
caído de las Brigadas Internacionales" was accorded a state funeral
in Barcelona in October 1938. The volunteers did not die only at
the hands of fascists. Among those murdered by Soviet agents were
Erwin Wolf, a former secretary of Leon Trotsky, and Mark Rein, son
of the Bundist-Menshevik politician Rafael Abramovich.

The Best Tunes

Established in 1897, the Bund was the first Jewish political party and
the first constituent in what became the revolutionary Social Democrat movement in the Russian Empire. As Arkady Kremer, one of
its founders, declared in a speech at its first meeting, the Bund's
ideology was based on the perception that "Jewish workers suffer
not only as workers but also as Jews" and on a desire to defend them
on both fronts simultaneously.[24] This dual purpose remained the
leitmotif of the Bund throughout its existence. Driven underground
and eventually out of existence in Soviet Russia, the Bund regrouped
elsewhere, especially in Poland. It established branches in other
European countries and in the Americas. The Brussels chapter held
meetings at the Salle Matteotti and the Maison des Huit Heures,
at which members heard lecturers such as Angelika Balabanov,
who spoke on "Fascism and the Working Class." In Amsterdam and
Vienna (until the Nazi takeover in 1938) the local sections raised
funds for the Yiddish schools in Poland. But these were more in the
nature of supporters' clubs and *landsmanshaftn*. Only in one country

did the Bund develop into a significant political force in the interwar period.

In Poland the Bund vigorously contested the ground between Communism and socialist Zionism. Against the former it formulated the slogan "proletarian dictatorship equals proletarian democracy."[25] Against the latter it denounced "dreams of a Jewish state built on sand and English guns."[26] The Bund rejected emigration to Palestine or anywhere else as a solution to the Jewish problem, insisting on *dokayt* (the here and now). The "father of Russian Marxism," Georgii Plekhanov, had once called Bundists "Zionists who are afraid of seasickness." But whereas *Gegenwartsarbeit* was a tactic for the Zionists, *dokayt* was a matter of deep principle for Bundists. "Fate has placed us here in Poland," declared one of the party's leaders, Wiktor Alter, in 1938, "and it is here in Poland that we shall fight. We are bound to our country with all that is dear to us in life."[27]

The Bund shared many of the ideas of Austrian socialists who had striven before 1918 to reconcile proletarian solidarity with the multinational composition of the Habsburg empire. There was one critical difference: the Austrian socialists, whose leadership was heavily Jewish, refused, on that very account, to recognize Jews as a nationality; the Bund insisted that, as a matter of sociopolitical reality, such recognition was vital. Rejecting integration into the Polish Socialist Party, the Bund sought cultural autonomy for the Jews in Poland, and in particular, separate schools and the right to use Yiddish in official business.

The national issue went to the very core of the Bund's self-conception. Before the First World War, Vladimir Medem, one of the party's foremost ideologists, had enunciated a doctrine of "neutrality" on the issues of collective Jewish survival or assimilation that so engaged other Jewish political movements. Later, however, he abandoned "neutralism" in favor of a more positive attitude toward Jewish national survival, while still maintaining deep hostility to Zionism. The tensions within the party between nationalism and internationalism led to constant internal debate and frequent secession of splinters either to Communism or Zionism.

The concentration of most of the Jewish proletariat in small units

of production made both labor union and party political organization an uphill struggle and hampered the ability of the Bund to
mobilize Jewish workers. On the other hand, their relative isolation
from the rest of the working class rendered the national elements in
the Bund's doctrine attractive to many Jews who might otherwise
have made common cause with non-Jews in the Polish Socialist or
Communist parties.

The Bund's strict insistence on the priority of class struggle
prevented it from cooperating easily with other Jewish parties. At
the time of its fortieth anniversary commemoration in 1937, Simon
Dubnow reproved it for its "greatest sin . . . its tendency toward
isolation."[28] But the party's hostility to what it saw as nationalist
"chauvinism" generally precluded cooperation with even the socialist
Zionists. Political realities led it to conclude a temporary pact with
Poalei Zion in elections to the Sejm in 1930. But the combined bloc
failed to win any seats. Infuriated by the Bundists' attitudes, Poalei
Zion set up its own labor unions in the 1930s. Each side blamed the
other for the lack of unity.

Even more than other Jewish parties, the Bund was wracked by
internal divisions: its left wing, about 40 percent of the membership in the 1930s, was in constant danger of being sliced off by the
Communists, while the right was closer to central or west European social democracy. In 1930, after much internal wrangling, the
Bund decided to join the Second International, the social democratic
federation of opponents of Communism. At heart, for all its revolutionary bluster, the party was deeply committed both to internal
democracy and to a peaceful, parliamentary road to socialism. But
it regarded that path as blocked by the forces of reaction that
turned Polish parliamentarism after 1926 into the façade for a quasi-
dictatorial regime.

The two best-known leaders of the Bund, Henryk Erlich and
Wiktor Alter, were social democrats, bitterly hostile to Communism. Erlich, a lawyer, orator, and editor of the party newspaper,
Folks-tsaytung, "a man who felt history in his bones,"[29] represented
the party on the Warsaw Municipal Council. Alter, the party theorist, leader of the Bundist trade unions, an eternal optimist, and
"happy warrior," was "strikingly handsome . . . the Cary Grant of

Jewish labor."[30] Both were of bourgeois origin, although the party's supporters came mainly from the urban working class in large cities such as Warsaw and Łódź.

The Bund never secured the election of a single member in the Sejm. It boycotted the election to the first (constituent) Sejm in 1919. In 1928, in its best performance in a parliamentary election in Poland, it won just one hundred thousand votes out of half a million cast for Jewish parties. Its formal membership was tiny: only twelve thousand in 1935. In the late 1930s it gained ground thanks to its resolute opposition to fascism and anti-Semitism. By 1939 it could plausibly claim, on the basis of municipal election results, to be the largest Jewish party in Poland.

Like most Jewish political parties, the Bund was something more: a social-cultural movement that served as a secular religion for its adherents. Its network of affiliated institutions—labor unions, schools, women's groups, newspapers, the Morgnshtern sports club, the SKIF children's organization, and the Kultur-Lige cultural organization and publishing house—together constituted a miniature society that shaped its members' working and recreational lives and their values and aspirations. The party anthem, "Di Shvue" ("The Oath"), with words by S. An-sky (Shloyme Zaynvl Rapoport), was a "Marseillaise"-like call to arms with its chorus:

Himl un erd vet unz oyshern,
  Heaven and earth will hear us.
Eydes veln zeyn di likhtike shtern
  The stars will bear witness,
A shvue fun blut un a shvue fun trern—
  An oath of blood and an oath of tears
Mir shvern, mir shvern, mir shvern!
  We swear, we swear, we swear![31]

Whatever might be its failings in other spheres, the Bund could at least claim to have the best tunes in Jewish politics.

During the early 1930s, when the Comintern decreed that social democracy was "social fascism," conflict between Communists and Bundists in Poland degenerated into name-calling, brawls, affrays, and at least one political murder—of a young Warsaw Bundist by Communist gunmen. The switch to a popular front strategy in 1935 by Communists everywhere, on orders from Moscow, did not improve relations. The Bund rejected the idea of a popular front in Poland. "We do not change our convictions like gloves," wrote Erlich in the *Folks-tsaytung*.[32] The popular front might be suitable for France, Erlich argued, but not for Poland. In the later years of the decade, shocked by the Moscow trials and Stalinist repression, of which many former Bundists were victims, the Bund became even more anti-Communist.

The three main forces in Polish-Jewish politics, the Aguda with other orthodox elements, the Zionists of various hues, and the left (Communists, Bund, and Left Poalei Zion), each commanded a base support of around a quarter of the Jewish population. The remainder fluctuated in their views or supported minor groups. Three of the latter, although much smaller, represented significant currents of opinion in Jewish society both in Poland and elsewhere.

Folkists

Simon Dubnow, the leading Jewish historian of the age, was the foremost exponent in his time of diaspora nationalism, for which he founded a political vehicle, the Yidishe Folkspartey (Jewish People's Party), in the Russian Empire in 1906. A liberal, latter-day *maskil* (enlightened thinker), he propagated the concept of a worldwide Jewish *Kulturgemeinschaft* (cultural community). Dubnow shared the Zionists' organic conception of Jewish peoplehood but regarded the idea of a Jewish state as utopian. While rejecting the Marxism of the Bund, he shared its idealization of the Jewish masses and of the Yiddish language as the natural expression of the folk soul.

During the First World War the Folkist party was reborn in Poland and came to play a minor part in interwar politics. Like the Bund, the Folkists were influenced by the Austro-Marxists' conception of national-personal autonomy within the multinational Habsburg dominions. The Folkist program demanded national autonomy for Jews, a separate Yiddish educational system, and equal rights for Yiddish in public administration and the courts. Unlike the Bundists, who insisted on the class basis of politics, the Folkists emphasized *klal yisroel* (all-Jewish unity).

The Folkists' leader, Noyekh Prytucki, represented the party in the Warsaw Municipal Council and in the Sejm. An intellectual who made significant contributions to Yiddish linguistics, he wrote dramatic criticism, political tracts, and erotic poetry, collected Yiddish folksongs, and edited *Der moment*, one of the main Yiddish dailies in Warsaw. Dr. Tsemakh Szabad, the party's leader in Vilna, where he presided over the Jewish community, won election to the city council and, in 1928, to the senate of the Polish Republic. Thanks to such figures, the Folkists exerted a broad influence even though electorally they never managed to move beyond their narrow base of mainly middle-class, Yiddishist intellectuals.

Freeland

Somewhere out on a limb beyond the Zionists stood the territorialists. They shared the Zionists' recognition that the prospects for successful integration of Jews in eastern Europe were bleak. They also agreed that what was required was the concentration of Jews in a cohesive settlement where they could form a majority and therefore command their own destiny. But they regarded the Zionists as blindly sentimental in their insistence that Palestine must be the focus of Jewish state building.

Territorialism traced its origins back to efforts such as those of the millionaire philanthropist Baron Maurice de Hirsch around the turn of the century to settle Jews in Argentina. The territorialist idea had taken political form in 1905 following the Zionist Congress's rejection of a British government proposal for Jewish settlement in East Africa (the so-called Uganda project). At that time the Anglo-Jewish writer Israel Zangwill split away from the Zionist Organization and formed the Jewish Territorial Organization with the object of seeking opportunities for Jewish settlement under British auspices in some territory outside Europe. So long as Palestine remained subject to Ottoman rule, the territorialists could justify their position by pointing to the resistance of the Turkish imperial authorities to anything that smacked of Jewish self-government there.

In the 1920s, however, during the early years of the British mandate in Palestine, when the imperial power's support for the Jewish National Home seemed firm, the territorialist idea lost much of its allure. As Jacob Lestchinsky, who was sympathetic to their cause, pointed out, the territorialists were caught in a double bind: they could never be taken seriously by governments that might perhaps offer them a tract of land for settlement unless they formed a mass movement; but it was difficult for them to gain mass support so long as no country was willing to offer them such a territory.[33] After 1936, Arab opposition to Zionism, manifested in a three-year-long countrywide revolt, led the British to restrict Jewish immigration to Palestine and eventually reverse the Balfour Declaration policy. Against that background, territorialist ideas once again became attractive to European Jews.

The territorialists' leader in the 1930s, Dr. Isaac Steinberg, was a former Socialist Revolutionary in Russia, who had served as commissar of justice in Lenin's short-lived coalition government from December 1917 to March 1918. He resigned in protest against the Treaty of Brest-Litovsk and left Russia in 1922. An outstanding orator, who unusually combined revolutionary socialism with orthodox Jewish observance, Steinberg was described in later life as having a "thick, short body," a "black beard bristling from a pale, fine-grained face," and "quizzing eyes beneath that broad dome of forehead." He "talked with great passion, laughed explosively," and "gave way to abrupt splurges of anger if his ideas were challenged."[34]

In 1934 Steinberg established the Freeland League for Territorialist Colonization, based in London. Freeland was a little more than a one-man band but a lot less than a genuinely popular movement. It boasted branches in several countries as well as two youth associations in Poland, Shparber ("Hawk") and YUF (an acronym for "Young Freeland").

A wealthy sympathizer funded an agricultural training farm near Vilna. Territorialism, like Zionism, Bundism, and Communism—and Judaism—could inspire energy and faith in its adherents. The trainees at the farm included not only youths ("sparrows") but some older men, such as Gershon Malakiewicz, a porter, former Socialist Revolutionary, and editor of the Yiddish socialist magazine *Baginen* (Dawn). His friend the Vilna Yiddish journalist Hirsz Abramowicz, also a Freeland supporter, later recalled that Malakiewicz

> was always so poorly dressed that he could almost be taken for a beggar. He was half-blind and wore dark glasses (one eye had been wounded by Cossacks during an anti-Tsarist demonstration), but when he was in a field or meadow his face shone with pleasure. . . . I remember a bright autumn day in the middle of Sukkot [the feast of Tabernacles] in 1938, when a group of us visited the farm . . . Gershon was busy with the cows. He cleaned the stable, then went to dig up potatoes in the field . . . [He] seemed to be happier than anyone else. He had found his purpose in life at last.[35]

But whereas the Zionists, on their more numerous training farms, prepared their adherents for *aliya* (literally "ascent") to Palestine, Freeland could offer only the dim prospect of emigration to . . . somewhere.

Freeland did not contest elections but, thanks to the vivid personality and itinerant diplomacy of Steinberg, it was taken semiseriously as a player in Jewish political life. As pressure from refugees in central and eastern Europe intensified in the late 1930s, the territorialist message chimed with the thinking of a small segment of Jewish opinion and even of governments.

Shedding Encumbrances

"Assimilation" was a loaded word in Jewish polemics and remains so in Jewish history—so much so, indeed, that some historians abstain altogether from using it. If applied mechanically as referring to a uniform and one-way process, it can be seriously misleading. But the word was part of the vocabulary of Jewish controversy at the time and to avoid it altogether is to ignore an important dimension in

Jewish social development and self-understanding in an age of rapid transition.

Throughout Europe, many members of the Jewish middle class in the nineteenth and early twentieth centuries embraced the idea of assimilation to the surrounding society and culture as a positive value. They might well retain a fondness for certain Jewish customs, rituals, foods, or ideals. But while adopting the philosophy of the open society, in which many of them had advanced or hoped to advance on a meritocratic basis, they felt a duty to shed what they regarded as exclusivist encumbrances that might stand as barriers between them and their fellow citizens.

In eastern Europe most assimilationists were liberals who hoped to apply there the west European model of civic integration of Jews as individual members of a religious minority within the nation-state. They therefore wished to reform religious practice, adopt the national language, and temper social differences between Jews and non-Jews. Their emphasis on loyalty to the state and on religious reform often led to accusations that they were renegades, ashamed of their origins. But this was by no means always so. A more sympathetic approach is to see them as "integrationists" (to use a term proposed by Ezra Mendelsohn).

The assimilationists, for the most part, were not organized in a distinct political party, save in some local communal elections. But they included the wealthiest and most powerful elements in Jewish communities almost everywhere. Moreover, they found some common ground with otherwise far-removed sectors of society. For example, they shared with the Agudists an insistence on a religious rather than ethnic definition of Jewishness and with both the Agudah and the far left a rooted opposition to Zionism, indeed to any form of Jewish nationalism.

"Knocking Off Inconvenient Individuals"

Jewish politics, particularly in Poland, where it reached its fullest development, was far from decorous. Debate within and between parties was no-holds-barred, rough-and-tumble. Personal rivalries were often vicious. There was little room for give-and-take.

Venomous antagonisms between members of different political parties led not infrequently to violence. The youth movements of several parties, among them the Revisionist Zionists and the Bund, organized uniformed militias that did not scruple to use force against their opponents. In 1923, when Zionists in Poland celebrated the inauguration of the Hebrew University (Albert Einstein had just delivered its first public lecture in Jerusalem), Communists received instructions from above to disrupt the proceedings. But Moshe Zalcman, who was among the disrupters, ruefully complained, "there were just a handful of us confronting an ecstatic crowd of young people and adults; we emerged from the fight physically and morally bruised; although we had obeyed the orders of our chiefs, we could not understand why we had to oppose a Jewish school or university."[36]

In 1930 the Bundist *Naye folks-tsaytung* reported that Communists had "pogromized" (*hobn pogromirt*—a very provocative expression) the Mikhalovitch School (under the wing of the TSYSHO Yiddish school system, affiliated to the Bund) at Mila 51 in Warsaw. Paving stones were thrown at windows. Doors were torn out and there was a "murderous attack on a teacher."[37] This was only one of several incidents, which included the invasion by Communists in 1933 of the Bundist-sponsored Medem children's sanatorium, near Warsaw. Such episodes rent the Jewish left into warring factions.

The rise of the Popular Front in France led the Communists to halt attacks on socialists and Bundists and to attenuate their antireligious propaganda. At a funeral of one young Communist militant, it was reported, the late comrade had been honored by renditions of both the kaddish (the prayer for the dead) and the "Internationale."[38]

For all the mutual elbow-jabbing and recriminations, the large number of political parties necessitated coalition-building, which often led to incongruous alliances. In elections for communal rabbis in Poland, for example, the Mizrachi might join with secular Zionists and hasidic groups in order to block Agudist candidates. The latter were not above seeking, when it suited them, the removal from electoral lists of antireligious Jews who openly denied the faith. In such expedients they sometimes enjoyed clandestine government encouragement. A "strictly secret" circular to provincial authorities, issued by the Polish Ministry of Interior in 1936, suggested

that while "mass application" of a regulation permitting the exclusion from voting in *kehillah* elections of "persons who publicly come
out against the Mosaic faith" "would not be a clever move," the
clause might be utilized for "knocking off certain inconvenient . . .
individuals."[39]

The multifarious complexity of their politics in the interwar period
reflected the rapidly shifting and polymorphous social structure of
the European Jews. As their traditional society was shaken, they
sought new bearings and grasped hold of the nearest available bul-
warks of security. Their disorientation was accentuated by rapid
urbanization and the end of an archetypal way of life that had long
been associated with their residence in small country towns, particularly in eastern Europe.

4

FROM *SHTETL* TO *SHTOT*

A People in Motion

In the early twentieth century, Jews were already the most urbanized people in Europe, but in the course of the interwar period they became even more so. They also became the most metropolitanized, as they concentrated not merely in urban areas but ever more densely in the capitals and largest cities of each country: Moscow, Leningrad, Warsaw, Budapest, Bucharest, Paris, and until the Nazis began to push them out, Vienna and Berlin.

The successive catastrophes between 1914 and 1921 of the First World War, the Russian Civil War, and the Russo-Polish War had led to the deaths of vast numbers of Jews from battle, pogroms, and disease in the area of the former Russian Empire. The disasters had also dealt something close to a death blow to the traditional Jewish way of life in the region. During the war, entire populations of Jews in *shtetlakh* of the Pale and Austrian Galicia fled their homes for fear of the depredations of undisciplined armies. At the conclusion of hostilities many, having settled elsewhere, decided not to return. Altogether, death and emigration resulted in Jewish population loss in the former Pale of Settlement of as much as six hundred thousand.[1]

Jewish migration out of small towns and villages was visible all across the continent. In Germany, especially Bavaria, Baden, Hesse, and Würtemberg, Jews were leaving rural areas and concentrating in Berlin and other big cities. Largely in consequence, the number of Jewish communities in Germany declined from 2,359 in 1899 to 1,611 by 1932.

A similar process was in train in France. The small towns of Alsace, in particular, had once held many flourishing small communities. In Herrlisheim (Bas-Rhin), where Jews, like gentiles, wore wooden sabots, the number of Jewish inhabitants declined from 202 in 1890 to 80 by 1936. Such communities were on the verge of disappearance. A contemporary observer lamented: "The great human reservoir of Alsatian Jewry, the countryside, is exhausted; there remain there, above all, old people waiting to die, caretakers of the beautiful synagogues that were once filled with the vibrancy of youth."[2]

The village Jews of Lithuania—pedlars, estate managers (*arendarn*), innkeepers, millers, blacksmiths, tinsmiths, shoemakers, lime and pitch burners, wheelwrights, carpenters, and lumbermen—had begun in the 1890s to move in large numbers to cities such as Vilna or Kovno or overseas, particularly to South Africa. "By the time World War II broke out," we are told, "the Jewish villager was virtually extinct in Lithuania."[3]

In the USSR and interwar Poland, movement out of *shtetlakh* attained large dimensions. In the period 1917–27 a million Jews, particularly young people, left Soviet *shtetlakh* for the big city. The exodus continued over the next decade. The proportion of Soviet Jews living beyond the former Pale rose from 32 percent in 1926 to 43 percent in 1939. The number of Jewish residents in Moscow rose from 28,000 in 1920 to 250,000 by 1939 and of Leningrad from 52,000 in 1923 to 202,000 by 1939. At least 87 percent of Jews in the USSR now lived in urban areas. More than a third lived in five cities: Kiev, Odessa, Kharkov, Moscow, and Leningrad. Just 442,000 Soviet Jews still lived in *shtetlakh*.[4] This was a colossal migration that exceeded even the great flight from the Tsarist dominions that had transformed the American Jewish community in the years between 1881 and 1914.[5]

One reason for this movement was the desire of those labeled *lishentsy*, or threatened with being so labeled, to escape into the relative anonymity of urban life. There they stood less chance of being compromised by disclosure of embarrassingly "bourgeois" origins, though "bourgeois" in such cases might have involved no more than peddling, petty trading, or ownership of a small workshop. As a result of the "passportization" of the Soviet population in 1932, however, when all citizens were required to carry identity documents, unauthorized internal migration slowed down and, with it, the pace of Jewish movement out of the former Pale.

What was achieved by a planned system in the USSR was replicated, if more slowly, in a free-market one. In Poland too, *shtetlakh* thinned out as Jews moved to cities. Although the *shtetl* survived in a diminished form in Poland, the Soviet Union, and a few other parts of eastern Europe, it was no longer the model Ashkenazi Jewish settlement. Instead it came to seem a static, outmoded relic of a bygone age.

Why did the Jews leave and what exactly were they leaving?

The Living Dead

The *shtetl* is easier to describe than define. It had no fixed size, save that it was smaller than a city (*shtot*) and larger than a village (*dorf*) or a hamlet (*yishuv*). The *shtetl* had a characteristic social geography, centered on the *rynek* (town square). This was the site of the weekly market, a manifestation of the *shtetl*'s essential function as the hub of the rural economy in eastern Europe. Nearby would be the main synagogue and the Jewish bathhouse. Jews lived mainly in houses around the square, in which they often kept stores or taverns. The better-off built their houses of brick, occasionally of more than one storey. Most homes, however, were primitive, single-storey wooden structures, grouped hugger-mugger in unpaved lanes near the square. Fires were frequent. Many towns had all-Jewish volunteer fire brigades, but in the absence of piped water supplies, their capabilities were limited. Often whole towns burned down, sometimes several times.

Every *shtetl* had its cast of characteristic types, including the rabbi, the *magid* (itinerant preacher), and the *melamed* (elementary Hebrew school teacher, generally despised as good for nothing better). Often functions were combined: the *hazan* (cantor) might act as *shohet* (meat slaughterer) and sometimes additionally as *mohel* (circumciser). The *shames* (synagogue beadle), another lowly figure, was often also responsible for looking after the *besmedresh* (religious study hall) and bathhouse. The *shul-klaper* would go round the town on Friday before dark with a big stick, hammering three times on each doorpost to indicate that the time for the lighting of Sabbath candles was imminent.

The *badkhn* was a jester and master of entertainments at weddings. In his role as comedic master of ceremonies, he offered improvisational humorous advice to the bride and groom. Traditionally the first line was "Weep, bride, weep!" An ancient Jewish institution, the *badkhn* is mentioned in the Babylonian Talmud (Ta'an 22a). Later *badkhones* developed a satirical edge and sometimes great dramatic intensity. Although fading away by the 1930s, the *badkhn* could still be found performing at marriages in country places. The visiting card of Jacob Zismor of Vilna, one of the last of the *badkhonim*, advertised his availability for "concerts, weddings, barmitzvahs, and all kinds of entertainments, with music or without, always at moderate prices."[6]

The *shrayber* (scribe) would go from place to place acting as a letter writer and teaching children, especially those girls who did not attend a *heder* (elementary Hebrew school), to write in Hebrew and Latin or Russian scripts. The Yiddish writer Sholem Asch was such a letter writer in his youth in Włocławek (Russian Poland) in the 1890s. In order to supplement their meager incomes, any or all of these figures might also run a small business on the side.

The *shtetl* was a location as much in the imagination as in the real world. In the paintings of Marc Chagall it seemed poised almost halfway behind heaven and earth, its inhabitants floating off into the clouds. "The '*shtetl*,' " it has been written, "is always a synthesis of facts, memory, and imagination."[7] Drawing in varying quantities on ingredients of nostalgia, idealization, mythification, and repulsion, Yiddish writers from Shalom Aleichem to Sholem Asch depicted the *shtetl*, depending on their ideological stance, as the hearth of traditional virtues or a nest of reactionary vices, as "a little Jerusalem," an almost timeless, paradisiacal home ground in which the Jew communed intimately with his Lord, or as a stagnant repository of ignorance, filth, and backwardness. The literary historian Mikhail Krutikov notes that while realism was the dominant literary style in interwar Yiddish literature, "yet, when it came to depicting the shtetl, the clarity and confidence of realistic representation would often be blurred by sentimentalist nostalgia or disfigured by expressionist fragmentation."[8]

Shmuel Yosef Agnon's Hebrew story "Oreah natah lalun" (A Guest for the Night), based on his return visit in 1930 to his birthplace, Buczacz, in eastern Galicia, famously visualized a town of the living dead. Around the same time Isaac Babel, writing in Russian, described the departure for Moscow of a recently bereaved widow from a Soviet *shtetl*. Her son, who has arrived from Moscow too late for his father's funeral, roams around his birthplace at night: "His native *shtetl* was dying. The clock of the centuries chimed the end of its defenceless life. 'Is this the end, or is it a rebirth?' Boris asked himself." Like Agnon, Babel viewed the decline of the *shtetl* with an ambivalent mixture of sadness and resigned submission to what seemed inevitable social forces. "He walked past the ruins, past the squat, crooked, sleeping houses, a hazy stench of poverty seeping out of their gates, and bade them farewell."[9]

Such depictions were not restricted to fiction. A letter written in 1933 by a poverty-stricken Jew in Łódź, Wolf Lewkowicz, records how, out of desperation, he momentarily considered moving to the nearby small town of Opoczno: "But what will I do in Opoczno when 95% of the people are poor, naked and barefoot? The town looks like a cemetery; the people resemble corpses; the houses look like tombstones. What will I do there? After all, Łódź is a city with a population of 600,000, with factories, and I am not able to find work."[10]

A visitor to Ostrog in Volhynia (in eastern Poland) in 1937 reported on his impressions. Jews had lived there since the fifteenth century and constituted more than half the population. The town had a rich Jewish history and had been the home of famous rabbis, Hebrew printing presses, and *yeshivot*. In the interwar period, Ostrog's location close to the Soviet border hastened its economic decline. The writer reported that shops were shuttered, Jewish inhabitants were "hungry and pale shadows," and "grown-up girls [were] walking without shoes and gowns for they have none." "Ostrog," he wrote, "is perishing."[11] Such descriptions undoubtedly reflect one facet of reality.

The average Polish *shtetl* in the 1930s, however, was far from the sleepy, one-horse town portrayed by these writers. The *shtetl* might be in retreat, economically and demographically, but it did not lie down and die. Local Yiddish newspapers in dozens of such towns record the intense associational life, fierce controversies, festivities, amateur theatricals, lectures, and sports events. At the spring festival of Lag Ba'Omer, the fire brigade band would lead a march through the town. On May Day the Bund would hold its own parade and demonstration. Many medium-sized and larger *shtetlakh* boasted a movie theater that would show Yiddish, Polish, and American films. Thus was inserted into each of these towns a powerful telescope into the starry, secular heaven being conjured up by children of the *shtetl* in faraway Hollywood.

Around half of all Polish Jews in the 1930s still lived in *shtetlakh*. The Jews would typically constitute a quarter to half the inhabitants, but since they mainly lived near the center of the town and owned most of the shops and inns, they tended to imprint a Jewish character on the *shtetl*. For example, a socioeconomic survey of Probuzhana, a small town in the Tarnopol district of southeast Poland with a population in the early 1930s of 3,550, of whom one-third were Jews, reported, in passing: "We may also remark here that when we speak of the commercial structure of the Jewish community we mean the commercial structure of the entire town, since there is only one Christian business establishment in town. This is a stationery store in the Public Library." Jews also formed the great majority of skilled workers in Probuzhana. But the report pointed to severe economic distress. A large category of persons in the town was "the group of families who have no occupation at all. This group includes 44 families or 14.4% of the total Jewish population. Of this number, 10 are beggars."[12]

A visitor in the mid-1920s to another *shtetl*, Wysoki Dwór, near the border of Poland and Lithuania, noted:

> Little attention was paid to the rules of hygiene. Only about 60 per cent of the women made use of the *mikvah* [ritual bath]. Both the *mikvah* and the bathhouse were very seldom cleaned. The water in the *mikvah* was changed infrequently and gave off a foul odour. . . .

Religious spirit did not appear particularly strong in the town. It was more a matter of tradition than religion. . . . About 35 per cent of the male population prayed every day. . . . On the Sabbath, however, everyone attended without exception, although not a Sabbath went by without some controversy in the synagogue. : . .

In this provincial atmosphere any tendency towards left-wing politics evaporated. This could be seen in the young married men. On the Sabbath, even those of them who were Bundists went dutifully to the synagogue with their prayer-shawl bags.

This town too was desperately poor. Of its 65 Jewish families, 55 received money or other help from abroad. Modernity was nonetheless making some inroads: "Wysoki Dwór," we are told, "had fallen under the influence of the outside world and was obsessed with soccer." Moreover, "recently, the younger men could be seen going bareheaded outdoors."[13]

As Samuel Kassow has pointed out, the *shtetl*, bathed in a warm nostalgic glow in the collective Jewish memory, could be a harsh, unforgiving place, especially for those on the lowest social rungs: shoemakers, water carriers, or unmarried girls from poor families.[14] In the rainy season it was muddy, in the dry season dusty and smelly, and throughout the year filthy, at any rate by contemporary bourgeois standards.

The small scale and intimate nature of social relations did not preclude class distinctions. If anything, it magnified them. "In our town [Gliniany], there was more democracy but in Premishlan [Peremishliany] they had castes like that. A tailor didn't talk to a shoemaker, a shoemaker didn't talk to a bathhouse attendant, a bathhouse attendant didn't talk to a carpenter."[15] The stock exchange of local opinion, fed by malicious gossip, could be merciless in its scolding of deviants and of those who committed minor peccadilloes. Cruel nicknames, highlighting personal defects, were common. One woman, recalling her *shtetl* in the 1930s, mentions such names as "Faivel cold sore," "Eli big belly," "Meishl Pick the stutterer," "Crutch the one-legged tailor," and "Yosl Latrine (smelliest man in town)."[16] In Opoczno, a resident wrote to his nephew in Chicago: "Here . . . can be found a Shmiel Pipil (belly button) . . .

Meyer Petzke (small penis), Yisroel Sralash (defecator). . . . It's simply terrible to live in a town where everyone has a nickname."[17]

The fragile economy of the Jewish poor in the *shtetl* was to some degree buttressed by aid from America and western Europe. This came from the Joint, from ORT, and from *landsmanshaftn*, as well as from individuals who helped support their relatives. Loan societies were a traditional feature of Jewish life throughout east-central Europe. They were revivified in the interwar period by the decision of the Joint to support existing or new *gmiles khesed kassas* (cooperative loan funds) in Poland, Lithuania, and Romania. The Joint insisted, however, that half the capital for each fund must come from the town itself. Some were small, local mutual aid societies; others developed into full-fledged cooperative banks. By the mid-1930s there were more than eight hundred *kassas* in Poland alone. The *kassas* helped tide small businesses and families over rough patches. As a report in 1936 put it, the non-interest-bearing loans provided by these funds were, for many, "practically the last escape from complete destitution."[18]

Even in the traditional environment of the *shtetl*, the hold of orthodox religion was beginning to fray in interwar Poland. While Jewish shops would remain closed, Sabbath observance was no longer universal. In April 1936 the local Yiddish weekly newspaper of Baranowicze, in Polish Byelorussia, announced the performance in the hall of the Apollo movie theater on the first day of Passover, of a play by Sholem Asch, starring the celebrated Yiddish actor Maurice Schwartz. On later days of the festival, the paper advertised "dancing-tambola" and other events similarly out of keeping with strict observance of the holiday. In July of the same year, the paper announced appearances "today, Friday, and tomorrow, *shabbes*," by a visiting theatrical troupe who would perform the "Di umgezetslekhe froy" (The Illegal Wife), billed as "a sensational picture of life in three acts."[19] That such spectacles could not merely be staged on a major festival and the Sabbath but find an audience (the performances were sellouts) in a town with a reputation for orthodoxy and with two large *yeshivot* and the courts of two hasidic *rebbes* is an indication of the profound change in mores. Nor was Baranowicze in this respect exceptional.

The decline of religious observance in the *shtetl* was also registered in other ways. In 1934 a letter in the local Yiddish weekly in

Wołkowysk, a little to the west of Baranowicze, lamented the "spiritual decline" that led the local Maccabi organization to hold football matches on the Sabbath. Yet the correspondent was clearly in a minority, since he complained that community leaders seemed not to take the matter very seriously, regarding it as akin to the venial offense of not washing hands before saying the grace after meals, rather than recognizing it as a cardinal sin, akin to "eating carrion and *treyf* [nonkosher food] on Yom Kippur." [20]

In the Soviet Union the *shtetl* was seen as primitive and socially backward, a "malignant tumour on the body of the young, weak Soviet country." [21] Like the Zionists, the Soviets wanted to productivize the *shtetl* Jews and wean them away from what were seen as parasitic occupations. Young, small-town Jews, lacking a future in the trades that had sustained the previous generation, saw their salvation in the cities, and moved away to colleges, government jobs, or factory work. The *shtetlakh* were now disproportionately inhabited by old people, although the Byelorussian and Ukrainian authorities tried in the 1930s to encourage the creation of cooperatives of craftsmen as a way of providing some economic rationale for the continued existence of the *shtetl*.

Unable, after the termination of the New Economic Policy, to continue to trade as pedlars or shopkeepers, Jews who remained in the Soviet *shtetl* concentrated in the traditional craft occupations of Russian Jews: as tailors, furriers, smiths of tin, copper, or gold, watchmakers, hatters, and bookbinders. Or, in increasing numbers, they packed the tools of their trade together with their miserable household goods and joined their brethren in the exodus to their promised land—the big city. The Soviet Yiddish poet Dovid Hofshteyn recorded its dangerous lure:

Shtot!
> City!
Du host mir fun vaytn gerufn
> You called me from afar.

. . .

. . .
Du host mir fun vaytn getsoygn
> You drew me from afar

mit tsvangen
> With forceps
fun shayn un fun shimer.
> Of gleam and gloss.
Du host mikh farnart
> You seduced me,
un du host mikh gefangen![22]
> You captured me!

Captivated by the big city, the Jews would not return, save in their imaginations, to the *shtetl*.

Rus in Urbe

Much changed on arrival in the city. Traditional garb gave way to modern dress. Except among the older generation and the strictly orthodox, the long black *kapote* (gaberdine coat) was replaced by worker's clothing, indistinguishable from that of gentiles. Whereas most Jewish males in the *shtetl* still wore some form of head covering at all times, only the orthodox did so in the city. Even many Hasidim tended to restrict wearing of the *shtreimel* (fur-trimmed hat) to the Sabbath, though they would, of course, wear a *yarmulke* (skullcap) at other times.

The orthodox held on determinedly to the old ways, fearful of the corrupting influences of the big city "with its attendant phenomena that have torn away our young people from their roots and turned them into 'people of the twentieth century' . . . who allow their lowest instincts to dominate them, and who throw away their few years of youth on the momentary gleam of over-extended 'pleasure' "—as an Agudist publication in Antwerp editorialized in 1936. They therefore erected "defensive walls against the engulfing tides of social life."[23] But increasingly their communities came to be little island *shtetlakh* in a spreading urban ocean of modernization and secularization.

The majority of immigrants from the *shtetl* to the city did not immediately transform all their social and cultural habits and conventions. Where there seemed no pressing need to change, they retained many of the attitudes, customs, and institutions of their places of origin.

Although they might become less punctilious about the minutiae of *kashrut*, most east European Jews still favored the traditional dishes: chicken soup with *lokshen* (noodles) or *kneydlach* (dumplings), *gefilte fish*, *kreplach* (pasta dough triangles, filled with ground meat), *varnitshkes* (dumplings filled with cheese or jam), *tsimmes* (sweet casserole), *knishes* (flat potato dumplings covered in dough), *blintzes* (pancakes), chopped liver, herring, salt beef, and pickled cucumbers, *challah* (braided white bread, eaten on the Sabbath), as well as special holiday dishes such as *latkes* (potato pancakes for Hanukah), *hamentashen* (on Purim), and various *matzah*-based foods on Passover. Above all, even nonreligious Jews tended to avoid pig meat.

The volume of the influx to cities in the interwar period was such that many of them were no less Jewish than the *shtetlakh* the Jews had left. In Warsaw, Lwów, and Kiev, Jews constituted a third of the population. In Białystok and Grodno, they formed close to an absolute majority. The immigrants tended to concentrate in those areas of the cities where Jews already formed a large proportion of the population. In Warsaw, Jews were concentrated in the Muranów district, which was 91 percent Jewish in 1939, as well as in other white- and blue-collar areas in the center and west of the city. As a result, according to Mordechai Altshuler, "the assimilationist impact of the metropolis on the Jews . . . was less pronounced than in the large cities outside the Pale. Thus the *shetl* continued to exert an influence on the Jews of these cities."[24]

Nearly every city in east-central Europe had its Jewish quarter, generally near the center of town. In Tomaszów Mazowiecki, an industrial town in central Poland, the main street in the heart of the Jewish quarter had 625 inhabitants, of whom 565 were Jews. Here were Jewish institutions, synagogues, and shops. Here too was the Odeon cinema, owned by Adolf Bernstein, which catered to a general audience but often showed films of Jewish interest, for example one on the opening ceremony of the Hebrew University in 1925. Nearby was the bathhouse (eighteen tubs, a steam bath, and five showers: nine thousand customers each year). Part of the reason for such concentration was a feeling of greater security. In the Karpathy neighborhood of Tomaszów Mazowiecki, where Jews were a small minority, local hooligans "looked after their own" Jews (that is, those from the district) but were said to threaten those they did not know. Jews moved out of the area when they could.[25]

The teeming street life of the Jewish districts imported the sounds, images, and smells of the *shtetl* marketplace into the heart of the city. The Yiddish novelist Isaac Bashevis Singer later recalled Krochmalna Street in the Jewish area of Warsaw, where he spent his childhood years: "Women still peddled handkerchiefs, needles, pins, buttons, and yard goods of calico, linen—even remnants of velvet and silk. . . . The nostrils were assailed by the familiar odour of soap, oil, and horse manure."[26] Another observer noted how street sellers there would call out the merits of their wares in Yiddish: "Oylem, oylem ests bikhinem, ests bekhinem! Fir beygl a tsenerl, fir tsenerl! fir tsenerl!" ("Everybody! Everybody! Eat for free! Eat for free! Four bagels for ten groszy!")[27]

Housing and health conditions in the immigrant areas were generally grim. The Jewish working class in the cities of central and eastern Europe lived, for the most part, in overcrowded, insanitary slums. Conditions for the urban poor in Warsaw may be gauged from a survey of applicants for places in the Medem children's sanatorium in the mid-1930s. More than 80 percent of the children who applied lived in homes with a density of more than five persons to a room. In one case four families, twenty-four persons, were living in one cellar.[28]

Among the surviving application forms for 1936 is that of Nachme Rozenman. Aged fifteen, Nachme lived in a barely furnished basement with six others. One of his siblings had died of "lung disease," from which he too had suffered. His father, a tailor, stitched together clothes that his mother sold in the street. She was illiterate. Nachme had spent only four years in school and had started working with his father at the age of ten. The sanatorium noted that he was dirty, stubborn, and angry but also timid, gloomy, lazy, and apathetic. He quarreled with his sisters and cried a lot.

Another application was from Moshe Kotlorski, aged fourteen. His father had left home before he was born. Moshe did not speak until he was nine years old. His mother died when he was twelve.

Since his mother's death, his father had begun to interest himself in Moshe and from time to time sent him small sums of money. The previous year Moshe had suffered from typhus. He worked as a cobbler and lived in one room with his aunt, her seven children, and two lodgers.[29]

The east-European Jewish immigrant community in Paris in the 1930s, some 90,000 out of a total Jewish population of 150,000, was still heavily concentrated in certain districts in the heart of the city, in particular the Pletzl (the Marais) and Belleville. When Moshe Zalcman arrived there from Poland in 1929, he had the impression of being back in the Jewish quarter of Warsaw: "the same small shops, the same simple restaurants, the same tumult. My heart beat faster on recognizing my native language. From a shop door emerged the sad melodies of popular Yiddish songs."[30]

Some of the immigrants to Paris were pedlars, shopkeepers, or craftsmen but the majority worked in the clothing industry and were employed in small workshops. Others were semi-independent *façonniers* or fully independent *ouvriers à domicile*, often drawing on family members for supplementary labor. Most lived on the edge of penury. Many had arrived quite recently from Poland after the United States imposed severe restrictions on immigration in 1924.

They had not received a warm welcome from the established French-Jewish community, from which, as a result, they felt deeply alienated. Mutual resentment was heightened by political division: in general, the immigrants were left-wing, whereas the more bourgeois, French-born Jews tended to the political center, particularly the Radical Party, or even the moderate right. In religious practice too there were differences: the observant among the immigrants hewed to more traditional forms of practice, often worshipping in small *shtiblakh*. They found the solemn ceremonials of the synagogues under the control of the Consistoire de Paris, such as the grand temple in the rue de la Victoire, austere, cold, and, for all their surface orthodoxy, somehow un-Jewish. The *haute bourgeoisie*, for the most part, adhered only superficially to traditional practice. On high holy days, we are told, "the doors to the rue de la Victoire synagogue were blocked . . . by the chauffeurs of wealthy congregants who stood around smoking cigarettes and talking."[31]

The immigrants were much more likely than the natives to be closely involved with Jewish institutions. They formed networks of *landsmanshaftn* and mutual aid societies, some of which were bound together in the Fédération des Sociétés Juives de France. The Fédération, which was mainly Zionist in orientation, and its Communist rival, the Union des Sociétés Juives de France, ran Yiddish libraries as well as night classes, youth clubs, and sports groups. In the late 1930s, inspired by the Popular Front, left-wingers formed organizations such as the Parizer Yidisher Arbeter-Teater (PYAT), which sought to represent onstage the needs of the Jewish masses, "the tragedy of their lack of rights, protests against oppressors, and their struggle for bread, justice and freedom."[32]

Jews did not just concentrate in particular districts of cities. They also tended to frequent specific cafés, clubs, and resorts: in Munkács, the Csillag, next to the Tündérkertje ("Wonder Garden"); in Cracow, Szmatka Kawiarnia; in Prague, the Jugendstil-designed Slavia, both the latter favored haunts of the intelligentsia. The café was a gathering place for literary coteries, a rendezvous for lovers, a place to play cards, to read the paper, to argue about politics, to observe and display. In larger cities each profession would have its own gathering place. The regular (generally male) would have his *Stammtisch*, where he would take refreshment at the appointed hour every day. Sometimes a group would reserve such a table, as at the Europa in Czernowitz, where Hebrew speakers would gather in a special corner. Back rooms would often be rented for political meetings.

In Paris each of the Polish-Jewish *landsmanshaftn* had its designated locale. Yiddish actors and actresses assembled at the Espérance on the Place de la République. On the other side of the same square, Yiddish journalists held forth at the Thenint. There too the "Amis de Varsovie" held their annual ball. Immigrants from Łódź met at the Taverne de Paris. At the Istamboul, Sephardi Jews would exchange gossip in their native Judeo-Espagnol. Political parties met in the back rooms: the Bund in a café on the rue des Francs Bourgeois, Left Poalei Zion on the first floor of Le Georges, a bistro on the rue de Belleville.[33]

Workers United and Disunited

The Great Depression hit Jews in east-central Europe particularly hard. In Warsaw 34 percent of Jews in the labor force were without work in 1931. Jewish unemployment was much higher than non-Jewish—partly accounted for by the low participation of Jews in the civil service, where jobs were relatively secure. In Lwów, for instance, 29 percent of Jews were out of work in 1931, compared with 16.5 percent of non-Jews. The east European economies enjoyed a hesitant recovery in the late 1930s but Jewish unemployment persisted.

The Jewish proletariat in Poland, in the sense of workers employed in big industrial enterprises, was small. Few Jews worked in the extractive industries such as coal mining and petroleum production or in heavy industries such as steel. Altogether only 3 percent of Jewish wage-earners worked in large-scale industry, whereas 83 percent were employed in small artisanal workshops, with not more than five workers. Increasingly in the late 1930s these were home-based family enterprises. More than half of all Jewish employees worked in textile or garment manufacturing. Certain crafts such as cap-making, haberdashery, shoe-making, goldsmithery, and wig-making were predominantly Jewish. Jews were also to be found in large numbers in a few other industries such as printing and bookbinding. In Poland, as elsewhere, Jews were much more likely than non-Jews to be economically independent. Nearly half of all self-employed workers in the country were Jews. Such conditions were not auspicious for labor union organization.

Most unionized Jewish workers belonged to exclusively Jewish labor unions. The Bundist unions, with 98,810 members in 1939, half of these in Warsaw and Łódź alone, comprised at least two-thirds of the Jewish union membership. Competition between rival unions was fierce. The socialist Zionists bitterly accused the Bundist unions of "ideological terrorism" and "boundless self-interestedness."[34] For their part, the Bundists complained that the Zionists were "corrupting" workers with "mendacious promises that they would receive certificates [for emigration to Palestine]."[35]

In Warsaw there were Jewish trade unions for porters, shop assistants, furniture makers, needle workers, photographers, office workers, hairdresser and barbershop employees; metal, soda water, general provisions, and leather industry workers; as well as one for "home-workers and not well-off handicrafts workers." Adopting a broad definition of the proletariat, the Bund organized not only employed but also self-employed workers. For example, the transport workers' union recruited large numbers of porters, carters, draymen, cabdrivers, chauffeurs, and deliverymen who, after repeated strikes, succeeded in setting minimum tariffs for their services.

In Warsaw thousands of porters, more often Jews than Christians, since Jewish merchants preferred to rely on other Jews for their deliveries, carried loads on their backs, in wheelbarrows, and sometimes in carts to which they were yoked like horses. These men generally had little or no education. Some had failed in petty trade but most had worked as porters since childhood. Political competition in the porters' unions was particularly intense. The union of *playtse-tregers* (porters who carried loads on their backs), for example, changed allegiance successively from the Communists, to the Bund, and then to the left faction of the Polish Socialist Party, after which it split into three.

In December 1936, the porters' union newspaper reported on the plight of Jewish *drozhkazhes* (horse-cab drivers) in Lublin. They had joined the union in the hope of resisting what they saw as pressure by non-Jewish competitors, aided by the local authorities, to eject them from what had once been a commanding position in the profession. The municipal inspector, they alleged, was enforcing regulations against them in a discriminatory and merciless manner. They were being fined for trawling illegally for customers, when in fact, so they said, they were merely turning their cabs around. Their licenses were being withdrawn for punitive periods on the ground that their cabs were dirty—this in winter when, so they maintained, it was hard to keep them clean. An anti-Jewish boycott had reduced their incomes so severely, they complained, that they could barely afford to feed their horses, let alone their families.[36] Whether the union was able to help them much is doubtful but the episode illustrates how economic pressures and anti-Semitism in the late 1930s were combining to impel some Jews into collective self-help.

Although Jewish workers in Poland were more unionized and more militant (they engaged in more strikes) than non-Jews, their conditions of work were generally worse. Since most worked in small-scale workshops, they were not subject to the eight-hour law that protected workers in large enterprises. As a result, they often worked ten or twelve hours a day—in the busy season even longer. A survey of Jewish barbers in Warsaw in 1937 found that they worked an average of eleven hours a day, six days a week.[37] For the same reason, most Jewish workers were not covered by the unemployment insurance law. Often they had no health insurance either and lived in dread of a lengthy or disabling illness.

And then there was the lowest stratum of the Jewish poor: the unemployed or unemployable, the disabled, widows, tramps, and street people. Their lot, of course, was often no worse than that of the poorest segments of the surrounding population, with the important difference that Jewish poverty was mainly urban and gentile poverty mainly rural. The degradation of pauperdom in the big city was different in character from that of the rural poor: urban hunger was less readily assuaged; dirt and pollution in the city were more intense; diseases there were more swiftly transmitted.

Bildung

For all the thunderous rhetoric of the Jewish labor movement, this was, for the most part, a bourgeois people, at least in the sense that even Jewish workers generally owned what Marxists called the "means of production," namely the capital equipment and tools of their trade. Since most were self-employed, they fell more naturally into the petty bourgeoisie than any other class. Furthermore, given their relative economic independence, some among them were able to acquire the two essential conditions for upward social mobility: resources for investment and/or education. With easier access to financial and social capital than the great mass of peasants and industrial workers around them, growing numbers of Jews throughout the continent succeeded in advancing rapidly into the entrepreneurial and professional classes.

In Romania, for example, Jews owned nearly a third of all private

commercial and industrial enterprises in the late 1930s. Jewish ownership was particularly marked in the provinces of Bukovina (77 percent), Bessarabia (63 percent), and Moldavia (56 percent). The
largest industrial company in the country was the Reşiţa Iron Works
and Properties, headed by Max Ausschnitt. It employed 17,000
people, producing 90,000 tons of steel per annum, as well as loco-
motives, machinery, motors, and armaments. Similarly in Hungary,
40 percent of industrial firms were Jewish-owned. Many wealthy
Hungarian-Jewish industrialists had been granted patents of nobility
under the Habsburgs. Among these was Manfred Weiss, founder of
a giant heavy industrial combine, producing iron, steel, aircraft, and
motor vehicles. Manfred's sons, Alfons and Eugene, both barons,
headed the concern after his death in 1922.

Jews were also strongly represented in the professions. In Vienna,
as many as 65 percent of doctors in the 1930s were Jews. In Poland,
more than half of all private physicians and lawyers were Jewish.
Similarly in Hungary, where Jews were 5 percent of the total population, half the lawyers and a third of the journalists were Jews.

As Jews moved up the social scale, they left central districts of
cities and headed for more salubrious and genteel quarters in the
suburbs. In Berlin in 1933 only 15 percent of the Jewish population, then numbering 161,000, lived in the old Jewish area in and
around the Scheunenviertel in Berlin Mitte. More had moved out to
districts such as Wilmersdorf, Schöneberg, and Charlottenburg: out
of Berlin's twenty districts, these three now held 44 percent of the
city's Jewish population. But there, as elsewhere, they continued,
for the most part, to live among fellow Jews. A certain separateness
continued to characterize Jews' social life, even as they moved into
the middle class.

The middle and upper Jewish bourgeoisie distinguished themselves from other Jews not only by their choice of residence but by
language and mode of life. Most abandoned Yiddish and adopted
the language of high culture of surrounding society. In Germany
and Austria this was German; in Hungary, Hungarian. In eastern Europe, the language of choice was not necessarily that of the
greater part of the surrounding population or of the nation-state.
In Romanian-ruled Transylvania, in Slovakia, and in the Vojvodina

province of Yugoslavia, Jews, especially the bourgeoisie, spoke Hungarian. In Bucharest the educated classes cultivated French rather than Romanian. In Soviet Ukraine, the rising Jewish professional class, as they left Yiddish behind, preferred Russian to Ukrainian. Richard Pipes, growing up in a middle-class family in Warsaw in the 1920s and 1930s, spoke Polish with his mother but German with his father and his nannies.

The Jewish bourgeoisie of Germany was, until 1933, the largest, proportional to the rest of the Jewish population, and, considered en masse, the most prosperous in Europe. It set the tone for Jewish elites in the continent as a whole by its liberal religious and political outlook, its patriotism, its cultural sophistication, its charitable activities, and the sense of security and optimism that it felt about its place in the world.

The distinct flavor of middle-class life, as it was developed and refined among German-speaking Jews throughout central Europe, is conveyed in the hundreds of unpublished memoirs of German Jews (not all, of course, from the bourgeoisie) that are preserved in the archive of the Leo Baeck Institute in New York. These testify to their preoccupation with the ideal of *Bildung* (an untranslatable concept, involving, among other things, education, civilization, tolerance, and cultivation of the arts), their pride in their respectability, their stress on good manners, cleanliness, and personal grooming, their formality, their deep love and affinity for German literature, their respect for learning, their elevation of music to the height of a religious experience, their horror at fanaticism of all kinds, and their disdain for the lifestyle and "jargon" (that is, Yiddish) of the *Ostjuden* from whom most of them were themselves descended. These accounts of life in the 1920s and 1930s also bear witness to the outer cloak of dignity and self-confidence that the German-Jewish middle class felt it important to maintain in the face of adversity as well as to their inner disorientation and disillusionment in the late 1930s as their material and psychological world crumpled.

5

NEW JERUSALEMS

Jews felt at home in most of the great cities of continental Europe but there were a few with which they had a special relationship. These were places that, without necessarily abandoning faith in the heavenly Jerusalem (*Yerushalayim shel ma'lah*), they transmuted in their imagination into an earthly one (*Yerushalayim shel matah*) that might serve as a place of sojourn, pending their return to the true Zion—for the irreligious among them it might even be a replacement for that.

Jerusalem of the West

"Amsterdam is the city of the Jews and cyclists," wrote the journalist Egon Erwin Kisch.[1] Like the cyclists, the Jews were totally at home in the Dutch capital. Siegfried van Praag called it the "Jerusalem of the west" in a book of that title published in 1961 but the phrase was in common use long before.[2] Both Jews and non-Jews called the city by the affectionate slang name Mokum, allegedly derived from the Yiddish/Hebrew word for "place."

Jews had first arrived in the late sixteenth century, many as Marranos (converts to Christianity who secretly preserved the old faith) from Spain and Portugal. Later the Sephardim were joined and eventually greatly outnumbered by Ashkenazi immigrants from central and eastern Europe. In the seventeenth and eighteenth centuries Amsterdam flourished as a major Jewish cultural center, the home of Hebrew printers, scholars, poets, and thinkers (though the

greatest, Baruch Spinoza, had been expelled from the community).
Jews in Amsterdam had long played a significant role in Dutch cultural, economic, and political life and probably encountered less
hostility from their fellow citizens than in any other major city in
Europe.

In 1939 about seventy-nine thousand Jews lived in Amsterdam,
constituting more than half the Jews in the Netherlands. But here
as elsewhere the Jewish birthrate was declining, the population was
aging, and, recent historians have concluded, "the demographic prospects for the Jewish population . . . looked sombre. Had the trends
apparent in the 1930s continued, then this population group would
have been doomed to extinction."[3]

Most Dutch Jews were still nominally orthodox, though secularism was making steady progress among Jews, particularly on the
left. Although many Jews were nonpracticing, the community's
institutions were orthodox-dominated and traditional Judaism had a
stronger hold than in most west European cities. The small Liberal
congregations in The Hague and Amsterdam, founded in the 1930s,
drew support mainly from refugees from Germany and remained on
the periphery of the community.

The substantial Dutch-Jewish middle class "was characterized
by a kind of dry, stolidly bureaucratic mindset"—the judgment of
Benno Gitter, who grew up in Amsterdam in the interwar period.[4]
Most of the Jews in the city, however, belonged to the working class
and were poorer than the rest of the city's population. In 1930,
whereas 18.5 percent of taxpayers in the city paid tax on income
higher than three thousand florins, for Jews the proportion was only
8.9 percent. In 1932, although they formed less than a tenth of the
population, they were a quarter of all those receiving poor relief.[5]

As in most European cities, Jews were heavily concentrated in
retail trade. At least a third worked in this sector, compared with
21 percent of the general population. This statistic, however, concealed a huge range of economic power and social standing, from the
gilded patriciate, such as the owners of the fashionable de Bijenkorf
department store, founded by the Goudsmit family, to the mass of
petty street traders and itinerant hawkers.

The Jewish proletariat, in the strict sense of the term, was concentrated, here as elsewhere, in the garment manufacturing industry, in which 20 percent of Jews worked, compared with just 5 percent of the general population. At the lowest levels of skill and pay, women, in particular, often worked very long hours in small workshops.

The aristocracy of labor in Amsterdam was to be found in another part of the skilled working class, the diamond industry, in which Jews had played an important role since the seventeenth century. As in tailoring, they predominated in the industry both as employers and workers. Jews had founded both the diamond employers' organization, the Algemeene Juweliers-Vereeniging, and the Diamond Workers' Union, established in 1894. This was the first Dutch labor union and Henri Polak and others among its leaders became working-class heroes and played an important role in the Social Democrat Party. The union built an imposing headquarters on the Franschelaan in the affluent Plantage district.

Before the First World War, more than half of all the diamond workers in the world had been Dutch. In the 1920s, however, the Amsterdam diamond industry suffered a severe downturn. The city ceded its preeminence in the industry to Antwerp, where labor was cheaper. Unlike Amsterdam, where stones were cut in large factories, Antwerp developed a system of cottage outworkers who cut and polished at home. The Great Depression diminished diamond production and trade everywhere. In consequence, employment in Amsterdam declined even further. Many unemployed diamond workers were driven to setting up market stalls on the Waterlooplein, the large square near the old Jewish quarter, or miserable, small shops elsewhere. By the 1930s, just 6 percent of the Jewish labor force worked in the industry.

What survived of diamond production in Amsterdam remained mostly Jewish: at least 80 percent of the employers and 60 percent of the workers were Jews. The diamond bourse still closed on Saturdays, as it had since its inception in 1890. Members could attend *mincha* (afternoon) services in a special prayer room set aside for the purpose. A kosher restaurant in the building offered Amsterdam-Jewish delicacies like ginger cakes and marzipan tarts. At Passover *matzot* were served, spread with thick butter and brown sugar.[6] Diamond merchants there, as throughout the world, still used the Yiddish phrase *a mazel un a brokhe* ("luck and a blessing") when they closed a deal.

With the exception of this phrase, plus a few others that had been absorbed into the local Jewish working-class dialect, Yiddish in Amsterdam, a branch of the Western variant of the language, had been dead since the end of the nineteenth century. In the interwar period, however, some recent eastern European immigrants reintroduced it, now in its Polish-Russian form. Most of the immigrants were leftists—Communists, Bundists, or Labor Zionists—and they established the An-sky East European Jewish Workers' Cultural Society, with its own library.

These Jewish immigrants, like those to most European cities, congregated initially in the center of the city. The heart of Jewish Amsterdam was in and around the Waterlooplein flea market, a large proportion of whose traders were Jewish. *Heet iis te gèèf* ("I'm *giving* it away!") was a characteristic stallkeeper's cry. Jews were conspicuous among the sellers of old clothes, bric-a-brac, fruit, fish, flowers, vegetables, and ice. From here ragpickers, itinerant barrowmen, and pedlars radiated out to the rest of the city.

The area is remembered nostalgically in picturesque sepia photographs, but the reality of life there was harsh:

> Waterlooplein. A battlefield. A struggle for existence. Never an armistice. There is nothing more cruel. From early morning to late in the evening, eternally. . . . Everyone fights for himself. Need dictates the onslaught. . . . Hear those cries—one continuous sound all day long. The stench of garbage and the reek of decomposition; moldly dregs and the color of decay. . . . On the battlefield of Waterloo one learns the value of the worthless. Shoes you would not even hurl at a mangy cat are fought over. Rags you wouldn't dare give a beggar cause quarrels.

And yet, with it all, sparks of the human spirit burst forth: "Laughter, laughter! The struggle for existence does, after all, have its own humor."[7]

In the Jodenbuurt, the old Jewish quarter nearby, were located

the main communal institutions and places of worship, including
the great Portuguese Esnoga, completed in 1675. In the surrounding
streets one could buy traditional delicacies: fried roe, ginger buns,
and smoked fish. In 1930 the city had eighty kosher food stores,
including thirty-two butchers and twenty-four bakeries and cake
shops. The *volksrebbe* (people's rabbi), Meijer de Hond, part old-
style *magid* (popular preacher), part populist controversialist, part
modern social worker, became a tribune of the working class in the
district, or at any rate of those among the poor with some sentimental attachment to Jewish tradition.

The German-Jewish social worker Gertrude Cohn (later van
Tijn), who settled in Amsterdam in 1915, was fascinated by the
Jodenbuurt:

> The streets there were rabbit-warrens; the houses incredibly old.
> I learned later how much poverty, inter-marriage [she meant mar-
> riage between close relatives] and sickness there was in the ghetto;
> but it did not hit the eye as it did in London. There seemed to be
> no slums. I was fascinated by the Jewish markets, which were held
> in front of the two beautiful old synagogues. Everything was sold
> there from old rusty nails to silk underwear.[8]

Housing conditions in the Jewish quarter in the 1930s remained
overcrowded and unsanitary. The area was rife with social problems,
including drunkenness and prostitution.[9]

By then, however, only a remnant, consisting of the very poorest
Jews, still lived in the district. Most of the rest had moved to east-
ern parts of the city: better-off elements of the working class to the
Transvaalbuurt, the affluent middle class to the Plantage.

Jonathan Israel has pointed out that the so-called pillarization of
Dutch society facilitated "both acceptance of a separate Jewish identity within Dutch national life and, simultaneously, a remarkably
smooth quasi-segregation of Jewish existence from the mainstream
of Dutch politics and public affairs."[10] Not having their own "pil-
lar," Jews tended to identify politically with the Liberals or Social
Democrats. By the early twentieth century the "quasi-segregation"
had diminished and Jews were playing a full part in Dutch public

life, particularly in the socialist movement. Four out of six aldermen in Amsterdam (one Liberal and three Social Democrats) in the early 1930s were Jewish.

At the same time, Dutch Jewry had its own internal divisions, in this case into three groups: Sephardim, Ashkenazim, and, after 1933, immigrants from the Third Reich. The Sephardim looked down on the Dutch Ashkenazim and both adopted a patronizing attitude toward the refugees from Germany.

Tempering condescension was a sense of responsibility. The community boasted an impressive set of educational and social welfare institutions. In most cases, however, these were divided not only according to function but also between Sephardim and Ashkenazim.

The "Portuguese" population of no more than 4,500 persons had its own hospital in the Plantage, two orphanages (one for boys and another for girls), three old-age homes (one for men, one for women, and one for couples, provided they had been married at least twenty years), as well as a society for giving fifteen winter coats a year (to men only), and another for giving blouses to women above the age of fifty. Two Portuguese-Jewish societies gave help to women after childbirth, one after the birth of a son, the other after that of a daughter. These bodies "withstood any attempt at fusion and [kept] vigorously to their independence."[11]

Two other Jewish hospitals were primarily for Ashkenazim. The main one, on the Nieuwe Keizersgracht, had three hundred beds. The Joodsche Invalide, a home for elderly, blind, or otherwise disabled people, founded on the initiative of Maijer de Hond, earned a worldwide reputation and in 1937 opened a fine modern building, known as the Glass Palace, on the Weesperplein. Largely supported by private donations, it was unusual among Jewish institutions in securing donations from non-Jews as well as Jews. It raised money by means of collection boxes, the sale of calendars, social events, free advertising in *De Telegraaf*, several popular touring revues with dancing girls, specially recorded gramophone records, and films. It also ran lotteries on the AVRO radio station, endorsed by well-known personalities, including the Dutch prime minister, Hendrikus Colijn.[12] As such non-Jewish backing indicated, Amsterdam

Jewry's links with its neighbors were generally harmonious and un-marked by the hostility that prevailed in much of the rest of Europe.

But the arrival in or passage through the Netherlands between 1933 and 1940 of about thirty-five thousand Jewish fugitives from the Third Reich tested this relationship and revealed its limitations. As J. C. H. Blom puts it, the refugees "were as unwelcome in the Netherlands as in most other countries."[13] The minister of social af-fairs noted that the refugees exhibited "a totally different mentality from the Jews here."[14] The government offered little material help to the uninvited guests.

By 1935 the pressure on the Amsterdam committee for Jewish refugees was almost unbearable. It had dealt with 5,400 arrivals in the Netherlands since 1933. Of these, 2,200 were dispatched to overseas destinations, principally Palestine. About a thousand were sent back to Germany, supposedly on the basis that they would no longer be in danger there.[15] In April 1935 the committee's secretary, Gertrude van Tijn, wrote to James G. McDonald, the League of Na-tions high commissioner for refugees: "We shall have to close down within a couple of months as it is quite impossible to get the funds required for this work either locally or internationally."[16]

Most of the refugees who remained in Holland lived in Amster-dam. Among them was Otto Frank, his wife, Edith, and daughters Margot and Anne. His business in Frankfurt was already in serious trouble in 1933 when he decided to settle in Amsterdam, which he already knew from a brief earlier sojourn. He set up a small com-pany there for the "production and sale of fruit products, especially pectin" (a natural gelling agent derived from fruit and used in the manufacture of jam and jellies).[17] Later he also sold spices used in the making of sausages. This enterprise was a comedown for a man who had been a reasonably prosperous private banker in the 1920s. The Franks settled in the Rivieren district of south Amsterdam, where many other German-Jewish refugees lived.

Like refugees the world over, those who arrived in Amsterdam clustered together, socialized in their own language, and set up shops, clubs, and places of worship. By 1939 a third of the popula-tion of the Rivieren district was Jewish. The nearby Beethoven-straat, a focus for German-Jewish shops and cafés, became known

as Brede Jodenstraat (a play on the Jodenbreestraat near the Waterlooplein), and tram number 24, which traveled down it, was dubbed
the "Berlin express."

Dutch-Jewish historians have vigorously debated the degree of
integration of Jews in Dutch society in the interwar period. Viewed
in contemporary comparative context, the Amsterdam community
seemed more firmly anchored than almost any other European Jewish community. No doubt, as some have alleged, there were elements of self-deception in the general Dutch-Jewish feeling of
security and acceptance in the Netherlands. Henri Polak declared in
1930: "Anti-Semitism is in our country of no political significance;
it doesn't exist as a political slogan; it doesn't figure in any party
program and few people will admit that they have anti-Semitic
feelings."[18] But by 1933 he was sufficiently concerned to publish a
lengthy refutation of "scientific" anti-Semitism, advocating the establishment of a detention center for anti-Semites.[19] The birth of a
small Dutch Nazi movement, the NSB, which garnered 8 percent of
the vote in provincial elections in 1935, seemed cause for concern,
but not for alarm. At first not anti-Semitic, it adopted an anti-Jewish
policy in 1938, calling for the removal of Jews to a colony such as
Surinam.

As pressure from events in the Third Reich intensified, the outlook for Amsterdam Jewry began to darken.

Yerusholoyim d'Lite

The "Jerusalem of the North," or Yerusholoyim d'Lite (Jerusalem of
Lithuania), was said to have derived its handle from Napoleon's remark when he passed through Vilna on his way to Moscow in 1812:
"Gentlemen, I think we are in Jerusalem!" Probably he was alluding
not to the physical aspect of Vilna but rather to its intensely Jewish
character (its population at that time was more heavily Jewish than
that of Jerusalem).

Like Amsterdam, Vilna (the Russian name; the city was known
to Poles as Wilno, to Lithuanians as Vilnius, and to Yiddish speakers as Vilne) had a proud Jewish heritage. In the 1930s it remained

a center of religious and secular scholarship but, again like Amsterdam, the community was living in large measure on accumulated cultural capital of the past.

Jewish settlement in Vilna dated back to the fifteenth century and by the early sixteenth a quarter of the population was Jewish. The city's fame in the Jewish world arose chiefly from its association with the revered rabbinic figure of the Vilna Gaon, who countered the ecstatic populism of the Hasidic movement with a more rationalistic, scholarly sobriety. In the nineteenth century Vilna was a center of the *haskalah* (Hebrew Enlightenment). It was also a hub of Hebrew publishing: the so-called Vilna Shas, the edition of the Talmud published by the Rom family house and completed in 1886, became a prized possession in orthodox homes throughout the world. By 1914 Jews constituted close to half the city's population. Vilna's prestige among Jews was not limited to the religious sphere. Alluding to the city's role in the early history of Russian socialism, Semen Dimanshteyn, the leading Soviet party official responsible for Jewish affairs, declared in 1919, "For us Jewish revolutionaries, Communists, Vilna long ago became a historic centre, the heart of the Jewish spiritual liberation."[20] The Jews here felt, said one of their number, "not a trace of the well-known innermost feeling of Jewish inferiority" so common elsewhere.[21]

During and after the First World War, Vilna and its Jews underwent a series of disastrous vicissitudes, successive occupations, civil strife, and waves of refugees flowing in and out. Lithuania proclaimed the city its capital but in 1920 it was captured by Polish forces. The Poles remained in control until 1939. They claimed to be the largest ethnic group in the city: in 1916 50 percent of the population had reported Polish as their first language, 42 percent gave Yiddish, and only 2.5 percent Lithuanian. The Lithuanians refused to accept the Polish coup de main and relations between the two states were poisoned. The frontier between them was closed for most of the interwar period, with severe effects on the economy of Vilna, particularly on the large Jewish mercantile class. The closure also affected Jewish cultural life: not only people but books and newspapers were prohibited from crossing directly between Vilna and Kovno or other places in Lithuania.

Forced wartime evacuations to the Russian interior had led to a reduction of nearly half in the number of Jews in Vilna to just 47,000 in 1920. Eight thousand emigrated between 1926 and 1937, mainly to South America, South Africa, and the United States (in that order of magnitude). The Jewish population nevertheless recovered somewhat, reaching 60,000 in 1939, but by then Jews were little more than a quarter of all residents.

Vilna Jews were heavily concentrated in certain occupations: they were tailors, bookbinders, tinsmiths, hatters, and carters. They also held an important place in the professions: three-quarters of the doctors in the city were Jews. In many lines of work, Jews formed their own unions or professional associations, among them the barbers, shoe stitchers, waiters, and construction and woodworkers' unions.

Interwar Vilna remained a city of five nationalities: Poles, Lithuanians, Byelorussians, Russians, and Jews. It evoked in its inhabitants a special affection and, in some, an unusual breadth of mind. The Polish poet Czesław Miłosz, who lived there, recalled in his mind's eye

Wilno of the Enlightenment or Romanticism. Those stinking piles of garbage, the sewage streaming down the center of the roadways, the dust or mud that one had to wade through. . . . [T]he narrow lanes of the Jewish quarter . . . preserving the memory of Walentyn Potocki, a righteous man, who had converted to Judaism in Amsterdam and was burned at the stake in Wilno; and also, *sha sha*, talk about Officer Gradė, who had been hidden in a pious Jewish household, and about how he had already recovered from his wounds and decided to become a Jew, had himself circumcised, and intended to marry the daughter of the house. This was the man whose descendant would be a poet in the Yiddish language, Chaim Grade, a member of the Yung Vilne poets' group, which was parallel to our Polish language group "Żagary."[22]

Actually, the story about the Polish nobleman Potocki is certainly false and the supposed ancestry of Grade is probably no less legendary. No matter: people believed it. Such myths clustered about Vilna. More pertinently, Miłosz wrote that the city's different communities in his youth lived "within the same walls yet as if on separate planets."[23]

Between the wars, Vilna's Jews endured commercial boycotts supported by the Roman Catholic Church, defacement of Jewish signs, and anti-Semitic student riots. In one such disturbance, in 1931, a Polish youth was killed by a Jewish student, Samuel Wolfin, acting in self-defense. Wolfin was sentenced to two years' imprisonment by the county court for "participation in stoning to death the Polish student."[24]

The leading Jewish political figure, until his death in 1935, was Dr. Tsemakh Szabad, who served on the city council and from 1928 as a senator in the Polish parliament. A man of broad cultural horizons, Szabad enjoyed a personal following that transcended his association with the Folkists.

For the most part, however, political loyalties here, as elsewhere in Poland, were mainly party-based. The Agudists, the Zionists, and the left all enjoyed support in the city. Vilna was, in particular, a stronghold of the Bund, which had been founded there in 1897 and was popular among the poverty-stricken working class.

The old Vilna ghetto was picturesque in the eyes of some (and in the sentimental folk memory of later years) but to contemporary visitors it often seemed "disgusting and unhealthy, the antithesis of modernity and of progress."[25] Its decrepit buildings, general aura of decay, its slum and cave dwellers, and its jostling street population of pedlars, vagrants, crazies, organ-grinders, and deformed beggars shocked rather than charmed tourists. Many Jewish institutions, including several synagogues and *yeshivot* and the famous Strashun Library, were located in or near the Alte Kloyz (old courtyard). The Hebrew and Yiddish teachers' colleges, the Leyzer Gurvitch Yiddish primary school, a museum, and the offices of the *kehillah* all occupied another yard at 7 Azheshkove Gas (*gas* meaning passage).

With its innumerable synagogues, the city remained a citadel of non-Hasidic orthodoxy. There were separate congregations of chimney sweeps, printers, and gravediggers. Vilna's Vaad Hayeshivot (committee of *yeshivot*) presided over orthodox Jewish education in a wide area of northern Poland and Lithuania. The influence of its leading rabbis extended throughout orthodox Jewry. But the power of the orthodox even in Vilna was declining. In 1928 a coalition of Zionists and leftists, who already controlled the *kehillah*, captured the *tsedoko gedoylo*, the main Jewish charitable body, hitherto under orthodox direction, and appropriated it for general communal use.

Until the collapse of the Russian Empire, modernized, educated Jews in Vilna tended to speak Russian rather than Yiddish. With the end of imperial rule, Russian gradually lost its attraction. Vilna Jews did not, however, adopt Polish, which they tended to use only on formal or official occasions.

Instead Vilna became the capital of *yidishkayt*, what the journalist Hirsz Abramowicz called "the city of the most intimate Jewishness in the world" and "the most Yiddishist city in the world."[26] According to the census of 1931, 86 percent of Jews there claimed Yiddish as their mother tongue. Bank checks and doctors' prescriptions were issued in the language. The Yiddish gymnasium (academic high school) competed with a Hebrew one. The Yiddish scout organization Bin (Bee) held summer camps, sporting jamborees, and soirées, and issued its own songbook. The VILBIG (Vilner Yidishe Bildungs Gezelshaft) "people's university" organized lecture series in Yiddish on history, languages and literature, geography, physics, chemistry, and sociology. It also organized a choir (of both sexes) and a mandolin orchestra.

YIVO, the Jewish Scientific [in the European sense of scholarly] Institute, was conceived by Yiddish-speaking intellectuals in Berlin in the early 1920s but established in Vilna in 1925. Its primary purpose was research but it had the ambition of serving as a national academy of the Yiddish language and as a teaching institution. Its supporters saw it as "the crown of the building of Yiddish secular culture," a modern "Sanhedrin of scholars."[27] Ambitious to construct an intellectual engine for the collective self-understanding of east European Jewry, YIVO set up departments of philology, history, economics and statistics, and psychology and pedagogy. Its ethnographic commission, with a network of several hundred volunteer *zamlers* (collectors), gathered material on Ashkenazi Jewish folklore, building on the work before the First World War of S. An-sky. YIVO also created a major library and archive. Determinedly secularist, the institution's leaders were nevertheless inspired by what has been described as a "mixture of latent religious inspiration and overt secular content."[28] As Joshua Karlip has written, the Yiddish revivalists of the early twentieth century "sometimes consciously and sometimes unconsciously . . . borrowed their belief in the redemptive role of culture from the traditional emphasis on the study of Torah and the performance of *mitzvoth* [commandments/good deeds]."[29]

The *spiritus rector* of YIVO was Max Weinreich, "a short man with a highly expressive face that was marred by the loss of one eye, the souvenir of a pogrom."[30] He married the daughter of Tsemakh Szabad. A cosmopolitan, progressive, and wide-ranging scholar, Weinreich studied at the universities of St. Petersburg and Berlin, earned a doctorate in linguistics from the University of Marburg, lived for a short time in Vienna, and also spent a year as a visitor at Yale. Under Weinreich's guidance, YIVO moved beyond "a salvage effort towards inter-disciplinary social research, [shifting] its research focus from the past to a concern with the present and the future."[31]

Although YIVO was nominally nonpartisan, most of its leading figures were close in their outlook to the Bund (Weinreich), the Folkists (Prylucki) or the Left Poalei Zion (Ringelblum). As a result, YIVO was viewed with suspicion by Communists, Agudists, and Zionists. The institute's work, while reflecting the leftist outlook of its leadership, tried to steer clear of direct political involvement.

YIVO—and Yiddish secular culture in general—lived in a state of chronic financial crisis. In 1929 a Yiddish journalist deplored the trouble YIVO encountered in raising the $3,500 needed to erect its building in Vilna, noting that orthodox Jews had been able to raise much larger sums in Poland and, in addition, $53,000 overseas, for the new Lublin *yeshiva*. "Where," he asked plaintively, is the pride in the building of Jewish secular culture?" In Lublin itself, the writer added, a secular Yiddish school building could not be completed for lack of a paltry sum of money.[32] Such funds as YIVO did manage, with great difficulty, to scrape together came mainly from small contributors in eastern Europe rather than the relatively affluent Jewish communities of North America.

Against the odds YIVO succeeded by 1933 in raising the $10,000 required to renovate a modern, spacious building on a hilltop beyond the crowded streets of the old Jewish quarter. A young American visiting scholar, Libe Schildkret, who arrived to spend a year working at YIVO in 1938, later described it: "Everything about the YIVO—its location, its landscaped setting, its modern design, the gleaming immaculateness of the place—delivered a message. I interpreted it to mean that the YIVO had class, was no moldering institution, but a place from which distinction and excellence would issue. Even more: The YIVO was no seedy relic of the past; it belonged to the future."[33]

From its modernistic headquarters, YIVO sought to establish itself as the flagship of a forward-looking Yiddish culture. Yet while it enjoyed considerable prestige and respect among intellectuals, YIVO's reach into broader society was limited. It succeeded in the 1930s in opening branches in Paris and New York and support groups elsewhere. But as Simon Dubnow sadly concluded after a visit in 1934, YIVO in Vilna remained "a small island of culture in a sea of beggary."[34]

Several Yiddish newspapers were published in Vilna, notably the "non-partisan, democratic" (in fact, leftist, fiercely anti-Zionist) *Vilner tog* (1919–39, with short gaps), edited by the philologist and literary scholar Zalmen Reyzen, and the nonparty, Zionist, and anti-Yiddishist *Di tsayt* (1924–39, also with occasional intervals). Most popular was the sensational *Ovent-kuryer*, which, like many Yiddish papers, held readers in tantalized suspense with its serialized cliffhanger novels. Some of these were translated from the American yellow press. When the importation of foreign papers was suddenly banned midstory, the paper found a solution: the entire cast of characters embarked on a ship that foundered in a storm with no survivors.

The group of writers and artists known as Yung Vilne would meet at the Café Velekh, at the corner of Yidishe Gas and Daytshe Gas, welcomed by the proprietor, Wolfie Wolf. A special page in the *Vilner tog* on October 11, 1929, announced the *araynmarsh* (festive entry) of the group into Yiddish literature. Although non-Communist, the Yung Vilne writers inclined to the left. They were inspired by the personality and works of Moshe Kulbak, whose poem "Vilna" (1927) was a hymn of praise to the spiritual qualities of the city from a modernist, secular writer: "Du bist a tehilim oysgeleygt fun leym un ayzn . . ." ("You are a psalm, spelled in clay and iron . . .")[35]

Yung Vilne included several poets and writers who became prominent figures of the last phase of Yiddish literary creativity, among them Chaim Grade and Avrom Sutzkever. Unlike other Yiddish literary groups, Yung Vilne adopted no uniform programmatic stance or style. One of its members, Leyzer Volf, claimed a world record in 1930 for writing 1,001 poems in a month. Between 1934 and 1936 Yung Vilne produced three issues of a literary annual (the second was confiscated by the censor and had to be issued in a revised form). In the late 1930s Volf helped a number of aspiring teenage writers, among them Hirsh Glik (later to become well-known for his "Song of the Partisans"), form another group, Yungvald (Young Forest). They began issuing their own magazine, of which just four numbers appeared (January to April 1939).

By the mid-1930s Jewish Vilna collectively shared in Polish Jewry's general sense of gloom and foreboding. Borekh "Vladek" Charney, a leading Yiddish writer in New York, who had lived in Vilna in his youth, wrote in 1934:

> Since the world war the name of Vilna has acquired a doleful tone. When someone says "Vilna" that generally means trouble [*tsores*]. And even the small amount of satisfaction [*nakhes*] that we can derive from Vilna, like the Yiddish schools or YIVO, is merely spiritual satisfaction. It smacks of an effort to preserve, conserve, and defend what little remains against the attacks of hostile surroundings.[36]

Vladek had long left the old country behind and his impression was no doubt colored by the emigrant's nostalgia for past glories. But his comment reflected the pervasive sense of depression that was descending over the Jewish population of the city.

Red New Jerusalem

Minsk, a hundred miles southeast of Vilna, was another old center of Jewish religious scholarship, a former stronghold of *haskalah* and later of political radicalism. Although founded in Vilna, the Bund had set up its first headquarters in Minsk and the first congress of the Russian Social Democratic Workers' Party had convened there in 1898. At that time Jews constituted over half the population of the city. Zionism was also strong there. In the elections to the Russian Constituent Assembly in December 1917, to the Minsk Soviet, and to the *kehillah* in 1918 and 1920, Zionists and their allies secured decisive majorities of Jewish votes.

In the final stages of the First World War and during the Russian civil and Russo-Polish wars, Minsk, like Vilna, was occupied and re-occupied several times by Bolsheviks, Germans, and Poles. Although ideologically little attracted to Bolshevism, Jews in Minsk generally sided with the Soviets during the civil war, seeing them as a lesser danger than the anti-Semitic "Whites" or the Poles, both of whom were credited with responsibility for pogroms in territories that they captured. A minority of Jewish activists—Bundists, Mensheviks, and Bolsheviks (the latter at first few in number)—played a significant role in revolutionary activity in Minsk in 1917. In the early 1920s Jews were well represented in the leadership and membership of the Communist Party in the city. Thereafter many were purged as *lishentsy*, Zionists, Bundists, or Trotskyists.

Under Bolshevik rule, Minsk became the capital of the Soviet Socialist Republic of Byelorussia. The *kehillah* was dissolved. Most synagogues, *yeshivot*, and *hadorim* (elementary Hebrew schools) were closed. The last congress of the Bund on Soviet soil took place in Minsk in March 1921 and resolved on a merger with the Communist Party. Some Zionist groups remained active in Minsk until the mid-1920s, when they were penetrated by the GPU (Soviet secret police) and nineteen activists were arrested and sentenced to expulsion from the Soviet Union. An underground cell of Poalei Zion, with eight members, was, however, still operating in Minsk in 1935.[37]

In the 1920s and 1930s Jews moved to the city from surrounding *shtetlakh*. But many moved out of the former Pale altogether, especially to Moscow and Leningrad. The Jewish population of Minsk (fifty-four thousand in 1926), as a result, grew more slowly than the Byelorussian, and by the end of the 1920s Jews were no longer the largest ethnic group.

The traditional Jewish quarter, located in the heart of the old city, remained heavily Jewish until the Second World War, though because it lacked many institutions of the kind that existed in Vilna, its Jewish character became less visible.

In Minsk, as elsewhere in the USSR, Jews, who were concentrated in mercantile occupations, suffered disproportionately after the end of the New Economic Policy in the late 1920s. More than a fifth of adult Jews in Byelorussia in 1930 were classified as *lishentsy*. Most businesses in Minsk had been Jewish and were forced to close. In her study of the city's Jews between the wars, Elissa Bemporad reports that of 482 people listed on the city council's "black board" of *lishentsy* in 1930, "nearly all had Jewish names."[38] By the mid-1930s there were, at any rate officially, no Jewish traders left in Minsk. The Jewish working class of the city was heavily represented in the skilled and semiskilled sectors of the garment, leather, printing, and woodworking industries. Meanwhile, Jews were entering in large numbers into professions such as medicine and law.

In spite of a decree, issued in 1922, banning Jewish religious instruction to minors, save in the home, some clandestine Hebrew schools and a secret *yeshiva* continued to exist until the early 1930s, with financial support from the Joint. But by the late 1930s only a handful of the 120 synagogues in the city were still open for prayer and just five rabbis remained.

Cut off from its traditional links with the vital heartbeat of Jewish life in the new states of Poland and Lithuania, interwar Jewish Minsk fell back on its own resources and became a proving ground for the definition and creation of new forms of Jewish culture, Soviet-style. Under the policy of *korenizatsiia* (literally "rooting," that is, indigenization or nativization), pursued in non-Russian regions of the USSR between 1921 and 1933, local languages and cultures were promoted. The policy did not give free rein to non-Russian cultures. Rather, the official hope was, by working through other languages, to implant Communism more effectively in the non-Russian-speaking segments of Soviet society.

As in Vilna, the Jewish bourgeoisie had by the turn of the century embraced Russian as their main language of cultural discourse. Yiddish, however, remained the day-to-day tongue of the Jewish working class. Until 1938 it was recognized as one of the four official languages of Byelorussia. A large sign at the main railway station in Minsk displayed the name of the city in Byelorussian, Russian, Polish, and Yiddish. Citizens had—and exercised—the right to use Yiddish in courts and in official business. Schools, trade unions, and party cells all used the language. The local radio station broadcast regularly in Yiddish. The title cards of silent films shown in cinemas appeared in Yiddish. And we are told that Byelorussia was "the only area in Eastern Europe throughout which letters could be addressed in Yiddish."[39]

As a result, Minsk developed into the USSR's main center of Yiddish culture in the 1920s. A Yiddish theater in the former Choral Synagogue on Volodarskaia Street, a college to train teachers for Yiddish schools (in a former *talmud torah*), a "Jewish Workers' University" (an evening school), and a Jewish Central Party School for the training of cadres were all established in the 1920s. So too was a Jewish section of the Byelorussian Institute for Culture, later upgraded into an Institute for Jewish Proletarian Culture of the Byelorussian Academy of Sciences. A chair in Yiddish, the first anywhere in the world, was inaugurated at the new Byelorussian State University. A Jewish section of the university for a time taught courses in science and mathematics—probably the only instance in history of university teaching through the medium of Yiddish.[40] Lack of suitable textbooks and the preference of many Jewish students for study in Russian, however, prevented the innovation from lasting long.

A number of Yiddish writers and intellectuals, some from other countries, moved to the city and established the Yiddish journal *Tsaytshrift* in 1926. It printed contributions from some non-Communist, non-Soviet scholars. The fifth volume, which appeared in 1931, contained standard Soviet subject matter such as "Style and Genre in Proletarian Literature." But it also published texts of letters by the founding figure of modern Yiddish literature, Mendele Moykher Sforim (S. Y. Abramovitsh, 1835–1917). Mendele is also regarded as a father of modern Hebrew literature and the letters included some written in Hebrew. This was a very rare instance of modern Hebrew publication in the Soviet Union—perhaps the last. It was certainly the last in *Tsaytshrift*, which henceforth ceased publication.

The end of NEP in the late 1920s produced crude, anti-Semitic attacks on alleged Jewish speculators.[41] The campaigns against Bundism and Trotskyism from 1926 onward, partly a reflection of national rivalries between Byelorussians and Jews in the local power structure, also degenerated in Minsk into a coded form of anti-Semitism.[42] Bundism and Trotskyism indeed commanded significant support among Jewish workers and party members in the city. Jews were heavily represented both among those accused of these heresies and those who dared to defend them, for example by speaking up in defense of the Bund or by voting against the expulsion of Trotsky from the Communist Party.[43]

In the 1930s, however, as they were offered opportunities for integrating into Russian, as distinct from Byelorussian, culture, Minsk Jews increasingly internalized the values of Soviet society—a trend depicted in the novel *Di zelmenyaner* (1931–35), by Moshe Kulbak, who had moved there from Vilna in 1928.

Jerusalem of the Balkans

For the Sephardic Jews of Salonica, their city too was a Jerusalem, a "holy city, where the traditions and language carried from Spain were tenaciously perpetuated across the centuries, seducing by their intact purity," as a former resident wrote nostalgically in the 1950s.[44] Visitors gained a similar impression. An Italian journalist wrote in 1914 that the city "gives the impression of being a strange Jerusalem, very modern, very Macedonian, a little international, but Jerusalem to be sure, because of the great quantity of Jews who inundate her, so much so that they make all the other nationalities of secondary importance."[45]

In 1913 the Jewish population of Salonica was estimated as 61,000 out of a total of 158,000. Only 37,000 residents were Greeks, and the Jews were the largest single group in the population. Jewish merchant princes, owners of banks, and textile entrepreneurs did not need to seek entry into the city's social elite: they *were* the elite. Most of the Jews, however, were petty traders, artisans, or laborers. A survey in 1918 found that the "occupational pyramid" of Salonica Jews contained 750 professionals, 1,900 businessmen, 6,100 small shopkeepers, 7,450 office and shop clerks, 7,750 craftsmen and workers, and 9,000 porters, dockers, boatmen, and fishermen, the latter divided between *moros* (deep-sea fishermen) and *gripari* (who fished in shallow waters).[46] The large number of manual laborers was unusual for a Jewish community. A majority of workers in the port were Jews and Saturday rather than Sunday was observed there as the day of rest.

The main language of the community was Judeo-Espagnol, though from the 1870s onward, as a result of education in the French-language schools of the Alliance Israélite Universelle, many of the younger generation, especially those from more affluent backgrounds, were turning to French. Over the centuries the community had tenaciously and lovingly preserved its distinctive customs. Different synagogues existed for families whose ancestors originated in various regions of Spain, such as Aragon and Catalonia. Popular local songs, known as *cantigas*, were sung at events known as *caffé aman* or *caffé chantant*. During Passover women would serve aromatic *galettes d'azyme* (round *matzot*).

Cultural life was less intense than in comparably sized Ashkenazi communities. The Jewish press displayed little of the intellectualism of the more serious Jewish papers in Poland. There was no professional Judeo-Espagnol theater, though plays were occasionally performed in the language, including *Los Maranos* by T. Yaliz (a pseudonym for Alberto Barzilay), the French playwright Henry Bernstein's adaptation of S. An-sky's Yiddish play *Der dybbuk*, and, in 1938, "a sensational event—the first Greek-Jewish artistic performance," Racine's *Esther*, adapted into Judeo-Espagnol as a musical.

In Salonica, as in other communities, Jewish institutions proliferated. The nineteen (in 1938) concerned with some form of social welfare included: the hospital, founded with a gift from Baroness Clara de Hirsch in 1898, which had twelve doctors (presumably part-time, since they all gave their services free of charge) and ninety-seven beds, of which fifty-five were for nonpaying patients; the Asilo de Locos (mental asylum), with eighty inmates, fifty of them women, supported in large part by Salonicans in New York; the Matanoth-Laévionim, providing free meals to 675 children and old people; and the Tora Oumlaha, which distributed schoolbooks to poor children.

With little help from the municipality and against increasing odds, the community also somehow supported the Allatini orphanage and the Aboav girls' home (holding fifty *guerfanos* and forty-five *guerfanas* respectively), the Bené Berit fraternal order (which provided bursaries to ninety-five *protégéados* studying at high schools and universities), the Asilo de Viejos (old-age home, with thirty-five *protégéados*), the Benosiglio maternity home (which looked after 311 *mujeres povres* that year), and the Bikour Holim (society for medical visitation of the sick and poor and a free dispensary, founded in the sixteenth century).[47] The secular associational life of the community also included women's groups, Zionist societies, several libraries, and youth clubs.

Salonican Jews had been comfortable with Ottoman Turkish rule. The conquest of the city by Greece in 1912, however, deprived them of the imperial protection they had enjoyed for 482 years. That was merely the first in a series of calamities that befell them over the next generation. In 1917 a terrible fire destroyed much of the central area of the city, including the densely populated Jewish neighborhoods. The conflagration rendered half the population of the city, including fifty-two thousand Jews, homeless. Many institutions, including thirty-two synagogues (with 450 Torah scrolls), ten rabbinical libraries, eight schools, and five *yeshivot*, were destroyed and others badly damaged. The Jews were not allowed to return to their former districts in the heart of the city. Instead, most were left to rot in "cheerless, barrack or tin-shack places" on the periphery.[48]

The succession of blows led to large-scale Jewish emigration to France, Italy, the Americas, and Palestine. In Paris the more affluent among the immigrants congregated in the IXth arrondissement, where they formed the Association Amicale des Israélites Saloniciens and in 1932 opened their own synagogue. Many of the emigrants prospered in their new homes. Among them was the family of the young Daniel Carasso, who brought to France in 1929 a small yogurt manufacturing company, Danone, that by the time of his death at the age of 103 in 2009 had grown to be the world's number one seller of fresh dairy products.[49]

The demographic composition of Salonica was revolutionized in the 1920s by the so-called exchange of populations, in reality mutual expulsions, between Greece and Turkey. Nearly all Muslims, including all the Dönmeh (descendants of Jewish converts to Islam in the seventeenth century who had retained a distinctive identity), were expelled to Turkey. In their place, 150,000 Greeks from Turkey arrived in the city, imposing huge pressure on housing and resources and damaging relations between residents and newcomers. Suddenly the Jews found themselves the largest and most conspicuous minority in Salonica. In an atmosphere of heightened nationalistic feeling, they became a target for xenophobic attack.

Like all the national states of eastern Europe, Greece was determined to break what was seen as alien dominance over its commerce and culture. Although most Jews acquired Greek citizenship, they were not fully accepted as Greek nationals. Commercial enterprises were no longer permitted to keep account books in languages of their own choosing. Greek-owned ships arriving at the harbor sought out Greek stevedores in preference to Jews, who were confined to working with foreign-owned vessels. A law was passed in 1924, specifically aimed at Salonican Jews, requiring Sunday rest by shops, offices, and factories and forbidding any exception for Jews. The port too was compelled to switch from Saturday to Sunday as its rest day. Compulsory hellenization entailed compulsory secularization. "Everybody says you cannot live on five days work a week," reported one observer. "The stevedores and porters in the port, the carriage-drivers and tobacco-factory workers, and the shopkeepers: and even members of families of *dayanim* [judges in the religious court] and rabbis—all open their businesses or go to work on Saturdays."[50]

In 1928, in an act of legislative ghettoization at that time unique in Europe, Jewish citizens of Greece were placed in a separate electoral college. In December 1928, an Association of Jewish Assimilationists was formed. This sought to repeal the electoral law and to harmonize relations between Jews and Christians by opposing Zionism and encouraging Jewish children to attend Greek schools. The local Zionist press called the association "the work of the devil" and an unholy alliance of "*faubourgistes* and *je m'en fichistes.*"[51]

Following the fall in 1933 of the Liberal prime minister, Eleftherios Venizelos, who had backed the electoral college, it was abolished. An angry Venizelos declared, "The Greeks do not want the Jews to influence Hellenic politics. . . . The Jews of Thessaloniki [Salonica] follow a national Jewish policy. They are not Greeks and do not feel as such. Hence they ought not to involve themselves in Greek affairs."[52]

All Jewish schools were required to appoint teachers of Greek to ensure that the student body acquired full proficiency in the national language. This gave rise to tension. About half of Jewish children attended communal schools, most of the remainder the Francophone schools of the Alliance. When a public school inspector visited the Talmud Torah school in 1929, he told the fourth-form Greek teacher that he found the class feeble in the language. The teacher, presumably a Greek non-Jew, replied: "We can't get better results because these Jews only like French and won't apply themselves to learning Greek." The Jewish community's school inspector was furious and complained (in French) of the teacher's "odious calumny." The main problem, he said, was not the pupils but the Greek teachers, many of whom did not take their job seriously and were frequently absent from class. He added that, with few exceptions, they took absolutely no interest in school activities apart from their own lessons and all disciplinary measures had to be handled entirely by the Jewish teachers.[53] In 1937 the headmaster of a Jewish communal school demanded the dismissal of a Greek teacher who, he said, was lazy, sought to undermine the authority of the teachers of French and Hebrew, and "lacked all professional conscientiousness." His pupils were learning nothing from him "and have even unlearned what they knew." Moreover, the complaint continued, "Mr. Economides, I must tell you, does not like us" ("ne nous aime pas").[54]

In the early 1930s Greek became the compulsory medium of instruction. Schools maintained by foreign governments were proscribed, save for non-Greek citizens, who constituted only about 10 percent of the Jewish population, and for a time the teaching of Hebrew as a living language was forbidden. Twelve hours a week were permitted to be reserved for Jewish subjects. The Alliance schools were handed over to the direction of the Jewish community and the teaching of Judeo-Espagnol and French was prohibited. From 1935 a government-designated curriculum was imposed. Some Jewish children started attending Greek government schools rather than Jewish ones: from 140 pupils in 1934–35, the number climbed to 836 by 1938–39.[55] The suggestion was raised in 1939 that the community schools should be handed over altogether to governmental control.[56]

Anti-Semitic agitation by Greek ultranationalists erupted in 1931 in a violent anti-Jewish riot in the working-class Campbell district. In a subsequent trial of alleged rioters, the court found that they had committed arson but ruled that they had been motivated by patriotism and therefore acquitted them.[57] This latest in the succession of disasters plunged a large part of the Jewish population into despair.

Meanwhile their economic position deteriorated further. In 1933, 70 percent of the Jews in Salonica were on relief rolls. Pauperization and violence led a further ten thousand Jews to emigrate between 1931 and 1934.

Under Ottoman rule Zionism had not been very strong in Salonica. When the future Zionist leader David Ben-Gurion lived there in 1911, as a student of law, he was severely critical of what he saw as the Salonican Jews' absence of national spirit.[58] But the series of blows that rained down on the community from 1912 onward fed the rise of Zionism. Zionist publications in Judeo-Espagnol painted idyllic pictures of the Holy Land: "Yerushalayim! Que attraccion majica!" ("Jerusalem! What magical allure!")[59]

The community council became the arena for fierce conflict among Zionists, "moderates" (assimilationists), and Communists. In 1928 the Zionists won an absolute majority of votes (61 percent). The Zionist-dominated council actively encouraged emigration to Palestine, hoping thereby to alleviate unemployment in the city. When the new port of Tel Aviv opened in 1936, Jewish stevedores from Salonica moved there to enable the port to function. But the limitation of Jewish immigration to Palestine after 1936 reduced the flow from the city.

Salonican Zionism, however, was focused as much on straightening the backs of Jews in their deepening predicament in the diaspora as on promoting emigration to Palestine. Deprived of the safety valve of emigration, the community leadership in Salonica, as elsewhere, tried to steer Jews toward what were held to be productive occupations. The program of the newly elected council in 1934, in which the Zionists, with twenty-one seats, were the largest party but depended on support from others for a majority, provided for the "encouragement of the Jewish population towards productive careers: agricultural and artisanal work etc. in order to arrest the tendency towards commercial occupations."[60]

Unlike most of the authoritarian regimes of eastern Europe, the military dictatorship of Ioannis Metaxas, who seized power in Greece in August 1936, was relatively friendly toward Jews, who, except for the Communists, generally reciprocated, at least in public, with cordiality. But behind a veneer of amity, the government undermined the community's democratic structures, abolishing internal elections and imposing a new administrative council composed of yes-men.

Culturally and ideologically the Jews were tugged in several directions: by the Alliance school system toward French; by Communists and assimilationists toward Greek; and by the Zionists toward Hebrew. Unlike Vilna with its Yiddishist movement, there was no powerful cultural force working to maintain and revive Judeo-Espagnol. In the 1930s assimilationism seemed to be gaining ground. One sign of this could be seen in local birth announcements as non-Jewish names, such as Alberto and Sarina, began to replace Jewish ones, such as Avram and Sara.

By the 1930s there was not a single rabbinical seminary left in Salonica. When the last Sephardi chief rabbi of the city, Ben-Zion Uziel, left for Palestine in 1923 to take up the position of Rishon le-Zion, or Sephardi chief rabbi of the Holy Land, Salonica, like Sephardi communities elsewhere in Europe, found it necessary to turn to Poland for spiritual leadership. After an interregnum of several years, the Polish-born Zvi Koretz was appointed chief rabbi in 1932. A graduate of the Hochschule für die Wissenschaft des Judentums in Berlin, he held a doctorate from the University of Vienna. A proud, autocratic figure, Koretz cultivated good relations with Metaxas and with the royal family, but his relations with his flock were tempestuous.

Ashkenazim were only a tiny minority of the Jewish population of the city—dubbed *Mashemehas* (possibly, it has been surmised, because when they arrived they asked in Hebrew for the names of local Jews: *ma shimcha?* means "What is your name?")—and Koretz's

6

HOLY MEN

Tohu-bohu

The hundreds of thousands of Jews who served in the European armies during the First World War were, like all conscripts, torn abruptly away from their communities. Most Jewish soldiers from eastern Europe were also torn away from their culture, often definitively and irretrievably. Whatever theoretical right to religious practice they might possess while in uniform, in practice they found such basic *mitzvot* as Sabbath observance and *kashrut* difficult to maintain in armies in the field. If they survived at all, the soldiers returned home utterly changed men. The masses of Jewish civilians who fled their homes in the western parts of the Russian Empire as well as in Austrian Galicia faced different but often hardly less devastating upheavals that similarly loosened the moorings of their inherited value systems. The first stage of the dejudaization of the Jews of Europe had begun with the Enlightenment; the second started here.

In the accelerating flight of Jews from Judaism, the orthodox suffered more losses than other streams of Judaism, first because there were more of them and consequently more to lose; second because orthodoxy placed greater demands on its adherents than the rest and was, as a result, harder to reconcile with the requirements of modern life, whether military or civilian. An orthodox Jew, once he had ceased to lay *tefillin* (phylacteries) every weekday morning, pray in a *minyan* (quorum of ten men) three times a day, celebrate the Sabbath and festivals, and obey the remainder of the 613 positive and negative commandments, would generally find it more difficult to resume his previous practices than a Liberal Jew whose observances would in any case have been less punctilious from the outset.

The decade after 1914 therefore led to a sense of crisis in east European orthodoxy. Not only orthodox leaders but ordinary Jews with no axe to grind saw religion as in rapid retreat. "The only ones who pray are the middle class, the poor and the aged," wrote an observer in Łódź in 1928.[1] By the late 1930s many shops on Nalewki Street in the heart of the Jewish area of Warsaw were open on the Sabbath.

Ben-Zion Gold, in his memoir of his youth in Radom, recalls that the orthodox milieu in which he grew up was generally felt to be in a state of decay. The pressing demands of the secular world had impinged on the culture of the *bet hamidrash*, the study hall that was a fixture in every Jewish community of some size, and in which, in the previous generation, laymen would occupy their spare time in study of holy texts. Before the First World War this "unique, voluntary system of higher education without formal appointments, salaries, budget, or administration," as Gold terms it, had been at the center of orthodox Jewish life and had been frequented round the clock by Talmudic autodidacts. But, Gold recalls, "what had recently been the norm became in my time an exception." In his hometown, only one *shtibl* (prayer-hall) out of twenty was a place of study for young Talmudists; the rest were used for prayer but otherwise stood empty most of the time. "In cities with large Jewish populations such as Warsaw and Łódź," he writes, "one could still find *shtibls* full of young men studying, but on the whole the traditional community was on the defensive and losing ground."[2]

A Jewish religious map of Europe between the wars would show orthodoxy as still the dominant trend in much of east-central Europe. Elsewhere, however, it was weakening. In the Soviet Union religion was in the process of being eliminated altogether. In Germany the orthodox were no more than one-eighth of the community in the interwar years. In Hungary the dominant form was Neolog, a variant of Liberal Judaism. In areas where orthodoxy was nominally the main religious stream, it was either, as in France, besieged by secularist forces, or, as in Italy and the Balkans, more flexible than the Polish-Lithuanian variety.

Even in Poland, although orthodoxy predominated, non-orthodox elements controlled many central Jewish religious institutions. In Warsaw, for example, the Great Synagogue on Tłomackie Street was known, like such synagogues throughout the continent, as the "German *shul*," on account of what was seen as the modernized and excessively formal nature of its services.

In western Europe roles were reversed. Here most Jews were non-orthodox but the orthodox maintained nominal control of major Jewish religious institutions, notably the Consistoire in France. Jewish religious observance was fading. An orthodox writer in Antwerp in 1936 spoke of the orthodox as *she'erit ha-pleitah* ("the surviving remnant") who had "saved themselves from the tohu-bohu, the wild commotion of surrounding society."[3] Growing numbers of Jews there, as well as in France and Italy, were ignoring the minutiae of religious practice and in some cases abandoning the faith altogether.

"The Torah Forbids Anything New"

The term *orthodoxy*, as applied to conservatively religious Jews, dates back only to the early nineteenth century. One of the earliest orthodox ideologists was Moses Schreiber (1762–1839) of Pressburg (Bratislava), known as Hatam Sofer. His uncompromising resistance to change, encapsulated in the dictum *hadash asur min hatorah* ("the Torah forbids anything new"), continued to serve as a lodestar to orthodox Jews in succeeding generations.

Their most revered Torah sage of the early twentieth century was Yisrael Meir Hakohen (1838–1933), known as Hafets Hayim, after a book he published in 1873, dealing with Jewish laws concerning gossip and slander. A leading figure in the Agudist movement, he opposed Zionism and fiercely criticized emigration to America, which he regarded as a den of modern iniquities.

After the death of Hafets Hayim, the most influential rabbi of the *misnagdic* tendency was Hayim Ozer Grodzenski of Vilna, who served as president of the rabbinical board of Agudas Yisroel. Recognized as an *ilui* (genius) from his youth, Grodzenski was an opponent of Zionism, though for a time he sought some accommodation with the Mizrachi party. He also opposed secular education, Reform

Judaism, indeed any form of religious innovation. Assimilation and Reform Judaism, he argued in responsa issued in 1939, were responsible for the disasters that were befalling the Jewish people.[4]

Orthodox leaders such as Grodzenski felt that the only way to stem the modernist tide was to mount the ramparts of unyielding conservatism. This led them to expound a doctrine known as *daas toyre*, whereby they arrogated to themselves the power to go beyond the mere recital of Talmudic sources and precedents and, on their own authority, to issue rulings that would have the force of law. Yet in Grodzenski's own family there were deviants from the straight path. His nephew left his *yeshiva* studies, embraced secularism, and became editor of the *Ovent-kuryer* newspaper in Vilna.

An even more painful domestic embarrassment confronted another orthodox eminence, Rabbi Joseph Rozin of Dvinsk (1858–1936), known as the Rogatchover Gaon. A renowned scholar, he was reputed to know the entire corpus of rabbinic literature by heart. Rozin was presented with an awkward dilemma when his son-in-law died and his daughter consequently found herself obliged to undergo the ceremony of *halitzah*. According to Jewish law, this must be performed by a surviving brother, who renounces the right to marry the deceased's widow, leaving her free to wed whom she might please. The problem facing the gaon was that of his two remaining sons, one was a Communist in Leningrad, the other a convert to Christianity in Königsberg. Talmudists debated which should perform the ceremony. In the end the gaon decided that, since both sons were equally bad, he might as well select the Communist. The judgment, however, gave rise to controversy since it seemed to open the way to branding all nonobservant Jews as apostates.[5]

In Germany a radically different interpretation of orthodoxy had developed since the late nineteenth century. The two dominant figures in the formulation of this German neo-orthodoxy were Esriel Hildesheimer (1820–99) of Berlin and Samson Raphael Hirsch (1808–88) of Frankfurt. While regarding themselves as strictly orthodox, they embraced secular as well as religious studies and sought to reconcile Judaism with enlightened thought. Although they and their followers engaged in sometimes bitter rivalry, their outlooks were, in fact, quite similar. Both embraced the concept of *torah im derekh-eretz* ("Torah combined with common sense") that had been advocated by thinkers of the *haskalah*. Hirsch had permitted some modest innovations: choirs (men only) could sing in the synagogue and weddings might be performed there; rabbis could wear robes and might preach sermons in German.

The twentieth-century epigones of Hirsch stiffened their resistance to change or accommodation to the modern world. But German neo-orthodoxy remained distinct from east European ultra-orthodoxy. It has been termed "a kind of stabilized dualism" or, as Hildesheimer put it, "a faithful adherence to traditional teachings combined with an effective effort to keep in touch with the spirit of progress."[6]

"There Is No Room for Two of Us"

Although Hasidim and *misnagdim* cooperated in Agudas Yisroel and other such organizations, and although most followers of each would have found it difficult to identify hard-and-fast doctrinal differences between the two camps, the historic animosities between them had in no way softened. Hasidic *rebbes* retained vast, if inchoate, followings, especially in central and southern Poland and parts of Hungary, Romania, and Czechoslovakia, as also in destination lands of Jewish emigration, above all the United States.

The two dynasties with the largest support in central Poland were those of Gur and Aleksandrów. In Galicia the Belzer Hasidim predominated. Other Hasidic groups ranged in numbers from thousands to a few dozen. They were generally not members of any formal organization, save for an inner core who might enroll as students in the *rebbe*'s *yeshiva*. His most devoted followers would gather as a loyal retinue in his court, generally in the *shtetl* in which the dynasty had its origin or to which the current *rebbe* had moved. In the cities to which many Hasidim migrated from their *shtetlakh*, each Hasidic group would establish its own informal *shtibl*, often in a private house or apartment, rather than a synagogue. Followers would visit the *rebbe* or write to him, seeking spiritual inspiration, business advice, permission to marry, solutions to problems, and cures for diseases.

Among the Hasidic leaders, the one who earned a reputation for the most vociferously uncompromising piety in this period was Hayim Eleazar Shapira, *rebbe* of Munkács in Subcarpathian Ruthenia. An excitable man, with a cracked, squeaky voice, he became notorious for his shrill maledictions against Zionism, other *rebbes*, Communism, America, and all existing governments, as well as visiting theatrical troupes, sports, and "any sort of festivity."[7] Nor were the Agudists exempt from his anathemas: "Di Agudisten, yimakh shmom vezikhrom, vos zenen erger als di klovim di Tsiyonisten . . ." ("The Agudists, may their name be blotted out, who are worse than those dogs the Zionists . . .")—as he referred to them in a sermon in Marienbad, where he was taking the waters in the summer of 1930.[8] He enjoyed undiscriminating, sometimes frenzied support from his followers. When he ventured forth in public, his carriage would be mobbed by enthusiasts who would have to be beaten off by his guard of honor.

Whereas most modernist Jewish ideologies placed a high value on labor, many of the strictly orthodox explicitly accorded it a secondary status: only Torah study was worthy of human endeavor, as opening the path to the messianic era. As the Munkácser *rebbe* put it: "One may not rely on any natural effort or on material salvation by human labor. One should not expect redemption from any source other than God." In the same spirit he opposed all forms of secular education as well as modern medicine, technology, engineering, and architecture, since, after all, the revived Temple would be designed by God himself and "handed down to earth fully built and completely decorated and appointed."[9]

The *rebbe* opposed emigration to the Holy Land or America, insisting that his followers remain in Europe to await the messiah, who would arrive at the time of the apocalypse, which he predicted would occur in 1941 (the *rebbe* died in 1937). "May the Lord rebuke you, O Satan, who choose Jerusalem!" he wrote.[10] The much-sought-after immigration certificates to Palestine were *shmadtsetlakh* or *toytnshayn* (certificates of apostasy or death).[11] The *rebbe* visited Palestine in 1930 but returned only more convinced of the satanic character of the Zionist enterprise. When Zionists persuaded the city council of Munkács to name the main street of the Jewish district after Yehuda Halevi, the twelfth-century Spanish-Jewish poet famous for his verses expressive of yearning for the Holy Land, the *rebbe* got the decision reversed and the street was instead named Ways of Repentance Street, after the title of a work by the *rebbe*'s late father.

The miracle-working capabilities and prophetic powers attributed to Hasidic *rebbes* were derided by *misnagdim* as well as by neo-orthodox, Reform, and secular Jews. Marriages between scions of different dynasties were celebrated like royal weddings between offspring of absolute monarchs. Festivities would last several days and would be attended by thousands. Some Hasidic customs aroused particular scorn, for example, the practice of *khapn shirayim* (grabbing leftovers) from the *rebbe*'s plate at festive meals.

The *rebbes* received voluntary donations (*pidyoynes*) from their followers and a few as a result became wealthy men whose courts acquired palatial accoutrements. The Munkácser *rebbe*, for example, enjoyed an assessed taxable income in 1928 of 621,500 crowns (equivalent at the official exchange rate to $18,833—then a considerable sum in Czechoslovakia).[12] His revenues were the more impressive in that, unlike many other *rebbes*, who were happy to accept contributions from all and sundry, he would take money only from the "Torah-true," in his narrow definition of the term.

Enlightened central European Jews regarded Hasidism with a mixture of horrified repulsion and yet, often in the early twentieth century, fascinated attraction. In the German-speaking lands, most became acquainted with it only indirectly through the medium of the writings of Martin Buber, whose foggy, *völkisch* romanticism briefly attracted even the future Marxist Georg Lukács.

An unusually far-reaching case of such attraction was that of the Czech-Jewish writer Jiří Langer, who embraced Hasidism wholeheartedly and for a time lived in Belz at the court of the *rebbe*. In Marienbad in 1916 Langer introduced his friend Franz Kafka to the Belzer *rebbe*. *Introduced* is perhaps the wrong word, since the *rebbe* was a virtually unapproachable figure, but Kafka was permitted to accompany the *rebbe*'s entourage as the great man went for his constitutional in the woods, all the while reciting to himself the Talmud (he too was said to know the entire work by heart). Every now and again, the *rebbe* paused to chat with ornamental wooden gnomes. Kafka was amused by the almost royal decorum that was enforced in the *rebbe*'s presence. He was fascinated by this encounter with Hasidic Judaism and talked and wrote about it extensively. The *rebbe* reminded Kafka of a sultan in a Gustav Doré illustration of the adventures of Baron Münchhausen.

The Hasidim were highly territorial and fanatically devoted to their respective dynasties. Some frowned on intermarriage with followers of other rabbinical *rebbes*, feuded bitterly with them, even engaging in physical violence, and, worst of all, impugned the *kashrut* of a rival *rebbe*'s *tish* (table). When the third Belzer *rebbe*, Isachar Dov Rokeach, fled from Galicia to Munkács in 1920, the Munkácser *rebbe* refused to countenance the presence of a rival on his turf. "There is no room for the two of us in this one place!"[13] A war of "excommunications and bans, libels and slanders, propaganda and even violence" ensued.[14] Eventually the Munkácser not only drove his competitor out of town but succeeded in mobilizing influence on the government to secure his expulsion from Czechoslovakia. The Belzers never forgot this slight.

Herr Doktor or Rov?

In Judaism the rabbi is not, like the Christian priest, a mediator between man and God. He is rather a scholar, a teacher, and (but only since the nineteenth century) a preacher. Sometimes he may also be a judge (*dayan*) in a rabbinical court; but the authority of this institution by the early twentieth century was much more restricted than in the past. Under modern conditions, the rabbi, whether orthodox or not, also bore responsibility for seeking to ensure that his flock did not stray too far from the fold.

In interwar Europe the status of the rabbi was generally held to have declined over the preceding century. Save among the strictly orthodox, rabbis were no longer usually regarded as leaders of their communities. Nor were they, for the most part, seen as intellectual mentors.

Rabbis came in many forms and guises. The type of the Hasidic *rebbe*, revered as a miracle worker by his followers, remained little

changed from earlier times. Liberal rabbis often wore clerical habits, similar to those of Christian clergy. In late imperial Russia the
government had appointed "crown rabbis," government officials who
were required to know Russian, were responsible for population reg-
isters, and received secular as well as religious education. They were
regarded by the orthodox as religiously unsatisfactory and by others
as government stooges. The suspicion endured: after 1917, Soviet
rabbis, whose appointments similarly depended on the government,
were commonly regarded with intense mistrust by those Soviet Jews
who still cared about such matters.

The office of chief rabbi existed in some cities, regions, or countries but not in all. Both Paris and France had a chief but Germany
had none, though some regions had a *Landesrabbiner* and some cities
an *Oberrabbiner*. In the Balkans, the title of *haham bashi*, equivalent
to chief rabbi, was bestowed by the Ottoman imperial government
and its successors on the religious heads of Jewish communities. For
most Jews, especially the orthodox, the prestige of a rabbi depended
not on such handles but on his reputation for learning.

The Sephardic Jews of the Balkans did not, by this time, retain
much spiritual vitality. Few Sephardi *yeshivot* could rival in prestige
the great Talmudic academies of Poland and Lithuania. The organ
of the Union Universelle des Juifs Sépharadim complained in 1935
that the Sephardi rabbinate, "once upon a time so flourishing and
which produced so many eminent men," was now "diminishing day
by day and the few worth-while rabbis who remain are getting older
and older." The journal warned that "it is to be feared that the rabbinate may disappear altogether one day."[15] The dearth of trained
Sephardi rabbis was such that communities in southern Europe were
obliged to import Ashkenazi rabbis from Poland. Israel Zolli (originally Zoller), for example, born in Austrian Galicia, was appointed
rabbi of Trieste in 1929 and of Rome in 1939. In Bulgaria the three
chief rabbis between 1889 and 1914 were all Ashkenazim. A Sephardi from Salonica was appointed between 1920 and 1925 but
then Bulgaria had to do without a chief rabbi altogether until after
the Second World War.

In German-speaking Europe, under the influence of the Enlightenment movement *Wissenschaft des Judentums*, a modern
type of rabbi had emerged. Graduates of rabbinical seminaries and

universities rather than *yeshivot*, the German rabbis were deeply affected by the German intellectual tradition, especially by Hegel and Goethe.

Traditionalists of the old school complained that "Herr Doktor" was not a *rov* (rabbi) and quipped that since rabbis had become doctors Judaism had become sick.[16] Hayim Ozer Grodzenski compared the combination of university and Talmudic studies to the mixture of poison with water and maintained that Poland was "not in need of rabbis with doctorates."[17]

A formidable rabbinical combination of secular and religious learning was Hirsch Perez Chajes, chief rabbi of Vienna from 1918 until his sudden death in 1927, at the age of fifty-one. Of Galician origin, he was in the difficult position of being the orthodox-inclined leader of a largely Liberal community. A man of unremitting energy and wide culture, an outspoken Zionist as well as a pacifist, he exemplified the modern, activist rabbi-politician. Chajes aroused both admiration and criticism for his impassioned sermons and speeches. "I do not speak what I want to speak but what I must speak, that which my inner being dictates," he declared.[18] His participation in 1925 in the opening ceremony of the Hebrew University of Jerusalem prompted one of his more orthodox Vienna colleagues to proclaim a fast day. Chajes nonetheless enjoyed the unusual distinction of being recognized as not only the religious but also the secular leader of Austrian Jews. At his death he was acclaimed, in a glut of mixed metaphors, as "a lambent flame, a glowing torch, a banner and a battle-cry."[19]

Even before the accession of Hitler to power, German Jewish orthodoxy was becoming inclined to defer to rabbinical authorities in eastern Europe. An early test of relative authority came in May 1933, when the Nazi government, in one of its first actions against Jews, restricted *shechitah* in Germany, requiring that all animals be stunned before being slaughtered. In religious law, the matter was debatable. Some German rabbis favored compliance with the new regulation, lest German Jews turn to nonkosher meat; properly slaughtered meat imported from Holland or Denmark was expensive and in short supply. But Grodzenski feared that compliance would lead other countries to follow the Nazi example and pass similar legislation, as some, including Poland, in fact did. He accordingly used his influence to persuade German orthodox rabbis not to issue a ruling that would permit compliance with the new law.

After 1933, rabbis such as Joseph Carlebach in Hamburg, Joachim Prinz in Berlin, and, above all, Leo Baeck as head of the Reichsvertretung, overshadowed the lackluster secular leadership of German Jewry. In the early months of Nazi rule, Prinz's lectures on Judaism attracted audiences of over five thousand people. But this enthusiasm, which led to talk of a renewal of Judaism, did not last. By 1937, in a farewell article on his departure from Germany, Prinz was lamenting the shallowness and brevity of the phenomenon: "The 'return to Judaism,' " he wrote, "was no 'proud march of the up-right' but a procession of the lame and the blind, as described by the prophet in his vision of the Return: *veshavu ligvulam* ['and they shall return to their own borders']."[20]

Heder

Traditional Jewish education, central to the practice and perpetu-ation of the faith, had generally been conducted at three levels: it began in the *heder*, continued in the more advanced *talmud torah*, and culminated in the *yeshiva*, the summit of religious learning.

No Jewish institution suffered from a worse reputation than the *heder*. The *melamed* was a pathetic figure, often of little intellectual ability (since the gifted would seek more respected positions, such as rabbi), miserably remunerated, and the butt of practical jokes by his pupils. From the Enlightenment onward, the *heder* was the object of withering social criticism. A common trope in autobiographies was exposure of it as a den of cruelty, filth, and superstition. Failing memory might have added some embellishments to these literary horror-stories but the reality was often dreadful enough. Classes were large and hours long, generally from 8 A.M. to 6 P.M. with an hour off for lunch. Pedagogic methods were old-fashioned, involving rote learning and sometimes violence. Inquiring young minds were bullied into submission rather than stimulated or inspired.

The youngest pupils, generally boys, though girls sometimes

joined the lower levels, studied the Hebrew alphabet, reading and prayers, as well as the weekly portion of the *humash* (Pentateuch). From the age of eight they would add Rashi and other medieval biblical commentators and soon thereafter the Onkelos *targum* (translation) of the Pentateuch into Aramaic.

At the age of ten, they (boys only by this stage) embarked on the Talmud, starting with the seventh tractate of the order Mo'ed in the Mishnah. This deals with the laws concerning Jewish festivals and starts with the words "The egg that was born on a Sabbath." The text discusses what should properly be done with such an egg, the product of labor by a chicken, given that all work by persons and animals alike is forbidden on the Sabbath. Dan Porat, who spent four years of his childhood after 1929 in Kuty, at the foot of the Carpathian Mountains, on the Polish-Romanian border, attended an old-style *heder* there: "I was awed," he writes, "and it would never have occurred to me to ask for the relevance of these tractates to our daily existence."[21]

Around the turn of the century in Russia, efforts to modernize Jewish elementary education had produced the *heder metukan* ("reformed *heder*"). Zionist in orientation, it used Hebrew rather than Yiddish as the medium of instruction. But such innovations gained only limited traction and the supposed improvements were superficial. Enemies of religion, for their part, regarded the reformed *heder* as more of a threat than the traditional version.

Even defenders of the *heder* recognized the need for reform. Joseph Carlebach, director of the Jewish high school in Hamburg in the early 1920s, had got to know and respect east European Jewry, during his service as a military chaplain with the German army on the eastern front in the First World War, when he had established modern Jewish high schools in Kovno and Riga. In a pamphlet published in Berlin in 1924, he proposed a program for root-and-branch reform of the *heder:* proper physical space and educational tools; separation of the classroom from the living quarters of the teacher; preparation of syllabi for religious and secular teaching; raising of the standard of the *melamdim* through better training and security of employment; provision of suitable Jewish educational literature; prohibition of corporal punishment "and other unpedagogic disciplinary methods"; and permanent supervision of *hadorim* by professionally qualified religious authorities.[22]

But change percolated slowly down to the *shtetl*. Dan Porat's *heder* was in the home of the *melamed* who was also the rabbi of the town.

> This was a very modest wooden structure, with a ceiling so low that even to a child it appeared stifling. The floor was compacted soil, and two rough-hewn tables plus four benches and a bookshelf complemented all the furnishings. The *Rebbe's* wife was often doing the laundry in the adjacent room, filling the house with the smell of tallow soap, while his daughter, who suffered from tuberculosis, was always diligently working away at a weaving loom making kilims. We *cheder* [*heder*] children witnessed that scene daily since a big opening was cut in the wall between the study room and the kitchen-living-weaving room to let light into the latter from the only windows in the house.[23]

Porat's education was multilingual, reflecting the multiethnic society in which he grew up. His general schooling was in Polish, all other daily activities being conducted in Ukrainian. He learned four alphabets: Latin for Polish, Cyrillic for Ukrainian, Hebrew for Yiddish, Aramaic, and Hebrew, and, in the *heder*, Gothic, "the latter a remnant from the old Austrian empire . . . to make the Jewish population literate in German. The Austro-Hungarian empire had collapsed a decade earlier but the custom of teaching Gothic script remained as part of the *heder* curriculum."[24]

Porat's experience was by the 1930s exceptional. The traditional *heder* was in its death throes—and not only in the Soviet Union. In interwar Poland it was strictly regulated by government legislation. On hygienic grounds it was no longer supposed to be in a private home but in a public building. In some areas it was modified into a part-time afternoon and Sunday school. In others it remained a full-time elementary school, still with very long hours. The legislation required that secular subjects such as history, arithmetic, and Polish language and literature be added to the curriculum. Since the *melamed* was rarely qualified in those, another teacher, often a nonreligious Jew or a gentile, would teach them. But religious education remained the core of the curriculum, occupying at least twenty-seven hours a week as against a minimum of twelve hours for secular subjects. After 1932, when the school week was restricted to thirty-six hours, religious study was further limited but could still occupy a large portion of the school week.

Legislation, however, was not always translated into reality. In 1938 a school inspector's report on the *heder/talmud torah* attended by 1,200 boys in Cracow complained of overcrowding, damaged premises, plumbing problems, lack of electricity, and dirt and filth everywhere.[25]

In many places the *heder* disappeared altogether, save as a supplementary afternoon school, since parents preferred to send their children free of charge to state elementary schools, rather than pay to send them to a full-time *heder*. In Warsaw, according to official statistics, the number of *hadorim* declined between 1931 and 1935 from 108 to 62.[26] In Białystok just one *heder* remained.[27] In the *shtetl* of Wołkowysk the thirteen *hadorim* that had existed before the First World War had all closed by the 1920s, leaving only a seven-grade *talmud torah* "with a more updated modern curriculum which included modern Hebrew, history, geography, natural science, Polish, and arithmetic."[28]

Proposals for reform, whether inspired from within or imposed from without, probably came too late to save the *heder*. Reflecting on his boyhood experience in Radom, Ben-Zion Gold writes that the system led to an adversarial relationship between the *melamed* and the pupils and an alienation from religion. The result was that "children who came from homes that lived by the tradition, had contempt for *heder*, and those who came from homes where tradition was neglected came away from *heder* with contempt for tradition."[29]

Yeshiva

The two hundred or so *yeshivot* in Poland in the 1930s included some independent institutions but most were grouped in two federations. The first, the Khoyrev system in central Poland, was founded in 1924 as an offshoot of Agudas Yisroel. Its 103 *yeshivot* enrolled

10,200 students in 1934–35. The second federation operated under the aegis of the Vaad Hayeshivot, founded at a rabbinical confer- ence at Grodno in 1924. Its executive director, and after the death of Hafets Hayim, also its titular head, was Hayim Ozer Grodzenski. From his base in Vilna, he coordinated the activities of sixty-four *yeshivot* in the five eastern provinces of Poland, with 5,700 students.

The total number of *yeshiva* students in Poland in the 1930s has been estimated at no more than 20,000, representing around 14 percent of Jewish male teenagers. These figures, as Shaul Stampfer has pointed out, clearly indicate that "traditional Jewish society in Poland was declining in the 1930s."[30] A few thousand more were studying in other countries, particularly Lithuania, Hungary, Roma- nia, and Czechoslovakia, but they did not change the overall picture.

In earlier times, Hasidim had not established *yeshivot*, which re- mained the preserve of their opponents, the *misnagdim*. But from the early twentieth century many Hasidic leaders, notably the *rebbes* of Gur, Aleksandrów, Bobowa, and Lubavitch, founded *yeshivot* in Poland and elsewhere, though the Belzer dynasty remained resistant.

The pride of Polish orthodoxy was Rabbi Meir Shapiro's Lu- blin *yeshiva*, a Hasidic institution, opened in 1930. Its six-story, 120-room building contained a large dormitory, an infirmary, a forty-thousand-volume library, and a scale model of the Temple. Shapiro's program for daily study of the Talmud, known as *daf yomi* (daily page), attracted wide attention and the support of the influential Gerer *rebbe*. Thousands of students all over the world studied the same page each day in a seven-and-a-half-year cycle (the second ended in 1938). This was an innovation, but in pedagogy and dissemination, not substance. Even so, the Munkácser *rebbe* pro- nounced it impermissible.

The Musar movement inculcated an intense spirituality, asceti- cism, and ecstatic religious experience. Founded by Rabbi Israel Lipkin (1810–83, better known, from his place of residence, as Salanter), Musar, in Ben-Zion Gold's later description, "was dedi- cated to deepening moral sensitivity in religious practice and in personal relations." Its adherents "engaged in exercises that were designed to curb lust, arrogance and indolence and to nurture gra- ciousness, fearlessness and generosity." They tried to free themselves from the corruption of *di gas* (the street).[31] The Slobodka *yeshiva* in Lithuania, founded in 1881, was the citadel of Musar. Its adherents further differentiated themselves from other *yeshiva* students in their manner of dress. Denizens of the *yeshiva* world had an unenviable reputation for poor hygiene and slovenly clothing but followers of Musar "were to be impeccably groomed and dressed in the manner of contemporary bourgeois society."[32] In contrast, some followers of Musar went to the other extreme, insisting on poverty, appearing in tattered clothing, eating sparse meals, and cultivating a doctrine of *prishus* (separation from the world).[33]

The *yeshiva* system of education did not allow for a large number of instructors. The 326 students of the Lublin *yeshiva* had ten teachers in 1937 and the 477 of the Mir *yeshiva* just four. In most *yeshivot* there was very little direct instruction and there were no exams. Occasionally there might be a lecture but usually students studied by themselves or with classmates. There was no particular point at which students had to leave a *yeshiva* and some remained for many years. At the Telz *yeshiva* in Lithuania, for example, which was regarded as one of the best organized, students ranged from sixteen to as high as twenty-eight years of age.

The *yeshiva* was not only an educational institution; it was also a disburser of welfare. Wealthier *yeshivot* provided dormitories and refectories for their students. Elsewhere, students found lodgings nearby or even slept on benches in synagogues or study halls. Many "ate *teg*," meaning they were granted free meals on a particular day each week as an act of benevolence by pious families in the town. But the practice came to be frowned on as threatening students with exposure to untoward outside influences—another sign of the defensive posture of orthodoxy in this period.

The largest single item in the Lublin *yeshiva*'s budget for 1939 was not, as in most educational institutions, salaries of staff but provision of meals for students. They literally consumed 39 percent of the institution's costs. The Lubavitch *yeshiva* in Otwock, the budget of which revealed a similar pattern, provided students "free of charge with food, clothing, and accommodation; also medical aid, convalescence etc."[34] Most of the students there also received free housing. Students' fees, however, brought in only 0.5 percent of revenues. Other *yeshivot* such as those of Ponevezh and Slobodka had similar patterns of income and expenditure.

If, as was once maintained, the British Empire was a gigantic system of outdoor relief for the younger sons of the British aristocracy, then the *yeshiva* might with no less plausibility be viewed as a large-scale system of indoor welfare for offspring of the Jewish petty bourgeoisie.

The *yeshivot* had always relied on financial support in various forms from the wealthy. The dislocations of the years after 1914 rendered them heavily reliant on external support, particularly from the United States. The onset of the Depression accentuated this dependence. Many *yeshivot* were in precarious financial shape in the late 1930s. The Ponevezh *yeshiva* reported an income of $10,279 in 1938, but expenditure of $16,582.[35] The accounts of the Mir *yeshiva* for 1937–38 show income amounting to less than half of expenditure; not surprisingly, the *yeshiva* was heavily indebted.[36] Less distinguished *yeshivot* were even worse off, although, since many did not keep proper accounts, it is impossible to say how deeply they were mired in debt. In 1938 and 1939 the Vaad Hayeshivot was in deficit to the tune of half of its expenditure. By this time the entire *yeshiva* system was on the verge of bankruptcy.

Seminaries

Before the First World War, orthodox German Jews would not have dreamed of sending their sons to study in east European *yeshivot* though in 1918 a few did so. Gradually *torah im derekh-eretz* was replaced or admixed with Musar and religious-Zionist influences. In 1937, twenty-nine German-born students were enrolled at the Telz, Lithuania, *yeshiva* alone.

For the most part, however, German orthodoxy trained its religious leaders in rabbinical seminaries rather than *yeshivot*. The seminaries were permitted to function after 1933, although Gestapo agents attended meetings of their supervisory boards.

In Berlin the two main seminaries had long existed in a state of permanent religious tension with their surroundings. The

Hochschule (Lehranstalt) für die Wissenschaft des Judentums, supposedly serving the whole Jewish community, in fact catered to
more liberal elements. Originally intended less as a seminary than
as a teaching and research institution at university level, it stressed
the application of the highest scholarly standards to Jewish studies. The dismissal of all Jewish university teachers as a result of the
Nuremberg Laws in 1935 led the Hochschule to hire several of the
suddenly unemployed faculty members. The additional staff enabled it to broaden its curriculum so as to provide university-level
teaching in a wide range of subjects in the humanities and social
sciences. Such courses were open to Jewish students, all of whom
faced increasing restrictions on admission to German universities.
The objective was "to transform the Hochschule gradually and in a
non-obtrusive manner into a Jewish university."[37]

The neo-orthodox supported the Rabbinerseminar für das Or-
thodoxe Judentum, popularly known as the Hildesheimer Seminary,
after its founder, Esriel Hildesheimer. His successors maintained the
tradition of *torah im derekh-eretz*, combining adherence to *halachah*
(Jewish law) with respect for the canons of contemporary scholarship. Secular studies were a required part of the curriculum. The
seminary was on that account regarded with suspicion by the super-
orthodox.

The appointment of the Lithuanian-born Jehiel Jacob Weinberg
as rector of the Hildesheimer Seminary in 1931 did not bring peace.
Weinberg had studied at Lithuanian *yeshivot* and held a doctorate
from the University of Giessen. In the course of a long sojourn in
Germany, he had gradually moved away from the closed world of
Lithuanian Judaism toward the more sophisticated intellectual outlook of German modern orthodoxy. The suspicions of the strictly
orthodox increased in 1937 when, in an unprecedented exercise in
cooperation, students of the Hildesheimer Seminary joined those of
the Hochschule in attending joint lectures on non-Jewish subjects.
As a concession to critics, however, these lectures took place not on
the premises of the Hochschule but in a "neutral place."[38]

The Breslau Jüdisch-Theologisches Seminar, founded in 1854,
and the Budapest Rabbinical Seminary, founded in 1877, were non-
orthodox but traditionalist, akin to Conservative Judaism in the

United States. They taught "positive historical Judaism."[39] The rules of conduct at these institutions were quite different from those at *yeshivot*. Raphael Patai, who studied at both Breslau and Budapest in the 1930s, recalled that he and other students went regularly to the cinema and even attended dance halls, both of which would have been regarded as scandalous behavior by a *yeshiva bokher*.[40]

"To Make It More Edible"

Orthodoxy and Reform were two deeply entrenched camps but, as the records of the seminaries illustrate, there were all sorts of gradations within and between, as well as regional variations.

Reform Judaism had originated in Germany in the early nineteenth century. It sought to rid Judaism of what were seen as obsolete accretions. *Halachah* (religious law) was no longer regarded as changeless. The messiah was no longer expected imminently. The vernacular replaced Hebrew in services. Choirs, organs, and sermons were introduced into synagogues. Many strict observances were relaxed. In some cases the Sabbath was moved to Sunday.

Not only the orthodox despised the accommodationist tendency of the German Reformers. Joseph Roth wrote of them in 1933 with contemptuous insight: "Because they didn't have the courage to convert, *they preferred instead to have the entire Jewish religion baptised.*"[41]

In the United States, Reform Judaism eventually became the largest Jewish denomination. Yet in the land of its origin it barely existed: in Berlin there was just one Reform synagogue.

Instead, the great majority of German Jews belonged to *Einheitsgemeinde* ("united communities") that generally adhered to a Liberal form of worship. Liberal Jews, while sharing many of the basic principles of Reform Judaism in the United States, were less radical in their rejection of tradition. Liberal congregations, although most common in Germany, spread to many other parts of Europe. Neolog congregations in Hungary, about two-thirds of the community there, as well as in formerly Hungarian regions such as Slovakia, were similar in outlook and, as in Germany, attracted the more affluent, assimilatory class as well as those who aspired to join it.

One should not imagine that all Jews were equally concerned about the differences among these various denominations. Most, indeed, simply thought of themselves as Jews tout court. Some adopted positions that cut across established lines, for example ultra-orthodox Zionists, and many adapted their practice to external exigencies.

Few devoted much attention to issues of faith or belief: what counted in Judaism was practice, though that too was often flexible. The writer Primo Levi recorded that in his youth in Turin in the 1920s, his father, "a fundamentally secular man, did not eat pork 'out of a kind of superstitious fear'; yet he ate ham, albeit 'with a guilty expression.' "[42] Robert Kanfer recalls that in his semi-assimilated home in Vienna in the 1930s, although the family ate *matzot* on the Passover, his father, "to make it more edible, turned it into a sandwich with butter and ham."[43]

Sour Cream in the Slop Bucket

In Soviet Russia, all religious activity was subjected to an intense official campaign of antireligious propaganda. In 1917 there had been an estimated 12,000 *hadorim* in the Russian Empire, with 170,000 pupils.[44] But in December 1920 the Central Jewish Bureau of the Department of Public Education issued an order for "the liquidation of *hadorim* and *yeshivot*": "The children must be liberated from the terrible prison, from the full spiritual demoralization and from physical deterioration."[45]

The following year a show trial of the *heder* took place at Vitebsk. Appropriately, given their performative character, the proceedings took place not in a court of law but in a local theater. The defendants included a former *talmud torah* teacher, a Yiddish poet, and a former left-Bundist. The opening of the trial was disrupted by a crowd of religious Jews, who assembled to defend the *heder*. After a postponement of several days, the trial reopened in the town's main theater, which was filled to the rafters. Both sides brought claques of supporters to the theater, which resounded to the laughter, applause, and partisan cries of rival factions in the audience.

The prosecutor declared that pretrial investigations had disclosed the existence in the town of thirty-nine *hadorim* with forty-nine *melamdim*, most of them elderly, and 1,358 pupils, ranging in age from five to seventeen. Four hundred of these also attended a public school; for the rest the *heder* was their only source of education. The prosecution portrayed the *heder* as an institution that was faulty by every criterion—hygiene, personnel, pedagogy, and curriculum. The *melamdim* had a "medieval" outlook. Premises were filthy, some veritable pigsties. Pupils were said to have been "terrorized" by sadistic beatings. The *heder* was injurious to the physical and spiritual development of the pupils. It inculcated chauvinism and hatred for non-Jews. The prosecutor called for a "death sentence" against the *heder*.

In the course of the proceedings, conducted in Yiddish, the court heard testimony from witnesses for the prosecution who quoted from the works of writers such as Salomon Maimon, Peretz Smolenskin, and Y. L. Peretz, recounting the horrors of the *heder* system. One witness accused a *melamed* of pederasty. Witnesses for the defense were permitted to dispute the prosecutor's contentions and counterquoted Philo and Maimonides, Froebel, Pestalozzi, and others, all to no avail. When one witness tried to defend a *melamed* who was present in the theater, the prosecutor retorted with the old adage "You can't whiten a slop bucket with a spoonful of sour cream."

Rabbi Shmaryahu Leib Medalia, appearing for the defense, complained that the trial was unequal, since one side, the prosecution, was supported by the political power. Medalia, according to the trial transcript, worked himself up into a state of "religious ecstasy," declaiming several times in thunderous tones: "Di toyre iz min hashomayim" ("The Torah comes from heaven"), and invoking martyrs of old who had sacrificed their lives in its defense. The president of the court assured him that the Soviet state recognized freedom of religion. But Medalia would not be stilled. "You think you have already passed judgement on the *heder* and the Torah and that the Torah, God forbid, has been rendered null and void, that you've already torn up the Torah: no! *Di toyre hot gelebt un vet lebn!*" ("The Torah has lived and shall live!") Medalia's declaration undoubtedly reflected a significant part of Jewish public opinion in the town, as shown by frequent complaints by the prosecution, in the course of the trial, about demonstrations of support for the defendants.

The result, however, was not in doubt. After five days of proceedings, the final session lasted from six o'clock in the evening until five the next morning. A tensely hushed court heard the judges pronounce a verdict of guilty. They ordered all *hadorim* to be closed. *Melamdim* were required to sign statements undertaking that they would no longer teach. Pupils were to be transferred to Yiddish secular schools. The verdict, greeted with an enthusiastic mass singing of the "Internationale," was hailed as a victory over "Jewish clericalism, Zionism, and nationalism." But the transcript concluded by recording that the defense counsel sang in unison the second stanza of the Zionist anthem, "Hatikva: Od lo avda tikvatenu . . ." ("Our hope is not yet lost . . .").[46]

In 1922 the Russian criminal code made the teaching of religion to groups of more than three children under the age of eighteen an offense punishable by up to a year's hard labor. *Melamdim* were put on trial and, in at least one case, in Polotsk, near Vitebsk, pupils were called as witnesses against their former teacher.[47] Some *hadorim* lingered on, especially in the *shtetlakh* of the former Pale. In 1928–29 they were reported still to be active in 183 towns.[48] But by the late 1930s they had been altogether eliminated from Soviet territory.

The Vitebsk trial was the first of many such quasi-judicial, antireligious morality plays that were mounted in these years. In Minsk in 1925 the trial of a *shochet*, accused of attempted murder of a rival, provided the occasion for attack on another central Jewish institution: kosher slaughter. Attended by three thousand people, the trial was widely reported in the press and formed the subject of a Yiddish play used in antireligious propaganda.[49] A further trial, in Kharkov in 1928, placed in the dock yet another feature of traditional Jewish life, the practice of circumcision. That trial was brilliantly satirized by Isaac Babel in his story "Karl-Yankel" (1931), a vignette peopled with vivid grotesques.

The trials were partly propaganda from above. But they also reflected real internal conflict for the heart and soul of the Jewish population. Bolsheviks sought to portray this as a war between revolutionary activists and bourgeois upholders of the traditional order. In fact, they were struggles not so much between protagonists of the past and the future as over rival conceptions of the Jewish here and now.

These episodes were part of a larger campaign of antireligious warfare waged by *Evsektsiia* in the 1920s. Feasts were held on fast days and a "red *bris*" sometimes replaced the circumcision ceremony, though a majority of males in the 1920s were probably still circumcised. Religious Jews responded to government orders to close down synagogues with protests, petitions, and demonstrations, but to little effect.

In 1928–29, rabbis, like priests, together with their families, were deprived of rights to housing, social security, and higher education. Over the next decade, most synagogues and ritual baths were closed and kosher meat became almost unavailable.

In the small town of Slutsk, in Byelorussia, nearly all Jewish institutions, except Yiddish schools, were closed in 1926 and the synagogue was turned into a military warehouse. The rabbi of the town, Yehezkel Abramsky, a noted Talmudic authority and author of *Hazon Yehezkel*, a commentary on the Tosefta ("Additions" to the Mishnah), was able, in 1928, to publish the only rabbinical periodical ever to appear in the USSR, *Yagdil Torah*, but it was banned after just two numbers. Abramsky was arrested in Moscow in 1930 and accused of having provided information to a visiting ecclesiastical delegation from the United States that was investigating religious persecution in the USSR. He was sentenced, without trial, to five years' hard labor in Siberia. After intercession by German rabbis with Chancellor Heinrich Brüning, he was released in 1931 in exchange for a Communist held in Germany and was put over the border to Latvia.

The closure of *Evsektsiia* in 1930 did not end antireligious propaganda, which was taken up with even greater intensity by other bodies, such as the League of Militant Godless, which published the Yiddish magazine *Der Apikoyres* (The Heretic) between 1931 and 1935.

A Yiddish *Antireligiezer literarisher layenbukh* (Antireligious Literary Reader) appeared in Minsk in 1930, designed, so the editors affirmed, "to illustrate the fact that religion, in all its historical metamorphoses, maintains its subversive and cannibalistic character."[50] The selected texts included the early-nineteenth-century anti-Hasidic satire of Yosef Perl; Yiddish socialist writers such as Morris Winchevsky, Morris Rosenfeld, and Dovid Pinski (all residents of the United States); and the familiar genre of dire memoirs of violence and filth in the *heder*. As for Yiddish literature, the editors had some trouble identifying suitable passages. Classical Yiddish literature, with the exception of the young Peretz, they explained, had been almost barren of antireligious, as distinct from anticlerical, themes. They therefore looked further afield, to authors such as Lucretius, Heine, and Sinclair Lewis. More surprisingly they included passages by two of the founders of modern Hebrew literature, Peretz Smolenskin and Yehuda Leib Gordon, whose works by this time were scarcely acceptable for publication in the USSR in any other context. Anticipating possible objections to such a contents list, the editors explained that, since some of the texts by "bourgeois" authors were defective in their approach, they had omitted certain words, phrases, or passages. With a few exceptions such as Shmuel Halkin, Peretz Markish, and Dovid Hofshteyn, and (translated from Russian) Ilya Ehrenburg, Soviet writers were lightly represented. Soviet literature, Yiddish and Russian alike, the editors lamented, had not tackled the subject directly: there was an urgent need, they declared, for it to do so.[51] One Soviet writer was conspicuously absent: the former seminarian who now ruled the country.

Many Jews no doubt considered it possible to reconcile continued Jewish observance with loyalty to, or at any rate acquiescence in, the Soviet system, like Old Gedali in Isaac Babel's story, who inquires: "So let's say we say 'yes' to the Revolution. But does that mean that we're supposed to say 'no' to the Sabbath?"[52]

Meanwhile, however, the introduction of a compulsory six-day workweek in 1929 made Sabbath observance by Jews virtually impossible. Failure to turn up for work on Saturdays or Jewish holidays became a punishable offense.

Such basic religious practices as observance of the Sabbath, kosher slaughter, and circumcision nevertheless continued to be practiced in the Soviet Union, albeit often surreptitiously and on a decreasing scale, particularly in large cities such as Minsk and in *shtetlakh* of the former Pale. The young Polish Communist Moshe Zalcman, who immigrated to the USSR in 1933, reports that on Yom Kippur in Kiev in the mid-1930s, Jewish factory workers would turn up for work but abstain from smoking or eating in the canteen.[53] When he visited his uncle in Moscow, he found him teaching the *humash* to his two sons.

Yeshivot were not, initially, considered illegal by the Soviet regime, so long as students were over eighteen years of age. But in practice they were hounded out of existence. By 1928–29 they functioned in only twelve towns, with a total of just 620 students.[54] Of these, 150 were in Minsk, but the single remaining *yeshiva* there closed at the end of 1930. The last report of the exposure of an underground *yeshiva* in the USSR came from Berdichev in 1938.[55]

The Chabad movement of the sixth Lubavitcher *rebbe*, Yosef Yitshak Schneerson, who had succeeded his father in 1920, was active in the USSR until the early 1930s. The family had left Lubavitch in 1915; the *rebbe* lived in Rostov until 1924, then in Leningrad. At a conference of Soviet rabbis in 1926 he was elected president— though he did not attend. In 1927–29, as Lubavitch *yeshivot* in other towns were closed, their students moved to a new, clandestine *yeshiva* in Vitebsk, which held classes in synagogue buildings. The number of students reached 150 but it proved hard to find Jewish homes ready to offer them the traditional free meals, especially after the authorities started seeking the names and addresses of such generous householders. In early 1928 the head of the *yeshiva* was arrested. For a time it continued to function secretly in private houses but shortly before Passover in 1930 it closed altogether and the remaining instructors were imprisoned.

The prisoners, with their long beards, *peyes* (sidelocks), and *kapotes*, were held in jail for several months. They managed to smuggle in *talesim* (prayer shawls) and even a *shofar* (ram's horn), to be used in the celebration of the high holy days. But at New Year they were suddenly told they could go, provided only that they signed a receipt for all their belongings. This they refused to do on a holy day. Accordingly, they were held until the end of the feast, when they were released. Twelve students fled to Georgia, where Soviet control over religious activity was more lax.[56] The Lubavitcher *rebbe* had meanwhile been imprisoned in 1927 but after foreign pressure on the Soviet authorities, he was released and permitted to leave for Latvia.

Claims of clandestine Chabad activity in the Soviet Union under Stalin may be exaggerated but we have at least some corroborating evidence. Isaac Bashevis Singer, then a little-known Yiddish journalist in Warsaw, on a visit to the USSR in 1926, was present at a "secluded midnight celebration" of Lubavitch Hasidim and "was surprised to find among them engineers, students, and other enlightened men" who had become pious *after* the revolution.[57]

In Uman and Tul'chyn, in Ukraine, remnants of the Bratslav Hasidim continued to maintain a religious life until the late 1930s. This was a unique sect of mystics who, unlike all other Hasidim, had no living leader: instead, they followed the teachings and gloried in the memory of their founder, Nahman of Bratslav (1772–1810), who died without issue. Hence they were known as the "dead Hasidim." The Bratslavers regarded Nahman as the messiah and expected his imminent return from the dead, an event that would herald the dawn of the messianic era. Some moved to Poland (mainly Lublin and Warsaw) after the Russian Revolution but, given the central importance to the sect of the annual pilgrimage to their founder's tomb in Uman, a few elected to remain there. Their *kloyzl* (small prayer hall) there was requisitioned, however, in the mid-1930s, and after a denunciation was sent to the authorities, several of the Hasidim were arrested.[58]

Two distinguished rabbis, members of the Twersky Hasidic dynasty, remained active in the Soviet Union throughout the 1930s: Shlomo Ben-Zion Twersky, the *admor* (a high rabbinic title) of Chernobyl, had moved to the United States after the revolution but returned to live in Kiev because, as it was said, "the materialistic life in America did not suit him."[59] The authorities even returned his apartment, which had been nationalized. He died in 1939. In the *shtetl* of Makhnovka (known from 1935 as Komsomolske), near Berdichev, Avraham Yehoshua Heschel Twersky, the *admor* of Makhnovka, maintained a Hasidic court, the last in the Soviet Union, though the local Jewish community had dwindled by 1939 to just

843 persons, a third of its size in 1897. These two cases, however, were exceptional.

In 1936–38, several of the most prominent remaining rabbis in the Soviet Union were arrested. Some were released after a short time. But Rabbi Shmaryahu Leib Medalia, secretary of the Bet Din (rabbinical court) in Moscow, who had been such an outspoken witness for the defense in the Vitebsk *heder* trial, was arrested with his family, accused of counterrevolutionary activities, and executed. Mordechai Feinstein, rabbi of Shklov, who had headed a *yeshiva* there until 1930, was arrested while seated at the festive table of Shavuot (Pentecost) and sent to Siberia, where he died. His brother Moshe Feinstein, rabbi of Luban, a *shtetl* near Minsk, and a contributor with Abramsky to *Yagdil Torah*, was permitted to leave for the United States. By 1939, fewer than 250 Jewish "clerics" remained in the whole of the USSR.

The secularization of Soviet Jewry was part and parcel of its rapid urbanization and modernization and was most strongly felt among the young. Jewish religious practice became almost exclusively the preserve of the prerevolutionary generation. Any form of religious observance by party members was regarded, by the mid-1930s, as deviant behavior.

In 1937, apparently in order to demonstrate the progress of the antireligious campaign, a question about religious belief was included in the Soviet census. The result was embarrassing: no less than 57 percent of the population as a whole declared themselves believers. Yet in this, as in other respects, Jews revealed themselves as the most perfectly sovietized Soviet nationality: just 10 percent of Jews pronounced themselves believers. Twice as many Jewish women as men did so.[60]

Yet here lay a double paradox, since while women were, in traditional Judaism, second-class citizens (actually, not citizens at all), in much of the rest of Europe they were in the vanguard of modernization and acculturation of Jewish society.

7

UNHOLY WOMEN

Chained Women

"The inferior status of women was not merely an inherited folk prejudice but a tradition rooted in the Talmud and the Codes, the sacred sources of Judaism."[1] Ben-Zion Gold's observation on the attitude of orthodox circles of his youth in Radom finds support in rabbinic sources. According to a much-quoted dictum by the Talmudic sage Rabbi Eliezer, he who teaches his daughter Torah is teaching her promiscuity.[2] This view was endorsed, if in less colorful terms, by such venerated authorities as Maimonides in the twelfth century and Joseph Karo in the sixteenth. In its most extreme form, it was pressed by the Munkácser *rebbe* into a questionable interpretation of the Talmud. Referring to a famous passage in which Beruria, the learned wife of a rabbi, is commended for urging her husband to pray for the repentance rather than the destruction of evildoers, the *rebbe* declared that since it was "both obvious and certain that the Talmud did not take the opinions of a woman seriously," the text could safely be set aside.[3]

The woman in traditional Jewish society in eastern Europe was usually dependent for most of her life on her father or husband. She was good for bearing children, for household work, sometimes also for helping to run the family business, but not for the most serious department of Jewish life, religious scholarship. Folk doggerel might express some ambivalence about her exact status:

> *Finef finger hot a khap!*
> Five fingers in a catch!

fir fislakh hot a betl,
>Four legs on a bed

dray ekn hot a krepl,
>Three corners on a dumpling

tsvey ekn hot a shtekn,
>Two ends on a stick

eyns iz a yidene
>One is a Jewish woman

nit zi lebt, nit zi shvebt
>She neither lives, nor floats in the air

nit afn himl, nit af dr'erd.[4]
>Neither in heaven, nor on earth.

But as between a son or a daughter there could be no doubt about a father's preference: "Beser a zun a beder, eyder a tokhter a rebbetzin!" ("Better a son, even one who is a bathhouse attendant, than a daughter, even one who is a rabbi's wife!")

A girl might attend the early classes of *heder* but she was barred from higher levels of Jewish study. As an adult, she could not be counted toward a *minyan*, nor play an active role of any kind in the synagogue. Indeed, strictly orthodox women in eastern Europe seldom attended services, save on a limited number of festivals, such as Simhat Torah, and when they did so, were confined behind a screen or, in larger, modern synagogues, in a gallery. The *bat mitzvah* confirmation ceremony, initiated in the United States in 1922, did not become common there until the 1940s and was almost unknown in interwar Europe, save in isolated cases such as that of the future painter Charlotte Salomon in Berlin in about 1929.

Among the neo-orthodox in Germany and elsewhere, the female sex was granted a little more latitude. Their womenfolk attended synagogue more frequently, for example on the Sabbath morning, but not on the eve of Sabbath or festivals, as they would be at home preparing the festive meal. Whereas in eastern Europe women did not sing *zmires* (*zemirot*, Sabbath hymns) at the table with their menfolk, in neo-orthodox families in Germany they often did so.

One of the major innovations of non-orthodox congregations was to enhance the role of women, although in the interwar period they still sat separately from men at most Liberal services. The

Prinzregentenstrasse synagogue in Berlin, opened in 1930, was the first in the city in which men and women sat together.

In the nineteenth century the main purpose in life of a young woman in the *shtetl* and in Sephardic communities of the Balkans was marriage, usually before the age of twenty. An unmarried daughter in her late twenties was a shame to her family and an object of pity. Arranged marriages were common and the *shadkhan* (matchmaker) performed a vital social function into the early twentieth century. For a time, the profession had its own magazine, published in Vilna. Among the Romaniotes (Greek-speaking descendants of Byzantine Jews) of Ioannina, in northern Greece, in 1939 "it was still the custom for parents to select the mates for their children. After the two sets of parents had come to an agreement, generally through the matchmaker (*proxenitis*), the father announced the betrothal to his son or daughter as a fait accompli."[5] Even in the relatively modernized environment of a city such as Cracow, the matchmaker was still "an indispensable institution" in the 1930s.[6] Jewish migrants from Galicia took their marriage customs with them and in the interwar period strictly orthodox girls in Vienna were often married off to spouses chosen for them by their parents. In new environments the *shadkhan* was transformed into a modernized equivalent, as in the matchmaking section of the Paris Yiddish newspaper, *Parizer haynt*.

By the 1930s, Jewish women, even in the *shtetl*, were marrying later than a generation earlier and Jews were marrying later than gentiles all over Europe. By 1931 the average age of marriage for Jewish women in Poland was twenty-seven.[7]

In earlier times nearly all Jews had married. But by the 1930s this was no longer the case. In western Europe a growing minority of men and women remained single throughout their lives. The numerical imbalance of sexes after the First World War, particularly in the Soviet Union, led, for the first time in modern history in eastern Europe, to the presence in Jewish society of large numbers of never-married women. In Byelorussia in 1939, for every 1,000 unmarried Jewish men between the ages of twenty and twenty-nine, there were 1,687 unmarried Jewish women.[8]

Upon marriage, Ashkenazi Jewish women in eastern Europe had traditionally shaved their heads and henceforth worn a wig (*shaytl*).

Actually, the practice was relatively modern, probably dating only from the late eighteenth century, and had been opposed by the Hatam Sofer as an innovation. By the 1930s it was confined to the strictly orthodox. The form of female head covering varied according to location, milieu, and degree of religiosity. For some, a headscarf covering all the hair was deemed adequate. In the case of wives of Hasidic rabbis, wigs were regarded as unsatisfactory and a headscarf was de rigueur. The maternal grandmother of Fritz Worms, child of a middle-class orthodox family in Frankfurt in the 1930s, wore a *shaytl*, "a tightly woven, upside-down bird's nest," but his mother did not.[9]

Regular recourse to the *mikveh* (ritual bath), required of women in preparation for marriage, after menstruation, and after the birth of a child, was confined to similar circles. On the Sabbath afternoon orthodox women in the *shtetl* would read the *Tsene-rene* (literally "Go Forth and See," from Song of Songs 3:11), a popular Yiddish adaptation of biblical tales, designed "for women and uneducated men," as the earliest extant edition, published in 1622, put it.[10] Some would recite *tkhines* (supplicatory prayers in Yiddish) at home. At the conclusion of the Sabbath they would say the Yiddish prayer "Got fun Avrom" (God of Abraham) to greet the new week.

Among Hasidim the separation of women remained quite strict: men would dance only with other men. But in broader society, even in the *shtetl*, such customs were changing. A memoirist from the town of Piotrków-Trybunalski in central Poland recalls that at wedding feasts in the 1930s, although men and women sat at separate tables, often in separate rooms, they would dance together.[11] To the traditional folk dances, the *freylekhs*, the *sher*, and the *skotshne*, were now added the foxtrot, the Charleston, and the rumba. Even a small town such as Baranowicze boasted a "dancing academy."

There is no evidence that Jewish men behaved worse than other men toward their womenfolk. Given that drunkenness was much less common among Jews than gentiles, Jewish wives probably suffered less physical harm than others. But as the sensational press and the courts showed, they were by no means immune from violence at the hands of their husbands. The plight of the maltreated wife was a common theme in *shund* ("trash") literature and in popular song:

A gut ovent, brayne
        Good evening, Brayne
di beste shkheyne, mayne! . . .
        My dearest neighbor! . . .
nekhtn hot er mikh geshlogn.
        Yesterday he beat me
broyn un blo hot er mikh gemakht. . . . [12]
        Left me brown and blue. . . .

Those women who suffered ill treatment had limited options. Religious divorce was entirely in the gift of the husband. Civil divorce was hard to obtain almost everywhere, save in the Soviet Union.

The divorce rate among Jews nevertheless rose rapidly in the interwar period. The increase was marked in eastern as well as western Europe. In Kovno, for example, it rose, as a proportion of marriages, from 60 per thousand in 1925 to 140 in 1937.[13] This figure is presented with a caveat: a *sofer* (scribe) competent to prepare a *get* (religious bill of divorce) was not available elsewhere in Lithuania, so most would-be divorcers from the provinces came to Kovno to obtain the document, thus elevating the statistics for the city. All the same, the trend was clear.

In the Soviet Union, where divorce was easier to obtain than anywhere else in Europe, the Jewish rate rose dramatically: in Leningrad in 1936 it reached 298 per thousand of all Jewish marriages.[14] Rates such as this were much higher than for non-Jews and also higher than for Jews in earlier times. They demonstrate that the supposed cohesion of the Jewish family was by this time conventional myth, not social reality.

A unique form of distress was experienced by *agunot*, "chained women," who could not remarry because they were unable to obtain a *get*. Some such women had been abandoned; others were widows of soldiers who had fallen in wars but whose deaths were unrecorded; and in a few cases husbands were incompetent or stubbornly refused to grant a *get*. Jewish law required that a husband must either be proven dead or consent to a divorce before a wife might remarry.

Similar problems arose in the case of a widow whose husband

had died without offspring. The brother of the deceased (the *levir*) was required, according to rabbinic law, to perform the ceremony of *halitzah*, releasing the widow from the requirement to marry him and thus enabling her to marry another person. Problems arose where the *levir* was absent, mentally ill, an apostate, or simply refused to perform the ceremony.

Although the problem of *aginut* affected the orthodox most acutely, many moderately religious widows balked at the prospect of defying Jewish law and tradition blatantly by ignoring these requirements, thus not only rendering themselves ineligible for religious remarriage but also marking any children of a future marriage indelibly with the stigma of bastardy.

The word *mamzer*, generally translated as "bastard" though often used as a general term of opprobrium, was, in Jewish law, reserved for children of forbidden degrees of marriage. Children simply born out of wedlock were not technically regarded as *mamzerim*. The *mamzer* was, in effect, an outcast from the Jewish community ("A *mamzer* shall not enter the congregation of the Lord," Deuteronomy 23:3). Hence the peculiar horror of women in the awful limbo of *aginut*. Rabbinic authorities had wrestled with the issue unsuccessfully for centuries. It remained a stark reminder of the second-class status of women in orthodox Judaism.

Thousands of women in eastern Europe were affected, because of the upheavals between 1914 and 1921 and because large numbers of young men had emigrated, mainly to the Americas, promising, but often failing, to return later to collect their wives. In Vilna a Committee for Women's Defense sought to alleviate that problem by trying, in cooperation with similar bodies in other cities and countries, to locate missing husbands. But they had limited success.

The difficulty of obtaining divorce from a recalcitrant husband gave rise to many tragic cases and sensational newspaper stories. Desperate women might resort to a "corner-shop rabbi" (*vinkl-rov*) who sold his services for dubious purposes. In 1939 a special session of the Warsaw rabbinical court heard a case concerning a certain Yaakov Yagodnik. A few years earlier, as a *yeshiva bokher* in Ostrów, he had married a rich young woman from Białystok. He became chronically ill and she asked him for a divorce, which he declined to grant. She and her relatives were alleged to have held him in a Warsaw hotel room with a corrupt cleric in attendance. There they induced Yagodnik to sign a *get* without his being fully conscious of what he was doing. Subsequently the validity of the document was challenged by the rabbi of Ostrów. Such, at any rate, was Yaakov's side of the story. Unfortunately, we do not have his wife's version, nor the decision of the court.[15]

Fewer Jewish than non-Jewish women bore children outside marriage. In Budapest in 1929 only 4 percent of Jewish births occurred out of wedlock, compared with 22 percent among non-Jews. The very rarity of Jewish illegitimacy, in the sense of births to unmarried parents, however, meant that cases, when they occurred, particularly in the small community of the *shtetl*, were a source of scandal and shame.

An unmarried Jewish mother who could not persuade the Jewish father of her child to marry her before the birth could hardly remain in the *shtetl* and would be compelled to leave for the sheltering anonymity of a city or for America. Before departure, she might hand over the illegitimate child to nearby peasants (who might see the gift as an extra pair of laboring hands) or place the infant in an orphanage, if one were available. Under a false name, perhaps claiming to be an aunt, she might send money periodically to cover expenses for the child's upkeep.[16]

If, however, the father were not Jewish and she married him (illegitimate children being the most common catalyst of such, still relatively infrequent, outmarriages in the *shtetl*), she would dishonor her family twice over: exogamy, after all, was hardly less of a disgrace than illegitimacy. Such couples too, with the child, would often move away—and appear from time to time among the arriving lists of steerage passengers on ships docking at Ellis Island and other ports of disembarkation in North America.

Liberated Women

In the early twentieth century, Jewish women in much of Europe threw off many of the shackles that had previously bound them. They played a role quite out of proportion to their numbers in the feminist movement all over the continent. They moved into previously all-male spheres, acquired political rights inside and outside Jewish communities, and often preceded male Jews in opening doors to acculturation in non-Jewish societies.

The reasons for all this were probably connected to the Jews' high level of urbanization and to the decline in fertility, which occurred earlier and faster than among surrounding populations. Early and widespread use of artificial birth control among Jews was both a cause and a symptom of women's ability to free themselves from the constrictions of traditional Jewish society.

In Germany, in particular, Jewish women were much more mobilized than non-Jews into women's organizations. Bertha Pappenheim (1859–1936), who headed the moderately feminist Jüdischer Frauenbund, founded in 1904, was a founding figure in German-Jewish and international feminism. (She later became famous as Freud's case study "Anna O.") Her organization combined feminism with Jewish communal activism. It organized resistance to "white slavery" and engaged in social work among the sick, the elderly, children, delinquents, prostitutes, and female Jewish convicts. By 1929 the Frauenbund had a membership of fifty thousand women, drawn mainly from the middle class.

Both Pappenheim and the organization were quite conservative in their social attitudes, embracing the concept of motherhood as a primary function of the female sex. On religious grounds, the Frauenbund rejected birth control and abortion, though, given the demographic data, there can be no doubt that many of its members utilized artificial contraceptives. At the same time, it sought to open career opportunities to women. While formally neutral in politics and religion, the Frauenbund campaigned for women's rights, combated anti-Semitism, and was sympathetic to the international feminist-pacifist movement, in which Jewish women from several countries were leading participants. It was not actively hostile to Zionism but kept its distance. Pappenheim's obituary, written by herself, supposedly for a Zionist paper, called her "an old and active enemy of our movement, though one cannot deny that she had Jewish consciousness, and strength. She believed herself a German but was an assimilationist. What a pity!"[17]

Unlike many women's associations, the Frauenbund was not

dissolved upon the Nazi takeover of power, since it could hardly be absorbed into the Nazi women's organization, but it functioned after 1933 under police surveillance. Between then and 1938, when, like most Jewish organizations, it was closed down by the government, it focused on helping Jews in need and on assisting prospective emigrants to prepare for their departure.

Alice Salomon, "the German Jane Addams," was a pioneer of women's social work in Germany and another major figure in the international women's movement. In 1908 she established the Soziale Frauenschule in Berlin and in 1925 the German Academy for Women's Social and Pedagogic Work. Salomon had grown up in an enlightened, secularized household in which religion played next to no role. "We never celebrated anything other than the Christian festivals at home and knew nothing of Jewish laws or customs."[18] In 1914 she converted to Lutheranism—"the most important decision I have ever taken, a decision that I took out of belief." During the Nazi period she belonged to the anti-Nazi Bekennende Kirche (Confessing Church). Like many converts, she continued to regard herself as in some sense Jewish. In 1933 the government forbade her to enter her school. Faced with demands for the dismissal of Jewish teachers and students, she chose to close down the academy. She annoyed the Nazis by continuing to play a public role in international women's affairs until her expulsion from Germany in 1937.

In the Netherlands too, Jewish women were prominent in the feminist movement, through both the Council for Jewish Women and general women's organizations. Aletta Jacobs (1854–1929), a suffragist, pacifist, and advocate of birth control, was the first woman to enter a Dutch university (Groningen in 1871). Insisting that she was a "world citizen," Jacobs withheld support from the Council of Jewish Women, whether "out of political [or] out of religious conviction."[19]

The next generation of Dutch Jewish feminists, however, were less inclined, or found it less easy, to shrug off Jewish identification, as the issues of anti-Semitism and Palestine became impossible to avoid. Like some male Jewish politicians, they sometimes deliberately chose to remain in the background for fear of provoking anti-Jewish reactions. Occasionally, they nevertheless felt it necessary to take a stand on Jewish issues. In 1939, for example, Rosa Manus, one of the leaders of the Women's International League for Peace and Freedom, established during the First World War, engaged in a wrangle with an Egyptian delegate at an International Woman Suffrage Alliance meeting in Copenhagen on the subject of Jewish refugee immigration to Palestine.[20]

Within Jewish communities no less than outside, women had to fight hard to obtain equal rights, including the right to vote. Nearly all orthodox authorities in eastern Europe and Germany in the interwar period strongly opposed women's involvement in politics in any form, whether as voters or as candidates for office inside or beyond the community.

In Poland only those who were taxpaying heads of household could vote in *kehillah* elections. The exclusion of women from participation in the political life of the *kehillot* was challenged by women's groups such as the Farband fun Yidishe Froyen, a left-Zionist organization, but they had no success in changing the law. Although both sexes could vote in parliamentary elections in interwar Poland, the turnout of Jewish women at the first general election, in 1919, was lower than that of Jewish men and of non-Jewish women. Some Hasidic *rebbes* permitted women to vote in elections to the Polish parliament (to have done otherwise would have greatly reduced the influence of the orthodox) but the general orthodox approach remained in principle unchanged. Of the total of 107 Jewish deputies and senators elected to the two houses of the Polish parliament in the interwar period, just one was a woman.

The socialist movement was theoretically committed to equality of the sexes but, in this period, rarely practiced what it preached. Whereas men of Jewish origin played a major role in the leadership of the Austrian Social Democrat Party, women, whether Jewish or gentile, occupied only secondary roles. In the Bund, theoretically committed to sexual equality, women remained distinctly secondary. Its women's organization, Yidishe Arbeter-froyen Organizatsye, never amounted to very much and in 1939 only about 10 percent of the party's members in Warsaw were female. The best-known woman in the Bund's leadership after the Russian Revolution, Ester Frumkin, joined the Com-Bund and later became a leading figure in the Soviet Communist Party and in the *Evsektsiia*.

In Germany, vigorous campaigning by women's groups gained

them the vote in communal elections in all the major communities except Cologne by 1929. But women rarely played more than a subordinate role in communal life, generally finding themselves confined to what was regarded as the female sphere—charitable activity, care of children, and so forth. After 1933 the Jüdischer Frauenbund was unsuccessful in its demand for representation in the leadership of the Reichsvertretung. Its head, Leo Baeck, explained that women and men differed in their capacities: "While men possessed perspicacity and foresight, women had the gift of being good listeners . . . of being able to recognize the needs of mankind . . . and of shaping an evening with warmth, dignity and substance."[21]

Women had had the right to vote within the Zionist Organization since 1898 but nearly all the Zionist leaders were men. Though some Mizrachists felt that the election of women candidates would breach the walls of modesty between the sexes, the religious Zionist movement decided to support women's suffrage and the right of women to be candidates for political office. Women did not, however, play any significant part in Mizrachi politics or in the affairs of other Zionist parties in Europe.

The Women's International Zionist Organization (WIZO), founded in 1920, had branches in all the European communities. Its membership was generally middle-class and it devoted its efforts mainly to fund-raising. Women Zionists, while active in their own sphere, were often regarded as exotic intruders if they ventured into broader domains. Dora Gross-Moszkowski, who used to travel around Polish towns in the 1930s, lecturing on behalf of the Zionists, recalled one occasion when, arriving in a town to speak in the local synagogue, she was told that "as a woman I could not lecture on the platform, in front of the altar [sic], without special permission from the rabbi. I waited outside for three hours for his consent."[22]

In the Soviet Union, the subjection of women was a frequently voiced item on the Communist charge sheet against Judaism. At the heder trial in Vitebsk, one of the expert witnesses for the prosecution cited with relish the oft-quoted daily prayer in which the orthodox Jewish man thanks God that he was not born a woman.[23] The Russian Revolution opened up political life to women. It also provided them with new educational opportunities and, in principle, enabled them to participate on an equal basis with men in the workforce. Jewish women such as Rosa Luxemburg and Clara Zetkin had played a full, indeed disproportionate, role (as compared with non-Jewish women) in the revolutionary movement before 1917. After the revolution, however, they disappeared from leadership positions. Ester Frumkin, one of the last representatives of the type, was sidelined after the dissolution of the *Evsektsiia* in 1930 and imprisoned in 1937.

Notwithstanding the work of women like Pappenheim, efforts to build an international Jewish women's movement met with only halting success. The first world congress of Jewish women met in Vienna in 1923. A second, in Hamburg in 1929, was attended by delegates from fourteen countries, eleven of them European. The orthodox German-Jewish newspaper *Der Israelit* opposed the demand of the congress for women's voting rights in communities, quoting the psalmist's adage *"kol kevodah bat melekh pnimah"* (Psalms 45:13, "The king's daughter is all glorious within"), traditionally interpreted as meaning that the woman had no place in public life.[24] The congress resolved to form a World Federation of Jewish Women, "to unite Jewish women of the whole world, without wishing to disturb the national feelings of individuals or their practical activity in their homelands." The Depression and the rise of Nazism, however, eliminated any prospect of realizing the resolution.[25]

Yet if the record of political achievement by Jewish feminists was nugatory, Jewish women spoke more loudly and confidently in their own voices in this period. Even the strictly orthodox started to assert themselves. In 1938 the Lublin *yeshiva* celebrated the *siyyum* (conclusion) of the seven-and-a-half-year cycle of study of the *daf yomi* of the Talmud. Thousands of rabbis, *yeshiva* students, and pious delegates from all over the world gathered for the festivity. But an unprecedented note was sounded when a group of women tried to attend the ceremony, stirring male opposition. They were eventually permitted to enter a closed-off balcony. The assembled crowd waited impatiently for the proceedings to begin. After a while, the presiding rabbi mounted the platform and announced, "The *siyyum* will not take place so long as the women won't leave the *yeshiva*."

They refused to budge. Eventually a compromise was agreed: the ceremony took place in the open air. After the formalities, fireworks were set off and singing and dancing (males only) continued until four the next morning.[26]

Educated Women

"The assimilation of a people," wrote Joseph Roth in 1927, as he observed east European Jewish immigrants in Paris, "always begins with the women."[27] Roth, whose ear was peculiarly attuned to the social nuances and cultural cadences of the Habsburg lands (he was a native of Brody, eastern Galicia), expressed a view that, at least in the case of the Jews, concords with historians' findings.

In some societies women may be more resistant than men to modernizing influences, but among east European Jews, the reverse seems often to have been the case. In orthodox circles until the early twentieth century, the very fact that females were automatically excluded from many *hadorim*, from the *talmud torah*, and from the *yeshiva* meant that such education as girls received was likelier to include elements of modern, secular, non-Jewish culture. As a result, Jewish women in eastern Europe, it has been argued, turned into "engines of acculturation."[28] This remained true in the age of compulsory elementary education. In Poland, in particular, Jewish women, educated in Polish rather than Yiddish, often became actively engaged in Polish culture. The Zionist leader Yitzhak Gruenbaum, for instance, recalled that while his father shut himself in his study to read a Hebrew newspaper, his mother "opened a window" for him "to Polish literature."[29]

Even among the orthodox, however, attitudes to girls' education were beginning to change. The German neo-orthodox thinkers Hirsch and Hildesheimer had approved of girls' education—within certain limits: girls were not, for example, judged fit to learn Talmud. In 1933 the revered Hafets Hayim issued a similar ruling, though he went so far as to permit girls to study Pirkei Avot, the most popular and accessible tractate of the Talmud (also one of the shortest).

The advent of universal compulsory primary education confronted the orthodox with a challenge. If they did nothing, girls would receive an entirely secular education. Yet the very notion of incorporating girls into the *heder/talmud torah/yeshiva* system seemed unthinkable.

The solution was the network of Beys Yankev (Bet Yaakov) religious girls' schools, the first of which was founded in Cracow in 1917. Its initiator, Sarah Schenirer, was anything but a rebel. Influenced by the ideas of Hirsch and blessed in her endeavor by the Belzer *rebbe*, she persuaded the Agudist movement to support the creation of a countrywide system of such schools. Beys Yankev developed rapidly in the 1920s and eventually spread to Czechoslovakia, Lithuania, and Romania. Teachers, all of whom were female, were trained at a seminary in Cracow established in 1931. The main focus of study in the schools was on the Bible, Jewish religion, and Hebrew language and literature. The language of instruction for these subjects was Yiddish. Secular subjects such as literature, history, geography, music, handicrafts, and gymnastics were studied in Polish (or other local language). The curriculum also provided vocational courses in bookkeeping, typing, sewing, child care, nutrition, home economics, and nursing—a telling commentary on the limited occupational opportunities available to most girls, especially those from orthodox homes. Pupils were obliged to dress modestly and to say prayers twice a day. Some religious authorities, notably the Munkácser *rebbe*, disapproved of what they regarded as Beys Yankev's too progressive approach to female education, but in general the orthodox took pride in the movement's achievements.

Much has been made of the significance of these schools. Ben-Zion Gold, whose sisters attended them, argues that Beys Yankev "liberated its members from the inferior station that tradition had assigned them, turning the gender difference from inferiority to distinctiveness."[30] By 1937, two years after Schenirer's death, the 250 Beys Yankev schools taught 38,000 pupils. But none was a gymnasium and only fourteen were full primary schools. All the rest were afternoon classes that cocooned Jewish girls in an orthodox environment after they had finished the day's study in state primary schools.

Very few such girls progressed to a gymnasium and only a handful to university.

In 1932 the *Beys Yaakov Journal* conducted a survey of its girl readers, asking questions such as "What problem troubles you most?" "Would you like to be materially independent?" and "Would you prefer not to work at all and just to be a housewife?" The responses were revealing of the extent to which, even in this traditionalist milieu, many girls had absorbed advanced social views:

> I am for the emancipation of women; therefore we must be financially independent. A woman must worry about her own destiny, just the way a man does.
>
> After marriage, the husband and the wife must both strive to fulfil themselves.
>
> I'd like to earn my own living.

With despairing realism, however, the last respondent added, "—but does what I want matter?"[31]

Many Jewish young women in this period, though mainly from non-orthodox backgrounds, managed to take control of their own lives, in particular by gaining admission to colleges or universities. Even before the First World War, Jewish women had been disproportionately represented in central European universities. By the 1930s their numbers increased further—at any rate until their exclusion from German higher education under the Nazis and their limitation by the *numerus clausus* elsewhere. In 1928–29 women made up 38 percent of Jewish students in Polish universities whereas the proportion of women in the general student population was 27 percent. It often took considerable perseverance for girls to obtain university places and then even more for them to proceed into professional careers.

Working Women

In traditional society in eastern Europe, it was not customary for Jewish women to go out to work, though they might engage in some

form of economically productive activity in the home. In the interwar period, however, force of circumstance compelled even women
from orthodox homes to join the workforce, particularly in various
branches of clothing manufacture. In the textile factories of Łódź in
the early 1930s, a third of the Jewish workers were female. Women's
wages there, as almost everywhere else, were lower than men's. In
the USSR, in spite of nominal equality of the sexes, women's wages
for unskilled work in the late 1920s ranged between 67 and 85 percent of that for equivalent work performed by men.[32]

In western and central Europe between the wars, most married Jewish women did not work outside the home. In Germany in
1925, for example, only 17 percent did so. Jewish women nevertheless made rapid inroads into the professions and constituted a large
proportion of women lawyers and doctors in Germany before 1933.
Some characteristically Jewish occupations, however, remained
closed to women. In Amsterdam, for instance, only men could be
members of the diamond exchange throughout the interwar period.

Nor were Jewish women able to make much headway in another
profession that had traditionally been a male preserve: literature. Of
forty-nine Yiddish writers represented in the leading Yiddish literary periodical, *Literarishe bleter*, in 1930, just five were women.[33]
Only half a dozen or so out of the 102 official delegates to the leftist
Congress of Yiddish Culture in Paris in 1937 were women and the
assembled writers paid next to no attention to women's issues.

In May 1927 the Yiddish writer Melech Ravitch published
an article deploring the absence of women among Yiddish writers. This evoked a bitterly sardonic response from the poet Kadya
Molodowsky.[34] A slight but intrepid young woman who bore the
burdens of the world heavily on her shoulders, she won acclaim for
her early poems about poor women in Warsaw. Molodowsky indignantly rejected the condescension implied in the lumping categori-
zation of "women's poetry." When a Yiddish journalist introduced
her to his wife as "a good poetess," she responded with some heat, "I
want to persuade you to say 'a great poetess.' " When he responded
with a smile, "I don't know whether a woman can ever be a great
poetess," she slapped him on the cheek, though she quickly regretted it and added three kisses. "She wanted to make it a hard slap,"

he recalled patronizingly, "but she couldn't. She's a *klayninke* [a little slip of a girl] . . . and can't administer a slap. She's better as a singer."

Moving from her person to her verse, the same critic, writing in the *Literarishe bleter* in 1933, praised her as expressing and exemplifying the "crisis in the psyche of the Jewish woman" and pronounced her "the champion of the Jewish woman and their poetess." He detected in her verse the "rhythm of the recitative of the *tkhines* and the *Tsene-rene*." She was an initiator of Jewish women's revolt but she was "suffocated with fear: the shade of her *bobe* [granny] has terrified her."[35] Molodowsky found a more sympathetic ear in her fellow poet Rokhl Korn, who maintained that women's subjugated role placed them in closer contact with day-to-day realities, rendering them best able to achieve, as in the case of Molodowsky, a "happy synthesis of life and poetry."[36]

Jewish women writers in other languages had a little more success in breaking through the male-dominated literary establishment. The German expressionist poet Else Lasker-Schüler, for instance, was one of a group of bohemian artists and writers in Berlin in the early years of the century who adopted a conception of Judaism as a modernist, countercultural expression of protest against the assimilatory conventions of their parents. She called her friends "wilde Juden." Aged sixty-three at the time of Hitler's accession to power, she was beaten up with an iron rod by a gang of Nazis. She left Germany immediately and spent the next six years in Switzerland.

One profession remained completely closed to women: the rabbinate. The very idea of women rabbis was laughably unthinkable in the eyes of the orthodox, even though rabbis, unlike priests, were not empowered to administer sacraments or have care of souls. The main Liberal Jewish seminary in Berlin numbered 27 women among its 155 students in 1932 but none was granted *semikhah* (ordination) there. The first woman rabbi in the world, Regina Jonas, who had graduated from the Hochschule in 1930, was refused *semikhah* there. In 1935, however, she was granted it privately by a Liberal rabbi in Frankfurt. Although she was never allowed to serve as a congregational rabbi, she preached in Liberal synagogues in Berlin in 1938–39, replacing rabbis who had been arrested or had fled abroad.[37]

By contrast with this newest Jewish profession for women, the oldest continued, in the uncertain and often desperate conditions of the 1920s and 1930s, to admit and attract recruits.[37]

Fallen Women

The effort to counter prostitution and the traffic in Jewish girls, particularly from eastern Europe to south America, stretched back to the early years of the twentieth century. An international conference on the subject had taken place in 1910 but the outbreak of the First World War and the ensuing political and social chaos in eastern Europe had precluded much effective action.

A second conference convened in London in 1927 with seventy delegates from the Jewish communities of seventeen countries, including most of those in eastern and central Europe, but not the USSR, where commercialized sex was held to have disappeared. Speakers alternated between a desire to emphasize the seriousness of the moral danger represented by Jewish prostitution, and anxiety, lest, by painting too alarmist a picture, they might provide material for anti-Semitic propaganda. Thus a delegate from Łódź reported that, according to police records, only 36 out of 218 registered prostitutes in the city were Jewish (one-third of the population of Łódź was Jewish). But a delegate from Vilna pointed out that most prostitution in Poland was unregistered and clandestine. Rabbi Felix Goldmann of Leipzig asserted that it was "dangerous to talk so much about the Traffic and to be incessantly proclaiming our sins to the world." On the other hand, feminists such as Bertha Pappenheim stressed the untoward effects of *agunah* and *shtile khupe* ("silent," that is, clandestine and/or irregular religious marriage, often organized by recruiters for prostitution) and called for reform in religious law. The proceedings soon deteriorated into altercations between supporters and opponents of orthodoxy.[38]

The conferees had to contend with the fact that prostitution was legal in several countries and tolerated in many others. There was little doubt that the transoceanic traffic in Jewish girls had not ceased. The conference was credibly informed that in Czernowitz white slave traffic "belongs to three families who have been in the profession for some generations." It was impossible to touch them. Nor had Jewish prostitutes vanished from European cities. Jewish prostitution may have been no more prevalent than gentile but its very existence punctured another hole in the myth of Jewish family values.

One explanation for the persistence of prostitution had been offered by a writer in a Hebrew journal in 1901. He attributed it to the deleterious effects of "Jargonish [that is, Yiddish] literature of a certain type" as well as "American novels and especially the disgusting scenes they put up on the Jargonish theater [which] deeply subverted the morals of the masses . . . [casting a] pall on the daughters of our masses, erasing from them any sentiment of shame or modesty."[39]

Dubious if taken seriously as analysis of the effects of literature on society, this is surely wrong on one point. Shame seems not to have been erased: how else to explain the fact that the testimonies of the women themselves are lost to history? If we wish to hear them, we can do so only at second hand, mediated through fiction and poetry. Yet the whores who populate the novels of Sholem Asch, the early Warsaw stories of Isaac Bashevis Singer, the sensational Yiddish press, and the Yiddish stage were more than imaginary figments.

And sometimes an authentic-sounding voice breaks through. In Mordkhe Gebirtig's song "Di gefalene" (The Fallen Woman), a prostitute bewails her lot:

> *Ergets shlogt shoyn tsvey der zeyger*
> Somewhere the clock's striking two,
> *s'iz shoyn lang nokh halber nakht*
> It's already deepest night
> *un keyn groshn, keyn fardinstl*
> And not a penny, not a single job
> *hot biz itst zikh nisht gemakht.*[40]
> Has so far come my way.

This woman stood alone. But she was part of a larger mass of deviants from the conventional norms and values of Jewish society and another sign that these were cracking under the growing pressures from within and without.

8

LUFTMENSHN

Living on Air

Floating in the air, suspended above the *shtetl*, visible but power-less, buffeted hither and thither by gusts from all directions, Marc Chagall's *luftmensh* becomes an archetype for Jewish weightlessness in this period. He is, at the same time, a convenient catch-all for the deviants, marginals, and outcasts who constituted a minor but revealing part of Jewish society. Chagall's was the archetypal "fiddler on the roof."

The *luftmensh* could be defined, in the words of Lewis Namier, as a man "without solid ground under [his] feet, without training or profession, without capital or regular employment, living in the air, and, it would seem almost on air."[1] It might almost be said that the Jew, almost any Jew, was by definition a *luftmensh*, since, virtually alone among the peoples of Europe, he and his kind were not rooted in the land but operated in an ethereal, commercial stratosphere. This indeed was a view shared by anti-Semites and many modern-izing Jewish ideologists, including Zionists and socialists.

The *luftmensh* can be more specifically located in certain sectors of Jewish society. Loafers, flâneurs, and boulevardiers, respectable if unsuccessful businessmen, *yeshiva* students dependent for sup-port on charity, imaginative but impractical inventors and financial speculators, charlatans, con-men, smugglers, denizens of the crimi-nal underworld, whores, tramps, beggars, the physically disabled, the simple-minded, and lunatics might all be regarded, in some sense, as *luftmenshn*. So too might unpublished poets, café philosophers, wandering minstrels, organ-grinders, fairground characters, circus performers, "resting" actors, and amateur sportsmen, though they would all probably have shrunk with horror from the idea of any commonality.

A stock character in Yiddish fiction, the *luftmensh* also existed in real life. In poorer parts of Europe, the phenomenon was all-pervasive. In Subcarpathian Ruthenia, the primitive, easternmost province of Czechoslovakia, in the 1920s, more than half of the Jewish population was said to consist of *luftmenshn*, at least in the sense that they had no visible source of income.[2]

Some *luftmenshn* took advantage of the religious precept of *tsedakah*, particularly the custom of inviting strays and wanderers to partake of the festive meal on the Sabbath or holidays. Sometimes such guests assumed semi-permanent rights of visitation. At Ben-Zion Gold's home in Radom a chronic presence at the Passover *seder* was one Leibl "Shteklman." He always carried a long walking stick (*shtekl* in Yiddish)—hence his nickname. A short man with a gray beard and ruddy complexion, he had "a mustache the color of amber from heavy smoking and snuff." On the occasion of Leibl's first visit, he arrived when the *seder* was almost over, knocked on the door, and shouted, "You already had your Seder, ha? Has it occurred to you to ask whether *I* had a Seder?" Thereafter, he arrived every Passover, assumed his reserved place, and regaled the company with Hasidic stories. Leibl was not exactly a beggar: generally he would supply his own *matzah* (unleavened bread) and wine at Passover; and in the autumn he might turn up bearing a gift of an old watch or copper weights—from which Ben-Zion deduced that he was some sort of "dealer in used objects."[3]

The *luftmensh* was not necessarily poor. He might even live in a certain style. Gerhard Schreiber, a schoolboy in the 1930s, recalled his family's mode of life in Czernowitz:

My father, who didn't really have an actual job, nevertheless lived a life that on the looks of it was one of constant leisure. He lived in a hotel, was served breakfast by a maid, and left around nine. Every day around 11.30 he would meet with friends or business associates for a second breakfast. There were special restaurants (similar to New York delis) which catered to this all-male crowd. Food consisted of delicious morsels of different appetizers and the drinks were usually a few shots of rye or plum brandy, in the summer cold beer on tap. One of these places, "Lucullus," was famous all over Romania. Lunch followed at about two o'clock at my grandfather's restaurant. . . . Sexual mores were quite loose. I heard of different extramarital affairs that existed in my parents' circle and also among relatives. Abortions, which were quite common, I had to infer only. After lunch, my parents' routine was always the same. My mother would go home across the street for a two-hour nap while my father would go to a café "Leopold-stadt" for his card game. He played a game called Tarok (with Tarot cards) for about two hours. He would then be "in town" until 8, when we gathered for dinner at the restaurant. After dinner, I would be sent off to bed with my nursemaid while my parents together with my aunt and uncle would go out. Most times, this would be to the "Russian Club" (a private club catering to Russian-speaking Jews coming from Bessarabia), where they were joined by my paternal grandfather. My mother played rummy and my aunt poker. My uncle, the only one with a university degree, played bridge. . . . This totally unreal lifestyle . . . was somehow not so strange in central Europe. . . . Now, almost sixty years later I still wonder how my family lived, where they got the wherewithal to maintain their lifestyle, apparently oblivious of the world around them.[4]

Of course, this way of life was neither peculiar to Jews, nor common among them. Yet this most urbanized and socially mobile segment of society was exceptionally open to such conduct.

The chaos of war and revolution in Russia, followed by the period of the quasi-liberal New Economic Policy, provided a rich field of activity for *luftmenshn*. The imposition of greater social discipline under Stalin tamed some of their excesses. Lev Kopelev recalled that his uncle "Mishka the Bandit" had served "in both the White and Red armies, commanded a fort at Sevastopol, stolen the daughter of a former tsarist officer, deserted, been a criminal, later given himself up and gotten a job somewhere. . . . Eventually he 'came to his senses,' studied and became an engineer specializing in farm equipment."[5]

In the Soviet Union the term *luftmensh* acquired specific and, for those to whom it was affixed, potentially dangerous connotations, close to the second-class status of *lishentsy*. The *luftmensh* in socialist society was viewed unforgivingly as a parasite and asocial element. A report on a *shtetl* in the Mozyrsk region of Byelorussia in 1926, for example, referred to "a typical group of people in the shtetl . . . without defined occupations, the so-called 'people of air.' " Some were "unqualified artisans" who wandered about in search of work; others were former shopkeepers who engaged in illegal trade; and then there were "loafers" who were economically superfluous in the *shtetl* but who lacked the means to leave.[6]

Tricksters, Pranksters, and Chancers

The *luftmensh* had acquired folk celebrity in the late eighteenth century in the person of Hershele Ostropolyer, a wit and prankster, *der freylekhster yid in der velt* (the merriest Jew in the world), who became court jester to a Hasidic *rebbe*. He developed into the stuff of legend, bobbing up repeatedly in Jewish literature down to the interwar period, for instance in Isaac Babel's short story "Shabos Nakhamu." Another real-life humorist who acquired quasi-immortality was the *badkhn* Motke Chabad (a pseudonym), who had been active at the end of the nineteenth century but whose tomfoolery was still being celebrated in collections of stories published in Vilna in 1940. Often fact and fiction became inextricably confused. Hershele and Motke were suspected of being inventions while fictional tricksters, like Mordkhe Gebirtig's "Avreml the Swindler" (a *voyler yat*—a playboy), were fondly believed to be real-life characters.

Two grand-scale confidence tricksters whose exploits left wreckages of lives in their wake were Serge-Alexandre Stavisky and I. T. Trebitsch Lincoln. Stavisky, a Russian-born Jew who became a shady financier in interwar France, almost brought down the Third Republic when his jerry-built financial-political empire crumpled. His downfall and suicide, accompanied by revelations of corruption in high places, provided, as the historian of the affair has observed, "a bonanza for antisemites." Stavisky was "the poisoned gift of rabble-rousers and scandalmongers."[7]

Trebitsch Lincoln (whose bizarre story has been told in full in another place[8]) was a Hungarian-born Jew who became successively a Presbyterian missionary in Canada, an Anglican curate in Kent, Member of Parliament for Darlington in 1910, a promoter of speculative oil companies in Romania, a German spy in the First World War, a fugitive from justice in the United States, a member of the short-lived, extreme-right government of the Kapp Putsch in Germany in 1920, a political adviser to warlords in north China, a Buddhist monk in Shanghai, and finally a Japanese agent in the Second World War. Nazi propaganda always stressed Trebitsch's Jewishness. Both he and Stavisky were exploited by Joseph Goebbels as prime exhibits in the Nazi bestiary of Jewish political-financial tricksters.

Trebitsch and Stavisky were no doubt as atypical of interwar European Jews as the disgraced MP Horatio Bottomley was of Englishmen or the "match-king" swindler Ivar Kreuger of Swedes. But in the 1930s Jews generally felt a shudder of anxiety when any person of Jewish origin was accused of a major offense. They feared that Jews *en bloc* (unlike the English or Swedes) would share in the obloquy and perhaps also in the punishment administered by angry societies.

Criminals

It is hard to attach much credence to most contemporary assessments of the extent of Jewish crime in this period, bound up as they were with anti-Semitism on the one hand and Jewish apologetics on the other.[9] But we can build up some sort of picture from a variety of sources. According to official statistics, the overall rate of Jewish criminality in Poland in the late 1920s was about half that of non-Jews. Crimes against persons or property were rare among Jews. In Warsaw, for example, those against persons were committed nine times less frequently by Jews than by non-Jews. The disparity in murder rates was even wider. Recorded rates of theft and embezzlement were also disproportionately low among Jews. So were those

for most sexual crimes—rape, bigamy, and "unnatural sexual relations," a category that included pederasty, sodomy, and incest. On
the other hand, more Jews than non-Jews were convicted as *soute-
neurs* (pimps). The only other offenses for which the recorded rate
for Jews was higher than for non-Jews were illicit speculation, smuggling, contraband distilling, fraud, vagabondage, begging, avoidance
of military service, and "other crimes against social order."

Surprisingly, and contrary to the received view at the time, political crime by Jews in Poland was registered at only four-fifths the
level for non-Jews, notwithstanding the high involvement of Jews in
illegal left-wing activity, principally as members of the Communist
Party. Part of the explanation may be that in the smallest (in terms
of absolute number of convictions) but most serious segment of this
category, treason and espionage, the Jewish rate was higher than the
general one, whereas it was lower for such crimes as "resistance to
and insulting the authorities."[10]

All these figures must be treated with caution. They relate only
to recorded crime and presumably only to cases resulting in convictions. Moreover, as defenders of the Jews pointed out, cases involving alleged avoidance of military service might be partly accounted
for by the notorious prevalence of anti-Semitism in the Polish army.
And the disproportionate Jewish rate of economic criminality could
no doubt be explained by high Jewish participation in commerce.

These statistics may nevertheless probably be taken as broadly
indicative for Poland and for east European Jewry as a whole. A
similar pattern of low Jewish rates for crimes of violence or drunkenness and higher ones for "speculation," smuggling, or trading in
proscribed goods is suggested by an analysis of court cases in Soviet
Byelorussia in the 1920s.[11]

For other areas, only sporadic data are available. In interwar Amsterdam, recorded crime by Jews was higher than for non-Jews under
the rubrics of "swindling, embezzlement and refusing to co-operate
with authority." Reports in 1934 at the police station on the Jonas
Daniël Meijerplein, in the heart of the Jewish district, dealt mainly
with "common economic criminality," bicycle thefts, and "a considerable amount of what can be described as 'verbal aggression.' "[12]
The murder of a young Jewish girl in the district that year initially

kindled Jewish fears that the crime was motivated by anti-Semitism. The revelation that the perpetrator was a disturbed Jewish man produced feelings of "dismay and relief at the same time."[13]

In Czernowitz, however, there was dismay but no relief following a sensational crime in the 1930s. Two Jewish beggars killed a Jewish prostitute and cut her body into pieces. Romanian newspapers covered the case for weeks, pronouncing it "a typical Jewish ritual murder."[14]

Of course, official data do not tell the whole story. For further clues as to the nature and extent of Jewish criminality, we may turn to language and literature. The underworld slang of German, Dutch, English, and Russian incorporated words drawn from Yiddish, for instance *ganef* (thief), which appears in several European languages. In Odessan Russian, the Hebrew/Yiddish word *hevrah/khevre* (group, society) denoted a gang. Such borrowings are suggestive, though whether they were adopted directly from Jewish inhabitants of this milieu or at some remove is impossible to ascertain.

A rare instance of Jewish criminal autobiography is that of "Urke Nakhalnik" (a gangland alias, meaning, in Polish, "impudent thief"). Born Yitzhak Farberowic in 1897 in a village near Łomza, northeast of Warsaw, the son of a well-off miller, Urke dropped out of *yeshiva* at around the time of his *bar mitzvah*. After robbing his own family, he fled to Vilna, where he found a job as assistant *shames* of the gravediggers' congregation in the old synagogue courtyard in the city. Soon afterward, according to a recent study, he "entered the criminal underworld, where he passed through all the stages of initiation from *konik* ("little horse," i.e. apprentice) to seasoned criminal."[15] In the course of his career, he committed a wide range of offenses, including a bank robbery in Warsaw.

By 1933, Urke had spent more than half his life in Russian, German, and Polish prisons. Behind bars, he started writing memoirs. His manuscripts came to the attention of a visiting professor, who submitted them to a publisher and also interceded on Urke's behalf with Marshal Piłsudski. Granted a pardon, Urke retired from crime and became a full-time writer. His autobiography, written and published in Polish in 1933, was a succès de scandale. It appeared in Yiddish as *Mayn lebensveg: Fun der yeshive un tfise biz tsu der literatur*

(My Life: From *Yeshiva* and Prison to Literature). A second volume, *Leybedike meysim* (The Living Dead), gave a vivid picture of prison existence. Later he produced more memoirs, a novel, short stories, and poetry. His works were serialized in the Yiddish press in Warsaw, Riga, New York, and Buenos Aires.

Returning to live in Vilna, Urke visited the YIVO Institute and provided valuable additions to its philological division's collection of Yiddish criminal argot. He met a nurse at the Jewish hospital and, in spite of her mother's hostility to this *shmendrik* (good-for-nothing), married her. Supported by his literary earnings, he settled down to family life in Otwock. By 1939 Urke had become something of a celebrity. His life story was adapted for the stage. He made public appearances to promote his books and frequented the writers' club in Warsaw. The members did not quite know what to make of him: they were used to ex-prisoners—but of the political, not the criminal, variety.

No doubt Urke embellished his narratives with fictional plums. Many of his fellow authors moved in the other direction, seeking to depict criminality fictionally in a realistic way. Sholem Asch's novel (later dramatized) *Mottke ganef* (Mottke, the Thief, 1916), a mixture of social comedy and melodrama, told the picaresque tale of a young scallywag from a *shtetl* who commits murder, becomes a pimp in Warsaw, and finally is betrayed by the girl he loves. In his novel *Shosha* (1974), Isaac Bashevis Singer portrayed denizens of the criminal underworld of the Warsaw he had known in the 1930s. On the most disreputable section of his native Krochmalna Street, "the gutters seemed even deeper, the stink even stronger."[16] Notorious denizens of the area included "Blind Itche, chief of the pickpockets, proprietor of brothels, a swaggerer and a knife carrier" and "Fat Reitzele, a woman who weighed three hundred pounds, [and] was supposed to conduct business with white slavers from Buenos Aires."[17]

Several collections of Yiddish folk music included a genre of underworld ballads, among them "love-songs of thieves" and "songs from the abyss," grim jailhouse laments in which prisoners complain of their miserable lives and confess their sins. Some were self-justifying:

Dos ganevishe lebn
> The life of a thief
hot got mir gegebn . . . [18]
> was given me by God . . .

Others were self-dramatizing, as in this long moan, supposedly from an orphan purse snatcher in Vilna:

Der yold iz mir mekane.
> The guy is jealous of me.
Der yold iz mir mekane.
> The guy is jealous of me.
Der yold iz mir mekane mit mayn layd shtikl broyt
> He's jealous of my miserable bit of bread.
Er vil fun keyn zakh visn
> He doesn't want to know anything
Vi ikh ver oysgerisn
> about how I suffered,
Vi shver es kumt mir on mayn shtikl broyt!
> How hard come by was my piece of bread!

mayn mame un mayn tate
> My mother and father
zi zeynen geven blate
> were lowly folk.
far a rov tsu makhn mir geven iz zeyer farlang.
> They wanted to make a rabbi out of me.
fun zibn yor keseder
> For seven years regularly
bin ikh gegangen in kheyder
> I went to heder
biz draytsen yor hob ikh gekvetsht di bank!
> Until I was thirteen I squirmed at the bench!

mayn tate shikt mir esn,
> My father sent me food,
mayn tate shikt mir trinkn,

My father sent me drink,
shikt mir tsu a hipshe bisel gelt.
Sent me a nice small amount of money.
geshtorben iz der tate,
My father died,
nakhher oykh di mame,
After that my mother too.
geblibn bin ikh elnt oyf der velt!
I remained alone in the world!

a yerushe iz mir farblibn,
A legacy was left to me.
a yerushe iz mir farblibn.
A legacy was left to me.
a katerinke hob ikh mir gehat.
I got myself a barrel-organ.
farkoyft di katerinke
Sold the barrel-organ
genumen bronfn trinkn,
And took to liquor,
un far a ganef hot men mir gemakht!
So that people took me for a thief!

Ikh gey aroys in markt,
Out I go to the market
derzeh a fetn kark,
And see a fat neck,
a mise moyd mit dolarn hob ikh mir dertapt.
Snatched at a dirty old woman with dollars.
Do geyt farbey a yente
But a woman passerby
un firt mir tsu a mente,
Reported me to a cop,
un firt mir glaykh in tsirkl arayn!
Who put me straight in clink!

Ikh zits mir in di krates,
I sit behind bars

ongeton in shmates,
> Clad in rags.
zumer ze ikh regn geyn un vinter shney.
> In summer I see rain, in winter snow
Avek di yunge yorn!
> Begone youth!
Avek di yunge yorn!
> Begone youth!
A ganef tsu zayn iz dokh vind un vey! [19]
> To be a thief is but misery and woe!

Although it was presented as a folk song, we should not imagine that a real prisoner, a Yiddish-speaking Silvio Pellico, composed the dismal dirge. Some ballads of this kind originated in Yiddish musical theater, others in the Tsarist or Polish armies, and a few were Yiddish renderings of popular songs from other languages. Many were preserved by conscientious Yiddish *zamlers* who scoured the cities and *shtetlakh*, recording folklore on the edge of its disappearance.

Smugglers and Horse Thieves

Smuggling offered special attractions to a mobile and commercial people who often found themselves in border regions such as Alsace or the former Pale of Settlement. In the eighteenth century, Jewish horse thieves had been characteristic types in Alsace.[20] Joseph Opatoshu's *Roman fun a ferd ganef* (Tale of a Horse Thief, 1912) depicts the world of cross-border horse smuggling on the eastern marches of Germany. Although written in New York by an emigrant, the novel went through many printings in eastern Europe and remained popular in the interwar period, perhaps because it reflected reality (it was based on a true story).

In *shtetlakh* near the border of the USSR and its western neighbors, such smuggling continued well into the Soviet period. In Probuzhana, a small town in southern Poland, ten miles from the frontier, in the 1920s: "Russian peasants would arrive daily and buy up goods, especially cloth and leather and smuggle it across the border into Soviet Russia. With their help, large shipments of saccharine, potash and matches would be smuggled into Russia and horses would be smuggled out of Russia. The peasants paid with gold or silver Rubles." Later, however, border security became tighter and smuggling became more difficult. "Merchants [in Probuzhana] who had large stocks of goods solely intended for that purpose were completely ruined, either losing their capital or simply eating it up. The worst sufferers were the horse dealers."[21] Similarly, on the border between Romania and Czechoslovakia in the 1930s, it was reported that "the Jews here live from smuggling. They bring silk and other fabrics to Romania and return with food items. . . . It is mainly children who are involved in these activities. They all have stories of how they were shot at or escaped away."[22]

A more up-to-date form of smuggling, with a Jewish flavor, was uncovered in 1938 in a joint operation by the Paris Sûreté and the New York Police Department. A Polish-born Jew, Isaac Leifer, conceived a scheme for transporting stashes of heroin and cocaine from France to the United States. Posing as "chief rabbi of Brooklyn," Leifer, "long-bearded, bespectacled, rather lugubrious-looking," persuaded a simple-minded Jewish bookbinder in Paris to insert secret compartments inside *siddurim* and *makhzorim* (prayer books).[23] He explained that these would hold "holy earth from the Land of Israel," to be shipped to America as a folk remedy for ailments. The naïve workman (or so he later presented himself to the police by way of self-exculpation) accepted the explanation.

The arrest of Leifer and an alleged accomplice caused great excitement in the Pletzl. A search for a "third man" rumored to be in the nearby area of the rue de Rivoli heightened the furore.[24] Clad in a *kapote*, Leifer had established his credentials in the area as an orthodox rabbi by frequenting a strictly kosher restaurant but eating only fish and fruit compote: he refused to touch meat, claiming to be dissatisfied with the standard of *kashrut* of the Parisian *shechitah* inspectorate.

The world's press covered the case with avid interest. It was also followed with fascination by the Yiddish press in Paris, with spiteful glee by the anti-Semitic *Action française*, and with pseudo-scholarly interest in the *Mitteilungen über die Judenfrage*, published in Berlin.[25] The publicity alarmed Jewish leaders. The chief rabbi of Paris informed *Le Petit Parisien* that there was no such position as "chief rabbi of Brooklyn." And the Association of Rabbis in Poland issued a statement denying that there was any rabbi named Isaac Leifer in Brooklyn and pronouncing the arrested man an impostor.[26]

Subsequent investigation disclosed that Leifer had a long record of involvement in rackets in Warsaw, Vienna, and Palestine. Moreover, his orthodoxy had evidently waned and waxed in the past. In Warsaw, he was said to have enjoyed a meal in the (nonkosher) Hotel Bristol. On the other hand, during a period of residence in Haifa, he had bought a car and driven himself each Friday to the nearby orthodox settlement of Kfar Hasidim in order to bathe in the *mikveh*: in Haifa, he said, there was no properly kosher *mikveh*. Suspicious characters had been seen entering and leaving his "villa" in Haifa with parcels containing, he said, holy books that he was dispatching at his own expense all over the world.[27] Leifer was sentenced to two years' imprisonment in June 1939. In August, the French Judicial Board approved a request for his extradition to the United States. His lawyer announced an appeal but that was still pending in September 1939, so Leifer remained in a French prison.[28]

The Capital of the Luftmensh

A characteristically Jewish gangland, with its own codes, methods of operation, and forms of speech, developed in certain areas of high Jewish density. The historian Arcadius Kahan, who grew up in Vilna in the 1930s, recalled that the underworld there "had its well-functioning organizational forms, and keen observers of the streets could watch the introduction of methods of schooling and collective training in pickpocketing that superseded the previous system of individual apprenticeship in this trade."[29]

By general consent, however, one city held first place in this sphere. Odessa was the capital of the *luftmensh* or, in its Russianized form, *liudi vozdukha*. From the late nineteenth century onward, especially in the interwar period as a result of Isaac Babel's stories about Jewish bandits and gangsters, the city became notorious in literature and popular mythology as a "Jewish city of sin." "Zibn mayl

arum ades brent di gihenum" ("The fires of hell burn for seven miles
around Odessa"), went the Yiddish saying. "In Odessa," wrote Babel
in 1916, "the destitute *luftmenschen* roam through coffeehouses trying to make a ruble or two to feed their families, but there is no
money to be made, and why should anyone give work to a useless
person, a *luftmensch?*"[30] Babel's underworld boss character, Benya
Krik, the subject of a Russian film in 1926, was supposedly based
on the real-life gangster Moisei Vinnitskii, aka Mishka Iaponchik
("Mike the Jap," so called, it is said, because of his slanting eyes).
Around 1919, this "King of Odessa" allegedly controlled the city's
demi-monde of vice and organized crime from his headquarters at
the Monte Carlo restaurant. He led a detachment of 2,400 bandits
who fought on the Bolshevik side in the civil war; he was later shot
by the Bolsheviks.[31] No doubt there are elements of the fabulous
in the story but a recent historian has verified that "there is ample
documentation to demonstrate their [Jews'] leading role in the city's
underworld" in the late imperial and early Soviet periods.[32]

Odessa was a byword for *bosyakes, hultayes, zhulikes, karmant-
shikes,* and *sharlatanes* (vagabonds, rogues, swindlers, pickpockets,
and charlatans).[33] Jewish forgers and fencers, counterfeiters and confidence tricksters were standard Odessa lowlife figures, especially
in the heavily Jewish Moldavanka district of the city, known as
"Odessa's moral garbage can."[34] Analysis of crime reports, at any rate
for the period up to 1917, suggests that criminal activity in the city
then may indeed have been disproportionately Jewish.[35]

The city spawned cheerful songs of Jewish criminality, mainly
in the Odessan Russian dialect, some in a macaronic mixture of
Russian and Yiddish. The immensely popular jazz musician and
cabaret artist Leonid Utesov transported Odessan Jewish criminality into legend in the 1920s and 1930s. A prudish Leningrad critic
complained: "There is nothing more vulgar, nothing smuttier, than
Jewish anecdotes and third-class bar-room gypsy romances. And
Utesov is a master of both these genres. He is a master of vulgarity
and obscenity."[36] Utesov, however, enjoyed the useful sponsorship of
Lazar Kaganovich, "friend of the jolly" and the last Jew in the senior
leadership of the USSR.[37] Utesov and his music prospered and he
even performed his song "From the Odessa Jail" (loosely based on

a poem of Heine that was set to music by Schumann) at a private concert in the Kremlin in the presence of Stalin.[38] Only in the late 1930s, when jazz fell out of favor, was he obliged to take the edge off his musical style and his lyrics.

Beggars

Begging was one of the few areas of what was seen at the time as criminality in which Jews probably outnumbered most other segments of society. One reason was, no doubt, the Jewish religious imperative of charity. Another was the high urbanization of Jewish society and the concentration of poor Jews in city centers, where they might hope to rub shoulders with the better-off.

In this world of ubiquitous poverty and incessant assaults on human dignity, minor distinctions of vocabulary helped people hold up their heads. *Proste yidn* (the common people) were not necessarily *kaptsonim* (paupers); nor were *batlonim* (idlers) always *betlers* (mendicants) or *schnorrers* (beggars). A *treger* (porter) or *medine-geyer* (pedlar) might look almost indistinguishable from a *shleper* (tramp), but the latter, having no occupation at all, was at the bottom of the heap.

The beggar might be a cabaret artist manqué, as in the case of the blind street singer, E. Weissman, aged eighty-two, encountered in Kiev in 1932 by the Soviet musical ethnographer Moisei Beregovskii. Weissman traveled around cities performing in streets and sometimes in private houses. He had learned his repertoire from Peretz Volekh, an Odessa troubadour of the 1880s who sang his own compositions in wine cellars, at parties, and at weddings.[39]

In Soviet society, begging, like unemployment, was officially supposed to have been abolished. But in Russia and Ukraine after the revolution, large numbers of orphans turned into beggars. In the former Pale, many of these were Jews. "You see them all over the cities and towns, and in the villages, in the railroad stations, hungry . . . naked, shoeless. . . . They wander about first with a bewildered, forlorn expression, then with a hand stretched forth for a handout, and finally in a camp of little criminals, embittered, degenerate," reported the Moscow Yiddish daily *Emes*.[40] In response, the Soviet authorities set up the Third International Jewish School-Camp for War Orphans at Malakhovka, near Moscow. Chagall worked there for a while as a drawing teacher. He later recounted the misery of his young charges: "They had seen their fathers' beard savagely torn out, their sisters raped, disembowelled. Ragged, shivering with cold and hunger, they roamed the cities, clung on to the bumpers of trains until, at last—a few thousand among so many, many others—they were taken into shelters for children."[41] With the end of the civil war and the gradual restoration of stability in Russia, the problem of orphan beggers eased. But a few years later, when NEP came to an end, a new wave of Jewish beggars appeared, composed of former NEP-men, now driven out of petty commerce and, without occupation or means of support, marginalized and vilified as *lishentsy*.

Jewish beggars were most visible in east-central Europe. They swarmed in the main streets of older Jewish districts of cities like Vilna and Munkács, congregating especially at cemeteries, where they would implore mourners for *tsedoko*. They would gather outside synagogues and prayer halls on Friday nights, hoping to be invited to a free meal. In some towns the *besmedresh* would remain open all night and homeless people might sleep on the hard benches. Certain especially poverty-stricken regions were held to be particularly productive of beggars. Subcarpathian Ruthenia, for instance, came to be known as the "Land of the Schnorrers." A historian of Jewry in this area remarks that begging there was "an accepted and even honourable way to make a living."[42]

Often masters of the verbal putdown, beggars were not to be antagonized lightly, as a woman in Vasily Grossman's story about his native Berdichev learns when, "tearing the very smallest onion off her string," she throws it into the bowl of "a blind beggar with the white beard of a wizard." "He felt it, stopped praying, and said angrily, 'May your children be as generous to you in old age.' "[43]

The beggar was a standard type in Yiddish fiction, drama, and poetry. The popular Yiddish poet Itzik Manger wrote the wandering mendicant's refrain:

Oremkayt, du mayn kinigraykh!
    Poverty, you are my kingdom!

Du bist i di verbe i der taykh.
>You are both the willow and the river.

Du bist mayn opru un du bist mayn ol,
>You are my rest and you are my burden,

mayn likhtik gezang oyf a tunkl kol.
>My bright song in a dark voice!

Du bist di tfile in krey funem hon
>You are the prayer in the chicken's cluck

un di goldene bin oyfn roytn mon.[44]
>And the golden bee on the red poppy.

Here is a voice of self-respect and of integration into the natural world. The beggar expected, and often was accorded, a certain respect in Jewish society. We can see and hear this too in a famous scene in the classic 1937 Yiddish film *Der dybbuk*, where the beggars dance with chaotic abandon but also with a marked dignity.

From time to time, Jewish communities would take action against begging, for example, by setting up night shelters. But the problem would not disappear. In 1935 plans were afoot in Vilna to publish a newspaper, *Der yidishe schnorrer*, that would represent the interests of beggars.[45] It seems never to have appeared, presumably owing to lack of support. Efforts the following year to remove beggars from the streets of the city led a sympathetic paper to comment: "Nobody has addressed the question of how these living creatures should exist when they are not capable of work, when they are not permitted to beg, and when neither charities nor the community is willing to support them."[46]

Meshugoim

In both Jewish and other societies, begging was often closely associated with mental and physical disability. In the absence of adequate welfare provision for the disabled, many of them were reduced to begging as a way of life. Jewish attitudes to the mentally ill, however, were probably somewhat more humane than those of many other societies, a tendency accentuated by the pioneering role of Jews in modern psychiatry.

Jews were widely thought to suffer from higher incidences of certain mental illnesses, especially depression, schizophrenia, and paranoia, than non-Jews, although there were few solid statistics to support this belief. Jews were, however, to be found more often as patients in psychiatric hospitals. In the Netherlands, for example, the number of Jewish patients was two and a half times as high as non-Jewish. Of course, this did not necessarily reflect differential rates of mental illness. It may simply indicate a higher level of care for the Jewish mentally ill, at any rate among wealthier communities such as those of the Netherlands.

Het Apeldoornsche Bosch, the "Jewish Central Asylum for the Insane" in the Netherlands, was founded in 1909. It occupied a large building in spacious grounds near the village of Apeldoorn and had a reputation for professional excellence and progressive care. In 1934–35 its 664 patients were cared for by six doctors and 192 nurses. The arrival in Holland in the 1930s of large numbers of Jewish refugees from Germany, some of whom suffered from psychological problems as a result of their experience under Nazi rule, led to a sharp increase in the number of patients, to over 800 by 1938. A related school for mentally disturbed or retarded Jewish children, the Pedagogium Achisomog, opened in Apeldoorn in 1925, with about seventy-four pupils by 1938.

Het Apeldornsche Bosch was a model institution of its kind. Germany, with an estimated 2,500 to 3,000 Jewish mentally ill in 1939, had similar hospitals. But in the much poorer countries of eastern Europe, treatment of the mentally ill was less generous. Such institutions as existed were generally inadequate and many disturbed people remained in society with little support. Almost every village had its *dorf nar* (village idiot) and each town its *eygene shtetl-meshugoim* (its own town crazies). In Vilna, a well-known figure in the 1930s was *Rokhel di meshugene* (Crazy Rachel), "a wispy figure capped by a curious headpiece."[47] In the Romanian *shtetl* of Ştefăneşti, there was a "synagogue of the *meshugoim*"—literally "lunatics" but here perhaps denoting "eccentrics" or Hasidim.

In the Land of the Deaf

As with mental illness, it was thought in this period that Jews were especially susceptible to deaf-mutism. The main causes were held to be inmarriage and consequent congenital defects. Jewish deaf-mutes in interwar Europe suffered more than their gentile fellow disabled. As children they would attract taunts from other children that would be redoubled because of their Jewishness. As adults in Nazi Germany and in much of east-central Europe, they found themselves the victims of a double exclusion from general society, and their capacity to resist or fend for themselves was limited.

Hereditary deaf-mutes were traditionally classed by Judaism with the insane. Orthodox Jews did not recognize them as fully responsible members of the community. They were not called up to the reading of the Torah, consequently could not celebrate *bar mitzvah*, and could not be counted as members of a *minyan*. Whatever their mental attributes, they were regarded as retarded, were subject to special rules regarding marriage and divorce, could not sue or be sued in Jewish courts, were treated as infants from the point of view of criminal responsibility, and could not be accepted as converts. These far from enlightened attitudes changed only slowly, although their practical application by orthodox Judaism began to ease in the modern period.

Jews had been among the pioneers of special education for the hearing-impaired. The first Jewish school for the deaf, founded in Nikolsburg in Moravia in 1844, moved to Vienna in 1852. It set a standard for later establishments in Warsaw, Cracow, Berlin, and Budapest. The Vienna school closed for financial reasons in 1928 but others continued.

The Israelitische Taubstummenanstalt (Israelite Institution for Deaf-Mutes) in Berlin-Weissensee, in particular, acquired a sterling reputation as a progressive center for deaf education. At the time of its foundation in 1873, Jews had numbered just 52 out of Berlin's recorded deaf population of 672. The need for a Jewish school arose from the fact that existing institutions for the deaf in Germany were all confessionally based. The school was so successful that it attracted pupils from all over Germany and beyond. It was supported by a charitable society that had eight thousand members in 1929. The school's founder, Dr. Markus Reich, remained at the helm until his death in 1911. His son Felix took over in 1919, serving until 1939. The school had its own synagogue with a cantor who faced the congregation rather than, as in other synagogues, facing Jerusalem. In the 1930s, however, the Depression and Nazism adversely affected the institution. Foreign pupils withdrew. Membership of the supporting society shrank to 4,500 by 1936. The number of pupils fell from 58 in 1930 to 38 in 1938.

A conference of societies of the Polish-Jewish deaf-mutes in Warsaw in 1931 was told that in the Polish capital alone there were at least three hundred Jewish deaf-mutes. The Jewish societies had originally formed part of a general Polish Association of the Deaf but the Jews had been excluded in 1925. At the 1931 conference, a tentative arrangement for cooperation between Jews and gentiles was nevertheless approved. Outside big cities in Poland, educational opportunities for deaf-mute children were limited, with the result that many remained illiterate. The proposal by a delegate from Vilna that a Yiddish-language school for deaf-mutes be established in that city gave rise to a "lively discussion" and there was unanimity that there could be no question of such an enterprise save as the exclusive responsibility of the Vilna group.[48] But the branch there was in a parlous condition. In 1937 its officers reported that 90 percent of its members were illiterate and most were too poor to pay a membership fee.[49]

The Reichs were pioneers of an international movement for the rights of the Jewish deaf. A World Congress of the Jewish Deaf in Prague in 1931 aroused criticism from an organization of the German deaf that censured the separatism of the Jewish deaf. Two years later, however, all Jews were expelled from the German society of the deaf. Efforts to establish an international organization of the Jewish deaf foundered. Thereafter the Jewish deaf, isolated and defenseless, faced a world of ominous and threatening silence.

Sport

And then there was another kind of *luftmensh*, who, like Shake-speare's Ariel, challenged the physical world by striving "to swim, to dive into the fire, to ride on the curl'd clouds." Jews in this period were widely regarded as physical weaklings, unfit for demanding athletic activity. Many Jews themselves shared this perception. The Polish-Jewish beauty queen "Miss Judea 1929," for instance, deplored the fact that "the Jewish nation stands lower than other nations with regard to physical fitness."[50] As the Jewish former sports editor of the Berlin newspaper the *Vossische Zeitung* put it in 1935:

> It is regrettable but true and characteristic that a very great athlete is today not less but more useful to his people than a great poet or scientist. That goes not for enduring value but for the immediate benefit of the current generation. If, however, we want to apply the highest standard, we must also admit that physical culture is actually a necessary complement to spiritual culture, so necessary, indeed, that spiritual culture alone may not present any claim to the name of culture.[51]

As spectators Jews took an interest in much the same sports as non-Jews in this period, especially football and indoor cycling. But as players rather than fans, they exhibited special characteristics.

Seeking to revolutionize the Jew's wimpish self-image, the turn-of-the-century litterateur and Zionist Max Nordau called for the creation of a *Muskeljudentum* ("muscular Jewry"), a slogan that evoked a keen response, especially among Revisionist Zionists. Jews took special pride in sporting achievements that demanded demonstrations of physical prowess.

The wrestler Zishe Breitbart, known as "the strongest man in the world," became a hero to east European Jews. The son of a black-smith, he performed onstage and in the circus ring, bending iron rods and breaking chains. He also "pounded nails into boards with his fist." He met an unfortunate end in 1925, at the age of forty-two, when he contracted blood poisoning from a rusty nail.[52]

His successor to the title of *Shimshn-hagibr* (Samson the Mighty) was Szymon Rudi, born in Białystok, who, so it was said, could take apart chains with his teeth. He emigrated to Palestine but returned to Europe for an exhibition tour in 1938. Such characters were more fairground attractions than sportsmen but they addressed an evident psychological need for European Jews in the 1930s.

Boxing, a sport with long Jewish connections, aroused no less enthusiasm. Salamon Arouch, born to a family of Salonica stevedores, was trained as a pugilist by his father and won his first bout at the age of fourteen. Subsequently the stocky five-foot, six-inch, 135-pound middleweight enjoyed a successful amateur career in Greece and farther afield. He compensated for his size with speed, skipping around much taller opponents and earning the sobriquet "the ballet dancer." By 1939 he had scored twenty-four knockouts.[53] Arouch's exploits lifted the spirits of Salonican Jews in a period when they were suffering a serious crisis of morale.

Like other sports favored by Jews, boxing ran into a variety of political problems. The Bundist Morgnshtern sports organization, formed in 1926, at first discountenanced boxing, both on account of its violence and on ideological grounds: competitive sports, particularly those involving individual rather than team competition, were held to transgress socialist principles. By the late 1930s, however, Morgnshtern relented. Upon investigation it concluded that boxing was, after all, permissible, since it was not damaging to health, taught workers to defend themselves, and (a strange argument, perhaps, in the mouths of twentieth-century socialists) had been practiced by the ancient Greeks.[54] But in 1938 politics imposed itself from another direction when Morgnshtern boxers found themselves excluded from the Warsaw Boxing Federation by Polish anti-Semites.

Szapsel Rotholc, a national boxing champion of Poland, encountered other political difficulties. At the time of the 1936 Olympic Games, held in Berlin, he faced conflicting pressures from Jewish organizations, which opposed having any truck with games hosted by the Nazis, and from the Polish army, in which he was serving. He decided to participate. Later he competed against several German fighters and was cheered on by Polish audiences with calls of

"Szapsel, beat the German, beat him into the swastika!" In April 1939, however, he was dropped from the Polish team in the European championships in Dublin, apparently because he was Jewish.

Among east European Jews, other popular sports included *glitshn* (ice-skating), table tennis (all the Polish national champions in the interwar period were Jews), and weight lifting (the Bar Kochba club in Łódź alone produced four national champions in the 1920s).

Another sport in which Jews excelled was chess. Jews constituted a majority of grandmasters in the interwar period. Among the most notable was Andor Lilienthal, born in Moscow to Hungarian parents in 1911. His family moved to Hungary in 1913 but he emigrated to the USSR in 1935 and became a Soviet citizen in 1939. The intellectuality and nonphysicality of chess seemed to mark it out as a peculiarly Jewish pursuit. On that very account, Jewish sports enthusiasts tended to dismiss it as a game or hobby rather than a genuine sport. But its popularity among Jews transcended ideological and social divisions.

Several Jewish youth organizations were devoted primarily or partly to sport. The largest was the Zionist-oriented Maccabi, which had branches in every country. In Poland it had forty thousand members in 1936, organized in 150 clubs. In 1933 the Maccabi World Union head office was moved from Berlin to London. Thereafter the organization banned any contact with German clubs, including German-Jewish clubs, a prohibition to which it adhered throughout the 1930s.

Morgnshtern had barely a tenth as many members as Maccabi. Its socialist ideology led it to prefer noncompetitive gymnastics, swimming, and cycling. Similar scruples led it for a time to disapprove of football (soccer). In 1929 it proposed unsuccessfully at the International Congress of Socialist Sport that the rules of the game should be amended so as to provide points not only for goals but also for "aesthetic" performance and "fair play." Eventually, in the case of football, as of boxing, popular opinion compelled it to set aside such reservations.

In eastern Europe, sport was often organized along ethnic lines. In Czernowitz, the city's pronounced multinational character was reflected in its Romanian, Ukrainian, German, Polish, and Jewish sports clubs. The Jewish ones were Maccabi, which appealed mainly to the middle class, and Jask, a socialist-Zionist club, later renamed after the Marxist-Zionist theoretician Ber Borokhov. Occasionally such clubs, generally leftist ones, admitted non-Jews: the Lublin Morgnshtern football team, for example, included non-Jewish players from the Polish Socialist Party youth movement.

Some Jewish football teams, such as Bar Kochba in Berlin and Hakoach in Vienna, attained general renown. Hakoach's glory days were in the 1920s, when it twice won the Austrian national football championship. By the mid-1930s, however, it encountered trouble in finding top-quality players. After a disastrous season in 1937, culminating in a 6–0 loss in its final game, it even considered liquidating. It decided to carry on, though after the annexation of Austria to Germany in March 1938 it could play only against other Jewish teams. The limitation did not, however, prevent matches against non-Jewish teams abroad. In the summer of 1938 Hakoach visited Warsaw to play against the Polonia football team. The visitors won 3–0, scoring a goal in the final second of the match. The referee's whistle at the end of the "friendly" was the signal for a ferocious onslaught by Polonia fans against Jewish spectators in the stadium.

One reason for the existence of Jewish clubs was the prevalence of anti-Semitism in many sports. The Klein family of Czernowitz included three brothers, all good athletes. The first, a middle-distance runner, was stoned while running for his military unit during national service; he was forced to drop out of the race. The second brother, observing the incident from the stand, was so disgusted that he decided there and then to emigrate: soon afterward he settled in Peru. The third, the most talented, competed on behalf of Maccabi in the national championships in Bucharest and was awarded a bronze medal by the king. Since his name sounded German, the local pro-Nazi German newspaper hailed the triumph of the "German" athlete. But the item was dropped after the first edition, presumably because Klein's unsatisfactory racial pedigree became known.[55]

In 1936 Jews celebrated the snub administered to Hitler when thirteen Jews (at any rate as defined by Nazi standards) won medals at the Berlin Olympics. Some of these victories, however, were double-edged. Four of the medals were for fencing, in which Endre Kabos won a gold in both the individual and team events. The sport had acquired an allure among Jews in Hungary and Austria because of its aristocratic origins and connection with dueling. But anti-Semites considered Jews unworthy opponents. Kabos offended on ground of both his Jewish and his petit bourgeois origin (he owned a grocery store) and he suffered discrimination and humiliation as a result.

An even more spectacular triumph in Berlin was that of another Hungarian, Ibolya Csák, who became the first Hungarian woman to win an Olympic gold medal. Her main rival for the high-jump championship, the German Gretel Bergmann, was withdrawn from the German team shortly before the event because she was Jewish. She was replaced by an "Aryan," Dora Ratjen. Two years later, at the European games in Vienna, Ratjen defeated Csák for the European crown. But shortly afterward the judges disqualified Ratjen on the ground that she/he was a hermaphrodite. Csák was declared the winner and held the European high-jump record for the next twenty-four years. After the war, Hermann Ratjen announced he was a man and claimed he had been forced by the Nazis to pose as a woman.[56]

Passing as a different sex was no doubt perilous. But many Jews undertook what was, in the interwar period, the no less difficult enterprise of trying to pass as gentiles.

9

NON-JEWISH JEWS

Passing

Pride and shame mingled incongruously and uncomfortably in many Jews' attitudes to their Jewish heritage. Nowhere were these internal contradictions more often evident than in Germany. Martin Stern, son of a wealthy Jewish industrialist in Essen, recalled his family home in the 1930s:

> Mother often admonished us to be and act as "proud Jews." That did not make much sense to me. After all, we were born as Jews. It was our inheritance, not our choice, and therefore not of our doing and thus nothing to be proud of; just a fact of life. It did not seem to be consistent with an attitude on the part of my parents of wanting to lie low, to be inconspicuous in order not to attract attention or anti-semitism.[1]

Lying low, however, was not always easy. Jews therefore resorted to a variety of stratagems in order to avoid standing out in the crowd.

One of the most common, particularly in Germany and Hungary, was name-changing. In much of Europe in the 1930s, ears were subtly attuned to the Jewishness or otherwise of names. The traditional tripartite division of Jews into priests (*cohanim*), Levites, and Israel (the rest) gave rise to surnames such as Cohen, Cohn, Kagan, and Katz (short for *kohen tsedek*, "holy priest"), as well as Levy, Loewensohn, and Isserlis (son of Israel). All were recognizably Jewish, though some non-Jews in Germany, to their discomfort, were called Kohn. Other common Jewish names were derived from occupations: for example, Cantor, Sofer (scribe), Dayan (judge), or Schneider (tailor). From matronyms: Dworkin (offspring of Dvorah), Rivkin/Rifkind (of Rivkah/Rebecca), and Sorkin/Serkin (of Sarah). From names of flowers, animals, or precious minerals: Rose, Wolf, Wolfsohn, Silber, Gold, Goldman, Perl, and Diamant. Or from places: Ashkenazi (from the Hebrew word for Germany; but the name could also be found among Sephardim), Pollak (Polish), Litvak, Frankfurter, Wilner, Prager, Shapiro and Spiro (from Speyer).

In the modern period, many Jews were given two sets of forenames, one Hebrew, used for religious purposes (*shemot ha-kodesh* in Hebrew, *oyfruf-nemen* in Yiddish), the other secular (*kinuyim, rufnemen*). The former were mostly biblical Hebrew names such as Abraham, Isaac, Jacob, and Moses. As for the latter, Abraham might be called Arnold, Isaac could be Ignaz, and Moses Moritz. In the Soviet Union, Russian names came to replace Hebrew ones altogether: for instance, Arkadi for Aron.

Name-changing was nothing new in Jewish history. The Talmud records that "most Jews in the Diaspora bear non-Jewish names."[2] Often the change was a commercial decision: the German-Jewish singer Paula Levi, for instance, decided in 1926 to adopt the stage name Lindberg. A new name might be politically expedient: Moshe Faintuch, for instance, a leading figure in the French Communist Party's bureau for aid to the Republican cause in Spain, gallicized himself as Jean Jérôme.

In Hungary, where name-changing was particularly common, Joseph Lőwinger, a banker, changed his name, upon ennoblement, to Lukács de Szeged. His son, György, born in 1885, was therefore known as von Lukács. In 1919, when he served briefly as deputy commissar for education in the short-lived Communist regime of Béla Kun, he dropped the *von*. Writing mainly in German, it was as Georg Lukács that he became the best-known Marxist literary critic of the age.

The Frankfurt School social theorist Theodor Adorno, whose father, Oscar Wiesengrund, was a Jewish-born convert to Protestantism, was registered Wiesengrund-Adorno at birth but later called himself Theodor W. Adorno (from his mother's maiden name

Calvelli-Adorno della Piana—she claimed descent from Corsican nobility). He was baptized a Catholic, although he practiced no religion. Some students of his thought have detected what Martin Jay calls a "muted, but nevertheless palpable Jewish impulse" within it, including echoes of the philosopher Franz Rosenzweig.[3] But Hannah Arendt sneered at him for what she and others saw as a snobbish (and futile) effort to conceal his Jewish origin.

Anti-Semites often complained that Jews adopted new names in order to hide their Jewishness. In Poland the Sejm passed a motion to limit such changes. They occurred all the same: for example, the Yiddish theater director Mark Arnshteyn, who also directed on the Polish-language stage, used for the latter purpose the name Andrzej Marek.

Not all name-changing was for the purpose of concealment: Béla Presser, a rabbinical student in Budapest, magyarized his surname to Béla Berend and became a rabbi. Occasionally name-change could even constitute an act of defiance. In 1932, Günther Stern, a journalist on the leading German liberal paper, the *Frankfurter Zeitung*, was approached by his editor, who suggested that, given the growing influence of the Nazis, it would help the paper to avoid the charge that it was a Jewish mouthpiece if he changed his surname: "Warum nennen Sie sich nicht etwas anders?" ("Why don't you call yourself something else?") Stern took the advice literally: he changed his surname to Anders.[4]

Converts

Apostasy had been a significant feature of Jewish life in most of Europe since the Enlightenment. Even in Poland, conversion on a small scale was recorded from at least the sixteenth century onward. As Jews acculturated, as they moved up the social scale, and especially as exogamy grew, conversions increased. Adoption of Christianity might be a matter of social convenience or of religious conviction or a mixture of the two. Whatever the motive, it was a step fraught with consequence and rarely undertaken lightly.

The surrealist French poet and painter Max Jacob decided to

become a Christian in 1909 after a series of visions, apparently precipitated by reading a translation of the medieval Jewish mystical work the *Zohar*, in the Bibliothèque Nationale in Paris. On one occasion, he witnessed what he took to be an apparition of Christ on the wall of his room. Jacob sensed that his defection from Judaism would cause his family pain: when revealing to his cousin Jean-Richard Bloch in 1915 that, after a long period of instruction, he was about to be baptized, he adjured Bloch not to breathe a word to his family: "my father would die if he knew."[5]

Jacob's conversion was certainly one of faith; yet like that of many other authentic converts, it went along with a continuing, intense self-conception of Jewishness, expressed in his later writings. This lack of any feeling of contradiction between Judaism and Christianity, a sense of *anima naturaliter Christiana*, was a common trope of Jewish converts.

A bohemian and a homosexual, Jacob retreated to eremitic isolation in the 1920s, while continuing to write and paint. In the following decade he was subjected to venomous anti-Semitic attacks, especially by his former friend the writer Marcel Jouhandeau. In January 1939 the Egyptian-Jewish poet Edmond Jabès asked Jacob to speak out against racism. He declined, saying the matter was in the hands of the pope, the cardinals, and the bishops who would intervene with Hitler and Mussolini. In any case, he said, suffering alone was what preserved a race or a society. It was necessary to find again "the martyr whose blood revives" (*le martyre dont le sang féconde*). As for himself, he averred, "I am prepared for it both as a Jew and as a fervent Catholic."[6]

Most conversions, especially in central Europe, were more a matter of facilitating social mobility. Some Jews, while no longer believers, disdained so-called career baptism (*die Karrieretaufe*), asserting a defiant *Trotzjudentum*, a refusal out of pride to convert merely for convenience. A few, like Heine, converted in haste and repented at leisure. But most converts tried to put their Jewish pasts behind them and got on with their lives, even if their enemies subsequently dug up their origins for use against them or their descendants. In cases of intermarriage, conversions were usually of the Jewish spouse to Christianity, rather than in the other direction.

In Germany, Austria, and Hungary conversion had long been common as a means of social advancement. The critic Walter Benjamin's great-uncle Gustav Hirschfeld (1847–95), for example, converted in order to be eligible for appointment as professor of classical archaeology at the University of Königsberg. Of another great-uncle, the mathematician Arthur Moritz Schoenflies (1853–1928), who became a professor at Göttingen in 1892, Benjamin wrote that he was the "kind of Jew with a strong Germano-Christian leaning."[7] Another well-known German intellectual, the journalist Maximilian Harden (1861–1927), adopted Christianity as "the way of life corresponding to the higher culture."[8] This attitude was common among German converts.

German Jewry, in particular, suffered large-scale losses to Christianity throughout the early twentieth century. Even the preeminent German-Jewish religious thinker of the period, Franz Rosenzweig (1886–1929), had seriously considered baptism until he experienced a spiritual crisis during the synagogue service on Yom Kippur in 1913.[9] In 1933 conversions in Germany reached an unprecedented level: 1,440 were recorded. The anti-Semitic political climate no doubt was a major cause. It evidently took some time for the harsh reality to sink in that under the new dispensation baptism brought no relief from the effects of racist legislation.

Elsewhere in central Europe too, the conversion rate rose in response to the growth of anti-Semitism. As religion throughout this region was a matter of civil status, registered with the state, we have precise figures on changes of faith. In Hungary in the late 1930s, as anti-Semitism became part of the official policy of the state, thousands thought to escape persecution by leaving Judaism. Outside rabbinical offices in Budapest, long lines formed of those seeking the necessary preliminary paperwork. The net loss to Judaism through conversions in 1938 reached 8,486, compared with 318 ten years earlier.[10] The census of 1941 found no fewer than 61,548 persons who fell into the category "Christians of Jewish Descent."[11]

It was not unusual in Hungary to find that some members of a family had converted and others had not. For example, in the wealthy Hatvany family, owners of large industrial enterprises and patrons of the arts, Baron Lajos, a celebrated writer, one of whose central literary themes was the issue of Jewish social assimilation, and his brother Baron Ferenc, an art collector, were baptized. So were their cousins the baronesses Lili and Antonia, both also writers. The baronesses' brother Baron Bertalan, however, remained Jewish and expressed sympathy for Zionism.

In Poland and Lithuania, conversions remained rare. An estimate for Poland reckons the number of baptisms in the interwar period at no more than 2,000 to 2,500 per annum.[12] In Warsaw in 1928 only ninety-seven Jews formally abandoned Judaism.[13] Yet even in Poland, many Jews in the 1930s, particularly in the less traditional western regions, opted out of the community, though without necessarily changing religion. Converts included a number of prominent figures, such as Benjamin Mond, the sole Jewish general in the Polish army. The Cracow Polish-Jewish daily *Nowy Dziennik* caused a sensation when it published the names of all the Jews in the city who had left the faith, including "physicians, lawyers, artists . . . and a long list of Jewish women who had become nuns."[14] In Katowice, in Polish Silesia, a single issue of the local newspaper in 1933 contained the formal announcements of seventeen persons who had left the Jewish community, which numbered about nine thousand at the time.[15]

Even in more traditional Sephardi society in the Balkans, conversion, particularly in order to facilitate intermarriage, was increasing. In Bitolj (Monastir), in Yugoslav Macedonia, a Judeo-Espagnol song in the 1920s lamented:

> *Laz fijiques di ağore*
>> The girls nowadays
> *no querin noviu ğidió.*
>> Do not want a Jewish groom.
> *Cuandu salin a la puerte*
>> When they go out the door
> *in todos miren pur conesir.*[16]
>> They look to meet anyone.

In Salonica, *L'Indépendant* reported in January 1939 that a young Jewish girl, Riqueita Benveniste, had disappeared from her home and was suspected of having eloped with her Christian boyfriend with a view to marrying him after converting to Orthodox Christianity.[17] In July that year another girl, Renata Beraha, was reported to have been baptized, taken the new name Marina, and immediately thereafter married to a Christian.[18] (Civil marriage between Jews and Christians became legal in Greece in 1934 but remained very uncommon; hence these conversions prior to weddings.) Such news items were not uncommon in the Jewish press in southern and eastern Europe; in western and central Europe, on the other hand, such events rarely reached the press: they were so common that they hardly merited newspaper reports—and the girl, in such circumstances, might well not have felt any need to flee her family.

In Italy, where the Jewish community felt relatively relaxed in its relations with non-Jews, conversions were rare but not unknown. Primo Levi recounted that one of his uncles converted, supposedly in order to escape an impossible wife, became a priest, and went to China as a missionary. Levi's grandmother, like other members of the family, married a Christian and in old age "was torn between Judaism and Christianity, so much so that she sometimes attended the synagogue, sometimes the parish church of Sant' Ottavio, where she went to confession."[19]

Few converts returned to the fold. But external events sometimes led to the discarding of Marrano-like cloaks. In Russia in 1917, as in Amsterdam three centuries earlier, the new freedom accorded to Jews is said to have resulted in at least a hundred retroversions to Judaism in Petrograd alone.[20] Sometimes reversion was a public act undertaken in order to make a political point. For example, the bestselling German writer Emil Ludwig, who had been baptized at the age of twenty-one, returned to Judaism after the assassination in 1922 of his friend Walther Rathenau.

Conversion to Judaism of persons with no previous connection with the religion and no Jewish marriage partner was very unusual and, in the 1930s, almost unheard-of. Perhaps the most remarkable case of this kind was the mass conversion of an entire community of Italian peasants from the mountain village of San Nicandro Garganico in Apulia. Eighty followers of a local visionary embraced Judaism, braving the hostility of local ecclesiastics and government officials, Fascist anti-Jewish laws, and the skepticism of Italian Jewish leaders, among them the chief rabbi of Rome (who himself later converted to Christianity). This was not a case of proselytization, since the converts had had next to no contact with Jews or Judaism. The peasants, primitive illiterates, seem to have found their own way to Zion and, once arrived, stuck with remarkable pertinacity and refused to budge.[21]

Christian missionaries, often themselves converts, were deeply unpopular among Jews. Discussion of the issue in the Jewish press often recalled the role of apostates in medieval polemics against Judaism. Accused of predatory enticement of Jews from their faith, missionaries were sometimes subjected to violence. In Vilna they handed out cups of cocoa and sugar buns to poor children in winter, sponsored a children's summer camp, and, according to Max Weinreich, were "detested by every member of the Jewish community."[22]

Most Jews, whether religious or secular, regarded converts with distaste as something close to traitors. Isaac Babel, in his first published story, "Old Shloyme" (1913), describes how an old *shtetl* Jew, on hearing that his son has decided to "leave his people for a new God," hangs himself at night outside the door of his house. In 1938, when two Jewish women in Rotterdam were reported to be contemplating conversion in return for an offer of housing, a Jewish resident of the city persuaded a policeman to intervene and ask them whether they were being baptized of their own free will. But, as the chief rabbi of Rotterdam wrote sadly, "it was useless to ask this question in the church."[23]

Integration of converts into Christianity did not proceed without obstacles. In Poland they were not always welcome in the Church. A current of Catholic opinion urged caution in admitting Jews, advising that the motives of the would-be convert should be carefully examined to ensure that baptism was not being sought for opportunistic reasons.

Most converts, especially recent ones, rarely mentioned their Jewish roots, generally regarding them, if not as shameful, then as something they wanted to forget and leave behind. Jacob Bock, for example, was an Austrian socialist schoolteacher who converted to Catholicism with his wife soon after their marriage. Their son,

Rudolf, born in Vienna in 1915, did not become aware of his Jewish background until he was sixteen years old.

Often, ex-Jews resorted to elaborate measures to conceal their origins. But they seldom did so with total success. As Gustav Mahler observed, the converted Jew remained an object of suspicion. He himself felt "thrice homeless: as a native of Bohemia in Austria, as an Austrian among Germans, as a Jew throughout the world. Everywhere an intruder, never welcomed."[24]

Not all former Jews, however, wished to abandon every vestige of their backgrounds. Family ties, common interests and tastes, as well as lack of acceptance by non-Jewish society often pulled them back into Jewish social frameworks. Even after two or three generations as Christians, some continued to mix largely with Jews or descendants of Jews, as in the case of the family of Felix Gilbert in Berlin. Descended through his mother from Moses Mendelssohn, his family, Christians since the beginning of the nineteenth century, remained "conscious and proud of their Jewish heritage."[25]

Dora Israel, born in Vienna in 1894 to Jewish parents, was converted to Protestantism in 1897 together with her siblings, as her father "was very worried that we would be subjected to anti-Semitism as children, especially with the name 'Israel.' " At the same time the family name was changed to the non-Jewish-sounding Iranyi. The family never set foot in a synagogue and had a Christmas tree at home every year until 1938. Yet they continued to move in almost wholly Jewish social circles. Dora did not recall any non-Jewish friends of the family, apart from some literary acquaintances of her father, a writer and translator.[26]

Conversion, indeed, was not incompatible with a deep sense of fellow feeling with Jews. Few Jewish writers of the interwar period can match the sensitivity with which Joseph Roth wrote about the mentalities of Jews from small towns like his native Brody. He unerringly depicted their rootedness in the *shtetl* and their rootlessness in the big cities of Europe to which so many of them, like him, migrated. His novels, travelogues, and *feuilletons* (he was a master of this *mitteleuropäisch* literary form) look back nostalgically to the Habsburg dual monarchy and to the traditional world of east European Jewry, particularly that of the Habsburg lands. He admired the solid, inherited values of the *Ostjuden* and despised what he saw as the hypocrisy of the assimilationists. An elegiac melancholy and gentle irony infuse his writing.

Toward the end of his life Roth appears to have converted to Catholicism, possibly out of deep identification with the cause of Habsburg restoration. He died in Paris in May 1939 of a heart attack prompted by news of the suicide in New York of his friend and fellow exile, the playwright Ernst Toller—or, according to other accounts, the attack was a consequence of too many glasses of Pernod. "I've known many Jews and I've known many drunkards," commented the attending doctor, "but I've never known a Jewish drunkard."[27]

Since no witness could definitely verify Roth's baptism, he was accorded a "conditional" Catholic funeral. Jewish friends caused a stir among the assembled Habsburg loyalists, Communists, exiled writers, and former drinking companions of the dead man by reciting Hebrew prayers at the grave. The headstone, in the Catholic section of a suburban Paris cemetery, bears neither a cross nor a Star of David.

In general, Jews, even in mainly Catholic countries, preferred to convert to Protestantism rather than Catholicism. Dora Israel notes that "since Catholicism was the state religion of Austria, it would have been much more sensible to convert to Catholicism as my father's uncle . . . had done with his family. Father couldn't bring himself to do that." So Dora found that she exchanged one form of exclusion for another: "instead of belonging to a Jewish minority in school, we belonged to a Protestant one. There were never more than two or three Protestants in our classes, and they never accepted us."[28]

Some Jews converted in order to escape anti-Semitism; for others, apostasy involved an embrace of it. The philosopher Simone Weil, born in Paris to well-off Jewish parents, both freethinkers, beat Simone de Beauvoir into first place in the entrance exam to the Ecole Normale Supérieure in 1928. She sympathized with Marxism in the early 1930s and served briefly as a volunteer with the Republican fighters in the Spanish Civil War. In 1937 she experienced a mystical vision in the chapel of Saint Francis in Assisi and moved close to Christianity, though she never adopted it formally. She wrote in early April 1938 that she would prefer German hegemony over France to war. If the price of that were "certain laws of exclusion against Communists and Jews," she, in common, she thought, with the majority of the nation, would have no objection.[29] Weil's interpretation of public attitudes in France in the late 1930s was probably correct. She lived "a life, absurd in its exaggerations and degree of self-mutilation," as Susan Sontag later put it.[30] What was both absurd and contemptible was not her readiness to court martyrdom for herself but her willingness to drag others en masse onto her sacrificial pyre.

A different and more impressive kind of self-sacrifice was sought by another woman convert, Edith Stein. Born in Breslau in 1892 to a Jewish merchant family, Stein too had a brilliant university career as a philosopher. She was baptized in 1922, a few months after reading the autobiography of Saint Teresa of Avila, founder of the Carmelite order of nuns. Whereas Weil wrote that she had felt Christian all her life, Stein declared, "I had given up practising my Jewish religion when I was a 14-year-old girl and did not begin to feel Jewish again until I had returned to God."[31] In 1930 she wrote: "After every encounter in which I am made aware how powerless we are to exercise direct influence, I have a deeper sense of the urgency of my own *holocaustum*."[32] (The word, of course, had a more restricted meaning then, conveying the ancient sense of a sacrificial offering.) Stein's conversion caused acute pain to her mother. In 1933, insisting on her unity of destiny with the persecuted Jews, Edith entered the cloistered community of Discalced Carmelite nuns at Cologne-Lindenthal.

Not all Jewish conversions were to Christianity. In a few celebrated (or reviled) cases, Jews were attracted to other religions, such as Buddhism or the Baha'i faith. One of the most colorful apostates of the period was Leopold Weiss. Born to a Jewish family in Lwów, he traveled as a journalist in the Middle East in the 1920s, reporting for the *Frankfurter Zeitung*. In 1926 or 1927 he converted to Islam and was henceforth known as Muhammad Asad, living for much of the 1930s in Saudi Arabia. He has been called "the twentieth century's most influential European Muslim."[33] His book *The Road to Mecca* (1954) became the most celebrated work of its time by a Muslim proselyte.

Halfway House

Converts made a conscious choice not to be Jewish. But there were those who had no choice: these were so-called half-Jews, born to non-Jewish mothers or fathers. In accordance with Jewish law, the former were not recognized as Jewish by religion. According to the Nazi racial taxonomy, however, humanity was divided into Aryans, non-Aryans, and *Mischlinge* (persons of mixed race), that is, persons with one non-Aryan parent or between one and three non-Aryan grandparents. In many countries, even before explicitly racist laws were enacted, a certain social stigma often attached to people of partly Jewish origin. In Germany under the Nazis they formed their own association, which sought to emphasize their loyalty to all things German, in the hope thereby to escape the full measure of persecution meted out against so-called full Jews.

Many *Mischlinge* had never, before the advent of the Nazis, thought of themselves as Jewish. Gerhard Langer, whose father was a gentile and whose mother was "¾ Jewish," was a teenager in Jena in the 1930s. In spite of his tainted racial background, which was either concealed or overlooked, he was accepted into the Hitler Youth, was assigned to a communications unit, and took part in an *Aufmarsch* in Weimar in which, with his comrades, he passed in review before visiting Nazi dignitaries Rudolf Hess and Heinrich Himmler. In August 1939, after receiving clearance from the Hitler Youth, he left with his mother for the United States, ostensibly on a tourist visit.[34]

Both the Nazis and the "half-Jews" themselves conceived various gradations of affiliation of *Mischlinge* to Jewishness. Gerhard Neuweg, son of a Jewish father and a Protestant mother, was born in 1924 in Landsberg an der Warthe, a small town in the province of Brandenburg. Although his father was nonobservant, attending synagogue only on the high holy days, Gerhard was circumcised and for a few years was sent to Hebrew classes. In school he was given the offensively derisive nickname Itzig and subjected to (by the standards of the day) mild anti-Semitic abuse by one of his teachers. Nazi maltreatment of such children led relief organizations also to deal with them as if they were Jewish. Gerhard thus became eligible for a program that sent German-Jewish children to certain British private boarding schools. But the various procedures for securing permission to leave Germany were time-consuming and at the end of August 1939 Gerhard was still waiting for the green light to go to England.

Jews Without Judaism

In countries such as France and the Soviet Union that officially paid little or no attention to the religion of their citizens, it was possible for Jews to cease practicing Judaism without taking any formal step out of the Jewish community. But in Germany, Austria, and other central Europe states, matters were more bureaucratically organized. Each citizen was assigned a religion by parents at birth. On that basis, a small *Kirchensteuer* (church tax) was levied and shared among the institutions of each faith. It was possible to declare oneself *konfessionslos*, thereby opting out of the Jewish community. This demonstrative act of dissociation was a minority choice but the number taking it increased in Germany to about sixty thousand (more than 10 percent of the community) in the Weimar period.

Marie Jahoda, a Viennese-born middle-class socialist and agnostic (later a pioneer social psychologist), decided to resign from the Jewish community in 1933 at the early age of sixteen. She spoke for many when she declared, "My Jewish identity only became a real identification for me with [the rise of] Hitler. Not earlier. It played hardly any role in my thinking and feeling."[35] Jahoda's resignation was an affirmative act, based on her secular, left-wing Weltanschauung. Others left the community for opportunistic reasons, hoping to ease their way into general society while at the same time avoiding the renegade status accorded by many Jews to those who underwent baptism.

In western Europe and the Soviet Union, where no such formal exit was required, growing numbers of Jews were opting for civil marriage and refrained from circumcising their sons. For many Jews throughout the continent, Christian holidays, often in a secular guise, accompanied or superseded Jewish ones. Christmas was widely celebrated among non-orthodox Jews. Richard Koch, who grew up in Frankfurt in the 1880s and 1890s, recalled that "it was no longer an exclusively Christian holiday but had become a really cosmopolitan feast."[36] His family ate plum pudding and exchanged presents. At Easter there were colored eggs and a sponge-cake bunny. By contrast, "Passover was not much of an event. There was some saltbeef and a packet of Mazoth as well as Matzoball soup." On the Day of Atonement only his grandmother fasted, though the entire extended family joined her for the celebratory meals before and after the fast.

Yet even completely secularized Jews often felt a backward tug to the old customs and loyalties. In December 1930 in Vienna, Sigmund Freud wrote in a preface to a projected Hebrew edition of his book *Totem and Taboo*:

> No reader of [the Hebrew edition of] this book will find it easy to put himself in the emotional position of an author who is ignorant of the language of holy writ, who is completely estranged from the religion of his fathers—as well as from every other religion—and who cannot take a share in nationalist ideals, but who has yet never repudiated his people, who feels that he is in his essential nature a Jew and who has no desire to alter that nature. If the question were put to him: "Since you have abandoned all these common characteristics of your countrymen, what is there left to you that is Jewish?" he would reply: "A very great deal, and probably its very essence." He could not now express that essence clearly in words; but some day, no doubt, it will become accessible to the scientific mind.[37]

Another Viennese Jew, Franz Bienenfeld, a lawyer, expressed a similar outlook in a lecture to the Sociological Society of Vienna in 1937: nonreligious Jews, he argued, notwithstanding their abandonment of religious belief, retained a common "mental attitude" that set them apart from non-Jews and bound them to other Jews: "Most of them, and especially their intelligentsia, present to the world a common countenance since the foundations of their spiritual life are identical."[38] In support of this theory, Bienenfeld cited, among others, the examples of Marx and Rathenau, in each of whom, he maintained, "the principles of the Jewish religion, apparent in their doctrines without their knowledge and against their will, have broken through the cloud of unconscious memory."[39]

This reductionist proposition may be hard to sustain but what is undeniable is that even many thoroughly secularized Jews in the 1930s adhered to the main rites of passage of Judaism: circumcision, religious marriage, and burial.

Another stubbornly maintained component of traditional culture was food. Helene Ziegelroth, daughter of a cantor in Warsaw, who became one of the earliest woman doctors in Germany, declared herself *konfessionslos* as a young woman, was baptized upon her marriage in 1904, and thereafter refused to discuss Judaism and discouraged her daughter from associating with Jewish children. Yet, we are told, she baked "egg bread" (*challah*) on Friday and ate "flat bread" (*matzot*) around Easter-time until her dying day. Her daughter was baptized but returned to Judaism late in life.[40]

Soviet Jewish attitudes to Jewishness were often a complex and inconsistent jumble. Lev Kopelev, in 1932 a worker in a locomotive factory in Kharkov, later recalled that the secretary of his local Komsomol (Communist youth organization) committee was astonished to find that Kopelev, on receiving his first internal passport, which from that year had to show the holder's nationality, had registered himself as Jewish. The man pointed out that he could just as easily have registered as a Russian, thereby (went the half-spoken implication) avoiding much trouble. But Kopelev insisted that "so long as I knew I would hear the reproach, 'Aha! You're ashamed, you're hiding it,' I would count myself a Jew." Yet Kopelev was far from being any kind of "nationalist chauvinist," as Soviet Jews who laid too much stress on their nationality were often called. In his role as editor of the factory newspaper, Kopelev insisted it should appear only in Ukrainian: "I was absolutely convinced of the need for

Ukrainianization—socialist culture should be 'national in form.' "
When a co-worker asked to issue a page in Yiddish, pointing out that
fifteen hundred of the employees in the factory were Jews, Kopelev
strongly objected, maintaining that many of them probably did not
know Yiddish, and anyway "why artificially unite them and separate
them from their other comrades? Purely on the basis of nationality?
Ridiculous!" The applicant, who claimed unimpeachable proletarian
credentials, angrily berated him as a bourgeois intellectual, whereupon Kopelev "lost [his] self-control and let out such a roar that at
the next meeting of the Komsomol cell . . . I received a reprimand
'for making statements of an anti-Semitic nature.' "[41]

Anti-Jewish Jews

Could a Jew be an anti-Semite? In the early twentieth century,
many Jews, across all social and ideological boundaries, internalized
elements of anti-Semitic discourse. Not a few succumbed to what
Theodore Hamerow has called psychological surrender. "The most
destructive result of anti-Semitism," he writes, "was that so many of
its victims, while vehemently disagreeing with their victimizers in
public, agreed or half-agreed with them in private."[42] In some cases,
the agreement was not so private. The conservative, French-Jewish
cultural critic Julien Benda, for example, though a former Drey-
fusard, was capable of writing about Jews and their relationship to
French culture and society in terms more commonly associated with
anti-Semites like Charles Maurras.[43]

Jewish anti-Semitism was often termed "Jewish self-hatred," a
phrase popularized, though not coined, by the German-Jewish philosopher and sexologist Theodor Lessing, who wrote the classic
study of the subject, *Der Jüdische Selbsthass*, in 1930. In his early
life, Lessing, who converted to Christianity in 1895, himself exhibited many symptoms of the pathology that he later diagnosed in
others.

Perhaps the best-known case of this sickness was the Viennese
writer Otto Weininger (1880–1903), who converted to Protestantism in 1902. His *Sex and Character* (1903) was an incoherent

mishmash of misogynism, anti-Semitism, and penetrating psychological observations. A guilt-ridden homosexual, Weininger took the
logical ultimate step of the militant, Jewish anti-Semite: at the age
of twenty-three, he committed suicide.

Whereas Weininger despised both women and Jews, Lessing
sought to regenerate both and developed into a feminist and a Zionist. Arthur Trebitsch (1880–1927), also from Vienna, was a follower
of Weininger. He converted to Christianity and became a violent
anti-Semitic propagandist. Both Weininger and Trebitsch were discussed by Hitler and furnished useful material for Nazi anti-Jewish
theorizing.

Self-hating Jews undoubtedly existed but Lessing's book gave
the concept a popular currency that outpaced reality. Most Jews
afflicted by some form of anti-Semitism were not so much haters of
themselves as haters of *other* Jews. Often they attributed to others
characteristics that they feared brought down upon all Jews, including themselves, undeserved disrepute. Among the most complex and
controversial cases of this kind were the two most hated German
writers of the age.

The savage and inspired Viennese satirist Karl Kraus renounced
Judaism and resigned from the Jewish community in 1899, was
received into the Catholic Church in 1911, but then left it in 1923.
His attitude to Jews and Judaism was always tortured and often
contradictory. He attacked the "Jewish press" and mocked Yiddish-
inflected German. Yet, like Kafka, he expressed admiration for Yiddish "jargon-theater," such as the Budapester Orpheum, a comedic
troupe that performed in hotels in Jewish districts of Vienna. *Die
Fackel*, the magazine that he edited from 1905 until his death in
1936 (in later years he wrote it single-handedly) was full of crude
anti-Semitic jokes, sneers, and imagery. Kraus was influenced by
the racist doctrines of Houston Stewart Chamberlain and helped
draft an anti-Semitic article by Chamberlain that he published in
Die Fackel.[44] He poked fun at Jewish-sounding names and at those
Jews who changed their names the better to conceal their origin;
yet he deplored Jewish resistance to assimilation. He assailed Jewish solidarity, as at the time of the Dreyfus Affair; yet he bewailed
the "unspeakable horror" of the assassination of Walther Rathenau.

He was an early opponent of Nazism and was himself vilified as a "syphilytic Jew."[45]

Kraus's expressions of anti-Semitism have often been interpreted as self-hatred, though he himself rejected the concept. "His criticisms of Jews," Ritchie Robertson writes, "have an incoherent, flailing quality which suggests that they originate, not from observation and judgement, but from a personal source too intimate and deep-seated for Kraus ever to examine it."[46] Kraus's biographer, Edward Timms, interprets his outlook not as self-hatred but rather as "the desire to liberate the self from compromising affiliations."[47] As a searing critic of bourgeois society, Kraus earned the deep admiration of Jewish intellectuals such as Elias Canetti and Walter Benjamin.

He was an opponent of Zionism, which, he said, would merely create a new ghetto. The Zionist writer Max Brod wrote, "I am disgusted and repelled by such types of my race as Karl Kraus, because I regard them as the embodiment of everything that has abased my people for thousands of years."[48] Yet the German Zionist Gershom Scholem detected in Kraus's work echoes of Hebrew prose and poetry (though Kraus knew no Hebrew) and considered that "this Jew" had discovered "undreamed-of Jewish provinces" in the German language.[49] If the judgment seems far-fetched, it is one that, coming from this source, must be considered seriously.

Similar questions are raised by the career and writings of the other great German-language satirist of the age. The antimilitarist, antireligious, anti-almost-everything Kurt Tucholsky was the most feared German writer of the period. He attacked nationalism, philistinism, respectability, and much else, including the Jews. He too had abandoned Judaism in 1911, although, as he put it, "I know one can never do that."[50] In 1918 he underwent a Lutheran baptism. In the Weimar period he was viciously attacked by right-wing anti-Semites as a typical case of poisonous Jewish subversion of German culture and society.

Tucholsky's attitude toward things Jewish has been fiercely debated. In the character of Herr Wendriner, who appears in a number of his stories and sketches, he created a model of the despicable, philistine, German-Jewish bourgeois compromiser. In a prophetic piece that he wrote in 1930, he predicted the reaction of Wendriners to a

Nazi takeover. A group of them have gathered in a cinema with SA men (brownshirts) outside and are chatting in whispers. Jews must wear the yellow star. But after all, things are not so bad. At least now they know where they stand. One of them points out a man whom they take to be an *Ostjude*. Anti-Semitism directed against that sort, they agree, is certainly justified. "What a repulsive type! I'm surprised he's still here and that they haven't thrown him out yet!"[51]

Scholem saw the Wendriner sketches as "a sinister document of the German-Jewish reality" and Tucholsky as "one of the most gifted, most convinced and most offensive Jewish anti-Semites."[52] To such criticism there was an obvious response that had been voiced years earlier by Theodor Lessing in his own "self-hating" phase. Taxed with having written an anti-Semitic diatribe, he wrote to Martin Buber: "I am alarmed by the weaknesses of our kind. What should be done with this race of ghetto-heroes who feel incapable of standing naked in front of a mirror?"[53]

Tucholsky, however, did more than take embarrassing social snapshots. He evinced bottomless contempt for the submissiveness, as he saw it, of Jews, a "slave-people," toward their persecutors: "Now I understand," he wrote in his diary in early 1935, "how this race has been able to survive for so long: they guzzled their own shit."[54]

Apparently repressing memory of the scurrilous attacks to which he had been subjected, he claimed, in his last letter, written from Hindås in Sweden to Arnold Zweig on December 15, 1935, that he had never personally experienced anti-Semitism. He assailed the Jews' cowardice, lack of dignity, and "absolute inability to grasp what heroism even is." It was also untrue, he continued, that the Jews were fighting back. "They don't fight at all." Contrary to the pabulum they were often fed, the Jews should not comfort themselves that they were "attacked but undefeated." "Jewry *is* defeated—no less defeated than it deserves."[55]

The letter has been called a "political testament."[56] Marcel Reich, a bookish young Polish-German Jew (later the foremost literary critic in postwar Germany), read a shortened version of it in a Nazi paper in Berlin a few months later: "We could not believe that these implacable and occasionally hate-filled remarks, now and then turning into open abuse, could have been written by Tucholsky. . . . This letter had been written by a man in whose life the pain of Jewishness, and an uncanny self-hatred, had played a major, possibly the decisive part."[57] Tucholsky committed suicide two days later. The news was received by Nazi propagandists with a chorus of splenetic abuse: *hebräischer Schmutzfink, jüdischer Paralytiker,* and so forth.[58]

In spite of all this, the historian Walter Grab has argued that, unlike Weininger and Rathenau, Tucholsky was free from any sense of shame or stain arising from his Jewish birth. True, Grab argues, he criticized Jews, but he lambasted Germans much more fiercely. As for his admittedly sharp words against German Jews in the final weeks of his life, Grab sees these as arising from contempt for the weak-kneed response of the German-Jewish establishment to the rise of Nazism. According to Grab, Tucholsky's words spoke "sorrow and pain, despair and resignation but no Jewish self-hatred."[59]

The satirist speaks with many forked tongues and the first error of the reader is to take him literally. Kraus and Tucholsky cannot be pigeonholed in simple categories. Their ferocious, guns-blazing-in-all-directions assaults on contemporary icons and their breaches of all manner of taboos and mannerly conventions of civilized discourse were what rendered them so powerful as social critics—and so attractive particularly to Jewish intellectuals among their readers. At least they were both unswerving in their abhorrence of Nazism— which was by no means true of all Jews.

Jewish Nazis?

Otto Rudolf Heinsheimer, aged twenty-five, a Jewish student in Berlin, heard a speech by Hitler on the radio in May 1933. He found it "shocking, crushing—yet at the same time uplifting. . . . Is there really no possibility for a Jew to take part in this thing here?"[60] Heinsheimer soon realized that there was not: a few weeks later he left for Palestine.

The architectural historian Nikolaus Pevsner had converted to Lutheranism in 1921, but, like other converts, was categorized by the Nazis as a "non-Aryan." In the spring of 1933 he said: "I love

Germany. It is my country. I am a Nationalist, and in spite of the way I am treated I want this movement to succeed. . . . There are things worse than Hitlerism."[61] Pevsner sided with Goebbels against the conductor Wilhelm Furtwängler, who wanted to employ Jewish musicians. All this availed him nothing: his application for admission to the Reichskulturkammer (the state-controlled "cultural chamber" set up by the Nazis) was rejected and he was compelled to leave Germany.

The attraction of some "non-Aryans" to Nazism could take erotic form. Werner Warmbrunn, a teenager in Frankfurt, recalls that

> my anti-Semitism after 1933 was to a large extent "identification with the aggressor." I accepted/shared some of the Nazi view of the Jews as being commercial, un-soldier-like, clever, cowardly, physically unattractive etc. (I never bought the view that Jews were evil, or vermin to be exterminated.) I took great pleasure in the fact that I did not look Jewish, that I could (and did) "pass," that my passport issued in 1933 listed "dunkel blond" (dark blond) as the color of my hair. Blond, blue-eyed and athletic has been my idea of beauty . . . I would have given a lot to become an officer in the German army.

His closest friend was a member of the Hitler Youth who took him riding at an SA riding academy. This friend became his "first love" about whom Werner had "erotic daydreams."[62] Another acquaintance, Hans-Joachim Schoeps, a young Jewish theologian, monarchist, ultranationalist, and homosexual, took Warmbrunn under his wing, accompanying him on bicycling trips and on a visit to his friend Martin Buber.

Exaggerated nationalism was a common Jewish characteristic throughout Europe. What gave the German-Jewish superpatriots their special character was not so much their hyperventilated devotion to the country of their birth but rather the fact that some of them maintained their faith even when the German state turned decisively against them. The Verband nationaldeutscher Juden, founded in 1921, was one of a number of marginal organizations that attempted to reconcile Jewishness with German ultranationalism. Its leader, Max Naumann, a Berlin lawyer and former army officer, considered German Jews to be one of the "tribes" that formed part of the German *Volk*. He attacked Tucholsky as a recruiting sergeant for anti-Semites. At its height, the Verband boasted no more than 3,500 members, drawn mainly from the professional classes, particularly in Berlin. Strenuously patriotic, it refused to admit *Ostjuden* and opposed Zionism. Naumann bewailed the "flood [of *Ostjuden*] that threatens to devour us."[63] The *Ostjuden* were "pitiful creatures . . . of a not quite human level."[64] He blamed their conspicuously Jewish lifestyle for evoking anti-Semitism and called for their expulsion from the country. Naumann rejected the God of Israel, calling instead for faith in a "German God." In 1932 he hailed the "popular movement," of which the Nazi Party formed a part, as promising a "rebirth of *Deutschtum*."[65] After 1933 his movement sought unsuccessfully to ingratiate itself with the Nazis by means of *Verständigungsarbeit* (work for understanding). All this availed the Verband nothing after the Nazi advent to power. Although it sought to position itself as a "loyal opposition" to the new regime, its stress on assimilation led it to be regarded as dangerous by Nazi ideologues bent on racial separation. As a result, in 1935 it was one of the first German-Jewish associations to be banned.

Another such ultrapatriotic organization was the Deutscher Vortrupp (German Vanguard), a youth movement established by Schoeps, then aged twenty-four, in February 1933. It was anti-democratic, anti-Marxist, antiliberal, and anti-Zionist but, unlike other such bodies, had a positive attitude toward Jewish religion. Schoeps considered anti-Semitism peripheral to the Nazi program, with much of which he was in sympathy. In November 1935, several months after the promulgation of the Nuremberg Laws, Schoeps wrote that he still felt closer to Hitler than to Mussolini, Laval, or Baldwin. "I would rather be hungry here than elsewhere," he wrote. He deplored the *Jammergeschrei* (wailing) of his fellow Jews.[66] The slogan of the organization was *Bereit für Deutschland* ("Ready for Germany"). Men like Naumann and Schoeps were mortified when, in March 1935, Jews were excluded from the German armed forces. Notwithstanding a restaurant meeting with Ernst Roehm, head of the SA, Schoeps, like Naumann, was rebuffed at every turn in his efforts to persuade the Nazis that Jews could be good Germans.

Were Jews such as Naumann and Schoeps, like Milton, "of the

devil's party, without knowing it"? Perhaps—with the critical difference that Satan in *Paradise Lost* was a figment of the imagination,
whereas Adolf Hitler was flesh and blood.

"A Burden for France"

Jewish ultranationalism was not unique to Germany. It could be
found throughout the continent. In France, for example, the Union
Patriotique des Israélites Français stressed that French Jews must
have only one loyalty—to France. The union's leader, Edmond Bloch,
was almost a mirror image of Neumann: a lawyer and *ancien combattant* who had earned the Croix de Guerre in the First World War,
he was close to rightist circles and an outspoken opponent of Communism, the Popular Front, and Zionism. The more it registered an
increase in anti-Semitism, the more his group insisted that French
Jews must demonstrate unconditional patriotism. The union mus-
tered only about five hundred members (though it claimed many
more) but its ideas were representative of a larger body of French-
Jewish opinion.

Such views, at least so far as they concerned Jewish immigrants,
were not restricted to the right. The prominent French-Jewish journalist Emmanuel Berl was a left-winger, ardent pacifist, and "Mu-
nichois." In an article in November 1938, two weeks after the
Kristallnacht pogrom in Germany, he insisted that France could not
admit all the Jewish refugees who might want to come there. There
were in Poland no fewer than three million Jews, "dans l'ensemble
peu désirables" ("taken as a whole not very desirable"), who would
pour in if the frontier were open to them.[67] Berl assailed the "crazy
generosity" of granting speedy naturalization to refugees. "I find it
incomprehensible that immigrants who three years ago weren't even
thinking that they could become French, some of whom have not
even learned the language, enjoy the same political rights as a French
peasant." The German-Jewish immigrants, he declared, were of "low
quality" and "a burden [*un fardeau*] for France."[68]

In an attack on warmongering international financiers in March
1939, Berl ventured this historical reflection: "I see very few

millionaires among the victims of the wars of the twentieth century. No Austrian Rothschild died in 1866. No French Rothschild died in 1870. No English Rothschild, to my knowledge, died in 1914"— though he quickly added, "The same goes, I think, for the Morgans and the Vanderbilts."[69] Unforgiving of Jewish plutocrats, Berl displayed greater charity toward literary anti-Semites. He could forgive even Céline, announcing that he was prepared to "wipe a sponge over *Bagatelles pour un massacre* so as to retain only the inventor of a new language."[70]

Berl's attitude has been interpreted as masochistic and as a product of self-hatred.[71] But he never sought to hide his own Jewishness. His utterances can more plausibly be seen as a product of self-regard and self-protection by way of separating himself from and vilifying *other* Jews.

In France, as elsewhere, literary anti-Semitism spilled over from gentile into Jewish writing. The French writer Irène Némirovsky was born in Kiev in 1903 and moved with her parents to France in 1919. Her wealthy father was a banker. Her family resembled that of Zachary Mirkin, a central character in Sholem Asch's trilogy *Three Cities*, set in St. Petersburg, Warsaw, and Moscow before and during the Russian Revolution. Whereas Asch, for all his hostility to socialism, showed deep sympathy for *amkho* (the common [Jewish] people), Némirovsky felt an almost convulsive repulsion from them, from her Jewish origins, and from her family, especially her mother.

In her quasi-autobiographical novel *Le Vin de solitude* (1935), Némirovsky painted a merciless portrait of her parents, viewed through spectacles of adolescent rage: a mother interested only in her love affairs and a father only in making money. Everything in the daughter revolts against her parents and all they stand for. "I have spent my life fighting against an odious bloodline, but it is within me. It flows inside me."[72] The anger is directed here at her mother, but critics have discerned discomfort too with her Jewish origin. This was clearly expressed in her first novel, *David Golder* (1929). The title character, an unscrupulous Jewish businessman, having pushed a business associate over the edge into suicide, is depicted unsparingly as a profit-obsessed misanthrope. The novel, a *succès fou*, was adapted for stage and screen. Némirovsky was compared to

Balzac and Proust. During the 1930s her subsequent novels enjoyed continuing acclaim.

At the same time, however, and even more so after their rediscovery in recent years, they were attacked for their unflattering, stereotypical portrayal of Jewish characters. Némirovsky has been accused of "crude anti-Semitism," of creating "portraits of Jews depicted in the most cruel and pejorative terms, whom she observes with a kind of horrified fascination, even though she recognizes that she shares with them a common destiny."[73] In her defense, Frederic Raphael has contended persuasively that "the mercilessness directed at 'her own people' concealed a much wider scorn. The underlying topic was the interplay of emotion and callousness, the alternations of vanity and despair, in all the players of the world's game."[74] The controversy echoes the similar debates about Kraus and Tucholsky, with the difference that the extra latitude that may be accorded to the satirist cannot readily be claimed for Némirovsky, a middlebrow, conventional storyteller. Némirovsky herself conceded, in an interview with a Jewish newspaper in 1935, that "if there had been Hitler [at the time], I would have greatly toned down *David Golder*."[75]

In November 1938, Némirovsky and her husband, also a Russian-born Jew, no doubt alarmed by the growing anti-immigrant clamor in France, applied for French citizenship, to which they were entitled by virtue of long years of residence. They never received a response. In February 1939 they and their daughters underwent baptism. Némirovsky's motive seems to have been at least partly spiritual, though the simultaneous conversion of her husband and children suggests the presence of a prudential motive too.

Whatever view may be taken of Némirovsky's personal conduct or her literary strategies, it is plain that she did not consider Jewishness as something to be affirmed or celebrated. For her, as for many others in the 1930s—it was rather something to be concealed, glossed over, or jettisoned, a source of anxiety rather than of inspiration, a burden rather than a badge of pride.

10

THE LINGUISTIC MATRIX

Tongues Holy and Unholy

"I was brought up in three dead languages—Hebrew, Aramaic and Yiddish," recalls the narrator of Isaac Bashevis Singer's semiauto-biographical novel *Shosha*, set in Warsaw of the late 1930s.[1] Jewish Europe then was a multilingual world in which most Jews spoke a Jewish vernacular, generally Yiddish or Judeo-Espagnol, plus at least one language of the surrounding non-Jewish society, and in addition knew at least the rudiments of Hebrew and Aramaic. Apart from all those, many Jews also spoke one of the languages regarded as conveyors of high secular culture. In much of the former Russian Empire, including the Baltic states, that was Russian. Elsewhere it was German or French.

In Romania, for example, the Jews were divided into several linguistic groups. Those of the Regat or Old Kingdom (Moldavia and Wallachia) generally spoke Romanian in daily intercourse. In Bucharest intellectuals spoke French as well as Romanian. Most Jews in Transylvania, culturally magyarized as a result of rule from Budapest until 1918, spoke Hungarian. In the small *shtetlakh* of Bessarabia, Yiddish still prevailed. In Czernowitz, most educated Jews spoke Viennese German, though "knead[ing] it" with an admixture of words in Yiddish and Ruthenian. The Jews there saw themselves as the bearers "of German culture into the heart of eastern Europe."[2]

Taking the continent as a whole, one non-Jewish language was preeminent as the lingua franca of Jews in the 1930s. That was the foremost *Kultursprache*, German. "From the Baltic to the Balkans," wrote the Yiddish poet Itzik Manger, "the Jewish intelligentsia had faith in the German poetic and theoretical word, as it spoke to them of Europe."[3] German was the language of science, of philosophy—and of Zionism. The first official organ of the Zionist Organization, *Die Welt*, published between 1897 and 1914, appeared in German. Theodor Herzl, the founder of the movement, did not speak Hebrew and wrote his programmatic *Der Judenstaat* in German, which he predicted would be the language of the Jewish state. At Zionist Congresses until the 1930s German, rather than Hebrew or Yiddish, was the most generally used language, although often in a highly Yiddishized form that came to be known derisively as "Congress-Deutsch." This was often barely distinguishable from the *Daytshmerish* that had been used on the Jewish stage in Tsarist Russia after Yiddish was banned in theaters there in 1883.

Many Jews, especially in Germany, renounced and despised Yiddish as the "jargon" of the *Ostjuden*. In the eighteenth century Moses Mendelssohn had written, "I am afraid that this jargon has contributed not a little to the immorality of the common people."[4] In the nineteenth, Herzl called it a "stunted, shrivelled-up jargon . . . the furtive tongue of prisoners."[5] During the First World War, when the German occupation authorities in Poland used Yiddish in their propaganda among Jews in Poland, a German-Jewish leader pronounced: "To consider this jargon as a cultural German product is an insult to German culture."[6]

A distinctive Jewish way of talking in other languages was given a derogatory name in several of them. In German it was called *mauscheln* (meaning to jabber in Yiddish-style German, with implications of fiddling and cheating), in Polish *żydłaczyć* or *szwargot*. These terms were used by Jews as well as non-Jews. Indeed, as Edith Stein noted, "that unpleasant intonation common to the uneducated Eastern Jews . . . irritated the German 'assimilationists' even more than it did the 'Aryans.' "[7] In Russian, Jews were assumed by some to be unable to pronounce the letter *r*. Disparagers of Yiddish often criticized the "sing-song" intonation of its speakers. The same complaint was made of Judeo-Espagnol: "This kind of sing-song left a disagreeable impression with those who heard Judeo-Espagnol spoken for the first time."[8]

Since Jewish languages still formed part of the cultural experience, for many the main medium of communication, of a majority of European Jews, why did Singer's literary alter ego speak of these tongues as dead? This was not mere hindsight in a novel written in the 1970s. It reflected the reality of the 1930s. A century earlier nearly all Jews in Europe had spoken a Jewish language: Yiddish, Judeo-Espagnol, Hebrew (then used only as a language of prayer and religious scholarship), or a dialect such as Judeo-Greek or Judeo-Italian. By the 1930s all these were in retreat in Europe.

While all religious Jews as well as many others knew some Hebrew, most could not have carried on a conversation in the language. A few keen Zionists spoke it at home, but they were a tiny minority. Otherwise, apart from products of the relatively new and small network of modern Hebrew secondary schools in east-central Europe, few could easily handle the modern Hebrew that was developing in Palestine. Moreover, as Iris Parush points out in her study of Jewish women's reading in nineteenth-century eastern Europe, Hebrew was seen in traditional society as "an exclusively male language."[9]

One of the innovations of the Zionists and modern Hebrew revivalists was the switch from the Ashkenazi pronunciation of Hebrew, redolent of Yiddish, to the supposedly purer Sephardi pronunciation, said to be more authentically rooted in ancient Hebrew speech. The differences between the two were slight (*shabbat* instead of *shabbes*, *adon olam* instead of *adoyn oylem*, and so on) but most of the orthodox balked at the change and acrimonious arguments broke out over attempts to change the practice in synagogue ritual or schools.

Although modern Hebrew was closer to its ancient form than modern to ancient Greek, it remained a strange yet at the same time intimately familiar tongue to most Jews. The best index of that is the publication and circulation of Hebrew books and newspapers. Modern Hebrew book publishing in Europe never really got off the ground. Even in Poland, with its three million Jews, formidable Zionist movement, and vigorous Hebrew education network, successive attempts to establish a Hebrew daily newspaper failed for lack of readers. Hebrew remained a holy tongue but, like Aramaic, the language in which much of the Talmud is written, it remained, so far as use for purposes other than study and prayer were concerned, barely alive.

Mameloshn

If Hebrew, as a spoken language, was struggling for existence in Europe, albeit newly a-birthing in Palestine, what of Yiddish—that "language crackling with cleverness and turmoil," as Irving Howe lovingly describes it, "ironic in its bones . . . this street tongue, this disheveled creature wearing the apron of the Jewish week, this harum-scarum of a language?"[10] How could Singer, who lived in and by Yiddish, regard it too as already "dead"?

Most east European Jews, after all, still spoke Yiddish in the 1930s. The language boasted a lively press, impressive literary and theatrical activity, and, in the YIVO Institute in Vilna, a scholarly institution dedicated to its preservation and regeneration. By some measures Yiddish was growing rather than declining. The Polish census of 1931 reported that 80 percent of Polish Jews claimed Yiddish as their mother tongue (*mameloshn*) as against 70 percent in 1921. Yet Singer's character glimpsed beyond all this the path, inclining downhill, on which Yiddish was already embarked.

The 1931 Polish census certainly exaggerated the number of Yiddish speakers. In drawing up the census questionnaire, the government, not wishing to give a handle to minority nationalisms, decided that this census, unlike its predecessor, would not inquire into the ethnicity or "nationality" of respondents. The questionnaire did, however, ask for the "mother tongue" and religion of respondents, specifying that the latter was not a matter of belief but rather of formal adhesion. The decision to exclude any question about nationality aroused protests from all the national minorities. The government announced that, for the purposes of the census, each respondent was at liberty to declare a mother tongue for which he or she had a preference, irrespective of whether they spoke these languages in daily discourse. In the absence of a question on nationality, Jewish political parties called for respondents to declare a Jewish language, Hebrew or Yiddish, as their mother tongue. Many Jews heeded such calls. In Poland as a whole, 8 percent of Jews declared for Hebrew. Yet Hebrew was hardly spoken at all in normal intercourse anywhere in Europe. The census returns, which have often been cited as evidence of the survival, indeed resurgence, of Yiddish, must therefore be regarded with suspicion as a guide to actual linguistic practice. They are evidence not so much of any arrest in the ongoing process of linguistic assimilation as of the extent to which, in the face of general rejection by Polish society, Jews felt driven to affirm their ethnic particularism.[11]

In western Europe Yiddish survived only among immigrant groups and in the form of words, phrases, and occasional turns of speech, constituting a patois used by Jews among themselves. But this too was in decline. In Alsace and Lorraine, for example, the remnants of Yiddish dialect were dying out. As for the Netherlands, a middle-aged Jew in The Hague, writing in 1930, recalled that in his youth "the use of Yiddish was still rather common, especially among the lower classes" but now it was limited to the use of a few expressions, mainly by Jews in Amsterdam.[12]

In Hungary spoken Yiddish was limited to the ultra-orthodox. In Czechoslovakia it was current only in the small towns of eastern Slovakia and among the traditional Jews of Subcarpathian Ruthenia. In the Romanian *shtetl* of Ştefăneşti, we are told, "the better-educated youth of a post First World War period prided themselves on their inability to speak Yiddish and in the purity of their Romanian accent."[13]

Socially aspiring and upwardly mobile Jews often tried to elevate their Yiddish into something that sounded more like High German. Benno Gitter, whose family spoke German in his home in Amsterdam, writes: "Any Jew intent on fitting in with the European way of life strove to expand his knowledge of the language [German] and fine-tune his pronunciation in an effort to erase all traces of the sing-song Yiddish intonation."[14]

Already before the First World War, Yiddish and Polish had co-existed among Jews. The journalist Bernard Singer recalled the Sabbath in Warsaw in his youth: "On Muranowska, Mila, and Nalewki the couples spoke exclusively in Yiddish. On Bielańska these same strollers mixed Polish with Yiddish, and in the Saxon Gardens and on Marszałkowska they spoke exclusively Polish. Towards evening they returned to their quarter. And again on Bielańska Polish was mixed with Yiddish, and on Nalewki Yiddish ruled."[15] The question

should therefore not necessarily be seen as *either* Yiddish *or* Polish.
Polish Jewry in the early twentieth century lived in a trilingual environment in which Polish, Yiddish, and Hebrew were all known to
some degree by most Jews, for whom each language served a specific
function.[16]

Yiddish in the 1930s, however, like the people who spoke it,
was on the defensive, as emerges from the spirited assertiveness of
a former leader of the secular Yiddish school system in Poland who
insisted that for him and his colleagues, "Yiddish was more than just
a language . . . it was a weapon for instructing the people, for arm-
ing it with a new national consciousness. Yiddish was the symbol of
a steadfast determination to live and fight in *golus* (the diaspora)."[17]
Polish, however, was making inroads even among strictly orthodox
Jews. A defensive tone is audible in an article in 1931 by the orthodox women's educational leader Sarah Schenirer, urging orthodox
girls to speak only Yiddish rather than Polish. Yiddish, she points
out, is a holy tongue since it was spoken by many Torah sages over
the centuries: "Show that you are indeed Jewish daughters. Don't
be ashamed anywhere of your own Yiddish language and, with the
help of the Holy One Blessed be He, that will surely hasten the
redemption!"[18]

In spite of the requirements of the minorities treaty, the Polish
government had declared in 1921 that, while Hebrew would be
accorded a measure of recognition, "the so-called 'jargon' will not
be recognized as a separate language but [merely] as a sort of local
dialect."[19] Contrary to the provisions of the treaty, no government
primary schools operated in Yiddish. Polish, as a result, made rapid
headway among Jewish youth. In 1926, a survey of books borrowed
from Jewish libraries in Poland found that 44 percent were in Yiddish and 41 percent in Polish.[20] Since assimilated Jews would tend to
use non-Jewish libraries (or, since they were better-off, to buy their
own books), these figures suggest that Jews were already reading
more Polish than Yiddish. Even in Vilna, the citadel of Yiddish, just
8 percent of the loans from the Mefitsei Haskalah Library in 1934
were of Yiddish books.[21] The decline of Yiddish was also registered
on the Jewish street. In 1937 the *Vilner tog* deplored a drift from
Yiddish to Polish street signs in the Jewish district. On the Daytshe
Gas only 17 out of 129 store signs were in Yiddish.[22]

Yiddish was, in any case, by no means the language of all Polish or Russian Jews. The ethnographer and playwright S. An-sky, creator of *Der dybbuk*, wrote most of his early work in Russian, adopting Yiddish as his primary mode of literary expression only later in life. Vladimir Medem and John Mill, two of the Bund's most respected leaders in the early decades of the century, spoke Russian, not Yiddish, in childhood. Erlich and Alter, who led the party in the 1930s, similarly mastered Yiddish only as adults. Neither used Yiddish as the language of his own home. The Yiddish scholar Max Weinreich's first language was German, not Yiddish, which he learned when he joined the Bundist youth movement in his late teens. Bella (Rubinlicht) Bellarina, one of the foremost actresses of the Yiddish stage in the 1920s, "felt most comfortable in Polish, more comfortable, in fact, than in Yiddish."[23]

Even in Vilna the Bund, which prized the Yiddish language as the thew and sinew of Jewish working-class culture, found it necessary to produce election literature in Polish as well as Yiddish in the late 1920s and 1930s. The American Yiddish writer Joseph Opatoshu, on a return visit to Poland in 1938, noted that when he visited a Yiddish theater in Warsaw, Yiddish resounded to the rafters from the stage yet the audience in the stalls and the actors behind the scenes all whispered to one another in Polish.[24]

In the interwar period, Yiddish was endowed for the first time with a kind of academic status. Yiddishism, an ideology that sought to defend, enhance, revivify, and codify the language, traced its origins to a conference at Czernowitz in 1908 that declared Yiddish "a national language of the Jewish people." (In deference to Zionists and others, the *in*definite article was used.) Although Yiddish was the language of most orthodox Jews in Poland and the Baltic states, Yiddish*ism* was primarily a secular movement, often, though not always, with a leftist orientation. The Yiddishists were keen to prove that their language was not the *Kauderwelsch* (gibberish) scorned by both assimilationists and Zionists. They wanted to show that it was more than a debased dialect of German but in fact a language in its own right, with a lengthy pedigree and a thriving literary tradition. They went further. For the Yiddishists, the language was not merely a medium; it was raised into what the sociolinguist Joshua Fishman has called "a value and a cause in its own right."[25]

In 1936–37, YIVO issued a set of orthographic rules for the language that were adopted in most Yiddish schools in Poland, though many writers, publishers, and newspapers ignored them. YIVO was particularly concerned to reduce the *daytshmerizms* (Germanisms) in the language. Ironically, given the Yiddishist conflict with the Zionists, the YIVO experts emphasized the language's Semitic roots, which they valued as evidence of its Jewish character.

But YIVO's capacity to enforce its rulings was limited. By the 1930s the center of gravity in the Yiddish cultural world was moving rapidly toward New York, which had a Jewish population five times that of Warsaw. One sign of this shift was the absorption into Yiddish, including east European Yiddish, of a number of English terms.

Soviet Yiddish

Meanwhile, another European pole of attraction for Yiddish emerged, one that for a time seemed to offer bright prospects for the language. Whereas Yiddish in Poland received next to no state recognition or encouragement, it enjoyed large-scale government support in the Soviet Union. In fact, the USSR was the only state in history ever to make a substantial investment in Yiddish institutions, including schools, book publishing, newspapers, academic departments, and the stage.

Soviet promotion of Yiddish should be seen in the context of a general policy, inaugurated by Lenin, of supporting the languages of national minorities. In contrast to Polish official attitudes in the same period, Soviet policy discountenanced Hebrew while promoting Yiddish. Hebrew books did not appear in the USSR after the mid-1920s—one of the last was a 1926 edition of translated stories by Isaac Babel, who, since he knew the language, checked the proofs himself. Thereafter, "bourgeois-clerical-nationalist" Hebrew, regarded as triply dangerous on account of its supposed class character, religious connotations, and connection with Zionism, achieved the distinction of being the only national language that was virtually proscribed in the USSR in the 1930s, even as obscure tongues with tiny numbers of speakers, such as Budukh and Kryts, spoken in Daghestan, were mandated for use in schools and local government offices.

The Judeo-Tat language of the thirty thousand or so "mountain Jews," recognized as one of the five national groups in Daghestan, was also nourished by the Soviets: Judeo-Tat newspapers appeared, a literary circle was formed, and a drama troupe was active in the late 1930s. But like other non-European languages in the USSR, Judeo-Tat was forced to change its alphabet, first in 1929 to Latin, then in 1938 to Cyrillic.

The struggle between Hebrew and Yiddish was portrayed by the Communist Party as a "class struggle" between the "Jewish bourgeoisie" and the "aspirations of the proletarian masses to free themselves from spiritual slavery," as the prosecutor in the Vitebsk *heder* trial put it.[26] Soviet officialdom embraced Yiddish as the "language of the Jewish toiling masses." At the same time they tried, subtly and not so subtly, to change it.

From the early 1920s they projected an orthographic reform of Yiddish. This decreed that words of Hebrew origin would henceforth be spelled phonetically rather than in their traditional Hebrew form. In 1932 the special end-of-word forms of certain Hebrew letters were eliminated in favor of their regular equivalents. Also in the 1930s Soviet language planners sought to replace Hebrew-origin words in Yiddish with Slavic ones. These efforts had transparent anti-Zionist and antireligious motives, though they may be set in the context of general Soviet efforts in this period to standardize national minority languages.

Unlike YIVO, which had no means of enforcing its efforts at linguistic standardization, the Soviet Yiddishists could ensure that their edicts were obeyed, at any rate eventually (compliance was at first spotty). The reforms were little observed, however, outside the Soviet Union. Although YIVO too seriously considered dehebraicization of Yiddish, Weinreich fiercely opposed such changes: "the naturalized spelling," he wrote, "means that somebody is exterminating the Jewish tradition, is tearing the language from its Jewish source."[27] The new orthography's Soviet defenders countered with the Stalinist slogan that the reform was "socialist in content and national in form."

Nokhem Shtif, who had been the initiator and foremost figure among the founders of YIVO but who subsequently moved to the Soviet Union and became head of a Yiddish academic center in Kiev, established in 1926, proclaimed:

> This is not an ordinary reform. It is a Soviet reform. It is imbued with the spirit of October, the spirit which conducts a cultural revolution . . . [without] being afraid of tradition. . . . In the Yiddishist scholarly camp . . . [they are] afraid to touch the "delicate" spelling of the "exalted" [Hebrew] words, they are afraid to touch even such an everyday traditional nuisance as the final letters. . . . With the first steps in the reform—to spell the Hebrew words in the Yiddish way—we hit reaction and opportunism like a thunderbolt. This, the whole pious and Hebraistic-Yiddishistic reaction cannot forgive us to this day.[28]

Even in the argumentative little world of Yiddish intellectuals, Shtif was exceptionally quarrelsome. Denouncing his former YIVO colleagues, Shtif not only urged the dehebraicization of Yiddish but also inveighed against the *balebatish* (bourgeois) Lithuanian form of the language used in Yiddish schools in Poland, advocating instead what he maintained was the more *ameratsish* (working-class) Byelorussian dialect.

In the case of Yiddish, as of other languages, some Soviet linguists proposed romanization of the alphabet. Anatoly Lunacharsky, the first Soviet commissar for enlightenment, had suggested the romanization of Russian, so the idea had progressive credentials. Ayzik Zaretski, a member of the Kiev group of Soviet Yiddishists, considered this matter too a form of class struggle: "the Roman alphabet is ideologically closer to communism; Yiddish letters are full of harmful associations with religion, Hebrew, and national isolationism."[29] But in the early 1930s latinization of Cyrillic alphabets was condemned as counterrevolutionary and the idea of applying it to Yiddish was abandoned. New political contingencies led to reprobation of any stress on the Germanic roots of Yiddish as "serving the interests of German fascism."[30]

Such brawls mattered little to most ordinary Yiddish speakers,

who no doubt observed them with the amused detachment of simple medieval monks contemplating the impassioned debates of scho-
lastics over abstruse doctrinal issues. The orthographic conflict,
however, proved to be merely the opening salvo in a bitter war of
words between Yiddishists in the Soviet Union and those in Poland.
The conflict reached a low point in 1930, when the Jewish department of the Byelorussian Academy berated YIVO in a pamphlet
entitled *Fashizirter yidishizm un zayn visnshaft* (Fascisticized Yiddishism and Its Scholarship).

The Soviet Yiddishists, unlike YIVO, could count, at least for a
while, on substantial financial support from the state. Shtif's center
in Kiev, renamed the Institute for Jewish Proletarian Culture of the
Ukrainian Academy of Sciences, became a red replication of YIVO,
with its historical, literary, philological, pedagogic, ethnographic,
and bibliographic sections. It attracted some Marxist scholars from
abroad. Among these were Meir Wiener, a Cracow-born Yiddish
writer who lived in Vienna, Berlin, and Paris as a Communist intellectual before settling in the USSR in 1926, and Kalmon Marmor, a
well-known American Communist intellectual. In 1929 the literary
historian Max Erik moved from Vilna, where he had earned a precarious living as a Yiddish secondary school teacher, to the Institute
for Jewish Proletarian Culture in Minsk and later to its counterpart
in Kiev. After Shtif's death in 1933, Erik became the Kiev institute's
leading figure.

By 1934–35 it claimed to be the largest Jewish scholarly enterprise in the world with one hundred researchers. Shifting ideological
currents, however, destabilized it and led some of its projects into
dead ends. Shtif had been demoted when he proposed to invite
Simon Dubnow to attend its opening ceremony (the invitation was
declined). Wiener was compelled to admit to methodological er-
rors in his literary criticism. Marmor went home after two years.
A Russian-Ukrainian-Yiddish dictionary, prepared for publication,
was banned on account of "sabotage in the Ukrainian terminological
work."[31]

Although Yiddish enjoyed a brief academic vogue in the USSR,
it was in decline as a spoken language in most of the country. In
1926, 70 percent of Soviet Jews had declared a Jewish language as

their mother tongue. By 1939 only 40 percent did so.[32] Since that figure included Georgia and the central Asian republics, where Jews still lived in traditional milieux and spoke Jewish languages among themselves, the proportion of Jews speaking Yiddish in the European republics of the USSR must have been even lower. In the 1939 census no major city recorded a majority of Jews as declaring Yiddish their mother tongue. In Moscow 81 percent of Jews reported that as Russian. The highest percentage of Yiddish speakers was in Minsk: 50 percent.

Yiddish was already largely the language of the older generation of Soviet Jews. Only 20 percent of Jewish recruits in the Red Army in 1939 declared a Jewish mother tongue. We must beware, in any case, of assuming that declarations of mother tongue mean that that language was used regularly in everyday discourse. In the case of Yiddish, in particular, that was not necessarily the case. In Kiev, for example, although 93 percent of Jews had declared Yiddish their mother tongue in 1917, only 70 percent pronounced it their "everyday language."[33]

David E. Fishman has maintained that "by 1939, Soviet Yiddish culture was the target of creeping official liquidation."[34] It is true that in the late 1930s official enthusiasm for Yiddish definitely cooled. Several Yiddish writers were sent to prison camps. In 1938 the Department of Yiddish at the Moscow State Pedagogical Institute was closed after accusations of "isolationism" and "sabotage."[35] In the same year the language of instruction in Yiddish schools in Minsk was changed to Byelorussian. This required some adjustment since many pupils did not yet know the language. Accordingly, at first, teachers would address the class in Byelorussian but pupils were permitted to respond in Yiddish.[36]

Official repression was not, however, the main cause of the decline of the language in the USSR. This was a period when Soviet culture of all kinds operated under severe constraints. There is little evidence that Yiddish culture was, at that time, singled out for specially harsh treatment. Until the late 1930s, the Soviets had done more to promote Yiddish than any other government in history. Yet the substantial Soviet effort to encourage Yiddish in the 1920s and 1930s appears at most to have arrested a natural process of decline, the roots of which can be traced back to the last years of the Tsarist empire.

The pressure to abandon Yiddish seems to have come more from below than above. The Jews of the Soviet Union, for the most part, preferred Russian, which offered them brighter economic and social prospects and broader cultural horizons. A telling sign of the nature of the acculturation of Jews in the Soviet Union was the fact that Jews preferred to acculturate to Russian rather than to the majority languages of union republics such as Ukrainian or Byelorussian. In this they followed the practice of Jews throughout history, from Byzantium to the Habsburg dominions to British India, who had found it wiser to adopt the language of the imperial power than that of their colonized neighbors.[37]

In the spring of 1939 considerable Soviet state support was given to the celebration of the eightieth birthday of Shalom Aleichem. In Ukraine two hundred local committees worked to organize festivities. New editions of the writer's works were issued and critical studies and a memoir by his brother were published. The Ukrainian Academy of Sciences in Kiev mounted an exhibition in honor of the anniversary. On April 19, in the Hall of Columns of the House of Trade Unions (the former Nobles' Club) in Moscow, Shlomo Mikhoels and other actors from the State Yiddish Theater performed scenes from a play, and several of the best-known Yiddish writers and poets in the country, among them Peretz Markish, Itsik Fefer, Dovid Bergelson, and Dovid Hofshteyn, delivered speeches and readings.[38] Thousands of people attended. The occasion was a sign that Soviet state support for Yiddish had not altogether abated, even if its speakers in the former Ashkenazic heartland were abandoning it in droves.

The decline of Yiddish everywhere was primarily a consequence of decisions taken by Yiddish speakers themselves rather than of policies imposed from above. The downward trend was similar whether in western Europe, Poland, or the Soviet Union. It is striking that in the United States census of 1940, the proportion of the estimated Jewish population declaring Yiddish as mother tongue, 43 percent, was only slightly greater than the proportion of Soviet Jews we have noticed answering the same question in 1939.[39] Soviet Stalinism,

American capitalism, and Polish nationalism all, it seems, made little difference on this front.

Los españoles sin patria

Judeo-Espagnol (also known as Judezmo or Ladino, though some linguists insist that the latter name should be reserved for the form of the language used in sacred works), the tongue of the descendants of Jews expelled from Spain and Portugal at the end of the fifteenth century, was still spoken in the 1930s among the Sephardic communities of the Balkans and Turkey. It was traditionally printed in the Rashi form of the Hebrew alphabet rather than the square lettering commonly used for modern Hebrew. It was handwritten in Solitreo, a special form of Hebrew writing. By the 1930s, however, it was often printed and written in Latin characters, particularly in Turkey after the 1920s, when Kemal Atatürk dictated a switch from the Arabic to the Latin alphabet for Turkish.

Whereas Yiddish underwent a process of continuous evolution, absorbing elements from the surrounding linguistic environment, whether in Holland or Lithuania or later in the United States and Argentina, Judeo-Espagnol was held to have preserved, in something close to a fossilized form, the language of the fifteenth-century Iberian peninsula in Castilian or Portuguese variants: "This archaic, savoury language had always shown itself resistant to foreign words and furthermore it was spoken with the singing, melodious modulated inflexions in which there palpitated the ardent languorousness of faraway Andalusia," one romantic enthused.[40]

A group of Spanish writers who visited Salonica in the 1880s was enthralled to discover Sephardi Jews who still used many archaic Spanish expressions that had disappeared from the language in its homeland. The writer and Liberal Spanish senator Angel Pulido, in a series of books and articles between 1904 and 1923, promoted the conception of the Sephardim as a kind of lost tribe of fellow countrymen, *los españoles sin patria* ("the Spaniards without a fatherland," also the title of one of his books). He visited Salonica and other Sephardi centers and urged his government to provide official support for the language of "this brother people who preserve in the world something of the possible sovereignty of our language."[41] In 1931 the Spanish government sent a delegation, headed by Ernesto Giménez Caballero, editor of *La Gaceta Literaria* and "the first Spanish fascist," to Salonica, Constantinople, Skopje, and elsewhere in the Balkans. Ostensibly his purpose was to explore ways to sustain Judeo-Espagnol; in reality he was charged with examining the possibilities of exploiting the Sephardim to further Spanish commercial ties and political influence. The mission does not appear, however, to have led to any action by the government.

In fact, Judeo-Espagnol was far from being the embalmed tongue of Ferdinand and Isabella. It absorbed syntactical and expressive elements from other languages. Archaic terms that had been abandoned in modern Spanish were indeed preserved in Judeo-Espagnol, but the supposed purity of the language was a legend or at best an exaggeration that had been cultivated for separate reasons of collective egotism by both Sephardim and Spaniards.

Judeo-Espagnol evolved over the centuries, most especially in its last century. Under pressure from the speech of neighboring peoples, it was open to loanwords and morphological change, calques, and hybrid constructions. The Jews of each city or region where it was spoken had their own dialect of the language, reflecting local sociopolitical realities. Speakers in Monastir and Skopje had fewer Slavic elements in their speech than those in Belgrade and Sarajevo. The Sarajevo dialect had more Turkish elements than that of Belgrade. The presence in Salonica of an influential Livornese-Jewish merchant elite infused the language there with Italianisms.

From Hebrew the language ingested biblical phrases associated with religious ritual and words such as *sedakah* (charity), *edut* (witness), *ani* (poor), and *safek* (doubt). *Brit*, the Hebrew word for ritual circumcision, the strict meaning of which is "covenant," became in Judeo-Espagnol, by a process known to linguisticians as metonymy, *biri* (penis), often used with a diminutive suffix, *biriniki*. Some Hebrew words acquired Spanish prefixes or suffixes, sometimes both: for example, *malmazalozú* (meaning unfortunate, from the Hebrew *mazal*, meaning luck). Some Spanish words acquired Hebrew endings, for example, *ladrones* (thieves) became *ladrunim*. Some of the same Hebrew words that made their way into Yiddish were also found in Judeo-Espagnol, for example *sehel* (intelligence). Occasionally Hebrew words changed their meaning in Judeo-Espagnol, for example, the word *hamotsi* (literally meaning "who brings forth"), taken from the blessing over bread or cake, as in the Judeo-Espagnol phrase "Daki un hamotsi" (Give me a piece of cake).

From Ottoman Turkish, Judeo-Espagnol adopted much of the vocabulary of government (*vali, paša,* and so forth), the names of some occupations such as *kasap* (butcher) and *berber* (barber), as well as expressions of everyday interchange such as *bashtiné* (with pleasure, from *başüstüne*) and *mutla* (absolutely, from *mutlaka*). From German or Yiddish came such words as *móler* (painter) and *šnajder* (tailor). From Greek, *clise* (church—εκκλησια). And from Arabic *alhá* or *alhád* (Sunday), found not only among Sephardic communities in the Arab world but also in the Balkans, for example, in Monastir. English appears to have supplied just two words: *penéz* (penny), and, strangely, *winč* (winch), no doubt reflecting British commercial and engineering connections.

The processes of mutation and naturalization accelerated from the middle of the nineteenth century as Sephardim, like Ashkenazim, integrated into emerging national societies. In the independent Balkan states, local languages replaced Turkish in official usage and in government schools. The evolution of Judeo-Espagnol reflected these new realities. In Bulgaria not only were Bulgarian words absorbed into everyday Judeo-Espagnol speech but Slavic roots were given romance inflections and vice versa. In Sarajevo, we are told, Serbo-Croat influences "started entering all spheres of Bosnian Judeo-Spanish, its lexicon, morphology, phonology, syntax, and even grammar." The arrival of compulsory education ended "four hundred years of educational autonomy in Bosnia" and reduced Judeo-Espagnol "to the language of intimacy, spoken only at home or in the Jewish milieus."[42]

French influences predominated from the mid-nineteenth century onward, reflected in the adoption of such words as *randavu* (*rendezvous*), *malorozo* (*malheureux*), and *suetar* (*souhaiter*). As early as the 1880s the activity of the Alliance Israélite Universelle was said to have "succeeded in the difficult task of *de-Judeo-Espagnolicizing* oriental Jewish youth."[43] In Salonica the Alliance schools, the presence of a French expeditionary force between 1915 and 1918, and more general French cultural influence all helped inject Gallic vocabulary into Judeo-Espagnol. It became chic to use words such as *restorán* (restaurant), *mayonés* (mayonnaise), *kilotas* (culottes), *manikyur* (manicure), *foburgos* (faubourg), and *apremidís* (afternoon gathering of friends). Hairdressers now offered their customers a *permanent* or an *ondulasyon*. A hybrid language emerged that some called "Judéo-fragnol."[44]

Whereas Yiddish became, for many Jews in eastern Europe, a vehicle for social, cultural, and political modernization, Judeo-Espagnol never made the leap toward modernism. Max Nordau called it "a degenerate, anemic, atrophied dialect of Castilian . . . a dead branch of Castilian that has become corrupt and boggy."[45]

Unlike Yiddish, Judeo-Espagnol did not develop a rich secular literature though a few novels and short stories appeared in the language up to the 1930s. Some recent historians, however, have portrayed it as a modernizing force on the ground that it brought Western literature to Sephardic Jews in translation.[46] Translations of popular works from other languages, such as Eugène Sue's *Mystères de Paris*, began to make an appearance in Judeo-Espagnol in the late nineteenth century. Altogether an estimated 150 such translations were published in Judeo-Espagnol between 1901 and 1938.[47] Yiddish works, including those of Shalom Aleichem, Peretz, and Asch, were among them. Newspapers in the language were published all over the Balkans, especially in Salonica. But the volume of publishing, whether of books or periodicals, in Judeo-Espagnol was only a tiny fraction of that in Yiddish.

By the 1930s Judeo-Espagnol was considered, even by many of its speakers, as incorrigibly old-fashioned, a manifestation of cultural backwardness that the younger generation sought to shrug off.

It still retained some creative vitality, however, expressed, for example, in the *cantes populares*, sung-poems composed in Salonica by Sadik Nehama Gershón ("Maestro Sadik") and Moshé Cazés (under the joint pseudonym Sadik y Gazóz), which were performed in cafés and at family celebrations.[48] But cultivated Francophone sections of Sephardic society in the Balkans regarded Judeo-Espagnol rather in the way German Jews looked down on Yiddish: as a vulgar jargon of the masses.

By the late 1930s Judeo-Espagnol, even more than Yiddish, was losing ground to the national languages of the states where Jews lived. In Bulgaria and Bosnia only about half the Jews spoke Judeo-Espagnol and in Serbia fewer than a third did so. To some extent this was a result of nationalist pressures on education and business.

In Romania at the turn of the century, Judeo-Espagnol had still been the lingua franca of the small Sephardi community. But when an academic investigator from England, Cynthia Crews, visited Bucharest in 1930 she could not find a single family that spoke the language in their daily lives and only a few who knew it at all. Not only the language but also much associated folklore had been forgotten: local Sephardim no longer knew any of the traditional *romanses* (ballads) or *konsenzas* (stories). When Crews visited other Romanian cities where the language had formerly been current, such as Ploieşti, Constanţa, and Craiova, she discovered that there too it had virtually disappeared. Its extinction was hastened by the fact that it was close enough to Romanian to preclude its use, as elsewhere in the Balkans, as an intimate, semisecret means of communication among Jews.[49]

Contemporary analysts in the 1930s were pessimistic about the future of the language. "As for judéo-espagnol, which has known such glories and such misadventures, it is in its death agony," wrote one observer.[50] The descent to rigor mortis can be observed in the surviving archives of the Salonica community, where, until 1932, correspondence between the community council and the Matanoth-Laévionim charity was largely conducted in Judeo-Espagnol, written in Solitreo script; from 1932 to 1939 it was still in Judeo-Espagnol, but written in Latin characters; from 1939 onward it was all in Greek.[51]

By the end of the decade *El Mesajero*, published in Salonica, was the last Judéo-Espagnol newspaper left in the Balkans and its circulation had diminished to around a thousand. Acknowledging that the language was probably on its last legs, it advertised in 1939 the publication of "A REAL TREASURE! A collection of *romansos* and stories in Judeo-Espagnol is a real treasure that every reader should have in his home. All the more so since it is impractical to publish new ones, and the existing ones will be the last."[52]

Secret Languages

Hebrew, Aramaic, Yiddish, and Judeo-Espagnol were the only Jewish languages current in Europe. But these did not exhaust the distinctive forms of speech that Jews almost everywhere used.

Although Dutch-Yiddish had long since died out, the Jews of Amsterdam, particularly the working class, still spoke their own patois, from which general Dutch slang had derived a number of words and expressions. Benno Gitter recalled from his teenage years in Amsterdam in the 1930s such cases as *Het majimt* (It's raining—from the Hebrew *mayyim*, meaning water) and *jajim* (alcoholic drinks—from the Hebrew *yayin*, wine). A more subtle derivation was the phrase *oisseh sholem*: Gitter relates that he heard this used by a non-Jewish driving instructor to mean "reverse a little": these Hebrew words, given here in the Ashkenazic pronunciation, occur at a point in the *Amidah* prayer, recited by the pious Jew three times a day, where he takes three token steps backward.[53]

Another precariously surviving dialect was a Jewish variant of Greek. Before the arrival of Sephardi refugees in the Ottoman Empire following the expulsions from Spain and Portugal in the 1490s, Greek-speaking Romaniote communities had lived all over the former Byzantine lands. Gradually, however, the greater wealth and more dynamic culture of the Sephardim overwhelmed the Romaniotes, most of whom merged with the newcomers. By the early twentieth century only a handful of Romaniote communities survived. The largest were in Ioannina, the capital of Epirus in northwestern Greece, and on the islands of Chalcis, Corfu, and Zante.

In Ioannina the continued predominance of Romaniotes had resulted in the assimilation of Sephardi and Italian immigrants to the existing community. With the incorporation of northern Greece into the national territory in 1912–13, the Romaniotes in that area "became a minority within a minority, while being at the same time majority-language users."[54] But in the early twentieth century the distinctiveness of the Romaniotes was slowly fading away. In 1904 there were four thousand Jews in Ioannina, "so poor that the Greek Christians called them *spangoraménous* ('tied with strings') because they used string for shoelaces."[55] By the 1930s, emigration to Romania, Alexandria, Istanbul, Jerusalem, and New York had reduced their numbers by half.

The Judeo-Greek dialect was a form of demotic Greek, with a few Hebrew and Aramaic words and phrases, written in Hebrew characters (in modern times also in Roman or Greek script). In its written form it was not used for secular purposes: at any rate, no published texts of a nonreligious character exist. It contained a few loanwords from other languages, such as Arabic, Turkish, Italian, and Judeo-Espagnol. An example was *kassátes* (cheese patties) from the Italian *cassata*: this, we are told, "appears to be the only Italian word used by Greek Jews and not by others speaking Greek."[56]

The late Rae Dalven, an American scholar born in Greece to a Romaniote family, studied the Ioannina community and its language and recorded its characteristic expressions. These included words with Hebrew roots and Greek suffixes (*Sabbathiou*), phrases that were half-Hebrew and half-Greek (*i psychí't sto ganéden*, May his soul go to the Garden of Eden), and some with both Hebrew and Turkish or Arabic words (*inshalláh na s'ríkso to taleth*, literally "God willing, I will throw the prayer shawl on you," in other words, see you get married).

Several Hebrew expressions were used only among Ioannina Jews, as a kind of secret language when they did not want Christians to understand: for example, *ayin ara* (the evil eye), and *mi ditzers dibourim* (meaning "don't speak"—*mi* being the Greek negative; the second word derived from the French *dire*; and the third from the Hebrew for "words").[57] Similarly, the Ioannina Jews used curses and words of abuse such as *kelev* (dog), *hamor* (ass), *zona* (prostitute), *shakran* (liar), *goy* (non-Jew), and *mamzer* (bastard), all Hebrew loanwords.

The Romaniote Jews incorporated a few Judeo-Greek elements into their liturgy, called *minhag Romania*, that is, the liturgy of (the eastern) Rome, namely Byzantium. At the third Sabbath meal, on Saturday afternoon, Ioannina Jews would sing Judeo-Greek songs by local hymnists: "Ye Sons of Israel" ("Eseís, Paidiá tou Israel") and the thirteen distiches (rhyming couplets) of "God is Great" ("Megalos Einai O Theós"). On the New Year they sang at home "The Creation of the World" ("I Demiourghía tou Kósmou"), consisting of sixty-four distiches. And on the afternoon of the Day of Atonement, they, like other Jews, would read the book of Jonah in the synagogue—but in their own Judeo-Greek translation.[58]

Judeo-Italian in the modern period was not so much a dialect of Italian as a series of Jewish variations on local dialects of Italian in areas in which Jews lived. In the late nineteenth century the Ghettaiolo of Jews in Ferrara, the Lason Akodesh of Primo Levi's ancestors in Piedmont, the Bagito of Livorno, and the argot of the Rome ghetto were as mutually unintelligible as the dialects of the general population of those areas.

Primo Levi and Dan Vittorio Segre recall in their memoirs the Piedmontese Jewish dialect that their elders spoke as they were growing up in the 1920s and 1930s. Levi took pleasure in collecting Judeo-Piedmontese vocabulary. Many words were derived from the liturgy or quotidian religious practice and were common among Jews everywhere. Other words from Hebrew included *ruah* (unpleasant odor, fart), *khumayom* (oppressive heat), and *besim* (testicles, from the Hebrew *betzim*, eggs). Levi also recorded some words and expressions of more obscure origin, such as *meruzav* (marriage broker).[59] The dialect included expressions in which Hebrew words were treated morphologically as if they were Piedmontese, for instance by the addition of Piedmontese prefixes or suffixes. Levi and Segre were among the last generation to hear such talk used naturally and unself-consciously.

In the 1930s the Roman-Jewish poet Crescenzo del Monte (1868–1935) published sonnets in the antique dialect of the Roman ghetto.[60] But this was a self-conscious exercise in cultural retrieval rather than a manifestation of a living language. By 1939 the Jewish-Italian dialects were all on the verge of extinction.

The Jewish underworld also generated its own jargon. In Czernowitz, for example, the word *bombien* was used to signify pimping or white slaving. "You can hear people, when asked about some of the finest houses in the centre of the town, say about their properties: 'Where does he get his money from?' 'From *bombien*, of course.' " The word was said to derive from Bombay, the destination to which many of the victims of the white slave traffic were allegedly sent.[61]

Finally, Jewish words in other languages sometimes served as signals of mutual recognition. Just a phrase or a subtle inflection might suffice for the purpose. This was important in the 1930s particularly in contexts, such as the Soviet Union, where it was considered bad form to refer overtly to such matters.

Language was the matrix from which Jewish culture in Europe was formed. As Jewish languages declined, so the vitality of the culture to which they gave expression diminished. As Jews abandoned their own languages for those of the surrounding majority populations, they entered the cultures of their neighbors, often with a passion and intensity that aroused suspicion and antagonism rather than welcome. In the interwar period European Jewry thus found itself at a delicate point of transition between sustaining its own culture and embracing that of others. Nowhere was the resulting tension more clearly registered than in the Jewish press.

11

THE POWER OF THE WORD

Judenpresse

Anti-Semites accused the Jews in all countries of controlling the press. The accusation had little substance in France, where it had been loudly expressed at least since the time of the Panama Canal scandal in the 1880s. In central Europe, however, matters were different. Before the rise of the Third Reich, the German-language press in Vienna, Berlin, Budapest, and other major cities of central Europe had indeed been to a considerable degree owned and produced by Jews—although not by *the* Jews, since the Jewish pressmen did not act in concert.

The foremost example of such a newspaper was the *Neue Freie Presse*, the leading daily newspaper of Vienna from the late nineteenth century until 1938. Moritz Benedikt, its editor-in-chief from 1881 until his death in 1920 (in his final years also its proprietor), developed it into the chief organ of the Viennese liberal bourgeoisie. Benedikt was said to be able to make or break Austrian ministries and in 1917 was appointed to the upper house of the Austrian parliament. The paper's liberalism aroused the ire of Karl Lueger, the anti-Semitic Christian Social Party mayor of Vienna at the turn of the century: "The main creator of Austrian anti-Semitism," he said, "was the Jewish-Liberal press with its depravity and terrorism."[1]

The influence of the *Neue Freie Presse* was not restricted to politics. In the heyday of Viennese cultural efflorescence between the 1880s and 1914, it was also a legendary arbiter of taste in literature, opera, theater, music, and art. The founder of the Zionist movement, Theodor Herzl, worked for the paper as a foreign correspondent and as editor of its much-admired *feuilleton* section. Stefan Zweig, who as an aspiring writer was thrilled to be invited by Herzl to contribute to the paper, called it "the oracle of my fathers and the temple of high priests."[2]

The *Neue Freie Presse*, it was said, was written by Jews for Jews. Hitler, who had conceived a loathing for the paper during his time as a down-and-out in Vienna before the First World War, called it the "Judenblatt" (Jews' paper). Nearly 80 percent of the editorial staff in the interwar period was Jewish. Sigmund Freud read it every day. The Viennese joke went that one Jew said to another: "So you no longer observe *Shabbes* or any of the holidays. Do you subscribe to anything Jewish anymore?" "Why certainly," came the reply, "to the *Neue Freie Presse*."

Such papers did not, however, see themselves as Jewish publications. Notwithstanding their heavily Jewish ownership, staff, and readership, they held to a universalist, liberal outlook, sought a general audience, and bent over backward to avoid making special claims on behalf of Jewish interests. Herzl's involvement with the paper led Benedikt to take extra care to avoid any pleading in its columns on behalf of Zionism.

The *Neue Freie Presse* nevertheless became a prime target not only for anti-Semites but also for the satirical poison pens of Kraus and Tucholsky. They charged Benedikt with hypocrisy, cowardice, self-satisfaction, and complacency and accused him of bearing partial responsibility for the outbreak of the First World War. Kraus's dramatic masterpiece *Die letzten Tage der Menschheit* (The Last Days of Humanity) consisted in large measure of verbatim clippings from the newspaper.

The collapse of the Habsburg dual monarchy and the demotion of Vienna from a great imperial *Weltstadt* to the capital of a minor, central European rump republic deprived the *Neue Freie Presse* of much of its earlier importance. Like other papers it lost circulation and advertising in the Great Depression and in 1934 the owner-editor, Ernst Benedikt, son of Moritz, was forced to sell it to the Austrian government. Thereafter it dwindled into an official propaganda mouthpiece and in 1936 its new owners truckled to the Nazis by offering to dismiss all their Jewish employees.

In Budapest the venerable German-language *Pester Lloyd* occupied a position analogous to that of the *Neue Freie Presse* in Vienna. Although it appeared in German, the *Lloyd* was the leading newspaper of Hungary and a respected liberal political voice. After 1933 it published a number of anti-Nazi German writers, including exiled German Jews. But in 1937 the *Lloyd*'s editor, Josef Vészi, a member of the upper house of the Hungarian parliament, was forced, on account of his Jewishness, to relinquish his direction of the paper.

These papers, and others like them throughout east-central Europe, were more than just liberal mouthpieces. In states in which the greater part of the press was government-controlled and/or highly colored by party-political considerations and/or corrupt, and in which broadcasting was entirely under the direction of the state and the airwaves closed to unconventional opinions, the existence of independent, pro-democracy papers was of great importance to those who sought objective news coverage. Precisely for this reason, such papers became hated targets of right-wing, nationalist forces, whose animosity extended beyond the producers of the newspapers themselves to Jews in general.

What Goebbels called the "Judenpresse" therefore had a certain basis in reality. And nowhere more so than in Germany itself, where, as Joseph Roth wrote in 1933, "the magazines and newspapers were edited by Jews, managed by Jews, read by Jews."[3] And in Germany too, precisely because they did not wish to be identified, or rather stigmatized, as Jewish papers, the great liberal organs refrained from taking overly strong positions on issues of Jewish concern.

The *Frankfurter Zeitung*, long regarded as Germany's most serious newspaper, had enormous influence, although its circulation was no more than seventy thousand, mainly among businessmen and professionals. For most of its history the paper had been owned and run by the Sonnemann-Simon family. Heinrich Simon, grandson of the founder of the paper, had been baptized as a child but subsequently left the church, without, however, returning to Judaism. A cultivated patron of the arts and a convinced liberal, he maintained the paper's formidable reputation. But in the face of severe financial difficulties in the 1920s, the family's control weakened. In 1930 they were compelled to surrender 49.5 percent of the shares in the newspaper to a front for the I. G. Farben chemical combine. After

January 1933 the paper quickly kowtowed to the new order. On March 27, 1933, Goebbels crowed in his diary: "The Jewish press is whimpering with alarm and fear. All Jewish organizations are proclaiming their loyalty to the government."[4] In June 1934 Simon was forced to sell the family's remaining shares in the newspaper.

Hans Lachmann-Mosse, head of the Mosse press and advertising conglomerate, which owned several major papers, including the liberal *Berliner Tageblatt*, left Germany shortly after Hitler attained power. He was enticed back a few weeks later by a personal assurance of safe conduct from Hermann Goering. When he returned to Berlin, the press baron was forced at gunpoint to sign over all his German assets to a supposed foundation to benefit war veterans. He was then escorted to the French frontier by the chief of the Gestapo.

The Ullstein family was similarly forced out of its dominant position in its company, the largest publishing business in Germany. Among the leading titles in the Ullstein group were the *Berliner Zeitung*, the *Berliner Morgenpost*, the loss-making *Vossische Zeitung* (nicknamed "Tante [Aunt] Voss," the country's oldest newspaper), and the immensely profitable *Berliner Illustrirte Zeitung*, which, with a circulation of 1.5 million in the late 1920s, was the bestselling illustrated paper in Germany.

These papers catered to a broad non-Jewish as well as Jewish market. All of them were committed to a liberal worldview and supported the Weimar constitution. They did not lose significant market share to Nazi papers prior to Hitler's assumption of power. In 1933 the Nazi press in Germany reached barely 2.5 percent of newspaper readers. But as Hermann Ullstein later wrote: "Although our readers seemed superficially to remain loyal to us, there was little doubt that in their hearts they were no longer on our side. Inwardly a good half of them, persuaded that 'things cannot go on as they are,' were already in Hitler's camp. Day after day we criticized their idol . . . and it had not the slightest effect on them."[5]

In truth, quite apart from its personnel and audience, the German-language liberal press in central Europe was Jewish in another and deeper sense. For all the protestations of its proprietors, their papers' adhesion to democratic values represented a commitment to the type of society in which Jews could best prosper, one based on the rule of law, in which minorities need not fear the tyranny of the majority, in which social mobility could proceed on a meritocratic basis, and in which the rights of freedom of expression, association, and conscience were respected. The failure of the liberal press to stand up and fight for those values was what earned them the contempt of Kraus and Tucholsky. The pusillanimity of these newspapers in their death throes was far from impressive. It was part and parcel of the larger failure of German and European liberalism in the 1930s in a struggle that Jews could not hope to fight and win alone.

In October 1933 a decree law in Germany excluded Jews from employment in journalism, save on Jewish papers. But even before that, most Jewish journalists had been dismissed. Many writers fled abroad, initially to other German-speaking lands, then, as the Nazi empire expanded, to Moscow, Paris, London, New York, Tel Aviv, or Mexico City. Among the exiles were several of the big names of contemporary German literature such as Lion Feuchtwanger and Arnold Zweig. They could no longer publish at all in Germany, unless they did so using noms de plume in Jewish publications or in the few remaining periodicals not directly under Nazi control. If they still wished to appear in print in their own language, they could do so only in exile newspapers or German publishing houses in Switzerland. But their sales were greatly reduced and the fees or royalties they could hope to command were likewise slimmed down.

The exile German-language press in cities such as Prague and Paris was endowed with fine, experienced writers but lacked much of an audience. "Today we are writing in a vacuum. The people who read us are of our own opinion to begin with, and we don't reach those who have no opinion or who are vacillating," laments a German-Jewish journalist in Paris in 1935, a character in the novel *Paris Gazette* by Feuchtwanger.[6] Save for the refugee publications, the German-language press not just in Germany but throughout Europe had been largely "Aryanized" by 1939.

Choking in the Stinking Sea

The first Jewish newspapers, among the earliest of any kind, had appeared in Amsterdam: the *Gazeta de Amsterdam*, published in Judeo-Espagnol between 1675 and 1702, and the Yiddish *Dinstagishe un Fraytagishe Kurant* in 1686–87. Their modern successors, especially the *Nieuw Israelitisch Weekblad*, penetrated most Jewish homes in the Netherlands and provided a forum for the fierce controversies that characterized this and all European Jewish communities.

In the early twentieth century the Jewish press played a vital role as a glue joining together scattered communities, as a mobilizing force for political and religious movements, as a means for the importation into Jewish discourse of ideas from the non-Jewish world, and as a source of entertainment, solace, and news of special interest to Jews, for example from Palestine.

The dispersion of the Jews rendered newspapers a necessary tool of cohesion but at the same time weakened the ability of the press to survive financially. Jewish newspapers proliferated but, like day lilies, often flowered briefly and then withered. Censorship and frequent government harassment throughout central and eastern Europe added to their difficulties.

Despite all this, the Jewish press was a vibrant, multilingual reflection of the lives of its millions of readers in every country in which Jews lived. At least 854 publications, ranging from daily newspapers to specialized periodicals, were published in Yiddish, Hebrew, and Judeo-Espagnol, as well as in the national languages of every country between the Urals and the Pyrenees.[7]

The Yiddish press was an important force in the Jewish community. In Warsaw eleven Yiddish dailies competed strenuously for readers in the mid-1930s. They ranged from sensationalist afternoon papers, such as *Der varshever radio* (Warsaw Radio) to *Haynt* (Today), a morning paper that was close to the General Zionists, and *Der moment*, which, in its final period, tended toward the Revisionist Zionists.

Haynt was a serious paper, with high intellectual standards and a cosmopolitan outlook, that managed to achieve a mass circulation. Its editor until 1933, when he emigrated to Palestine, was the leading Zionist politician Yitzhak Gruenbaum, who helped build it into the most influential Yiddish paper in Europe. *Haynt* published not only articles by Yiddish journalists but also syndicated features by such figures as André Maurois and Winston Churchill. Yet, like most Yiddish papers, it depended on serialized novels as circulation boosters and it often printed sensational stories under headlines such as "Four months 'after his death' the man suddenly returns" (an old journalistic standard), or (inserting a Jewish angle) "Who is the young hasid who killed himself?"[8]

Noyekh Pryłucki, editor of *Der moment*, was a well-known and popular figure in Jewish Warsaw. A Yiddish philologist, ethnographer, and bibliophile (he owned the largest private library of Yiddish books in the country), he was elected to the first Sejm as a representative of the Folkist Party. He also served on the Warsaw municipal council for several years. *Der moment* was the first Yiddish daily to publish regular sports reports. Its sports reporter, who came from a Hasidic family, was conspicuous on the press bench at sporting events (sport was an unusual avocation in Hasidic circles).

Both *Haynt* and *Der moment* claimed to sell over 100,000 copies at their peak but in the late 1930s the circulation of both was in decline. According to Polish police records, *Haynt* sold an average of only 27,000 copies in 1932–38 and *Der moment* 23,000. By the summer of 1939 both papers were in serious financial trouble. *Haynt* had to appeal to the Zionist Organization for a loan to wipe out its debts.[9]

Official interference and economic pressures undermined the stability of the Yiddish press. Several smaller papers, particularly those suspected by the authorities of Communist inclinations, led a fly-by-night existence. The big Warsaw titles were close to being national newspapers: in the 1930s as much as half of their circulation was outside the city. In many cases special editions were published for provincial cities. Independent Yiddish dailies were published in some provincial cities, such as Vilna and Lwów. Weeklies appeared in smaller towns.

Polemics in the Jewish press, especially in Yiddish papers, were

waged without gloves and with red-hot pokers. Sometimes the conflicts were ideological. Often, in what was largely a commercial
press, they were viciously competitive circulation battles. Even in a
shtetl such as Baranowicze, no holds were barred in the struggle between the *Baranovitsher kuryer* and the rival *Baranovitsher vokh*. In
1936 the two papers conducted a bitter war of words over whether
a Jewish-owned press agency, apparently connected with the *Vokh*,
should distribute a Polish anti-Semitic paper and over whether the
local Jewish gymnasium should teach German, "the language of Hitler and Goebbels." The editor of the *Kuryer* might deplore the "lack
of culture and tact" of participants in the public arena and condemn
the personalization of conflicts.[10] But the same writer had no compunction in a subsequent issue about launching into a vituperative
tirade against the "vile, ugly, lying, and malicious stammerings and
insinuations from that person [his competitor] with his unhealthy
ambition to be a 'supporter of culture' in spite of his more than
semi-illiteracy."[11] Baranowicze (Jewish population at the time ten
thousand, about half the total) was small enough that the protagonists in this epic struggle would, no doubt, pass each other regularly
in the central square.

Ideological divisions seem, at least in some instances, to have
been more easily set aside than personal ones. When it came to practical matters there could be remarkable cooperation across political
boundaries. Thus Warsaw's Agudist *Togblat* was printed on the ma-
chines of the Bundist *Folks-tsaytung*, even as the latter waged a war
of words against the *frumakes* (orthodox)—who responded with no
less acerbity against the *apikorsim* (heretics). The *Togblat* always appeared with the Hebrew letters ב'ה (signifying "with the help of the
Almighty") at the head of the paper; the *Folks-tsaytung* was wont to
appear with slogans such as "Down with clericalism." On one occasion a printer's error (or practical joke) led them to switch the two,
causing consternation and merriment.[12]

The Yiddish press, more than the Polish, was subject to official
censorship, as in many other countries, after rather than before
printing of the paper. Presses were closed down on the ground that
"the machinery is defective" or for no stated reason at all. Editors
learned to anticipate the official blue pencil and exercise a measure

of self-censorship. The *Folks-tsaytung*, in particular, occasionally appeared with blank spaces and found it prudent to change its name several times. In 1937 the entire press run of the paper was confiscated eighty times. The three censors of the Yiddish press in Warsaw were two right-wing Zionists, "pathetic timeservers who would beg the editors to accede to their requests and save everybody *hartsveytok* (heartache)," and a permanent inebriate, who gave the least trouble.[13]

The popular Yiddish papers published plenty of sensational news items, especially on crime and underworld activities, often with a Jewish twist: typical items included Goering's alleged marriage to a Jewish woman, a brothel that employed fourteen-year-old girls, and Hitler's supposedly incurable illness. These papers also devoted considerable space to competitions, raffles, jokes, puzzles, and columns on graphology.[14] But the chief selling point for the whole of the Yiddish press was fiction: nearly all the major papers published short stories and episodic novels, often featuring one or more of these cliffhangers in each issue. Some were major works of literature; most were what came to be called *shund*—the uncomplimentary term derived from a German word used in abattoirs to denote the stench of a skinned carcass. Serious writers often wrote fiction at speed on a formulaic pattern, publishing under assumed names, concerned lest their reputations suffer from association with literary junk. Among these pseudonymous writers was the at the time little-known Isaac Bashevis Singer. The popularity of such potboilers aroused concern and earnest debate among Yiddish writers.

Kadya Molodowsky was one of those who called for sanctions against writers who debased Yiddish literature by churning out shameless trash. The Yiddish reader, she insisted, must be saved from "choking in the stinking sea" of *shund* that rendered him "incapable any longer of picking up a good book." Surely the profit-seeking press could find room for serious literary novels, even perhaps for the occasional poem? At least, she pointed out, they published no *shund* poems: "all honour to the poets!" Exactly how one might determine the fine distinction between what passed for literature and *shund*, she disdained to explain.[15]

A large number of special-interest Jewish publications, mainly in Yiddish, sprouted up in interwar Poland. Almost every profession and occupation had its own paper, such as the *Leder un shikh-tsaytung* (the newspaper for the leather and shoe industry). Several Yiddish satirical magazines came and went in Warsaw. Even the orthodox, fearing pollution by the secular press, felt compelled to found newspapers; some *yeshivot* produced their own journals.

Publications for women included a Polish-language weekly off-shoot from *Nasz Przegląd*, entitled *Ewa: Tygodnik*, which began appearing in Warsaw in 1928. Mildly feminist in tone, it campaigned for women's suffrage in *kehillah* elections and for family planning, the right to abortion, and against prostitution.[16] But its circulation reached only about two thousand and it closed after five years. The strategy of injecting feminist ideas into the popular mix of serialized fiction and features on home and family was tried by, for example, *Di froy*, published in Vilna in 1925—but that paper lasted only for a few issues.[17] In Holland *Ha'Ischa* (The Woman, and in spite of its Hebrew name, a Dutch-language paper) was the organ of the Council of Jewish Women. Unlike many women's periodicals, it did not restrict its content to matters relating to the domestic sphere but printed articles on a broad range of Jewish political, religious, cultural, and social issues.

The Bundist *Folks-tsaytung* was the only Yiddish daily with a regular children's section. Yiddish children's publications included *Grininke beymelekh* (after a poem of Bialik). For older children, *Der khaver*, a monthly magazine published in Vilna, offered stories, poems, songs, and jokes. Both of these were aligned with the Yiddish secular school system. The rival Tarbut educational network published magazines in Hebrew. Each youth movement issued its own magazine, for example, the Bundist *Der yugnt-veker* (The Youth Sentinel). But these publications, for all their openness to juvenile self-expression, were largely controlled and edited by adults. Janusz Korczak's children's paper, *Mały Przegląd*, published from 1926 to 1939 as a weekly supplement to *Nasz Przegląd*, took a different tack: it was written exclusively by children themselves and published stories, articles, notes, and letters.

At the heart of the Yiddish cultural-journalistic scene was the weekly *Literarishe bleter*, published in Warsaw from 1924 to 1939.

Under the editorship of Nakhmen Mayzel, it became the main organ of Yiddish literature in its final years of flowering. With excusable self-puffery, the paper claimed to be the "veritable, pulsating center" of Yiddish cultural endeavor.[18] It was open to the world. Contributions were drawn not only from Poland but from the United States, Canada, Palestine, Belgium, France, Germany, and Romania. At first some Yiddish writers from the USSR appeared there, too, but after a while Soviet officials discouraged them from writing in a non-Communist publication. In 1929 one such contributor confessed: "While living in a provincial town, I didn't realize what the *Literarishe bleter* is. . . . But now [I know] that the *Literarishe bleter* is a bourgeois publication, which is certainly not the place for our sort of people, I admit my error."[19] Subscribers were to be found as far afield as Grenoble, Czernowitz, Tel Aviv, New York, Rio de Janeiro, Montreal, Vienna, Buenos Aires, and Chicago. There were hardly any in the USSR, save for a handful in Moscow and Minsk (probably institutions rather than individuals).[20]

Nonparty, although sympathetic to the left in the 1930s, *Literarishe bleter* was an important microphone for Yiddish poetry from all over the world. In 1936, 79 Yiddish poets were published in the paper, of whom 42 were from Poland, 12 from the USA, and the rest from elsewhere. The following year 38 were from Poland, 22 from the United States, and 4 each from Palestine, Romania, and the USSR (in the last case whether with or without the writers' consent is not clear), as well as a few others from elsewhere. The growing number of American bylines, reflected also in prose contributions, was a further sign of the extent to which, by the late 1930s, New York was replacing Warsaw as the fulcrum of Yiddish cultural vitality. Mayzel moved to New York in December 1937. The paper limped along without him until its last issue in July 1939.

In spite of the growth of support for Zionism, the Hebrew press in Europe led a checkered existence. The Warsaw paper *Hatsfirah*, founded as a weekly in 1862, became a daily in 1910, ceased publication in 1914, and was revived in 1920, but did not last. It appeared again as a daily from 1926 but found only a modest audience and finally collapsed altogether in 1931. The weekly *Baderekh* was made compulsory reading in Hebrew-language schools but even with such a guaranteed base it failed to make ends meet. With its closure in 1937 the spluttering Hebrew periodical press in Poland came to an end.

Top Hat and White Gloves

More formidable was the Jewish press in the Polish language, particularly the daily papers *Nasz Przegląd*, published in Warsaw, which, according to police figures, sold an average of twenty-two thousand copies in the 1930s, *Chwila* in Lwów, and *Nowy Dziennik* in Cracow, the last two with smaller circulations. All three were moderately Zionist in orientation. Unlike most of the Yiddish press, these papers appeared on the Sabbath. They were founded with the intention of fostering good relations between Jews and non-Jews and, at least initially, were aimed at both. Their audiences, however, were mainly Jewish, generally from the assimilated middle class. Circulation of Polish-Jewish as of Yiddish dailies declined in the late 1930s, whereas that of other Polish papers rose sharply, suggesting that Jewish readers were turning from a Jewish to a general press.

The content of the Polish-Jewish press was geared toward Jewish interests, about which, unlike the German liberal papers, they were quite outspoken. Bernard Singer, who wrote for the Polish as well as for the Yiddish press under the barely disguised pen name Regnis, was one of the most influential political commentators in Poland. An anti-Zionist former Folkist but sympathetic to the left, he set aside his private opinions when writing in the bourgeois press. The Polish-Jewish papers did not, however, achieve much by way of improving Polish understanding of Jews.

Instead one of their main effects, though by no means their original intention, was to wean their Jewish audience from Yiddish to Polish. So much so, indeed, that in 1929 the editor of *Literarishe bleter*, Nakhmen Mayzel, complained that these papers in Lwów and Cracow had "displaced Yiddish." The Galician Jews were not "nationally" more assimilated than before the First World War, he claimed. Nevertheless, "Polonization ha[d] made rapid strides over the past ten years—and this thanks to the Jewish-Polish press."

Mayzel recalled that the founder of *Chwila*, Dr. Gershon Cyper, who was also one of the founders of the Yiddish *Lemberger togblat*, had said, "After the Lemberg pogrom [of 1918], I founded *Chwila* as a sign of mourning. When times became better and Jews felt more free, I would shave off the beard and return to the Jewish press." But the "temporary sickness" that gave birth to the Polish-Jewish press had become a "permanent illness." Before the war only a few Jews had been polonized. Now "not only the intelligentsia but even the Hasidic Jew, the merchant, the businessman, the pedlar and the worker read and trust the Polish paper as a Jewish one."

Warming to his theme, Mayzel lamented that the result was the polonization of the whole of Jewish social life. Jewish institutions in Galicia now conducted their affairs largely in Polish, even though their central offices in Warsaw might still use Yiddish in communication with individuals and organizations. The Polish-Jewish press, he concluded with a flourish, was thus not only *folksfeyntlekh* (an enemy of the people), it was tearing off living limbs from the Jewish masses.[21]

Over the following decade the process of linguistic decline accelerated. At a conference of Yiddish journalists in 1937, Zalmen Reyzen, editor of the *Vilner tog*, proposed that staff members of the Polish-language press should be excluded from membership in the Jewish journalists' union. Shortly afterward another Yiddish writer, Yoshue Perle, issued an unrestrained philippic against the Polish-Jewish press. It amounted, he wrote, to nothing less than "a disguised means of destroying the whole of modern Yiddish culture." The leaders of this press were not drawn from the heart of the people but from the "semi-assimilated or wholly assimilated salons." They wore "top hats and white gloves." They were not fit exponents of Jewish thinking. They barely printed Yiddish writers and when they did so they paid them only a humiliating pittance. They employed "semi-converts, actual converts, and *goyim*, yes, yes, there are no Yiddish writers working in the Polish-Jewish press today, just *goyim*!" And so on.[22]

The Polish-Jewish newspapers, however, insisted that they represented a social necessity. "It is not possible," one of their writers declared, "to fight the laws of nature. . . . A Polish Jew is doomed to knowledge of three languages: Yiddish, Hebrew, and the language of the state."[23]

"Stink Bird Moyli"

The Soviet Yiddish press (there were hardly any Jewish publications in other languages of the USSR) was a pale shadow of the Polish, whether measured by circulation or number of publications. Already in the 1920s official reports noted that, even in *shtetlakh*, readers showed a preference for Russian over Yiddish papers, the former being regarded as more authoritative.[24]

After an initial flurry of activity in the early 1920s, Soviet Yiddish newspaper publishing declined fast in the remainder of the interwar period. In 1931 the total circulation of the seventeen main Soviet Yiddish newspapers and periodicals was under 150,000.[25] Some copies no doubt had multiple readers. On the other hand, some subscribers, particularly the many institutional ones in the USSR, probably took multiple papers. By 1935 a total of only forty-one Yiddish newspapers and periodicals appeared in the Soviet Union. It is clear, therefore, that in the 1930s only a small minority of Soviet Jews were regular readers of the Yiddish press. Even in Minsk, the most concentrated center of Yiddish speakers, the circulation of the local Yiddish newspaper declined to just 8,350 by late 1933.[26] In the Soviet Union circulation levels were set centrally but there is little doubt that demand for Yiddish newspapers in the USSR, as elsewhere, was falling rapidly.

Minsk was meanwhile yielding preeminence as a Soviet Yiddish cultural hub to Kharkov and Kiev. Kharkov, which had not fallen within the Tsarist Pale of Settlement, had not hitherto been a significant Jewish center. But as capital of Ukraine from 1919 to 1934 its Jewish population, just 11,000 in 1897, grew fast, reaching 130,000 by 1939. A Yiddish daily, *Der shtern*, appeared there from 1925, with a circulation of twelve thousand, the highest for any Soviet Yiddish paper at the time.

A number of other Yiddish papers and magazines appeared in Kharkov over the next decade, including a literary journal, *Di royte velt*. Although this had a small print run (never more than two thousand, except for a special issue on collectivization in 1930), it attracted contributions from several important writers. In 1925 it declared the outbreak of a "civil war" in Soviet Yiddish literature.[27]

While characterized by much ideological posturing, the conflict seems to have been essentially a struggle between different cliques in Moscow, Kiev, Minsk, and Kharkov for dominance in the little world of Soviet Yiddish literature. A low point in the war of words was the portrayal by the poet Leyb Kvitko of the editor of the Moscow daily, *Emes*, Moyshe Litvakov, as "stink bird Moyli," sitting on a roof and poisoning surrounding lives.[28] Kvitko was subsequently reprimanded for his "anti-Communist pasquinade" and sent to work in a tractor factory. Litvakov gave as good as he got, denouncing "literary mutinies against Communist guidance."[29] Kvitko, however, survived and his books, mainly for children, sold millions of copies in translation.

In 1933 *Di royte velt* was incorporated into a journal published in Kiev. The following year the capital of Ukraine was moved to Kiev and many Yiddish writers from Kharkov, among them Kvitko, moved there, too. But in 1936 the Kiev Yiddish institute, like other Jewish institutions in the USSR, including the institute in Minsk, fell victim to the purges and closed down. *Der shtern* continued to appear but by 1939 it was one of only a handful of remaining Yiddish papers in the Soviet Union.

The Moscow Yiddish daily, *Emes*, was always dependent on the vagaries of Soviet policy toward national minorities. Its circulation, only twelve thousand in 1927–28, was limited by the relatively small proportion of Yiddish speakers in the capital and by difficulties of distribution to more distant subscribers. In 1937 the editor, Litvakov, was arrested, accused of terrorism and of being a Gestapo agent, and shot. The paper closed in 1938.

The fate of Litvakov and his paper may have been linked to a general assault on minority cultures at the time. But in spite of the sinister political atmosphere, the death of *Emes* need not be attributed to anything other than market forces, which operated to a residual degree even in the socialized economy. Toward the end, demand for the paper was so small that it was impossible to find on newsstands. Yiddish dailies continued to appear in Minsk, Kiev, and Kharkov for a little longer but by 1939 no more than seven Yiddish newspapers, with a combined circulation of just 38,700, remained in the USSR.[30]

Wolf Wieviorka, a writer in the *Parizer haynt*, penned a sardonic but not unjust obituary for *Emes*, which, he predicted, would not be much mourned. It had been a "Bolshevik crown rabbi" (referring to the officially appointed rabbis in Tsarist Russia) or a "red Kelmer Magid" (after a famous nineteenth-century "terror *magid*" who had fulminated against all manner of vices). *Emes* had "unmasked" Trotskyists and other "enemies of the people." It had been written in a rebarbative (*otz-kotzik*) style and did not "dream the dreams" of the Jewish masses in the USSR. On the contrary, Wieviorka alleged, its main task had been to enable its readers to "work through" Stalin's latest speeches and letters. But "that in itself was enough for the Yiddish world to turn away" from *Emes*. After all, there would soon be no Jews in the USSR who didn't understand Russian and, if they wished, they could "work through" Stalin's teachings in the original without the help of a Yiddish nursery school teacher. In the end, according to Wieviorka, the paper had become little more than an echo chamber for the party line, which it propagated to Yiddish Communist papers throughout the world. From *Emes* they learned how much dirt to fling in this or that direction and "how much poison and bile to mix into their lampoons."[31]

Little Frankitos

This last accusation was implicitly aimed at a target closer to home. In Paris there were three Yiddish dailies catering to the immigrant community. All were financially precarious and relied heavily on contributions from supporters. The smallest and shortest-lived was the Bundist *Unzer shtime*, which appeared between 1936 and 1939. The pro-Zionist *Parizer haynt*, founded in 1923 and a daily from 1926, was an outgrowth of the paper of the same name in Warsaw. Its first editor, Shmuel Yatzkan, had been the editor and proprietor of *Haynt* in Warsaw. A lively little paper that, like its parent, syndicated many big-name writers, *Parizer haynt* sold ten thousand copies daily.

Its main competitor was the Communist *Naye prese*, founded as a weekly in 1923. It was obliged to change its name ten times to beat the censor before settling down as a daily in 1934. The daily's first editor, Leo Katz (whose pseudonyms included Joel Ames, Franz Wich, Leo Weiss, and "Maus"), was the former *feuilleton* editor of the German Communist Party's organ *Rote Fahne* (Red Flag). His wife meanwhile worked as a Comintern agent in Paris. After his expulsion from France in 1938, he was succeeded by Louis Gronowski (writing under the pen name Lerman) and Abraham Rajgrodski (Adam Rayski), refugees respectively from Radziejów (central Poland) and Białystok. The paper took its editorial line directly from the party's French organ, *l'Humanité*, at the daily editorial meetings of which the editor of *Naye prese* or one of his staff was generally present. *Naye prese*'s circulation may have reached eight thousand at the height of public enthusiasm for the Popular Front in 1936 but later declined to five thousand or less. Still, here as elsewhere, the influence of the Yiddish papers was probably greater than their circulations might indicate.

Thanks to the large Polish-Jewish immigration to Paris in the 1920s, the Yiddish press in Paris held out longer than in any other European city. But its audience aged and shrank as the second generation, educated in French schools, abandoned the language and embraced French culture.

At the other end of Europe, in the Sephardi communities of the Balkans, French influences wrote *finis* to four centuries of Judeo-Espagnol cultural experience in the region. Judeo-Espagnol newspapers had never attained the importance or influence gained by the Yiddish press elsewhere in Europe. Most had already died out before the First World War. One reason was the comparatively smaller concentrations of Sephardic Jews in Europe. Only in Salonica was there a critical demographic mass that might support a Jewish press in a Jewish language.

By the 1930s, however, the Judeo-Espagnol press in Salonica was being overtaken by French papers. Three Judeo-Espagnol newspapers, the anti-Zionist *El Tiempo,* the socialist *Avanti,* and the Zionist *El Pueblo,* had all closed by 1935. Two daily papers in the language remained in the late 1930s. *Acción,* which appeared from 1929 to 1941, was initially leftist, later Zionist. Its peak circulation was three thousand (plus another one thousand to overseas subscribers). *El Mesajero,* the last Judeo-Espagnol newspaper in the city (and the last anywhere to appear in Rashi Hebrew characters) was founded in 1935 and lasted until 1941, but with a small and declining circulation. In 1939 the combined circulation of the remaining Salonican Jewish newspapers, *L'Indépendant* and *Le Progrès* in French and *Acción* and *El Mesajero* in Judeo-Espagnol, had shrunk from over 25,000 in 1932 to around 6,000.[32] The fashion among the younger generation was now to speak French or, among the very youngest, Greek, not Judeo-Espagnol. Disapproving elders scoffed at the *frankitos* (little Frenchies) or *musyús* (messieurs).[33] But by 1939 in Salonica, as in Paris, the drift away from Jewish languages seemed inexorable.

Wear It with Pride, the Yellow Star!

Before 1933 German Jewry had had a flourishing press. Its finest moment, perhaps, came shortly after the advent of the Nazis to power, in the twice-weekly Zionist organ, *Die Jüdische Rundschau.* Its editor, Robert Weltsch, was at first not exactly an anti-Nazi militant. A few months earlier his paper had even suggested that Zionists might, in spite of everything, be able to find a common language with so-called *Edelnazis* ("noble Nazis"): "Jewry with its national consciousness will be able to find the way to a *modus vivendi* with a German nationalism strengthened from within and relieved of the dross of mob anti-Semitism."[34]

Yet in April 1933 Weltsch gave heart to German Jews with what became a famous front-page article under the challenging headline: "Tragt ihn mit Stolz, den gelben Fleck!" ("Wear it with pride, the yellow star!") It concluded: "They remind us that we are Jews. We say yes, and we bear it with pride."[35] The piece was written in response to the Nazis' boycott of Jewish businesses, when yellow stars were ordered to be affixed to the fronts of Jewish-owned stores. This turned out to be one of the rare moments between 1933 and 1939 when Hitler suffered a setback, since the boycott proved abortive. For all the Führer's savage utterances, it still seemed inconceivable at that stage that within a decade German Jews would be forced to wear such a badge of humiliation on their own persons. The article created a sensation and the paper had to print an extra edition. The *Rundschau's* circulation rose from 5,000 to 38,000 by the end of 1933. Weltsch and his paper are today chiefly, if at all, remembered for this single, brave declaration—which he subsequently regretted.[36] As he later recollected, the reaction was a "remarkable, unique manifestation of psychic euphoria in a tragic situation."[37]

Unlike the great regional and national newspapers formerly owned by Jews, the specifically Jewish press was neither taken over nor closed by the Nazis in 1933. Apart from the *Rundschau*, two other main papers, both weeklies, sought to uphold the spirits of German Jewry between 1933 and 1938: the *C.V. Zeitung*, organ of the Centralverein deutscher Staatsbürger jüdischen Glaubens (before 1933 an assimilationist body—but now there was not much left to assimilate to), and the independent, Hamburg-based *Israelitisches Familienblatt*, which had been the most widely read Jewish paper in pre-Hitler Germany.

Altogether the German-Jewish press in these years consisted of some 120 publications. It is interesting to compare this number with the grand total of 47 Jewish newspapers and periodicals appearing at the time in the Soviet Union for a community five times the size of German Jewry. As an index of the comparative degree of repression, these raw statistics should not be taken altogether at face value. Nor should the hundreds of papers appearing in Poland be regarded, merely by virtue of their number, as a measure of freedom for Jews in that stunted democracy. Still, it can be said that, thanks to its press, German Jewry between 1933 and 1938 retained a limited area of public debate and, within certain boundaries, the capacity to voice authentic expressions of individual and collective opinion.

Jewish papers, of course, like all others in Nazi Germany, had to bow to the censor's blue pencil—strictly speaking to postpublication *Nachzensur*. In 1935 the *Jüdische Rundschau* went too far and had

the temerity to respond to an anti-Jewish tirade by Goebbels with
an article entitled "Der Jude ist auch ein Mensch."[38] The *Rundschau*
was banned for six weeks and the authorities administered a stern
warning to Weltsch. Four weeks later the Propaganda Ministry or-
dained that Jewish publications must no longer be sold from news
kiosks.

In November 1938 the ultimate form of *Nachzensur* was imposed: the official seal on the door. The *Jüdische Rundschau*, together with the whole of the German-Jewish press, was summarily
closed. Almost the only permitted Jewish periodical in Germany
thereafter was a thin, twice-weekly information bulletin, the *Jüdisches Nachrichtenblatt*. This was published from the former office
of the *Rundschau* but issued under the auspices of the Jüdische
Kulturbund, one of the few Jewish organizations still permitted to
function. The first issue, delayed for a day because of intervention
by the censor, appeared on November 23, 1938. The editor, Leo
Kreindler, had earlier been editor of the Berlin edition of the *Israelitisches Familienblatt*. The paper's two main functions were to diffuse
official orders affecting Jews and to provide information about opportunities for emigration. The paper also published personal advertisements and reviews of events organized by the Kulturbund. It was
like a prison bulletin with the difference that, until October 1941,
the prisoners were being urged to escape. Its print run of seventy-six
thousand was distributed to subscribers of the closed-down papers,
whose former staff members furnished its staff of forty.

If the Jewish press had, since 1933, helped maintain the morale
of German Jews, the sudden abolition in November 1938 of this
semi-autonomous area of semi-free speech had a depressing effect
and heightened feelings of disorientation and helplessness. With
their newspapers gone, German Jews who valued the written word
(and taken as a whole they were probably the most culturally sophisticated and literate part of the population) were driven back to the
last refuge of a persecuted intelligentsia—the book.

12

A PEOPLE OF MANY BOOKS

The Jewish Book

The written word was at the core of traditional Jewish life. In the synagogue the most sacred objects were the handwritten scrolls of the law. The printed volumes of the Talmud, the Shas, occupied a place of honor in the *talmud torah* and, where he could afford his private copy, in the home of the orthodox Jew.

In the eighteenth and nineteenth centuries, publishers of Hebrew books, mainly on religious themes, developed a system of prepublication subscription, whereby they could cover their costs in advance. The lists of subscribers, printed in such books, give their names and towns of residence. They show that book collectors could be found even in the smallest *shtetlakh*, remote from cultural centers.

Almost everywhere, Jews were the most literate section of the population. The discrepancy between Jewish and non-Jewish literacy was particularly marked in east-central Europe, where between a quarter and a third of the general population was still illiterate in the 1930s. In the Soviet Union in 1939, 94 percent of Jews were literate, the highest figure for any Soviet nationality. The high rate was partly a function of urbanization, but even compared with other city dwellers, Jews were much more literate.

Polish census figures in 1921 that showed higher Jewish than non-Jewish illiteracy rates cannot be taken at face value, since the Polish census takers, like their Russian predecessors, did not include ability to read or write Yiddish or Hebrew as evidence of literacy.[1] In fact, most Jewish males in eastern Europe were literate twice over, since they could read and write in both Hebrew/Yiddish and at least one other language; most Jewish women could also do so, though pockets of female illiteracy survived among the older generation.

Given their high rate of literacy and their disproportionate participation in commerce, it is hardly surprising that Jews played an important role in book as in newspaper publishing. Firms such as S. Fischer in Germany, Calmann-Lévy in France, and Emilio Treves in Italy were in the vanguard of literary publishing in the early twentieth century. These published in the national languages of their respective countries. In eastern Europe Jews were also heavily involved in the publishing as well as the printing industries. But there they produced books not only in languages such as Polish and Romanian but in Yiddish and Hebrew (and in much smaller quantities in Judeo-Espagnol).

The advent of the *haskalah* had broadened the scope of Hebrew literature and brought a wave of secular publishing of fiction and nonfiction on cultural, social, and political themes. Meanwhile, the Yiddish press in the late nineteenth century churned out cheap editions of popular literature.

In the *shtetl*, itinerant booksellers would offer for sale *sforim* (religious books in Hebrew or Aramaic), calendars, *mayse-bikhlekh* (collections of stories), the *Tsene-rene*, the classic Yiddish novels and stories of Mendele Moykher Sforim, Shalom Aleichem, and Y. L. Peretz, popular fiction by authors such as Ayzik Meyer Dik, and perennial favorites like the *Centura Ventura*, a Yiddish translation of the adventures of Sinbad the Sailor. As a result, all but the poorest Jewish homes contained at least a few books.

Reading began early. Jewish children read the same books as their neighbors, except perhaps for Christian biblical tales, but being close to 100 percent literate and members of a bookish civilization, they read more. Often they also read books specifically directed toward Jews, including books in Yiddish: simplified versions of the stories of Shalom Aleichem, Jewish folk tales, biographies of figures such as Nansen and Caruso, or translations of Grimm's fairy tales, Oscar Wilde's Dos Shternkind ("The Star-Child"), or Lucy Fitch Perkins's Stone Age fantasy, *The Cave Twins* (the Yiddish version was published in Vilna in 1939).[2]

Such books percolated to every level of Jewish society. They often evoked deeply felt responses. It was a common practice for young booklovers to keep reading diaries in which they recorded impressions and reactions to what they had read. Poor people often spent significant sums on books. And where they could not afford to buy, they borrowed them.

Libraries

By the early twentieth century even quite small Jewish communities in eastern Europe boasted libraries. Sometimes these were promoted by the *kehillah* and attached to the synagogue or study house, as in Buczacz in eastern Galicia. There the twelve-year-old Shmulik Czaczkes (later known as Shmuel Yosef Agnon, the name under which he wrote, in Yiddish and Hebrew, the works that won him the Nobel Prize for Literature) was commissioned by the *gabai* (warden) to arrange and catalogue the books, a task he is said to have performed with great professionalism.[3] But he also committed the cardinal sin of the overenthusiastic librarian: he wrote comments in the margins of the books.[4]

Other libraries were associated with societies or movements, orthodox, Zionist, or leftist/Yiddishist. In Poland the Bund-affiliated Kultur-Lige alone claimed to operate no fewer than nine hundred libraries in the mid-1930s. The Hebraist Tarbut school network operated another 370. Big city communities established their own major libraries. In 1936, for instance, the Jewish Central Library in Warsaw, dating back to 1866 and holding thirty-five thousand books, opened a new building next to the Great Synagogue on Tłomackie Street.

Such institutions became poor men's universities and inspired deep affection among their readers. Of the Strashun Library in Vilna, an important repository for Hebrew and Yiddish books and manuscripts, the poet Avrom Sutzkever wrote: "There were many libraries in Poland, but the Strashun Library, with its warmth and folksiness, and the friendly smile and charm of its librarian, Khaykl Lunski, . . . [was] unparalleled."[5] The library had an average of

230 visitors a day but only a hundred chairs. Often readers had to share a seat. Like many other Jewish libraries, the Strashun was open on the Sabbath, though no writing was permitted on that day.

Too much should not perhaps be made of the sheer number of libraries. Some lasted just a few years and had a pitifully small and tattered stock, composed mainly of popular fiction. Few could afford to buy new books and many were reduced to begging for them. In 1929, for example, the Y. L. Peretz Library in Czortków, Galicia, wrote to a Yiddish publisher in Chicago, pleading for donations of books on the ground that the dollar prices were "so exorbitant that we cannot even dream of buying them."[6] A number of gifts were, in fact, received from overseas.

A report issued by the Czortków library in 1937 provides evidence of the evolution of language use and literary tastes. By this time the library had collected 2,500 books. Unlike many secular-Jewish libraries, this one acquired only books in Yiddish, citing the existence of other libraries, private and public, that offered books in Polish. Interest in Yiddish culture in Galicia, however, was said to be weak. The report pointed out that unlike other libraries, where readers were mostly schoolchildren and women, here 78.5 percent of the users in 1936 were adult men. The explanation, it suggested, was that children in the town who attended Polish state schools were "far away from Yiddish." As for women, many could not read the language.

The library had conducted a survey with other Jewish libraries in the town to determine the extent of demand for Yiddish and Polish books: it found that Polish readers were 2.4 times as numerous as Yiddish ones. Nearly a third of the books in the library were translated into Yiddish from other languages. The most popular book, as measured in number of loans of an individual title, in 1934, 1935, and 1936, was a collection of short stories by the little-known Chicago-based Yiddish writer Moisey Ghitzis (perhaps his Chicago publisher had, as requested, supplied it free of charge). The library also counted the number of loans per reader: the champion had read, or at any rate borrowed, 206 books in 1934.[7]

A revealing index of linguistic preference comes from a survey of the inventories of Jewish libraries in Warsaw in 1934. Just over half

"A battlefield. A struggle for existence. . . . There is nothing more cruel." Hard bargaining in the Jewish marketplace on Waterlooplein, Amsterdam, c. 1930.

"The thousand-year history of German Jewry has come to an end." Rabbi Leo Baeck, leader of the Jewish community in Nazi Germany, addressing a meeting, c. 1933.

Polish-Jewish parliamentarians, 1920s. Among those shown are Noyekh Pryłucki (*second from left*) and Yitzhak Gruenbaum (*fifth from left*).

Vladimir Jabotinsky (*seated, center*), with uniformed members of his Revisionist Zionist movement, Poznań, Poland, 1937.

Guerfanas (orphan girls) of Meir Aboav orphanage, Salonica, 1926/27.

Jews forced out of their homes after the anti-Jewish riot in the Campbell district of Salonica, 1931.

7

Debatte im Oberhaus

Einzelnummer 0,25 Goldmark

JÜDISCHE RUNDSCHAU

Erscheint jeden Dienstag u. Freitag. Bezugspreis bei der Expedition monatlich 2,– Goldmark, vierteljährlich 5,75 Goldmark. Auslandsabonnements werden in der Währung der einzelnen Länder berechnet. Anzeigenpreis: 8 gesp. Nonpareillezeile 0,50 G.-M. Stellengesuche 0,25 G.-M.

Redaktion, Verlag und Anzeigen-Verwaltung: Jüdische Rundschau G. m. b. H., Berlin W 15, Meinekestr. 10. Telefon: J 1 Bismarck 7165-70. Anzeigenschluß: Dienstag und Freitag nachmittags 4 Uhr. Redaktionsschluß Sonntag und Mittwoch nachmittag.

Postscheck-Konten: Berlin 17392, Basel V 9355, Belgrad 68032, Brüssel 39433, Budapest 59693, Danzig 1973, Haag 140470, Prag 59410, Riga 4155, Straßburg 16430, Warschau 190708, Wien 156030. Bank-Konten: Dresdener Bank, Depositen-Kasse Berlin, Kurfürstendamm 52; Rumänische Kreditbank, Cernauti (Rumänien); Anglo Palestine Co. in Haifa, Jerusalem, Tel-Aviv.

Nummer 27 | Berlin, 4. IV. 1933 | ח' ניסן תרצ"ג | XXXVIII. Jahrg.

Der Zionismus erstrebt für das jüdische Volk die Schaffung einer öffentlich-rechtlich gesicherten Heimstätte in Palästina. „Baseler Programm."

Tragt ihn mit Stolz, den gelben Fleck!

Der 1. April 1933 wird ein wichtiger Tag in der Geschichte der deutschen Juden, ja in der Geschichte des ganzen jüdischen Volkes bleiben. Die Ereignisse dieses Tages haben nicht nur eine politische und eine wirtschaftliche, sondern auch eine moralische und seelische Seite. Ueber die politischen und wirtschaftlichen Zusammenhänge ist in den Zeitungen viel gesprochen worden, wobei freilich häufig agitatorische Bedürfnisse die sachliche Erkenntnis verdunkeln. Ueber die moralische Seite zu sprechen, ist unsere Sache. Denn so viel auch die Judenfrage jetzt erörtert wird, was in der Seele der deutschen Juden vorgeht, was vom jüdischen Standpunkt zu den Vorgängen zu sagen ist, kann niemand aussprechen als wir selbst. Die Juden können heute nicht anders als als Juden sprechen. Alles andere ist völlig sinnlos. Der Spuk der sogenannten „Judenpresse" ist weggeblasen. Der verhängnisvolle Irrtum vieler Juden, man könne jüdische Interessen unter anderem Deckmantel vertreten, ist beseitigt. Das deutsche Judentum hat am 1. April eine Lehre empfangen, die viel tiefer geht, als selbst seine erbitterten und heute triumphierenden Gegner annehmen.

Es ist nicht unsere Art, zu lamentieren. Auf Ereignisse von dieser Wucht mit sentimentalen Salbadereien zu reagieren, überlassen wir jenen Juden einer vergangenen Generation, die nichts gelernt und alles vergessen haben. Es bedarf heute eines neuen Tones in der Diskussion jüdischer Angelegenheiten. Wir leben in einer neuen Zeit, die nationale Revolution des deutschen Volkes ist ein weithin sichtbares Signal, daß die alte Begriffswelt zusammengestürzt ist. Das mag für viele schmerzlich sein, aber in dieser Welt sich behaupten kann nur, wer den Realitäten ins Auge sieht. Wir stehen mitten in einer gewaltigen Umwandlung des geistigen, politischen, sozialen und wirtschaftlichen Lebens. Unsere Sorge ist: Wie reagiert das Judentum?

Der 1. April 1933 kann ein Tag des jüdischen Erwachens und der jüdischen Wiedergeburt sein. Wenn die Juden wollen. Wenn die Juden reif sind und innere Größe besitzen. Wenn die Juden nicht so sind, wie sie von ihren Gegnern dargestellt werden.

Das angegriffene Judentum muß sich zu sich selbst bekennen.

Auch an diesem Tage stärkster Erregung, wo im Angesicht des beispiellosen Schauspiels der universalen Verfemung der gesamten jüdischen Bevölkerung eines großen Kulturlandes die stürmischesten Empfindungen unser Herz durchzogen, haben wir vor allem Eines zu wahren: Besonnenheit. Stehen wir fassungslos vor dem Geschehen dieser Tage, so dürfen wir doch nicht verzagen und müssen uns ohne Selbsttäuschung Rechenschaft ablegen. Man müßte in diesen Tagen empfehlen: daß die Schrift, die an der Wiege des Zionismus stand,

Theodor Herzls „Judenstaat",

in hunderttausenden Exemplaren unter Juden und Nichtjuden verbreitet wird. Wenn es noch Gefühl für Größe und Adel, für Ritterlichkeit und Gerechtigkeit gibt, müßte jeder Nationalsozialist, der dieses Buch zu Gesicht bekommt, vor seinem eigenen blinden Tun erstarren. Aber auch jeder Jude, der es liest, würde beginnen zu verstehen; und würde daraus Trost und Erhebung schöpfen.

Theodor Herzl, dessen reiner Name in diesen Tagen durch ein Zitat aus einer Fälschung vor der gesamten deutschen Oeffentlichkeit befleckt wurde, schrieb in der Einleitung der genannten Schrift:

> „Die Judenfrage besteht. Es wäre töricht, sie zu leugnen. Sie ist ein verschlepptes Stück Mittelalter, mit dem die Kulturvölker auch heute beim besten Willen noch nicht fertig werden konnten. Den großmütigen Willen zeigten sie ja, als sie uns emanzipierten. Die Judenfrage besteht überall, wo Juden in merklicher Anzahl leben. . . .
>
> **Ich glaube den Antisemitismus, der eine vielfach komplizierte Bewegung ist, zu verstehen. Ich betrachte diese Bewegung als Jude, aber ohne Haß und Furcht.** Ich glaube zu erkennen, was im Antisemitismus roher Scherz, gemeiner Brotneid, angeerbtes Vorurteil, religiöse Unduldsamkeit — aber auch, was darin vermeintliche Notwehr ist. Ich halte die Judenfrage weder für eine soziale, noch für eine religiöse, **wenn sie sich auch noch so und anders färbt. Sie ist eine nationale Frage, und um sie zu lösen, müssen wir sie vor allem zu einer politischen Weltfrage machen, die im Rate der Kulturvölker zu regeln sein wird."**

Man müßte Seite um Seite dieser 1897 erschienenen Schrift abschreiben, um zu zeigen: Theodor Herzl war der erste Jude, der unbefangen genug war, den Antisemitismus im Zusammenhang mit der Judenfrage zu betrachten. Und er erkannte, daß nicht durch Vogel-Strauß-Politik, sondern nur durch offene Behandlung der Tatsachen vor aller Welt eine Besserung erzielt werden kann. Gegen nichts hat er so leidenschaftlich Stellung genommen als gegen das, was ihm jetzt unterschoben wird, nämlich gegen den Gedanken, die Juden könnten eine nichtöffentliche Weltverbindung herstellen oder irgend etwas tun, was bei den anderen Völkern irrtümlicherweise solche Vorstellungen erwecken könnte. In seiner Schrift „Leroy-Beaulieu über den Antisemitismus" schreibt er:

> „Wir Zionisten sind auf das deutlichste und entschiedenste gegen jede internationale Vereinigung von Juden, die, wenn sie wirksam wäre, den mit Recht verpönten Staat im Staate vorstellte und, da sie machtlos und nichtssagend ist, nur Nachteile bietet. . . . Nur das sei gesagt, daß wir zur Lösung der Judenfrage nicht einen internationalen Verein, sondern eine internationale Diskussion wünschen, das heißt: nicht Bündeleien, geheime Interventionen, Schleichwege, sondern die freimütige Erörterung unter der beständigen und vollständigen Kontrolle der öffentlichen Meinung."

Wir im Geiste Theodor Herzls erzogenen Juden wollen auch heute nicht anklagen, sondern verstehen. Und uns fragen, was unsere eigene Schuld ist, was wir selbst gesündigt haben. Immer hat das jüdische Volk in kritischen Tagen seines Schicksals sich zunächst die Frage vorgelegt, was seine eigene Schuld ist. In unserem wichtigsten Gebete heißt es: „Um unserer Sünden willen wurden wir aus unserem Lande vertrieben". Nur wenn wir kritisch gegen uns sind, werden wir gerecht auch gegen andere sein.

Die Judenheit trägt eine schwere Schuld, weil sie den Ruf Theodor Herzls nicht gehört, ja, teilweise verspottet hat. Die Juden wollten nichts davon wissen, daß „eine Judenfrage besteht". Sie glaubten, es komme nur darauf an, als Jude nicht erkannt zu werden. Man wirft uns heute vor, wir hätten das deutsche Volk verraten; die nationalsozialistische Presse nennt uns, und wir sind dagegen wehrlos, den „Feind der Nation".

Es ist nicht wahr, daß die Juden Deutschland verraten haben. Wenn sie etwas verraten haben, so haben sie sich selbst, das Judentum, verraten.

Weil der Jude sein Judentum nicht stolz zur Schau trug, weil er sich um die Judenfrage herumdrücken wollte, hat er sich mitschuldig gemacht an der Erniedrigung des Judentums.

Bei aller Bitterkeit, die uns beim Lesen der nationalsozialistischen Boykottaufrufe und der ungerechten Beschuldigungen erfüllen muß, für eines können wir dem Boykottausschuß dankbar sein. In den Richtlinien heißt es in § 3:

> **„Es handelt sich . . . selbstverständlich um Geschäfte, die sich in den Händen von Angehörigen der jüdischen Rasse befinden. Die Religion spielt keine Rolle. Katholisch oder protestantisch getaufte Geschäftsleute oder Dissidenten jüdischer Rasse sind im Sinne dieser Anordnung ebenfalls Juden."**

Dies ist ein Denkzettel für alle Verräter am Judentum. Wer sich von der Gemeinschaft wegstiehlt, um seine persönliche Lage zu verbessern, soll den Lohn dieses Verrats nicht ernten. In dieser Stellungnahme gegen das Renegatentum ist ein Ansatz zur Klärung enthalten. Der Jude, der sein Judentum verleugnet, ist kein besserer Mitbürger als der, der sich aufrecht dazu bekennt. Renegatentum ist eine Schmach, aber solange die Umwelt Prämien darauf setzte, schien es ein Vorteil. Nun ist es auch kein Vorteil mehr. Der Jude wird als solcher kenntlich gemacht. Er bekommt den gelben Fleck.

Daß die Boykottleitung anordnete, an die boykottierten Geschäfte Schilder „mit gelbem Fleck auf schwarzem Grund" zu heften, ist ein gewaltiges Symbol. **Diese Maßregel ist als Brandmarkung, als Verächtlichmachung gedacht. Wir nehmen sie auf, und wollen daraus ein Ehrenzeichen machen.**

Viele Juden hatten am Sonnabend ein schweres Erlebnis. Nicht aus innerem Bekenntnis, nicht aus Treue zur eigenen Gemeinschaft, nicht aus Stolz auf eine großartige Vergangenheit und Menschheitsleistung, sondern durch den Aufdruck des roten Zettels und des gelben Flecks standen sie plötzlich als Juden da. Von Haus zu Haus gingen die Trupps, beklebten Geschäfte und Schilder, bemalten die Fensterscheiben, 24 Stunden lang waren die deutschen Juden gewissermaßen an den Pranger gestellt. Neben anderen Zeichen und Inschriften sah man auf den Scheiben der Schaufenster vielfach einen großen Magen David, den Schild König Davids. Dies sollte eine Entehrung sein. Juden, nehmt ihn auf, den Davidsschild, und tragt ihn in Ehren!

Denn — und hier beginnt die Pflicht unserer Selbstbesinnung, — wenn dieser Schild heute befleckt ist, so sind es nicht unsere Feinde allein, die dies bewirkt haben. Viele Juden gab es, die sich nicht genug tun konnten in würdeloser Selbstverhöhnung. Das Judentum galt als überlebte Sache, man betrachtete es ohne Ernst, man wollte sich durch Lächeln von seiner Tragik befreien.

Aber es gibt heute bereits den Typus des neuen, freien Juden, den die nichtjüdische Welt noch nicht kennt.

Wenn heute in der nationalsozialistischen und deutschnationalen Presse häufig auf einen Typus des jüdischen Literaten und auf die sogenannte Judenpresse hingewiesen wird, wenn das Judentum für diese Faktoren verantwortlich gemacht wird, so muß immer wieder gesagt werden, daß dies keine Repräsentanten des Judentums sind, sondern höchstens geschäftlich von den Juden zu profitieren versucht haben. In einer Zeit bourgeoiser Selbstgerechtigkeit konnten diese Elemente auf Beifall auch bei jüdischen Zuhörern rechnen, wenn sie Juden und Judentum verhöhnten und bagatellisierten. Wie oft wurden uns Nationaljuden von dieser Seite die Ideale eines abstrakten Weltbürgertums gepredigt, um alle tieferen Werte des Judentums zu vernichten. Aufrechte Juden waren stets entrüstet über die Witzeleien und Karikaturen, die von jüdischen Possenreißern genau so oder in noch höherem Maß gegen das Judentum wie gegen Deutsche oder andere gerichtet wurden. Das jüdische Publikum beklatschte seine eigene Erniedrigung und viele versuchten, dadurch ein Alibi für sich zu schaffen, daß sie in den Spott miteinstimmten. Auch jetzt, in diesen schweren Tagen, glauben manche sich durch Fahnenflucht oder Anschmeißerei retten zu können. Der „Völkische Beobachter" vom 2. April berichtet schmunzelnd, daß die Boykottleitung von jüdischen Geschäftsleuten überlaufen wurde, die für sich eine Ausnahmebehandlung wünschten. Viele, so behauptet der „V. B.", hätten sich schnell taufen lassen, um sagen zu können, sie seien Christen. Glücklicherweise geht selbst aus der Darstellung des „V. B." hervor, daß solche Fälle vereinzelt waren. Aber die Zeit des Druckes ist noch nicht vorüber, wir stehen am Anfang, und darum muß von dieser Gefahr die Rede sein.

Denn die Gefahr, die größte Gefahr, die dem Judentum droht, ist die einer Verderbnis und Verkrüppelung des Charakters. Die Nationalsozialisten erklären in ihren Reden und in ihren Kundgebungen, daß sie Charakterlosigkeit mehr verachten als alles. Dr. Goebbels hat sich in seiner Rede am Freitag über die Wandlung der „jüdischen Presse" lustig gemacht, die so schnell umgelernt habe, daß die Redakteure des „Angriff" vor Neid erblassen müßten.

Wenn der Nationalsozialismus diese Sachlage erkennt, dann müßte er sich als jüdischen Partner ein Judentum wünschen, das seine Ehre hoch hält.

Er dürfte nicht jüdische Charakterlosigkeit fördern, um sie dann brandmarken zu können. Er dürfte dem Juden, der sich offen als Jude bekennt und der nichts verbrochen hat, seine Ehre nicht bestreiten. Ob dem so ist, wird sich bald erweisen: Man hat jetzt eine Prozentnorm für gewisse Berufe angekündigt

"Wear it with pride, the yellow star!" Front page of the *Jüdische Rundschau*, Berlin, April 4, 1933.

8

Khaykl Lunski, librarian of the Strashun Library, Vilna. This was one of the greatest of the hundreds of Jewish libraries in eastern Europe.

9

"A short man with a highly expressive face marred by the loss of one eye, souvenir of a pogrom." Max Weinreich, director of YIVO in Vilna (drawing by S. S. Prawer).

10

"She believed herself a German . . . " The pioneer feminist Bertha Pappenheim (drawing by Joseph Oppenheim).

"A klayninke . . . can't administer a slap!" The Yiddish poet (she objected to being patronized as a "poetess") Kadya Molodowsky (drawing by Feliks Friedman).

11

"He wrote Yiddish as if the language were his personal enemy." Sholem Asch and other delegates at the first assembly of the World Jewish Congress, Geneva, 1936.

The bibulous novelist and *feuilletonist* Joseph Roth at the Café Le Tournon, Paris, shortly before his death in 1939 (drawing by the Viennese caricaturist Bil Spira).

Bruno Schulz, artist, author, and mordant fantast whose *The Street of Crocodiles* was written largely from the point of view of "a small east European Jewish boy in the corner of the room."

The director Max Reinhardt, "presiding genius of European theater."

"Only now . . . do I understand why we have no Lear worthy of the name in Britain." Shlomo Mikhoels as King Lear, Moscow, 1935.

"I will never again forget . . . that I am not a German, not a European, indeed perhaps scarcely even a human being . . . but I am a Jew." A self-portrait of the composer Arnold Schoenberg.

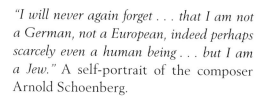

Marc Chagall, Paris, August 1934.

"*Welt, gute Nacht!*" The singer Paula Lindberg-Salomon, c. 1928.

Two Jewish schoolgirls, Hetty d'Ancona de Leeuwe (*left*), and her best friend, Judith Konyn, on their first day in an Amsterdam public school, September 1, 1936.

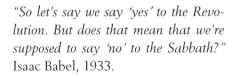

"*The right of the child to die.*" Janusz Korczak, pioneer child psychologist and Jewish orphanage director in Warsaw.

"*So let's say we say 'yes' to the Revolution. But does that mean that we're supposed to say 'no' to the Sabbath?*" Isaac Babel, 1933.

Dienstag, den 30. August 1938, 20³⁰ Uhr

WESTEND-SYNAGOGE, FREIHERR VOM STEINSTR.

STIMMEN IM TEMPEL

Mitwirkende:

Erna Gross,	Sopran
Paula Levi,	Alt
Sofie Seligmann,	Rezitation
Martel Sommer,	Orgel
Hans Assenheim,	Bariton
Alfred Auerbach,	Rezitation
Max Firnberg,	Klavier
Rudolf Ganz,	Rezitation

Gesamtleitung: Alfred Auerbach

Einlösung der September- Mitgliedsmarke und Eintrittskarten:
Montag, den 29. August bis Donnerstag, den 1. September!

Auch in der Spielzeit 1938-39:

„Jeder Jude im Kulturbund"

Preis 20 Pfg.

Jüdischer Kulturbund (Jewish Cultural Association) program, Frankfurt am Main, August 30, 1938. Paula Lindberg-Salomon appears here under her maiden name, Paula Levi.

The Bobover *rebbe* Ben-Zion Halberstam (*seated, second from right*), greeted by followers at the resort town of Krynica in Poland, 1937.

Group of Soviet Yiddish writers in the Literature Museum, Kharkov, 1933.

"The people sing! The people dance!" The slogans on the board are a play on the popular song, *"Az der rebbe zingt un az der rebbe tantst"* ("When the *rebbe* sings and when the *rebbe* dances"): Yiddish-language school in Zhitomir, Ukraine, 1938.

"Home evening" at the Jewish school for the deaf, Berlin-Weissensee, December 4, 1934.

28

Presidium of the Institute for Jewish Proletarian Culture, Kiev, 1934. Among those shown are the visiting American Communist Kalmon Marmor (*front row, third from right*), the musicologist Moisei Beregovskii (*back row, fourth from right*), and the literary historian Max Erik (*back row, fifth from right*).

29

Jewish colonists at a collective farm in Stalindorf, Jewish autonomous subdistrict, southern Ukraine, reading the Moscow Yiddish newspaper *Emes*, 1937.

"AND SO THEY HAVE MUSIC WHERE'ER THEY GO." —
A Jewish band of Rathin, Galicia.

א אידישע קלעזמער־קאפעליע פון ראהאטין, גאליציע.

A *klezmer* band at Rohatyn, Galicia, 1912.

The historian Simon Dubnow (*third from left*) and the sociologist Jacob Lestchinsky (*fourth from left*) at the grave of the Jewish communal leader Tsemakh Szabad, Vilna, 1935.

Jews waiting outside the Polish consulate in Vienna, on March 16, 1938, four days after the *Anschluss*.

"Ooouuut!" Roll call for newly arrived prisoners at Buchenwald concentration camp, November 1938.

Work detail in the "isolation camp" for refugees from Nazi Germany at the state workhouse for vagrants, Merxplas, Belgium, early 1939.

Jews flee Memel following its annexation by Germany from Lithuania, March 1939.

Meeting of the Executive Committee of the Jüdische Kulturbund, Berlin, July 1939. The Kulturbund's musical director, Rudolf Schwarz, is fourth from left.

"I have no prayer but this—that we shall meet again, alive." Parting words of the Zionist leader, Chaim Weizmann, to the World Zionist Congress, Geneva, August 24, 1939, after news arrived of the Nazi-Soviet pact. Among those shown are (*front row, left to right*) Moshe Shertok, David Ben-Gurion, and Weizmann.

the total number of books stocked were in Polish. Yiddish came far behind with just over a quarter.[8] Here was yet another telling indication of the decline of Yiddish, even in its largest center in Europe.

We should not imagine that the main goal of all these libraries was furthering a disinterested search for knowledge. Nearly all of them had an ideological flavor that governed the selection of materials they made available. So broad-minded a scholar as Emanuel Ringelblum, while conditionally approving the decision of his party, the Left Poalei Zion, in 1931, to end censorship in its libraries, set limits: Bundist and anti-Soviet propaganda should not be admitted.[9]

A more dramatic instance of attempted library censorship, one that exhibited the depth of mutual loathing between religious and secular Jews, took place in the *shtetl* of Radin, near Vilna. In 1926 students in the *yeshiva* of Hafets Hayim removed all the books from a secular Jewish library in the town. Like cats presenting mice tails to their mistress, they tore off all the bindings from the books and deposited them in the sage's "throne room." They then set fire to the pages in ovens in the *yeshiva*. A police investigation, while disclosing these facts, failed to unearth the culprits. Far from criticizing the perpetrators, Hafets Hayim issued a decree forbidding disclosure of their names by his followers to the detectives.[10]

Secularists in the town and far beyond denounced the "vandals" and vowed to reconstitute the library. Contributors gave money and books, including a Yiddish edition of Marx's *Capital*. For their part, the supporters of Hafets Hayim angrily rejected the accusation of book burning as a politically motivated slander by persons bent on disparaging "our ancient Jewish culture, the mother of all world cultures."[11] Max Weinreich, of the YIVO Institute, who went to Radin to inquire into the affair, found that the incident was the culmination of a long struggle by *yeshiva* students in the *shtetl* against the library, against a modern Hebrew Tarbut school, against an amateur dramatic group, "in short, against anything that does not fit in with the spirit of the Aguda."[12]

The commotion was whipped up beyond Radin by secularists who saw the incident as a godsend (as it were) for antireligious propaganda. Opinion in the town itself seems to have been more blasé. A report nine years later stated: "The local youth receives little benefit from this library. Because of the crisis and the dark prospects for the future, the young people are generally apathetic and show little interest in literature or study."[13]

In the Soviet Union Hebrew books remained available in some public libraries in the early 1920s but thereafter they were withdrawn from all save specialist collections. In Kiev in the early 1930s Moshe Zalcman discovered a Jewish public library but there were few readers, mainly "aged persons or scholars engaged in historical or literary research." "The catalogues were being continually revised: the number of legal books diminished. People were frightened to go and look for a book. Who could guarantee that the book would not be forbidden the next day? And then there would be a document attesting that such-and-such a person had read the now illegal book."[14] In Minsk, the Y. L. Peretz Library was ordered in 1924 to remove its collection of 2,900 Hebrew books, although it did not actually do so until three years later.[15] By the late 1930s even private ownership of Hebrew books, particularly any by authors deemed anti-Soviet, became hazardous.

Jewish libraries could also be found in most of the larger Jewish centers in Europe. Paris had six, each associated with a different political group, in addition to the substantial library of the establishment Alliance Israélite Universelle. In Salonica many of the old Jewish libraries were incinerated in the great fire of 1917. But new ones were established, including the Biblioteka Sosyalista, which held Judeo-Espagnol editions of Marxist classics. Smaller Sephardic communities were less well endowed. A visitor to Monastir in 1927 noted, "Superstition and ignorance are rife. . . . Books are few and far between and no library is maintained by the Jews."[16]

Who used the libraries, how much, and to what effect? We are told that, apart from a few girls, the readers in the Y. L. Peretz Library in Minsk in 1926 were exclusively male.[17] Ten years later a survey of users found that 1,016 people visited the library in the course of a month. They read the Yiddish classics and the major Soviet Yiddish authors, as well as the works of Shakespeare and Nansen.[18]

In Poland libraries were much frequented by the young. Warsaw Jewish teenagers, it has been estimated, read, on average, a book a week.[19] For these young people, according to one analyst, "reading opened up a path to communion with the self but also conduced to sundering of communion with family and community."[20] Books and their characters often became the best friends of their readers, revealing broader horizons, suggesting new values, introducing taboo subjects, and advertising forbidden but enticing worlds.

As books became cheaper, more readily available, and public rather than private property, attitudes toward them changed. The traditional attitude of the Jew to the Hebrew written word was one of reverence: religious books were never destroyed, nor written in; when dropped, they were picked up and kissed; when no longer of use, they were decently retired and buried like human beings. But the modern Jew seemed to treat books differently. The head of the Grosser Library in Warsaw complained in 1933 of "the terribly lawless attitude of Yiddish readers towards books. The physical condition of a book in a Yiddish library cannot be compared with that of a book anywhere else. The book gets torn, smeared with grease, and defaced with graffiti by people who either curse the author or argue against a political opponent."[21]

Yet this brutal intimacy with the book, deplorable in the eyes of the preservationist librarian, was perhaps a barometer of the passion invested in literature by Jews of all classes, outlooks, regions, and ages.

Sovetish

As the Yiddish critic Shmuel Niger pointed out in 1939, war and revolution in the period 1914–21 had destroyed "the unity and homogeneity which had been characteristic of Yiddish literature" before the First World War.[22] What came to be regarded, in retrospect, as the "golden age" of Yiddish literature had come to an end with the deaths of Peretz, Shalom Aleichem, and Mendele during the war. Henceforth there were three main centers of Yiddish publishing: Poland, the United States, and the USSR, with the last becoming isolated from the others.

For a brief period in the 1920s it seemed as if the Soviet Union offered the brightest prospects for the survival and regeneration of

Yiddish literature. The difficulties of making ends meet in the narrow and harshly competitive Yiddish literary market in capitalist countries led several major writers to return from exile to the Soviet Union. They were lured there by the promise of a secure income, low-cost housing in privileged accommodation, and guarantees of publication and wide dissemination of their works. As for censorship, did that not exist also in Poland, the only other European country with a comparable Yiddish-reading population? And was not the USSR more free of anti-Semitism than Poland? Among those who cast their lots with the Soviets on the basis of such reasoning were four major figures, all of whom paid for their decision with their lives.

The poet Dovid Hofshteyn had left Russia in 1924 after being subjected to official criticism for advocating the teaching of Hebrew. He lived abroad for two years, first in Berlin, then in Palestine. In 1926 he moved back to the USSR. He generally hewed to the official line and his work was widely admired. But his eminence did not protect him or his work from interference. In 1929 he found himself attacked as a nationalist. In the following year, when he received the gift of a Hebrew-Yiddish Corona-brand typewriter from America, it was taken away by secret police for a week's inspection. Early poems of his reappeared with Hebraicisms deleted. A dedication to Bialik was removed. "Later," his widow wrote, "all dedications were removed. There was no knowing what might happen on the morrow to a man to whom one had presented a poem the previous evening. . . ."[23]

Dovid Bergelson, born in Okhrimovo, a *shtetl* in Ukraine, had lost his parents at a young age and was brought up in Kiev by older siblings. He began publishing Yiddish stories before the First World War. In 1921 he moved to Berlin, where he became a central figure in the small circle of Yiddish writers. Although he sympathized with Communism, he remained in Germany for the time being. The rise of the Nazis, however, made his position there uncomfortable and potentially dangerous. As a temporary measure, he moved to Denmark in 1933. He toyed with the idea of emigrating to America but opportunities did not beckon. He might have gone to Palestine: he knew Hebrew well and in his youth had considered becoming a

Hebrew rather than a Yiddish writer. But the outlook for Yiddish in Palestine was even less promising than in America.

In 1934 he returned with his family to Moscow. The decision was partly ideological and partly practical. Bergelson had been Berlin correspondent for the Moscow Yiddish daily *Emes* and his wife had worked for the Soviet trade mission in Berlin. She strenuously opposed their return to Russia. When they arrived at the station in Moscow, she said, "Where have we come? We shall all die here."[24]

The poet, novelist, and playwright Peretz Markish, born in a *shtetl* in Volhynia, had worked in Kiev in the early years after the revolution but settled in Warsaw, where he became one of the founders of the *Literarishe bleter*. He moved to Moscow in 1926. A popular writer in translation as well as in Yiddish, he became a faithful adherent and articulate spokesman of the Soviet system, earning the Order of Lenin in 1939.

The last of the four was perhaps the greatest writer: Pinhas Kahanovich, who wrote poems and prose fiction in Hebrew and Yiddish under the pen name Der Nister (The Hidden One). The explanation of this name has been much debated. It may have arisen from his evasion of military service in Tsarist Russia or it may have had a quasi-kabbalistic significance in the mind of a writer whose early works, sometimes labeled symbolist, were full of mystical allusions. Der Nister had left Russia in 1921 and, like the others, lived for several years in Berlin. In 1926 he returned to the USSR, settling in Kharkov.

Der Nister's great, probably unfinished, family saga, *Di Mishpokhe Mashber* (The Mashber Family), of which the first volume appeared in Moscow in 1939, has been described as "one of the peaks of all Yiddish fiction" and "the most non-Soviet, and internally the freest work in Yiddish prose in the Soviet Union."[25] Set in the 1870s, the novel describes the mutual relations and spiritual struggles of three brothers, one of whom, portrayed with sympathetic insight, is a follower of the Bratslaver Hasidim. Quite why Der Nister was attracted to them (as he clearly was) is unknown. Perhaps it was their mysticism. Or he may have thought that the Bratslavers would be more acceptable to the Soviet censor since they, uniquely free of allegiance to a dynasty or court, had held closer than any other

Hasidic sect to the democratic wellsprings of the early phase of the movement. (Ilya Ehrenburg, bellwether of the limits of the acceptable in Soviet literary circles, had admired the Bratslavers when he visited Poland in 1927.)[26] That a novel with such a theme could be written and published in Stalin's Russia at the height of the purges is extraordinary. Der Nister enjoyed the patronage and protection of the editor of *Emes*, Moyshe Litvakov. But after Litvakov was shot in 1937, that connection turned into a dangerous liability. That Der Nister was able to survive and continue to write (for the time being) was almost miraculous.

In recent years there has been a tendency to rediscover and celebrate the Soviet Yiddish writers of the 1930s. Intrinsically there is much to be said for that: these four are among the giants of the silver age of Yiddish literature. And there were others. But the Soviet Yiddish writers' ranks, readership, and impact should not be exaggerated. As Mordechai Altshuler points out, of the 6,376 Jewish prose writers, poets, journalists, and editors recorded in the 1939 Soviet census, "only a tiny fraction worked in Yiddish."[27] The great majority wrote in Russian for the Soviet population as a whole rather than for their fellow Jews.

The peak year of Yiddish publishing in the USSR was 1932, when 668 books and pamphlets appeared. In 1935 the number declined to 437. Of these, however, 213 were translations from Russian. Many of the books were Soviet political literature or schoolbooks. Imaginative literature published in the original was a relatively small component of Soviet Yiddish publishing. Leaving aside fiction, hardly any was on Jewish subjects. For example, of thirty-six works on history that appeared in 1932, just three were on Jewish topics.

In 1934 twenty-four Yiddish writers participated in the first Soviet writers' congress, which was preceded by the first all-union congress of Yiddish writers. Itsik Fefer, a former editor of *Di royte velt* in Kharkov and of its successor journal in Kiev, delivered a characteristically party-line oration. An exponent of supposedly proletarian values and *proste reyd* (simple speech), he seized the occasion to denigrate Sholem Asch and other non-Soviet Jewish writers, including Bialik, who had recently died. It was left to Maksim Gorky, the untouchable éminence grise of Soviet literature, to pay tribute to the memory of Bialik, "a poet who was almost a genius."[28] Joseph Opatoshu, visiting from the United States, attended the preliminary meeting but otherwise Yiddish writers from abroad were notable for their absence, a sign of the growing isolation of Soviet Yiddish—and of Soviet Jews. In the 1920s Soviet Yiddish writers had often engaged in vigorous correspondence with confrères in other countries. By the mid-1930s they hardly dared to send or receive a postcard.

This was a sealed and self-contained cultural world, since living non-Soviet Yiddish authors, other than Communist Party members or fellow travelers, could now almost never be published in the USSR. Nor could their works normally be imported. Even publication in the Soviet Union did not necessarily indicate easy availability. A writer in the Yiddish literary journal *Sovetish* in 1939 complained that the main Yiddish publishing house in Ukraine was so bad at advertising and distribution that "one rarely sees even a simple announcement in our Yiddish papers and journals, not to speak of catalogues, bulletins, fliers, or posters."[29] By this time book publishing, like newspaper publishing, in Yiddish was fading. The total number of Yiddish books issued in the USSR in 1939 was 339.

The isolation of the Soviet Yiddishists was demonstrated in 1937 when an international Yiddish cultural congress convened in Paris. It attracted 102 delegates from twenty-three countries. Four thousand people attended the inaugural session at the Salle Wagram. Although it was organized mainly by left-wingers (but not the Bund, which, in a characteristic display of ideological purism, boycotted the event), at a time when the left was supposedly still committed to the concept of the Popular Front, one country was notable by its absence: the USSR. When Wolf Wieviorka complained that a "mysterious veil" had descended over the assembly on the subject, the chairman twice tried to shut him up.[30]

The congress announced the establishment of an international organization, IKUF (Alveltlikher Yidisher Kultur Farband). Regarded by some as a Communist front organization, its leaders included non-Communists such as Zalmen Reyzen, editor of the *Vilner tog*. In its proclamation of the unity of the Jewish people, its affirmation that no law could deny Jewish national existence, and its declaration that "the present Jewish culture is the continuity of all the human and progressive traditions of the Jewish people, whose language is Yiddish," IKUF sounded almost Zionist (save for the final word).[31] The New York *Forverts* (or *Jewish Daily Forward*) dismissed IKUF as a "Communist maneuver to take over Jewish souls."[32] But Communism without Soviet support was not a viable proposition in the 1930s. IKUF did not last long.

The Doghouse

Meanwhile, the other main European hub of Yiddish literary activity was also in decline. Until the 1920s Poland had been the center of Yiddish and Hebrew book production. But the publishing industry in Poland was severely affected by the Depression, and the number of Yiddish books produced fell to 222 in 1932. A limited recovery in the following years was reflected in an increase to 443 in 1939. As in the Soviet Union, many of these were translations into Yiddish: one of the last to appear was *Der gelibter fun lady chatterly*.

Titles produced did not, however, necessarily mean books sold, and the Yiddish publishing world in Poland remained in the doldrums: print runs were greatly diminished and several publishing houses collapsed. New York was eclipsing Warsaw as the Yiddish cultural capital, even as the main center of Hebrew creativity was moving to Palestine.

In 1933 the poet Elias Sheps, who wrote under the pen name A. Almi, gave an interview to the *Literarishe bleter* in which he bewailed the state of Yiddish culture on his return to Warsaw after an absence of twenty years: "I listen here to the same sighs of resignation as in America . . . here too Yiddish books lie mouldering on shelves, here too cynicism, lack of faith, and apathy have taken over." He described the situation unapologetically as a *khurbn* (an extreme term used to denote a catastrophe or a holocaust): "Let's call things by their real name," he insisted.[33] The interview evoked a furious, defensive riposte from Kadya Molodowsky: yet two years later she herself decided to leave Warsaw, hoping for better things in America.

She was not alone. Many prominent Yiddish writers had moved to North America by the late 1930s, notably the brothers Israel Joshua Singer and Isaac Bashevis Singer. Increasingly, contributors to the *Literarishe bleter* were writing not in Poland but from New York, Los Angeles, Denver, Montreal, or Toronto.

The ticking heart of Yiddish literature, nevertheless, remained in Europe. More specifically it resided at 13 Tłomackie Street in Warsaw. This was the *bude* ("den" or "doghouse"), home of the Yiddish writers' club. Situated in the center of Jewish Warsaw, adjacent to a brothel, the club was a rendezvous for gossip, rumors, bitter quarrels, and incessant argument among its four hundred members. Its inner sanctum, dominated by a portrait of Y. L. Peretz, was later transmuted into literary legend by repeated evocation in the works of Isaac Bashevis Singer. Melech Ravitch, who had learned organizational skills by working for ten years in a bank in Vienna, served as club secretary from 1924 until his emigration from Poland in the mid-1930s. A considerable writer on his own account, he imposed some order on the quarrelsome and unbusinesslike literary rabble. On visits to the club Singer would be joined by other fledgling scribblers,

> each with his own plans, complaints, vexations. One had been left out by a critic who had compiled a list of prose writers of the younger generation in a literary journal. A second had been promised to have his poem printed by an editor but months had gone by and the poem still lay in the editor's drawer, or possibly he had lost it.[34]

Membership of the club was limited to accredited writers. The standard criteria for accreditation were numerical rather than aesthetic: ten published poems, two stories, fifty newspaper articles, or the translation of a book. Once elected, members settled into a life of ease. The balcony of the club became their "summer residence." Food was cheap and the young Singer was able to obtain extended credit for his meals from an obliging waitress.

Yiddish writers in Poland and elsewhere attached considerable importance to the decision in 1927 by the International PEN Club for writers to constitute a "Yiddish Center"—the only nonterritorial group of its kind in the organization. The center was originally chartered in Vilna, apparently to avoid antagonizing the Polish Writers Association in Warsaw. But it soon established a presence in Warsaw at 13 Tłomackie. The recognition was a bittersweet victory, since it exacerbated the already difficult relations of Yiddish writers with the Polish PEN club, from which they were effectively excluded.

Most of the important Yiddish writers of the period spoke at the writers' club at one time or another. One visitor who created a sensation was Itzik Manger, probably the most popular Yiddish poet of the 1930s. He was born in Czernowitz in 1901—or rather, as he put it, "I was born in a station, between one town and the next. From that, perhaps, derives the 'wandering-demon' in me."[35] Manger has been called "the last Yiddish troubadour."[36] In 1929 he visited Warsaw and was feted at the club as a new voice of Romanian *yidishkayt*. Interviewed by the *Literarishe bleter*, he deplored the lack of contact between Polish and Romanian Yiddish literary worlds. "The first *salta mortalis* [death leap] over that mythic-fantastic curse," he said, "is my present visit to Poland."[37] He liked it so much that he spent most of the next nine years in Poland.

The atmosphere at the club was rarely placid. Isaac Bashevis Singer, for example, would engage in heated discussions with the journalist Isaac Deutscher, a Marxist who wrote for the bourgeois, moderately Zionist *Nasz Przegląd*. Deutscher had been expelled from the Polish Communist Party in 1932 for advocating left-wing unity against the danger of fascism, thus becoming one of the earliest "premature anti-fascists." He later moved to Trotskyism and defended his position in a rowdy meeting at the writers' club.

> The Stalinists tried to outshout him. They called him the renegade, fascist, sellout, capitalist bootlicker, imperialist murderer, provocateur. But Deutscher had a powerful voice. He pounded his fist on the podium and his audience of Trotskyites encouraged him with thunderous applause. He hurled sulphur and ashes at Stalinists and right-wing Socialists, at Fascists, and at such alleged democracies as America, England, and France.[38]

In 1939 Deutscher took refuge in one of the "alleged democracies," living contentedly in England for the rest of his life.

In the late 1930s the club verged on collapse as conflicts erupted between leftists and bourgeois writers. Old-timers were annoyed when earnest young radicals told them to switch off the *patephon* (gramophone) because it was interfering with their political discussions. The restaurant closed as writers preferred to eat at the Piccadilly café. In the summer of 1938 the club moved into new quarters at 11 Graniczna Street. The opening of its new home was a star-studded festivity. The film star Molly Picon and the actress Ida Kaminska lent the occasion glamour. But within a few months the club was again in severe financial straits and on the edge of dissolution.

The bibliographic scholar Brad Sabin Hill has investigated the last Jewish books published in Poland in 1939 just before the outbreak of war. The final work of rabbinic scholarship, he reports, was *Barukh she-amar*, a collection of Hebrew liturgical studies, including a commentary on the Talmudic tractate *Avot*, issued in Pinsk by Baruch Epstein, one of the leading Talmudic sages of the period. As for works of secular Yiddish literature, probably the last to appear was a collection of literary essays entitled *Kritishe minyaturn*, the first publication by a young German-born critic, Joseph Wulf. Printed in Warsaw in the summer of 1939, apparently intended for later distribution, it bears the date 1940. A copy sent to a Yiddish writer in America in advance of publication appears to be the only one to have survived.[39]

Villa Shalom

By far the most popular Yiddish writer of the period was Sholem Asch. In the Czortków library his works, taken as a whole, were the most requested every single year over the decade to 1937.[40] He was one of the few Yiddish writers whose royalties enabled him to live comfortably by the pen. He was the only one who could, as a result, afford to buy a villa on the French Riviera (named Villa Shalom), where, clad in his flowered dressing gown, he would greet morning visitors in his garden overlooking the sea. He was indeed the only Yiddish writer in the 1930s who was regarded as a celebrity.

Asch's life exemplified the transition from traditional Jewish society to modernity. He had started writing in Hebrew, had then (so at any rate went the legend) been persuaded by Y. L. Peretz to turn to Yiddish, and ended up being read mainly in translation into German and English. His earliest novella, published in 1904, was called *A Shtetl*. Later novels and plays explored more adventurous (some said salacious) themes. His play *Got fun nekume* (God of Vengeance), produced by Max Reinhardt in Berlin in 1907, depicted lesbianism and prostitution and caused scandal in several countries. "Burn it, Asch, burn it!" had been the first reaction of Peretz when Asch read it to him.[41]

Asch's writing had tremendous narrative thrust; vivid, if often crude, characterizations; an eye for social distinctions; and an ear for colloquial turns of speech. Perhaps because of his immense popularity, some critics looked down on Asch as a sensationalist, moralizer, and literary middleweight. It was said of him that he wrote Yiddish as if the language were his personal enemy.[42] Isaac Bashevis Singer considered him "a rustic" whose stories "personified the pathos of the provincial who has been shown the big world for the first time."[43] According to Irving Howe, "Asch brought together two strands of the Yiddish tradition: the tendency to idyllicize the past, bathing it in a Sabbath light, and the tendency to enlarge upon the pathos of romanticism." Howe dismisses him as an author of "middlebrow narratives with the kind of 'power' certain to endear him to popular audiences" and he adds that "under the shrewd hand of his translator, Maurice Samuel, he often read better in English than in Yiddish."[44]

Asch also came under attack on other grounds. The orthodox were infuriated by his condemnation of the rite of circumcision (though he was not alone in this view—Simon Dubnow, for example, shared it and did not attend his own son's *bris*). Moshe Zalcman, who once visited Asch in France with a party of young Communists, taxed him with his "glorification" of the Piłsudski regime and his failure to endorse the proletarian struggle in his fiction. Asch, who had a short temper, was offended and sent them packing: "I don't know you and don't want to know you. I don't see you and don't want to see you."[45] Zalcman was joined in his strictures by Isaac Deutscher, who complained in the Communist *Miesięcznik Literacki* (Literary Monthly) that "the cult of the Jewish bourgeoisie [was] building up around Asch." According to Deutscher, this was to be explained "not only by the fascist values in his fiction" but by Asch's activities "in the arena of so-called Polish-Jewish relations."[46]

In 1938 Asch moved to the United States and in the following year published *The Nazarene*, the first volume of a trilogy on the founders of Christianity. The novel was widely praised in the general press and became a huge bestseller in English. But its reception among Jews was deeply hostile. *Haynt*, which had previously serialized most of Asch's novels, rejected this one. The New York *Forverts* stopped publishing it halfway through and the paper's editor led a vitriolic campaign against Asch that permanently damaged his reputation. Asch was accused of Christianizing tendencies and of virtual betrayal at a time of extreme danger to the Jewish people. Asch, whose naïve intention was to further a vague, ecumenical coming together of faiths, felt badly bruised. He regarded the book as his "crowning work" and called himself "a sacrifice to my writing."[47] A few Yiddish critics, notably Shmuel Niger, shared this estimation, but their voices were drowned in the storm of abuse.

Something more was at work here than mere religious defensiveness. Neither Joseph Klausner's *Jesus of Nazareth*, first published in Hebrew in 1922, nor the French-Jewish writer Edmond Fleg's *Jésus, raconté par le Juif Errant* (1933) had aroused such a violent reaction. Nor did Chagall's painting *White Crucifixion*, which was created almost simultaneously with Asch's novel. Most of Asch's detractors were nonreligious Jews. Their venom, it has been suggested, arose less from a feeling that he had betrayed Judaism than that he had betrayed *yidishkayt* by publishing the book first in English translation.[48]

Asch, however, insisted that he was not merely a Jewish but a universal artist. At least in terms of his large international audience in many languages, he could make this claim with greater justice than any other Yiddish writer of the period. But both the criticism and the defense raise the larger issue of what exactly constituted a

Jewish writer and what, if any, special responsibilities might attach to such a label.

Escape to the Modern

Poets and novelists in Jewish languages such as Hebrew and Yiddish were in some sense the builders of Jewish culture. But could a writer who did not use a Jewish language also be regarded as one of the construction workers? Was such a writer of Jewish origin who wrote on non-Jewish subjects part of the work crew or regarded as working on a separate building site? Did one even have to be Jewish to be a Jewish writer?

These theoretical conundrums, at which scholars and critics have gnawed lengthily, if not always productively, become easier to resolve if viewed in biographical and historical context. The notion of a special Jewish sensibility is a fata morgana that has often led critics down paths to nowhere. Jewish writers of the period who did not write in Jewish languages were generally regarded as Jewish writers, though, like Asch, most did not subscribe to a narrow or exclusive understanding of that label and some preferred not to think of themselves as Jewish writers at all.

The greatest of them declared in his diary in January 1914: "What have I in common with Jews? I have hardly anything in common with myself and should stand very quietly in a corner, content that I can breathe."[49] Yet the life and work of Franz Kafka are incomprehensible without relation to his self-understanding of his Jewishness, his involvement in Jewish issues, and his insights into the Jewish condition. In 1923 (probably—we do not have an exact date) he wrote to his lover Milena Jesenská:

> I've spent all afternoon in the streets, wallowing in the Jew-baiting. "Prašivé plemeno"—"filthy rabble" I heard someone call the Jews the other day. Isn't it the natural thing to leave the place where one is hated so much? (For this, Zionism or national feeling is not needed.) The heroism which consists of staying on in spite of it all is that of cockroaches which also can't be exterminated from the bathroom.[50]

Kafka was not alone in comparing the Jew to a giant insect. The image was a commonplace of anti-Semitic propaganda. The difference was that Kafka, unlike the anti-Semites and unlike other Jewish writers in German who sometimes wrote in such terms of the *Ostjuden*, was squarely on the side of the cockroaches. As Nahum Glatzer writes, "The West European Jew had shaken off the burden of tradition. But Kafka does not—at least with part of his being—consider himself as belonging to that traditionless, uprooted community."[51] He identified much more with the *Ostjuden*. At one point, coming upon a hundred east European Jewish war refugees in the Jewish Town Hall in Prague, he wrote: "If I'd been given the choice to be what I wanted, then I'd have chosen to be a small East European Jewish boy in the corner of the room."[52]

Kafka's shade hung over modernist Jewish writers in Europe in the 1930s, perhaps over none more than the mordant fantast Bruno Schulz, whose quasi-autobiographical writings in Polish are written largely from the point of view of "a small East European Jewish boy in the corner of the room." A teacher, artist, and author of stories such as *The Street of Crocodiles*, in which he constructed a magical, imaginary version of his Galician hometown, Drohobycz, Schulz transmutes the mundane into the exotic and then back again. Although Schulz rarely refers directly to Jewish issues, his works are full of allusions to the problems of small-town Polish Jews and to the larger existential issues facing Jews in the 1930s. Of all Polish-Jewish writers of the period in any language, his work, like Kafka's, conjures up an imaginary that is at the same time Jewish and universal.

Schulz was one of several important Jewish writers in Poland who preferred to write in Polish rather than Yiddish. Indeed, the main Warsaw cultural weekly, *Wiadmości Literackie*, had so many contributors of Jewish origin that it was sometimes described as a Jewish paper.

Three other Polish writers of the period found themselves compelled, whether they liked it or not, to address the question of their Jewishness. The poet and satirist Julian Tuwim also made frequent appearances in *Wiadmości Literackie*. He criticized the "black Hasidic rabble" yet attacked anti-Jewish stereotypes.[53] "I do not deny that I am a Jew, but only [by] origin," he declared in an article in *Nowy Dziennik* in 1935.[54] "My greatest tragedy—that I am a Jew," he wrote, though later in the same poem he declared his pride in being "a son of the oldest people—of the embryo of messianism."[55] Was this irony or ambivalence? As in many such cases, probably a mixture of the two.

A sharper double edge may be felt in the work of Bruno Jasieński, a futurist poet and novelist who converted to Christianity and then became a Marxist. In 1925 he emigrated to Paris, where he consorted with Ilya Ehrenburg and other left-wingers at the Café du Dôme. Although he wrote in Polish, he was sympathetic to Yiddish, declaring that he had been "estranged from [Yiddish] by my father."[56] Expelled from France in 1929, he was not permitted to return to Poland and took refuge in the USSR. In 1937, however, he was arrested there and sentenced to five years' imprisonment.

Together with Tuwim, Jasieński, and others, Aleksander Wat became a leading member of the "Skamander" group of young futurist poets in Poland in the 1920s. Wat had grown up in a moderately observant family but received little Jewish education. Although he chose assimilation to Polish culture, his early poetry, blasphemous and grotesque, contains traces of kabbalistic mysticism and some of his early fiction was on Jewish themes. He later summarized his attitude toward his origins: "I have never felt myself either a Polish Jew or a Jewish Pole. . . . I always felt myself a Jew-Jew and a Pole-Pole (as they would say in French). It is difficult to explain, yet it is true. I have always been proud (if one is permitted at all to be proud of belonging to this or that group) that I am a Pole, that I am a Jew. And simultaneously driven to despair that I am a Pole, that I am a Jew. What a lot of bad luck!"[57]

A similar avowal might have been made by Ilya Ehrenburg, apart from Isaac Babel, the best-known Soviet-Jewish writer of the period. Ehrenburg enjoyed the unusual privilege of being able to travel with relative ease between Moscow and Paris, where he spent most of his time between 1921 and 1940. In the 1930s he served as a correspondent for *Izvestia* in Paris and during the civil war reported from Spain. When his friend the poet Osip Mandelstam was arrested in 1934, Ehrenburg, together with Boris Pasternak, helped prevent his execution. Stalin instead sent Mandelstam into internal exile with the instruction "isolate but preserve."[58] Ehrenburg's intervention was certainly not an act of Jewish solidarity (all three writers were of Jewish origin). The extent to which Ehrenburg stuck his neck out has been disputed, though Joshua Rubenstein has argued ably the case for Ehrenburg's defense. Insofar as he tried to use his influence to soften the edges of Stalinist terror, he did so as a writer, not a Jew. But there is no doubt that the depth of Ehrenburg's loathing for fascism was connected to his strong Jewish identification.

Ehrenburg, who did not know Yiddish, wrote exclusively in Russian. Like Babel, he wrote for a general, not a Jewish audience. Only one of his novels, *The Stormy Life of Lasik Roitschwantz* (1928), has a specifically Jewish theme, narrating the story of a hapless small-town Jew in his encounters with Communism, Hasidism, and Zionism. Lazar Kaganovich considered the book an expression of "bourgeois Jewish nationalism" and it was banned in the USSR.[59]

Ehrenburg, unlike Babel, survived the terror and his reputation suffered as a result. He came to be regarded as an unprincipled compromiser. Abraham Brumberg wrote of him that "his cynicism was as acrid as his sentimentality was poignant."[60] But his Russian-Jewish duality was open and unapologetic. For all his political maneuvering, Ehrenburg seems to have had less of a complex about his Jewishness than most other Jewish writers of his time.

A rather different case was that of the Romanian writer Mihail Sebastian. Educated as a lawyer in Paris, he returned to his native land, where he achieved success in the 1930s as a novelist and playwright. Like Romanian intellectuals in general, he admired French culture and regarded Paris as the intellectual capital of the world. But like most Romanian Jewish writers, he wrote in Romanian and sought integration and recognition within Romanian culture. He chose as his nom de plume the more Romanian-sounding name by which he is remembered. As was the fate of many Jewish intellectuals in the highly nationalistic states of east-central Europe between the wars, he bumped repeatedly against resentment and hostility on the part of those who regarded themselves as guardians of the national culture.

His reactions, recorded with candor in his diary, published only long after his death, were perplexed and often contradictory. Blessed with a great zest for life in all its infinite variety, Sebastian was a democrat who at times flirted with Communism. Yet he remained close to radical-right intellectuals such as the philosopher Nae Ionescu and the religious thinker Mircea Eliade, whose attitudes were strongly infected with anti-Semitism and who were close to the Romanian fascist movement. "Under all circumstances, and especially the present ones, the Jewish writer, quite aware of reality, clings to an imagined integration into national life, while knowing that actual integration has been denied him" was the comment, after a meeting with Sebastian, of his fellow Jewish writer and diarist Emil Dorian in February 1938.[61]

The Last Mohicans

Bordering the literary kingdom but separate from it was the realm of scholarship. In the interwar period researchers on Jewish issues applied the methodologies of the social sciences to Jewish historical study. The effort to create a general understanding of past and present Jewish societies and cultures gave birth to two great scholarly enterprises, the *Encyclopaedia Judaica*, several volumes of which appeared in German before the project was aborted by the rise of Nazis, and the Yiddish *Algemeyne entsiklopedye*, which limped to a conclusion after the Second World War.

The head of the latter project was Simon Dubnow, the most influential Jewish historian of the time, a protean scholar whose *World History of the Jewish People*, published in many languages, shaped Jewish historical self-consciousness in his generation and beyond. He had no university education and his only formal academic appointment was at a short-lived "Jewish People's University" in Petrograd in 1919–22. Dubnow called for a new focus in Jewish history. Whereas the scholars of the nineteenth-century *Wissenschaft des Judentums* had researched Judaism and others had written about exemplary individuals and their relation to men of power, he and his followers would research the "folk."[62]

Dubnow, who lived in Berlin and then in Riga during the interwar period, served as an inspiration to the founders of YIVO. He also influenced the group of young students in Warsaw, headed by

Emanuel Ringelblum, who formed a seminar that collected materials on Polish-Jewish history. This "Young Historians' Circle" intended, wrote Ringelblum, "to impart a new spirit to the writing of Jewish history," liberating it from "nationalist and religious attitudes" and applying the methods of historical materialism.[63] The enterprise won the support of Polish-language scholars such as Majer Bałaban, head of the Institute of Jewish Studies in Warsaw, founded in 1927, and from 1936 occupant of the chair in Jewish history at Warsaw University, the only professorship in the subject at a Polish university.

In the Soviet Union the prerevolutionary Jewish intelligentsia was either bolshevized or went into exile. The "last Mohican" of non-Marxist Jewish scholarship in Russia was the literary historian Yisroel Tsinberg. A chemist by profession, he had been an ardent Yiddishist in his early years. Between 1929 and 1937 he succeeded in publishing in Vilna eight volumes of his Yiddish *History of Jewish Literature*, a remarkable feat for a Soviet citizen. His home in Moscow became a "cultural outpost" of secular Jewish scholars and intellectuals. But he was arrested in April 1938 and died in a transit camp in Vladivostok at the end of the year.[64]

Scholars and poets, avant-garde modernists and journalistic hacks, visionaries, pedants, and purveyors of fairy tales—these writers responded variously to the Jewish predicament, *their* predicament, but, considered collectively, their lives and works expose the dark heart of the Jewish experience in Europe of the 1930s.

13

MASQUES OF MODERNITY

"The entire cultural renaissance of Central Europe was made possible," it has been said, "by the emancipation and urbanization of Central European Jewry."[1] Whether there was anything specially Jewish about the culture they produced is another matter. The Judaic ingredients in early-twentieth-century European culture cannot be isolated like chemical elements. That does not mean, however, that they were not there at all. We cannot speak of a Jewish collective imagination, let alone of a Jewish mind. Yet there were characteristic milieux, mentalities, relationships, obsessions, hypocrisies, delusions, and preoccupations that were exhibited not only on the printed page but in the visual, plastic, and performative arts, particularly on the stage, the cinema screen, the concert platform, and the painted canvas.

The School of Fame

"The school of fame that the Jewish youth of Vienna attended," according to Hannah Arendt, "was the theater."[2] As individuals rather than a collectivity, Jews played a vital part in the theater in much of central and eastern Europe.

Max Reinhardt, the presiding genius of European theater in the early twentieth century, born to orthodox Jewish parents in Vienna, made his name as director of the Deutsches Theater in Berlin. In the 1920s and 1930s he directed plays and opera in Berlin, Vienna, and Salzburg, where he revived the annual festival of music and drama, and in Hollywood. His range extended from small, intimate studio performances to giant spectacles, such as his production of Büchner's *Danton's Death*, presented in an arena that seated five thousand spectators. Reinhardt was one of the hundreds of playwrights, directors, actors, cabaret artists, and critics of Jewish origin who transformed the European stage, especially in the German-speaking *Kulturraum*, in these years.

In one other essential respect, too, the theater in these lands was disproportionately Jewish: the audience. In Poland, it was said that without the Jewish audience the theater "could save itself the expense of turning on the lights."[3] Anti-Semites accused Jews of dominating and perverting the theater of central and eastern European nations to their own purposes. The extent to which Jewish components can be detected in German, Austrian, Hungarian, Polish, and Romanian drama in these years has been much debated. But of the Jewishness of one branch of the theater, which, through various subterranean connections, infused many of these others, there can be no doubt.

From its origins in the festive *purimspiel* and for long after the establishment of the first professional Yiddish theater at Jassy, in Romania, in 1876, Yiddish drama flourished in a direct relationship with its popular audience, eschewing any pretension to artistic or literary sophistication. But the standard repertoire, developed in the late nineteenth and early twentieth centuries, included plays with biblical, historical, social, or nationalist themes that resonated with a population that, as it was losing absolute faith in traditional religion, sought meaning elsewhere.

"Whatever was noble, and much of what was coarse and decadent in their culture," according to Irving Howe, "found its reflection on the stage." Yiddish theater, he writes, drew on "the *hazan*'s dramatism, the *magid*'s eloquence, the *badkhn*'s clowning" and on "the very depths of the Jewish past." And he claims for the Yiddish stage a uniqueness at any rate in its more serious manifestations: "It was a theater spontaneously expressionistic, for it set as its goal not the scrutiny of personal relationships or the probing of personal destinies, both of which have been dominant concerns of the modern and classical theaters of the West, but rather a mythic ordering of Jewish fate, whether through historical spectacle or family drama."[4]

The precarious economy of Yiddish theater prevented it from living up to such ambitious pretensions. In central and western Europe it led a hand-to-mouth existence. In Vienna, Yiddish drama, sometimes at a highbrow level, had flourished in the first quarter of the century. Two Yiddish theaters, the Jüdische Bühne and the Jüdische Künstlerspiele, continued to operate until 1938, performing the classic Yiddish repertoire as well as popular operettas and melodramas, translated plays by Strindberg, Arnold Zweig, and Ernst Toller, and newly written comedies with contemporary themes, such as *On tsertifikat ken palestina* (Without a Certificate to Palestine). While these Yiddish theaters functioned at some distance from the neighboring German-language stage, important figures in the latter, such as Arthur Schnitzler, often attended Yiddish plays.

In eastern Europe Yiddish theater suffered under political as well as economic constraints. Dramatic censorship in Poland and Romania, although not laced with terror as in the USSR, was a constraint on adventurous, particularly left-wing, drama. Most companies were short-lived and financial pressures led to endless rows among actors, proprietors, directors, and unions, not to mention critics and audiences. A few companies battled on regardless: the longest-lasting, in Lwów, was founded by Yankev-Ber Gimpel in 1889 and kept afloat under his family's control until 1939.

In Warsaw, the center of European Yiddish theater between the wars, four main dramatic companies as well as several popular music halls competed for audiences. The leading serious company in the early 1920s was the Vilna Troupe. Founded during the First World War in Vilna, it later set up its base in Warsaw. In its heyday it excelled in ensemble performances. It had no permanent director and did not pursue a clear artistic direction. Rather it moved from realism to naturalism and from romantic mysticism back to social realism. The Troupe was welcomed on tour in Poland, Romania, Germany, western Europe, and the United States. "When Einstein saw them in Berlin," it was said, "he changed his views on gravity."[5] Reinhardt went backstage after a performance by the troupe of An-sky's *Der dybbuk* in Vienna and told the cast, "Das ist nicht ein Schauspiel. Das ist ein Gotte[s]spiel!" ("This is not mere acting; it's divinely inspired!")[6] In New York, however, the troupe disintegrated and, although some of its members returned to Europe and reconstituted the company, it never recovered its original luster, disbanding altogether in 1935.

Der dybbuk (originally entitled *Between Two Worlds*) was not only the greatest success of the Vilna Troupe but the most-performed and best-known Yiddish play ever written. Its original version was not in Yiddish. With the encouragement of Stanislavsky, An-sky wrote it in Russian before the Russian Revolution and, only after it was banned by Russian censors, translated it into Yiddish. The first production, by the Vilna Troupe, was staged in December 1920, shortly after An-sky's death. It ran for over three hundred performances in Warsaw alone, was translated into many languages, and was widely performed throughout Europe.

The Habimah theater company staged a Hebrew translation by Bialik in Moscow in 1922. A critic found it "a very strange amalgam of prophetic fury and discipline, of the spontaneous and the artificial, of fantasy and observation."[7] After the company's departure from Russia in 1926, they took the production on tour all over the world. When they reached Paris, Chagall attended with delight. In extreme old age, Hanna Rovina, who had played the lead role in the Moscow production, was still performing it in the 1970s for Habimah (by then the national theater of Israel).

Termed a "mystery play" by contemporaries, *Der dybbuk* married Hasidic and kabbalistic imagery with modernist expressionism. Orthodox Jews boycotted it because of what they regarded as its insulting portrayal of Hasidim—but then they rarely attended the theater anyway. The play's very success became an embarrassment for Habimah and the Vilna Troupe, since audiences clamored for repeat performances but seemed interested in little else.

In the 1930s the leading Yiddish company in Warsaw was led by Ida Kaminska. She was a member of a famous theatrical family, daughter of Ester-Rokhl Kaminska (1870–1926), known as the "Jewish Duse" or "Di Mame Ester-Rokhl." Born in a theater dressing-room in Odessa, Ida first performed on the stage in Shakespearean comedy at the age of five and directed from the age of sixteen. Together with her first husband, Zygmunt Turkow, scion of another acting dynasty, she led the Warsaw Yiddish Art Theater from 1923 until 1931.

Thereafter she headed the Esther Kaminska Ensemble, which

often performed in the handsome Nowósci Theater. Built in 1926 in the heart of the Jewish area of Warsaw, it seated two thousand spectators and staged productions by Yiddish companies, including Kaminska's, until 1939. The company was, as her former brother-in-law later wrote, "in the fullest sense Ida Kaminska's, concentrating everything around her artistic individuality, . . . yet at the same time presenting harmonious ensemble performances."[8] Her appearance in the title role of Max Baumann's Glückel of Hamlyn, translated into Yiddish from the original German, was a huge success, presented more than 150 times in Łódź, Cracow, Lwów, and elsewhere, before reaching Warsaw in 1938.

Unlike many Yiddish actors, Kaminska was a minimalist rather than an exaggerator. An obituarist later recalled:

> She did not thunder in the declamatory tradition so often associated with Yiddish drama. She often spoke in a firm voice, very low, so low as to make the audience lean forward in unaccustomed silence to catch the power of her words. Although she was not leather-lunged, she rose to peaks of passion and anger that generated their own electricity. She could wheedle and coax on stage with a charm that attested to a rare stage presence.[9]

In the winter of 1938–39 she performed in *Flamen* based on a novel by Yoshue Perle, and in a Yiddish version of Lope de Vega's *Fuente Ovejuna* (The Sheep Well). The latter, an ambitious and expensive production with a huge cast, was a roaring success.

The experimental Young Theater, established by Michał Weichert, grew out of an actors' studio he established in 1929. It first performed in February 1933 in the hall of the Warsaw tailors' guild. Weichert, who had trained under Reinhardt in Berlin, drew together a collective of thirty young student-actors. They dispensed with curtain and footlights. The actors often stepped down from the stage to draw the audience into the midst of the action. In 1936, however, the company was closed down by government order, apparently on political grounds.

The Yiddish theatrical world was rent by conflict: bitter squabbles, fierce ideological argument, careless love affairs, and unforgiving personal rivalries. Actors flitted from one theater, city, country, and companion to another, rarely establishing a secure financial base. Those who aimed to perform serious modern Yiddish drama resented the cheap sensationalism of theatrical *shund*.

Such unashamedly entertaining stews, mixing vaudeville, music hall, burlesque, and cabaret, were often smash hits with the undiscriminating mass of theatergoers, even though they might be disapproved of by the more high-minded. The Bundist *Folks-tsaytung* declared in 1933: "We have no interest whatsoever in reviewing *shund* plays. Occasionally we make an exception but only in order to warn the Jewish workers against this claptrap which only warps their taste and distracts them from the superior Yiddish theater."[10] Yet however much they were "warned," Jewish audiences continued to flock to earthy comedies, vulgar musicals, and crude melodramas that social and cultural elites considered beneath contempt.

The Yiddish theater faced a struggle for existence, since it was regarded with disfavor by the orthodox and with disdain by assimilationists. It was nevertheless very popular and, according to the impressionistic estimate of the critic Nakhmen Mayzel, drew an audience in Warsaw three or four times the size of the readership of the Yiddish press.[11] The audience was generally working-class, since the Jewish bourgeoisie was moving rapidly toward Polish culture.

There was little direct connection between the Yiddish and Polish-language stage, although many actors and producers and much of the audience for Polish, as for Yiddish, theater was Jewish. Exceptionally, the director Mark Arnshteyn staged Yiddish plays in Polish in Warsaw in the late 1920s. His productions of *Der dybbuk* and of Jacob Gordin's popular *Mirele Efros* were critical and commercial successes but his other exercises in translation from Yiddish encountered resistance. Arnshteyn's dream of building "a bridge between Polish and Jewish societies" by way of the theater proved unrealizable, partly because of opposition from militant Yiddishists to the staging of Yiddish plays in another language.[12] "The Yiddish theater in Poland," wrote Mayzel, "lives apart, like the Yiddish cultural world in general, isolated in a veritable ghetto!"[13] A rare, quixotic "gesture of Polish-Jewish solidarity" was the production in 1938–39 in Warsaw and Łódź of a Yiddish version of Shakespeare's

The Tempest with a Jewish cast by the modernist director Leon Schiller, a leftist non-Jew.

In the Soviet Union, Yiddish theaters, subsidized by the state, were to be found in twelve cities in the late 1930s. Under the leadership of Shlomo Mikhoels, the Moscow State Yiddish Theater managed to survive the purges of the 1930s. Founded in Petrograd in 1918, the company was strongly influenced by modernist trends in Russian theater, in particular the expressionism of Eisenstein and the "biomechanics" of Vsevolod Meyerhold. In 1928 the company went on a tour of western Europe from which its founding director, Aleksandr Granovsky, decided not to return. Henceforth the authorities applied stricter discipline, reining in deviations from Socialist Realism. Walking a narrow line, Mikhoels, who directed the theater from 1928, maintained the artistic integrity of the enterprise. His performance as King Lear in 1935 was hailed as a triumph of Soviet as much as of Yiddish theater and ran for over two hundred performances. Gordon Craig wrote in *The Times* of London, "Only now, after having returned from the Theatre Festival in Moscow, do I understand why we have no Lear worthy of the name in Britain. The reason is quite simple: we have no actor like Mikhoels."[14]

The company's staging of *Boytre the Bandit* by Moshe Kulbak, based on Schiller's *Robbers*, about a proletarian Robin Hood–like figure who heads a gang of thieves, ran into trouble. Mikhoels explained that the production strove "to show the accumulation of rage and hate felt towards the oppressors." It was welcomed in the press but the most senior Jewish figure in the party leadership, Lazar Kaganovich, visited the theater, demonstratively failed to applaud, and after the show gave the cast a dressing-down: "It's a shame to me, a shame! . . . Look at me, at what I am . . . a Jew. My father was also one: exalted, bright, healthy. . . . Why do you drag down such Jews on your stage? Deformed, lame, crippled? . . . I want you to summon sensations of pride in today and yesterday with your plays. Where are the Maccabees? Where is Bar Kochba? . . . Where are the Birobidzhan Jews who are building themselves a new life?"[15] Shortly afterward Kulbak was arrested, subjected to a show trial, and shot.

Mikhoels took Kaganovich's guidance literally. He commissioned a play on Bar Kochba by Shmuel Halkin, who subtly altered the underlying Jewish nationalist theme, turning the hero into a model of socialist man. The second-century Palestinian Jews' revolt against the Romans was transformed into a proletarian rebellion. To avoid any hint of Zionist deviation, the locale of the play's action, the Land of Israel, was not mentioned in Halkin's text.[16] Remarkably, however, Rabbi Akiva was portrayed sympathetically, a rare such appearance for a religious figure on the Soviet stage. A critic commended the "grandfatherly, sincere, folk-lyricism—and, where necessary, manly severity and harshness" that Benjamin Zuskin injected into his portrayal of the rabbi.[17] *Bar Kochba* toured the Soviet Union in the spring and summer of 1939, securing enthusiastic receptions from Jewish audiences. Meanwhile, the theater prepared a production of an antifascist and anti-Zionist play by Peretz Markish, *The Oath*. But as Germany and the USSR moved toward diplomatic rapprochement, the play was out of tune with the mood of the times and was never produced.

Mikhoels, it is now known, came close to being purged in 1939. Isaac Babel, who was arrested in May that year, was induced to implicate him in a forced confession that he retracted before he was shot.[18] But by then the purges were winding down and for the time being Mikhoels remained free. The price of survival was some higher degree of conformism. The collective of the theater condemned those who had been unmasked as "enemies of the people" and Mikhoels issued ritual denunciations of religion, though he kept a Bible on his desk and traveled with one in his pocket.[19] Jeffrey Veidlinger, whose history of the theater is based on its archive, previously thought to have been destroyed, argues that "while sharing many aspects of the state's educational ideals and class-based worldview, the Yiddish theater successfully resisted all attempts to turn its stage into just another platform of Soviet propaganda."[20]

Golden Cinema

In film as on the stage, the role of Jews as entrepreneurs, directors, and players was enormous. The European and particularly the

German film industry were almost as much a Jewish creation as Hollywood. Directors like Ernst Lubitsch and Billy Wilder, lost to the United States thanks to Hitler, created a genre of light comedy that was deeply infused with Jewish humor. The Jewish imprint was so pervasive that some saw it when it was not there: the pathos of Charlie Chaplin's portrayal of the little tramp misled Hannah Arendt, among others, to assume that Chaplin was a Jew and to include him in her "thread of Jewish tradition."[21] In film, as on the stage, we tread on more solid ground in searching for the Jewish imaginary if we focus on Yiddish productions.

The short life of Yiddish cinema lasted for barely three decades. It suffered from even greater financial constraints than Yiddish theater. Production costs were no less than for films in languages with larger audiences. Subtitling might help but the potential appeal of Yiddish films was limited not only by language but by subject matter, since Jewish themes rarely appealed to non-Jews.

Some of the earliest Yiddish films, silent versions of stage performances by Ester-Rokhl and Ida Kaminska and others, were made before the First World War but have been lost. In 1912 Sholem Asch's *Got fun nekume* was filmed in Moscow, also without sound. But as early as 1913–14 a number of experiments were made in Russia with sound film, including a hundred-meter talking film, *Yidl mitn fidl*.

In the 1920s silent Yiddish films were made in Austria, Poland, and Soviet Russia. In 1925, shortly before they left the Soviet Union, Habimah filmed Shalom Aleichem's *Der mabul* (The Deluge). Considerable resources were lavished on the enterprise and scenes were shot on location in the Jewish quarter of Vinnitsa and in Litin, a nearby *shtetl*. But ideological problems and personality disputes arose in the course of the production, which was not judged an artistic success.[22]

The first Yiddish sound picture, *Nosn beker fort aheym* (Noson Beker Goes Home), starring Mikhoels, was released in the Soviet Union in 1932. Based on an original script by Peretz Markish, the film depicted a Jew returning to his *shtetl* from America and participating in the construction of the Dneprostroi power station. While it necessarily glorified the industrializing achievements of the first Soviet five-year plan and stressed the obsolescence of the *shtetl* way of life, the film included affectionate portrayal of Jewish folk themes. But this was the only Yiddish sound feature film ever made in the USSR.

The first actress to become a star of both Yiddish stage and screen was Molly Picon. Although born in the United States and possessing, initially, an uncertain command of Yiddish, she became hugely popular in Europe. She was sent there, she later recalled, "first of all to perfect my Yiddish which was none too good. . . . For three years we wandered over Europe to learn Yiddish."[23] She developed from a vaudeville performer into a star. In 1936 she was paid $10,000 (then a huge sum) to appear in a new version of *Yidl mitn fidl*, the first Yiddish musical feature film. It cost $50,000 to make and was the most commercially successful Yiddish film of all time. Itzik Manger wrote the songs. Outdoor scenes were filmed on location in Kazimierz, the Jewish quarter of Cracow.

Purists decried such confections as *shund*. But during its short heyday in the 1930s Yiddish cinema also produced work with greater claim to seriousness. "The first artistic talking film in Yiddish produced in Poland," *Al kheyt* (For the Sin), was produced in 1936 by a cooperative group called Kinor (*Kino-or*, golden cinema; as a Hebrew word it means harp) with actors drawn from the Warsaw Yiddish stage.[24] Several of those involved, including the director Aleksander Marten, were refugees from Germany. The film, which took its title from a solemn hymn recited on the Day of Atonement, was a melodrama about a young *shtetl* girl made pregnant by a German-Jewish officer stationed in her town during the First World War. He promises to marry her but is killed in battle. She abandons her child and flees to America. Twenty years later she returns, rediscovers her father and child, and is reconciled with them. The plot, while formulaic, struck several obvious chords with its audience.

The film version of *Der dybbuk* appeared in 1937. Directed by Michał Waszyński, it starred Lili Liliana and many other leading figures of the Yiddish stage. The play's mystical symbolism translated effectively to the screen and the film was an artistic and box-office success. A sour note was struck, however, by the prominent Polish (Jewish) critic Stefania Zahorska, who wrote in *Wiadmości Literackie* that the film left such "an insipid residue of pathetic kitsch that all the traditions on which it is based have not given birth to even one good scene."[25] Notwithstanding such criticism, *Der dybbuk* came to be generally recognized as the supreme achievement of Yiddish film-making and a masterpiece of the European cinema.

The last Yiddish feature film made in Poland before the war, *On a heym* (Without a Home), which appeared in the spring of 1939, was directed by Aleksander Marten, who also acted in it. Based on a classic play by Jacob Gordin, it dealt with the hardships of turn-of-the-century immigrants to America. The female lead was played by Ida Kaminska and the cast included the comedic duo Szymon Dzigan and Yisroel Schumacher. But the film was not a success. A reviewer in the *Literarishe bleter* complained, "What Jew, if he gets a visa to America, will complain that he has no home?"[26]

The Presence of the Lord

In music, more perhaps than in any other form of artistic expression, the question of Jewishness was much debated. Wagner's *The Jews in Music*, first published anonymously in 1850, maintained that Jews were incapable of genuine musical creativity, alleged that their control of the press had prevented proper recognition being accorded to major composers such as himself, and urged their complete removal from cultural life and the revocation of their civil rights. Wagner's central position in the pantheon of German *völkisch* ideology and Hitler's embrace of his legacy gave Wagnerian ideas about the Jews considerable currency in the 1930s.

Yet Jews in this period had few compunctions about performing or listening to Wagner's music. Marcel Reich-Ranicki reports that the bridal music from *Lohengrin* was played at his parents' wedding in Posen (then in Germany) in 1906. "Among Jews in Poland, at least among educated ones," he writes, "this was nothing unusual; indeed it was part of the ritual."[27] Edith Friedler, a child in Vienna in the 1930s, "grew up hearing my mother tell of the many times she and her cousin Lilly . . . as teenagers, stood in line for hours at the opera to attend Wagner performances."[28]

As with theater, so with music: Jews were the core of the audience for orchestral concerts and opera throughout central and eastern Europe. For German Jews in particular, classical music came to occupy a place in their spiritual life that amounted to an ersatz religion.

In a sense Wagner got it almost right: Jewish music, in the narrow sense of the term, was much less important than the role of Jews in music in general. Jewish popular entertainers, other than those associated with the Yiddish stage, commonly steered clear of Jewish themes. In the Netherlands, for example, where more than half the members of the Nederlandse Artiesten Organisatie were Jewish, almost the only performer known for a Jewish repertoire was Louis Contran, with such songs as "Moppen van Isaac." Among the most popular entertainers, Louis Davids recorded "Het Jodenkind" (based on the English "What's the Matter with Abie") and Sylvain Poons issued "Isaac Meijer's Wiegelied," but these were exceptions.[29]

Without collapsing into the pitfalls of contributionism, we may say that absent Jewish composers, conductors, players, singers, and impresarios, music in Europe in the early twentieth century would have been a much-diminished mode of expression.

The foremost Jewish instrument was the violin. Jews played it in disproportionate numbers in all the great orchestras of the continent, save for those that had been racially purged by the Nazis. Since the late nineteenth century, through such figures as Joseph Joachim and Eugène Ysaÿe, Jews had personified, and often come close to monopolizing, the virtuoso tradition. In the 1930s Fritz Kreisler, Jascha Heifetz, the young David Oistrakh, and countless others sealed the special relationship between the Jew and the violin. In later years Isaac Stern used to express wonderment that so many masters of the instrument had been born in the narrow confines of the former Russian Pale (he was one of them).

The celebrated teacher Petr Solomonovich Stolyarsky, who came from a family of klezmer players, trained a number of infant prodigies, including Oistrakh, one of the Stolyarsky pupils who scooped four of the top six prizes at the International Eugène Ysaÿe Violin Competition in Brussels in 1937. Isaac Babel was another early, though in his case unsuccessful, pupil: he wrote a story, "Awakening," about this "*Wunderkind* factory."[30]

In traditional east European society, instrumental music was not greatly respected or listened to, save for klezmer bands at weddings.

The preeminent musical genre among religious Jews was *hazanut*. In the course of the nineteenth century the office of *hazan* (cantor) had become professionalized, especially in the Habsburg lands. Congregants took enormous pride in the quality of their cantors. Some participated in *Vergnügungsabende*, social events at which they would sing sacred and profane melodies to raise money for charity or to supplement their generally meager salaries.[31] In non-orthodox congregations, the *hazan* would be accompanied by an organ. Opera singers in Vienna and elsewhere would come to the synagogue to sing solo parts. The celebrated cantor Moshe Koussevitsky was the star attraction in the Great Synagogue in Warsaw, accompanied by a fine boys' choir. Christian Poles, especially visiting émigrés, were said to visit the synagogue just to hear him sing.

In the nineteenth century a tradition of synagogal choir singing developed. "Choral synagogues" were established in Bucharest (1857), St. Petersburg (1893), Vilna (1902), Minsk (1904), and other cities. In liberal temples choirs would be mixed, in more orthodox ones they were male-only. Julius Braunthal, who sang as a boy in the choir of the Seitenstättentempel in Vienna before the First World War, did not enjoy the three hours every Monday to Thursday that he had to spend rehearsing:

> The master of the choir was then Professor Joseph Sulzer, a cellist of the illustrious Viennese Symphony Orchestra, and son of Salomon Sulzer, who was the first to compose and introduce liturgical music into the reformed Jewish service. It was an obsession with Professor Sulzer to produce perfect performances of his father's works. He was mercilessly exacting; he rehearsed every chant untiringly, shouting, and beating our fingers and heads with his baton when we failed him. He never allowed us wretched, ill-fed children a moment's rest, though there was always a shadow of pity in his big eyes when, entirely exhausted, he dismissed us at long last.[32]

The choirboys also had to be present for four services on the Sabbath, for the Friday evening *kabbalat shabbat*, and frequently for weddings on Sundays. The younger boys sang "for the glory of God"; older ones earned a very small stipend.

Singing was not restricted to formal or religious spheres. Like other small, downtrodden nations, the Jews of eastern Europe were a people of song. "Serving-wenches and apprentice tailors, middle-class young women and Hasidic young men, virtuous housewives and boorish barrow-boys—they all sang."[33]

Among the Hasidim, songs without words helped the devout attain high moments of exaltation. Ben-Zion Gold remembers the Lithuanian *nigunim* (melodies), "full of longing, reminiscent of Bye-lorussian folk songs," different from "the Hasidic *nigunim* of central Poland, which were influenced by Polish folk dances."[34] Noyekh Prylucki described the typical Hasidic singing style: "With the hands and with the feet, with the head, the eyes, the lips, every muscle moves, every vein beats to the rhythm, absorbing the holy content of the words, forming throughout the whole organism the soulful mood which joins man with the divine."[35]

No less important to the Hasidim than song as a pathway to the most intense feelings of spirituality, was the dance. Nakhmen May-zel witnessed one on a visit to the *shtibl* of the Bratslaver Hasidim in Warsaw in the late 1930s:

The essence of the thing was the dance, which came after prayers. They had hardly finished the afternoon or evening service than one of them began to sing the well-known tune of *reb* Nahman [of Bratslav, founder of the sect]. He began very quietly, slowly, shyly. Immediately others took it up, and soon all of them. Hands joined hands on neighbours' shoulders. They already formed a circle, like rings in a chain, around the reading-table, and the dance began. The Bratslav dance is quite unusual. They do not go round and round. The circle does not move. Each person dances in place. The ecstasy grows ever greater, hotter, more fiery. One hears shrieks of joy, sighs. It's as if one has thrown off all one's heavy burdens, all one's torments. Old and young, healthy and feeble—they all dance away their innermost joy and their love and their devotion to the holy memory of *reb* Nahman.[36]

Such moments were regarded by devotees as the very highest point of *dvekut* (bonding with God).

The storehouse of Hasidic music continued to fill in the interwar period. The Kuzmir-Modzits dynasty of *rebbes*, in particular, had manifested musical gifts for several generations. The Modzitser *rebbe*, Shaul Yedidyah Eliezer Taub, was said to have composed at least seven hundred *nigunim*, many of which became popular far beyond the confines of the Hasidic world. His *tish* in the summer resort of Otwock, near Warsaw, attracted visitors from near and far. Among them, at the festival of Shavuot (Pentecost) in 1939, was the young Ben-Zion Gold. He found a position that gave him a good view and watched as, halfway through the meal, the *rebbe* tapped his snuffbox with his finger and the whole assembly fell silent:

> After a moment he began to sing a new *nigun*. The composition consisted of four parts. The first and third were meditative, while the second and fourth were rhythmic and cheerful. The singing was pure melody without words, and the Hasidim who stood behind the *rebbe*'s chair supported him. They sounded like a powerful and well-trained choir. The effect was spellbinding. When they finished the *nigun* I felt as if I had awakened from a marvelous dream.[37]

Another visitor, a *hazan*, described the impact on the audience: "A deathly, mystical silence fell over the entire hall. Even the festive candles that had wavered symmetrically the whole time were stilled." The *rebbe* began to sing *pianissimo*. The crowd, who knew the tune, wanted to join in but the *rebbe* silenced them with an imperious glance. "His voice rose and I was astounded: a dramatic, heroic tenor . . . the *shekhinah* (the presence of the Lord) descended on him."[38]

The Soul of the Nation

Jewish music was not limited to the religious sphere. Folk songs were popular in the Yiddish-speaking heartland and among Judeo-Espagnol-speaking communities of the Balkans. They were of all kinds: cradle songs, love songs, children's songs, marching songs, and other types common to all nationalities—only drinking songs were hardly to be found among this sober race.

The first transcriptions of Jewish folk song in eastern Europe were not made until the end of the nineteenth century, unless one counts the occasion in the 1860s when the young Mussorgsky wrote down (and later incorporated into his opera *Salammbô*) a tune he had heard sung by Jewish neighbors during the festival of Succot (Tabernacles). In the early twentieth century, Jewish ethnologists embarked on intensive efforts to transcribe and record songs before they fell into oblivion. YIVO played an important part in this enterprise and its work was paralleled by folklorists in the Soviet Union. The latter, however, stressed songs with "proletarian" themes and accorded priority to Slavic over German elements in Jewish music, as in Yiddish folklore in general.

Among the most popular performers of Yiddish folk songs was the tenor Menachem Kipnis. An orphan from a family of cantors, he began as a boy singer accompanying itinerant *hazanim*. In later life he would publish much-feared reviews of prominent cantors. At the age of sixteen he entered the chorus of the Warsaw opera. He issued collections of folk songs, wrote short stories and a humorous column in the *Haynt* under various pseudonyms, and published photographic essays about street characters in Warsaw. His touring recitals of Poland, Germany, and France, with his singer wife, Zmira Seligfeld, won the hearts of their hearers.

Exactly what turned a song into a folk song, let alone a Jewish one, was a matter of dispute. "Is every expressive term that someone uttered out there to be called a folk-creation?" asked the socialist-Zionist theoretician Ber Borokhov.[39] Some experts accorded highest respect to antiquity, regarding the folk song as the repository of the soul of the nation. Noyekh Pryłucki, who, in addition to his roles as politician, newspaper editor, and bibliophile, was one of the leading collectors of Yiddish folk song in interwar Poland, located its roots "in the most secretive darkness of ancient society."[40] As late as 1970 a writer on the subject could still maintain, with unabashed primordialism, that it was music that came not "from above" but was "a spontaneous outpouring of feeling from the broad Jewish masses, a music whose roots lay in the distant past and grew on the soil of full-blooded, original, Jewish life."[41] Yehuda Leib Cahan, head of YIVO's folklore commission until his death in 1937, put it more simply: what made a song a folk song, he said, was the fact that the "folk" sang it.[42]

Folk songs were not all anonymous or ancient, nor spontaneous eruptions from the body of the people. New compositions by poets and professional songwriters could be "folklorized." Among the leading practitioners in Yiddish in the interwar period were Mordkhe Gebirtig and Itzik Manger. Gebirtig's songs bridged the worlds of the *badkhn* and the cabaret artist, appealing to sophisticates and sentimentalists and earning approval even in the *Literarishe bleter*. Often whole evenings would be devoted to concerts of his songs. But in spite of their huge popularity, there were noises off from the wider world of mass entertainment. We hear more than a hint of this in Kipnis's praise of Gebirtig in 1936: "Now, when empty rhythm and broken, foreign, negro, foxtrot and tango tunes fill the air, the suppressed souls of song and folklore are embodied in Mordekhai Gebirtig."[43]

Soviet Yiddish also generated what passed for new folk songs. Ideological pressures in the high Stalinist years required that songs composed by the "folk," that is, bona fide proletarians, be accorded highest respect, irrespective of quality. Surviving shreds of the archive of the Kiev Institute for Jewish Proletarian Culture, for example, contain the following wretched lyric from Kherson in Ukraine in 1939:

> *A yortsayt, khevre, kumt oprikhtn*
> > An anniversary, comrades, marks
> *nokhn vistn doles*
> > Another sad fate
> *lomir danken dem khaver stalin*
> > Let us thank Comrade Stalin
> *far frayhayt un far ales*
> > For freedom and for everything
>
> . . .
>
> > . . .
>
> *Kumt a tentsl, khevre, fraylekh*
> > Come dance a joyful jig, comrades

Un a krenk di sonim
    And down with the enemies
Zoln zay tsepiket vern
    May they be exposed
Zay hobn shoyn a ponim![44]
    They already have a face!

Whether folk songs or pièces d'occasion, such works by proletarian poetasters were judged worthy of publication in Soviet Yiddish newspapers.

Not all Soviet Jewish folk song was so despicable. In the 1930s the dedicated Soviet ethnomusicologist Moisei (Moyshe) Beregovskii, working out of the Jewish cultural institute in Kiev, recorded performances of folk songs in Ukraine and Byelorussia. The singers were seamstresses, bristle workers, tailors, teachers, shoemakers, an actor, a schoolboy, "three working girls in Belaia Tserkov," "a blind bandura [plucked instrument, similar to a guitar] player," and so on.

The first of Beregovskii's projected five volumes on Jewish folk music appeared in 1934. The introduction denounced "bourgeois-clerical-Zionist" approaches to the subject based on the concept of the "soul of the nation," dutifully quoted Lenin, and claimed to represent a new, advanced stage of "workers' and revolutionary folklore."[45] It assembled workers' and artisans' songs, including such items as "Oy, ir narishe tsiyonistn" (Oh You Crazy Zionists), revolutionary and military anthems, as well as family ballads. Beregovskii avoided much Hasidic or religious music, though some religious motifs, drawn from the traditional liturgy, crept in, as in the "Av hora-khamim" (Father of Mercy, first words of the prayer for the dead). A second volume was set in print in 1938 but, probably for political reasons, not published. A compilation drawn from this and other unpublished volumes appeared in the USSR after his death in 1962. That included seven melodies of the Bratslaver Hasidim. To what extent these were still being sung in the USSR in the 1930s must be a matter of conjecture but, as we have seen, the Bratslav Hasidim still maintained a presence in the Soviet Union at that time.

Folk song formed one strand of a broader genre of popular folk music. Elements of *badkhones* lingered in the Yiddish cabaret of Warsaw and Cracow, in the songs of the Soviet jazz musician and cabaret artist Leonid Utesov, and in the repertoire of klezmer players in interwar Poland and the USSR.

Klezmer (the word comes from the Hebrew term *klei zemer,* "musical instruments") bands traveled around the *shtetlakh,* performing at weddings and on the merrier Jewish festivals such as Purim and Hanukah. Klezmer music was viewed by many city folk as hopelessly old-fashioned and by the 1930s had given way, at most Jewish weddings in Poland, to "light-classical items or even popular songs in Polish or Yiddish, including new songs by Jewish composers, using Jewish themes but in Polish."[46] Klezmorim nevertheless continued to play throughout the former Russian Pale as well as in Galicia, Bukovina, Transylvania, and Subcarpathian Ruthenia.

The bands had their own hierarchies, customs, and argot. Each town's *klezmer-kapelye* had its own territory into which a rival would stray at its peril. Some players were full-time professionals; most were part-timers with other jobs, especially, by tradition, barbers. Typically the band comprised violins, flute, clarinet, horn, tambourine, and drum, sometimes also cembalom (hammered dulcimer), lute, double bass, and trumpet. Klezmer music was influenced by surrounding folk styles, especially Turkish and gypsy, and some bands included gypsy players. In cities they would play in theaters, dance halls, restaurants, taverns, and bordellos. On Soviet territory, klezmer musicians played in privately owned restaurants in the NEP period and at weddings in Ukraine and Byelorussia into the 1930s.

Since most folk music was not written down (many klezmer players could not read musical notation), much of it has been lost, though Beregovskii recorded some klezmer bands. With the violinist M. I. Rabinovich he also helped organize the State Ensemble of Jewish Folk Musicians in Kiev. Then in his late sixties, Rabinovich had learned his klezmer technique from his grandfather, a celebrated musician of the mid-nineteenth century, born as far back as 1807.[47] The ensemble began in 1937 as an old-fashioned band but was dissolved after a few months, apparently as a result of political convulsions in the Ukrainian Communist establishment.

In 1938, however, it was reorganized into a large orchestra that toured the Crimea and Ukraine. The musicians performed onstage with actors reciting *badkhones* responsively. When they appeared in Odessa, a reviewer in *Emes* praised their "real folk temperament" but criticized their attempt to "foxtrotize this or that folk motif."[48] *Der shtern* reported on their visit to the Jewish "national district" of Naye-Zlatopol in 1939: "hundreds of people from the collective farms of the district came together in automobiles and wagons. The summer theater was overfilled. From the other side of the fence a peculiar sort of loge seats were improvised on the trucks."[49] The ensemble gave at least eight radio concerts and issued recordings of klezmer music that were sold at the World's Fair in New York in 1939–40.

Folk musical traditions also survived and evolved in the Balkans. In Salonica the blind oud player Sadik Nehama Gershón (Maestro Sadik) performed in Judeo-Espagnol and achieved popularity, particularly with the songs of Moshé Cazés. The Greek singer Roza Eskenazi, who became the most acclaimed performer of *rembetika* (songs of the Greek demi-monde), began her career on the stage of the Grand Hotel in Salonica. She toured taverns all over the Balkans, singing haunting, Oriental, jazz-junky tunes in Greek, Turkish, Judeo-Espagnol, and other languages, accompanied on the bouzouki, zither, or *baglama* (small lute).

"Degenerate Music"

Contrary to the conventional anti-Semitic wisdom that held that such musical talent as they might have was merely performative rather than creative, Jews were also among the most innovative composers of the era. Ernest Bloch, son of a Geneva clockmaker, stood out as "incontestably one of the contemporary composers whose art may most legitimately be described as authentically Jewish," according to a writer in a French-Jewish newspaper in 1939.[50] Bloch had moved to the United States during the First World War but returned to Europe in 1930. He lived on the French-Swiss border until December 1938, when, alarmed by the rise of Nazism, he returned to America, eventually to be celebrated as "Oregon's most famous composer."

Bloch's music frequently employs liturgical forms, biblical texts,

and Hasidic or other folkloristic themes. His works on Jewish subjects included *Schelomo* (Solomon, 1916) for the cello and *Avodath
Hakodesh* (Sacred Service), an arrangement of the Sabbath liturgy
for baritone, chorus, and orchestra (1930–33). Bloch denied that it
was his purpose to "reconstitute" Jewish music "or to base my work
on melodies more or less authentic. I am not an archaeologist. It is
the Jewish soul that interests me, the complex, glowing, agitated
soul, that I feel vibrating through the Bible; the freshness and na-
ïveté of the Patriarchs, the violence that is evident in the Prophetic
books, the Jew's savage love of justice, the despair of the Preacher
in Jerusalem, the sorrow and the immensity of the Book of Job, the
sensuality of the Song of Songs."[51] Bloch himself, at any rate, had no
doubt about the Jewishness of his music.

The case of Arnold Schoenberg is more complex and, in view of
his centrality to musical modernism, more significant. Schoenberg
had become a Protestant in 1898. Unlike those of many of his Viennese intellectual contemporaries, however, Schoenberg's conversion
appears to have been one of conscience rather than convenience.[52]
Indeed, whereas anti-Semitism induced some Jews to opt out of
Judaism, for Schoenberg collision with anti-Jewish prejudice had
the opposite effect. In 1921 he and his family were forced to leave
a gentiles-only resort in an Austrian lake area. Two years later, after
discovering that his close friend the painter Wassily Kandinsky had
expressed anti-Semitic sentiments, he wrote to him that he would
"never again forget . . . that I am not a German, not a European,
indeed perhaps scarcely even a human being . . . but I am a Jew."[53]
Kandinsky's reply, in which he assured him of his love but stated, "I
reject you as a Jew," grieved him and, although they met again once
or twice, the two remained distant for the rest of their lives.[54]

In May 1933, anticipating the Nazis' racial cleansing of the Prussian Academy of the Arts, where he was director of a class in musical composition, Schoenberg left Berlin. Two months later, in a
ceremony at the Liberal synagogue on the rue Copernic in Paris,
formally witnessed by Marc Chagall, he was readmitted to the Jewish fold. "Now that I have returned officially to the Jewish religious
community," he wrote to his friend and pupil Anton Webern, "it is
my intention . . . to do nothing more in the future than work for the

Jewish national cause."[55] Over the next few years Schoenberg devoted considerable energy to formulating proposals for the creation of a "Jewish Unity Party," with an ultranationalist, nondemocratic program. He saw himself as its prophet and, perhaps, leader. Nothing came of these ideas but they testify to his suddenly inspired Jewish political commitment, an engagement that was registered clearly also in Schoenberg's artistic creativity.

The Nazis condemned Schoenberg's music, like that of all "non-Aryans," as "un-German" and banned its performance. Schoenberg reacted with defiance. At the time of his departure from Germany, he was working on the opera *Moses und Aron*, which, he wrote, confirmed his conception of himself as Jewish.[56] His *Kol Nidre*, based on the most solemn Jewish prayer, sung to a traditional tune on Yom Kippur, was composed in 1938 in exile in Los Angeles. Set for chorus, speaker (*Sprechgesang*), and orchestra, it was written in reaction to what Schoenberg saw as the excessive sentimentality of the (non-Jewish) Max Bruch's *Kol Nidre*. The latter remained the more famous rendering of the melody. Jewish music? Certainly in the eyes of the Nazis who consigned both to the realm of *entartete Musik* (degenerate music).

Not Nebbish

Entartete Kunst (Degenerate Art) was the title of an exhibition, sponsored by Goebbels, that opened in Munich in 1937. Supposedly illustrative of the corrosive effects on art of the Jewish and Bolshevik spirit, it included works by many non-Jewish and non-Communist artists, including one or two who had tried to curry favor with the Nazis. The 650 items in the exhibition were hung next to jeering slogans on the walls. It toured Germany over the next three years and was eventually seen by four million people. Among the stars of the show were artists whose life and works were deeply influenced by their Jewish origins and others whose Jewishness was detectable only by Nazi racial taxonomists.

If we reject the Nazi criterion, how might we define the Jewish artist? As in music and literature, the attempt to pin down a uniquely Jewish sensibility has led to palpably absurd conclusions. The German-Jewish artist Hermann Struck boldly declared Rembrandt a Jewish artist on the ground that the "sentiment underlying [his paintings] is Jewish" and Struck added for good measure that "he must have been of Jewish descent."[57] "Once beyond the representational," writes Irving Howe, "the 'Jewishness' of art by Jewish painters becomes an all but meaningless question, dissolved as it now is into the categories of the modern."[58] The sculptor Jacques Lipchitz, recalling his time in Paris in the early decades of the century, remembered anxious arguments over the question: "In Paris . . . we had a society of Jewish artists to which I belonged . . . We often had meetings to discuss the question of what is Jewish art. Did it exist? We concluded that Jewish art was a bit *nebbish*—you know, broken down and melancholy . . . I said that I was not *nebbish* and that it was time others outgrew such a feeling."[59] Whatever view may be taken of the problem of definition, there can be no doubt about the Jewishness of the work of at least one major artist of the period.

Marc Chagall's star has risen and fallen over the past century. With Lipchitz and others, Chagall participated in an exhibition of Jewish artists in Paris in June 1939: he showed *Ma maison natale*, in which a critic found "a grace, a simplicity of popular art, reality modified by poetic dreaming." The picture reminded the writer of Chagall's early works in which he had initiated "a Jewish style in modern painting."[60] A more recent critic, however, dismisses Chagall's work as original only in its subject matter, not its form.[61] This is an ungenerous and inaccurate judgment.

In Paris between 1911 and 1914, Chagall discovered and entered the world of artistic modernism. He was deeply influenced by his Hasidic background and in the "magical chaos" of his canvases returned endlessly to his hometown, Vitebsk.[62] Actually, he was by no means the first Jewish artist to seize on the life of traditional *shtetl* Jewry as subject matter for painting. Maurycy Gottlieb (1856–1879), from Drohobycz, was one of several precursors in this regard. What was original in Chagall's work was not at all his subject matter but on the contrary, what he made of it.

Chagall's early paintings included several versions of *Over Vitebsk* (1914–18), in which an old Jewish pedlar, literally a *luftmensh*, floats over the deserted, snow-decked city; *Die Erinnerung* (1914), in which the old pedlar reappears carrying on his back not a bundle but his entire home; *Newspaper Vendor* (1914), in which a sallow, thin-faced, bearded man in a peaked cap displays an array of papers, including the Yiddish *Moment*; and *Cemetery Gates* (1917), in which what appears to be the angel of death hovers batlike above the Hebrew-engraved gates of the burial ground. Drawings such as *The Jewish Wedding* (after 1910) and *Rabbi of Vitebsk* (1914) are valuable to the historian as social documents of the *shtetl* in its final moments before the shattering blows that began with the First World War. "That this 'Jewish hole,' dirty and smelly, with its winding streets, its blind houses and its ugly people, bowed down by poverty, can be thus attired in charm, poetry and beauty in the eyes of the painter— this is what enchants and surprises us at the same time," was the verdict of the critic Alexandre Benois.[63]

Chagall, however, was more than a nostalgic manufacturer of folksy, fantastical whimsy, though he could produce that, too, in huge quantities, and often on a high level, as in his illustrations of stories by Der Nister (1916) and his many depictions of klezmer musicians. In 1918, having fervently embraced the revolution, Chagall returned to Vitebsk after eleven years of absence and was appointed commissar for artistic affairs. This period of liberated, experimental artistic efflorescence in Soviet Russia was the most tumultuous, but also the most creative, of Chagall's life. Inaugurating the People's Art School in the city, he declared that "the doors to the scientific and artistic holy of holies" would be open to all workers, "these former outcasts of life."[64] Chagall himself directed and taught in the school for two years until political and aesthetic disputes led to his departure. In the early 1920s, he designed for the Yiddish theater in Moscow sets that still exist and that even his critics recognize as probably among his greatest achievements.

In 1923 he returned to France, where he remained until the Second World War. The 1930s were perhaps Chagall's most intensely Jewish decade. In 1931 he traveled to Palestine in the company of Bialik and became preoccupied with biblical themes. In 1935 he visited Vilna, where he attended a conference of YIVO, met Yiddish poets, and drew the Great Synagogue. In 1938 he published a long (not very good) autobiographical poem in Yiddish in the *Literarishe bleter.*[65]

Also in 1938 he painted the *White Crucifixion*, in which a Jew, with a loincloth like a *talles* (prayer shawl), is martyred on the cross, while around him are scenes of pogrom, arson, mayhem, plunder, and sacrilege, from which refugees are fleeing by land and sea. Although Chagall was inspired by contemporary events in Germany, the figures are clearly those of *Ostjuden*, reminiscent of those from Vitebsk in Chagall's early paintings. Benois rightly called this angry, eloquent, terrifying work "a document of the soul of our time."[66]

World, Good Night

After 1933, Jews in the Third Reich were expelled from German culture even before they were forced to leave German territory. Jewish authors could no longer publish books in Germany; actors and musicians could no longer perform, save before fellow Jews; playwrights and scholars were also silenced. Many were driven into exile.

On the evening of Quinquagesima Sunday (the last before Lent) 1933, the night before the ban on public performances by Jews took effect, the Jewish alto singer Paula Lindberg participated in a broadcast concert from the Thomaskirche in Leipzig of Bach's cantata 159, "Sehet, wir geh'n hinauf gen Jerusalem." The concert was one of a series broadcast live throughout Germany. The church, in which Bach had been choirmaster and in which he is buried, was full. Boy choristers wore swastika armbands. The bass aria "Es ist vollbracht" (It Is Fulfilled), ending with the words "*Welt, gute nacht*" ("World, good night"), Lindberg later recalled, "left not only me but many, many who heard the cantata on 19 March, 1933 on the radio, in particular the Jewish listeners, with the definite feeling that this was a *Menetekel*, a kind of sign of the danger that threatened the Jews."[67] "Many, many"—but by no means all, as she later sadly reflected.

To provide cultural production exclusively by and for Jews, the German government in June 1933 permitted the formation of a special body, the Kulturbund Deutscher Juden (later it was obliged to change its name to Jüdische Kulturbund, since Jews were not permitted to call themselves "German"). It operated for most of its history under the control of Goebbels's Ministry of Popular Enlightenment and Propaganda but was accorded a certain autonomy, so long as it followed general guidelines. The organization was founded at a meeting in the Fasanenstrasse Synagogue in Berlin in August 1933, attended by hundreds of artists, actors, musicians, and cultural workers of all kinds, presided over by the prominent drama critic Julius Bab. Each major city with a significant Jewish community had its own branch of the organization. Separate departments were established for theater, music, lectures, film shows, and other activities. At its height, the Kulturbund sponsored three theatrical troupes, an opera company, two symphony orchestras, choirs, and chamber music groups. It also organized lectures and art exhibitions. It employed, at one time or another, 2,500 artists for an audience of 70,000 (probably about half of all remaining adult Jews in the country by the end of the decade) in about a hundred towns.[68]

The organization's head from 1933 to 1938 was Kurt Singer. A small, silver-haired man with a bent for sarcasm, he had been trained as a medical doctor before becoming intendant of the opera house of Berlin-Charlottenburg. The musical director from 1936 to 1941 was the Viennese-born Rudolf Schwarz, former conductor of opera orchestras in Düsseldorf and Karlsruhe. Together with others, these men, under near-impossible conditions, created one of the bravest cultural phenomena of the era.

In the early years the opera and music sections of the Kulturbund performed Mozart and Richard Strauss as well as Handel's oratorios *Judas Maccabaeus, Israel in Egypt*, and *Saul*. "For reasons of tact," as Singer put it, they refrained from performing Wagner.[69] In later years the Kulturbund was not permitted to perform "German music." Exactly what was included or excluded under that rubric, however, was a matter for delicate interpretation. Eventually Bach, Mozart, and Beethoven were placed on the forbidden list. Mendelssohn, however, a non-Aryan by Nazi standards even though a Christian from birth, featured frequently in its programs. Schubert songs with texts by Heine were regarded as sufficiently Jewish to permit their inclusion in Kulturbund programs. And Handel, who had no Jewish blood, was never banned.

Recordings of some of these concerts survive. Sound quality is

often poor but there is a palpable tension that renders them unique
in the history of recorded music. Each player and singer seems to
perform (as any player and singer always must, though few can) as if
this were both the first and last time he or she interpreted the piece.
And the audiences, whose response can often be gleaned even from
the audio records, convey a sense, particularly after November 1938,
that these occasions were the few, precious moments of spiritual
freedom left to them in what was otherwise a caged existence.[70] It is
impossible for any sensitive person to listen to these records without
being deeply moved.

The drama section was headed by Bab, who, in a private letter
in June 1933, insisted that its performances must be so outstanding
"that the Germans would have to be ashamed of themselves."[71] In
October 1933 the Kulturbund's Jüdisches Kulturtheater presented,
as its first production in Berlin, Lessing's *Nathan the Wise*. Over the
next few years the repertoire included Shakespeare, Molière, Shaw,
and Ibsen, as well as plays by Jewish writers (Stefan Zweig, Sholem
Asch, S. An-sky, and others) and/or on Jewish themes. Gradually
censorship tightened. First works by Communists and other anti-
Nazis were prohibited. Then German playwrights such as Schiller
were prohibited on the ground that their performance by Jews was a
sacrilege. Eventually all works by "Aryans" were forbidden.

The Kulturbund provided a means for Jews to continue to explore realms of the mind and spirit. Enforced isolation from the
broader currents of German culture in which they had played such a
significant part was painful. Yet in a sense it was liberating, since the
muses in general were being poisoned by their new masters.

In all the arts, as in life, the Jews were thus being driven into
exile or back to the ghetto.

14

YOUTH

Secret Worlds

Jews were like everybody else, Chaim Weizmann used to say, only more so. Jewish children too were superficially similar to gentiles. Yet the moment one digs beneath the surface one finds differences that arose from the continuing influences of traditional Jewish culture, from the overwhelmingly urban nature of Jewish society, and from the socioeconomic conditions that impelled Jews into a quest for upward mobility through education.

If the daily life of Jewish children was similar to that of others, it was still often expressed in a different language—Yiddish or Judeo-Espagnol. Like others they would be given a pinch in the cheek (*a knip in bekl*) and a caress of the hair (*a glet ibern kepl*). They would listen to similar folk stories, such as "Babele-ber" (Grandmother Bear, a version of "Little Red Riding Hood"), and play similar games—but in their own tongue.

Jewish children in eastern Europe, like those the world over, had their secret worlds of rhymes, riddles, and chants, as in the Yiddish counting song from Warsaw:

> *Eyns-tsvey, politsey.*
> > One-two, police.
> *Dray-fir, ofitsir.*
> > Three-four, officer.
> *Finef-zeks, alte heks.*
> > Five-six, old witch.

Zibn-akht, a gute nakht.
> Seven-eight, good night.
Nayn-tsen, shlofn geyn.[1]
> Nine-ten, go to sleep.

Often these were simply Yiddish versions of nursery rhymes common in many languages, such as "Patshe, patshe, kikhelekh" ("Patacake, Patacake") or "Rode, rode rane," sung to the tune of "Ring a Ring a Roses."[2] Others were composed in Yiddish, such as a much-loved children's poem by Bialik, "Unter di grininke beymelekh" (Under the Little Green Trees):

Unter di grininke beymelekh
> Under the little green trees
shpiln zikh Moyshelekh, Shloymelekh.
> Moyshes and Shloymes are playing.
Tsitsis, kapotelekh, payelekh,
> Tsitsis*, long coats, sidelocks,
yidelekh frish fun di eyelekh. . . .[3]
> Little Jews fresh out of the eggs. . . .

"The Right of the Child to Die"

Making due allowance for the frequent romanticization and mythologizing associated with the Jewish family, it is probably true that most Jewish children encountered a particularly caring and sympathetic atmosphere in their homes. To some extent this can be measured in medical statistics. Infant mortality was lower among Jews than among surrounding urban populations, even allowing for differences in degree of urbanization and social class. In Budapest in the 1930s, Jewish working-class children were much less likely than non-Jewish to die in infancy; similarly in the case of the Budapest Jewish and non-Jewish bourgeoisies.[4] Jewish children had especially low mortality, we are told, "in respect of those gastro-intestinal,

---

* Fringed undergarments worn by pious Jewish males

infectious and respiratory diseases which were avoidable or ame-
nable to treatment with the methods and therapies then known, so
that the greater care of Jews for preserving and restoring the health
of the children could be largely credited with the observed mortality
differentials."[5]

Other data tell a similar story. The Jewish rate of infanticide was
much lower than that of the general population.[6] More Jewish mothers breastfed their children than gentiles. Illegitimacy rates were
lower among Jews. Corporal punishment of children, although still
widespread in the home as in the school, was probably less prevalent
and less brutal among Jews.

Why did Jews behave in these ways? The popular attribution of
such conduct to allegedly traditional moral norms is dubious, given
that it was precisely the less traditional sectors of Jewish society in
which these trends were particularly in evidence. Other possible explanations suggest themselves. The wider use of birth control among
Jews, especially the more modernized, and resultant smaller families
meant that Jewish children could command greater attention from
their parents. As we have already noticed, fewer Jewish fathers
were habitually drunk, especially in countries such as Russia where
alcoholism was a major social disease among gentiles. Possibly also
the powerful tendencies among urbanized, secularized Jews toward
social mobility and delayed gratification extended across generations
and led them to devote greater care to children as an investment in
the future.

Although Jewish children in eastern Europe enjoyed a much
lower rate of infant mortality than the general population, they
suffered many ills associated with extreme urban poverty. More
than half of those in Poland in 1922 were reported to be infested
with vermin. In Lithuania in 1928 more than a quarter exhibited
symptoms of rickets at the age of four to six years.[7] Their predominantly urban environment immured many Jewish children in
densely crowded conditions, often in miserable slums. In Kovno in
the late 1930s only 21 percent of Jewish children slept alone in bed;
the remainder had to share.[8]

In the worst position were orphans, particularly those in the
USSR and Poland in the early 1920s. Many orphanages were grim

places, little more than dumping grounds for abandoned children, often illegitimate births. Other institutions did their best but, with tiny budgets, faced near-impossible odds. The Allatini orphanage in Salonica, for instance, had to turn away several children every year, owing to its accumulated deficit, rendered more acute by an effective halving of the municipal subvention after 1934.[9]

A pioneer of progressive care of orphans was Zinovy Kisselgoff, who headed a Jewish Children's Home in Leningrad and an affiliated National Jewish School. For a time the school used Yiddish as the medium of instruction but that was soon abandoned as few of the pupils knew it well enough. Kisselgoff's dedication and liberal attitude to his wards were widely admired. In Stalinist Russia that did not save him. In 1937 he was arrested. He was released a year later and Shlomo Mikhoels lauded him at a celebratory party, at which, unfortunately, Kisselgoff caught a cold. He died a fortnight later. At any rate, that was the official explanation of his death. Another educational reformer was Vita Levin, director of a school for Jewish mentally ill or retarded children that was founded in Vilna in 1928 to cater for a group for whom the Polish state provided little assistance.

The most famous experiments in Jewish child development took place at 92 Krochmalna Street in Warsaw, where Janusz Korczak headed the Dom Sierot orphans' home. Korczak founded the orphanage in 1912 and designed its building, where he lived in an attic room. Trained as a physician and child psychologist in Warsaw, Berlin, Paris, and London, Korczak articulated what has been called a "passionate, almost religious reverence for the rights of children."[10] "The child," he wrote, "is like a parchment densely filled with minute hieroglyphs and you are able to decipher only part of it."[11]

Korczak called for a "Magna Carta" of children's rights of which the "three basic ones" were:

1. The right of the child to die
2. The right of the child to the present day
3. The right of the child to be what he is[12]

The first of these, arresting and shocking at first sight, in fact indicates his confidence in the ability of the young to confront reality.

He meant that children with terminal illnesses should not be deceived about the nature of their condition (Korczak wrote this passage years before he would lead his charges in a march toward the death camp).

In his stress on juvenile rights, Korczak followed other advanced child psychologists but took their ideas further in his writings and put them into practice in the several children's institutions with which he was associated. In the Warsaw orphanage children were encouraged to take responsibility from an early age to look after themselves, to clean and help in the kitchen, the dining room (where Korczak too worked, clearing away dishes), the library, or tending weaker, younger, or sick children. An elected parliament of the children formulated disciplinary rules. Infringements were adjudicated by a children's court of peers. Though never a member of any political party, Korczak developed some sympathy for Zionism and in 1938 delivered lectures to a seminar of the Marxist-Zionist Hashomer Hatsair (Young Guard) youth movement. His ideas and example exerted wide influence on Jews and on broader Polish society.

Arop Dem Rebbn!

Since the Enlightenment Jews had looked to secular education as a means of gaining an entry to and advancing in gentile society. Emancipation led Jews to embrace the opportunities now available to them to leapfrog into professional and technocratic elites. With the onset of the Great Depression and the consequently straitened domestic economies of Jewish petty traders and artisans, education was seized upon as the most promising escape route toward social survival. At every level, Jews became much better educated than gentiles, even than fellow urbanites, but in the process the schooling of Jews began to lose many of its formerly distinctive traits.

Most European Jewish children in the 1930s attended the *heder* only part-time or abandoned it altogether in favor of secular state schools. In France nearly all did so. In Poland at least 70 percent received their primary education in state schools (lower percentages, sometimes cited, are based on double counting of pupils who attended Jewish afternoon supplementary schools).[13] Higher levels of enrollment in Jewish schools were found in Lithuania, where over 90 percent of all Jewish children enrolled in such schools, and in the Slovak region of Czechoslovakia, where about half of Jewish children attended the seventy or so denominational Jewish elementary schools in the 1920s. But in both countries Jewish schools declined in the 1930s, even though they enjoyed state financial support. In Romania Yiddish schools died out altogether by 1939, though there were sixty Hebrew schools affiliated with the Tarbut network. That network was so beset by financial problems, however, and governmental obstruction was so pervasive that its copresidents in Romania declared in October 1937 that they were entering the new school year "with despair."[14]

The only country in interwar Europe to adopt a systematic, large-scale policy of promoting Jewish schools under state patronage was the Soviet Union. At least half of all Jewish children in Byelorussia and more in Ukraine attended Yiddish-language schools in the early 1930s. Altogether an estimated 1,800 schools using Yiddish as the medium of instruction in the USSR in 1931 educated around 130,000 pupils.[15]

The basis for this policy was not, of course, tenderness toward the Jewish (or any) religion. These were strictly secular schools. They emerged rather as a by-product of the policy of *korenizatsiia*, through which the Soviet regime in the 1920s sought to render itself palatable to non-Russian regions of the country by encouraging local languages and cultures.

Yiddish schools were established mainly in *shtetlakh* and cities in the former Pale with large Jewish populations. In Minsk in the 1920s attendance at such schools was not wholly voluntary: indeed, in 1924 Yiddish-speaking children in the city were ordered to attend Yiddish schools, though not all complied.[16] About half of the Jewish children in the city attended Yiddish schools in the late 1920s; the parents of the rest preferred to send them to Russian (not Byelorussian) schools that their parents thought would improve their life chances in Soviet society.

The main driving force in the growth of Soviet Yiddish schools was, in fact, less Jewish enthusiasm for Yiddish in itself than the extreme reluctance of Jewish parents in Byelorussia and Ukraine to entrust their children to schools in which the medium of instruction was Byelorussian or Ukrainian, both widely regarded by Jews as uncultured, peasant tongues. In Russia, where Russian-language schools were now open to Jews without restriction, Yiddish schools were found in the 1930s only in Crimea (at that time part of the Russian Federation) and in the Jewish Autonomous Region of Birobidzhan.

Classes in Soviet Yiddish schools were held on the Sabbath and on festivals, though in Minsk in the late 1920s many children refrained from writing on Saturday and attendance notably declined on the high holy days.[17] After 1929, however, antireligious pressure intensified: children were forbidden to bring *matzah* to school during the Passover holiday and instead were given bagels.

The curricula of these schools had little Jewish content. Antireligious propaganda and slogans were common: "Arop dem rebbn!" ("Down with the *rebbe!*"), "Against *matzoh*, against the *seder*, against Passover clothes!"[18] Jewish history was dissolved into general history and presented within a Marxist-Leninist perspective. Yiddish language and literature were taught but the number of hours per week devoted to these decreased in each grade—from nine in the first grade, to four in the sixth. In grades seven through ten, Yiddish was still used as the medium of instruction but the language and literature were not taught at all, replaced by Ukrainian or Byelorussian.

Set texts included the classic Yiddish writers, Shalom Aleichem, Mendele, and Peretz, as well as living authors, mainly Soviet or leftist, such as Dovid Bergelson, Dovid Hofshteyn, and Moshe Kulbak, but also some others such as Sholem Asch—at any rate until he was denounced as a "fascist mediocrity." Elye Falkovitch lost his teaching position at the Moscow Pedagogical Institute in 1938 for advocating the inclusion of Bialik and Asch in the literary heritage.[19]

The schools took care to steer clear of any implication of nationalist separatism. Moshe Levitan, director of the Bureau of Jewish Education of *Evseketsiia* until its dissolution in 1930, stressed that Yiddish education in the USSR was fundamentally different from that offered by "petty bourgeois" Yiddishists elsewhere. Yet historians have concluded that the Soviet Yiddish schools "had a nationalizing effect" and that their pupils "felt their Jewishness more than the Jewish children who did not attend Yiddish schools."[20]

From the early 1930s, however, the Soviet Yiddish school

network declined. A number of reasons have been proposed: the liquidation of *Evsektsiia*, which deprived Yiddish schools of patrons inside the ruling elite; continued movement of Jews from *shtetlakh* into big cities outside the former Pale, especially Moscow and Leningrad; and the purges of the late 1930s.

One reason, however, seems to have been paramount: the reluctance of large numbers of Jewish parents to send their children to Yiddish schools. A Russian-born visitor to the USSR in 1936

> saw how his uncles and cousins, whose language was Yiddish, spoke to their children and grandchildren in Russian. When asked, Why? They replied: "If we speak to them in Yiddish, the children will be sent by local school authorities to Yiddish-language schools, but if we talk to them in Russian, they can claim that their native language is Russian and they can enter a Russian-language school. There is more *takhles* [material benefit] in a Russian than in a Yiddish school."[21]

This lack of enthusiasm for Yiddish was both rational and natural. The path to success in Soviet society, particularly for those who aspired to rise in the new elites, was overwhelmingly through the Russian language. After the abandonment of *korenizatsiia* from 1933 onward, Russian-language schools became widely available in Byelorussia and Ukraine. In consequence, Jews, especially in large cities, quickly abandoned Yiddish schools. In Kiev, for example, three closed in 1935 because parents chose Russian-language education instead.

In July 1938 the Byelorussian Supreme Soviet abruptly terminated the official status of Yiddish in the republic and closed all Yiddish schools and cultural institutions. The local Yiddish newspaper in Minsk, until then a champion of Yiddish schools, suddenly started complaining that "enemies of the people" had been "trying to enforce artificial Yiddishization" and had been "compelling Jewish parents to send their children to Jewish schools."[22] In the school year 1938–39 about seventy-five thousand pupils remained in Yiddish schools in the USSR, an estimated 20 percent of Soviet Jewish children of school age. Yet some future seems to have been seen for them by educational planners in Ukraine, if only to judge by the fact that school textbooks continued to be published in the language until 1941.[23] Yiddish pedagogical institutes still functioned in Kalinindorf and Dnepropetrovsk in southern Ukraine, as did Yiddish sections in the institutes in Moscow and Odessa. But by this time the writing was on the wall for Yiddish education in the Soviet Union.

"Poland Will Provide"

The most highly developed Jewish educational provision—even though, like the Soviet Yiddish system, it catered to a minority of Jewish children—was to be found in Poland. By contrast with the Soviet system, however, it came into being without state support, largely as a result of private and communal initiatives.

Indeed, Jewish education in Poland had to contend with considerable obstruction from the state. This was in spite of article 9 of the Minority Treaty, imposed on the reborn state by the Allies in 1919, which stated that "Poland will provide in the public educational system in towns and districts in which a considerable proportion of Polish nationals of other than Polish speech are resident adequate facilities for ensuring that in the primary schools the instruction shall be given to the children of such Polish nationals through the medium of their own language."[24] In the matter of minority school funding, as in other spheres, the treaty was honored mainly in the breach. The only step toward implementation conceded by the government was the creation in areas of high Jewish concentration of *szabasówki* or *shabasurka* primary schools, which, unlike other state schools, were closed on the Sabbath. Instruction in these schools was in Polish, not Yiddish, and the curriculum was identical to the general system. In almost every respect indistinguishable from other schools, the *szabasówki* accelerated the polonization of Jewish youth rather than fostering a minority culture. They were phased out in the 1930s; by 1938 only about sixty remained.[25]

Meanwhile, in 1934, the Polish government announced at the League of Nations that it would henceforth refuse all cooperation with international organizations in the system of minority

protection. Although Britain and France declared that such unilateral treaty repudiation was invalid, there was nothing that they
could or would do about it and thereafter the treaty was, in effect,
defunct.

At least two-thirds of Polish-Jewish schoolchildren (primary and
secondary) in the mid-1930s studied in state schools. In Galicia,
where the Jewish population, especially in Cracow, was highly polonized, the percentage was as high as 95 percent. The lowest levels of
Jewish attendance at state schools were to be found in the least polonized parts of the country, the Kresy (eastern provinces), though
even there a majority attended state schools.

In response to the demand of many parents for Jewish forms of
education, three main types of school emerged in Poland and Lithuania: religious, Yiddish-secular, and Zionist-Hebrew. Each was associated with a particular ideological outlook and each drew on a
specific sector of Jewish society.

The largest of the three was the religious system associated with
the Agudists: Khoyrev for boys and Beys Yankev for girls. In 1937–
38 the 462 Khoyrev schools (not counting *yeshivot*) enrolled 57,000
and the 425 Beys Yankev schools 35,000 pupils.[26] These, however,
were all elementary schools or afternoon classes, often little more
than dressed-up *hadorim*. Jewish religious subjects, including Bible,
Talmud, Jewish history, liturgy, all taught in Yiddish, dominated the
curriculum, though under state pressure some secular subjects were
also taught, generally in Polish. Khoyrev was relatively decentralized
and there was little in the way of coordinated financial control. After
1929 the schools suffered from a collapse in financial support from
America. Both Khoyrev and Beys Yankev spent less per pupil than
the secular school systems. It is a telling indication of the relative
importance attached by the orthodox to girls' education that average
per capita expenditure in Khoyrev boys' schools was more than 60
percent higher than in Beys Yankev.[27]

Next in size was the Hebraist Tarbut system, with 543 schools
and 48,000 pupils in 1937–38. As in the case of the religious
streams, a large number of these schools (276) were merely afternoon classes. Tarbut was oriented mainly to the General Zionists. The language of instruction was Hebrew but, on government

insistence, Polish language, literature, and history were taught in Polish. The curriculum included instruction in the Bible by secular teachers who tended to accentuate the national-historical aspects of scripture. Unlike the religious schools, Tarbut emphasized physical training, reflecting the Zionist value placed on the regenerative effect of labor. Whereas the model for emulation proposed by the religious schools was the rabbi/scholar, Tarbut held up the ideal type of the *halutz* (the "pioneer" in the Land of Israel). Children in these schools tended to come from somewhat better-off homes, reflecting the middle-class base of much support for Zionism. The Tarbut schools accordingly derived a greater part of their revenue from tuition fees than did other Jewish schools.

Third in size was the secular-Yiddishist TSYSHO (*Tsentrale yidishe shul organizatsye*) network, associated with the Bund and Left Poalei Zion. Its 169 institutions, of which 65 were afternoon schools, educated 16,000 pupils. Yiddish was the language of instruction for most subjects but Polish language and literature occupied a prominent place in the curriculum. Hebrew was an elective in higher grades. Jewish religious subjects such as Bible and Talmud were not offered at all and Tsysho rejected demands by official inspectors that religion be included in the curriculum.[28] The first Yiddish secondary school in Poland, the Realgymnasium in Vilna, with three hundred pupils in 1938–39, was TSYSHO's greatest pride. In Warsaw, with its 375,000 Jews in the late 1930s, TSYSHO failed to establish a Yiddish high school. TSYSHO's historian, one of its former leaders, blames the city authorities for repeatedly refusing permission.[29] As a result, the only secondary school in the Polish capital at which Yiddish was taught was the independent Zofia Kalecka Gymnasium for Young Women.

The TSYSHO system faced hostility on all sides. The left-wing Com-Bund opposed Yiddish schools on the ground that the Jewish working class should not set itself apart from its Polish proletarian brethren. The orthodox despised TSYSHO as a nest of irreligion, the Zionists viewed it as a dangerous rival, and the government feared it as a nursery of revolution. Zionist representatives in parliament and municipalities sometimes voted against funding for Yiddish schools since they regarded them as emanations of the Bund.

Official inspectors often rejected the qualifications of teachers, ordered expensive repairs to buildings, required that governing boards
conduct their meetings in Polish rather than Yiddish, or even closed
schools down altogether.

The TSYSHO schools suffered from chronic financial difficulties
since they catered mainly for the poorest sections of the population. Whereas Tarbut derived 86 percent of its income from fees,
TSYSHO's income from this source yielded only 30 percent of its
revenue. The Great Depression accentuated TSYSHO's financial
plight and in 1932 the teachers' college in Vilna, which had trained
the system's instructors for the previous decade, had to close permanently (it had earlier been shut down for a time by the government
on the pretext that it was a breeding ground for Communism).

Like the *melamdim* of earlier generations, teachers were poorly
remunerated in all Jewish schools. Wages were often paid short or
in arrears. Surviving archives contain piteous letters from teachers,
pleading for a minimal, regular salary that would save them from
toppling into penury. In larger centers, such as Warsaw, they were
able to organize into unions and threaten rather than supplicate, but
the results were rarely satisfactory. TSYSHO teachers, in particular, were paid a pittance and often were close to starvation.[30] There
were sometimes angry exchanges between Communist teachers who
accused Bundist TSYSHO administrators of using foreign contributions to line their own pockets.[31]

Even in schools where Yiddish or Hebrew was the main language
of instruction, there is evidence of creeping polonization. A former
pupil in the Hebrew Gymnasium of Cracow, for example, recalls
that Polish was, in fact, the dominant language of the school. In
this private school, not part of the Tarbut network, Hebrew was the
medium of instruction only in Jewish subjects. Among themselves,
students spoke exclusively in Polish.[32]

Although school attendance in Poland was compulsory between
the ages of seven and fourteen, a considerable minority of children
did not attend school at all or did so only sporadically. Many thousands of Jewish children in the late 1930s were among the nonat-
tenders. In Ostrog, for example, a survey in 1937 found that out of
262 children of school age only 109 were attending school. Of the

remainder, 117 were absent owing to extreme poverty, since, according to the report, they had no clothes or shoes.[33]

Poverty forced many Jewish children in eastern Europe into work at an early age. In Subcarpathian Ruthenia, boys would take up apprenticeships at twelve, often working twelve- or fifteen-hour days. In Warsaw and other big cities in Poland and Lithuania, Jewish children often slaved for long hours as needleworkers or running errands for parents who worked as tailors or dressmakers in their own homes.

In Poland, as elsewhere in eastern Europe, schooling generally ended by the age of fourteen. Although more Jews than non-Jews received secondary education, still only a small minority did so: about 20 percent in 1939. Polish-language high schools were the choice of most Jews. Even in Vilna only 873 Jewish children attended a Jewish gymnasium in 1930 whereas 1,940 attended Polish private and public ones.[34] Tarbut operated ten high schools in Poland in 1937–38, Tsysho just two. Khoyrev had none at all, unless one counts *yeshivot*. Although there were several private Jewish high schools, most of these too taught in Polish and followed a curriculum with little Jewish content. These statistics highlight the limits of Jewish secondary education in interwar Poland.

Altogether, an estimated 172,000 pupils were receiving some form of Jewish religious education (in religious schools, *hadorim*, and *yeshivot*) in Poland in the late 1930s.[35] These figures are subject to a measure of uncertainty and interpretation but, since the total number of Jewish children of school age was about half a million, it is certain that a majority of them received no Jewish religious education whatsoever outside the home. For religious Jews, education was *the* critically important guarantee of the survival of Judaism. By this criterion, Judaism in its foremost European stronghold was clearly in retreat.

Civilizing Mission

Outside Poland Hebrew schools enjoyed little success and were often opposed by the orthodox. When the Hebrew Reformrealgymnasium was established in Munkács in 1925, the Munkáscer *rebbe* held a special ceremony with black candles in order to anathematize all associated with it. His campaign of curses against the school continued for years. When a typhus epidemic broke out in the town in 1934, the *rebbe* declared that the *Realgymnasium* was responsible. The school's directors sued him and, after lengthy litigation, the *rebbe* lost. He died shortly afterward.

In the Balkans traditional Jewish education was weaker than in Ashkenazi areas of Europe. The *meldar*, the Sephardi analogue of the *heder*, was generally no less rough-hewn in its physical conditions and instructional methods. It too was in decline by the 1930s. Higher-level religious education had dwindled and was found only in a few centers.

The dominant Jewish educational force in the region in the early twentieth century was the secular system of the Alliance Israélite Universelle, the supposedly international, in fact largely French, philanthropic organization based in Paris. Its schools in the Balkans, the Middle East, and North Africa represented a kind of imperialist *mission civilisatrice* of French Jews among their oriental brethren. The French Jews, while organizing Jewish schools for others, did not believe in them for themselves: most French Jews attended public schools.

"The World Will Hear the 'Shema Yisrael' Longer than 'Heil Hitler' "

In Germany most public elementary education was organized on a confessional basis (Catholic or Protestant). Many Jewish families therefore sent their children to the eighty private Jewish schools, which, in 1932, enrolled about a quarter of Jewish schoolchildren. Several of these schools attained high academic standards, for example, the Philanthropin in Frankfurt, founded in 1804, which provided education from kindergarten all the way to the *Abitur* (university entrance exam). In 1936 Jewish children were ordered to be segregated from non-Jewish in public elementary schools. By 1937 more than half of the forty thousand Jewish schoolchildren remaining in Germany were being educated in Jewish schools. Until March 1939 such schools continued to be subsidized by the state.

In Austria the Chajes Realgymnasium, named after its founder, the former chief rabbi of Vienna, earned a reputation as one of the best schools in the capital. In the central European educational system, the *Realgymnasium* had a more modern curriculum than the classical gymnasium, seeking to achieve a balance between the humanities and sciences. The only Jewish secondary school in Vienna, the Chajes, unlike most public schools, was coeducational.

Dan Porat, whose family moved to Vienna in 1933, attended the school. This was a world away from his *heder* in Kuty. Instruction was in German and Porat also had to learn Latin, his fifth and sixth languages (Yiddish, however, was frowned on here). The school had a strongly Zionist ideological flavor. Theodor Herzl's *Jahrzeit* (anniversary of death) was commemorated each year. Musical education included rousing Zionist marching songs.

Although it was not a secular school, and in spite of the *mezuzot* on the doors, religious instruction was limited. Otto Hutter, another former pupil, nevertheless recalls studying biblical passages from Joshua, Judges, Samuel, and Isaiah, learning the liturgy, and singing traditional religious songs such as "Shomer Yisrael, shemor she'erit Yisrael" and "Elijahu hanavi, Eliyahu Hatishbi, bimherah yavo elenu."[36] The prevailing atmosphere of the school was "Jeder soll nach seiner eigenen Façon selig werden" ("Let everybody attain heavenly bliss in his own fashion").[37] One boy brought ham sandwiches to the school every day.

Modern Hebrew language and literature were emphasized, though the municipal council, which, together with the Ministry of Education and Religion, had supervisory authority over private schools, sought for a time to curtail Hebrew instruction on the ground that it was "too taxing" for students.[38] The school had to struggle to be permitted to continue to teach Hebrew for four or five hours a week. Though it succeeded, a third former pupil, Moses Aberbach, maintained that in this sphere "the school never equaled the achievements of the Tarbut schools in Poland and Lithuania."[39]

In such Jewish schools pupils felt sheltered from the threateningly anti-Semitic atmosphere of general society. In the summer they would joyfully embark for the camp at the Keutschachersee in Carinthia, where they would play games, swim, and dance the *hora* round a campfire. Otto Hutter remembers fondly: "For city dwelling, sheltered twelve-year-old Jewish kids, to be faced on arrival with a rough Hessian palliasse and a pile of straw for stuffing as mattress on primitive wooden bunks in the small wooden huts, was an experience that taught us what it was to live primitively."[40] For many children this was the only vacation they ever experienced.

Like most Jewish schools, the Chajes suffered from endless financial difficulties. In spite of Jewish emigration, classes were large, sometimes between forty and fifty students, especially after the German annexation of Austria in March 1938 and the subsequent expulsion of Jewish pupils from non-Jewish schools. According to Sonia Wachstein, a teacher at the Chajes in the late 1930s, school life as a result "was hard and lacked compassion for the weaker or troubled students."[41]

The headmaster, Dr. Viktor Kellner, was dedicated heart and soul to the school. But teachers and pupils criticized his harsh personality. One recalled that his idealistic inculcation of Jewish values was "combined with ruthless and vicious attacks on students who were often insulted in class."[42] The "Direx" struggled against increasing odds to balance the school's budget. Adverse conditions undoubtedly brought out the martinet in him. The growing impoverishment of the Jewish community made it ever more difficult for parents to pay fees of forty schillings a month. Poor families were granted a reduction but even they had to pay something. In some cases that proved beyond their means. Aberbach recounts one occasion in the middle of a class when a boy whose parents had not paid the reduced tuition of five schillings was humiliatingly sent home by Kellner.[43] Wachstein related that, on the other hand, if Kellner was dealing with a child of wealthy parents, "he would always point out that this student . . . had to pay more than the highest fee, which he called 'stupidity money.' "[44]

At the school's last graduation ceremony, in 1938, in a building now compelled to fly swastika flags and policed by brownshirts, Kellner redeemed himself with a brave speech, declaring: "I don't know what the future holds for you. But I can assure you of one thing. The world will hear the 'Shema Yisrael' longer than 'Heil Hitler.' "

Numerus Nullus

All over the continent the university offered both glittering opportunities and frustrating obstacles to Jews. In Russia, where in 1917
higher education had for the first time become open to all on the
basis of merit, Jews flooded into the universities both as students
and professors. By 1935 there were 74,900 Jewish students in Soviet
institutions of higher education, many times more than in Poland,
which had a similar-sized Jewish population. Jews, although only
1.78 percent of the Soviet population, constituted 15.5 percent of
those holding university degrees in 1939. They formed 11 percent
of the student body in Soviet universities, to be found particularly at
the most prestigious ones in the Russian Federation.[45]

In Germany, by contrast, a *numerus clausus* for "non-Aryans" of
1.5 percent of admissions was set in universities in 1933 and Jewish
professors were dismissed. After 1935 Jews were forbidden to take
doctorates. And in 1938 they were barred from university altogether.

In Poland an active campaign by anti-Semites sought to limit
admission of Jews to higher education. In 1938–39 just 4,113 Jewish
students were studying at universities, less than half the number of
five years earlier. The proportion of Jews in the student population
had declined since 1921–22 from 25 percent to 8 percent.[46] In some
universities there was a drastic absolute as well as relative fall in
their number: at the Stefan Batory University in Vilna, for example,
from 1,192 in 1930–31 to 400 in 1938–39.

Restrictions on Jewish entry into Polish universities forced some
Jews to study abroad. Similar conditions in Hungary led the Jewish community there to set up a special fund to support about 250
students studying elsewhere. But when such students returned to
their home countries they often found that they faced a complex
bureaucratic process of "nostrification" (recognition of their foreign
qualifications). In Poland in 1937–38, only forty nostrifications were
granted to Jewish students.

Enforcement of the *numerus clausus* was aggravated by harassment of the reduced numbers of Jewish students who managed to secure admission to universities. In 1935 the Politechnika engineering

college in Lwów announced that Jews would be required to sit on specially designated benches. In spite of bitter struggles, such "ghetto benches" had become widespread in Poland by 1938–39.

The ghetto benches reflected a larger social reality: a young Jewish academic in Warsaw in the 1930s later recalled that "there was virtually no contact between Jews and non-Jews, especially in social life. . . . I conducted a poll among my students with an 'Aryan' friend. . . . It came out that my Jewish students knew no Poles except for the janitor. . . . And the results were the same for the Polish side. . . . None of my 'Aryan' colleagues attended my doctoral examination [traditionally a ceremonious public event in European universities]."[47]

Although many Jewish students were drawn from the middle class, others lived in abject poverty. A survey of the Jewish students' mutual aid organization at the Warsaw Politechnika in the mid-1930s showed that nearly half lived with their families; a third shared a rented room; another 9 percent "rent[ed] a corner in someone's room"; and 12 percent were so-called flyers who had no home whatsoever: "They sleep as they can, every night in another room belonging to some colleague."[48] Against this background of "growing pauperization of the academic masses," one observer detected a mood of obsessive pessimism. "The conditions of study are very difficult, and, furthermore, they see no hope in the future, no prospect."[49]

Little Nests

In this maelstrom of economic uncertainty, pervasive hostility, and ideological confusion, generational conflict increased, parental authority declined, and values, instead of being imprinted by the family or traditional sources of morality, were often sought elsewhere. Youth movements, still a relatively recent social phenomenon, offered disoriented young people a haven of safety and an arena for self-expression. Often parents encouraged children to join, viewing the movements as a productive way to channel youthful energy. But traditionalists worried. In 1933 the rabbi of the small town of

Szydłów, in southern Poland, wrote to the local authorities "on be-half of the complaining parents and the entire Jewish community" to ask for help in dealing with "the impudence of the young" and calling for measures to prevent them joining the Hehalutz (Labor-Zionist) movement "as it leads to the corruption of the youth, which is prohibited by our religion."[50]

In principle, youth movements may be a means of transmitting the values of the parental generation to children or a vehicle for youth revolt—or a mixture of both. But in the 1930s, according to Jeff Schatz, "it was the rule rather than the exception that younger Jews belonged to different political movements than did their par-ents." And he adds: "The divide between children and parents was deepening into an abyss."[51] He refers here specifically to Poland but the same was true throughout Europe.

Like so much else in these societies, youth movements were gen-erally organized along religious, political, and often ethnic lines. In the Soviet Komsomol and among leftist movements in other coun-tries, Jews participated on an equal basis with non-Jews. In Italy too, until 1938, they were welcome in the Fascist youth movement, which many Jews joined. Elsewhere, however, barriers were rising.

In Germany the model for most youth movements had been the Wandervogel, founded in the late imperial period as a romantic, nature-loving group that stressed hiking and camping. The Wan-dervogel were sexually segregated and former members sometimes speak of "a homoerotic tinge to the movement and the relationships between its members."[52]

During the First World War, völkisch (nationalist) youth move-ments tended to exclude Jews from membership. As a result, young Jews sought refuge in a Jewish movement, Blau-Weiss (Blue-White). Founded in Breslau in 1908, it spread throughout Germany. It was romantic, idealistic, antimaterialist, and oriented toward Zionism. Its founders maintained that Jewish young people faced special problems: they were "in general physically less capable and more nervous than youth in general. A relatively greater portion suffers from the damaging influences of big-city life."[53] Like the Wandervo-gel, Blau-Weiss stressed the virtues of contact with nature and orga-nized country hikes. After the First World War some of its members planned to emigrate as a group to Palestine, hoping, in the words of Norbert Elias, one of its leaders, to become "the germ . . . of the future tradition and custom and culture" of a new Jewish nation.[54] Although Blau-Weiss was wound up in 1927, its example affected many other Jewish youth movements in Germany and beyond.

After 1933, when nearly all German youth movements were amalgamated into the Hitler Youth, Jewish ones were permitted to continue, since "non-Aryans" were prohibited from belonging to the Nazi organization. Zionist youth groups enjoyed a surge in membership, although their meetings often took place under the eye of bored Gestapo agents.

By the late 1930s, even where Jews were admitted to non-Jewish movements, they were often discriminated against. In Romania, for example, the Straja Ţării, founded by King Carol, was the sole youth movement permitted to function after December 1938. Every high school pupil was automatically enrolled. One Jewish member later recalled:

> We wore uniforms and were organized in paramilitary fashion. Every class was a "century" (based on the name of a Roman military unit), divided into "nests" of six and "little nests" of three. In our class of forty plus there were only six Romanians, three Poles, one Ukrainian, one German and the rest Jews. The century chief had to be an ethnic Romanian, the nest chiefs Christian; only the little nest chiefs could be Jewish . . . I made it to little nest chief and was quite proud about it.[55]

But as the poisonous cloud of anti-Semitism settled over the continent, reaching Italy in 1938, Jewish youth tended to seek refuge in their own movements.

Each Jewish political party had its youth movement (sometimes more than one): Bachad (orthodox), Betar (Revisionist-Zionist), Bnei Akiva (Mizrachi), Dror, Gordonia and Habonim (Labor Zionist), Hashomer Hatsair (Marxist Socialist–Zionist), Tsukunft (Bundist), and many others. Often new recruits joined for reasons other than ideology, especially attraction to the opposite sex (even some orthodox movements mixed boys and girls).

We're on Our Way!

Many youth movements as well as the medical organizations OSE and TOZ organized summer camps to which city children would be sent to enjoy sports, contact with nature, and fresh air. The success of such camps gave rise to the idea of a permanent establishment for a rotating population of the sick or needy. The Medem sanatorium, established by the Bund at Miedzeszyn, not far from Warsaw, in 1926, was primarily intended for Jewish children suffering from or threatened by tuberculosis but it broadened admission to poor children in general, including a few from non-Jewish workers' families. The sanatorium attracted general admiration: "a veritable Garden of Eden for children," the Warsaw paper *Moment* called it.[56] In 1937 it cared for a total of 695 children, each for an average of three to four months, though many more applied. The sanatorium was partly supported by the Joint. For a time the Warsaw City Council and the Polish government also contributed but by 1937 almost all official support had been withdrawn.

In 1936 the sanatorium was publicized in a documentary film, *Mir Kumen On* (We're on Our Way), directed by Aleksander Ford, with a screenplay by the leftist, Polish, non-Jewish writer Wanda Wasilevska. The film contrasted the wretched lot of street children in Polish towns with the modern, hygienic facilities of the sanatorium, the democratic self-government of the children, their lessons and recreations, and their socialist spirit. The title and signature tune were taken from the stirring anthem of the Bundist children's organization, SKIF.

> *A yontev makht oyf ale merk,*
> > Let marketplaces fill with fêtes,
> *un fayern tsint on oyf berg!*
> > And fires be lit on every peak.
> *Mir kumen—shturems on a tsam,*
> > We're coming—storms without end
> *fun land tsu land, fun yam tsu yam.*
> > From sea to sea, from land to land.

Mir kumen on, mir kumen on!
> Here we come, yes, here we come!

Un fest un zikher undzer trot,
> Our gait is firm, strong and sound,

Mir kumen on fun dorf un shtot.
> We come from villages, from towns.

mit hunger fayern in blik,
> With hunger gleams in our eyes,

mit hertser oysgebenkt nokh glik!
> With hearts that long for happy days,

Mir kumen on, mir kumen on.
> Here we come, yes, here we come!

Mir geyen ale fest un greyt,
> We march forcefully and ready,

vi likhtik flatert undzer freyd;
> Our banners fluttering with joy,

mir shlogn fayer oys fun shteyn
> We fashion fire out of stone,

un ver s'iz yung muz mit undz geyn!
> And anyone young must join us.

Mir kumen on, mir kumen on!
> Here we come, yes, here we come![57]

The film was banned in Poland on account of its allegedly subversive content, in particular a scene in which children of non-Jewish striking workers were shown being welcomed into the sanatorium. A protest campaign in the press failed to overturn the decision. The film was, however, shown abroad and enthusiastically received. In the United States it was released under the title *Children Must Laugh*. But the New York censor also interfered with it, albeit for a different reason from his Polish counterpart: he ordered the elimination, on ground of indecency, of all views of a mother breastfeeding a baby.[58]

The children in the film no doubt spoke and sang in a vocabulary, an ideology, and a screenplay that was in large measure prescribed to them by their elders. But we have some other utterances by young people who speak to us, unmediated, in their own voices.

Speaking for Ourselves

Children's voices can be heard through a remarkable collection of essays composed in February 1939 by pupils, aged between seven and fifteen, in a Hebrew school in Jagielnica, a *shtetl* in the Tarnopol district of eastern Galicia. The essays were reproduced and bound in a booklet for presentation to the chairman of the town's *landsman-shaft* in America. Handwritten in childishly clear Hebrew letters, the essays ranged in subject from biblical heroes such as Abraham, Samuel, or Jeremiah (by younger writers) to historical or literary subjects such as "The Golden Age in Spain" and "Haim Nahman Bialik." A few of the older children chose to write on contemporary problems. Shimshon Tauber addressed the question "What is the cause of anti-Semitism?" Bat-Sheva Shapira wrote on "The Jews in the Contemporary Period." Their observations echoed common-places of the adult world around them but what is striking is the depressed tone of these essays. Both these fifteen-year-olds evinced a deep sense of pessimism about the prospects for a collective life for Jews free of hatred by surrounding peoples.[59]

Rawer personal articulation of adolescent gloom is to be found in the archive of three hundred autobiographical essays that survive out of an original nine hundred that were submitted to YIVO in competitions held in the 1930s.[60] Most were from Poland but entries were received from at least seven other countries. The competitors were a self-selecting group, marked by certain special characteristics: most tended to be psychologically introspective, intellectually active, secularist, and politically leftist or Zionist. Although submit-ted to the Yiddishist YIVO, a quarter of the surviving entries were written in Polish, another indicator of the rapid polonization of young Polish Jews in the period.

The format must have steered competitors to produce what they thought might impress or move the judges. Nevertheless, making all due allowances, the impression left by most of these narratives is of unstudied, naïve records of childhood and adolescence. A few are more sophisticated and some strive for effect, but by and large they are artlessly innocent accounts of family relations, schooling, friendships, romantic yearnings, intellectual interests, social and political engagements, Jewish-gentile relations, efforts to find work, and musings on the purpose of human existence and suffering. Often submitted semi-anonymously, the statements veer from confessional mode to self-analysis, self-critique, kvetching, and, in some cases, howls of anguish. Their very simplicity gives them an authority as historical evidence, as well as a human dignity that autobiographies of mature writers can hardly hope to attain.

The predominant motifs are pain, struggle, poverty, illness, hunger, conflict, frustrated ambitions, stunted lives. Yet what is striking and moving is the burgeoning life force that infuses most of these young people: they plan, hope, dream of a brighter future. These are juvenilia of would-be intellectuals—"would-be" because, by and large, their thirst for a life of the mind was thwarted at every turn: whether by the ultra-orthodox father who would not let his daughter read secular books; or by the mother who said her daughter was better employed learning how to use a sewing machine; or by the Polish high school director who insisted that all pupils must attend classes on Saturdays; or by brute economic forces that turned youngsters who might, in other circumstances, in other times and places, have become scholars, teachers, or librarians into street people or refugees.

The narratives cast a shocking light on the hardships endured in these short lives: flotsam on the waves of the massive social upheavals of the period after 1914, the writers struggled to maintain mental equilibrium. Many underwent successive ideological conversions. Indeed, one conclusion to be drawn from these essays is that what counted for the authors was less the content of particular ideology than the sense of belonging that commitment to a group might offer. Only thus can one explain the readiness of so many of these deeply thoughtful and idealistic youngsters to flit to and fro, from Communism to Poalei Zion to Bundism to Revisionist Zionism.

These are young people who search for meaning in their lives with an earnestness and seriousness of purpose that belie the degradation of their everyday existence. They read voraciously, sometimes secretly by candlelight, the great classics of Yiddish literature and of contemporary European fiction translated into Yiddish and Polish.

Romain Rolland's *Jean Christophe* is the most often mentioned and plainly most loved book of the memoirists. The great Bildungsroman is obviously, in some cases explicitly, a model and inspiration.

Some of the essays read like short stories by Tolstoy. A seventeen-year-old girl, "Hanzi," blind in one eye, shares with the reader her girlish thoughts of love for the son of a cantor:

> Like me, he didn't stay in town all year but went off to study in a *gymnasium*. When I met him I had Nemilov's book *The Biological Tragedy of Women* in my hand. Together we read sections of it and afterwards discussed each section individually. He was very mature and gifted and I loved him more for his talents than for his looks. I looked for opportunities to run into him. He knew nothing of this, and I certainly didn't interest him. I was so lowly in my eyes that I couldn't imagine anyone falling in love with me.[61]

Another contestant, "the Stormer" writing in the spring of 1939, describes his long trek to the Black Sea Romanian port of Constanța, his arrest there, his experience of being dumped back over the Romanian-Polish frontier, and his forced return home. "My journey," he reflects, "left a deeper impression on my life than anything else. . . . I'm now looking for a way to emigrate from Poland. But all of my efforts run into a brick wall. . . . My future is as dark as a moonless night."[62]

On the vexed question of Polish-Jewish relations, the essays provide telling testimony: of the devotion to Polish literature, history, and national ideals of which young Jews educated in Polish state schools were capable; of the rejection that most encountered from gentile society, particularly in the late 1930s; of their sense of unrequited love and consequently hurt and embittered feelings; of the growing alienation, desperation, and sense of homelessness that ensued.

15

UTOPIAS

Hachsharah

As life for Jews in central and eastern Europe became more perilous, utopias that offered the prospect of extricating large numbers of them from their predicament became ever more alluring. Zionism, Communism, and territorialism each claimed to offer a solution to the problem of Jewish homelessness. Each acquired devoted followers, burning with zeal and determination to realize their dream.

The Zionist movement in the 1930s veered, in roller-coaster fashion, from success to failure, from glowing optimism to rancorous despondency. The arrival in Palestine of 164,000 Jewish immigrants between 1933 and 1936, mostly from Poland and Germany, enlarged the *yishuv* (the Jewish community in the Land of Israel) to over 400,000, not far short of a third of the population. A continued influx on such a scale would have produced a Jewish majority by the end of the decade. In 1936, however, Palestinian Arabs rose in revolt against the mandatory government and the Jewish National Home. The rebellion assumed major proportions and represented a serious challenge to British authority in the country.

The British responded with the time-honored recourse of governments faced with acute policy dilemmas: they appointed a committee of inquiry. The Royal Commission on Palestine, headed by Earl Peel, reported in 1937 that the mandate was unworkable. The Palestinian Arabs would not accept any further Jewish immigration and demanded immediate independence. The Zionists were determined that immigration must continue, with a view to the early establishment of a Jewish state. The only solution, according to the commissioners, was partition of Palestine into Jewish and Arab states.

The British government initially accepted the report in principle. But all the Palestinian Arab political parties rejected it. The Zionists, divided among themselves, temporized. Many of them, particularly the followers of Jabotinsky, rejected partition outright: they demanded a Jewish state in the whole country. Others, including the president of the Zionist Organization, Chaim Weizmann, and many of the Labor Zionist leaders, favored partition but sought a larger territorial base than the tiny Jewish statelet proposed by the Peel Commission.

Impressed by the scale and persistence of the Arab revolt, the mandatory government began in 1936 to limit Jewish immigration to a "political high level." The number of immigrants dropped precipitously, from 66,000 in 1935 (the largest number in any year before 1948) to under 11,000 in 1937. Large troop reinforcements were brought to Palestine and the British resorted to brute force in an effort to suppress the rebellion. With war clouds looming over Europe, they began to have second thoughts about the practicality of partition, fearing that to attempt to implement it against the will of the Palestinian Arab majority would rouse up the entire Arab world against Britain.

As conditions for Jews in Europe became more desperate, Zionist frustration with British restriction of Jewish immigration grew. Revisionist Zionists engaged in reprisal attacks against Arabs in Palestine and, together with freelance entrepreneurs, began to organize illegal migration of Jews from Europe to Palestine. The traffic had started in a small way in 1934 but grew larger from 1937 onward. The mainstream Zionists at first discountenanced such activities, advocating a policy of *havlagah* (self-restraint) in Palestine. They urged the British to implement partition, pressed for increases in immigration schedules, and organized the most dedicated of their young followers in Europe in *hachsharah* (training) farm schools in Germany and elsewhere to prepare for a future life as agricultural pioneers in Palestine.

The German government, far from opposing them, actively encouraged *hachsharot* in the hope of stimulating Jewish emigration.

The Berlin authorities persisted in this view in spite of frequent hostility from rural people in the neighborhood of such farms, who, indoctrinated by Nazi propaganda, feared that Jews would import syphilis and racial defilement to the countryside. More than twenty such farms operated in Germany by 1938, training over five thousand men and women.

Hachsharot were established in more than a dozen other European countries, providing agricultural education to over forty thousand students by 1939. Given the anti-Semitic climate in much of the continent, the Zionists found it prudent to locate the schools mainly in democracies such as Britain, the Netherlands, Denmark, and Sweden. But some were set up elsewhere. In Yugoslavia, for example, about two hundred *hachscharisten* were working in 1935 in six farm schools and two artisanal training workshops, one in Zagreb, the other in Osijek.

Although most such schools were Zionist in orientation, other Jewish political parties and organizations, ranging from territorialists to Agudists, also established them. In the summer of 1938 ORT opened a camp at Stadlau, outside Vienna, where 350 pupils took industrial and agricultural training courses with a view to emigration to Paraguay (they did not, however, succeed in reaching their destination). ORT planned in 1939 to expand such activities in Poland, Lithuania, Romania, and France.

A non-Zionist farm training school, supported by assimilationist elements in German Jewry, opened in 1936 at Gross-Breesen, an estate north of Breslau in Silesia. Local Nazis objected to the establishment of the "Jew farm" but the authorities overrode the opposition and approved it.[1] About a hundred trainees arrived, the majority of them boys. Parents of girls were reluctant to apply, though sexual abstinence was one of Gross-Breesen's "iron laws."[2] Like the Zionist farms, Gross-Breesen taught animal husbandry, crop rotation, carpentry, and so forth, aiming to turn city slickers into rustics. Girls did some agricultural work but were assigned mainly to household duties, cooking, cleaning, baking, laundry, and darning.

Unlike its Zionist competitors, Gross-Breesen shunned Jewish nationalism, inculcating an ethos that combined pride in Jewish tradition and respect for German culture. Food was not kosher and religious practice was "liberal and minimal."[3] Reflecting German Jewry's profound attachment to *Bildung*, each day ended with a short performance of classical music. There were weekly concerts, as well as play readings and lectures by visitors, including, on one occasion, Martin Buber, who led a discussion on the subject "Love thy neighbor."

The founders of Gross-Breesen hoped to organize the collective emigration of all the pupils in the school to a new settlement overseas. They pinned their hopes on the Paraná region of Brazil but, after lengthy negotiations, failed to secure Brazilian government approval for their plan. One former student, however, managed to get to the area and set up a plantation, named Nova Breesen. Others, with the help of the Joint, moved to a farm in Virginia and to a Jewish Colonization Association settlement, Avigdor, in Argentina. The remainder scattered to other destinations, including Australia, Kenya, and the Dutch East Indies.

In 1934 the Amsterdam Jewish Refugees' Committee established the Werkdorp [work village] Nieuwesluis on a polder, land reclaimed from the sea, at Wieringen on the Zuider Zee. The land was made available, rent-free, by the Dutch government, and Dutch companies donated equipment. The Werkdorp's primary purpose was to offer agricultural education, training in horticulture, building, furniture making, and metalwork, as well as domestic science for girls, in order to prepare young refugees, aged between sixteen (later fifteen) and twenty-five, for emigration to Palestine. Eventually 360 hectares of land were made available. The enterprise enjoyed financial underpinning from the Dutch Jewish community, the Joint, the Council for German Jewry, and, in the early years, payments from German Jewry.

In March 1934 the first group of eleven boys and four girls arrived in the wooden barracks of the forlorn landscape, "dark specks on the vast, treeless, still only sparsely inhabited new Polder," as Gertrude van Tijn, of the Amsterdam committee for Jewish refugees, described their new habitat. Eventually the "bleak collection of austere buildings, outlined against an immense horizon" was transformed into "a miniature garden city, surrounded by growing trees, each building the center of multicolored flowerbeds and shrubs."[4]

After some argument, it was agreed by the supervising committee that the kitchen would be strictly kosher. Living conditions were Spartan. Initially girls were directed to household duties but under the influence of a Zionist emissary from Palestine the policy changed: boys were required to share in household duties and girls to join work in the cowshed.

Wieringen maintained strict separation between the living quarters of the sexes and a so-called "sexual zone" of fifty kilometers was enforced around the farm. But emancipated young people refused to put up with such restrictions. As one girl from Berlin recalled, "all of us were in our early twenties and found a solution. We exchanged addresses of low-priced Amsterdam hotels where young couples could meet on weekends."[5] Altogether at least a thousand German-Jewish refugees received training in Wieringen, generally of about eighteen months.

Unlike *hachsharah* farms under the direct control of the Zionists, Wieringen recruited refugees of all political colors. The language of daily intercourse was German, not Hebrew. Political activity was forbidden, the students being required to sign a pledge to abstain from any demonstrations. Notwithstanding the rule, ideological dissension, even fighting, broke out in the Werkdorp between Zionists and non-Zionists, especially Communists. Gertrude van Tijn later recalled that "the presence of an active communist cell in the Werkdorp posed a real threat to its very existence in view of the stringent rules laid down by the host government and the official Dutch anti-communist policies. Yet, expulsion of the group was, of course, inconceivable. It would have meant deportation to Germany and almost certain death."[6] The problem resolved itself when the Communists decided to leave Wieringen to fight in the Spanish Civil War.

By the time the first group of would-be emigrants was ready to leave in 1936, immigration restrictions were already making it difficult for them to gain entry to Palestine. Precious certificates were preferentially distributed to young Zionists judged to be in greatest danger; those in the freedom of the Netherlands hardly qualified. Eighty-five students nonetheless succeeded in gaining admission to Palestine by October that year and a similar number emigrated to the Americas, Africa, Australia, or elsewhere.

The Zionists' failure to persuade the British to relax immigration restrictions in Palestine after 1936 left many members of *hachsharot* in a limbo at the end of their courses. They were trained for a future as *halutzim* (Zionist pioneers) on which they were now forbidden to embark. In many cases, their admission to countries in which the *hachsharot* were located had been conditional on their departing once they had completed their training, but a large number had nowhere to go. If the Zionists found it difficult to secure entry to the Jewish National Home even for this limited number of committed and qualified young people, how could the movement plausibly claim to offer a solution to the plight of the broad masses of the Jews in Europe?

KOMZET

The Communists shared with the tsars, the Zionists, and many others the diagnosis that Jewish concentration in commerce was socially unhealthy and that the remedy was settlement on the land. In the Russian Empire before 1917, only 2 percent of Jews were engaged in agriculture. The Soviet regime decided to correct the balance of what they saw as an unnatural Jewish social structure by moving Jews from *shtetlakh* to agricultural settlements. At the very time when the rest of Soviet society was about to set out on a great forced exodus from the countryside to the city, Jews were therefore being officially encouraged to move in the opposite direction.

From 1924 onward, the Joint joined with ORT in what became known as Agro-Joint. In partnership with the Soviet government, Agro-Joint promoted Jewish agricultural settlement, partly in existing areas of Jewish agriculture in Byelorussia and partly in newly established cooperative farms in southern Ukraine and Crimea. The Soviet government created two bodies, KOMZET (the Committee for Rural Resettlement of Jews) and OZET (Society for Settling Working Jews on the Land), to direct the enterprise. In 1926, at the first Congress of OZET Mikhail Kalinin, the Soviet head of state, declared: "The Jewish people stands before a great task: to preserve its nationality." To this end, he argued, a substantial part of the

Jewish population must be transformed into a compact, agricultural mass settlement of several hundred thousand souls.[7]

The new settlements were eventually organized into five "Jewish national districts" (*evreiskie natsional'nye raiony*): Kalinindorf, Stalindorf, and Naye-Zlatopol in southern Ukraine, and Fraydorf and Larindorf in Crimea (see map, opposite page). External support for the farms in Byelorussia ceased in 1930 as a result of the collectivization drive, but Agro-Joint was permitted to continue to support those in Ukraine and Crimea until 1938.

A former settler recalled the dismal conditions her family encountered upon their arrival in Fraydorf:

> It was a desolate, uninhabited area, an endless steppe of tall grass. In the center of the steppe stood a lonely broken-down shack, half-filled with water which had dripped down through the holes in the roof. It was the only shelter available in which to spend the night. . . . We made beds out of fresh grass and straw and lay down to sleep on the ground. . . . In the middle of the night my mother uttered a terrified scream. A mouse had entangled itself in her hair. Thus the ten of us spent the first day in our new home.[8]

Every family received a shack, two cows, chickens, and pigs. Eventually they built small cottages out of *saman* (clay bricks mixed with chopped straw that had been dried in the sun). Nearly all the settlers were Jewish though there were a few Germans and Ukrainians among them, some of whom learned to speak Yiddish. The main crop was grain but they also cultivated vineyards and orchards.

Yiddish schools opened in the main towns of the national districts. Yiddish newspapers appeared and amateur drama troupes performed. "Ours was a real island of Judaism [*sic*], which functioned 100 per cent in the Yiddish language. The Jewish villages were permeated with a warm Jewish atmosphere," wrote the same settler.[9] In four of the five districts, however (Kalinindorf was the exception), Jews remained a minority and use of Yiddish, as a result, was limited.

Religious expression was not encouraged on the farms. *Kashrut* was rarely observed and pig-breeding was specially encouraged.

Jewish National Districts in Ukraine and Crimea, 1939

■ Jewish settlements

Dnieper

UKRAINIAN SSR

●Dnepropetrovsk

Krivoi Rog●

Stalindorf ■

■ Fraydorf

Naye-Zlatopol ■

■Friling

Kalinindorf ■ ■ Fraylebn
Emes ■ ■ Nayvelt
Kaganovich

●Kherson

●Odessa

Sea of Azov

Larindorf Kadima
Yudendorf ■ ■ Fraylebn
Fraydorf ■
Ikor ■ Friling Naylebn ■ Rotenshtot
■Lenindorf

■Kheyrus

Kerch●

CRIMEA ■ Beys Lekhem

●Simferopol

(RSFSR)

Sevastopol●

●Yalta

N
W E
S

Black Sea

0		50 miles
0	50	100 kilometers

Map 2

None of the settlements had a synagogue. On the other hand, older settlers often lit candles on Friday night. All the settlements observed the Sabbath. And in many places an informal *minyan* would gather for Sabbath services. An antireligious activist complained in 1931 about the "high percentage of religious resistance" among settlers in the Dzhankoi district of Crimea.[10]

Kalinindorf had its own klezmer band and the Soviet-Jewish farmers, like the Zionist *halutzim*, had their songs, but in Yiddish, not Hebrew:

> *Kegn gold fun zun, geyt oyf mayn gold fun veytsn.*
>> Toward the golden sun springs my golden wheat.
> *Kegn gold fun zun, geyt oyf mayn goldn glik.*
>> Toward the golden sun springs my golden joy.
> *Naye horizontn rufn mikh un reytsn,*
>> New horizons call me and beckon,
> *naye lider zing ikh, yidisher muzik.*
>> I sing new songs, Jewish music.

> *Geyt di arbet freylekh, fun gantsfri biz ovent.*
>> The work goes happily from morn to night.
> *Zun iz mayn hudok un feld iz mayn fabrik.*
>> The sun is my lyre, the field is my factory.
> *Nekhtn shkheynim vayte, haynt shoyn azoy noent,*
>> Yesterday distant neighbors, today so close,
> *ukrayner poyer, yiddisher muzhik.*[11]
>> Ukrainian farmers, Jewish peasants.

Even in this cocooned environment, however, Yiddish was fading away. As in the big cities, settlers preferred to send their children to Russian rather than Yiddish schools. In the Crimea they read the regional, Russian-language party organ, *Krasnyi Krym* (which gave good coverage to local Jewish news[12]), rather than local Yiddish papers, which began to fade away in the late 1930s.

The Jewish settlements were among the few sections of Soviet agriculture that, for the most part, embraced rather than resisted collectivization at the end of the 1920s. In general, collectivization of Jewish farm cooperatives went ahead relatively smoothly. After collectivization, each family was permitted to keep some livestock and a small amount of land, often as much as three acres, as a kitchen garden and orchard. In many cases formerly all-Jewish co-operatives simply turned into all-Jewish collectives. In Byelorussia several of the settlements were in any case collective from the out-set. In other places, conflicts erupted between Jews and non-Jews on newly established joint collectives when Jews refused to work on the Sabbath.

In 1929 the Odessa party sent Gershon Shapiro to work as a party official at a Jewish farming colony, Friling (Springtime), in the Odessa oblast, a hundred kilometers from the city of Odessa. Shapiro came from a desperately poor small-town background in Volhynia. Between 1919 and 1926 he had served in the Red Army and in a Soviet border guard unit. In 1920 he had been purged from the Communist Party, accused of having "idealized Poalei Zion."[13] But he expressed appropriate remorse and secured absolution. In 1922 he was readmitted to the party as a candidate member and in 1925 as a full member. After a year's training in a Communist Party school in Odessa, he obtained employment at a metalworking fac-tory. There he was made responsible, as a party member, for dealing with the affairs of "minority" employees. About a third of the eight or nine hundred workers were Jews. Unlike the gentile workers, they were mainly new employees, former pedlars and petty traders. They spoke Yiddish among themselves, read Yiddish newspapers, and visited the Yiddish theater. Shapiro organized cultural events, song recitals, lectures, and recitations for them.

Shapiro's mission at Friling was part of the great collectiviza-tion program for Soviet agriculture initiated by Stalin. He was one of twenty-five thousand trusted, socially conscious, urban party workers who were sent out to the countryside to overcome rural resistance to collectivization. They were known as the *dvadtsatipiati-tysiachniki* (twenty-five-thousanders).

Shapiro was instructed to take charge of a credit cooperative that dealt with the affairs of Friling and ten surrounding settlements. He was told that, as the only party member in Friling, he would be held responsible for the entire political, economic, and cultural life of the settlement. Although he was assured that the assignment would be entirely voluntary, he knew there was only one possible answer.

When he arrived at Friling, he encountered primitive conditions. The only substantial building in the place was an elementary school. The settlers had moved to Friling in the mid-1920s from three declining *shtetlakh*. Each family had been granted ten to fifteen hectares of land but most were in debt. The cooperative credit bank that he was supposed to head turned out to have no readily available funds, save those provided by ORT. All the houses in the colony, as well as the livestock, horses, and agricultural machinery, had been purchased with ORT money. Agronomists from ORT had helped the settlers to operate productively. Two years earlier they had agreed to form a cooperative that would use tractors and combine harvesters from a nearby Machine Tractor Station. Shapiro's task, like that of other party workers sent into the countryside, was to push through the complete collectivization of the settlement.

His autobiographical account, written in the 1970s, of his experiences and actions at Friling displays a certain retrospective ambivalence. On the one hand he takes pride in what was accomplished. On the other he evinces discomfort with what he candidly admits was the degree of coercion involved. At Friling collectivization evidently encountered some opposition from a truculent minority of individualists. "I have my little piece of land and my own business. I know when I need to plough and sow," insisted one. Shapiro tried to respond with reasoned argument. But in the end, he admits, there were "other methods": economic and social pressures of various kinds.[14] In Friling, as in the other Jewish settlements, opposition was overcome relatively easily and there was no resort to force.

One day at an advanced stage in the campaign, Shapiro visited the editor of the Yiddish newspaper in Odessa and chatted with him about life in the colony. In the course of the discussion, the editor asked him how many kulaks (rich peasants) had been unmasked in Friling. When Shapiro told him there were none, he was advised to go back and find some. He did as he was told. On his return, communal assemblies took place and two men held to be exploiters were denounced and expelled from the colony. During the famine that accompanied collectivization, Friling was ordered to hand over the greater part of its produce to the state. The colonists, as a result, were reduced to near-starvation. Most of the 481 settlers (as of 1931) stuck it out, in spite of all the difficulties, and were still at Friling a decade later.

Although trumpeted as a triumph of Soviet planning, the entire Jewish agricultural settlement project in the USSR was heavily dependent on external support, mainly from the Joint and ORT. By 1938 Agro-Joint had spent $17 million on 218 collective farms, housing 13,250 families, in Ukraine and Crimea. The enterprise also enjoyed the support of a network of Communist front organizations in several countries. The most important was IKOR (*Idishe Kolonizatsie Organizatsie*), which raised funds in the United States and elsewhere, including several European countries.

Thanks to the aid from overseas, the settlements were relatively advanced in their techniques, highly mechanized, and, by Soviet standards, productive: 150 of them were electrified. Some of the residents, particularly women, engaged in small-scale artisanal work such as hat and beret making, knitting, and the production of soft toys and brushes.

In the late 1930s, however, the effort to settle Jewish farmers in Ukraine and Crimea went into reverse. One reason was the abolition of the category of *lishentsy:* those formerly assigned to this category were no longer subject to restrictions on social advancement and many former *lishentsy* were among those who migrated from rural districts back to urban areas. The population of the Jewish national districts declined as a result of net emigration. In the three districts in Ukraine the number of Jewish residents fell from 30,700 in 1931–32 to 19,730 by 1939.

In 1938 the agreements with the Joint and ORT were wound up by the Soviet government. This was not exactly a unilateral decision, since the Joint had decided two years earlier to terminate its activities in the USSR. But by this time, at the height of the Stalinist terror, no Soviet politician who valued his head could advocate continued cooperation with foreign charitable organizations based in capitalist countries. In April 1938 Jacob Tsegelnitski, a Soviet citizen who had served since 1923 as plenipotentiary representative of ORT in the USSR, was arrested by the NKVD. Within a few months all Joint and ORT activity in the Soviet Union had ceased.

Jewish agricultural settlement in the USSR has recently received serious academic attention and more sympathetic appraisal than in the past.[15] By one comparative standard it might be judged a success. At its peak the Soviet effort could boast 150,000 Jews settled in 250 farming settlements: this was much greater than the number of Jews settled on the land in Palestine—just 89,000 in 1936. The total amount of land in Jewish ownership in Palestine in 1939 was 383,350 acres; the Soviet government by then had allotted over a million acres to Jewish settlement.

Exit, Pursued by a Tiger

Meanwhile, in 1928, the Soviet government had gone further and designated the remote area of Birobidzhan, on the Amur River, adjacent to the border with Manchuria, for Jewish settlement. About thirty-six thousand square kilometers in size, Birobidzhan was slightly larger than mandatory Palestine. The first 628 colonists arrived in 1928 and settled in rice plantations. By 1934, 12,000 Jews were living in Birobidzhan out of a total population of 52,000.

In that year the territory was elevated to the status of Jewish Autonomous Region. The object, declared Semen Dimanshteyn, the senior party official in charge of Jewish affairs, was to "strengthen the productivization of the Jewish poor."[16] A further twenty thousand settlers arrived over the next four years. But after the long trip on the Trans-Siberian Railway many were dismayed at the lack of preparation or planning that they found upon arrival. In the absence of permanent housing, they lived in *zemlianka* (dugouts) or mud huts. Towns had no sewage or public lighting. Hunger and disease were rampant. A majority of the pioneers left, discouraged, after a few months.

During the purges of the late 1930s, most of the leading figures connected with the project were arrested, accused of Trotskyite conspiracy, espionage, sabotage, or "bourgeois nationalism." The local party chief, Matvei Khavkin, had won the favor of Stalin, who reportedly announced after meeting him, "This Jew is smarter than most."[17] But in 1937 Khavkin was forced to admit in a self-criticism session that he had been a member of the Trotskyite opposition in the 1920s. He was alleged to have held sumptuous banquets amid general shortages and was accused of "toadyism, pomposity, political arrogance and intrigue."[18] His leadership style was likened to that of "an insulted *shtetl* synagogue elder."[19] Perhaps most incriminating of all, he was reported to have greeted a comrade with the words *Gut shabbes* (Good Sabbath).[20]

Khavkin was relieved of his position, expelled from the party, declared an enemy of the people, and arrested by the secret police. His wife was accused of trying to poison the Moscow party chief, Kaganovich, with homemade *gefilte fish* when he came to dinner during his visit to Birobidzhan in 1936. She too was arrested and was consigned to a mental asylum.

In 1938 KOMZET and OZET were wound up and the organization of settlement in Birobidzhan was placed under the direct control of a department of the secret police. Altogether, out of 319 delegates to the second Congress of Soviets of Birobidzhan in 1936, 227 had been arrested by the end of 1938 and of these 116 were shot. The region's only Jewish policeman was reported in 1937 to have been eaten by a Siberian tiger.[21]

The elimination of the Birobidzhan leadership coincided with the arrests of the three most prominent figures concerned with Jewish issues in the Soviet Communist Party: Moyshe Litvakov, Semen Dimanshteyn, and Ester Frumkin. These events need not necessarily be interpreted as evidence of a policy of state-sponsored anti-Semitism. The Jews were one of many minority national groups that found themselves victimized during the Great Terror. All the same, the fates of these Jewish Communists offered a stark warning of the dangers of any kind of specifically Jewish politics in the USSR and demonstrated that the Soviet utopia, like the Zionist one, faced a bumpy road to realization.

In spite of the purges, the autonomous region remained in existence, a Yiddish newspaper continued to appear, and a Yiddish theater performed in the main town. The local literary magazine trumpeted, in terms strikingly similar to those of contemporary Zionist propaganda, that the region was transforming "tailors, shoemakers, and carters" into physically fit, politically aware, and culturally engaged agricultural laborers.[22]

The third Soviet five-year plan had forecast the immigration of 130,000 Jews to Birobidzhan between 1936 and 1940. But far fewer arrived and many left after just a short time. The government allocated a record sum of 46.5 million rubles for colonization work in Birobidzhan in 1939.[23] Yet altogether in that year Jews numbered no more than 18,000 out of the 109,000 inhabitants and only 8 of the 64 collective farms in the region were Jewish. Settlers who remained gravitated from collective farms to towns. By 1939 three-quarters of Jews in Birobidzhan lived in towns. Just 4,400 lived in rural settlements.

So many settlers sought to return to European Russia that the secret police took special measures to prevent such an exodus. An official report in 1940 explained that the settlers included people who "did not measure up to the physical and moral qualities required for a sparsely populated area: ill people, invalids, egotistic grabbers and so forth."[24] Stalin later complained that the Jews were "natural traders" and that Jewish settlers in Birobidzhan had stayed only two or three years and then scattered to the cities.[25]

Birobidzhan aroused fierce controversy among Jews outside the Soviet Union. It was roundly attacked by the Zionists. The Joint refused to provide any support. On the other hand the World ORT Union decided to contribute funds for the construction of marble, furniture, and haberdashery factories, a brickworks, a sawmill, and basket-weaving workshops. Jewish Communists throughout the world celebrated the establishment of the Soviet "Jewish homeland." In the United States a support body, known as Ambidjan (American Birobidzhan Committee), was formed. In Britain, the chief whip of the Labour Party in the House of Lords, Lord Marley, became a fervent advocate of the autonomous region. He visited Birobidzhan, published laudatory accounts of what he had seen, complete with photographs of smiling Jewish pig farmers, and toured the United States to raise money for the cause. But in 1938 Ambidjan and IKOR were compelled to cease their activities in the USSR for fear of endangering their contacts there.

This Land Is Our Land

Some foreign Communists, lured by the prospect of the autonomous Jewish homeland, emigrated to the Soviet Union with a view to settling in Birobidzhan. And not only Communists. In Subcarpathian Ruthenia in 1935 "hundreds of families" of poverty-stricken Jews registered to move to Birobidzhan—as the Zionist Organization noted with displeasure.[26]

The World ORT Union helped Jewish refugees with applications to the Soviet authorities for settlement. For 1936 they agreed to allow ORT to organize the immigration from abroad of two hundred families. The Soviets set three conditions: the immigrants were required to take Soviet citizenship immediately upon crossing the frontier; they had to undertake to stay in Birobidzhan for at least three years; and upon receiving a Soviet entry visa, each applicant had to pay two hundred dollars. In return each immigrant family would receive tickets from the Soviet frontier to Birobidzhan. Upon arrival there, the local authorities would provide housing and all necessary work tools.[27]

Applications for 269 immigrants in 1936 were presented. Most came from graduates of ORT schools in Poland or Lithuania. Some were from German refugees and others from unemployed workers in western Europe and elsewhere. The approval process was laborious and, in particular, security checks by the NKVD took a long time. Eighty immigrants set off from France and more there applied to go. Thirty-two families went from Los Angeles. Others arrived from Argentina.

Altogether, an estimated 1,500 immigrants from abroad arrived but in 1938 the region was closed to settlement from outside the USSR. Most of the overseas immigrants in any case left Birobidzhan after a brief sojourn. Of those who remained, many were arrested and sent to labor camps and some were shot. The Yiddish writer Dovid Bergelson, on his return to the USSR in 1934, had initially envisaged living in Birobidzhan but he never settled there, though he wrote several works praising the project.

Among the immigrants in 1932, together with his wife and three sons, was Abraham Koval, native of a small *shtetl* near Minsk, who had emigrated to the United States in 1910 and settled in Sioux City, Iowa. Once established in Birobidzhan, he became a Stakhanovite (hyperproductive) worker as a carpenter. He wrote to supporters in America that he had "no words to express the joy which we experienced when we received the deed to our land, assigning this land to our collective in perpetual ownership. . . . We are proud of this deed which is printed in golden letters in our Yiddish tongue." Abraham's sister went to visit the family in Birobidzhan and was reported to have returned to Iowa City "overbrimming with enthusiasm" over what she had seen.[28] One of Abraham's sons became a champion tractor driver in Birobidzhan. The two others did not stay long in the Far East, pursuing a more characteristic Soviet-Jewish path of upward mobility. They enrolled as students at the Mendeleev Institute of Chemical Technology in Moscow. One of the two, George, was recruited, upon graduation, by the Soviet intelligence service and by 1939 was in the final stages of specialist training as a spy.

Overseas settlers were particularly suspect to the Soviet authorities and several suffered accordingly during the purges. Ilya Blecherman, a native of Brisk (the Yiddish name for Brest-Litovsk), who had emigrated to Argentina and arrived in Birobidzhan in 1931, was lucky. A secret policeman who had known his family in their original home in Brisk warned him that he was liable to arrest. He advised him to disappear and take a job in a sawmill in the forest where nobody would know who he was. He survived.

Straight for the Wailing Wall

Not all Jewish immigrants to the Soviet Union headed for Birobidzhan. A large group of far-left Jews from Palestine had returned to Russia in the 1920s, many of them settling in the Jewish colonies in Crimea. Gershon Shapiro records meeting one of them who arrived in 1928 and became chairman of a *kolkhoz* not far from Friling. After 1933 a few non-Communist refugees from Nazi Germany sought admission to the USSR. In 1934–36 the Agro-Joint organized the immigration of seventy German-Jewish doctors. The operation was facilitated by the Commissariat for Public Health, whose head, Grigory Kaminsky, was the brother-in-law of the Russian-born, American head of Agro-Joint, Joseph Rosen. The distinguished medical historian and theorist Richard Koch, warned of his impending arrest in Frankfurt in 1936, accepted an invitation the following year to move to the USSR. He was not a Communist but took Soviet citizenship and remained in the Soviet Union for the rest of his life. Until 1935 all foreigners who settled in the USSR automatically received Soviet citizenship. Thereafter, amid a rising tide of paranoia and xenophobia, bureaucratic barriers against naturalization were erected even for strict party-liners.

The Polish-Jewish Communist Moshe Zalcman was among the ideologically driven immigrants to the Soviet Union. In 1933 he was overjoyed to learn that he had received formal permission from both the French Communist Party and the Soviet authorities to live in the USSR. At a farewell reception in Paris a South American comrade, recently returned from a visit to the Soviet Union, took him aside and gently suggested that he reconsider his decision. An astounded Zalcman merely smiled. "May you never regret it," were the man's parting words.[29]

Armed with a forged French passport, Zalcman crossed Europe by train, and shed tears of joy upon attaining the Soviet frontier. In Moscow he visited the Lenin Mausoleum, "like a pious Jew," he later wrote, "newly arrived in the Holy Land who heads straight for the Wailing Wall."[30]

In Moscow he encountered a small knot of fellow Communists from his region of Poland. Like small-town Jews who found themselves in Paris, New York, and other big cities of emigration, they formed a kind of *landsmanshaft*, although informally and circumspectly, since any such association might automatically become suspect in Stalinist Russia.

Many years afterward Zalcman recounted the stories of some of his friends: one, a veteran Communist who had played an important role in the formation of the Polish Communist Party, had been sent by the party in 1927 to study in the USSR. He was later assigned to run a giant tractor station. In this position he saw at close hand the terror of agricultural collectivization. He told the newly arrived Zalcman: "It's harder to be a Communist here than abroad."[31] His wife advised him to be more discreet. But he was arrested in 1937 and murdered by the NKVD. His wife, taken away shortly afterward, was killed too.

Another member of the group, who had founded the local party branch in Zalcman's hometown, had moved to the USSR to avoid arrest in Poland. He remained a true believer in the cause. In 1937 he was nevertheless expelled from the party, arrested, and shot. His wife was sent to a camp in Siberia, where she died. His brother, meanwhile, had been dispatched to work for a provincial newspaper. He too had been horrified by what he witnessed of forced collectivization. He returned to Moscow and brazenly handed in his party card. He too was arrested and shot.

Yet another member of the group had been assigned to work in Ukraine. He was charged with Ukrainian nationalism and suffered the same fate. In the end nearly all the members of Zalcman's Moscow circle were devoured by the system to which they had dedicated their lives.

After a few months in Moscow, Zalcman was given a job in a clothing factory in Kiev, where he noted to his surprise that workers were paid much less than victims of capitalist exploitation in similar factories in France. With his wife, who followed him from Paris, and their newly born son, he adjusted to the depressed living conditions of the Russian proletariat in the period of Stalinist "primitive accumulation" in the mid-1930s. He volunteered to fight in the International Brigade in Spain but was not accepted. As the Soviet Union descended into the bloodbath of the Stalinist terror, he slowly began to shed some of his youthful illusions.

A Swahili Phrasebook

Territorialism never commanded the mass support enjoyed by Zionism and Communism. Yet the apparent logic of its argument that a home *somewhere* must be found for a homeless people kept it alive. The Freeland League's indefatigable leader, Isaac Steinberg, conducted peripatetic freelance diplomacy around the world and succeeded at least in being taken semiseriously by the foreign ministries of several countries.

In 1938 Steinberg approached the Australian government requesting approval for Jewish refugee settlement in the East Kimberleys region of Western Australia, where his organization had been offered a large tract of land for purchase. An international Freeland conference in Paris in March that year authorized Steinberg to visit Australia to negotiate with the government.

When he reached Perth in May, he was received by the premier of the Western Australian government, J. C. Willcock, who expressed conditional support for the scheme. Steinberg visited the proposed settlement area, extending to more than ten thousand square miles (about the same size as mandatory Palestine) between the Ord and Victoria rivers. Steinberg thought up to seventy-five thousand Jews might be settled there on ranches and farms. After further discussions with the authorities, Steinberg believed he had secured their approval for his project. On September 1, 1939, he cabled the Freeland offices in London and Warsaw: "Mazl-tov! Today government officially accepted principle Jewish colonization Kimberley. Proposes discuss conditions after approval Commonwealth [that is, the Australian federal government in Canberra]. Inform friends."[32] Steinberg's interpretation of the government's position, however, was over-optimistic and was overtaken by larger world events on the date of his telegram.

Other schemes for Jewish settlement overseas met similar fates. In London the Plough Settlement Association, formed by members of long-established Anglo-Jewish families, sought to organize the migration and placement in Africa of trained Jewish agriculturalists from Germany. The potential settlers were mainly men in their twenties, many of them from the training farms at Gross-Breesen and Wieringen.

In June 1938 proponents of the scheme held a preliminary discussion with Colonel C. F. Knaggs, a Kenya settler who had been appointed agent of the Kenya government in London. Knaggs was not unsympathetic. He drew attention to the high costs involved but said he did not "anticipate any racial opposition provided suitable

people are chosen and taught to live as respectable citizens."[33] The
British government approved plans for 150 settlers to go to East
Africa and money was raised to support their transport, equipment,
and maintenance for up to a year. The migrants were to be apprenticed to white farmers in Kenya for a year, after which they would
be helped to establish themselves on land of their own.

In January 1939 an advance group of fifteen left England for
Kenya. Walter Fletcher of the rubber firm Hecht, Levis & Kahn,
and chairman of the sponsoring group, promised that a local reception committee would provide all necessary gear, though he recommended that, in addition, "a suit of khaki or white drill . . . dark
glasses, a sun helmet, or double Terai" would be useful on the boat
near the equator. He further advised that "rope-soled canvas shoes
and a few tropical weight aertex underclothes" would be essential
and "an English-Swahili dictionary and a phrase-book would be a
good thing too."[34] The colonial secretary, Malcolm MacDonald, sent
his "good wishes for success and happiness." The organizers gave an
undertaking to the government "that no purely racial enclave will
be formed."[35] They also promised that the settlers would not move
into towns. A representative of the Plough Settlement Association
announced: "We have promised the Government not to form Jewish Communities in Kenya but to settle the refugees on different
places so that they may be absorbed into the general community.
Eventually we shall have a central training farm."[36] As with Zionists
in Palestine and Communists in Birobdzhan, the notion of redeeming Jews from the evils of urban life dominated the thinking of the
Plough Settlement benefactors.

The emigrant group included five young men who had passed
through Gross-Breesen. Among these was Gerald G. Frankel (formerly Gerhardt Fraenkel), who wrote back enthusiastically from
Kenya in July 1939 to his London sponsor, reporting that "we have
no doubts that we shall be able at the end of this year to run farms
of our own, because we have learnt here how to work pyrethrum
[a natural insecticide], cattle and pigs and because we know from
Germany how to grow the different kinds of cereals, flax, and potatoes." He inquired forlornly whether it might be possible to bring his
parents from Germany to Kenya: "They would not have this horrible

threat of a war over their heads all the time, but would be a great help to us in building our farm up."[37] Many similar letters, pleading for the admission to Kenya of family members, reached London.

The influential white settler community in Kenya, however, did not welcome the prospect of any large-scale Jewish influx. A generation earlier, in 1903–4, their opposition had thwarted Joseph Chamberlain's proposal for Jewish settlement in Kenya (the so-called Uganda project). In March 1939 the governor of Kenya noted that the Plough Settlement Association's subscribed share capital of ten thousand pounds was "clearly inadequate" to allow for the admission of further refugees.[38] The following month the all-white Kenyan Legislative Council passed a bill to regulate refugee arrivals: it specified that immigrants must be able to return to their countries of origin or supply a bond of five hundred pounds. Moreover, guarantors of such immigrants must themselves be residents of the colony.[39] The Kenyan enterprise never advanced further.

Nor did a similar venture that established a pilot settlement in the Itauguá district of Paraguay. Nor a project financed by Jewish philanthropists and approved by the French (and Jewish) minister for colonies, Georges Mandel, under which a group of ten refugees were to leave for French Guiana.[40] The Rothschild bank in Paris proposed the purchase of a large tract of land in the Mato Grosso in Brazil or, alternatively, a scheme for settling Jews in the Upper Nile Valley in the Sudan, between Malakal and Bor—"a huge territory . . . with no population . . . where Jews might organize themselves an important colony."[41] These bright ideas too led nowhere. One after another, territorialist schemes, like some exotic plant, blossomed for an hour and then shrivelled.

In 1937 a Polish inquiry commission, headed by a colonial expert, Major Mieczysław Lepecki, and including two Jews, traveled to the French colony of Madagascar to investigate settlement possibilities there. The Polish government advocated Polish-Jewish emigration there both as a means of reducing Poland's Jewish population and as a way of advancing Poland's claim to colonies. For his part, the French minister for the colonies, Marius Moutet, sympathized with the idea of providing an outlet on French colonial territory for "victims of political discrimination and racial prejudice."[42]

The commissioners were divided in their views on the suitability of the island for Jewish colonization. Lepecki was favorable; his two Jewish colleagues were unimpressed but were forbidden to publish their views in the Polish press. A new French government, meanwhile, cooled to the idea. The prospect of dumping Europe's surplus Jews on Madagascar nevertheless continued for several years to exert a strange fascination upon Polish anti-Semites and German Foreign Ministry officials.

For a while possibilities in British Guiana seemed more realistic. An Anglo-American Commission whose members included Joseph Rosen, former head of the Agro-Joint operation in the Soviet Union, reported that, while the country, most of which was uninhabitable forest or swamp, was admittedly "not an ideal place for refugees," a small-scale experimental settlement should nevertheless be planned.[43] The British government approved the proposal but no settlement was ever established.

Newspaper headlines reflected the surges of hope and despair in the search for asylum: "Prospects for Jews in Ecuador" (*World Jewry*, August 23, 1935); "End of an Illusion: Polish Explanations regarding Madagascar Project" (*Jüdische Rundschau*, December 31, 1937); "Settling Jews in Tanganyika: Committee Set Up" (*The Times*, September 14, 1938); "Alaska as Home for Jews" (*Daily Telegraph*, November 25, 1938). A French-Jewish paper commended the French Pacific territory of New Caledonia: "The climate there is ideal . . . a very healthy country . . . rich and diverse forests . . . abounding in mineral resources."[44] Dutch Guiana, Angola, Cyprus, the Philippines, the Belgian Congo, the Dominican Republic, Mexico, Haiti, Ethiopia—each was broached, researched, and hailed as a potential haven. In each case obstacles were discovered and globes twirled again, until eyes fixed anew on the latest, ever more improbable land of redemption.

16

IN THE CAGE,
TRYING TO GET OUT

"Complete Annihilation"

The Jewish refugee, long a familiar figure in Europe, mutated in the 1930s into a major social and political problem and a human catastrophe. Jewish homelessness assumed a sharper edge than ever before. Instead of the "portable homeland" of which Heine had written a century earlier, more and more European Jews found they had no homeland at all.

The *Anschluss* ("union") of Austria to Germany on March 12, 1938, brought another 180,000 Jews under Nazi rule (220,000 "non-Aryans," according to Nazi criteria), enlarging the Jewish population of the Reich to at least 540,000. The Nuremberg Laws were extended to Austria. "Jew-stores" were expropriated. Jews were required to declare all their assets. Many were arrested and sent to concentration camps. Some resigned from the religious community, though that did not help them in the face of Nazi racial legislation. Scenes of public humiliation of Jews became commonplace. Sonia Wachstein, still teaching at the Chajes Realgymnasium, found the atmosphere "more poisoned with every day that passed. There was no exchange of words or eye contact with our neighbours. The estrangement was not only hatred on their side but also fear." [1]

The Jewish suicide rate rose to unprecedented heights: at least ninety-six Viennese Jews committed suicide in the ten days immediately following the Anschluss. In response to the question of his daughter whether it would not be a good idea to commit suicide, Sigmund Freud responded: "Why? Because they would like us to?"[2] Shortly afterward they emigrated to London.

Jewish schoolchildren were expelled from state schools and the Chajes was compelled to take in many of them. The only gentile teacher in the school, who taught English at the highest grade, "expelled himself." Sonia Wachstein had to take over his class, which had ballooned to more than fifty pupils.

> The newcomers were more confused and traumatized by the situation in which they found themselves than the students of the Chajes Gymnasium, whose Jewish identification and sense of existential unease were a part of them. The newcomers were bewildered by the situation into which they had been forced. . . . They often came from completely assimilated families. [For them] the terrible misfortune that had befallen the Jews was a harder, more unexpected burden.[3]

The government's measures were more far-reaching than those taken until then in the "Altreich"—pre-Anschluss Germany—leading the headmaster, Viktor Kellner, in June 1938 to foresee an impending "liquidation" of Austrian Jewry and another observer to write that Austria's new masters might be aiming "at a complete annihilation" of the country's Jews.[4]

One effect of the Anchluss, and of the ruthless persecution of Jews that ensued, was to initiate a great wave of emigration from Austria. Within a year at least seventy thousand Jews, more than a third of the community, fled. Adolf Eichmann, dispatched to Vienna by the SS to take charge of Jewish affairs, set up a Central Office for Jewish Emigration to coordinate bureaucratic procedures. The British consular authorities were deluged with applications for visas to enter Britain. The head of the Passport Control Office in Vienna reported that his staff were "so overwrought that they will burst into tears at the slightest provocation."[5]

Zionism, hitherto weak in Austria, suddenly won large numbers of new recruits. Both the Revisionists and the mainstream Zionists organized more boatloads of refugees heading for Palestine, often aided by dubious underworld operators. They also found willing cooperation in another quarter: after the Anschluss, the SS assisted Zionist emissaries in organizing departures of Austrian Jews to Palestine, whether or not they had immigration certificates. Of the 40,147 immigrants who arrived in Palestine in 1938 and 1939, 17,240 were illegal.[6]

Many Jews in Austria, especially in Vienna, originated in what became Czechoslovakia in 1918 and still retained close family or other connections with their places of origin. After the Anschluss, therefore, large numbers sought refuge in their homeland. No fewer than sixty thousand applications for residence in Czechoslovakia were received from Austrian Jews. The government in Prague, however, tightened visa requirements and only a small number were approved. About six thousand Austrian Jews nevertheless found refuge in Czechoslovakia in the year after the Anschluss, most of them as illegal immigrants.[7]

Among these refugees was Hugo Jellinek, a Czechoslovak citizen resident in Vienna. On June 6, 1938, hearing that he was wanted by the Gestapo, he left on the afternoon train from Vienna to Brno (Brunn), capital of the province of Moravia. Brno had a substantial Jewish community and a strong Zionist movement. Jellinek was one among many who descended on the city at this time and the local authorities as well as the Jewish community struggled to cope with the influx. At first he was assigned a bug-infested bed in a barrack for refugees—a "den of thieves," as he described it.[8] In his first few weeks in Brno he "went to pieces."[9] He had money problems and looked undernourished. He complained bitterly of the lofty indifference of the local Jews: "It is scandalous how [Jewish] society in Brunn behaves towards us poor émigrés. How they live in the same danger as us but, in their narrowmindedness, are not even aware of this fact."[10]

On the evening of the same day as Hugo Jellinek fled to Brno, his eldest daughter, Nadja, left for Palestine with an illegal transport. Like her father she supported the Revisionist Zionists, having joined their youth movement, Betar. Soon after his arrival in Brno, Hugo's younger daughters, Bertha and Anna, joined him there. They both found jobs and settled down in the city. He was comforted by their presence but annoyed with Bertha for consorting with socialists. Reports in August of German troop concentrations near the Czechoslovak border worried him but he opined hopefully, "Bohemia is a tough nut to crack with which this pack of criminals will break their teeth."[11]

Refugee Tennis

The Munich agreement at the end of September 1938 had terrifying consequences for the twenty-five thousand Jewish inhabitants of the "Sudetenland" area that Czechoslovakia was forced to cede to Germany. More than half of them fled immediately, most exercising their right to opt for Czechoslovak citizenship and residence.

The rump of the country, now known as "Czecho-Slovakia," fell under German influence. Administration was split into three with autonomous regional governments in the Czech lands, Slovakia, and Subcarpathian Ruthenia. Slovakia, with 137,000 Jews, was ruled by a Christian-Socialist government that was openly anti-Semitic. Jewish officials were dismissed. In Bratislava, Jewish shop windows were smashed and walls smeared with anti-Semitic graffiti.

In Mikulov (Nikolsburg), Moravia, whose Jewish community, celebrated as a fortress of orthodoxy, dated back at least to the fifteenth century, the four hundred or so Jewish residents scrambled to escape during the few days before the arrival of German troops. Most loaded their movable belongings onto horse-drawn wagons and withdrew to what they hoped would be the safety of Brno. A few days later some of them slipped back across the new frontier to try to salvage more of their possessions. But when they arrived, they found that their homes were already occupied by German settlers. They were ordered to leave immediately. Hardly had they begun to find their feet in Brno than a new blow struck: the government decreed that they were no longer entitled to Czecho-Slovak citizenship. They were obliged to pack up again and move to a camp for stateless, displaced persons at Eibenschitz (Ivančice), near Brno.[12]

In Subcarpathian Ruthenia, whose 103,000 Jews constituted 14 percent of the population, the government promised to protect minorities. But in November 1938, Hungary, with German approval, annexed part of the province, including Munkács, as well as southern Slovakia. The Jews in those districts accordingly found themselves subject to Hungary's anti-Jewish law, passed the previous May. The licenses of Jewish small-business owners were canceled. Jews in the professions were subjected to the *numerus clausus*. Non-Hungarian citizens were ordered to leave. Those who failed to do so were placed in camps or expelled. In the winter of 1938–39 some were deported to and fro across the new frontier between Hungary and Ruthenia. In desperation, a few fled across Poland to the Soviet Union.

Along the new border of the Third Reich, Jews fleeing the Nazis and refused admission to Czecho-Slovakia spent weeks in ditches in open fields. At the frontier post of Mischdorf invalid refugees took shelter in four furniture vans provided by the Jews of Bratislava.

In Brno, Hugo Jellinek observed all this with increasing gloom. His confidence that the Czechs would resist Hitler had been belied by the events that followed the Munich agreement. "All we Jews around the world are terribly worried and unnerved," he wrote to his daughter Nadja in Palestine. The Zionists there, he declared, were "the only star of hope for all brave Jews truly intent on fighting." [13]

As the rush to emigrate from the Third Reich became a frenzied stampede, tens of thousands of people were bounced across frontiers in what came to be called "refugee tennis." They escaped by any means available. The top swimmer in Hakoach sports club swam down the Danube from Vienna to Bratislava, arriving with only his pair of bathing trunks. [14]

Another young Viennese Jew, Paul Winckler, decided to walk from Vienna to the Czecho-Slovak frontier. He got a temporary *permis de séjour* in Czecho-Slovakia but after three months was arrested as an illegal resident and escorted to the Hungarian border. Guards advised him to swim across a river to Hungary. He was caught on the other side by Hungarian border patrols and forced to swim back. Czech guards were waiting for him. He swam back and forth from one country to the other five times. Finally he was allowed to enter Hungary and traveled to the Romanian border, where he surrendered to police and was given a temporary permit.

He went to Constanţa to try to board a ship to Palestine but was arrested as a spy. Acquitted of that, he was sentenced to twenty days' detention for illegal entry to Romania but was kept in prison for two more months. Released on condition he leave Romania, he embarked as a stowaway on a freight steamer heading for Palestine. On arrival at Haifa, he was arrested and spent two days in the Haifa lockup, after which he was put on the same boat back to Constanţa. He was forbidden to land and remained on board the ship, which returned to Palestine. There he was again handed over to the police and again locked up. In January 1939 he was ordered to be deported but an adverse medical report saved him and he was sent to a hospital.[15]

A black market developed in U.S. and Latin American visas and immigration certificates to Palestine. The British Secret Intelligence Service uncovered three cases of document-trafficking in the Passport Control Office at the Warsaw embassy. In Breslau the U.S. vice consul accepted a bribe of 500 marks (equivalent to $200 at the time or about $3,000 in 2011 values) in order to grant a visitor's visa to the father of ten-year-old Abraham Ascher. The boy was sent along to hand over the envelope, since the consul, presumably to avoid notice from prying eyes, had specified a Saturday morning for the transaction, and Ascher senior, who was strictly orthodox, would not handle money on the Sabbath. Abraham Ascher, today a historian in the United States, has conducted research into the consul's activities, concluding that, in return for financial inducements, he probably issued large numbers of such visas, not only to the United States but also to the Philippines, then under American rule. This was merely one of many cases of self-interested benevolence by consuls of many nationalities, whose conduct Ascher qualifies with the phrase "the banality of virtue."[16]

Britain, the United States, and Palestine took in the largest numbers of refugees. But demand for entry visas vastly outpaced supply. In the course of 1938 the Hebrew Immigrant Aid Society in New York received 590,963 letters requesting information or appealing for help in securing admission to the United States.[17] Only a small fraction of the inquirers could gain entry before the outbreak of war in Europe.

Hitler's "gift" to the democracies of scientists driven into exile who later aided in the war effort is well-known. The familiar list of names, beginning with Albert Einstein, who was abroad at the time of Hitler's accession to power and wisely decided not to return to Germany, will not be recited here. Less well-known are those who were unable to leave and whose names remain obscure, if only because they did not survive to personal or scientific maturity.

As anti-Semitism became the order of the day in the expanded Third Reich, other countries in Europe, where it had even deeper roots, joined what appeared to be the wave of the future. In December 1937, King Carol II of Romania invited A. C. Cuza, head of the League of National Christian Defense, and Octavian Goga, leader of the National Christian Party, to form a government. Both were outspoken anti-Semites and the new regime announced an exercise euphemistically called "examination of citizenship." The government fell after six weeks, to be replaced by a royal dictatorship. But the citizenship review continued. At least 150,000 Romanian Jews were rendered stateless as a result. Since only citizens were permitted to work in certain professions and trades, the legislation had the effect of throwing thousands of Jews suddenly out of work. In the province of Bukovina, 60 percent of Jewish artisans were affected. Restrictions were placed on Jewish lawyers, doctors, stockbrokers, and pharmacists. The liquor licenses of Jewish innkeepers were revoked. In May 1938 the diarist Emil Dorian noted: "All the Jews endlessly chew over the one preoccupation: leaving Romania. But this is merely an obsession, a neurotic symptom of powerlessness and despair. For in actuality, nobody moves—since there is nowhere to go and no salvation in sight! . . . There is no way out. We scream, we groan, blood mixes with earth, and a whole generation is destroyed."[18] The utter despair manifest in such outbursts was shared by Jews elsewhere.

In April 1938 the Polish deputy prime minister and minister of finance, Eugeniusz Kwiatkowski, in a speech in Katowice, declared that "in order to achieve internal unity, within a comparatively short period of time half the population should live in towns whose character should be made predominantly Polish."[19] The speech was interpreted as lending support to the view, long voiced by the nationalist right, that Poland suffered from a blight of "overpopulation"

by Jews, whose mass emigration was an urgent necessity. Kwiatkowski was an economic expert rather than a racist rabble-rouser.
The fact that a politician of his comparatively moderate color could
utter such sentiments was a disturbing portent.

The rising tide of verbal aggression against Jews in Poland in
1938–39 fed the growth of murderous physical violence, whose
only apparent motive was anti-Semitism. At least 242 Jews were
wounded and four killed in assaults in a single month between June
15 and July 15, 1938. In the Saxon Garden, the well-frequented
public park in the center of Warsaw, hardly a day passed at this time
without several unprovoked attacks on passing Jews.[20]

The spillover effect of German anti-Semitism was felt directly
in the western border regions of Poland. The expiration of the
Polish-German Convention on Upper Silesia in May 1937 freed the
German government to apply the full force of anti-Jewish measures
in the German-ruled portion of the territory. In early 1938 it went
further and started summary expulsions of Jews, all long resident in
the area, claiming they were Polish citizens. For a while the expellees were obliged to remain in no-man's-land between the German
and Polish frontiers, since the Poles would not admit them and the
Germans would not allow them back. Eventually most were allowed
to enter Poland.

As signs of anti-Jewish feeling proliferated, even those west European democracies that had traditionally welcomed fugitives from
oppression began to put up shutters. In France, a decree law of May
1938 severely restricted the right of sojourn by foreigners. Buildings in the center of Vichy were daubed with anti-Semitic slogans
and Jewish visitors taking the waters in the summer of 1938 found
themselves the butt of harassment by hooligans. The police inter-
vened and the prefect vowed to prevent a recurrence. But throughout the country hostility to Jewish immigrants spread to threaten all
Jews.

In Belgium the country's medical association, citing the danger
of an alien invasion of the profession, moved to ban foreigners from
practicing medicine. The Flemish Lawyers' Association in Antwerp
barred Jews from membership. When the Nazis dispatched forty-
four Jews across the Dutch-German frontier on a Rhine barge, they
were returned by the Dutch police.

In early October 1938, the German government, in friendly compliance with a request from the Swiss authorities, who were anxious about the arrival of large numbers of German Jews claiming to be tourists, ordered that the passports of all German Jews must be stamped with a large red *J*. This fateful decision ensured that, even before the institution of the yellow star, all bearers of such documents became marked persons, not only in Germany but everywhere in the world where they traveled—or tried to.

Interlude at Evian-les-Bains

Eleven days after the Anschluss, President Franklin Roosevelt, under pressure to take some action to alleviate the plight of German and Austrian Jews but without any hope of persuading Congress to loosen United States immigration laws, called for an international conference to address the refugee crisis. In spite of the urgency of the problem, however, preparations for the meeting proceeded at a leisurely pace, lasting more than three months.

It eventually convened on July 6, 1938, at the pleasant French resort of Evian-les-Bains, on Lake Geneva. Roosevelt himself did not attend. Twenty-nine countries sent relatively low-level representatives and a number of voluntary organizations were permitted to make submissions.

The level of oratory was high. Hélio Lobo, representing Brazil, affirmed his country's readiness "to respond to the noble appeal of the American government . . . within the limits of her immigration policy." The delegate from Belgium, "a small country with a very dense population," drew attention to "her traditional reputation as a hospitable people and a country of refuge" while at the same time emphasizing that "Belgium esteems it a point of honour not to assume fresh international obligations whose consequences she cannot estimate." The Australian representative pointed out that his country had "her own peculiar difficulties": immigration had hitherto "naturally been predominantly British; nor is it desired that this be largely departed from while British settlers are forthcoming." He added that "as we have no real racial problem, we are not desirous of importing one." "Statistics," explained the Argentinian spokesman,

"prove that no country has done more than the Argentine in wel-
coming immigrants, regardless of their original nationality, political
beliefs and religious creeds." His government therefore undertook to
"collaborate in studying and solving the problem."

Other delegates expressed similar mixtures of sympathy, restric-
tionism, and lack of precision: Ecuador, "an essentially agricultural
country," could not envisage "too great an influx of intellectual workers." Mexico found herself unable to "go beyond the official action
which takes the form at present of including annually in the national
budget a sum of more than 10,000 pesos (about $3,000) for the
work of the Immigration Board." Ireland confessed that she could
"make no real contribution." Switzerland considered "it essential
to exercise very stringent control over the admission of any further
foreigners." Peru, while conscious that "Jewish influence, like leaven
or ferment, is of value to all nations," was obliged to "fix limits to its
enthusiasm."[21]

All this was much as had been expected. The conference was
surprised, however, by the announcement of the representative of
the Dominican Republic that his government was willing to accept
one hundred thousand refugees. The expectations thus aroused
turned out to be exaggerated: the Dominican government's first act
toward implementation was the imposition, in December 1938, of
an "entrance tax" of five hundred dollars for all immigrants. By 1942
a total of 472 Jews had been admitted to the republic for settlement,
at a cost of three thousand dollars each, paid by the Joint Distribution Committee.

The conference decided to create an Inter-Governmental Committee on Refugees to negotiate with Germany an orderly exodus
of Jews from the Reich. The committee's work over the following
year produced a mountain of memoranda but next to no effective
action. The real decisions, in the form of an understanding between
the United States and British governments, had been taken before
the Evian conference even met. The British insisted that the question of immigration to Palestine must not be raised. The Ameri-
cans set a similar bar against any interference with existing quota
restrictions on entry to the United States. The result was that the
conference, far from alleviating the hardships of refugees, hardened

existing barriers to their admission. As a cynical wit noted, Evian spelt "naive" backward.

Expulsion

Approximately twenty thousand Jewish residents in Austria at the time of the Anschluss held Polish nationality, most of them natives of Galicia or their descendants. It was during his period as an unsuccessful artist in Vienna in the years before the First World War that Adolf Hitler had conceived his obsessive loathing for the *Ostjude* and specifically for Jews from Galicia (then a province of Austria), who were moving to Vienna in large numbers.

Immediately after the Anschluss many of these, fearful for their future in the Third Reich, fled to Poland. The Polish government, already irritated by the German expulsion of Jews from the German part of Upper Silesia, reacted with dismay. On March 18, five days after the Anschluss, the government presented a bill to the Sejm providing that Poles who had lived abroad for more than five years could be deprived of their citizenship. Such persons would consequently no longer hold any automatic right to reenter Poland. The bill passed through all its stages in parliament within eleven days. A communiqué issued by the semi-official Iskra news agency explained that the purpose of the law was "to make all Polish citizens residing abroad realize that the Polish state requires them to maintain an actively favourable attitude and not a passive and indifferent one towards it."[22] The head of the consular department of the Polish Foreign Ministry frankly explained to a conference of Polish consuls in Berlin that "the bill's aim was to elevate the dignity of a Polish citizen by excluding all those who had not been deserving, . . . above all, . . . representatives of national minorities, especially Jews, who are destructive elements."[23]

The Polish legislation was plainly a reaction to the events in Austria and was clearly aimed at Jews. Although this was obvious to all, the Poles were evidently somewhat embarrassed about the law's reception overseas, for an official of the Foreign Ministry, in conversation with a British diplomat, "denied that there was any connection between events in Austria and the Polish Government's decision to proceed with this law, which he described as only an installment of a long overdue revision of the Polish nationality laws." He admitted that the new law "might apply amongst others to persons of nominally Polish citizenship resident in Austria, but he denied that it had any specific anti-Semitic significance." In any case, he added, "it was intended to apply the new law, if and when it came into force, with moderation."[24] This statement was soon to be tested in an unforeseen manner.

On the night of October 28, 1938, German police abruptly arrested eighteen thousand Jews of Polish citizenship in cities throughout the Reich. These included many who had been born in Germany, since citizenship was not automatically acquired by birth on German territory. In Breslau two hundred Jews sought asylum at the Polish consulate, until the consul told them to leave or he would call the police. Marcel Reich, aged eighteen, was among those seized in Berlin:

> I was only allowed to take five marks with me, as well as a briefcase. But I did not quite know what to put in it. In the hurry I put in a spare handkerchief and something to read. I was reading Balzac's *Woman of Thirty*—so I packed that.... Before long the policeman and I had reached our destination: the district's police headquarters. Here I immediately found myself among ten or perhaps twenty fellow victims.... They were speaking perfect German and not a word of Polish. They had either been born in Germany or had come to Germany as small children and attended school there. But like me they all, as I soon discovered, had Polish passports.[25]

The prisoners were put on board trains heading for Poland. The trains from Berlin took men only. Those from other cities carried women and children as well. The Gestapo even rounded up children from orphanages. When they reached the border, the Jews were driven out of Germany with bayonets and whips. The Polish government refused to admit them, so most were left stranded in no-man's-land between the two frontiers.

A British diplomatic report, based on information from Jewish sources, described the scene at the border:

> The worst conditions were at Zbąszyń on the main line from Berlin to Poznan. Here some 6,500 arrived, of whom a proportion were women and children. They had been compelled to detrain at the German frontier station and to proceed on foot across the frontier. Germans are alleged to have fired a machine-gun into the air, causing utter confusion and panic, so that families scattered and lost what few belongings they had been able to bring with them. The local Polish authorities showed goodwill, but had no accommodation and many of the Jews had, of course, no idea where to go, having had little connexion with Poland. After some delay the military authorities provided tents. I understand that 1,500 have now left for various destinations, but that 5,000 still remain, since the Polish authorities hope that the negotiations with Germany may result in their being allowed to return to their homes.[26]

The American embassy in Warsaw reported to Washington: "It has been learned that the refugees were handled very roughly and that as a result they arrived in Poland in great disorder. Many had lost what few belongings they had managed to bring with them including their travel documents. Many were hysterical, and it is said that a few died of fright and several cases of temporary insanity were reported."[27]

The next day the German news agency issued an official statement explaining that the expulsions had been precipitated by the Polish government's decision to recall passports for special endorsement. If this endorsement were refused to the estimated 150,000 Poles in the Third Reich, "they would become a permanent burden to Germany, and the German Government would no longer be able to avail itself of the possibility, which is the legal right of all States, to expel them as undesirable aliens."[28]

In Poland the episode evoked mixed reactions. Polish Jews rallied to offer succor to the refugees stranded at the frontier. On the other hand, an article in the *Kurier Poznański*, an anti-Semitic paper aligned with the nationalist Endecja party, declared: "The population relies on the state authorities not to let a further ten, or more, thousand Jews enter the Polish republic."[29] Fearing that the far-right would exploit the episode, the government censored much of the press reporting on the subject.[30]

The deportations had far-reaching consequences. The Polish government protested vigorously against the German deportations. It arrested a thousand Germans in Łódź in order to impress the German government with the prospect of counter-deportations—but that idea was soon dropped. Competitive brutality was not a productive policy when dealing with Nazis. The alleged threat to German nationals in Poland became a menacing theme of German propaganda over the next ten months.

Among the deportees was the family of Herschel Grynszpan, a young Polish Jew, who had lived in Hanover all his life and who was in Paris at the time of the deportations. Anguished by the wrong done to his family, Grynszpan went to the Germany embassy in Paris on November 7, obtained access to the embassy counselor, Ernst vom Rath, and shot him. The diplomat died in a hospital two days later.

The murder was denounced by the Nazis as an intolerable provocation. On the night of November 9–10, the so-called Reichskristallnacht, synagogues all over Germany were burned down; Jewish-owned shops, businesses, and homes were ransacked; and at least twenty thousand Jews were arrested and thrown into prison or concentration camps. Most Jewish organizations and publications were closed down. The threadbare pretense was maintained that the violence was a spontaneous upsurge; in fact, it was directly organized by the German government and the Nazi Party.

As punishment for the murder of vom Rath, the German Jewish community was levied a huge collective fine of one billion Reichsmarks. In addition Jews were deprived of compensation for the massive damage caused during Kristallnacht, since their insurance policies were confiscated by the German state. Already before the Kristallnacht, Jewish property and businesses, large and small, were being "Aryanized," with the help of a decree "on eliminating the Jews from German economic life." Jews' bank accounts were blocked. The great art collection of the Rothschilds in Vienna was seized. Jewish-owned department stores were expropriated. The great names of the German-Jewish business community disappeared from economic life. Nearly two hundred private banks, including M. M. Warburg in Hamburg, Rothschild in Vienna, and Mendelssohn & Company in Berlin, were forced to transfer ownership to "Aryans" or close their doors. Their former owners scattered to the winds.

Further discriminatory measures were introduced. Jews were forbidden to own cars. They were barred from using restaurant or sleeping cars on trains. All Jewish children remaining in non-Jewish schools were excluded. Jewish orphans, including those who had been baptized, were moved from state children's homes and gentile foster parents to Jewish institutions.

Jews were prohibited from attending cinemas, theaters, or any other public performance, apart from those of the Kulturbund. Its head, Kurt Singer, was visiting the United States in November 1938 and was invited to stay. He insisted on returning. But on a stopover in Holland, he was persuaded that it would be dangerous for him to return and decided to remain in Amsterdam.

After November 1938, gentiles generally kept their distance from Jews. Jewish children found that former playmates would not visit their homes. Now, indeed, as one Viennese Jew put it, "we had all become *Luftmenschen*."[31]

Foreign diplomats and journalists from the democracies reported on the Kristallnacht in detail, evoking a certain disquiet and distaste among their readers. The French Foreign Ministry nevertheless received the German foreign minister, Ribbentrop, in Paris in early December, taking care to exclude from the official reception two Jewish ministers, Georges Mandel and Jean Zay (the latter was actually a Jew only by repute and by Nazi criteria: his father was Jewish).

For Jews in Germany, Kristallnacht and its aftermath produced a sudden realization of the illusory nature of the idea that it would be possible somehow to ride out the Nazi storm by keeping one's head down and submitting to the imposition, for a while, of a second-class status. Hundreds committed suicide. Hedwig Jastrow, a seventy-six-year-old former teacher, was among them. In a suicide note she wrote:

Nobody must undertake any attempts to save the life of someone who does not want to live! It is not an accident, nor an attack of depression. Someone leaves her life whose family has had German citizenship for 100 years, following an oath, and has always kept this oath. For 43 years, I have taught German children and have helped them in all misery and for much longer, I have done welfare work for the German *Volk* during war and peace. I don't want to live without a Fatherland, without *Heimat* [native home], without a flat, without citizenship, being outlawed and defamed. And I want to be buried with the name my parents once gave me and [bequeathed] to me, which is impeccable. I do not want to wait until it gets defamed. Every convict, every murderer keeps his name. It cries to heaven.[32]

As Christian Goeschel comments, this was an example of suicide as an act not of despair but "of self-assertion of her right to keep control over her life and body."[33]

"What Can They Do to Me?"

Foreign consulates and embassies were besieged by hordes of would-be emigrants. Uruguay, Siam, Tangier—no conceivable destination was ignored. In almost every case the word came back that visas were unobtainable. Even before the Kristallnacht, the U.S. consul general in Berlin had reported: "During September we had to deal with thousands of desperate people who stormed the Consulate General every day. . . . The quota is now insufficient to accommodate the applicants who number about 125,000 against the available numbers of 27,300 for the fiscal year. Applicants who newly apply must now wait three or four years."[34] At the U.S. consulate in Stuttgart "the stairway, from top to bottom, was filled with faces, patient, waiting faces, eager yet despairing, hopeful yet distrustful, waiting, hoping, waiting."[35] Clutching at straws, would-be emigrants wrote to strangers in America bearing the same surname, whose addresses they had somehow ascertained, pleading for an affidavit containing the financial guarantee that might eventually enable them to gain admission to the United States.

Dismissed from their jobs, forbidden to practice their professions, their businesses "Aryanized," the forcibly unemployed hopefully took courses in English or sought to retrain as butlers, gardeners, cooks or in other lines of work that might open doors for them overseas. The London *Jewish Chronicle* carried a flood of advertisements such as "Viennese married couple, educated, understanding English, seek posts as chauffeur-valet and maid or similar work.—Apply to Stierer, Vienna 9, Glasergasse 22" and "For Viennese Jewish girl (13½), still in Vienna, of good family, very well brought-up, nice manners and appearance, parents forced to proceed immediately to Shanghai, hospitality urgently required. References in London.— Write Box 532, Frost-Smith Advg., 64, Finsbury Pavement, E.C.2."[36]

Yet even after the Kristallnacht, a minority of German Jews, particularly the elderly, saw no need to leave. In late 1938 the parents of the young sociologist Norbert Elias, who had emigrated to England, visited him there from their home in Breslau. He begged them not to return. His father replied: "All our friends are in Breslau, and in London we don't know anyone." He added, "Ich habe nie etwas Unrechtes getan. Was können sie mir tuen?" ("I have never done anything wrong. What can they do to me?")[37]

Uneasy Refuge

In exile in Britain, France, the Netherlands, or even further afield, the refugees deeply missed their native landscape, culture, and society. Some comforted themselves by referring to Hugo Bettauer's novel *Die Stadt ohne Juden* (*City Without Jews*, 1922), which portrays a Vienna that expels the Jews but then, finding it cannot do without them, invites them to return. Others, remembering Heine, erected a kind of portable fatherland of idealized German culture.

A few could not bear to stay away. Werner Warmbrunn, exiled with his parents in Holland after 1936, returned on trips to Frankfurt at weekends and during school vacations, traveling on secondary trains across minor border posts manned by customs officials rather than the Gestapo. Astonishingly, his parents facilitated his trips by exchanging guilders for German marks at an advantageous rate. He was arrested only once, fortunately by the Dutch police, who suspected him of being a runaway.[38] Most returning Jews were not so fortunate: in 1935 the German police had begun arresting all returning emigrants and sending them to concentration camps.[39]

In exile the old distinctions between German Jews and *Ostjuden* continued to count for a great deal. Even so sensitive a person as Gertrude van Tijn could not altogether discard the prejudices of her Berlin upbringing when she came into contact with east Europeans among the refugees in Amsterdam: "Their mentality was so foreign to me, I found it hard to deal with them. After something had been decided, they would come right back and start to argue all over again at interminable length, while outside the waiting-rooms were crowded with people all waiting to present their case."[40]

Since 1933, van Tijn had not only been responsible for the day-to-day work of the Amsterdam Jewish Refugees' Committee but had also acted as representative in Holland of the League of Nations High Commission for Refugees and of the American Jewish Joint Distribution Committee. Since the Dutch government, like most European governments, required that, save in special cases, refugees pass on elsewhere rather than take up permanent residence, she also ran a committee that sought to organize emigration.

After the Kristallnacht, the flood of refugees arriving in the Netherlands became overwhelming. Van Tijn reported that public opinion at the time was relatively favorable to the refugees.[41] The generosity of the Dutch was widely applauded. A Yiddish newspaper in Riga, Latvia, declared that in its spontaneity and virtual unanimity it was without parallel anywhere.[42]

On closer inspection Dutch policy emerges as somewhat less benevolent. Only certain categories of refugee were granted legal admission and the government insisted that no costs of refugees must fall on public funds. While the border was formally closed to refugees, the government allowed any who arrived up to December 17, 1938, to remain. Thereafter, illegal arrivals were to be returned to Germany, unless they could prove that their lives were in danger. In effect, few were sent back. But both the government and the Jewish Refugees Committee neared the end of their tether. Although half of all the arrivals moved to other countries after a while, at least twenty-three thousand Jewish refugees were estimated to be in the Netherlands by early 1939.[43]

Institutions as Refugees

Not only people but institutions became refugees. After the Kristallnacht, the heads of Jewish homes for the blind and deaf in Germany desperately appealed for help in transferring their "unfortunate, absolutely helpless" inmates to England.[44] Most were unsuccessful, though some achieved limited results, as in the case of the head of the Jewish school for the deaf in Berlin, Dr. Felix Reich. He tried to secure entry for his pupils to England. Some had emigrated since 1933 but most countries were unwilling to accept deaf children. During the Kristallnacht, Reich was arrested and sent for several weeks to the Sachsenhausen concentration camp. He was released on December 20, just in time to return to the school for the Hanukah festival. The staff and students were shocked at his appearance, "with shaven head and limping."[45] After his release he intensified his efforts to organize the emigration of his charges. In March 1939 the British Home Office agreed to admit six boys and four girls from the school, provided they were all under the age of ten. In July Reich went to England with ten children, aged between two and eleven, whom he arranged to place in a Jewish school for the deaf in London. He had hoped to return to Berlin to fetch more but was stranded in Britain by the outbreak of war.

The orthodox Berlin Hildesheimer rabbinical seminary, like most other Jewish institutions in the Reich, was forced after the Kristallnacht to close forever. Its proposed transfer abroad had been discussed for several years. In a letter to Dr. Meir Hildesheimer, son of the seminary's founder, in December 1933, the Vilna orthodox authority Rabbi Hayim Ozer Grodzenski had opposed its removal to Palestine. He noted that Reformers had taken over the German communities in the time of the elder Hildesheimer "and they elected freethinking bad-sons/rabbis [ra-banim—a Hebrew pun] with higher education."[46] The implication, apart from the puerile insult to Hildesheimer junior, appears to have been that the seminary would be a bad influence if removed to the Holy Land. Most of its teachers and many of its students succeeded in leaving Germany by the summer of 1939. But the closure of the seminary left its rector, Jehiel Jacob Weinberg, "a broken man, crying over what had occurred."[47] In the spring of 1939 he was expelled from Germany and took refuge first in Kovno, then in Warsaw.

In June 1939, Leo Baeck, with support from the Cambridge Hebraist Herbert Loewe, made strenuous efforts to transfer the liberal Berlin Hochschule für die Wissenschaft des Judentums to Cambridge. But the idea was opposed by, among others, Rabbi Alexander Altmann, a former teacher at the Hildesheimer Seminary who had emigrated to Manchester in 1938 (his reasons are not known). Nothing had come of the proposal by the outbreak of war.[48] Baeck visited England in the summer of 1939 in an effort to advance this and other projects. He was invited to stay in England or move to the United States. He declined, declaring that he would depart from Germany only when he was the last Jew left there.[49]

More successful was the transfer plan for the technical school that had been operated by British ORT in Berlin since the beginning of 1937. The school trained locksmiths, blacksmiths, mechanics, electricians, plumbers, and welders in the hope of equipping them for emigration. It enjoyed official British protection that provided some degree of security: as a result it was almost the only Jewish institution in Berlin to emerge unscathed from the Kristallnacht pogrom. With the approval of the British government, 215 of its teachers and pupils migrated to Leeds in August 1939.

Other institutions that were not formally Jewish but had largely Jewish personnel also went into exile. The Institute for Social Research, founded in 1923 as an affiliate of the University of Frankfurt, had developed into the foremost center of social science in Europe, pioneering what later came to be called critical theory. Nearly all the leading figures of what became known as the Frankfurt School were Jewish or of Jewish origin, although, as leftist secularists, most had little or nothing to do with Judaism or the Jewish community. Two exceptions were Norbert Elias, a research assistant at the institute, and the psychoanalyst Erich Fromm. Elias had been an active Zionist in his student days in Breslau. Fromm wrote his doctoral dissertation on Jewish law and taught at Franz Rosenzweig's Freies Jüdisches Lehrhaus (Free Jewish House of Learning), the influential adult education center that operated in Frankfurt in the 1920s.

Before the Nazis gained power, the institute had moved its endowment to the Netherlands and transferred ownership of its library to the London School of Economics. In July 1933 the new regime closed the institute and confiscated its premises as "Communist property."[50] Most of the social scientists who had been associated with it, including Franz Horkheimer, Herbert Marcuse, Walter Benjamin, and Karl Mannheim, left Germany. Theodor Adorno followed a little later, after writing music criticism calculated to find favor with the Nazis but failing to ingratiate himself with the new regime. Some of the exiled social scientists regrouped in New York, where they resumed work under the aegis of Columbia University (not, as is commonly thought, the New School for Social Research).

"Exporting Children"

The Youth Aliya movement, established in 1932–33, was the brainchild of Recha Freier, a German-Jewish Zionist activist. Contrary to another received legend, she envisioned it initially as a response more to the unemployment crisis of the early 1930s than to the rise of Nazism. Hitherto, young Zionist "pioneers" had been required to undergo two years of training before the Zionist Organization would sponsor their emigration. Freier proposed the immediate large-scale transfer of Jewish teenagers to Palestine, where they would receive training in kibbutzim. She encountered initial opposition. Bertha Pappenheim criticized Youth Aliya as "exporting children."[51] But as prospects for Jewish young people in Germany became ever more dismal, Freier beat down the skeptics. A vital partner, although she had been doubtful at the outset, was the veteran American Zionist Henrietta Szold, whose Hadassah Women's Zionist Organization provided essential support.

Between 1933 and 1939, Youth Aliya brought 5,400 immigrants, mainly aged between fourteen and seventeen, to Palestine from

Germany, Austria, and Czechoslovakia, plus another two hundred from Poland, Romania, and elsewhere. The emigrants enrolled in short-term *hachsharah* courses, lasting six weeks, on farms and in *batei-hehalutz* (pioneer houses). But with the stiffening attitude of the British government to Jewish immigration to Palestine, the organizers were obliged to reject a large proportion of candidates from Germany and Austria. The movement in any case continued to be influenced by the traditional Zionist emphasis on selective immigration of ideologically motivated enthusiasts. As late as 1939 the head of Youth Aliya in Berlin insisted that such selectivity should not be abandoned even in favor of children whose fathers had been sent to concentration camps.[52]

In the last nine months of the peace the British government, influenced by public sympathy for German Jews after the Kristallnacht and hoping to defuse opposition to its Palestine policy, agreed to admit unaccompanied, "non-Aryan" children from Germany to Britain. The Children's Movement, or Kindertransport, as it came to be known, moved ten thousand children aged between five and eighteen to Britain by September 1939. Smaller numbers went to Belgium, Holland, and Sweden. France adopted a double-faced policy. The French prime minister publicly stated that France would join these other democracies in admitting refugee children. Shortly afterward the minister of the interior sent urgent telegrams to prefects of the northeastern border departments ordering them to prevent the entry of German-Jewish children.[53]

For all its humanity and generosity, the Kindertransport managed to evacuate only a fraction of the children endangered by Nazi persecution. In some households, one child in a family was approved for departure while another was not. In Vienna, in February 1939, the youth department of the Jewish community was being "stormed daily" by desperate parents seeking places for their children.[54]

Gertrude van Tijn was at the station in Berlin when the first train left carrying children to Holland. "The scenes were heartbreaking. With their husbands in concentration camps and their children leaving, the mothers tried hard to appear cheerful, but many broke down as the train pulled out. Many of the children cried too."[55] In May 1939 Gertrude reported that 1,586 "non-Aryan" children (including 45 Protestants and 36 Roman Catholics) had arrived in Holland.[56]

The letters to their children in Britain of parents stranded in Germany and Austria in 1938–39 are poignant, sometimes almost unbearably moving documents. Many were preserved by their recipients as the last, sometimes the only physical reminders of their families.

A father in Vienna in March 1939, writing to his teenage daughter in England, described how every door to emigration seemed closed: he pleaded with her to exploit any opportunity to persuade anyone she might meet to help her parents and younger brother to join her in England. In these times, he noted, the normal structure of family relations was overturned: instead of parents caring for their children, children had to try to do something for their parents—"it's perhaps hard for a young person to do but it is necessary. Don't let any passing opportunity go. . . ."[57] A few weeks later, after hearing a rumor in Vienna that someone had secured the financial guarantee required for a British visa by advertising in the *Daily Mail*, he asked his daughter to borrow the money to place such an advertisement in the paper.[58]

Perhaps the most saddening aspect of these exchanges is the way in which, slowly but inexorably, the reader sees physical separation leading to mental and spiritual estrangement, this in spite of the heartfelt efforts of both parents and children. "Our exchange of ideas by letter is the only form of connection and so we want to make this connection as intimate as possible. Your letters are balm for all our afflictions," declared the same father.[59] Such letters, though generally written with deep feeling, were often white lies in which parents sought to spare their children the full horror of life for Jews in the Third Reich—also, conscious of censorship, no doubt tempering their description of harsh realities. Children overseas, for their part, constantly reassured their parents that they were coping well with a strange country, people, language, and customs. Between the lines it is easy to see that for both sides the effects of these forced separations were traumatic.

Walking Toward the Enemy

One after another, in the late 1930s, European countries rushed, copycat-style, to follow the apparently successful Nazi model and pass anti-Jewish laws. The blaring organs of Nazi propaganda applauded such measures and called for more. Even Italy, where the small Jewish community had long enjoyed relatively harmonious relations with the rest of society, succumbed.

In its early days, fascism had not been anti-Semitic. "The Jewish problem does not exist in Italy," declared the undersecretary for foreign affairs, Count Grandi, in 1926.[60] Mussolini showed few public signs of racism. In 1932 he appointed a Jew, Guido Jung, as minister of finance. The Duce praised Jewish-gentile intermarriage in a newspaper article as proof of the "perfect civil, political, and above all 'moral' equality between all Italians"—though he objected when his own daughter proposed marrying a Jew.[61]

Many Italian Jews had rallied to the Fascist movement: 230 participated in the March on Rome in 1922 and by 1938 more than ten thousand, about a third of the adult Jewish population, were members of the Fascist Party. Until 1938 it was possible to be Fascist and at the same time Jewish, without in any way compromising or apologizing for one's Jewishness, as Dan Vittorio Segre relates in his evocative memoir of his "Fascist-Jewish childhood."[62] On the other hand, several Jews were active in the anti-Fascist resistance, notably the Rosselli brothers, Carlo and Nenno, founders of the movement Giustizia e Libertà. Both were assassinated in France in 1937 by *cagoulards*, French fascists, acting at the behest of the Italian government.

Italian policy toward Jews began to change in the early 1930s and especially from 1937 when Mussolini cast his lot with Germany in European diplomacy. Anti-Semitism was not, as was once widely believed, imposed on Mussolini by Hitler.[63] Rather it was a matter for the Duce of diplomatic convenience and shameless imitation. In July 1938 a *Manifesto of Fascist Racism*, issued by initially anonymous "scientists" and sponsored by the Ministry of Popular Culture, postulated the existence of a pure Italian race and explained that Jews, who could not be part of it, constituted a danger to Italy.

The racial laws promulgated in September 1938 and over subsequent months, although not as severe as German measures, represented a decisive turning point. In October the rector of the University of Rome, Giorgio Del Vecchio, a Fascist, and ninety-six other Jewish faculty members were dismissed. Many foreign-born Jews were deprived of Italian citizenship. More than four thousand Jews sought succor in baptism or resignation from the Jewish community. But a further decree law on November 10 extended the racist provisions of the earlier legislation. Mussolini dropped his Jewish mistress, the art critic Margherita Sarfatti. She had already converted to Catholicism in 1928 but judged it prudent to leave for Argentina.

Italian Jews reacted to the racial laws with confusion, insouciance, or indignation. Nearly four thousand emigrated. A female teacher, dismissed under the new legislation, wrote to Mussolini:

> Dismayed by the step taken against the Jewish teachers, which places me in an extremely painful situation, I dare to address Your Excellency. . . . I always tried to give my pupils pure Italian love, a truthful Fascist faith and endless love for their Duce; for You, Duce, whom I have always admired and loved. . . . I am no longer young and I don't have any other means of income. I have an old mother and a deaf and disabled father. What do I have left in life without my pupils to whom I have dedicated my life? Most of all I am hurt and humiliated in my honest and real Fascist faith.[64]

Dante Lattes, editor of the Zionist magazine *Israel*, called on Italian Jews to suffer with dignity and mutual steadfastness.[65] In his last editorial, published on September 22, 1938, he expressed the "great and profound sense of being Italian" that existed among Jews of the country and their "great and tragic sorrow that it is possible to throw doubt on the reality and grandeur of this feeling."[66] The magazine's Florence office was ransacked by Fascist Jews and closed by the authorities. In early 1939, Lattes left for Palestine.

Another editor, Angelo Fortunato Formiggini, who had produced the monthly literary review *L'Italia che scrive* since 1918, was ordered by the government to remove his name from that of his distinguished publishing firm. In despair, he jumped to his death from the Ghirlandina bell tower of Modena Cathedral.

Giorgio Morpurgo, an officer in the Italian military forces engaged in support of Franco in Spain, chose a different form of suicide. On hearing that, in accordance with the racial laws, he would be deprived of his commission and obliged to return to Italy, he "discarded his cover and went towards enemy positions, walking slowly and ignoring the calls to halt coming from the other side; though wounded, he continued to advance until he was shot through the heart."[67]

17

CAMPING

By January 1939 the Jews of Europe were being transformed into a people without fixed abode. All over the continent, Jews, evicted from their homes and homelands, were forced into temporary accommodation in so-called "camps." Sometimes, as in Germany, these were prisons where they were subjected to slave labor and torture. Elsewhere, as in France, Poland, or the Netherlands, they were places of internment designated for refugees, illegal immigrants, or political undesirables. What all these countries shared was the notion that the camp dwellers did not belong in normal society. The Jews were not alone in these places. In the USSR, selection for incarceration in the labor camp system was almost arbitrary. In Germany any political opponent of the regime might be rounded up. But the Jews, more than any other group in Europe, were already on the way to becoming a "camp people."

"Not a Bad Place"

The primary cause was Nazi anti-Semitism. Yet in the late summer of 1939 far more Jews were being held in camps outside the Third Reich than within it, most of them in countries that were subsequently to wage war against Germany.

The first major Nazi concentration camp was established in March 1933 at the site of a disused munitions factory at Dachau, near Munich. In May a twenty-seven-year-old Bamberg attorney, Wilhelm Aron, became one of the first victims of the Nazi camp

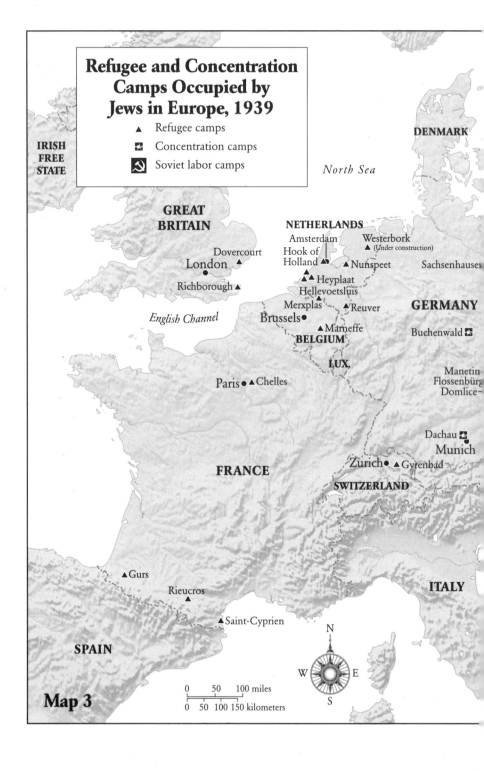

Refugee and Concentration Camps Occupied by Jews in Europe, 1939

▲ Refugee camps

✠ Concentration camps

☭ Soviet labor camps

IRISH FREE STATE

DENMARK

North Sea

GREAT BRITAIN

NETHERLANDS

Amsterdam
Westerbork ▲ (Under construction)

Dovercourt
Hook of Holland ▲

London ●   ▲ Nunspeet   Sachsenhause▮

Richborough ▲   ▲▲ Heyplaat
Hellevoetsluis

English Channel   Merxplas   ▲ Reuver   GERMANY

Brussels ●   ▲ Marneffe
▲   Buchenwald ✠
BELGIUM

LUX.

Manetin
Paris ● ▲ Chelles   Flossenbürg
Domlice▬

Dachau ✠
Munich

Zurich ●   ▲ Gyrenbad
FRANCE   SWITZERLAND

ITALY

▲ Gurs

Rieucros
▲

SPAIN   ▲ Saint-Cyprien

N

W   E

S

Map 3

0   50   100 miles
0   50 100 150 kilometers

system. He had been arrested a few weeks earlier "on suspicion of subversive activities" and was reported to have died suddenly in Dachau. The death certificate gave the cause of death as pneumonia. The body was returned to his family in a sealed coffin that "by order of the criminal police . . . was not to be opened."[1]

The two other important prewar Nazi camps were Sachsenhausen, near Berlin, which opened on July 12, 1936, even as preparations for the Olympic Games were in their final stages, and Buchenwald, near Weimar, which opened in 1937.

In the concentration camp system as a whole, until the outbreak of the war, Jewish prisoners constituted a minority of prisoners, save for a period between the spring of 1938 and early 1939. At first the number of prisoners was, by comparison with the wartime period, relatively small: in mid-1935 there were altogether 3,555 inmates in German concentration camps. Until 1938 there were never more than about 2,500 at Dachau. Many times that number, however, passed through the camp as, each year, newcomers were roughly balanced by releases—and deaths. In 1938, 18,000 prisoners were admitted, mainly after the Anschluss and the Kristallnacht, but most of these too were released after a short time so that in the summer of 1939 the camp held about 5,000 people.

Sachsenhausen, the largest concentration camp in the late summer of 1939, contained more than 6,000 prisoners: of these Jews numbered 250, as compared with 360 Jehovah's Witnesses. The Jewish inmates included political opponents of the Nazis, persons accused of "racial pollution" by virtue of sexual intercourse with non-Jews (many of these were sterilized), so-called asocial elements (including unemployed persons), and returning emigrants sent to camps to undergo "re-education."[2]

When Sonia Wachstein's brother Max disappeared in police custody in the spring of 1938, she went to Gestapo headquarters in Vienna to try to find out what had happened to him. An official told her he had been sent to Dachau. She began to cry. "Why are you carrying on like that?" he said. "Dachau is not a bad place."[3]

The organization and regimen of Dachau served as a template for all later Nazi concentration camps (as distinct from the wartime death camps). Upon arrival at Dachau prisoners were lined up and forced to stand and wait for a long time. Their heads were shorn and they were given cold showers. Camp uniforms were distributed: Jews were assigned blue-and-white striped cotton; gentiles had warmer clothing. Then the prisoners were marched off to wooden blockhouse barracks, each with fifty-four straw-covered bunks. When large groups of Jewish prisoners arrived after the Kristallnacht, the arrival procedure was augmented with a preliminary forced running of a gauntlet of SS guards who belabored the prisoners with sticks and seized their money.

A bugle call at six o'clock every morning woke them. At six-thirty there would be a roll call inspection on the main parade ground followed by another one or two later in the day. Some prisoners engaged in specialized work, such as shoemaking, but most Jews were assigned to labor on the camp's *Heilkräuterplantage* (herb garden). Apart from bread and ersatz coffee, they received only one meal a day, in the evening: it typically consisted of whale or lentil soup, potatoes served out of large tin cans, a piece of sausage or cheese, or a herring.

Relatives or friends were at first permitted to send parcels or money to prisoners in the camp. But the money was lodged in an account from which the inmate was forbidden to withdraw more than fifteen marks at a time. With this he might buy supplementary rations: salami, cheese, butter, honey, preserves, stationery, cigarettes, or coffee. Since these were priced much higher than in the outside world, the system amounted to an officially sponsored racket. Prisoners could write and receive letters at fixed periods. Both Dachau and Buchenwald boasted a lending library, shown off to impressionable visitors as a sign of the enlightened nature of the system.

Small infractions of rules often resulted in savage punishment. A man who left his socks on the wrong shelf was sentenced to an hour of "tree hanging"—he was suspended by his arms on the branch of a tree, with his toes just above ground level.[4] Many prisoners were tortured and some murdered.

Most concentration camp prisoners in the early years were men. But from 1937, Lichtenburg castle at Prettin, near Wittenberg, operated as a camp for women, mainly political enemies of the regime. It was closed in May 1939 and the women sent to Ravensbrück, near the former Mecklenburg health resort of Fürstenberg. Ravensbrück henceforth became the only concentration camp in Germany designated exclusively for women.

Gross overcrowding in the concentration camps in the weeks after the Kristallnacht exacerbated the hardships of the prisoners. In Buchenwald an inmate found himself one of two thousand men in a single barrack: "we had no beds, no soap, hardly any water, no linen. Sanitary conditions were hair-raising."[5]

The sudden increase in the camp population in November 1938 affected male Jews all over Germany. The day after the Reichs-kristallnacht, the SS turned up in strength at the Gross-Breesen training farm and arrested the head of the school, the master carpenter, another instructor, and many older pupils. They were sent to Buchenwald. One of the SS men politely asked the master carpenter for a sledgehammer. When the younger students returned to their rooms later, they found that they had all been smashed up. One of the farmworkers, on orders from the SS, chopped up a Torah scroll into small fragments on a pile of manure.

Hermann Neustadt, one of the arrested students from Gross-Breesen, later recalled his experiences in November–December 1938 in the "special camp" adjacent to the main Buchenwald concentration camp:

> When we arrived, the call again, "Ooouuut!" and we had to jump down from the truck and run on the trot over very rough gravel. On both sides stood S.S. men, who struck at us. Those who could not run quickly enough over this rough area of land or even fell down were beaten. In the end, we had to line up in military formation and wait. We waited the next 48 hours! . . .
>
> We had to sleep on the wooden plank beds and there was neither straw nor any blankets. . . . During the first nights the S.S. came and took a few people away with them from the barracks, who had apparently been on a special list. What happened to them, I could not see, as I did not dare to get out of my sleeping place. However dogs and screams were heard and that people were beaten. . . .
>
> We were able to observe, from our "special camp," which was

separated from the rest of the camp by barbwire fences, how prisoners were punished. Some of them were strapped onto the "rack" and then received 10 or 25 strokes with the whip, perhaps even more. Then they were unstrapped and had to stay at attention, else it produced more strokes. . . . Besides the already mentioned Sergeant Zoellner, who had trod on me, I only remember still one S.S. man Sommer or Somers, who as far as I could see was a rather good-natured fellow.

Although the Gross-Breesener group numbered only about 20, who all knew each other very well, for days we were not able to recognize each other. With heads shaved bare, all of us looked quite different. . . . The six barracks were built in such manner, that one corner of number 6A stood in the so-called "death-strip," i.e. that was the strip of levelled off land in front of the electric fence, where under "normal" circumstances, the S.S. guards could shoot the prisoners without a special order, if they believed that they wanted to escape. . . . [6]

Neustadt was released after three weeks upon signing an undertaking to leave Germany as soon as possible. He crossed the border on December 15 and made his way to Amsterdam. From there the Amsterdam Jewish Refugees' Committee dispatched him to the training farm at Wieringen. About the same time the other arrested Gross-Breesen students were released on condition that they too left Germany immediately. With the help of the Amsterdam committee, some moved to Wieringen. Others were admitted to England to work on farms.

But many Jews who had been held in concentration camps could not leave Germany before the end of August 1939.

Jews in the Gulag

In the USSR, Jews were not, in principle, more in danger than any other citizens. In strictly statistical terms, indeed, they were underrepresented in the Soviet prison camp system. Of 3,066,000 people imprisoned in the Gulag (the acronym formed from the title of the chief administration of camps of the NKVD) in 1939, between 46,000 and 49,000 were Jews, slightly less than their proportion in the population.[7] Among the leading figures in the Gulag administration were many Jews, several of whom were themselves ultimately arrested and shot.

Jews' legal emancipation in Soviet Russia endowed them with a superficial equality, even if only one of fear, in what was no longer, as it had been under the tsars, a *Rechtsstaat*. But in practice Jews in the 1930s found themselves peculiarly targeted by the Stalinist regime. In 1934 an NKVD circular initiated the process whereby particular ethnic groups, regarded as suspicious, were to be accorded special attention. Germans, Lithuanians, and Poles were among those in the first rank, regarded as hostile to the Soviet Union and excluded from high positions. Jews, together with Armenians and others, were in a second category who were to be closely observed.[8] In the prevalent atmosphere of paranoia and spy fever in the late 1930s, persons with foreign connections were particularly prone to fall under suspicion. Jews, with their high degree of urbanization and large number of emigrant relatives, were consequently natural targets.

In June 1937, for example, Grigory Kaminsky was abruptly dismissed from his post as commissar for public health, arrested, and later executed. His brother-in-law, Joseph Rosen, feared that the reason was his connection with the Joint. In his "secret speech" to the Twentieth Party Congress in 1956 and in the memoirs he caused to be published abroad after his retirement, Nikita Khrushchev called Kaminsky "a forthright, sincere person, loyally devoted to the party, a man of uncompromising truthfulness." Khrushchev related that Kaminsky was arrested immediately after having taken the floor in a central committee meeting to accuse Lavrenty Beria, at that time a rising force in the NKVD, of having collaborated with British intelligence.[9] According to another account Kaminsky disappeared after confronting Stalin with the challenge: "If you go [on] like this, we'll shoot the whole party."[10]

Whatever the explanation of Kaminsky's fall, it immediately endangered all who had had any close connection with him. Of the seventy German doctors whose entry to the USSR he had facilitated, fourteen had been arrested by the following December. Sixty officials of Agro-Joint in the Soviet Union, including all its senior figures, were also arrested and accused of being Trotskyite, Zionist, and/or Nazi agents. Under interrogation they were compelled to confess to criminal contacts. For example, the manager of the Agro-Joint office in Simferopol declared that a group of foreigners who had visited Crimea "under a false pretext of familiarization with the Jewish *kolkhozes*" had "collected spy information and slanderous materials about economic conditions, population structure, and other information."[11] The accountant of the office was accused of being "a member of the counterrevolutionary, Jewish, bourgeois-nationalistic spy organization created by German intelligence."[12] Most of those arrested were sentenced to long spells in labor camps from which few emerged alive. Several were sentenced to death.

Even the most devoted Jewish Communists, often *especially* the most devoted, fell victim to the purges. Yitzhak Barzilai, born in Cracow in 1904, had been brought up as a religious Jew and a Zionist. In 1919 he emigrated to Palestine, where he converted to Communism and became one of the founders of the Palestine Communist Party. During the 1920s he roamed the Middle East as a Comintern agent, helping to found Communist parties throughout the region (indigenous Jews were prominent in the nascent Communist movement in countries such as Egypt and Iraq). In 1933, in recognition of his services, he was accorded Soviet citizenship, whereupon he took a new name, Joseph Berger. As head of the Comintern's Near East department, he entered the USSR's policy-making elite. But in 1934 he was summarily dismissed and expelled from the party. A year later he was arrested, charged with Trotskyism, and sentenced to five years in a labor camp (the term was later increased to eight). He was sent to Siberia.

Gershon Shapiro was lucky not to share the same fate. He had already survived one purge. In 1932 he was ordered back from Friling to Odessa to take charge of the Yiddish House of Culture there. In the early years after the revolution, Odessa had been an important center of Soviet-style Jewish culture. Yiddish and even Hebrew publishing flourished. There were twelve Yiddish-language schools, several Jewish libraries, and, from 1924 to 1933, the Mendele Moykher Sforim Museum. But by the early 1930s Jewish cultural life in the city was dwindling. Shapiro came to the conclusion that his career should take a different direction. In 1934 he entered the Jewish section of the agricultural institute in Odessa, where he studied for the next five years.

In 1936, however, he got into trouble again following an exchange in a class that he gave in the Odessa party school. Shapiro had explained, in correct Stalinist locutions, that Trotsky was no proletarian revolutionary. A student pointed out that Trotsky had played a major role in the revolutionary movement in Russia. Shapiro replied that that might be so but there were proletarian revolutionaries and petit bourgeois ones: Trotsky belonged to the latter category. Shapiro's reply was reported to party authorities who interpreted it as an affirmation that Trotsky was, after all, a revolutionary, whereas, according to Stalinist orthodoxy, he was to be consigned to the category of counterrevolutionaries and traitors. A party meeting concluded that Shapiro had been trying to smuggle Trotskyist ideas into his teaching in the party school. Accordingly, he was expelled from the party and forbidden to continue his studies at the institute. Although his exclusion from the party was confirmed by the district party committee, his dismissal from the institute was rescinded. In spite of its partly reassuring aftermath, the incident troubled him. As Stalin's terror engulfed the Soviet Union, Shapiro began to feel what he later described as "incomprehension and bewilderment."[13]

In August 1937, Moshe Zalcman was arrested in Kiev. He had committed no overt act of unorthodoxy and his seizure should probably be seen as part of a broad drive for stricter discipline in the world Communist movement, in which Jews' prominence now rendered them particular victims. The previous spring the Jewish section of the French Communist Party had been ordered to dissolve. In May–June that year the Executive of the Comintern resolved that Jewish Communists must combat "certain tendencies within their own ranks," not only "declared Jewish fascists" but also "Jewish nationalists" who were creating "ideological confusion."[14] In the spring of 1938 the heavily Jewish Polish Communist Party was closed altogether on orders from Moscow and many of its leaders who had taken refuge in the USSR disappeared. During these months other foreign Communist refugees in Moscow, among them Béla Kun and others of Jewish origin, were killed.

After interrogation, partly conducted in Yiddish, and torture, Zalcman was told he had been found guilty of espionage and sentenced to ten years' detention in a labor camp. Only twenty-seven of the forty men crowded with Zalcman, nine to a wagon, survived the six-week train journey to Karaganda in Kazakhstan.

Here was the largest network of slave labor camps in the Soviet Union, with tens of thousands of prisoners. Zalcman was initially assigned to the Central Agricultural Industry Camp, annexed to Karaganda. Conditions were atrocious. Danger lurked on every side—from malevolent guards, criminal overseers, thieves, and informers to extreme temperatures, bedbugs, fleas, and disease of every kind. Even official inspectors sustained prisoners' complaints against the camp administration, who were reproached for "not being interested in the fate of those persons entrusted to them."[15] But there is no evidence that the inspectors' reports brought any improvement or, indeed, that anything was done with them besides filing them away in the archives.

In the camp Zalcman met several other Jewish prisoners. Among them was Leyzer Ran from Vilna. Ran had worked in YIVO and was well acquainted with Yiddish literature. In 1936 the Communist Party in Vilna had sent him to study in the USSR but he was arrested immediately upon crossing the frontier, sent to the Lubianka prison in Moscow, and then to Karaganda. Zalcman managed to get himself attached to Ran's group of prisoners, who formed an eight-man, Yiddish-speaking work brigade. After a few months they were all sent for a new round of interrogation. In response to an NKVD officer who accused him and his Jewish friends of "forming a nationalist group," Zalcman replied: "Isn't it normal to seek out a neighbour when one finds oneself abroad. . . . We can't help each other much but just hearing one's mother tongue leaves a good feeling."[16] He and his friends were not punished but were separated. Zalcman was moved to another camp and swallowed up in the maw of the Gulag.

A Passing Episode?

The first concentration camp in Poland was established in 1934 at Bereza Kartuska, near Brest-Litovsk. Political prisoners of every stripe were detained there without trial: originally designed for Ukrainian nationalists and right-wing Polish extremists, it later came to hold many thousands of Polish Communists, of whom a large proportion were Jews. Among them was Leon Pasternak, a young Polish poet and cousin of Boris Pasternak.

By 1939, however, the largest number of Jewish camp detainees in Poland were the involuntary border crossers from Germany who the Poles continued to insist were no longer Polish citizens. After a few weeks of sleeping in stables, some of the deportees were allowed by the Polish authorities to rent rooms, or rather beds in crowded rooms, in the border town of Zbąszyń. The Joint and Polish Jewish relief groups organized rudimentary schooling, clinics, and cultural activities.

Max Weinreich visited Zbąszyń in late November 1938. He reported on the misery that he encountered but also worried about its larger implications: "Is Zbąszyń a passing episode? If not—the heart stops at the thought!" [17] Another visitor was the historian Emanuel Ringelblum, who represented the Joint. His report helped galvanize further aid to the refugees. As time went by, however, the flow of charitable support diminished and the position of the refugees became even more desperate.

In early 1939 Germany and Poland came to an agreement about the disposition of the deportees. They were to be allowed to return temporarily to Germany "to wind up their affairs." What this in effect meant was that they would be despoiled, in pseudo-legal form, of most of their property. What little remained they would be permitted to remove to Poland, which finally agreed to admit them with their families. The Germans did not want all the expellees to return at once: only a few thousand were to be allowed back at any one time, for up to a month each. The encampment at Zbąszyń therefore continued to exist for several months.

In July 1939 there were still at least two thousand refugees there.

Meanwhile the Germans were driving additional, smaller groups of Jews across the frontier. A report on a visit to Poland by two representatives of the American Friends Service Committee in late July 1939 described a conversation with a woman at Zbąszyń who, with many others, had been chased into the Polish-German no-man's-land by German police with dogs. She had set out with two children, one that she carried and another who fell behind. "She was not allowed to go back for it [sic], and the little thing perished in the swamp."[18]

More Border Camps

Meanwhile, other countries had followed the Polish-German example in forcing Jews into no-man's-land camps. By January 1939 there were reported to be at least twelve along the German, Slovak, Hungarian, and Polish frontiers. In March, following the German annexation of Memel from Lithuania, Jews fled or were driven out from that small territory. Within three weeks not a single person remained in the enclave out of a former Jewish population of seven thousand. Some found shelter in Kovno. Late arrivals had to camp in the fields near the border town of Kretinga.

The expulsion fever spread to southeast Europe. Yugoslavia started deporting Jewish refugees who had arrived from Germany and Italy. And the Romanian foreign minister announced that "it was necessary in the interest of the Jews themselves as well as in the interest of the country that a part of the Jewish population should emigrate."[19] He later explained that he had been referring only to Jews resident illegally in the country, although, since the government had recently withdrawn the citizenship papers of a large number of Jews, many of these would presumably count as illegal.[20] At the end of April the Bulgarian government ordered the expulsion of all alien Jews. About fifteen thousand people were affected, among them some long-term residents of the country. Many were Poles who had been deprived of their nationality.[21] Most had nowhere to go.

Western Europe

In western Europe too, refugees found themselves confined to camps, albeit not on the frontier. In Switzerland Jewish organizations in January 1939 were maintaining nine hundred refugees in a dozen camps. In Belgium, where, that winter, refugees were crossing the border from Germany illegally at the rate of four hundred a week, the government set up an "isolation camp" at Merxplas and a training camp at Marneffe in a castle that had formerly served as a Jesuit college. The Merxplas camp was housed in buildings of the state workhouse for vagrants; the refugees, however, were separated from the tramps. The inmates were allowed to visit Brussels for two days every three weeks. They were not permitted to enter the village of Merxplas.

In France, as early as 1934, the director of the Sûreté Nationale had told the press that, given the difficulties involved in expelling undesirable refugees, the only solution to the problem would be to send them to "a concentration camp" where they would be "subjected to hard labor for a fairly long period of time."[22] The idea was shelved for the time being. But by 1939 contrasting pressures of philanthropy and xenophobia produced two different kinds of camps in the country. The eleemosynary impulse led to the creation after the Anschluss of a refugee camp for Austrians at Chelles, near Paris. The residents lodged in a hotel or private houses and ate in a communal refectory. They were free to come and go but could not set up residence in Paris, nor in several neighboring departments. By September 1939, 1,400 refugees, including some from the Spanish Civil War, were living in Chelles.

Meanwhile, bowing to less benign pressures from public opinion, the French government in November 1938 issued a decree envisaging the internment of undesirable aliens, by which was meant primarily Communists. The first camp of this kind opened in the spring of 1939 at Rieucros (near Mende, Lozère) as a "special concentration center" for aliens. These were mainly political refugees, who had been unable to obtain a visa for another country and who were detained "in the interests of order and public security."[23] The sudden implantation of this alien presence in the heart of the French countryside aroused consternation among local people. Mayors and other officials in the neighborhood protested indignantly against the presence of these undesirables. The special commissioner in charge of the camp reported to the departmental prefect that a veritable panic had broken out in the area and that there was talk of setting the camp on fire.[24]

Five more such camps were, nevertheless, established in France in the course of 1939, all in the Pyrénées-Orientales, for the internment of 226,000 former Republican combatants in the Spanish Civil War who sought refuge in France. Among these were Jewish former soldiers in the International Brigades. At one of these camps, Saint-Cyprien, in April 1939, former combatants of the Botwin Company, mainly Communists from eastern Europe, produced a primitively printed Yiddish paper, *Hinter shtekhel droten* (Behind Barbed Wire).[25] After a few weeks these internees were moved to a camp at Gurs, while the French government tried to find another country that would take them all in. Some were released on enlisting in the French Foreign Legion. About forty thousand, mainly Spaniards, were admitted to Latin American states. A few of the Jews succeeded in escaping from the camps before September 1939. But the Communist Party appears to have disapproved of such escapes as smacking too much of spontaneous initiative. At the outbreak of war many of the Jewish prisoners were still in the camps.

In general, Dutch society accorded the refugees a relatively generous reception but here too there were rumblings of xenophobia and anti-Semitism. Attempting to mediate between immense pressure from potential immigrants and resistance from extreme-right elements, the government decided after the Kristallnacht to admit a limited number of refugees but to quarantine them in an internment camp at the Lloyd Hotel in Zeeburg (east Amsterdam) and at the Heyplaat Quarantine Station in Rotterdam. Camps were also established at Hook of Holland, Reuver, Hellevoetsluis, and Nunspeet. These were internment camps designed for male illegal immigrants and there was an element of punishment in the camp regime. As Bob Moore writes in his history of Dutch refugee policy in this period, these were "bleak places" and "for the majority of respectable refugees who found themselves in these camps, the conditions and their treatment as criminals was a traumatic and harrowing experience."[26]

Walter Holländer, Anne Frank's uncle, who had been arrested during the Kristallnacht in Aachen and sent to the Sachsenhausen concentration camp but then allowed to leave Germany, was among the internees at Zeeburg. "We were cut off from all contact in this refugee camp and kept under police supervision. We were not allowed—nor was it even possible—to engage in any income-producing work, but we had to pay for our stay in the camp. If I wanted to leave for any reason, I had to obtain written permission from the police officer in charge."[27] In April 1939 Holländer was able, with the help of his brother in the United States, to secure release from Zeeburg on condition that he departed for the United States in December, with the visa and ship's ticket that he had shown to the Dutch authorities.

In the little walled town of Hellevoetsluis on the Haringvliet (an inlet from the North Sea) in South Holland, the inmates of the refugee camp were guarded by military police. Overcrowding was such that internees were "stuffed like herring in a barrel."[28] Mail was censored and there was little freedom of movement. At first local shopkeepers were reported to be "rubbing their hands" at the prospect of revived trade.[29] The atmosphere among the inmates was less jovial. Hardly had the first batch of refugees arrived than one of them, a young "non-Aryan" Christian from Wuppertal, hanged himself.

In the spring of 1939 the minister of the interior refused permission for the refugees to leave the camps briefly to celebrate Passover as the guests of hospitable Jewish families in nearby towns.[30] By April 1939 a total of 1,517 refugees were being held in camps in Holland, pending their "transshipment" elsewhere.[31]

Viewing the problem as a potentially long-term one, the Dutch Interior Ministry initiated work on the establishment of a central camp for both legal and illegal refugees. The chosen site was at Westerbork, a low-lying heath near Assen in the north of the country. The location had originally been designated within the Veluwe national park but Queen Wilhelmina, whose summer palace was nearby, objected, so the government decided on Westerbork instead.

The establishment of this central camp "for Jewish refugees only" was supported "with something like real enthusiasm" by the Amsterdam Jewish Refugees' Committee, which thought that it would provide a temporary "refuge for emigrable people" and a "first-class training centre."[32] Work on construction began in August 1939. Nearby shopkeepers here looked forward to an increase in business. Other local residents complained that their district was being used as a dumping ground for refugees and that it was "common knowledge" that among the potential residents were asocial elements whose motives for fleeing to the Netherlands were other than racial or religious.[33]

Europe: A Concentration Camp

The motives that led to the establishment of camps in Nazi Germany, the Soviet Union, Poland, and western Europe were very different in each case, as were the camp regimes. But underlying them all, even those in countries such as France and the Netherlands, was the notion that the inmates did not fit into society and should be kept apart. The camps, indeed, were a microlevel manifestation of a European-wide phenomenon. By early 1939, much of the continent was being transformed into a gigantic concentration camp for Jews. For most of them, life was being made punitively repressive where they were and, at the same time, they were prevented from moving anywhere else. In the lapidary phrase of Chaim Weizmann, in his evidence to the Peel Commission, their world was "divided into places where they cannot live and places they cannot enter."[34]

In January 1939 a decree in Romania ordered all commercial and industrial enterprises to report to the minister of national economy the ethnic origin of owners, stockholders, and employees. Efforts to drive the Jews out of the professions accelerated. In Bucharest Emil Dorian confided to his diary that month: "I have been obsessed of late by the idea of a satirical novel, or at least a sad one, based on the present life of Romanian Jews. Its tentative title would be *Wanted: Homeland* or *For Rent: One Homeland, All Facilities Included.*"[35] Dorian, be it noted, was no Zionist.

A new law in Poland in 1938 made it almost impossible for Jews to enter the legal profession. Employment on the stage (except for the Yiddish theaters) and in the press (except for Jewish papers) was almost completely barred against Jews by 1939. The boycott of Jewish businesses by Poles and Ukrainians intensified. In November 1938 the Jewish Fishmongers' Association, which supplied 90 percent of fish consumed in the country, reported finding itself under serious challenge by cooperatives that had "set themselves the objective of tearing the fish trade out of Jewish hands."[36] Similar complaints were heard in almost every branch of the Jewish economy.

A report by the central committee of Bundist labor unions in Warsaw in April 1939 provided chapter and verse, industry by industry, of the exclusion of Jewish workers from large areas of employment. Zealous and discriminatory official enforcement of work rules against Jewish bakers, porters, and slaughterhouse workers, for example, was driving Jews out of those trades. The report concluded gloomily: "It does not take the same form in all trades—in some it is faster, in others slower—but everywhere the Jewish worker is under severe pressure."[37]

In 1938 a cabaret skit by the Yiddish comedian Szymon Dzigan, titled "The Last Jew in Poland," took its theme from Bettauer's novel about a *Judenrein* Vienna and portrayed Polish officials and citizens, after the entire Jewish population had emigrated, begging the last Jew to remain in the country. The sketch led to a summons from the censors. That the unimaginable was being imagined was evidently unacceptable.

In Hungary political debate over a new anti-Jewish law was temporarily suspended in February 1939 when the right-wing prime minister Béla Imrédy was forced to resign after it was revealed that he himself had a Jewish great-grandmother. His successor, the Transylvanian aristocrat Count Pál Teleki, however, persisted with the legislation. The president of the House of Magnates (upper chamber), Count Gyula Karolyi, a former prime minister, resigned in protest, but the bill took effect in May 1939. The new law differed from earlier legislation in adopting a racial rather than a religious definition of Jewishness. It severely curtailed Jewish economic activity and civil rights, restricted Jewish participation in the professions, and required the dismissal of Jewish civil servants, theater directors, and editors of the general press. Only those Jews whose ancestors had lived in the country before 1867 retained the vote. The 7,500 foreign Jews in the country were ordered to leave.

The German occupation of Prague on March 15, 1939, and the resultant elimination of what remained of Czech sovereignty brought all the Jews of Bohemia and Moravia under direct Nazi rule. Refugees from Germany who failed to escape in time were arrested in large numbers. Anti-Jewish measures, similar to those in the Reich, were extended to the "Protectorate." Jewish officials were dismissed, Jewish property "Aryanized," Jewish pupils expelled from German-language schools, Jews excluded from public baths, parks, and theaters. "Hauptsturmfuehrer Eichmann, who worked in this field in Vienna," was reported to have arrived in Prague to take charge of the organization of Jewish emigration.[38]

Czech Jews joined those of Germany and Austria in a stampede for the exit. As in the Reich, potential emigrants had to navigate an elaborate bureaucratic maze of forms, attestations, property declarations, visas, and travel arrangements, starting with a four-page questionnaire, with twenty-six supplementary questionnaires (a separate set for each family member) and continuing with interviews at the Jewish community, government offices, consulates and so on.

In Slovakia, now nominally independent under a pro-German, clerico-nationalist puppet régime, decree laws eliminated Jews from the bar, the civil service, and the medical profession. Jewish pupils were excluded from public schools. Militiamen broke into Jewish homes and plundered them. Jews were beaten and tortured. Thousands fled to Poland. Those who managed to evade border controls were looked after by charitable organizations in Cracow and Katowice but were liable to arrest and deportation as illegal immigrants.

In several countries, notably Poland and Romania, restrictions were placed on the right of Jews to acquire land, whether for new houses or for institutions such as schools. In Latvia, where Jews were being forced out of commerce, the professions, universities, and government jobs, a report to the Joint in May 1939 stated that "the Jewish population has become terribly depressed and has fallen into a kind of apathy."[39]

The vise was also tightening around Jews in Italy. Three more anti-Jewish decree laws were promulgated in June–July 1939. Jewish military officers were dismissed. Jews were banned from membership of the Fascist Party (enrollment was a requirement for many forms of employment or advancement). Jews were now supposed not to employ non-Jewish servants. School textbooks by Jews were banned. They were expelled from clubs. Jewish children were excluded from public schools. Jewish businesses were closed or subjected to restrictions. Newspapers were forbidden to publish death notices of Jews. La Scala opera house was closed to them. Although the anti-Jewish laws and regulations were only sporadically enforced and could often be avoided by subterfuges or bribes, Jews felt increasing social isolation and vulnerability.

In the early months of 1939 thousands of refugees converged on the Romanian port of Constanţa on the Black Sea, many of them sailing down the Danube on pleasure steamers. Others traveled on sealed trains from the Romanian frontier. The refugees from the Third Reich included former concentration camp inmates. They hoped to make their way as illegal immigrants to Palestine. Some held phony South American entry visas. Many had been sold tickets by Zionist agents or commercial racketeers but upon arrival in Constanţa found that bribes were required to make further progress. One large group was lodging in a cellar near the port. There was fighting to get on board ships.

According to a Zionist intelligence report in July 1939, the German chancellor's office had issued an order that illegal immigration of Jews to Palestine was to be facilitated by all possible means.[40] But the British government did everything it could to try to block such traffic. The Secret Intelligence Service (MI6) monitored ships carrying refugees from Black Sea ports through the Dardanelles. British diplomats pressed the Romanian, Bulgarian, and other governments to prevent passage of Jewish refugees. Those who surmounted the blockade and reached the shore of Palestine faced an unfriendly welcome.

One group of several hundred refugees arrived in early 1939 aboard a dilapidated Greek freighter, the *Agios Nikolaios*. When the ship arrived off the Palestinian coast, it was met by a British warship, which ordered it to stop. The captain ignored the order and turned back to sea. A warning shot was fired and when the ship still refused to halt, a second shot struck amidships, causing one death and leaving a hole in the hull. The listing vessel limped back across the Mediterranean to Athens, where the Greek government allowed it to remain while repairs were made. The passengers were forbidden to disembark but were provided with food and supplies by the local Jewish community. After it turned out that the *Agios Nikolaios* could not be made seaworthy with the passengers on board, the Athens community chartered another ship, whose captain agreed to take the refugees to the edge of Palestinian territorial waters. He would not go any further for fear of arrest by the British naval patrol. The ship therefore towed a barge that would be used to transfer the passengers to the shore. In mid-July, after a journey that for many of them had lasted almost five months from their original departure points, they eventually succeeded in landing in Palestine, where they were promptly installed in a quarantine camp at Athlit, near Haifa.[41]

As doors everywhere slammed shut, the search for some haven of safety became ever more frantic. Eyes focused on the most bizarre and exotic locations. The International Settlement in Shanghai was almost the only place on earth that required no entry visa. Moreover, as the leaders of one of the main German-Jewish organizations pointed out in February 1939, it was "possible to keep a person in Shanghai more cheaply than in any other civilized place we know of."[42] The Jewish organizations outside Germany disapproved of emigration to Shanghai, pointing out that "the situation in that City has become quite desperate."[43] But in default of any alternative, thousands of German and central European Jews set out on the long sea voyage to the Far East.

By the summer of 1939 at least eighteen thousand Jewish refugees from central Europe had reached Shanghai. What amounted to a refugee camp developed in the slum tenements of the Japanese-occupied Hongkew district in the International Settlement. The arrival of this penniless horde, however, provoked a local reaction. In August 1939 the Japanese naval authorities let it be known that "whilst displaying genuine sympathy with European refugees" they were obliged "owing to lack of accommodation . . . not to permit

further refugees to reside in Hongkew after the end of this month."
As a result the Jewish refugee organizations called an immediate
halt to all Jewish emigration to Shanghai.[44] In the event, individuals, acting on their own initiative in defiance of such instructions,
continued to head for the Far East. But the difficulties and costs of
getting there mounted and even this improbable refuge became, for
most, unattainable.

Surveying the prospects for the Jews in Europe in a long internal
memorandum in March 1939, Morris Troper, head of the Paris office of the Joint Distribution Committee, referred to the impossible
dilemmas that confronted his organization in trying to allocate its
limited funds. In Germany alone, the Joint's expenditure in the previous month had been 1,185,639 Reichsmarks as against an income
of just RM274,354.[45] Troper rejected the view that "since the majority of Jews are doomed . . . all resources must be turned towards the
safeguarding of those who still have some measure of protection."
Instead he advocated continuing efforts toward "the salvaging of
thousands upon thousands of lives." And he continued: "One can
hardly compare the situation to the attempt to save part of a burning
building, for the destruction of part of a people carries with it moral
and spiritual consequences so devastating as to shake the very foundation of their coreligionists wherever they may exist."[46]

18

ON THE EVE

Politics Without Power

Politics for the European Jews by 1938–39 was not the conventional struggle for power: they had next to none. Nor was it a competition for spoils of office: positions were few and pickings were meager. Rather it was an agitated search for some form of collective self-defense against the omnipresent threat to Jews' economic survival and increasingly to their very existence. Jewish politics was also a quest for self-respect in a world where the word *Jew* was, in the eyes of most people, an insult and degradation.

A sense of desolation pervaded the Polish Jewish population, especially its youth, in the last year of peace. This was a generation, wrote a journalist in the *Literarishe bleter* in January 1939, that was "naked and barefoot, a generation of fed up, poor little *menshelekh*, with no yesterday, no today, no tomorrow."[1] One of the youthful contestants in YIVO's autobiography contest for 1939 wrote: "Poland raised me to be a Pole but brands me a Jew who must be chased out. I want to be a Pole, but you won't let me. I want to be a Jew, but I can't; I've moved away from Jewishness. I don't like myself as a Jew. . . . Unless Poland's leaders change—as well as most Poles—then this sad process, which produces culturally disoriented souls, will not change for the better."[2]

Since 1935 Jewish participation in the Polish parliament had been greatly reduced. The main reason was a new constitution and an electoral law that limited the ability of minorities, including Jews, to win seats in the Sejm. In protest, several Jewish parties, including the Bund, Folkists, and General Zionists (except for those in Galicia), joined other opposition groups in boycotting national elections in 1935.

As the mirage of early establishment of a Jewish state faded, the stock of the Zionists fell and that of their rivals rose. The Bund achieved its most impressive electoral results in the late 1930s. It gained ground in spite of a "declaration of principles" adopted at a party congress in 1935, in which it reaffirmed its opposition to "any *klal yisroel* [Jewish unity] politics" and vigorously attacked the Jewish bourgeoisie, whom it accused of "directly support[ing] the fascist regime" and of trying to stupefy the Jewish masses with "dreams of Palestine or with religious fanaticism."[3]

The growth of anti-Semitism led the Bund to modify its isolationist policies somewhat. It decided to participate in elections to *kehillot* in 1936, attracting support for its role after the Przytyk pogrom in mobilizing a one-day national Jewish protest strike and community-wide defense against anti-Semitism. An Agudist newspaper at the time noted disapprovingly: "The whole truth is that the Bund received very many votes from the simple masses of the people, from the Jewish poor who still keep the Sabbath, still eat kosher, go to pray on the Sabbath, and put on *tefillin* every day."[4]

In late 1938 the Zionists called for a united electoral front of all Jewish parties but this was rejected by the Bund. In its electoral campaigns in 1938–39 it directed the main thrust of its campaigning less against the Polish anti-Semitic right, from whom, after all, it could hardly hope to win votes, than against its most immediate competitors, other Jewish parties. "The gentlemen of the 'General Jewish Bloc,' the merchants and the Zionists, present themselves now to the Jewish population in the name of 'national unity,' " declared a Bundist election leaflet in Vilna, "but how can there be unity between the rich and well-fed, who have never tasted hardship, and the poor *horepashnikn* [toilers]?"[5] Instead, it called on Jewish voters, in districts where Jewish candidates had no hope of winning, to vote for its ally, the Polish Socialist Party.[6] In the parliamentary elections of November 1938, which the Bund and other opposition parties again boycotted, Jewish parties secured just five members in the Sejm (two Agudists and three Zionists) and two (appointed) senators.

In municipal elections in December 1938 and January 1939, however, the Bund won striking successes: together with leftist allies it won 17 out of 20 seats held by Jewish parties in Warsaw and 11 out of 17 in Łódź In partnership with the Polish Socialist Party, it formed governing coalitions in several municipalities. Although its support was much weaker outside the big cities, this was still an impressive advance. In the country as a whole, the Bund received 38 percent of the votes cast for Jewish parties in these elections, beating both the Zionists, who obtained 36 percent, and the Agudists and other religious elements, trailing with 23 percent. At the same time, membership of the Bundist labor unions increased: in January 1939 they claimed 36,567 members in Warsaw, a majority of the organized Jewish workforce.

These victories did not lead the Bund to abandon its opposition to *klal yisroel* politics. On the contrary, insisting that the elections proved that it alone "represented the Jewish masses of Poland and that the other Jewish political bodies had practically no influence or representative capacity and would either gradually wane or die out completely," the Bund refused, for instance, to participate with other Jewish organizations in a general committee of Polish Jews to cooperate with the Joint Distribution Committee, even though many of its institutions, such as the Medem sanatorium, depended in part on the Joint's financial support. A Bund representative pointed out "that they could not jeopardize their position with the non-Jewish elements of labor groups by sitting with people known as representing capitalist groups." Their relationship with socialist brethren was "much more important to them than any assistance granted them by the JDC through the Central Polish Committee and they would rather maintain their principles even at the risk of sacrificing such assistance." Such high-minded expression of class solidarity did not, however, prevent the party from presenting importunate demands to the Joint for assistance for various Bund-associated projects and institutions.[7]

Too much should not be made of the Bund's electoral victories at this time. Although for the moment the largest Jewish party, it still represented only a minority of Polish Jewry, who remained divided along traditional lines into three main parts: orthodox, Zionist, and the left (including the formally nonexistent, electorally invisible but, among Jews, still significant Communists). The Bund's rejection of *klal yisroel* politics prevented it from breaking out far beyond its proletarian base. One indication of its limited appeal emerges from membership figures for the Bundist youth organization, Tsukunft, which recruited youngsters aged fifteen to eighteen: in the whole of Poland in March 1939 it could muster just 2,235 members.[8]

As their political support ebbed, Zionists of all stripes exploited the mood of public desperation to try to outshine their rivals in extremist rhetoric. In early 1938, at a conference of his organization in Prague, Jabotinsky had offered the unfortunate prediction: "Great Britain will no more let you, the Czechs, down than us. Her word is a rock and she will keep it, she will not let down the smaller nations."[9] After Munich, as Britain tightened restriction of Jewish immigration to Palestine, Jabotinsky's proposals seemed all the more utopian. Yet his ideas secured the support of the anti-Semitic Polish right and friendly interest from the Polish government. In response to the Kristallnacht, Jabotinsky arrived at apocalyptic conclusions. Foreseeing "elemental floods" that would engulf east European Jewry, he propounded, in place of his ten-year, 1.5 million Jews emigration policy, a new "evacuation" plan, whereby one million people would be transferred to Palestine within a single year.[10]

Once the British backtracked from the idea of partition of Palestine, as they did in the course of 1938, the mainstream Zionists had little to offer, by way of competition with the Revisionists, save rhetoric. If Jabotinsky proposed unfeasible policies, they could present little more than ineffectual protests. In February 1939 the chairman of the Jewish parliamentary club in the Sejm, Emil Sommerstein, a General Zionist, denounced "the extermination policy of the present Government and system."[11] When the Sejm passed a bill calling for a complete prohibition of *shechitah* in Poland, the Jewish community observed a "meatless fortnight" in protest. The gesture had little impact, save on kosher butchers and restaurants, which suffered a foretaste of the bill's likely consequences if it were to be approved by the senate. The Bund, in a further characteristic exercise in ideological posturing, disdained to participate "since the religious motives of the Jewish bourgeois parties were foreign to its views," while at the same time it did not oppose the protest since the ban "was obviously a means of oppressing the Jewish minority."[12]

A Zionist leader wrote from Poland in March 1939 that the Revisionist "danger" was increasing "day by day, hour by hour. They always raise their heads when times are difficult for us." Their massive propaganda efforts were aided, he suggested, by the widespread demoralization—"and they indeed are the biggest factor in this demoralization." They were attracting, in particular, the assimilated intelligentsia. Using the propaganda methods of Italy and the USSR, he wrote, there were "no lies too good for them." Weizmann was portrayed as a British agent. Jabotinsky's "evacuationism" found a ready audience.[13]

The mainstream Zionists continued to favor a policy of selective immigration to Palestine of indoctrinated cadres, though Yitzhak Gruenbaum, the former leader of the Polish Zionists, by then resident in Palestine, had occasionally spoken in larger terms: "We must depart. The hour of the exodus has struck for the broad masses of Jewry," he had declared in 1936.[14] That, however, was not intended as a serious policy proposal. Apolinary Hartglas, president of the Zionist Organization of central and eastern Poland, rejected Jabotinsky's plan vehemently: "To other than ideologically motivated emigration to Palestine, we say no, never!"[15] His outspoken hostility to the Revisionists earned him a death threat.

The acrimonious Zionist debate over Jabotinsky's evacuation proposal proved to be purely academic. Its implementation was predicated on somehow inducing the British to comply. But neither by diplomacy nor by the organization of illegal immigration did the Zionists prove equal to that task. Their failure became manifest in May 1939 with the publication by the British government of its White Paper on Palestine. This spelled out what were to be the guiding principles of British policy for the foreseeable future. Jewish immigration was to be limited to a maximum of seventy-five thousand over the next five years. Jewish land purchase was to be altogether prohibited or severely restricted in large areas of Palestine. And for the first time the British government declared that its ultimate aim in Palestine was the creation of a state that would be neither wholly Jewish, nor wholly Arab. The White Paper marked the end of the more than two-decade-old Anglo-Zionist alliance and represented an attempt by the British to freeze the Jewish National Home within its existing demographic and geographical limits.

Regarded by the Zionists as a betrayal in their darkest hour, the White Paper was enforced rigorously by the British authorities in Palestine. Naval patrols sought to interdict ramshackle steamers carrying illegal Jewish immigrants. Every possible pressure was exerted against countries that allowed Jews to leave or cross their territory and against states in whose ships refugees traveled. Illegal immigrants were threatened with return to their countries of origin, though hardly any such deportations could take place as refugees lacking immigration certificates threw away their passports before reaching Palestine.

Most Jewish opinion condemned the White Paper. But in France the Union Patriotique des Israélites Français opposed protest demonstrations and expressed the view that "for foreigners admitted to reside on our soil, it behooves them to abstain from agitation of any kind, most particularly when it is directed against the actions of the government of a power allied to France."[16] In Warsaw the Poalei Zion organized a protest strike but the Bundist unions refused to participate.

Palestine, in any case, did not seem so attractive to some potential immigrants. In the summer of 1939 a family of orthodox Jews in Palestine wrote to their old parents in a *shtetl* in Romania, urging them to immigrate to the Holy Land. The father, a desperately poor *shochet*, replied: "How beautiful and how pleasant it would surely be to be with you face to face and to fulfil the commandment to settle in the Land of Israel. But what shall I say? Given the number of bad rumours that we hear from the Land in the newspapers, we certainly cannot think of this now."[17]

Phantom Vessels

An index of the desperation with which many Jews viewed their situation by this stage was the readiness even of respectable organizations to resort to extralegal actions. In early 1939 the Amsterdam Refugees Committee agreed to cooperate with the Haganah (the Zionist underground militia in Palestine) in a plan to send a ship carrying illegal immigrants, many of them from the training farm at Wieringen, to Palestine. The Joint, on which the committee was heavily dependent, insisted that its funds must not be used directly for the purpose of *aliya bet* (illegal immigration to Palestine).[18] But much of the necessary money was provided sub rosa by Saly Mayer, a wealthy Swiss Jew who worked in close cooperation with the Joint. Gideon Rufer, a Jewish Agency representative from Palestine, arrived to coordinate the arrangements.

The *Dora*, a rickety little forty-year-old Panamian-registered coal freighter, with a Greek captain, left Amsterdam semisecretly on the night of July 15–16, 1939, supposedly for Siam. Crowded aboard were over three hundred passengers, mainly German Jews, among them about fifty from the Wieringen farm school and some from the Hellevoetsluis internment camp. More boarded at Antwerp. Officially the Dutch government knew nothing about the ship's departure; in fact, senior ministers and officials colluded in the enterprise.[19]

I had great doubts [Gertrude van Tijn wrote later] whether it was justifiable to send the refugees on that rotten little boat with the added risk of interception before they reached their destination. But I reasoned that I would have sent my own son had he been in a similar situation. . . . For four weeks I lay awake at night, worrying about the ship. Then we heard that she had reached Palestine safely, had not been intercepted by the English coastguard and that all the boys and girls—who had, according to instructions, thrown their identification papers into the sea—had been distributed among the old Palestine colonies and were now unrecognizable as newcomers.[20]

The *Dora* reached Palestine on August 11–12, 1939. She was one boat among many. That summer twenty "phantom vessels" carrying refugees from Nazism were wandering the oceans in search of a friendly port.

The actual stuff of novels, a film, and boundless human anguish was the saga, enacted on the high seas, of the 937 refugees who left Hamburg on May 13, 1939, on the Hamburg-Amerika company liner *St. Louis*. Anti-Semitic demonstrations greeted news of the ship's impending arrival at Havana. Although armed with Cuban entry visas, the passengers were refused permission to land. The director general of the Cuban immigration authority, who had squeezed at least half a million dollars in bribes from refugees, was forced to resign when his peculations became public. A few passengers were admitted but 908 were refused landing permission. The president of Cuba offered to allow them to enter, provided the Joint Distribution Committee posted a $453,500 bond. Its representative tried to negotiate about the price but in the meantime the ship was ordered to leave harbor and sailed toward Miami. The U.S. authorities rejected pleas for their admission there and on June 6 the ship turned back toward Europe. Eventually it docked at Antwerp, and the Belgian, British, French, and Dutch governments agreed to take in the passengers. In announcing its decision, the British government warned that it could not "be regarded as a precedent for the reception in future of refugees who may leave Germany before definite arrangements have been made for their reception elsewhere."[21] The 181 passengers who were admitted to the Netherlands were initially deposited in the quarantine camp at Heyplaat in Rotterdam, which by this time had become, in effect, a prison camp surrounded by barbed wire with guard dogs.

"An Excess of Old Furniture"

The distraught flight of these world wanderers was a direct result of the deteriorating position of Jews under Nazi rule. In January 1939 all "non-Aryans" still in the Reich were humiliatingly obliged to add Israel (for males) or Sarah (for females) to their names, if their current forenames did not appear on an officially issued list of supposedly characteristic Jewish forenames. In the same month the Gestapo established a Central Authority for Jewish Emigration in the main Jewish community center on Oranienburgerstrasse in Berlin. Nazi policy was by now directed to making continued existence for Jews in Germany unviable and seeking every possible means to expedite the emigration of remaining Jews.

All Jews in the Reich were ordered to give up their gold, silver, and jewelry to pawnbrokers for a fraction of its value, the only permitted exceptions being one silver watch, one wedding ring, and two four-piece sets of cutlery per person. Debts owed to Jews by private persons, businesses, or insurance companies were no longer paid and recourse to the courts was fruitless. An increased emigration tax and yet other measures ensured that those who left were stripped of most of their property.

Over the next eight months a further 62,000 Jews left the country. A census in May 1939 recorded 214,000 Jews "by religion" living in Germany (not including areas annexed since the Anschluss). There were 331,000 "non-Aryans" in the Third Reich as a whole plus at least another 100,000 so-called *Mischlinge*. The emigrants were disproportionately young, male, and able-bodied. Those left behind, conversely, were more often old, female (including many widows), and infirm. Nearly all were destitute. Only 16 percent were gainfully employed. Most of the remainder fit for work (and some not) were already reduced to semi-slavery as conscripted laborers. In the final months of the peace, thousands more scrambled to at least temporary safety. By September 1939 the number of Jews "by religion" in the Altreich had fallen to 185,000. Only 1,480 of the 1,610 religious communities that had existed in 1933 remained. Two-thirds of other Jewish institutions had disappeared. The once proud and seemingly secure edifice of German Jewry had been reduced to pathetic dependence on a state that was far advanced on the road toward mass murder.

On July 4 a decree law was issued whereby the Reichsvertretung was formally replaced by a body to be known as the Reichsvereinigung der Juden in Deutschland (Reich Union of Jews in Germany). The new body, established after lengthy internal discussions among the remaining Jewish leadership in Germany, united all existing Jewish communities (which no longer retained legal existence) and institutions. The change of name was intended to drive home the Jews' humiliation. No longer were they to be treated as if they had a right to represent their own interests. The new body, headed, like the old, by Baeck, was responsible for all Jews (racially defined). The government regarded the union's main task as facilitating their exodus from the country. Although it operated under Nazi supervision, the Reichsvereinigung initially managed to preserve a limited sphere of Jewish autonomy and self-help, raising funds from overseas, organizing educational, health, and welfare activities, supporting the Kulturbund, and seeking, albeit with little success, to mitigate the harsh implementation of the government's anti-Jewish decrees.[22] But the realization soon dawned that the representative body of German Jews had been transformed into a hapless instrument of Nazi policy.

Kurt Goldmann, head of the Zionists' "Palestine Office" in Berlin until March 1939, wrote scornfully in a letter shortly after he left Germany, that those who remained there were "an altogether decadent, demoralized Jewry, worn down by internal contradictions. . . . You see Jews in cafés, degenerate types behaving in revolting ways, living out their mindless, empty lives, and you become aware of the downfall of German Jewry from a cultured, liberal, sophisticated community into a conglomeration of repulsive, egoistical people."[23] This was the voice of a young fanatic but his view exemplified the arrogant self-confidence with which many Zionists, like adherents of other ideologies at the time, were convinced that they alone were in possession of the Ariadne's thread that would lead to salvation.

The remaining Jews in Germany concentrated in the big cities, hoping to find a greater measure of security there. By mid-1939, 36 percent of what was left of German Jewry lived in Berlin, the highest proportion ever. In some small towns, every single Jew had left and the last reminders of their presence were being eliminated. At Creglingen in Württemberg, for example, all the seventy Jewish residents were gone, though not all had managed to escape Germany: some had found refuge, as they thought, in Stuttgart. The synagogue had been burned down on Kristallnacht. The municipal council offered the Jewish bathhouse (*mikveh*) for sale—to be demolished for its salvage value, since, as the council announced, "the small building spoilt the view of the town and also the style of the building is quite reminiscent of the bygone Jewish times."[24]

The small city of Offenburg, near the Black Forest in the province of Baden, was one of many towns near the Rhine where Jews had lived since medieval times. The synagogue, like most throughout

Germany, had been destroyed in November 1938, and the three hundred or so Jews terrorized. By the summer of 1939 Jews here, as elsewhere, were being shunned by surrounding society and were desperate to escape. Among them was Eduard Cohn, a businessman in the town who had served in the army in the First World War. During the Kristallnacht pogrom he was arrested, tortured, and sent to Dachau. After six weeks he was released on condition that he arrange to leave Germany. He managed to get to England in May 1939, hoping to proceed from there to Palestine. He was compelled, however, to leave his wife, Silvia, and their three children, behind in Offenburg. In the summer of 1939 they were still waiting anxiously for visas to enter Britain. In the meantime they tried to dispose of their remaining assets, mainly household goods. In 1937, when a relative of Anne Frank left Dortmund for Peru, she had been compelled to sell her furniture for just a quarter of its value. Now such goods were almost completely worthless. In a letter to her sister in late June, Silvia Cohn wrote: "You know that we are not permitted to advertise and old furniture is being offered for sale all over the place but people aren't interested in buying anything anymore and will pay next to nothing for it, since there's an excess of old furniture being offered for sale by emigrants."[25]

The situation was similar in Austria, where the remaining Jews concentrated in Vienna. In the summer of 1939 two provinces, Styria and Carinthia, ordered the expulsion of all Jewish residents. Altogether 109,000 Jews emigrated from Austria between March 1938 and the outbreak of the war. Here too the Jews who remained were mainly the old. The refugees were preponderantly children and those of working age: two-thirds of all Jewish children between the ages of one and fifteen had been taken abroad by September 1939.[26]

On March 14, 1939, Wilhelmine Floeck, a blind, seventy-two-year-old widow in Vienna, formerly married to an "Aryan," appealed to Josef Bürckel, Reich commissioner for the reunification of Austria with the German Reich, for permission to retain her small pension.[27] The Nazi official's response (if any) is not recorded.

A decree law that took effect on April 30 removed all legal protection from Jewish tenants throughout the Reich. Many were evicted from their homes and forced to share apartments or rooms with other Jews. In Vienna the housing department of the Jewish community reported in mid-May that it was overwhelmed every day by crowds of despairing, weeping people to whom it could offer no help.[28]

Dissolution in Danzig

As the world's attention turned toward Danzig, seemingly the next object of Hitler's rapacity, that city's Jewish community engaged in enforced self-liquidation. Danzig and the territory around it, which had a largely German population, had been a Free City under the protection of the League of Nations since 1920. In May 1933 local Nazis won control of the city council and reduced the authority of the League's representative to a cipher. The mainly German-speaking Jews of Danzig had always supported German as against Polish interests there. But that availed them nothing after 1933. Over the next six years they were subjected to an ever-growing reign of terror. Signs indicating "Jews not desired" began to appear in shop windows. Arbitrary violence and police-sponsored intimidation of Jews became the order of the day. Jewish-owned businesses were ordered to close. A day or two after the Kristall-nacht, the synagogues in the suburb of Langfuhr and the nearby seaside resort of Zoppot were destroyed. Fifteen hundred Jews fled over the Polish border.

In December 1938 all Jews were ordered to leave the territory. Only old people and a few "protected Jews" would be allowed to stay. In order to camouflage the forcible nature of the expulsion, the Nazis invited the Jews themselves to prepare an evacuation plan to be approved by the city authorities. Their departure would then be presented to the world as a generous response to a request by the Jews themselves.

On December 17 the head of the Jewish community, Dr. Curt Itzig, addressed two thousand people crowded into the main syna-gogue and announced the expulsion order. "When Jews came together in this holy place in former times," he said, "we came to pray to God.

In good times we thanked God for the good he bestowed upon us. . . . To-day we are gathered together here because we are all fearful for our fate and, what is even more important, for the fate and future of our children." He urged his hearers to grant him and his colleagues full authority to conduct an orderly dissolution of the community in accordance with the orders of the Nazi authorities. His hearers approved the proposal unanimously. Afterward they wept.[29]

The synagogue itself was ordered to be torn down in May 1939 and the ground on which it stood was to be sold to help finance the Jews' emigration. Signs were erected on the building announcing, "The synagogue will be demolished" and "Hasten, dear May and render us free of the Jews." The Joint Distribution Committee negotiated an arrangement whereby the ritual treasures of the community—a total of 342 items, including 52 Torah scrolls, 11 Torah crowns, 9 *mezuzot* (amulets), 8 Torah mantles, and 4 ram's horns, as well as a memorial plaque for the 56 Danzig Jews who had died "for the fatherland" between 1914 and 1918—were exported to the United States for safekeeping. The Nazi police chief authorized their removal "on condition that the proceeds are applied to funding the emigration of the Jewish community."[30]

Like Jews elsewhere, those of Danzig found it almost impossible to secure immigration visas to any destination. The British consul general in the city, Gerald Shepherd, helped to arrange the departure of 122 children and a small number of working-age adult males to England as well as of some elderly persons to Palestine. But he warned community leaders to have nothing to do with illegal immigration to Palestine. They ignored the warning. In concert with Revisionist Zionist operatives, they organized a transport of refugees to Palestine. The Nazi president of the Danzig Senate complained to the League of Nations high commissioner that Shepherd was doing his utmost to "torpedo" their departure.[31]

In early March a group of 423 Jews left the city, heading for Palestine. They traveled overland by bus, truck, and train to the port of Reni in Romania, where they boarded a Greek-owned cargo-ship, the eight-hundred-ton SS *Astir*. Conditions on the ship were unsanitary, food was inadequate, and the vessel was dangerously overcrowded. When the Danzig refugees, who were now accompanied by 280 others from Romania and Hungary, arrived in Haifa, they were refused permission to land. The ship wandered around the Mediterranean for several weeks, finally returning to Palestine in late June. The passengers, by this time in poor physical and mental condition, were transferred to small, Arab-manned sailing-boats off the coast of Gaza and landed on the beach. The few British officers present were unable to prevent the theft of the greater part of the refugees' belongings by the Arab boatmen. On landing, the immigrants were transferred to an internment camp, where they were able to recuperate from their ordeal.[32]

Some Danzig Jews managed to obtain visas for Bolivia. Fifty took refuge in Shanghai. A group of 135 found shelter at the nearby Polish port of Gdynia. But rising tensions between Poland and Germany led the Polish government to decree that no Jew could live within fifty miles of the border. They were therefore ordered to move on. By the end of August 1939, no more than 1,400 Jews remained out of the 10,000 who had lived in Danzig in 1933.

Scenes from Jewish Life in Europe, Summer 1939

In July 1939, the association of French Jewish veterans of the First World War held their usual annual pilgrimage to Verdun and recited *kaddish* at the Jewish memorial at the ossuary of Douaumont. Throughout France that month, Jewish communities celebrated the 150th anniversary of the revolution that had brought them, for the first time in Europe, civil equality with Christians. One such ceremony took place in the spa town of Vichy, recently the scene of anti-Semitic incidents. A rabbi delivered an eloquent address, lauding Abbé Grégoire, whose efforts in the National Assembly had led to the emancipation. At a celebratory dinner of Jewish ex-servicemen in the restaurant "Max," the mayor of Vichy declared his sympathy for refugees, victims, he said, of ignoble racist theories.[33]

In Vilna, the calendar of events at the Yiddish theater for the spring and summer seasons offered a lively program of both high- and lowbrow shows:

March 29–31	Guest performances by Jonas Turkow and Diana Blumenfeld [a husband-and-wife team, stars of the Yiddish stage] in "Freud's Theory of Dreams"
April 18–23	Guest performances by Lola Forman in two revues and an operetta
May 5–June 6	Guest performances by Peysakhke Burstein and Lillian Lux [another stage couple, stars of the New York Yiddish stage]
May 23–June 11	Seventh Maydim programme [Maydim was a sophisticated marionette theater]: "From Seventh Heaven"
June 10	United Academy of Literary Societies, Vilbig, Maccabi, Theater Organization: "80 Years of Shalom Aleichem"
June 23–25 and July 7	Eighth Davke [a local cabaret] program: "Zaverukhes" (Blizzards)
June 30–July 2	Guest appearances by Ayzic Samberg [a well-known Yiddish actor] and others
July 18 and 19	Song recitals by Yosele Kolodny[34]

Outside the theater, however, it was dangerous for Jews to hang around in the streets too long after dark. Every day in the city Jews were being attacked in seemingly pointless onslaughts, explicable only as outbursts of anti-Semitism.

In Minsk the seventy-one thousand Jews, now reduced to under a third of the population, were no longer the showpiece of Soviet Yiddish secularism that they had been for two decades. The previous July the Byelorussian Supreme Soviet had terminated the status of Yiddish as an official language of the republic. This was more an anti-minority than an anti-Jewish decision: Polish was similarly demoted. But it spelled the end of Soviet promotion of a secular Yiddish culture. Yiddish writers and scholars in the city were arrested. Nearly all remaining Jewish institutions, apart from the Yiddish theater, were closed.[35] The practice of Jewish religion in the city had by this time been driven almost completely underground. An illicit manufacturer of *matzot* found himself in a labor camp in 1939 with a five-year sentence.[36]

Many of the Soviet Jews who had embraced Communism with such burning faith were by now bitterly disillusioned. Moshe Zalcman had been separated from his Yiddish-speaking friends and moved to another camp of the Gulag system. Gershon Shapiro, after his second narrow scrape with denunciation, was keeping his head low. In both cases selfless commitment to the cause had given way to a dull determination to survive.

In Salonica Jewish life was in a sorry state: "Jewish schools were empty; Jewish youth associations no longer attracted many members. . . . The Zionist Federation was almost non-existent."[37] The annual meeting of the Grand Cercle Sioniste, the main Zionist society, had to be postponed owing to the absence of a quorum.[38] The Jews, within living memory the largest population group in the city, now numbered 52,000 out of a total population of 240,000, the great majority of whom were Greeks.

Declining religious observance in Salonica was reflected in a story published in *Acción* in which a character criticizes mothers who bring parcels of food to the synagogue for their children on Yom Kippur.[39] Another story appeared in *Mesajero* in which a father fails to persuade his son to observe the fast of the tenth of Tevet, while the son's wife seems more concerned with buying a silk umbrella than with fasting.[40] There were just twenty rabbis left in the city, most of them elderly, ten *shochtim*, four *mohalim*, and four *sofrim* (scribes qualified to write Torah scrolls).

Nearly all the Jewish charitable bodies reporting to the Salonica community council in May 1939 lamented crippling deficits in their budgets.[41] The Asilo de Locos (mental asylum), for example, stated "El estado general de mouestra ovra à pounto de vista financario es de los mas criticos." ("The general state of our work, from the financial point of view, is in the utmost degree critical.")[42] Traditionally the community had depended financially on various internal taxes and fees, notably the *pecha*, a tax on purchasers of kosher meat, with exemption for the poor. The growing impoverishment of the community and a declining observance of *kashrut* led to a drop in the number of *pecheros* to fewer than 1,200 by 1939, producing an income barely a quarter that of two decades earlier. The prevalent feeling among Jews in the city was one of communal decay and personal foreboding.

In Amsterdam the number of new refugees had at last begun to decline: whereas 601 had arrived in the Netherlands in January, only 253 gained entry in August. Of these 187 held onward transit visas and tickets. These numbers reflected the stringent application of Dutch immigration policy. Indeed, in August more refugees left than arrived. The most common destination for these emigrants was Australia (77 cases), followed by the United States (55), Britain (49), and various South American countries; only eight were able to move to Palestine. The number of refugees in camps in Holland was also declining, from 1,556 on March 31 to 1,278 on August 31; as a result, three of the camps closed in August.[43]

On August 30 the Joint organized a meeting in Paris of experts dealing with the refugee problem. Gertrude van Tijn was among those attending. She returned to Holland with one of the German-Jewish leaders, Fritz Seligsohn, whose wife and children had taken refuge there the previous November. Seligsohn's wife and Gertrude begged him not to return to Germany but he felt it was his duty to go back to help the left-behind Jews, mainly old and infirm, for whom he felt a responsibility.

In Warsaw the atmosphere was a strange mixture of fear and patriotic elation. As the likelihood of war grew, Jews joined in the military and civil mobilization and were relieved to note that, at least in this supreme crisis, they could find a degree of acceptance as fellow citizens. Some facets of the mood of the time are conveyed by headlines in the *Vus hert zikh in varshe?* local news section of *Haynt* on August 25: "Another emigrant swindled" (two Jewish crooks took advantage of a woman from a *shtetl* who had come to Warsaw to seek a U.S. visa); "A special room for Polish advocates in the District Court" (Jewish lawyers were not to be admitted); "Festive reception for Shaul Tchernikhovsky in Writers' Club" (the Hebrew poet, visiting from Palestine, received a warm welcome).

The occupation of Brno by the Nazis in March had been followed by intensified anti-Semitic measures. The main synagogue in the city was burned down. Hugo Jellinek was still living there as a refugee.

"The future is clouded with impenetrable black cloths," he wrote to his daughter in Palestine.[44] On the personal level, he was happier than ever since he had fallen in love with a local widow. But his parents, brothers, and sisters and their families, all stuck in Vienna, were desperately seeking avenues of escape. "We are at our wits' end," wrote one of his sisters in late June.[45] His father, a former synagogue cantor, who had been used to being treated with great respect, was bellowed at and humiliated by a Nazi official when he went to lodge an application. One of Jellinek's brothers had succeeded in leaving for the United States. Another left for Shanghai. A sister managed to get to Australia. His daughters Bertha and Anna applied for visas for the United States. Bertha also applied for admission to Britain. In August, still without visas of any kind, the girls considered following their sister Nadja on an illegal transport to Palestine. But at the end of the month they and their father were still in Brno.

In spite of the depressing trends confronting Yiddishists in most of Europe by 1939, the director of YIVO, Max Weinreich, an enthusiast but also a realist, was not altogether disheartened. Summarizing prospects for the language in a paper that he prepared for the International Congress of Linguists that convened in Brussels on August 28, 1939, he struck a hopeful note. While acknowledging that "inherent in the position of a minority language are certainly many dangers for its existence," he set these aside as "facts of an extra-linguistic nature." "Insofar as the linguistic level is concerned," he concluded, "it can be stated that at no period of its history has Yiddish reached such a degree of independence, integration and expressiveness as today, and the present-day achievements, especially in the language of poetry and scientific literature, give us the certainty that the development is not to stop there."[46] Weinreich was, of course, sadly aware that the "extra-linguistic" factors might expunge everything else. They hit the language, its speakers, and Weinreich personally, almost immediately. Unable to return to Vilna at the end of August, he was compelled to seek refuge elsewhere.

In Geneva, on August 16, the Zionist Organization convened its twenty-first congress. In spite of the political setbacks that had befallen the movement, membership was at an all-time high. The total number of shekel purchasers in 1939 was a record 1.3 million. This was 25 percent higher than prior to the previous congress, in 1937, even though the shekel could no longer be sold in greater Germany or Italy. Sixteen delegates from Germany managed to attend. Elected representatives arrived from almost every other Jewish community in Europe, except the Soviet Union. Although actively organized Zionists remained a minority of world Jewry and although the Revisionists had excluded themselves from the organization, the congress could plausibly claim to be the closest the European Jews had to a parliamentary assembly.

On August 24 the delegates were shocked by news of the signature at 2 A.M. that day, of a Nazi-Soviet nonaggression pact. While the secret clauses, by which Stalin and Hitler agreed to partition Poland, remained as yet unknown, it was immediately understood that the treaty gave Hitler carte blanche to go to war with Poland.

Already in May the dismissal of the Soviet foreign minister, Maxim Litvinov, a Jew identified with the policy of "collective security" and his replacement by Vyacheslav Molotov gave an important clue to the change in Stalin's thinking. Litvinov, whatever his loyalties, would hardly have been an appropriate interlocutor with Ribbentrop. Stalin accused Litvinov of disloyalty and instructed his new foreign minister, "Purge the ministry of Jews."[47]

The Nazi-Soviet pact caused consternation among Jewish Communists. In Paris the initial reaction of the Yiddish Communist daily, *Naye prese*, was almost instinctively to parrot the Moscow line faithfully. But party members there and elsewhere were aghast. Ilya Ehrenburg, whose dispatches from Paris had suddenly stopped appearing in *Izvestia* in April, was beside himself with rage and could not eat solid food for months, losing forty pounds as a result.

In the light of the news from Moscow, the Zionist Congress closed a day earlier than planned in order to enable delegates to return to their homelands. Chaim Weizmann delivered a farewell address to the assembly in Yiddish. The mood of his hearers was one of deep depression and anxiety. He told them: "I have no prayer but this—that we shall meet again, alive." Then, using a biblical phrase that came, toward the end of the war, to be used of Jewish survivors in Europe, he said: "*She'erit ha-pleitah* [the surviving remnant] will continue to work, to fight, to live, until better days shall come." The official record of proceedings recorded that there was deep emotion in the hall and many of those present had tears in their eyes.[48]

19

EXISTENTIAL CRISIS

The Hanging Question

One of the most acute contemporary analysts of European Jewish politics and society, Jacob Lestchinsky, wrote from Berlin as early as March 1933 that the Nazis aimed at "a mass slaughter of Jews."[1] Lestchinsky was a Lithuanian citizen, a leading figure in YIVO, and a serious commentator not normally given to sensational statements. His report earned him expulsion from Germany. He moved to Poland but was expelled from there too in 1937, this time because his writings on Polish Jewry were regarded by the government as hostile to the regime. In 1938 he emigrated to New York but remained in close touch with Polish Jewry and continued to write for the Yiddish press.

Lestchinsky, who was not a Zionist, observed in 1938 that, by comparison with Jews in Palestine, the Jewish worker in the diaspora (he meant principally in eastern Europe) did not feel sufficiently secure and rooted to make sacrifices today for gains the day after tomorrow. "He rattles through life in the Diaspora the way one rattles through five o'clock prayers" ("Er khapt op dos lebn in golus vi men khapt op dos funfornt-davnen"), "the quicker to be rid of a burden."[2] Deferred gratification, in other words, made no sense in a world of no expectations.

In late July 1939, Lestchinsky published an article calling for Jews to cast aside shortsighted passivity and to display greater readiness to resist their oppressors. Large numbers of German Jewish exiles, he pointed out, had volunteered at the time of the Munich crisis to serve in the French and British armies. Some voices then had inquired whether the volunteers were willing to take responsibility for untoward consequences that might befall the Jews who remained in Germany. "After all, Hitler would simply slaughter them" (*zi oyskoylenen*). "The question," he continued, "remained hanging in the air." But nobody now, he said, came out against Jews volunteering for the British army or the French Foreign Legion with the goal of fighting against Hitlerism.[3] Although his article did not discuss the Polish-Jewish predicament directly, the call for a strategy of resistance to anti-Semitism was plainly not restricted to Nazi Germany.

But how to resist? And how to address the "hanging question"?

Return to the Ghetto

According to Hannah Arendt, one of the salient features of what she termed "totalitarianism" was the reduction of its victims to atomized, isolated individuals.[4] Perhaps. But at any rate as regards Germany between 1933 and 1939, heightened solidarity rather than atomization was more characteristic of Jews' reaction to persecution.

Joachim Prinz, the young rabbi whose preaching captured the imagination of thousands of listeners in Berlin between 1933 and 1937, argued in 1935 in the *Jüdische Rundschau* under the headline "Ghetto 1935" that the only place in Germany that was not a ghetto was the synagogue.

> Everything else [as he later summarized the article] was ghetto, and that meant persecution: the streets, the parks, the theatres, the schools, the place of work. But the synagogue was a place of security, or at least one in which people felt secure. The yearning to be with other Jews was overwhelming. It included all kinds of Jews. Among them were Jews who had converted to Christianity and thousands of marginal Jews who were so assimilated that they had never seen the inside of a synagogue.[5]

Victimization, while heightening personal feelings of vulnerability, could also produce this kind of instinctive, across-the-board fraternity. But were the Jews, notwithstanding what Prinz maintained (and he left Germany in 1937), really rising above the ghetto or huddling back into it?

Talk of a "return to the ghetto" became a commonplace of Jewish discourse of the late 1930s. Debate over the concept cut across conventional ideological lines and across borders throughout the Jewish world. At first the phrase was understood as denoting a rejection by Jews of the universalism of the Enlightenment and reattachment instead to the roots of Jewish culture. It came to embody a feeling of disappointment in the consequences of emancipation and a resigned turn inward. The idea seems to have originated in Germany, where some Jews, particularly the strictly orthodox minority who had always been suspicious of the dangers, as they saw them, of an open society, were not, at first, altogether averse to the re-erection by the Nazis of barriers between Jews and gentiles. In Poland too, as nationalists sought to shut Jews out of common fellowship in national society, some were attracted to the idea of retreating into a shell. Later, as Jews were driven into economic and social isolation, the phrase began to carry more sinister implications.

A reaction soon set in from those, particularly liberals and leftists, who retained faith in the Enlightenment vision of the brotherhood of men. In 1937 Roman Zilbershtayn, a Warsaw city councilor, told a meeting of the Jewish Merchants' Association: "We must burn out with a red-hot iron every kind of nonsensical thought of going back to the ghetto. We may perish but we will not perish in a ghetto."[6]

In April 1938, after the horrors of the Anschluss, the New York Yiddish poet Jacob Glatshteyn published his "Goodnight, world," a savage, unsparing, petulant cry of rage:

A gute nakht, brayte velt,
　　　Good night, wide world.
Groyse, shtinkendike velt. . . .
　　　Big, stinking world. . . .
Oyf mayn aygenem gebot—
　　　At my own command—
Gey ikh tsurik in geto.[7]
　　　I return to the ghetto.

Whether he was consciously echoing the Bach cantata, the performance of which had so moved Paula Lindberg in 1933, is not known.

As sometimes happens when an idea is already in the air, publication of the poem fanned smoldering embers into a fiery controversy. The acerbic Warsaw literary critic Yoshue Rapoport wrote that for several weeks he could "neither swallow nor spit out" Glatshteyn's poem. "So Glatshteyn goes willingly into the ghetto? Not me!" he thundered. And if the day should come that he (Rapoport) was confined in a ghetto, he insisted, he would go not with misplaced pride but shouting out loud that he was being shoved in by force and creating a great commotion in order to let in a breath of the wider world. The Jews, he argued, should not succumb to a "deathly egocentrism" but instead ally with their traditional allies, the forces of enlightenment, to overcome their common enemies.[8]

Meanwhile, the editor of *Parizer haynt* observed that the catastrophe that was befalling the Jewish people had left many fearful that entire Jewish communities would be annihilated and wiped off the face of the earth. But he too disapproved of any talk of a return to the ghetto, arguing instead for a Zionist solution of the Jewish problem.[9]

In early 1939 the head of the historical section of YIVO, Elias Tcherikower, at the time an émigré in Paris, founded a Yiddish journal, *Afn sheydveg* (At the Crossroads), in which he too advocated a return to the ghetto. The circle around the magazine took a pessimistic view of Jewish prospects in Europe. In the Soviet Union Jews had become *meysim khofshim* (liberated dead). In western Europe assimilation was drying up the wellsprings of Jewish culture. Despairing of his earlier belief that secular Yiddish culture might serve as a replacement for religion, Tcherikower wrote: "Our generation, a scattered camp of Jews, gazes with wonder and envy at the spiritual fortitude of past Jewish martyrs, who 'cherished their troubles,' as the Gemara [Talmud] permits itself to say, who accepted providence and elevated suffering to heroism, to *kiddush hashem* [martyrdom]."[10] Tcherikower lamented that the old world of diaspora life was rapidly disappearing:

The tragedy of our generation does not consist in the quantity of afflictions that have fallen to our lot but rather in that the generation has lost the old beliefs and despaired of the new. Through and through individualistic, skeptical, and rationalistic, our generation is devoured by assimilation—right or left—and has lost its past strength. It stands now empty, expelled, without the innocence of a believer and without the primitive strength of a fighter— without any consolation in its afflictions.[11]

This sense of lost cultural and moral bearings, widespread not only among Jews in Europe of the 1930s, was part of what sustained the idea of a return to the ghetto.

The controversy rumbled on until the last, most terrifying word went to the grand old man of *yidishkayt*. In a letter to the editors of Tcherikower's magazine, reprinted in the Warsaw *Haynt* on August 25, the seventy-nine-year-old Simon Dubnow commented: "The last two Hitler-years, 1938–1939, have left many people with the impression that we are at the beginning of the destruction [*khurbn*] of European Jewry." Hitler's "extermination-system" (*oys-rotungs-sistem*), he maintained, was a straightforward re-creation of Haman's plan "to destroy, to massacre, and exterminate all the Jews," with the difference that in Haman's case it had remained merely a plan.[12] The Jews, Dubnow argued, were standing "not at a cross-roads but on a *battlefield*."

What was to be done "*now*, when we face a struggle for our very physical survival, for our human dignity"? What could an unarmed people do? A great deal, he maintained. Alas, his prescriptions were hardly new: strengthening the economic and moral boycott of the two aggressive "bandit-regimes" (he meant Germany and Italy: the article was written before news of the Nazi-Soviet pact reached him), securing homes for Jewish refugees in Palestine and other havens, and combating anti-Semitism in countries where it threatened to engulf the Jews (he meant eastern Europe, including Latvia, where he was then living).

More significant than his immediate political prescriptions were Dubnow's thoughts on Jewish collective self-understanding. He had long argued that emancipation, tolerance, and open societies led to

Jewish assimilation and internal disintegration, whereas persecution and exclusion solidified Jewish collective self-consciousness, cohesion, and solidarity. In this age, he admitted, there was a temptation to abandon the very idea of emancipation: what, after all, had it brought? Yes, it had brought the Jews assimilation, but it had also "brought to life the free human being within the Jew." Jews must struggle against "counter-emancipation," against calls for "evacuation." They must not throw up their arms and sigh. They would stand or fall with humanity as a whole and with the "anti-aggressor alliance" that now included the east European states (here he meant Poland and Romania, which had recently received guarantees from Britain and France).

Dubnow rejected the call for a return to the ghetto as a collapse into passivity and resignation. He discountenanced the summons to repentance and reliance on God. He agreed that every great disaster in the life of a people called forth a "spiritual reckoning" (*heshbon nefesh*). But the proper time for that would come later. Now, in the very midst of the cataclysm, the urgent necessity was saving bodies, not souls: "first Jews, then Jewishness!" ("*Friher yidn, dernokh yidishkayt!*")[13]

Gateway to Annihilation

The ten million European Jews were by no means all of a kind. Indeed, they were probably the most internally variegated people of the continent. But they faced a common set of enemies and they shared a common destiny. In 1939 they all faced an existential crisis.

The challenges confronting them came from within no less than from without. They were heirs to a great civilization but one that showed only limited capacity for self-renewal or rejuvenation. The collective sum of millions of individual decisions by Jews themselves over the previous two or three generations had weakened the ligaments of their society to an extent that even a renewed sense of solidarity in the face of extreme danger could not redress. Long before their enemies turned from vilification and persecution to outright extermination, the Jews themselves were far advanced on a road toward what one of their most perceptive and sympathetic observers called "race suicide."[14]

The demographic trajectory was grim and, with declining fertility, large-scale emigration, increasing outmarriage, and widespread apostasy, foreshadowed extinction. Jewish cultural links were loosening. Use of the Jewish vernaculars, Yiddish and Judeo-Espagnol, was waning from Vilna to Salonica. Traditional religious practice had been eliminated among the greater part of the Jewish population in the Soviet Union, had given way to secularism among large sections of western and central European Jewry, and was in retreat in its Polish-Lithuanian fortress. Many Jews wanted to escape from what they saw as the prison of their Jewishness but found that, however hard they tried, they could not throw off their jailhouse uniform.

In much of Europe, particularly France, Germany, Hungary, and the Soviet Union, a majority of Jews had opted for acculturation and social assimilation, in the hope that these would lead ultimately to full integration into general society. In all these cases that hope was proving delusory. In most of central and eastern Europe, Jews were treated as pariahs. In Poland they were rapidly acculturating without assimilating, let alone integrating. In the USSR, where, more than any other nationality, the Jews had embraced the ideals of the new Soviet society, their position in the late 1930s underwent a sharp reversal. In France the revolutionary tradition of the rights of man, to which most Jews clung as a lifeline, proved gossamer-thin and snapped in the ultimate crisis.

Acculturation and assimilation, of course, were neither one-way streets nor linear processes. The European Jews gave at least as much as they took from surrounding societies and cultures. Their "contributions" (as they are often termed) to European culture earned them admiration and congratulation—particularly after they were gone. In Europe of the late 1930s writers, artists, composers, and scholars of Jewish origin were more commonly assailed as subverters or perverters of national cultures than acclaimed as donors in a mutually beneficial gift relationship.

The problem was not just Germany. The Nazis were the vanguard of a wider European phenomenon of stigmatization, expropriation, extrusion, and bloodshed. Anti-Semitism almost everywhere on the continent that Jews lived had risen to unprecedented heights and was directed against every section of Jewish society, even children, the elderly, and the disabled. Whereas Europe in general was recovering from the Great Depression, the economic position of Jews was catastrophic in German-dominated central Europe and under sustained attack in Poland and Romania. Christian morality, which in the past had set some limits to the worst excesses of Jew-hatred, showed no capacity (nor, in the case of the Roman Catholic Church, much readiness) to restrain racist brutality.

Liberalism and socialism failed in this period in the case of the Jews, as in so much else, to live up to the universalist, Enlightenment principles on which they were founded. As Zygmunt Bauman has written:

> There was an irreparable contradiction between the conditions which had to be met to obtain exit visas from the ghetto, and those which had to be observed to purchase entry tickets to universal humanity. As travelers were soon to discover to their dismay, the universal currency which bought exit visas was not honored by those selling entry tickets.[15]

Allies to whom the Jews had looked with assurance in the past now had other priorities. In France the decline of the Popular Front was accompanied by a growth, even on the left, of xenophobia and collapse of faith in liberal principles. In Britain the policy of support for the Jewish National Home had been replaced by an overriding concern for national and imperial security, held to be incompatible with continued support for Zionism or for large-scale reception of Jewish refugees, whether in Palestine or anywhere in the British Empire. The Soviet Union, which had posed as the most determined foe of Nazism, turned suddenly in August 1939 into Hitler's catspaw.

Increasingly, as we have seen, the Jews of Europe were being transformed from a community into a desperate horde of wandering refugees and into a paradigmatic "camp people."

None of this was news to contemporaries: "the struggle for existence" was one of the characteristic phrases of the period among the

Jews of east-central Europe. As we have seen, contemporaries spoke repeatedly about the threat of "extermination" of the Jewish people. If nobody could foresee Auschwitz, no serious observer of European Jewry in 1939 could be anything but deeply pessimistic about its future.

The Jews of Europe did not react to their predicament passively. They were actors in their own history. They sought by every possible means, individually and collectively, to confront the threats that loomed on every side. They tried emigration, but the exits were blocked. They tried persuasion, but few would listen, and anyway the barking loudspeakers of Nazi propaganda deafened ears. They tried political organization of every kind, but they were politically weightless. A handful, even before the war, tried violent resistance, but their enemies could wreak vengeance a thousandfold—as the Nazis demonstrated on Kristallnacht. Some tried prayer, but their God betrayed them.

They might be captains of their souls but they were not masters of their fate. Theirs was, for the most part, the agitated ineffectuality of flies sealed in a bottle, slowly suffocating.

Wholly defenseless, largely friendless, and more and more hopeless, the European Jews, on the eve of their destruction, waited for the barbarians.

EPILOGUE

FATES KNOWN AND UNKNOWN

Aberbach, Moses, librarian and scholar: born Vienna, 1924. Died Jerusalem, 2007.

Abramowicz, Hirsz, journalist: born near Troki (now in Lithuania), 1881. Left Vilna for a vacation in North America in late June 1939 and did not return. Died New York, 1960.

Abramsky, Yehezkel, Talmudic scholar: born Grodno, 1886. Moved from Latvia to London, where he served as head of the Bet Din (rabbinical court). In 1951 he emigrated to Israel, where he died in 1976.

Adorno, Theodor (né Wiesengrun), philosopher: born Frankfurt am Main, 1903. Died near Zermatt, 1969.

Agnon (né Czaczkes), **Shmuel Yosef,** writer: born Buczacz (Galicia), 1888; Nobel Prize for Literature, 1966. Died Rehovot (Israel), 1970.

Alter, Abraham Mordechai, third Hasidic *rebbe* of Gur (Góra Kalwaria, Poland): born there, 1866. Fled from Poland to Palestine in 1940. Died in Jerusalem during the siege of the city in 1948.

Alter, Wiktor, Bundist leader: born Mława, north-central Poland, 1890. Arrested by NKVD and sentenced to death for anti-Soviet activity, September 1939. Released September 1941 but rearrested December 1941. Executed by firing squad, Kuibyshev, 1943. Maxim Litvinov, at the time Soviet ambassador in Washington, announced the deaths of Alter and Henryk Erlich and said both had been guilty of seeking a separate peace with Germany. Alter's execution was personally approved by Stalin.

Altmann, Alexander, rabbi and scholar: born Kaschau (Košice, now in Slovakia), 1906. Emigrated to England, 1938, where he became communal rabbi of Manchester. From 1959 professor of Jewish philosophy at Brandeis University. Author of the standard biography of Moses Mendelssohn (1973). Died Boston, 1987.

Andermann, Martin, doctor: born Koenigsberg, 1904; took refuge in Switzerland in 1937. Later emigrated to the United States and lived in Buffalo, New York.

Anders (né *Stern*), **Günther,** journalist: born Breslau, 1902. First husband of Hannah Arendt. Fled Germany, 1933. Emigrated to the United States, 1936. Returned to Europe in 1950 and became a founding figure in the antinuclear movement. Died Vienna, 1992.

Arendt, Hannah, political philosopher: born Hanover, 1906. Fled from Germany to France in 1933 and to the United States in 1941. Published *The Origins of Totalitarianism* in 1951 and *Eichmann in Jerusalem: A Report on the Banality of Evil* in 1963. Died New York, 1975.

Arnshteyn, Mark (later Andrzej Marek), theatrical director: born Warsaw, circa 1879. In 1940 founded a Polish-language theater company in the Warsaw ghetto. Died in 1943 either in the ghetto or in Treblinka.

Arouch, Salamon (later Salamo), boxer: born Salonica, 1923. Survived Auschwitz by fighting competition bouts in front of camp guards, experiences that formed the subject of a film, *Triumph of the Spirit* (1989). Died in Israel, 2009.

Asad, Muhammad (né Leopold Weiss), writer and convert to Islam: born Lemberg (Galicia), 1900. In India in the Second World War, Asad was interned as an enemy (Austrian) alien. Later became a Pakistani representative at the United Nations and a propagandist for Islam. Died in Spain, 1992. Buried in the Muslim cemetery of Granada.

Asch, Sholem, Yiddish writer: born Kutno (Poland), 1880. He spent the war years in the United States and later moved to Israel. Asch's reputation among Jewish readers never fully recovered from the attacks on his "Christological" books. He died in London in 1957. His funeral was poorly attended.

Ascher, Abraham, historian: born Breslau, 1928. Left Breslau for England in July 1939. Immigrated to the United States in 1943. Later a professor of Russian history at the Graduate Center of the City University of New York.

Ausschnitt (later Ausnit), **Max,** industrialist: born Galați, 1888. In 1940 he was ousted from control of his company. He was imprisoned for a time and then held under house arrest. In 1944 he flew to Egypt. He later returned to Romania but, upon the Communist takeover of the country, he immigrated to the United States. In 1948 he was tried and sentenced to death in absentia in Romania on a charge of plotting revolution with American and British agents. He died in New York in 1957.

Bab, Julius, drama critic: born Berlin, 1880. Emigrated to the United States, 1940. Died Roslyn Heights, Long Island, New York, 1955.

Babel, Isaac, Russian writer: born Odessa, 1894. Arrested on May 15, 1939, accused of espionage, and, after a twenty-minute trial, executed in Moscow on January 27, 1940. His last recorded words were "Let me finish my work." Posthumously rehabilitated, 1954. His *Complete Works* could not be published until after the fall of the Soviet Union.

Baeck, Leo, rabbi, leader of German Jewry: born Lissa (Prussian Poland), 1873. Upon the dissolution of the Reichsvereinigung in 1943, Baeck was deported with his family to the Theresienstadt concentration camp. He survived to be liberated in 1945 by the Red Army. Died London, 1956.

Bałaban, Majer: historian: born Lemberg, 1877. Died in the Warsaw ghetto, 1942.

Barzilai, Yitzhak (party name: Joseph Berger), Comintern agent: born Cracow, 1904. Survived the war in Soviet prison camps. Released and rehabilitated after Stalin's death. Allowed to emigrate to Poland and thence to Israel, where he taught at Bar-Ilan University. Died in Israel, 1978.

Bellarina, Bella (née Bella Rubinlicht), Yiddish actress: born Warsaw 1898. Moved to the United States in the late 1920s. Died New York, 1969.

Benda, Julien, writer: born Paris, 1867. Lived in Carcasssone during the war. Died Fontenay-Aux-Roses, near Paris, 1956.

Benedikt, Ernst (wrote under noms de plume Erich Major, Ernst Marliss, and Ernst Martin), journalist: born Vienna, 1882. Imprisoned by the Gestapo from November 1938 to April 1939. In July 1939 fled to Sweden, where he survived the war. Returned to Austria in 1962. Died Vienna, 1973.

Benjamin, Walter, German writer: born Berlin, 1892. Died in Portbou, Spain, 1940, after illegally crossing the Franco-Spanish frontier. The cause of death remains mysterious: possibly he committed suicide.

Beregovskii, Moisei, ethnomusicologist: born Termakhovka (Ukraine), 1892. After the German invasion of the USSR, he was evacuated to Ufa in central Asia. In 1948 his section of the Ukrainian Academy was, like almost all other Jewish secular institutions in the Soviet Union, closed. He was sent to Siberia in 1950. Upon his release in 1955, he resumed work but was not granted access to his collection of recordings and was not able to publish. The remainder of his work on Jewish folk music appeared posthumously. Died Kiev, 1961.

Berend (né Presser), **Béla,** rabbi: born Budapest, 1911 or 1912. During the war served on the Jewish Council in Budapest. Later he was accused of collaboration and war crimes. He was acquitted of all charges in Hungary and emigrated to New York, where he changed his name again, this time to Dr. Albert B. Belton. Died 1987.

Bergelson, Dovid, Yiddish writer: born Okhrimovo (Ukraine), 1884. Arrested and tortured by the KGB, then executed on his sixty-eighth birthday in Moscow in 1952.

Bergmann, Gretel (later Margaret Lambert), athlete: born Laupheim (Württemberg), 1914. Emigrated from England to the United States in 1937. In old age she received many awards and honors from Germany and elsewhere. She was still alive in New York in 2011.

Bergson, Henri, philosopher: born Paris, 1859. Nobel Prize for Literature, 1928. After the enactment of anti-Jewish legislation in France in October

1940, he refused a government offer of personal exemption and stood in line for several hours to register as a Jew. Died Paris, 1941.

Berl, Emmanuel, French writer: born Vésinet (Seine-et-Oise), 1892. He wrote the speeches to the nation delivered by Marshal Pétain on June 23 and 25, 1940. Died Paris, 1976.

Bernstein, Adolf, cinema owner: fate unknown.

Bernstein, Henry, French playwright: born Paris, 1876. During the war lived at the Waldorf-Astoria hotel in New York. Died Paris, 1953.

Bettauer, Hugo, writer: born Baden (Lower Austria), 1872. In the early 1920s he campaigned for the rights of women and homosexuals, attracting fierce anti-Semitic hostility (he was a Protestant of Jewish origin). Shot dead by an Austrian Nazi in his office in Vienna, 1925.

Bienenfeld, Franz, lawyer: born Vienna, 1886. Fled to England in 1939. Died London, 1961.

Blecherman, Ilya, Birobdzhan settler: born Brest-Litovsk, 1904. In 1970 he was among the signatories of an anti-Israeli collective statement by Birobidzhan Jews. Survived in Birobidzhan beyond the fall of the Soviet Union.

Bloch, Edmond, lawyer: born 1884. Died 1975.

Bloch, Jean-Richard, writer: born Paris, 1884. In exile in the USSR, 1941–44, he worked as a French broadcaster on Radio Moscow. His mother, aged eighty-six, and his daughter, a *résistante*, were murdered by the Nazis. He died, possibly by his own hand, in Paris in 1947.

Blum, Léon, statesman: born Paris, 1872. Put on trial by Vichy regime and handed over to the Nazis. Survived the Theresienstadt and Buchenwald concentration camps. Served again briefly as prime minister, 1946–47. Died Jouy-en-Josas, near Versailles, 1950.

Bock, Rudolf, ophthalmologist: born Vienna, 1915. Left Vienna for Zagreb in 1939. Spent the war years in China. After the war settled in the United States. Died Palo Alto, 2006. His father, **Jacob Bock,** died in Vienna in 1941.

Braunthal, Julius, socialist politician: born Vienna, 1891. Expelled from Austria, 1935. Settled in Britain, 1938. Secretary-general of the Socialist International, 1951–56. Died Teddington, Middlesex, 1972.

Buber, Martin, Jewish thinker: born Vienna, 1878. Died Jerusalem 1965.

Carasso, Daniel, yogurt manufacturer: born Salonica, 1905. Moved to the United States in 1941, returning to Europe in 1959 and reestablishing his business there. By 2008 the company had annual revenues of nearly $19 billion. Died Paris, 2009, aged 103.

Carlebach, Joseph, rabbi and educator: born Lübeck, 1883. Appears in Thomas Mann's *Dr. Faustus*. Chief rabbi of Altona 1924–36 and of Hamburg from 1936. Declined offers of positions abroad. Deported with his community and murdered near Riga in 1942.

Chagall, Marc (Moisei Zakharovich Shagal), painter: born 1887, Liozno, near Vitebsk. In the United States 1941–46. Died Saint-Paul-de-Vence, France, 1985.

Cohn, Silvia, housewife: born Offenburg (Germany), 1904. Having failed to receive a visa to Britain in time to leave before the outbreak of war, she was sent in 1940 to internment camps at Gurs and Rivesaltes in France. She managed to get two of her daughters to safety in a children's home in Switzerland. Later she was deported to Auschwitz, where she was killed in a gas chamber in September 1942. Her third daughter was also murdered there. Her husband, **Eduard Cohn,** was reunited after the war with his two surviving daughters.

Csák (Kádárné), Ibolya, athlete: born Budapest, 1915. Died Budapest, 2006.

Deutscher, Isaac, writer: born Chrzanów (Galicia), 1907. Moved to London in April 1939. Worked there as a journalist and historian until his death in Rome in 1967.

Dimanshteyn, Semen, Soviet politician: born Sebezh (near Vitebsk), 1886; shot 1938.

Dorian (né Lustig), **Emil,** Romanian writer: born Bucharest, 1893. Survived war. Subsequently served as secretary-general of the Romanian Jewish community and then as director of its library and archives. Died Bucharest, 1956.

Dubnow, Simon, historian: born Mstislav (Byelorussia), 1860. Shot dead by a Latvian policeman during a Nazi roundup of Jews in Riga in 1941.

Dzigan, Szymon, comedian: born Łódź, 1905. In 1939 fled with his partner **Yisroel Schumacher** (1908–61) to Soviet-occupied Białystok. They performed for Soviet-Jewish audiences until they were sent to a prison camp. Dzigan returned to Warsaw in 1947. He settled in Israel in 1950. The duo were reunited for a time there. Dzigan died in 1980.

Ehrenburg, Ilya, Russian writer: born Kiev, 1891. After the German invasion of the Soviet Union in 1941, Ehrenburg returned to favor and published vitriolic anti-German articles in the Soviet press. He also collected evidence of Nazi war crimes against the Jews that, together with Vasily Grossman, he assembled in *The Black Book*. This was, however, denied publication in the USSR in his lifetime. Died Moscow, 1967.

Elias, Norbert, sociologist: born Breslau, 1897. His magnum opus, *The Civilizing Process*, was published in 1938–39. Worked at the universities of Ghana and Leicester in the 1950s and 1960s. Later lived in Amsterdam, where he died in 1990.

Epstein, Baruch, rabbinical scholar: born Bobruisk, 1860. Died in the Jewish hospital in Pinsk in July 1941.

Epstein, Moshe, rabbi: born 1875. Forced to resign as Leningrad rabbi in 1942. Arrested in 1949 and sent to Kazakhstan. Later returned to

Leningrad and served as unofficial rabbi, especially for followers of Chabad. In 1976, at the age of 101, he was permitted to emigrate to Israel, where he died the following year.

Erik, Max (né Zalman Merkin), Marxist literary scholar: born Sosnowiec, 1898. Arrested in 1937 and died in a prison camp hospital, supposedly after a suicide attempt.

Erlich, Henryk, Bundist leader: born Lublin, 1882. Arrested by Soviet secret police and sentenced to death, August 1941. Released the following month but rearrested in December. Committed suicide in a Soviet prison in Kuibyshev, 1942. In April 1943 Intourist presented the Polish government with a bill for 2,577 rubles for his and and his colleague Alter's hotel expenses in Moscow in October 1941.

Eskenazi, Roza, singer: born Constantinople, birth date unknown. Survived in Athens during Nazi occupation. Died 1980.

Farberovits (Farberowic), **Yitzhak** ("Urke Nakhalnik"), professional criminal and writer: born near Łomza, 1897. Killed in Otwock, November 1939.

Fefer, Itsik, Yiddish poet: born Shpola (Ukraine), 1900. Served on the Jewish Anti-Fascist Committee during Second World War. Arrested in 1948 with other members of the JAC (whom he denounced to interrogators). Executed in Moscow, 1952.

Feinstein, Moshe, rabbi: born Uzda (near Minsk), 1895. In the United States he became the most revered Torah authority of his generation. Died New York, 1986.

Feuchtwanger, Lion, novelist: born Munich, 1884. Shortly after the outbreak of war French police arrested him at his home at Sanary in southern France. He was released after a few days but in May 1940 was rearrested and placed in an internment camp. An American consul helped him to escape and arranged for an emergency visa, with which he was admitted to the United States that October. Died Los Angeles, 1958.

Filderman, Wilhelm, lawyer, head of Romanian Jewish Community: born Bucharest, 1882. Deported to "Transnistria" in 1943 but released after three months. Fled to Paris, 1948. Died there in 1963.

Floeck, Wilhelmine, housewife: born circa 1867. Fate unknown.

Floersheim, Hans (Chanan), kibbutznik: born Rotenburg, near Kassel, 1923. Sent to live with relatives in Amsterdam, 1937. In 1940–41 he lived in the Wieringern *werkdorp* and from 1941 to 1943 in Gouda. Fled to Belgium in 1943, then to France, and in April 1944 to Spain. In November 1944 he arrived in Palestine and settled in Kibbutz Hazorea. He moved to Kibbutz Yakum in 1947 and was still living there in 2007.

Ford, Aleksander (né Moyshe Lipschutz), film director: born Kiev, 1908. Died Naples, Florida, 1980.

Fraenkel, Gerhardt (later Gerald G. Frankel): born circa 1919. Remained in Kenya until at least 1966. He did not succeed in getting his parents out of Germany but they survived the war there.

Frank, Anne, diarist: born Frankfurt, 1929. Died of typhus in Bergen-Belsen concentration camp, March 1945. Her sister **Margot,** born 1926, died a few days earlier, also of typhus in Bergen-Belsen. Her mother, **Edith,** born in 1900, was murdered in Auschwitz in January 1945. Her father, **Otto,** born in Frankfurt, 1889, died in Basel in 1980.

Freier, Recha (née Schweitzer), founder of the Youth Aliya movement: born on Nordeney (in East Frisian Islands), 1892. Fled from Germany to Zagreb in 1940 and reached Palestine in 1941. Awarded Israel Prize, 1981. Died Jerusalem, 1984.

Fried, Eugen ("Camarade Clément"), Comintern agent: born Nagyszombat (northeast of Bratislava, then in Hungary), 1900. Shot dead by the Gestapo in Brussels in August 1943, while working underground as a Soviet agent.

Friedler, Edith: born Vienna, 1924. Sent to England in the Kindertransport in July 1939. Later moved to the United States.

Friedmann, Georges, sociologist: born Paris, 1902. Published *Fin du peuple juif* in 1965. Died Paris, 1977.

Fromm, Erich, psychologist: born Frankfurt, 1900. Emigrated to the United States in 1933. Died Muralto (Switzerland), 1980.

Frumkin, Ester (née Khaye Malke Lifshits), politician: born Minsk, 1880; Vice rector of University for Western National Minorities, Moscow, 1921–36. Arrested and imprisoned, 1937. Sentenced to eight years of forced labor in 1940. Died in a labor camp in Kazakhstan, 1943.

Gebirtig, Mordkhe (Mordekhai), Yiddish songwriter: born Cracow, 1877. In Nazi-occupied Poland he continued to write songs, including "Ayn tog fun nekome" ("A day for revenge"). He was shot dead by Nazis in 1942 while being marched to Cracow railway station for transportation to a death camp.

Gitter, Benno (né Moses Bernhard Gitter), businessman, art collector, and philanthropist: born Amsterdam, 1919. Died in 2004.

Glik, Hirsh, Yiddish poet: born Vilna, 1922. Wrote "Hymn of the Partisans," 1943. Died in Estonia in 1944.

Gold (né Zyserman), **Ben-Zion:** rabbi, born Radom, 1923. His father planned to emigrate to Palestine with the family in the late 1930s but the death of Ben-Zion's brother led them to remain in Poland for the year of mourning. Ben-Zion survived six years in a ghetto and concentration camps and emigrated to the United States after the war. He studied at the Jewish Theological Seminary in New York and served from 1958 to 1990 as director of Harvard Hillel (in effect, the university's Jewish chaplain).

Goldmann, Kurt (later Reuven Golan): born Kiel, circa 1915. Survived the war. Moved to Israel, where he died in 1983.

Goldmann, Nahum, Zionist politician: born Wisznevo (now in Lithuania), 1894. Moved from Paris to the United States in June 1940. After the war played a central role in negotiations with the Federal Republic of Germany that led to the Luxemburg agreement (1952) on reparations to Israel and the Jewish people. President of World Jewish Congress (1951–78) and World Zionist Organization (1956–68). Died Bad Reichenhall, 1982.

Grade, Chaim, Yiddish writer: born Vilna, 1910. Died New York, 1982.

Grodzenski, Hayim Ozer, rabbi: born, Ivya (now in Lithuania), 1863. Died in Soviet-occupied Vilna, 1940.

Gronowski (Gronowski-Brunot), Louis (Luke), journalist: born Radziejów (Russian Poland), 1904. Active in the Resistance during the war. Returned to Poland in 1949. Re-emigrated to France as a result of the officially sponsored anti-Semitic campaign in 1968. Died 1987.

Gross-Moszkowski, Dora, teacher: born Cracow, 1901. Fled to Soviet occupation zone of Poland at outbreak of war. Deported with her family to a labor camp in Siberia in 1940. Later they were evacuated with the Polish army to Iran and Africa. In 1950 they moved to the United States and settled in Berkeley, California, where Dora pursued a second career, working with developmentally disabled children. Died there in 1991.

Gruenbaum, Yitzhak, Zionist politician: born Warsaw, 1879. Moved to Palestine, 1933. First minister of the interior of Israel, 1948–49. Died in Israel, 1970.

Grynszpan, Herschel, assassin: born Hanover, 1921; arrested after the vom Rath assassination and held in prison until after the fall of France, when he appears to have been transferred from French to German control. His ultimate fate is unknown but he was probably murdered by the Nazis.

Halberstam, Ben-Zion, *rebbe* of Bobov (Bobovosk, Galicia): born there, 1874. Succeeded his father as *rebbe* in 1905. Murdered near Lwów, 1942.

Halkin, Shmuel, Yiddish playwright: born Rogachev (Byelorussia), 1897. Arrested in 1949 and held in a prison camp until 1955. Died Moscow, 1960.

Hamerow, Theodore S., historian: born Warsaw, 1920. Moved to the United States in 1930. Worked for many years on the faculty of the University of Wisconsin.

Hartglas, Apolinary, lawyer and politician: born Biała Podlaska, 1883. Left Nazi-occupied Warsaw in December 1939 and managed to reach Palestine. Died Jerusalem, 1953.

Hatvany, Baron Bertalan, orientalist: born Budapest, 1900. Moved to Paris in 1939 and died there in 1980.

Heifetz, Jascha, violinist: born Vilna, 1901. Emigrated with his family to the United States at the outbreak of the Russian Revolution. Died Los Angeles, 1987.

Hofshteyn, Dovid, poet: born Korostyshev (near Kiev), 1889. Member of Jewish Anti-Fascist Committee in the USSR during the Second World War. Arrested in 1948. Executed with other Soviet Yiddish writers, 1952.

Holländer, Walter, businessman: born Aachen, 1897. Left Holland for the United States in December 1939. Became a factory worker at Leominster, Massachusetts. Died New York, 1968.

Hond, Meijer de, rabbi: born Amsterdam 1882; murdered at Sobibor death camp, 1943.

Horkheimer, Max, philosopher: born Stuttgart, 1895. Died Montagnola, Switzerland, 1973.

Hutter, Otto, physiologist: born Vienna, 1924. Moved to Britain with Kindertransport in 1938. His parents were murdered by the Nazis. Regius Professor of Physiology, University of Glasgow, 1971–90.

Israel, Dora (later Iranyi, later Amann): born Vienna, 1894. Emigrated to France in 1939 and to the United States in 1941. Died Washington, D.C., 1993.

Itzig, Curt, Danzig community leader: left Danzig for England with a final group of Jewish children from the city on August 23, 1939.

Jabotinsky, Vladimir, leader of Revisionist Zionist movement: born Odessa, 1880. Died New York, 1940.

Jacob (né Alexandre), **Max,** writer and painter: born Quimper, 1876. Died Drancy prison camp, March 5, 1944. The collaborationist *Je suis partout* noted the death of a "Jew by race, Breton by birth, Roman by religion, and sodomite in his morals." His dying wish for a Catholic burial was fulfilled.

Jahoda, Marie, social psychologist: born Vienna, 1907. Emigrated to England in 1937. Professor at the University of Sussex. Died Hassocks, West Sussex, 2001.

Jasieński (né Zusman), **Bruno,** Polish writer: born Klimontów (near Sandomierz, Poland), 1901. Executed in a Soviet prison in 1938.

Jellinek, Hugo: born Mistelbach (Lower Austria), 1888. In October 1939 he married **Fritzi Fränkel** in Brno. Together with her and his daughters, **Bertha** (born Tashkent, 1922) and **Anna** (born Tashkent, 1924), he was sent to Theresienstadt from Brno in December 1941. All were transported to Auschwitz in June 1942 and murdered there. Hugo's eldest daughter, **Nadja** (born Tashkent, 1920), remained in Palestine. She was still alive in 2010.

Jonas, Regina, rabbi: born Berlin, 1902. Deported in 1942 to Theresienstadt, where she lectured on Jewish thought. In the camp, Leo Baeck confirmed her *semikhah*. She was murdered in Auschwitz in 1944.

Kabos, Endre, fencer: born, Nagyvarad, 1906. Died in Hungarian resistance, 1944.

Kaganovich, Lazar Moiseevich, politician: born near Chernobyl, 1893. In 1957 he was accused of forming part of an "anti-party group" and dismissed from office. Died Moscow, 1991.

Kahan, Arcadius, economic historian: born Vilna, 1920. Deported to Soviet labor camp in Vorkuta, 1940. Later served in Polish Division of Red Army. Emigrated to United States, 1950. Joined University of Chicago, 1955. Died Chicago, 1982.

Kahanovich, Pinhas Mendelevich ("Der Nister"), Yiddish writer: born Berdichev, 1884. Arrested by Soviet secret police in 1949 and sentenced to ten years in a corrective labor camp "for criminal ties with nationalists and for anti-Soviet propagandizing." Died in a prison camp hospital in the Komi Republic in 1950.

Kaminska, Ida, actress: born Odessa, 1899. Escaped to Soviet-occupied Lwów in October 1939 and spent war years in USSR. Returned to Poland in 1945 and directed State Yiddish Theater there. Nominated for Academy Award for her performance in the Czech film *The Shop on Main Street* (1965). In 1968 she was forced to leave Poland as a result of an officially sponsored "anti-Zionist" campaign. Died New York, 1980.

Katz, Leo, journalist: born Sereth (Bukowina), 1892. Expelled from France 1938. Moved to New York and, in 1940, to Mexico. After a brief sojourn in Israel in 1949, he returned to Vienna, where he died in 1954.

Kellner, Viktor, educator: moved to Palestine in December 1938. Died Kibbutz Ein Harod, 1970.

Khavkin, Matvei Pavlovich: born Rogachev, near Gomel, 1897. Remained in prison until 1941, suffering beatings and torture. Then sent to a labor camp. Released in 1956. Permitted to return to Moscow, he was rehabilitated and, in 1967, awarded the Order of Lenin. Died in 1980s.

Kinderman, Szaja ("Jorge," "Georg Scheyer"), veteran of Spanish Civil War: in Poland after the Second World War served as an army officer, retiring with the rank of colonel.

Kipnis, Menachem, Yiddish singer and writer: born Uzhmir (Volhynia), 1878. Died in Warsaw ghetto, 1942.

Kisch, Egon Erwin, writer: born Prague, 1885. In exile in Mexico during the Second World War. Died Prague, 1948.

Koch, Richard, medical theorist: born Frankfurt am Main, 1882. Died Yessentuki, USSR, 1949.

Koltsov (né Friedliand), **Mikhail,** journalist: born Kiev, 1898. Executed in Moscow, 1940.

Kopelev, Lev, Russian writer: born Kiev, 1912. Served as major in Red Army propaganda unit during the Second World War. Imprisoned for ten years in 1945 because he tried to defend Germans attacked by Soviet soldiers intent on rape and looting. Expelled from Soviet Writers' Union, 1970, for dissident activity. Moved to Germany, 1980. Deprived of Soviet citizenship. Created honorary German citizen, 1981. Died Cologne, 1997.

Korczak, Janusz (né Henryk Goldszmit), children's rights advocate: born Warsaw, 1878 or 1879. In occupied Warsaw he remained at the head of his orphanage. In 1942 he accompanied the children to their deaths at Treblinka.

Koretz, Zvi, chief rabbi of Salonica: born Rzeszów (Galicia), 1884. Appointed head of the Salonica Jewish Council by the Nazis during World War II. He was deported to Bergen-Belsen in 1943 and later to Theresienstadt, where he contracted typhus, of which he died, in Trebitz, Saxony, three months after liberation. Survivors of Salonica Jewry accused him of collaboration with the Nazis, a charge of which recent research has, in some measure, exonerated him.

Korn, Rokhl, Yiddish writer: born in eastern Galicia, 1898. Fled east in the USSR in 1941. Emigrated to Canada, 1949. Died Montreal, 1982.

Kotlorski, Moshe: born 1922. Fate unknown.

Koussevitsky, Moshe, cantor: born Smorgon (next to Vilna), 1899 or 1900. During the war performed in an artists' "brigade" in the Soviet Union and in the Georgian Opera in Tiflis (but not *hazanut*, except privately). Died Kings Point, Long Island, 1966.

Koval, George, Soviet spy: born Sioux City, Iowa, 1913. In 1940 he moved back to the United States, where he was recruited into the army and, with an army scholarship, studied electrical engineering at City College, New York. He subsequently worked on a branch of the atom bomb project at Oak Ridge, Tennessee, from which position he fed secret scientific information to the Soviets. In 1945 he fled to the USSR. Died Moscow, 2006. In 2007 he was posthumously declared a Hero of the Russian Federation by President Putin and lauded for "his courage and heroism while carrying out special missions." It is not known what became of his parents. His tractor-driver brother, who remained in Birobidzhan, died there in 1987.

Kreindler, Leo, journalist: born 1886. Continued to edit the *Jüdisches Nachrichtenblatt* after the outbreak of the war. As the Jews of Berlin were deported to their deaths, the circulation of the paper dwindled. In November 1942, during a visit to his office by Gestapo officials, Kreindler suffered a heart attack and died.

Kreisler, Fritz, violinist: born Vienna, 1875. Moved to the United States in 1939. Died New York, 1962.

Kulbak, Moshe, Yiddish writer: born Smorgon (next to Vilna), 1896. Arrested in Minsk and shot in 1937.

Kvitko, Leyb, Yiddish writer: born Holoskovo (near Odessa) circa 1890; during the Second World War a member of the Jewish Anti-Fascist Committee. From 1946 head of the Yiddish Section of the Soviet Writers' Union. Executed with other Soviet Yiddish writers in 1952.

Lachmann-Mosse, Hans, publisher: born Berlin, 1885. Died Oakland, California, 1944.

Landmann, Ludwig, politician: born Mannheim, 1868. Emigrated from Germany to the Netherlands in 1939. During the Nazi occupation he remained in hiding in Voorburg near The Hague. Died there of malnutrition and heart problems in March 1945. His remains were returned to Frankfurt in 1987.

Langer, Gerhard, physicist: born Jena, 1923. Served in U.S. Army during the Second World War. Later became a research scientist in Colorado.

Langer, Jiří (Mordekhai Giorgio Langer), writer: born Prague, 1894. Fled upon the German occupation in 1939 and reached Palestine six months later. He continued to write daringly homoerotic verse in Hebrew and to publish poems, essays, stories, and articles until his death in Tel Aviv in 1943.

Lasker-Schüler, Else, poet: born Elberfeld, 1869. Upon the outbreak of war in 1939, she was on a visit to Palestine. Unable to return to Europe, she remained in Jerusalem, where she died in 1945.

Lattes, Dante, journalist: born Pitigliano (Tuscany), 1876. Lived in Palestine from 1939 to 1948. Then returned to Italy, resuming work there as a writer and editor. Died Venice, 1965.

Leifer, Isaac, narcotics smuggler: born Brzeziny (near Łódź), 1893. In January 1940 the French Appeals Court confirmed his sentence to two years' imprisonment. His fate after 1940 is not recorded. He is not listed among those deported from France to death camps.

Lessing, Theodor, philosopher: born Hanover, 1872. Left Germany for Prague after Hitler's assumption of power. Assassinated by Nazis in Marienbad (then in Czechoslovakia) in 1933.

Lestchinsky, Jacob, sociologist: born Horodicz (near Kiev), 1876. Remained in New York during the Second World War. Moved to Israel in 1959. Died Jerusalem, 1966.

Levi, Primo, writer and chemist: born Turin, 1919. During the Second World War he joined the anti-Fascist resistance. He was captured in December 1943 and transported to Auschwitz. After his liberation he wrote his first book, *Se questo è un uomo* (*If This Is a Man*), describing his experiences in the camp. Committed suicide in Turin, 1987.

Lewkowicz, Wolf, tradesman: born Konskie (near Kielce), 1892. In 1939 he moved to Opoczno, where he lived with relatives. In September 1942, together with most of the Jews in Opoczno, he was deported to Treblinka and killed.

Liebermann, Herman, politician: born Drohobycz, Galicia, 1870. Found refuge in London in 1940 and in 1941 became minister of justice in the Polish government-in-exile, the first Jew to serve in a Polish cabinet. He died in London after only a few weeks in office.

Lilienthal, Andor, chess grandmaster: born Moscow, 1911. Remained in the USSR during and after the Second World War, winning the Soviet championship in 1940 and coaching several champions in the 1950s. Returned to Hungary in 1976. Died Budapest, 2010.

Lindberg, Paula (née Levi, after her marriage known as Lindberg-Salomon), singer: born Frankenthal (Bavaria), 1897. Survived the war years in the Netherlands (from 1943 to 1945 in hiding). Lindberg appears as a character in the famous series of 1,325 gouaches, *Leben oder Theater?*, created during the war by her stepdaughter Charlotte Salomon, who was murdered in Auschwitz in 1943. The pictures are now in the Jewish Historical Museum in Amsterdam. Lindberg died, aged 102, in Amstelveen in 2000.

Lipchitz, Jacques (né Chaim Jacob Lipschitz), sculptor: born Druskieniki (now in Lithuania), 1891. Fled to New York during the war. Died Capri, 1975.

Litvinov, Maxim (né Meir Wallach), Soviet statesman: born Białystok, 1876. Ambassador to United States, 1941–43. Died Moscow, 1951.

Ludwig, Emil (né Emil Cohn), German writer: born Breslau, 1881. Died near Ascona, 1948.

Lukács, Georg (né György Löwinger, then von Lukács), Marxist literary critic: born Budapest, 1885. Lived in the Soviet Union from 1933 to 1945, when he returned to Hungary. Participated in Hungarian revolution of 1956. Died Budapest, 1971.

Lunski, Khaykl, librarian: born Slonim (now in Lithuania), 1881. Died Vilna, 1942.

Malakiewicz, Gershon, porter: murdered during the Second World War at Ponary, near Vilna.

Mandel, Georges (né Louis-Georges Rothschild), politician: born Chatou (Seine-et-Oise), 1885. Murdered by French fascist *milice* in the forest of Fontainebleau in 1944.

Mandelstam, Osip, Russian poet: born Warsaw, 1891. Rearrested in 1938 and condemned to five years detention in a labor camp, he died in transit near Vladivostok later that year.

Manger, Itzik (né Isidor Helfer), Yiddish poet: born Czernowitz, 1901. Moved from Warsaw to Paris in 1938. During the war he managed to get to England. In 1951 he settled in the United States and in 1967 in Israel. Bereft of his former Yiddish-speaking audience, he described himself as "the loneliest poet in the world." Died Gedera, 1969.

Mannheim, Karl, sociologist: born Budapest, 1893. Died London, 1947.

Manus, Rosa, Dutch feminist: Born Amsterdam, 1880. Arrested in 1940 and sent to Ravensbrück concentration camp, where she died in 1943.

Marcuse, Herbert, social thinker: born Berlin, 1898. Died Starnberg (Bavaria), 1979.

Markish, Peretz, Yiddish poet and dramatist: born Polonnoye (Volhynia), 1895. From 1939 to 1943 he headed the Yiddish section of the Soviet Writers' Union. During the Second World War he was active in the Jewish Anti-Fascist Committee. Arrested in 1949 and executed in Moscow in 1952.

Marten, Aleksander (né Marek Tennenbaum), theater director: born Łódź, 1898. Died 1942.

Masarano, Stela, schoolgirl: born Salonica, circa 1924. Died Salonica, 1942.

Maurois, André (né Emile Herzog), writer: born Elbeuf, 1885. Elected to the Académie Française, 1938. In the United States, 1940–46. Died Paris, 1967.

Mayer, Saly, businessman and philanthropist: born Basel, 1882: died St. Moritz, 1950.

Mayzel, Nakhmen: born near Kiev, 1887. Moved to the United States in 1937 and to Israel in 1964. Died there in 1966.

Mikhoels, Shlomo, actor: born Dvinsk, 1890. During the Second World War he headed the Jewish Anti-Fascist Committee, appointed by the Soviet authorities. In 1948 he was murdered in Minsk in a state-organized "traffic accident."

Molodowsky, Kadya, born Bereze (Grodno province), 1894. Died Philadelphia, 1975.

Mosse, George, historian: born Berlin, 1919. Died Madison, Wisconsin, 1999.

Munk, Esra, rabbi: born Altona, 1867. Rabbi of the Adass Yisroel congregation in Berlin, 1900–38. Emigrated to Jerusalem in 1938 and died there in 1940.

Namier (né Niemirowski), **[Sir] Lewis Bernstein** (aka "Ulu"), historian: born Wola Okrzejska (Russian Poland), 1888. Died London, 1960.

Naumann, Max, lawyer: born Berlin, 1875. Briefly imprisoned by the Nazis. Died of cancer in Berlin, 1939.

Némirovsky, Irène, novelist: born Kiev, 1903. After the fall of France, she moved to the village of Issy l'Évêque in southern Burgundy. In July 1942 she was arrested by French police and sent to an internment camp at Pithiviers. From there she was transported to Auschwitz, where she died of typhus on August 19, 1942. Her unfinished masterpiece, *Suite Française*, was first published, to huge acclaim, in 2003.

Neustadt, Hermann (later Harvey P. Newton), agronomist: born Breslau, 1920. Emigrated from the Netherands to the United States in 1940. Served in U.S. Army during Second World War. In 1973 he moved to Costa Rica, where he died in 1998.

Neuweg, Gerhard (later Roger G. Newton), physicist: born Landsberg an der Warthe, 1924. Survived the war openly in Berlin with his "mixed-race" family. Later a professor of physics at the University of Indiana.

Oistrakh, David, violinist: born Odessa, 1908. Died while on a visit to Amsterdam, 1974.

Pasternak, Leon, poet: born Lemberg, 1910. Died Warsaw, 1969.

Patai, Raphael (né Ervin György Patai), anthropologist: born Budapest, 1910. Moved to Jerusalem in the mid-1930s and earned the first doctorate awarded by the Hebrew University. Later a professor in the United States. Died, Tucson, Arizona, 1996.

Pauker, Ana (née Rabinsohn), politician: born Codăeşti (Romania), 1893. Imprisoned in Romania for Communist activity from 1935 to 1941, when she was allowed to leave for the USSR. She returned to Bucharest in 1944 and served as Romanian foreign minister from 1947 until 1953. She was arrested on February 18, 1953, but released a month later, following Stalin's death. Died Bucharest, 1960. Her husband, **Marcel Pauker** (born Bucharest, 1896), perished while imprisoned in the Soviet Union in 1938.

Perle, Yehoshue (Yoshue), writer: born Radom, 1888. Fled Warsaw in 1939 and found refuge in Soviet-occupied Lwów. In 1941 he returned to Warsaw, where he was active in Yizkor, a Yiddish underground cultural organization. After surviving several roundups, he escaped from the ghetto to live on the "Aryan side" of Warsaw. He was lured out of hiding, deported to Auschwitz, and murdered there in 1943.

Pevsner, Nikolaus (né Nikolai Pewsner), architectural historian: born Leipzig, 1902. Moved to England, 1934. Created the classic *The Buildings of England* series (1951–74). Died London, 1983.

Pipes, Richard, historian: born 1923, Cieszyn (Polish Silesia). With his family, Pipes escaped from Poland across Germany to Italy in October 1939. They emigrated to the United States, where Pipes became a professor of Russian history at Harvard and, in 1981–82, an adviser on Soviet affairs to President Ronald Reagan.

Polak, Henri, socialist politician: born Amsterdam 1868. Died Laren, 1943.

Poons, Sylvain, entertainer: born Amsterdam, 1896. Died Amsterdam, 1985.

Porat, Dan, physicist: born Stanisławów, Poland, 1922. In 1939 he emigrated to Palestine. During the war he served in the British army in North Africa and Italy. In 1948 he served in the Israeli army. Studied at Manchester University and then moved to the United States, where he became a researcher in high-energy physics at Stanford University. Died in 1996.

Prinz, Joachim, rabbi: born Burkhardsdorf, 1902. Died Livingston, New Jersey, 1988.

Pryłucki, Noyekh, Yiddish writer and politician: born Berdichev, 1882. Upon the German occupation of Warsaw in September 1939, Pryłucki fled to Lithuania. During the Soviet occupation of the city, he briefly headed YIVO. After the German conquest of Vilna, the Nazis ordered him to catalogue treasures in the Strashun Library. Arrested in August 1941 and murdered in Vilna.

Rabinovich, Mark Isakovich, musician: born *c.* 1870, Brusilov, Ukraine. Died Kiev, 1940.

Ran, Leyzer, writer: born Vilna, 1912. Died New York, 1995.

Rapoport, Yoshue, literary critic: born Białystok, 1895. Upon the outbreak of the war, he took refuge in Vilna and then made his way to Shanghai. Died Melbourne, 1971.

Rappoport, Charles, politician: born Doutsky (near Vilna), 1865. Died Cahors, 1941.

Ravitch, Melech (né Zekharye-Khone Bergner), Yiddish writer: born Radymno (Galicia), 1893. Emigrated from Poland in the early 1930s. Died Montreal, 1976.

Rayski, Adam (né Abraham Rajgrodski), journalist: born Białystok, 1914. Participated in French Resistance after invasion of the USSR. Returned to Poland in 1949 and served as party press chief. He moved back to France in 1957. Arrested and found guilty of spying for Poland, he was sentenced to seven years' imprisonment but was released after two years. Died Paris, 2008.

Reich, Felix, educator of the deaf: born Fürstenwalde (Brandenburg), 1885. Reich had planned to return to Germany to organize the emigration of the other children in his school but the outbreak of the war prevented that. In 1940 he was interned for seven months on the Isle of Man as an enemy alien. In 1942, 146 pupils of the Berlin Jewish school for deafmutes, nearly all those who remained in Germany, were murdered by the Nazis. After the war Reich became a schoolteacher in England. Died Manchester, 1964.

Reich (later Reich-Ranicki), **Marcel,** literary critic: born Włocławek, Poland, 1920. Secretary and translator for the Jewish Council in the Warsaw ghetto. Survived later part of the war in hiding. After the war became a literary critic in Poland. In 1958 moved to West Germany, where he became the best-known and most influential critic in the country.

Reinhardt, Max, theater director: born Baden (near Vienna), 1873. Died New York, 1943.

Reyzen, Zalmen, scholar and journalist: born Koidanov (Byelorussia), 1887. His paper, the *Vilner tog*, was closed upon the Soviet occupation of Vilna in 1939 and Reyzen was arrested. In 1941, while being transported by rail to a place of exile in Russia, he was removed from the carriage and, together with his son, shot dead.

Ringelblum, Emanuel, historian: born Buczacz (Galicia), 1900. During the German occupation of Warsaw, he organized a circle of informants who gathered an archive of materials on every aspect of Jewish life in the ghetto. Much of this survived the war and forms an essential basis for historical research. Murdered by Nazis in Warsaw in March 1944.

Rokeach, Aharon, fourth Belzer *rebbe*: born Belz (Galicia), 1880. In 1943 he fled Nazi-occupied Poland and found refuge in Budapest. In 1944 he managed to get to Palestine. Later he was criticized for having advised his followers to stay put and trust in the Lord, while he himself escaped. Died in Israel, 1957.

Rosenheim, Jacob, Agudist leader: born Frankfurt am Main, 1870. After 1940, Rosenheim lived in the United States. In 1950 he moved to Israel, where he died in 1965.

Rotholc, Szapsel (Shepsl), boxer: born Warsaw, 1912. During the war employed in Jewish police force in Warsaw ghetto. After the war, he was accused of collaboration and excluded from the Jewish community and from sporting competition. The exclusions were later lifted. Died Toronto, 1996.

Rothschild, Robert de, mining engineer and banker: born 1880. Escaped to North America in 1940. Died 1946.

Rozenman, Nachme: born 1921. Fate unknown.

Ruppin, Arthur, Zionist leader and sociologist: born Rawitsch, Prussian Poland, 1876. Died Palestine, 1943.

Salomon, Alice, feminist: born Berlin, 1872. Welcomed to tea at the White House by Eleanor Roosevelt, Salomon nevertheless found it hard to adjust to life in the United States. Died New York, 1948.

Salomon, Ernst, metal trader: born 1923. In Brussels 1933–40. Escaped to United States and joined U.S. Army. Later a businessman in Tokyo.

Samberg, Ayzic (Ajzyk), actor: born 1889. Directed and performed in plays in Warsaw ghetto in 1942. Died Poniatowa concentration camp, 1943.

Sarfatti, Margherita (née Grassini), art critic: born Venice, 1880; returned to Italy in 1947. Died Cavallasca (Como), 1961.

Schneerson, Yosef Yitshak, sixth Lubavitcher *rebbe:* born, Lubavitch, 1880. In 1940 he managed to get from Nazi-occupied Warsaw to New York, where he died in 1950.

Schoenberg, Arnold, composer: born Vienna, 1874. Died Los Angeles, 1951.

Schoeps, Hans-Joachim, theologian: born Berlin, 1909. Fled to Sweden in December 1938. He tried but failed to establish a Deutsche Vortrupp in exile. Both his parents were murdered by the Nazis. After the war, retaining his conservative, German nationalist position, he returned to Germany and became a professor of theology at Erlangen. In 1955 the deposed Hohenzollern royal family awarded Schoeps the Knight's Cross in recognition of his efforts to secure the restoration of the monarchy. Died Erlangen, 1980.

Schreiber, Gerhard, chemical engineer: born Czernowitz, 1928. Interned in Tul'chyn, Ukraine, 1942–44. Emigrated from Romania to United States in 1962.

Schulz, Bruno, writer and artist. Born Drohobycz, Galicia, 1892. Upon the Soviet occupation of the town in 1941, he was consigned to the ghetto. For a time he was protected by an SS officer who appreciated his painting. But in 1942 a rival Nazi officer shot him dead in the street. From the 1960s onward his works enjoyed wide posthumous recognition. He appears as a character in David Grossman's *See Under: Love* (1989) and is the the subject of an idiosyncratic biography by Jerzy Ficowski, *Regions of the Great Heresy: Bruno Schulz: A Biographical Portrait* (2003).

Schwarz, Rudolf, conductor: born Vienna, 1905. Arrested by the Gestapo on the second day of the war, he was released after ten months and allowed to resume work as a conductor with the Jüdische Kulturbund until its closure in 1941. Thereafter he was deported to slave labor at Auschwitz. Later he was moved to the Sachsenhausen concentration camp and to Bergen-Belsen, from which he was liberated in 1945. After the war he moved to England, where he conducted the Bournemouth, City of Birmingham, and BBC Symphony Orchestras and the Northern Sinfonia. Died London, 1994.

Sebastian, Mihail (né Iosef Hechter), Romanian writer: born Brăila, 1907. Survived the war in Romania, only to be run over by a bus in Bucharest on May 29, 1945.

Segre, Dan Vittorio, writer and diplomat: born Rivoli, Piedmont, 1922. Emigrated to Palestine in 1939. Later an Israeli Foreign Service officer and a professor of political thought and international relations in Haifa and Lugano.

Seligsohn, Julius ("Fritz"), lawyer: born Berlin, 1890. In 1940, as one of the leaders of the Reichsvereinigung, he took responsibility for its protest against deportations of Jews. He was sent to Sachsenhausen concentration camp and murdered there a few months later.

Shapira, Bat-Sheva: born Jagielnica, 1923; murdered there in 1942 (or, according to another account, in the ghetto of the nearby town Tłuste).

Shapiro, Gershon, zoologist: born 1899 in Rivne (Rovno, Volhynia). He rejoined the Red Army in 1941 and served until 1946. Thereafter he worked for the Odessa planning department until 1959. In the late Stalin years he lost faith in Communism and became a Zionist. After retirement, he edited a *samizdat* publication in Odessa of materials on Israel, Jewish resistance to Hitler, and Jewish history in Russia. He emigrated to Israel in September 1973.

Sheps, Elias (pen name A. Almi), poet and critic: born Warsaw, 1892. Died Buenos Aires, 1963.

Shtif, Nokhem, Yiddish philologist: born Rivne (Rovno, Volhynia), 1879. Died Kiev, 1933.

Simon, Heinrich, newspaper proprietor: born Berlin, 1880. Left Germany in 1934 and eventually settled in Palestine, where he helped found the Palestine (later Israel) Philharmonic Orchestra. Murdered in Washington, D.C., in 1941. The assassin was never identified.

Singer, Bernard, political journalist: born Warsaw, 1893. Suspected of Trotskyism, he served time in Soviet labor camps, 1940–41. Then moved to London, where he died in 1966.

Singer, Isaac Bashevis, Yiddish writer: born Leoncin (near Warsaw), 1902. Awarded Nobel Prize for Literature, 1978. Died Miami, 1991.

Singer, Kurt, head of Jüdische Kulturbund: born Berent (West Prussia), 1885: "My life has become silent," he wrote shortly before the outbreak of the war. He remained in Amsterdam, hoping to be admitted as an immigrant to the United States. Deported to Theresienstadt, he died there in 1944.

Sommerstein, Emil, Polish Zionist leader: born Hleszczawa, near Tarnopol (Galicia), 1883. Member of the Sejm, 1922–27 and 1929–39. In September 1939 he was arrested by Soviet forces in Lwów. He was held in various Soviet prisons until 1944. Upon his release, he was recognized as a leader of the remaining Jews in Poland, and received by Stalin. In 1946 he fell ill while visiting the United States at the head of a Polish-Jewish delegation. He never recovered and died in New York in 1957. His remains were buried in Israel.

Stein, Edith (later Sister Teresa Benedicta a Cruce, OCD), saint: born Breslau on Yom Kippur, 1891. In December 1938 she moved to a convent in the Netherlands. She was arrested by the Gestapo in 1942 as a reprisal for a protest by Dutch bishops against the persecution of Jews. Murdered at Auschwitz, 1942. Beatified as "a daughter of Israel" by Pope John Paul II, 1987; canonized, 1998.

Steinberg, Isaac Nachman, politician: born Dvinsk, 1888. The outbreak of the war prevented his departure from Australia, where he remained until 1943. He failed to translate the Kimberley project, or any other such scheme, into reality but continued to head the Freeland League, reduced to a tiny core of enthusiasts, until his death in New York in 1957.

Stern, Martin, scientist: born Essen, 1924. In 1937 his family left for Turin. They moved to France a year later. In 1940 they fled to Algiers, then to Casablanca. From there they made their way to Portugal and finally to the United States.

Stolyarsky, Petr (Peisakh) Solomonovich, violin teacher: born near Kiev, 1871. Accorded many honors by a grateful Soviet state, Stolyarsky was evacuated to the Urals during the war. He died in Sverdlovsk in 1944.

Stricker, Robert, politician and journalist: born Brno, 1879. Declined opportunities to leave Austria after the Anschluss. Arrested and sent to Dachau and other concentration camps. Murdered at Auschwitz, 1944.

Sutzkever, Avrom, Yiddish poet: born Smorgon (next to Vilna), 1913. As a prisoner in the Vilna ghetto between 1941 and 1943, he was conscripted to work, organizing the YIVO library and other Jewish collections, for transportation to the Institut zur Erforschung der Judenfrage in Frankfurt.

With others, he hid many precious items that were recovered after the war. He escaped from the ghetto in 1943 and went to Moscow. In 1947 he emigrated to Palestine. From 1949 to 1995 he edited *Di goldene keyt*, the last important Yiddish literary periodical. He died in Israel in 2010.

Szyr, Eugeniusz: born Łodygowice (Silesia), 1915. Died Warsaw, 2000.

Taub, Shaul Yedidyah Eliezer, second *rebbe* of Modzits: born 1887. During the war escaped to America via Japan. Settled in Tel Aviv. Died 1947.

Tauber, Shimshon: born Jagielnica, 1923. Murdered there, 1942.

Tcherikower, Elias (Elye Tcherikover), historian: born Poltava, 1881. Moved to New York in 1940 and died there, 1943.

Teitelbaum, Yoel, *rebbe* of Satmar (Szatmárnémeti, then in Hungary): born there, 1887. Permitted to leave Bergen-Belsen concentration camp with others following agreement between the Hungarian Zionist Rezsö Kasztner and Nazi officials in 1944. Moved to Palestine and, in 1947, to New York. Denounced the State of Israel as an agent of Satan. Died Monroe, New York, 1979.

Theilhaber, Felix, sexologist and demographer: born Bamberg, 1884. Died Tel Aviv, 1956.

Tijn, Gertrude van (née Cohn), social worker: born Braunschweig, 1891. Remained in Amsterdam after German invasion and continued work on behalf of refugees. Sent to Westerbork and Bergen-Belsen but included in 1944 exchange of Germans from Palestine for some Bergen-Belsen inmates. Died Portland, Oregon, 1974.

Trotsky, Leon (né Bronstein): born Ivanovka (Ukraine), 1879. Expelled from USSR in 1929. Murdered by Stalinist agent, Mexico City, 1940.

Tsegelnitski, Jacob, ORT representative in Moscow: in September 1939 he was sentenced to five years' imprisonment. Died February 1942 in Uzhenskii corrective labor camp, Sukhobezvodnoye, Gorky Province.

Tucholsky, Kurt, satirist: born Berlin, 1890. Settled in Sweden in 1929 and committed suicide in Göteborg in 1935.

Turkow, Jonas, actor: born Warsaw, 1898. Survived the Warsaw ghetto. Settled in New York in 1947 and in Israel in 1966. Died Tel Aviv, 1988. His brother **Zygmunt Turkow** (1896–1970) emigrated to Argentina in 1940 and to Israel in 1952.

Tuwim, Julian, Polish writer: born 1894. Lived in Paris, Rio de Janeiro, London, and New York between 1939 and 1946. Died Warsaw, 1953.

Twersky, Avraham Yehoshua Heschel, rabbi: born Makhnovka, Ukraine, 1895. Emigrated to Israel in 1963, taking with him what was said to be the *sefer torah* (scroll of the law) of the Baal Shem Tov, founder of Hasidism. Died Bnei Brak, 1987.

Ullstein, Hermann, publisher: born Berlin, 1875. Left Germany, 1938. Died New York, 1943.

Utesov, Leonid (né Lazar Iosifovich Vaisbein), jazzman, singer, and cabaret artist: born Odessa, 1895. Performed in patriotic musical films during the war and continued to appear on Soviet stage and television into the 1970s. Died Moscow, 1982.

Vecchio, Giorgio Del, legal philosopher: born Bologna, 1878. Died Genoa, 1970.

Vészi, Josef, journalist: born Arad, 1858. Died "a broken man," 1940.

Volf (Wolf, né Mekler), **Leyzer,** Yiddish poet: born Vilna, 1910. Left Vilna with Soviet forces at the end of their forty-day occupation of the city in October 1939. Wandered to various cities until evacuated to central Asia in 1941. Died of starvation, Shakhrisabz, Uzbekistan, 1943.

Wachstein, Sonia, teacher: born Vienna, 1907. Escaped to England in October 1938. Later moved to the United States. Died New York, 2001. Her brother **Max**, a pathologist, born in Vienna, circa 1905, moved to England in 1939, after his release from Dachau and Buchenwald. He emigrated to the United States in 1940 and died in New York in 1965.

Warburg, Max, banker: born Hamburg, 1867. Emigrated to the United States, 1938. Died New York, 1946.

Warmbrunn, Werner, historian: born Frankfurt am Main, 1920. Returned from Holland to Germany in 1941, holding an American visa that enabled him to leave for the United States. Studied at Cornell and became a professor at Pitzer College in California. Died Claremont, California, 2009.

Wat (né Chwat), **Aleksander,** Polish poet: born Warsaw, 1900. After imprisonment in the USSR in 1940–41, he spent the remaining war years in Kazakhstan. Returned to Poland in 1946. Baptized in 1953. Moved to France in 1963. Committed suicide in Paris, 1967.

Weichert, Michał, theater director: born Podhajce (Galicia), 1890. During the Second World War, he headed the "Jewish Self-Help Organization" that was permitted by the Germans to function in occupied Poland. Accused of collaboration after the war. Moved to Israel in 1958. Died there, 1967.

Weil, Felix, leftist millionaire: born Buenos Aires, 1898. Returned to Argentina from Germany in 1931. From there moved to New York in 1935. After the war lived in California. Died Dover, Delaware, 1975.

Weil, Simone, philosopher: born Paris, 1909. Moved to London in 1942. Died of tuberculosis and self-starvation at Grosvenor sanatarium, Ashford, Kent, 1943.

Weinberg, Jehiel Jacob, rabbi: born Pilwishki (Grodno district, Byelorussia), 1884. In Warsaw at the time of the German occupation, he was treated as a Soviet citizen. Upon the outbreak of war with the USSR in 1941, he was imprisoned and then sent to a camp for Soviet POWs in Bavaria. Liberated by U.S. forces in April 1945, he lived quietly in Montreux until his death there in 1966. Greatly distressed at the state of postwar Jewry, he wrote in 1955, "Everything among us is rotten and stench-filled."

Weinreich, Max, Yiddishist: born Kuldiga (Goldingen), Latvia, 1894. Unable to return to Vilna at the outbreak of the war, he went to New York, where, under his direction, YIVO established its new headquarters. Died New York, 1969.

Weiss de Csepel, Barons Alfons and **Eugene:** both brothers, together with forty-four other members of the family, succeeded in bribing their way out of Hungary in 1944. They were permitted by the Nazis to leave in return for transferring their entire industrial assets to German control. Most of the family moved to the United States.

Weizmann, Chaim, Zionist leader: born Motol (near Pinsk), 1874. Elected first president of Israel in 1948. Died Rehovot, Israel, 1952.

Weltsch, Robert, journalist: born Prague, 1891. In 1939 moved to Palestine and in 1945 to London, where he worked as correspondent for the Tel Aviv daily *Haaretz* and became a founder of the Leo Baeck Institute for the study of German-Jewish history. Returned to Israel in 1978 and died in Jerusalem, 1982.

Wiener, Meir, writer: born Cracow, 1893. Died Viazma (Smolensk region), 1941, while serving in the Red Army's Yiddish "Writers' Battalion."

Wieviorka, Wolf, Yiddish journalist: born Żyrardów (near Warsaw), 1898. After the occupation of Paris in 1940, he took refuge in the south of France. Arrested in Nice in 1943 and transported to Auschwitz. He died on the "death march" out of Auschwitz in 1945. His granddaughter Annette Wieviorka is a historian of the *shoah*.

Wijnkoop, David, Dutch Communist leader: born Amsterdam, 1876. Imprisoned briefly in Hoorn after the German occupation of Holland in May 1940. Thereafter he went underground. Died of a heart attack in May 1941 while in hiding in Amsterdam. Hundreds attended his funeral at Driehuis-Westerveld.

Wolf, Wolfie, café proprietor in Vilna: fate unknown.

Wolfin, Samuel, student: born Vilna, 1911. On the eve of the war he was studying medicine in Italy. He perished in the war but the exact circumstances are unknown.

Worms, Fritz (later Fred), businessman: born Frankfurt am Main, 1920. Emigrated to England in 1937 and became a leading figure in the Jewish community there.

Wulf, Joseph, writer: born Chemnitz, 1912. Survived two years in Auschwitz. After the war he settled in Paris and later in Berlin, where he urged the establishment of a documentation center and memorial to the genocide of the Jews. Despairing of these efforts, he jumped to his death from his fifth-floor apartment window in Charlottenburg in 1974. The library in the Wannsee villa memorial center was later named after him.

Yagoda, Genrikh Grigorevich, Soviet secret police chief: born Iaroslavl province, 1891. After his demotion in 1936, on ground of alleged sluggishness in the struggle against counterrevolutionaries, he was appointed commissar of communications. Arrested in March 1937, he was found guilty of treason, and shot in March 1938.

Yagodnik, Yaakov, *yeshiva* student: fate unknown.

Zalcman, Moshe, tailor: born Zamość, 1909. Released in 1947 after ten years in Soviet labor camps. Settled in Georgia until permitted to leave USSR in 1957. Returned to Paris, where he died in 2000.

Zaretski, Ayzik, linguist: born Pinsk, 1891. Died Kursk, 1956.

Ziegelroth (later Stoeltzner), **Helene,** physician: born Warsaw, 1868. Died Berlin, 1961.

Zilbershteyn, Roman, Warsaw city councilor: fate unknown.

Zolli (né Zoller), **Israel,** rabbi and apostate: born Brody, 1881. Took refuge in the Vatican after the German occupation of Rome in 1943. Resumed office as chief rabbi of Rome, 1944. In synagogue on Yom Kippur that year, he saw a vision of Christ. He embraced Christianity soon after. Died Rome, 1956.

Zuskin, Benjamin, actor: born Ponevezh (now in Lithuania), 1899. Executed Moscow, 1952.

Zweig, Arnold, writer: born Gross-Glogau, Silesia, 1887. Left Germany in 1933 and eventually settled in Palestine. In 1948 he returned to Berlin, where he became president of the East German Academy of Arts. Died Berlin, 1968.

Zweig, Stefan, writer: born Vienna, 1881. Settled in England in 1938. In 1942, Zweig, depressed by the fate of Europe, committed suicide in Petrópolis, near Rio de Janeiro.

NOTES

ABBREVIATIONS

Bibl. Ros.: Archival materials in Bibliotheca Rosenthaliana, University of Amsterdam

BNA: British National Archives, Kew

CAHJP: Central Archives for the History of the Jewish People, Jerusalem

CZA: Central Zionist Archives, Jerusalem

DRCTAU: Goldstein-Goren Diaspora Research Center archive, Tel Aviv University

IISH: Archive of the International Institute of Social History, Amsterdam

JC: *Jewish Chronicle*

JDCNY: American Jewish Joint Distribution Committee archive, New York

JSS: *Jewish Social Studies*

LBINY: Leo Baeck Institute Archive, Center for Jewish History, New York

LBIYB: *Leo Baeck Institute Year Book*

WL: Wiener Library, London

YA: YIVO Archives, Center for Jewish History, New York

YV: Yad Vashem Archives, Jerusalem

1: THE MELTING GLACIER

1. George L. Mosse, *Confronting History: A Memoir* (Madison, Wis., 2000), 26.
2. Thomas Lackmann, *Das Glück der Mendelssohns: Geschichte einer deutsche Familie* (Berlin, 2007), 426–29.
3. Robert Weltsch, *An der Wende des Modernen Judentums* (Tübingen, 1972), 67.
4. Esriel Hildesheimer, *Jüdische Selbstverwaltung unter dem NS-Regime: Der Existenzkampf der Reichsvertretung und Reichsvereinigung der Juden in Deutschland* (Tübingen, 1994), 34.
5. Ben-Zion Gold, *The Life of Jews in Poland Before the Holocaust* (Lincoln, Neb., 2007), 80.
6. Theodore S. Hamerow, *Remembering a Vanished World: A Jewish Childhood in Inter-War Poland* (New York, 2001), 155.
7. Celia Stopnicka Heller, "Poles of Jewish Background—The Case of Assimilation without Integration in Interwar Poland," in Joshua Fishman, ed., *Studies on Polish Jewry 1919–1939* (New York, 1974), 258.
8. Jacob Lestchinsky, "Aspects of the Sociology of Polish Jewry," *JSS* 28:4 (1966), 195.
9. Estimate by ORT, cited in Léon Baratz, *La question juive en U.R.S.S.* (Paris, 1938), 14.
10. Francine Hirsch, "The Soviet Union as a Work-in-Progress: Ethnographers

and the Category Nationality in the 1926, 1937, and 1939 Censuses," *Slavic Review* 56:2 (1997), 264, 275.

11. Georges Friedmann, *De la Sainte Russie à l'URSS* (Paris, 1938), 187, 193.

12. Léon Baratz, "Le problème des réfugiés juifs et l'U.R.S.S.," *La Juste Parole* July 5, 1939; see also Baratz, *La question juive.*

13. Lewis Namier, "Zionism," *New Statesman,* Nov. 5, 1927.

14. C. Wijsenbeek-Franken, Report on the Conditions of Jewish Social Work in Holland, June 1936, WL doc 1240/2, 4–5.

15. *JC,* Feb. 24, 1939.

16. D. E. Schnurmann, "La mortalité de la population juive en Alsace," *Revue "OSÉ,"* April 1938, 7–8.

17. Rudoph Stahl, "Vocational Retraining of Jews in Nazi Germany," *JSS,* 1:2 (1939), 171.

18. Hannah Arendt, *The Origins of Totalitarianism* (New York, 1994), 4.

19. Felix A. Theilhaber, *Der Untergang der deutschen Juden: Eine volkswirtschaftliche Studie* (Munich, 1911).

20. Arthur Ruppin, *The Jews in the Modern World* (London, 1935), 72.

21. Arthur Ruppin, *The Jewish Fate and Future* (London, 1940), 82. The book was sent to press in October 1939.

22. Ibid., 76.

23. Yehuda Don and George Magos, "The Demographic Development of Hungarian Jewry," *JSS,* 45:3/4 (1983), 189–216.

24. L. Finkelstein, "L'état de santé de la population juive en Lithuanie," *Revue "OSÉ,"* May 1937, 2.

25. Mordechai Altshuler, *Soviet Jewry on the Eve of the Holocaust: A Social and Demographic Profile* (Jerusalem, 1998), 69 and 85. Most of the data in this chapter concerning Soviet Jewish demography are based on the Soviet census data of 1926, 1937, and 1939, as analyzed by Altshuler.

26. Ruppin, *Jews in the Modern World,* 264.

27. Ibid., 94–95.

28. Liebmann Hersch, "The Principal Causes of Death Among Jews," *Medical Leaves* 4 (1942), 56–77.

29. Jerzy Tomaszewski, "Jews in Łódź in 1931 According to Statistics," *Polin* 6 (1991), 198.

30. Finkelstein, "L'état de santé," 5.

31. Ibid.

32. Don and Magos, "Demographic Development."

33. Bruno Blau, "On the Frequency of Births in Jewish Marriages," *JSS* 15:3/4 (1953), 246.

34. Uriah Zevi Engelman, "Intermarriage among Jews in Germany, USSR, and Switzerland," *JSS,* 2:2 (1940), 165.

35. Sean Martin, *Jewish Life in Cracow 1918–1939* (London, 2004).

36. Jacob Lestchinsky, "Economic Aspects of Jewish Community Organization in Independent Poland," *JSS,* 9:4 (1947), 336.

37. Jacob Lestchinsky, *Vohin geyen mir? Idishe vanderungen amol un haynt* (New York, 1944), 30.

38. Ruppin, *Jewish Fate,* 304.

39. Hirsz Abramowicz, *Profiles of a Lost World: Memoirs of East European Jewish Life before World War II* (Detroit, 1999), Introduction by David Fishman, 13.

40. Evyatar Friesel, *The Days and the Seasons: Memoirs* (Detroit, 1996), 21.

41. Omer Bartov, *Erased: Vanishing Traces of Jewish Galicia in Present-Day Ukraine* (Princeton, N.J., 2007), 6.

42. Frances Glazer Sternberg, " 'Cities of Boundless Possibilities': Two Shtetlekh in Poland: A Social History" (Ph.D. diss., University of Missouri–Kansas City, 2000), 260.

43. S. Y. Agnon, "Betokh ayari," in Y. Cohen, ed., *Sefer butchatch* (Tel Aviv, 1955–56), 11.
44. David Bronsen, *Joseph Roth: Ein Biographie* (Cologne, 1974), 43.
45. Avraham Barkai and Paul Mendes-Flohr, *German-Jewish History in Modern Times*, vol. 4, *Renewal and Destruction: 1918–1945* (New York, 1998), 16–17.
46. David H. Weinberg, *A Community on Trial: The Jews of Paris in the 1930s* (Chicago, 1974), 76.
47. Itzik Manger, "Idn un di daytshe kultur," in *Noente geshtaltn un andere shriftn* (New York, 1961), 467.

2: THE CHRISTIAN PROBLEM

1. Jacques Maritain, *A Christian Looks at the Jewish Question* (New York, 1939), 16.
2. Ibid., 28–29.
3. Ibid., 29–30.
4. Anna Landau-Czajka, "The Image of the Jew in the Catholic Press during the Second Republic," *Polin* 8 (1994), 170.
5. Maritain, *A Christian Looks*, 82.
6. Ibid., 61–64.
7. Ibid., 29.
8. Eugen Weber, *Action Française: Royalism and Reaction in Twentieth Century France* (Stanford, Calif., 1962), 235.
9. Pawel Korzec, "Antisemitism in Poland as an Intellectual, Social, and Political Movement," in Fishman, ed., *Studies on Polish Jewry*, 83.
10. David I. Kertzer, *The Popes Against the Jews: The Vatican's Role in the Rise of Modern Anti-Semitism* (New York, 2001), 280.
11. Ibid., 251.
12. Georges Passelecq and Bernard Suchecky, *L'Encyclique cachée de Pie XI: Une occasion manquée de l'Eglise face à l'antisémitisme* (Paris, 1995); Anton Rauscher, ed., *Wider den Rassismus: Entwurf einer nicht erschienenen Enzyklika (1938): Texte aus dem Nachlass von Gustav Gundlach SJ* (Padeborn, 2001); Giovanni Sale, *Hitler, la Santa Sede e gli ebrei* (Milan, 2004); Frank J. Coppa, "The Hidden Encyclical of Pius XI Against Racism and Anti-Semitism Uncovered—Once Again!" *Catholic Historical Review* 84:1 (1998), 63–72.
13. Lynn Viola, "The Peasant Nightmare: Visions of Apocalypse in the Soviet Countryside," *Journal of Modern History* 62:4 (1990), 755–56.
14. Nicholas Hewitt, *The Life of Céline: A Critical Biography* (Oxford, 1999), 167–68.
15. Eugen Weber, *The Hollow Years: France in the 1930s* (New York, 1994), 106.
16. Shmuel Ettinger, "East European Jewry from Imperial to National Policy" (unpublished paper).
17. Carole Fink, *Defending the Rights of Others: The Great Powers, the Jews, and International Minority Protection, 1878–1938* (Cambridge, 2004), 248.
18. Ibid., 276.
19. Arkadi Zeltser, "Inter-War Ethnic Relations and Soviet Policy: The Case of Eastern Belorussia," *Yad Vashem Studies* 34 (2006), 87–124.
20. Joel Cang, "The Opposition Parties in Poland and Their Attitude towards the Jews and the Jewish Problem," *JSS* 1:2 (1939), 246.
21. "Letter from Poland," by Jacob Lestchinsky, in *Forverts* (New York), March 27, 1936.
22. Angela White, "Jewish Lives in the Polish Language: The Polish-Jewish Press, 1918–1939" (Ph.D. diss., Indiana University, 2007), 211.
23. Korzec, "Antisemitism in Poland," 90–91.

24. Martin Andermann, "My life in Germany before and after 30 January 1933," *LBIYB* 55:1 (2010), 315–28.
25. E. Rosenbaum and A. J. Sherman, *M. M. Warburg & Co. 1798–1938: Merchant Bankers of Hamburg* (London, 1979), 166.
26. Sebastian Haffner, *Defying Hitler* (New York, 2002), 122–23.
27. Speech by Friedrich von Keller, *American Jewish Year Book*, 36, 5695/1934–35 (Philadelphia, 1934), 106.
28. Speech by Henri Bérenger, ibid., 108.
29. Ibid., 118.
30. Christian Goeschel, *Suicide in Nazi Germany* (Oxford, 2009), 98–99.
31. Barkai and Mendes-Flohr, *German-Jewish History in Modern Times*, vol. 4, 211.
32. Abraham Ascher, *A Community under Siege: The Jews of Breslau under Nazism* (Stanford, Calif., 2007), 4.
33. Weber, *Hollow Years*, 305.
34. Memorandum of telephone conversation, Nov. 30, 1936, JDCNY AR 1933–44, file 695.
35. Max Horkheimer, "Die Juden und Europa," *Zeitschrift für Sozialforschung*, 8:1/2 (1939–40), 115–37.
36. Bernard Wasserstein, "Blame the Victim," *Times Literary Supplement*, Oct. 9, 2009: a fuller, annotated version is available in Dutch: Bernard Wasserstein et al., *Hannah Arendt en de geschiedschrijving: Een controverse* (Nijmegen, 2010).
37. Full text in Marc B. Shapiro, *Between the Yeshiva World and Modern Orthodoxy: The Life and Works of Rabbi Jehiel Jacob Weinberg 1884–1966* (Oxford, 1999), Appendix 2, 225–33.
38. David Sha'ari, "The Jewish Community of Cernăuți between the Wars," *Shvut* 7:23 (1998), 116.
39. Introduction to Wilhelm Filderman, *Memoirs and Diaries*, vol. 1, *1900–1940*, ed. Jean Ancel (Tel Aviv, 2004), 13.
40. Memoir of Chanan (Hans) Floersheim, LBINY ME 1300, 2.
41. Ibid.
42. Marci Shore, *Caviar and Ashes: A Warsaw Generation's Life and Death in Marxism, 1918–1968* (New Haven, Conn., 2006), 139.
43. Sinai Leichter, ed., *Anthology of Yiddish Folksongs*, vol. 5 (Jerusalem, 2000), 229–33. See Natan Gross, "Mordechai Gebirtig: The Folksong and the Cabaret Song," *Polin* 16 (2003), 107–17.

3: GRANDEES AND GRANDSTANDERS

1. Quoted in *Unity in Dispersion: A History of the World Jewish Congress* (New York, 1948), 13.
2. Brenda S. Webster, "Helene Deutsch: A New Look," *Signs* 10:3 (1985), 556.
3. Printed notice, 13 Marcheshvan 5691 (Nov. 4, 1930), IISH Bund 331; and sim. 2 Marcheshvan 5699 (Oct. 27, 1938), YA 28/2/Bobov.
4. Aviezer Ravitzky, "Munkács and Jerusalem," in S. Almog, J. Reinharz, and A. Shapira, eds., *Zionism and Religion* (Hanover, N.H., 1998), 71.
5. YA RG 28 Box 1, folder BELZ.
6. Marcus Moseley, "Bal-Makhshoves," in Gershon Hundert, ed., *The YIVO Encyclopaedia of the Jews in Eastern Europe* (New Haven, Conn., 2008), vol. 1, 116.
7. Dan Jacobson, "A Memoir of Jabotinsky," *Commentary* 31:6 (June 1961), 520.
8. Eran Kaplan, *The Jewish Radical Right: Revisionist Zionism and Its Ideological Legacy* (Madison, Wis., 2005), 28.
9. Melekh Ravitch, "Emanuel Ringelblum," in Cohen, ed., *Sefer butchatch*, 227–28.
10. Julius Braunthal, *In Search of the Millennium* (London, 1945), 5.
11. Jean Lacouture, *Léon Blum* (Paris, 1977), 205.

12. Selma Leydesdorf, "In Search of the Picture: Jewish Proletarians in Amsterdam between the Two World Wars," in Jozeph Michman, ed., *Dutch Jewish History* (Jerusalem, 1984), 326.

13. Marcel Pauker, *Ein Lebenslauf: Jüdisches Schicksal in Rumänien 1896–1938*, ed. William Totok and Erhard Roy Wiehn (Constance, 1999), 24.

14. Isaac Deutscher, "Who is a Jew?" in Isaac Deutscher, *The Non-Jewish Jew and other Essays* (London, 1968), 42–59.

15. Jeff Schatz, "Jews and the Communist Movement in Interwar Poland," *Studies in Contemporary Jewry* 20 (2004), 20.

16. Moshé Zalcman, *La véridique histoire de Moshé, ouvrier juif et communiste au temps de Staline* (Paris, 1977), 40.

17. A. Kichelewsky, "Being a Jew and a Communist in 1930s France: Dilemmas seen through a Yiddish daily newspaper, the '*Naye Prese*,' " in A. Grabski, ed., *Żydzi a lewica: Zbiór studiów historycznych* (Warsaw, 2007), 93.

18. Michel Trebitsch, " 'De la situation faite à l'écrivain juif dans le monde moderne': Jean-Richard Bloch entre identité, littérature et engagement," *Archives Juives* 36:2 (2003), 47.

19. Ibid., 53.

20. Joshua Rubenstein, *Tangled Loyalties: The Life and Times of Ilya Ehrenburg* (Tuscaloosa, Ala., 1999), 132.

21. Annie Kriegel and Stéphane Courtois, *Eugen Fried: Le grand secret du PCF* (Paris, 1997).

22. S. L. Shneiderman, "Notes for an Autobiography," http://www.lib.umd.edu/SLSES/donors/autobio.html.

23. Ibid.

24. Koppel S. Pinson, "Arkady Kremer, Vladimir Medem, and the Ideology of the Jewish Bund," *JSS* 7:3 (1945), 245.

25. Emanuel Nowogrodski, *The Jewish Labor Bund in Poland 1915–1939* (Rockville, Md., 2001), chapter 6.

26. Manifesto adopted at 1937 fortieth anniversary Congress, Nov. 1937, quoted ibid., 169.

27. Gertrud Pickhan, "Yidishkayt and class consciousness: The Bund and its minority concept," *East European Jewish Affairs* 39:2 (2009), 259.

28. Sophie Dubnow-Erlich, *The Life and Work of S. M. Dubnow* (Bloomington, Ind., 1991), 229.

29. Victor Erlich, *Child of a Turbulent Century* (Evanston, Ill., 2006), 39.

30. Ibid.

31. Sinai Leichter, ed., *Anthology of Jewish Folksongs*, vol. 6 (Jerusalem, 2002), 221–22.

32. *Folks-tsaytung*, July 5, 1935, as quoted in Nowogrodski, *Jewish Labor Bund*, 152.

33. Jacob Lestchinski, "Vu iz der oysveg?" *Naye shtime*, July 1938, 6.

34. The description, by the Australian journalist George Farmer, is quoted by Beverley Hooper in her entry on Steinberg in *Australian National Biography*, online ed., http://adbonline.anu.edu.au/biogs/A160362b.htm.

35. "Gershon Malakiewicz," in Abramowicz, *Profiles of a Lost World*, 289–90.

36. Zalcman, *Histoire véridique*, 29.

37. *Naye folks-tsaytung*, Dec. 2, 1930.

38. Weinberg, *Community on Trial*, 56.

39. Robert Moses Shapiro, "The Polish *Kehillah* Elections of 1936: A Revolution Re-examined," *Polin* 8 (1994), 210, 213.

4: FROM *SHTETL* TO *SHTOT*

1. Zvi Gitelman, "Correlates, Causes and Consequences of Jewish Fertility in the USSR," in Paul Ritterband, ed., *Modern Jewish Fertility* (Leiden, 1981), 45.

2. Schnurmann, "La mortalité," 7–8.
3. Hirsz Abramowicz, "Rural Jewish Occupations," in Abramowicz, *Profiles of a Lost World*, 76.
4. Altshuler, *Soviet Jewry on the Eve of the Holocaust*, 44.
5. Ibid., 15.
6. Reproduced in Leyzer Ran, ed., *Yerusholoyim d'Lite*, vol. 1 (New York, 1974), 92.
7. Arnold J. Band, "Agnon's Synthetic Shtetl," in Steven T. Katz, ed., *The Shtetl: New Evaluations* (New York, 2007), 234.
8. Mikhail Krutikov, "Rediscovering the Shtetl as a New Reality," in Katz, ed., *Shtetl*, 211.
9. Nathalie Babel, ed., *The Complete Works of Isaac Babel* (New York, 2005), 742. This fragment of an unpublished novel did not appear in print in Babel's lifetime.
10. Wolf Lewkowicz to Sol Zissman, May 14, 1933, English translation from Yiddish at http://web.mit.edu/maz/wolf/65-179/wolf134.txt.
11. "The Plight of Jewish Children in Ostrog," Oct. 1937, JDCNY AR 33-44/822.
12. "Probuzhana," report by Economic-Statistical Bureau of C.K.B. (Central Society for the Support of Free Credit and the Spread of Productive Labour among the Jewish Population of Poland), Warsaw, c. 1935, YA 116, Poland 1/6/26.
13. Abramowicz, "A Lithuanian Shtetl," in Abramowicz, *Profiles of a Lost World*, 77–98.
14. Samuel Kassow, Introduction to Katz, ed., *Shtetl*, 8–9.
15. Interview with Yermye Herscheles, born in Gliniany, quoted in Walter Zev Feldman, "Remembrance of Things Past: Klezmer Musicians of Galicia, 1870–1940," *Polin* 16 (2003), 29–57.
16. Samuel Kassow, "The Shtetl in Inter-War Poland," in Katz, ed., *Shtetl*, 125.
17. Wolf Lewkowicz to Sol Zissman, Oct. 8, 1926, English translation from Yiddish at http://web.mit.edu/maz/wolf/29-64/wolf61.txt.
18. International Conference on Jewish Social Work, London, July 1936, Synopsis of Reports, WL doc 1240/40, XVI/4.
19. *Baranovitsher kuryer*, April 17 and July 17, 1936.
20. Sternberg, " 'Cities of Boundless Possibilities,' " 223–24.
21. Gennady Estraikh, *Soviet Yiddish: Language Planning and Linguistic Development* (Oxford, 1999), 24, quoting a work by Ja. Kantor published in Moscow in 1935.
22. Dovid Hofshteyn, "Shtot," Yiddish text from Irving Howe, Ruth R. Wisse, and Khone Shmeruk, *The Penguin Book of Modern Yiddish Verse* (New York, 1987), 263.
23. *Yoyvel-heft gevidmet dem 5 yorikn yoyvel fun di pirkhey agudos yisroel in ontverpn* (Antwerp, Adar 5696/March 1936), 1.
24. Altshuler, *Soviet Jewry on the Eve of the Holocaust*, 40.
25. Beate Kosmala, *Juden und Deutsche in polnischen Haus: Tomaszów Mazowiecki 1914–1939* (Berlin, 2001), 90.
26. Isaac Bashevis Singer, *Shosha* (New York, 1978; first published in Yiddish, 1974), 70.
27. Itzik Nakhmen Gottesman, *Redefining the Yiddish Nation: The Jewish Folklorists of Poland* (Detroit, 2003), 134.
28. "Gezelshaft medem-sanatorye," c. 1937, YA 1474/1/1.
29. YA 1474/1/7.
30. Zalcman, *Histoire véridique*, 51.
31. Weinberg, *Community on Trial*, 37.
32. *Naye prese*, Sept. 12, 1935, quoted ibid., 41.
33. Shmuel Bunim, "Sur les traces de quelques cafés juifs du Paris des années trente," *Les Cahiers du Judaïsme* 26 (2009), 46–51.

34. *Arbet un kamf: Barikht fun tsentraln profesioneln rat fun di yidishe klasn-faraynen in Poyln* (Warsaw, August 1939), ii.
35. *Der transport arbeter*, Dec. 1936, 4.
36. *Der transport arbeter*, Dec. 1936, 11–12.
37. S. Glikson, *Der yidishe frizir-arbeter in varshe* (Warsaw, 1939), 24.

5: NEW JERUSALEMS

1. Egon Erwin Kisch, *Tales from Seven Ghettos* (London, 1948), 178.
2. Siegfried E. van Praag, *Jerusalem van het Westen* (The Hague, 1962).
3. J. C. H. Blom and J. J. Chaen, "Jewish Netherlanders, 1870–1940," in J. C. H. Blom, R. G. Fuks-Mansfeld, and I. Schöffer, eds., *The History of the Jews in the Netherlands* (Oxford, 2002), 236.
4. Benno Gitter, *The Story of My Life* (London, 1999), 17.
5. C. Wijsenbeek-Franken, Report on the Conditions of Jewish Social Work in Holland, June 1936, WL doc 1240/2, 11.
6. Simone Lipschitz, *Die Amsterdamse Diamantbeurs* (Amsterdam, 1990), 146.
7. Meijer de Hond, describing the area in the 1920s, quoted in Selma Leydesdorff, *We Lived with Dignity: The Jewish Proletariat of Amsterdam, 1900–1940* (Detroit, 1994), 42–43.
8. Gertrude van Tijn, supplementary memoir, LBINY ME 1335, 26.
9. Leydesdorff, *We Lived with Dignity*, 81.
10. Introduction to Jonathan Israel and Reinier Salverda, eds., *Dutch Jewry: Its History and Secular Culture 1500–2000* (Leiden, 2002), 6–7.
11. C. Wijsenbeek-Franken, Report on the Conditions of Jewish Social Work in Holland, June 1936, WL doc 1240/2, 15.
12. Karin Hofmeester, "Holland's Greatest Beggar: Fundraising and Public Relations at the Joodsche Invalide," *Studia Rosenthaliana* 33:1 (1999), 47–59.
13. J. C. H. Blom, "Dutch Jews, Jewish Dutchmen and Jews in the Netherlands 1870–1940," in Israel and Salverda, eds., *Dutch Jewry*, 221.
14. Bob Moore, *Refugees from Nazi Germany in the Netherlands, 1933–1940* (Dordrecht, 1986), 71.
15. Comité voor Bijzondere Joodsche Belangen, Amsterdam, circular, April 1, 1935, Bibl. Ros. Vereenigingen Comité-G.
16. Gertrude van Tijn to James G. McDonald, April 5, 1935, JDCNY AR 1933–44, folder 703.
17. Melissa Müller, *Anne Frank: The Biography* (London, 2000), 43.
18. Salvador E. Bloemgarten, "Henri Polak: A Jew and a Dutchman," in Jozeph Michman, ed., *Dutch Jewish History* (Jerusalem, 1984), 262.
19. Henri Polak, *Het "wetenschappelijk" antisemitisme: weerlegging en vertoog* (Amsterdam, 1933).
20. Gennady Estraikh, "The Vilna Yiddishists' Quest for Modernity," in Marina Dmitrieva and Heidemarie Petersen, eds., *Jüdische Kultur(en) im Neuen Europa: Wilna 1918–1939* (Wiesbaden, 2004), 102.
21. Franz Kurski, archivist of the Bund, quoted in Pickhan, "*Yidishkayt* and class consciousness," 250.
22. Czesław Miłosz, "Miłosz's ABCs," *New York Review of Books*, Nov. 2, 2000.
23. Czesław Miłosz, *Native Realm: A Search for Self-Definition* (New York, 1968), 92.
24. Ran, ed., *Yerusholoyim d'Lite*, vol. 1, 40.
25. Yves Plasseraud and Henri Minczeles, eds., *Lituanie juive, 1918–1940: Message d'un monde englouti* (Paris, 1996), 62–63.
26. Abramowicz, *Profiles of a Lost World*, 31.
27. Quotations from unidentified Latvian Yiddish newspaper and from article by Michał Weichert in Cecile Kuznitz, "The Origins of Yiddish Scholarship and

the YIVO Institute for Jewish Research" (Ph.D. diss., Stanford University, 2000), 78–79.

28. Joshua M. Karlip, "Between martyrology and historiography: Elias Tcherikower and the making of a pogrom historian," *East European Jewish Affairs* 38:3 (December 2008), 268.

29. Ibid., 272.

30. Memoir of Sonia Wachstein, LBINY ME 1068, 37.

31. Barbara Kirschenblatt-Gimblett, "Coming of Age in the Thirties: Max Weinreich, Edward Sapir, and Jewish Social Science," *YIVO Annual* 23 (1996), 87.

32. *Literarishe bleter*, Jan. 18, 1929.

33. Libe Schildkret (later Lucy Dawidowicz), quoted in Kuznitz, "Origins of Yiddish Scholarship," 144.

34. Dubnow letter to Jacob Lestchinsky, quoted in Dubnow-Erlich, *Life and Work of S. M. Dubnow*, 216.

35. Howe et al., eds., *Penguin Book of Modern Yiddish Verse*, 406–11.

36. "B. Vladek," "A blik oyf tsurik," in Yefim Yeshurun, ed., *Vilne: a zamelbukh gevidmet der shtot vilne* (New York, 1935), 211.

37. Elissa Bemporad, "Red Star on the Jewish Street: The Reshaping of Jewish Life in Soviet Minsk, 1917–1939" (Ph.D. diss., Stanford University, 2006), 121.

38. Ibid., 49.

39. Ibid., 176.

40. Ibid., 207.

41. See "Jewish pigs" and other cartoons reproduced in Andrew Sloin, "Pale Fire: Jews in Revolutionary Belorussia, 1917–1929" (Ph.D. diss., University of Chicago, 2009), 481 ff.

42. Ibid., 352.

43. Ibid., chapter 6.

44. Gentille Arditty-Puller, "Poésie d'une Salonique disparu," *Le Judaïsme Sépharadi*, n.s., 11 (July 1956).

45. Mark Mazower, *Salonica: City of Ghosts* (London, 2004), 304.

46. Rena Molho, *Salonica and Istanbul: Social, Political and Cultural Aspects of Jewish Life* (Analecta Isisiana, 83, Istanbul, 2005), 39.

47. "Memoire sovre los escopos, la activita etc. de las institutions de bienfaisencia," Jewish Community of Thessaloniki, May 16, 1939, YA 207/87; see also related documents in this record group.

48. Mazower, *Salonica*, 367.

49. *New York Times*, May 21, 2009.

50. Quoted in Gila Hadar, "Space and Time in Saloniki on the Eve of World War II, and the Expulsion and Destruction of Saloniki Jewry, 1939–1945," *Yalkut Moreshet* 4 (2006), 50.

51. Ioannis Skourtis, "The Zionists and their Jewish Opponents in Thessaloniki between the Two World Wars," in I. K. Hassiotis, ed., *The Jewish Communities of Southeastern Europe from the Fifteenth Century to the end of World War II* (Thessaloniki, 1997), 511.

52. Mazower, *Salonica*, 409.

53. L'Inspecteur des Ecoles Communales Israélites [unnamed on carbon copy] to M. Batsoutas, Inspecteur des Ecoles Publiques, Jan. 24, 1929, CAHJP GR/sa/47.

54. Letter [signature indecipherable] to a member of the community's Educational Commission, Salonica, June 27, 1937, YA 207/119.

55. *L'Indépendant*, May 8, 1939.

56. President of Community Council, Salonica, to Community Education Commission, May 20, 1937, YA 207/145.

57. K. E. Fleming, *Greece: A Jewish History* (Princeton, 2008), 99.

58. Yitzhak Bezalel, "Bikoret mahutanit shel mister green: ben gurion al yehudei saloniki," *Pe'amim* 109 (2006), 149–53.

59. Shmuel Raphael, "The Longing for Zion in Judeo-Spanish (Ladino) Poetry," in Minna Rozen, ed., *The Last Ottoman Century and Beyond: The Jews in Turkey and the Balkans, 1808–45*, vol. 2 (Tel Aviv, 2002), 216, quoting A. S. Recanati, "Los escariños por la Palestine," *Ben-Israel* (1923), 15.

60. "Salonique: Le nouveau Conseil Communal," *Le Judaïsme Sépharadi* 24 (December 1934).

61. Minna Rozen, "Jews and Greeks Remember Their Past: The Political Career of Tzevi Koretz (1933–43)," *JSS*, n.s., 12:1 (2005), 111–66.

62. Quoted ibid., 135.

63. *L'Indépendant*, June 3, 1939.

64. Protocol of Community Council meeting, Jan. 6, 1939, CAHJP GR/sa/59.

65. See *Acción* and *Le Progrès*, January 1939.

66. *L'Indépendant*, May 8, 1939.

67. *L'Indépendant*, July 12, 1939: see also testimony of Ruth Calfon, 1956, regarding Stela Masarano, YV.

68. Mazower, *Salonica*, 404.

69. *L'Indépendant*, Jan. 9, 1939.

6: HOLY MEN

1. Wolf Lewkowicz to Sol Zissman, Oct. 14, 1928, English translation from Yiddish at http://web.mit.edu/maz/wolf/65-179/wolf94.txt.

2. Gold, *Life of Jews*, 99–100.

3. Schmuel Osterzetser, "Agudistishe yugnt," *Yoyvel-heft gevidmet dem 5-yorikn yoyvel fun di pirkhey agudos yisroel in ontverpn* (Antwerp, Adar 5696/March 1936), 2.

4. Gershon Greenberg, "Ontic Division and Religious Survival: Wartime Palestinian Orthodoxy and the Holocaust (Hurban)," *Modern Judaism* 14:1 (1994), 51.

5. See Shapiro, *Between the Yeshiva World and Modern Orthodoxy*, 95–96.

6. Samuel C. Heilman, "The Many Faces of Orthodoxy," Part 1, *Modern Judaism* 2:1 (1982), 43, 45.

7. Yeshayahu A. Jelinek, *The Carpathian Diaspora: The Jews of Subcarpathian Rus' and Mukachevo, 1848–1948* (New York, 2007), 163.

8. Raphael Patai, *Apprentice in Budapest: Memories of a World That Is No More* (Salt Lake City, 1988), 306.

9. Allan L. Nadler, "The War on Modernity of R. Hayyim Elazar Shapira of Munkacz," *Modern Judaism* 14:3 (1994), 237.

10. Ravitzky, "Munkács and Jerusalem," 67.

11. Nadler, "War on Modernity," 256.

12. Jelinek, *Carpathian Diaspora*, 175.

13. Nadler, "War on Modernity," 250.

14. Jelinek, *Carpathian Diaspora*, 172–73.

15. *Le Judaïsme Sépharadi* 31–33 (August–September 1935).

16. Alexander Altmann, "The German Rabbi: 1910–1939," *LBIYB* 19 (1974), 31.

17. Christhard Hoffman and Daniel R. Schwarz, "Early but Opposed—Supported but Late: Two Berlin Seminaries which Attempted to Move Abroad," *LBIYB* 36 (1991), 267–304.

18. Harriet Pass Freidenreich, *Jewish Politics in Vienna, 1918–1938* (Bloomington, Ind., 1991), 124.

19. George Alexander Kohut, in Victor Aptowitzer et al., eds., *Abhandlungen zur Erinnerung an Hirsch Perez Chajes* (Vienna, 1933), lix.

20. Joachim Prinz, "Abschied von einer Arbeit," *Jüdische Rundschau*, July 27,

1937. The allusion is to the passage in Jeremiah 31:1–16, in which the prophet comforts the weeping people with the prospect of a return to their own borders from "the land of the enemy" (a phrase that would, no doubt, have been unprintable in Nazi Germany).

21. Dan Porat memoir, LBINY ME 1060, 4.
22. Joseph Carlebach, *Der Chederprozess im Stadttheater zu Witebsk: Ein kulturgeschichtliches Dokument* (Berlin, 1924), 31.
23. Porat memoir, LBINY ME 1060, 3.
24. Ibid., 2.
25. Martin, *Jewish Life in Cracow*, 160–61.
26. Sabina Lewin, "Observations on the State as a Factor in the History of Jewish Private Elementary Schooling in the Second Polish Republic," *Gal-Ed* 18 (2002), 65.
27. Y. Y. Inditski, "Vi hot oysgezen der amoliger kheder," *Unzer Lebn* (Białystok), July 14, 1939.
28. Sternberg, " 'Cities of Boundless Possibilities,' " 119.
29. Gold, *Life of Jews*, 46–47.
30. Shaul Stampfer, "Hasidic Yeshivot in Inter-War Poland," *Polin* 11 (1998), 23.
31. Gold, *Life of Jews*, 117–18.
32. Shapiro, *Between the Yeshiva World and Modern Orthodoxy*, 5.
33. David Fishman, "The Musar Movement in Interwar Poland," in Yisrael Gutman et al., eds., *The Jews of Poland Between Two World Wars* (Hanover, N.H., 1989), 251.
34. YA 767/1/Lublin *yeshiva* and 767/1/Warsaw-Otwock.
35. Information form on Ponevezh *yeshiva* submitted to Haffkine Foundation, Paris, YA 767/1/Ponevezh.
36. Information form on Mir *yeshiva* submitted to "Joint," March 1939, JDCNY AR 33–44/836.
37. Richard Fuchs, "The 'Hochschule für die Wissenschaft des Judentums' in the Period of Nazi Rule," *LBIYB*, 12 (1967), 10.
38. Ibid., 21.
39. Raphael Patai, *Apprenticeship in Budapest*, 320.
40. Ibid., 340–41.
41. Joseph Roth, "The Auto-da-fé of the Mind," in *What I Saw: Reports from Berlin 1920–1933* (New York, 2003), 210–11; this article first appeared in *Cahiers juifs* (Paris), September–November 1933.
42. Myriam Anissimov, *Primo Levi: Tragedy of an Optimist* (New York, 1999), 20.
43. Robert Kanfer memoir, LBINY ME 1518, 8.
44. Aryeh Yodfat, "The Soviet Struggle to Destroy Jewish Religious Education in the Early Years of the Regime, 1917–1927," *Journal of Jewish Education* 40:3 (1970), 33.
45. Elias Schulman, *A History of Jewish Education in the Soviet Union* (New York, 1971), 59.
46. Leyb Abram et al., eds., *Der mishpet ibren kheyder* (Vitebsk, 1922).
47. Yodfat, "Soviet Struggle," 37.
48. Aryeh Yodfat, "Jewish Religious Education in the USSR (1928–1971)," *Journal of Jewish Education* 42:1 (1972), 31.
49. Bemporad, "Red Star on the Jewish Street," 149–50.
50. K. Beznosik, M. Erik, and Y. Rubin, eds., *Antireligyezer literarisher leyenbukh* (Moscow, 1930), 4.
51. Ibid., 5.
52. "Gedali," in Babel, ed., *Complete Works of Isaac Babel*, 228.
53. Zalcman, *Histoire véridique*, 114.
54. Yodfat, "Jewish Religious Education," 31.
55. Ibid., 33.

56. Meir Mushkatin, "In der tsayt fun bolshevikes," in Grigori Aronson, ed., *Vitebsk amol: geshikhte, zikhroynes, khurbn* (New York, 1983), 593–602.
57. Clive Sinclair, *The Brothers Singer* (London, 1983), 117.
58. See correspondence from Aharon-Yosef Hershunov in Tul'chyn (July 10, 1936) and from Rabbi Nahman Sternharz in Uman and Berdichev (1934 and 1937), enclosed with commentary in letters from M. L. Hershunov (Montreal) to Max Weinreich (New York), March 24, and April 22, 1944, CAHJP RU/84.
59. Avraham Greenbaum, *Rabanei brit ha-moatsot bein milhamot ha-olam* (Jerusalem, 1994), 28.
60. Altshuler, *Soviet Jewry on the Eve of the Holocaust*, 98–101.

7: UNHOLY WOMEN

1. Gold, *Life of Jews*, 55.
2. *Mishnah Sotah* 3:4.
3. *Berakhot* 10a; Nadler, "War on Modernity," 253.
4. Ruth Rubin, "Nineteenth-Century Yiddish Folk Songs of Children in Eastern Europe," *Journal of American Folklore* 65:257 (1952), 240.
5. Rae Dalven, *The Jews of Ioannina* (Philadelphia, 1990), 132.
6. Rafael Scharf, *Poland, What Have I to Do With Thee . . . Essays Without Prejudice* (London, 1996), 18.
7. Lucjan Dobroszycki, "The Fertility of Modern Polish Jewry," in Ritterband, ed., *Modern Jewish Fertility*, 69.
8. Altshuler, *Soviet Jewry on the Eve of the Holocaust*, 67.
9. Fred S. Worms, *A Life in Three Cities: Frankfurt, London, and Jerusalem* (London, 1996), 13.
10. See Jordan D. Finkin, *A Rhetorical Conversation: Jewish Discourse in Modern Yiddish Literature* (University Park, Penn., 2010), 83.
11. Mayer Bogdanski, "Dos yidishe kultur-lebn in farmilkhomdikn pyeterkov," *Oksforder yidish* 1 (1990), 48.
12. Aharon Vinkovetzky, Abba Kovner, and Sinai Leichter, eds., *Anthology of Yiddish Folksongs*, vol. 2 (Jerusalem, 1984), 90–91.
13. S. Binder, "Di demografishe bavegung in yidishn kibuts fun kaunas," in S. Binder et al., *Yidn in kaunas* (Kaunas, 1939), 33.
14. Altshuler, *Soviet Jewry on the Eve of the Holocaust*, 78.
15. *Unzer ekspres*, Aug. 9, 1939.
16. Such a case is recorded in P. Anderman-Neuberger, "Bet ha-yetumim be-butchatch," in Cohen, ed., *Sefer butchatch*, 184–85.
17. Marion A. Kaplan, *The Jewish Feminist Movement in Germany: The Campaigns of the Jüdischer Frauenbund, 1904–1938* (Westport, Conn., 1979), 38–39.
18. Alice Salomon, *Charakter ist Schicksal: Lebenserinnerungen* (Weinheim, 1983), 139.
19. Marloes Schoonheim, "Stemming the Current: Dutch Jewish Women and the First Feminist Movement," in Judith Frishman and Hetty Berg, eds., *Dutch Jewry in a Cultural Maelstrom 1880–1940* (Amsterdam, 2007), 174.
20. Selma Leydesdorff, "Dutch Jewish Women: Integration and Modernity," ibid., 192.
21. Kaplan, *Jewish Feminist Movement*, 157.
22. Dora Gross-Moszkowski memoir, LBINY ME 834, 24.
23. Abram et al, eds., *Der mishpet ibren kheyder*, 36.
24. *Der Israelit*, June 13, 1929.
25. *C.V. Zeitung*, June 14, 1929.
26. *Yidishe bilder*, July 8, 1938.
27. Joseph Roth, *The Wandering Jews*, trans. Michael Hofmann (New York, 2001), 85.

28. Dahlia S. Elazar, " 'Engines of Acculturation': The Last Political Generation of Jewish Women in Interwar East Europe," *Journal of Historical Sociology* 15:3 (2002), 366–94.
29. Ibid., 385–86.
30. Gold, *Life of Jews*, 56.
31. Deborah Weizman, "Bais Ya'akov as an Innovation in Women's Education: A Contribution to the Study of Education and Social Change," *Studies in Jewish Education* 7 (Jerusalem, 1995), 294–95.
32. Wendy Goldman, *Women at the Gates: Gender and Industry in Stalin's Russia* (Cambridge, 2002), 16.
33. Anna Fishman Gonshor, "Kadye Molodowsky in *Literarishe Bleter*, 1925–1935: Annotated Bibliography" (M.A. thesis, McGill University, 1997), 67.
34. *Literarishe bleter*, June 3, 1927.
35. Yankev Botoshanski, "Kadya Molodowski," *Literarishe bleter*, Jan. 6, 1933.
36. Rokhl Korn, "Dzhike-gas un ir dikhterin," *Literarishe bleter*, Jan. 19, 1934.
37. Katharina von Kellenbach, "Denial and Defiance in the Work of Rabbi Regina Jonas," in Omer Bartov and Phyllis Mack, eds., *In God's Name: Genocide and Religion in the Twentieth Century* (New York, 2001), 243–58.
38. *Second Jewish International Conference on the Suppression of the Traffic in Girls and Women, 22–4 June 1927, Official Report* (London, 1927).
39. Iris Parush, *Reading Jewish Women: Marginality and Modernization in Nineteenth-Century Eastern European Society* (Hanover, N.H., 2004), 297, quoting a writer, "A," in *Hador*.
40. Leichter, ed., *Anthology of Yiddish Folk Songs*, vol. 5, 114–16.

8: LUFTMENSHN

1. Lewis Namier, "Introduction" to Ruppin, *Jews in the Modern World*, xxv.
2. Jelinek, *Carpathian Diaspora*, 125.
3. Gold, *Life of Jews*, 28–30.
4. Gerhard Schreiber, memoir, LBINY ME 1416.
5. Lev Kopelev, *The Education of a True Believer* (New York, 1980), 44–45.
6. Deborah Hope Yalen, "Red *Kasrilevke*: Ethnographies of Economic Transformation in the Soviet Shtetl, 1917–1939" (Ph.D. diss., University of California, Berkeley, 2007), 85–86.
7. Paul Jankowski, *Stavisky: A Confidence Man in the Republic of Virtue* (Ithaca, N.Y., 2002), vii.
8. Bernard Wasserstein, *The Secret Lives of Trebitsch Lincoln*, 2nd rev. ed. (London, 1989).
9. See Michael Berkowitz, *The Crime of My Very Existence: Nazism and the Myth of Jewish Criminality* (Berkeley, 2007).
10. Liebmann Hersch, *Farbrekherishkayt fun yidn un nit-yidn in poyln* (Vilna, 1937); Liebmann Hers[c]h, "Delinquency among Jews: A Comparative Study of Criminality among the Jewish and Non-Jewish Population of the Polish Republic," *Journal of Criminal Law and Criminology* 27:4 (1936) 515–38; Liebmann Hersch, "Complementary Data on Jewish Delinquency in Poland," *loc. cit.*, 27:6 (1937), 857–73.
11. Sloin, "Pale Fire," vol. 1, 130.
12. Jac. van Weringh, "A Case of Homicide in the Jewish Neighbourhood of Amsterdam 1934: Reactions in Dutch Society," in Michman, ed., *Dutch Jewish History*, 338.
13. Ibid., 340.
14. Zvi Yavetz, *Erinnerungen an Czernowitz: Wo Menschen und Bücher lebten* (Munich, 2007), 228–29.
15. Gwido Zlatkes, "Urke Nachalnik: A Voice from the Underworld," *Polin* 16 (2003), 382. See also Avraham Karpinovitch, "Sipuro hamufla shel urke

nachalnik," *Kesher* 18 (1975), 93–101; and Mikhl Ben-Avrom, "Urke nachalnik," *Forverts*, June 23, 2006.

16. Isaac Bashevis Singer, *Shosha* (New York, 1978), 72.

17. Ibid., 71.

18. Shmuel Lehman, ed., *Ganovim-lider mit melodyes* (Warsaw, 1928), 25.

19. J. L. Cahan, *Yidisher folklor* (Vilna, 1938), 84. A variant version, recorded in Zamość during the German occupation in the First World War, is in Lehman, ed., *Ganovim-lider*, 23–24.

20. See Richard Cobb, *Paris and its Provinces 1792–1802* (Oxford, 1975), 141–93.

21. "Probuzhana," report by Economic-Statistical Bureau of C.K.B., circa 1935, YA 116, Poland 1/6/26.

22. Undated, contemporary report, quoted in Yeshayahu A. Jelinek, "Jewish Youth in Carpatho Rus': Between Hope and Despair, 1920–1938," *Shvut* 7:23 (1998), 148–49.

23. *New York Times*, July 25, 1938.

24. *Parizer haynt*, July 25, 27, 1938.

25. *Action française*, July 29, 1938; Kurt Ihlefeld, "Das Judenportrait. Isaak Leifer. Oberrabiner und Rauschgiftschmuggler," *Mitteilungen über die Judenfrage* 2:26/7 (1938).

26. *Parizer haynt*, July 28, 1938.

27. *Parizer haynt*, July 29, and Aug. 2, 8, and 18, 1938.

28. *New York Times*, June 21 and Aug. 5, 1939.

29. Arcadius Kahan, "Vilna: The Sociocultural Anatomy of a Jewish Community in Interwar Poland," in *Essays in Jewish Social and Economic History* (Chicago, 1986), 152.

30. "Odessa," in Babel, ed., *Complete Works of Isaac Babel*, 77.

31. Jarrod Tanny, "City of Rogues and Schnorrers: The Myth of Old Odessa in Russian and Jewish Culture (Ph.D. diss., University of California, Berkeley, 2009), 204–5.

32. Jarrod Tanny, "*Kvetching* and Carousing under Communism: Old Odessa as the Soviet Union's Jewish City of Sin," *East European Jewish Affairs* 39:3 (Dec. 2009), 318.

33. Robert A. Rothstein, "How It Was Sung in Odessa: At the Intersection of Russian and Yiddish Folk Culture," *Slavic Review* 60:4 (2001), 791.

34. Tanny "City of Rogues and Schnorrers," 171.

35. Ibid., 152–53.

36. Ibid., 276–77.

37. S. Frederick Starr, *Red and Hot: The Fate of Jazz in the Soviet Union, 1917–1980* (New York, 1983), 127.

38. Rothstein, "How It Was Sung in Odessa," 794–95.

39. Moshe Beregovski, *Old Jewish Folk Music: The Collections and Writings of Moshe Beregovski*, ed. and trans. Mark Slobin (Philadelphia, 1982), 273.

40. *Emes*, Feb. 2, 1922, quoted in Jackie Wullschlager, *Chagall: A Biography* (New York, 2008), 270.

41. Marc Chagall, *My Life* (New York, 1994), 169.

42. Jelinek, *Carpathian Diaspora*, 27.

43. Vasily Grossman, "In the Town of Berdichev," in *The Road: Stories, Journalism, and Essays* (New York, 2010), 19.

44. "Betler-Legende," by Itzik Manger, in Sinai Leichter, ed., *Anthology of Yiddish Folksongs*, vol. 7, *The Itzik Manger Volume* (Jerusalem, 2004), 189–92.

45. *Dos naye emese vort*, June 21, 1935.

46. *Dos emese vort*, January 1936.

47. Odile Sugenas, "Ville et 'shtetl' au quotidien," in Plasseraud and Minczeles, eds., *Lituanie juive*, 74.

48. Protokoll des II. Kongresses des Verbandes Jüdischer Taubstummen der Republik Polen," March 8, 1931, YA 54/1/4.

49. Vilna branch to central association, Jan. 8, 1936, YA 54/1/21.
50. Eva Plach, "Introducing Miss Judea 1929: The Politics of Beauty, Race, and Zionism in Inter-War Poland," *Polin* 20 (2008), 384.
51. Article by Dr. W. Meisl, Maccabi World Union Press Bulletin, July 10, 1935 (issued in London in German).
52. Sharon Gillerman, "Zishe Breitbart," in Hundert, ed., *YIVO Encyclopedia of Jews in Eastern Europe*, vol. 1, 324–25.
53. *New York Times*, May 4, 2009; *Independent*, May 23, 2009; *The Times*, June 22, 2009.
54. Roni Gechtman, "Socialist Mass Politics Through Sport: The Bund's Morgnshtern in Poland, 1926–1939," *Journal of Sports History* 26:2 (1999), 326–52.
55. Memoir of Gerhard Schreiber, LBINY ME 1416.
56. *Daily Telegraph*, Feb. 13, 2006; *The Times*, July 13, 2009; *Haaretz*, July 29, 2009.

9: NON-JEWISH JEWS

1. Martin O. Stern memoir, LBINY, ME 1339.
2. *Gittin* 11b.
3. Martin Jay, *Adorno* (Cambridge, Mass., 1984), 19.
4. Rodney Livingstone, "Some Aspects of German-Jewish Names," *German Life and Letters* 58:2 (2005), 170.
5. Undated letter (January 1915), in Béatrice Mousli, *Max Jacob* (Paris, 2005), 158.
6. Undated letter (January 1939), in Max Jacob, *Lettres de Max Jacob à Edmond Jabès* (Pessac, 2003), 72.
7. Momme Brodersen, *Walter Benjamin: A Biography* (London, 1996), 18.
8. Todd M. Endelman, "Introduction" to Todd M. Endelman, ed., *Jewish Apostasy in the Modern World* (New York, 1987), 15.
9. David J. Wasserstein, "Now Let Us Proclaim: The Conversions of Franz Rosenzweig," *Times Literary Supplement*, June 20, 2008.
10. Don and Magos, "Demographic Development," 189–216, table 13.
11. William O. McCagg, Jr., "Jewish Conversion in Hungary in Modern Times," in Endelman, *Jewish Apostasy*, 142.
12. Celia Heller, *On the Edge of Destruction: The Jews of Poland between the Two World Wars* (Detroit, 1994), 196.
13. Kirschenblatt-Gimblett, "Coming of Age," 63.
14. David Lazar, "*Nowy Dziennik*," in David Flinker et al., eds., *The Jewish Press That Was: Accounts, Evaluations, and Memories of Jewish Papers in Pre-Holocaust Europe* (Tel Aviv, 1980), 267.
15. Josef Chrust and Yosef Frankel, eds., *Katovits: Perihatah u-shekiatah shel ha-kehilah ha-yehudit: sefer zikaron*, (Tel Aviv, 1996), 46.
16. Mark Cohen, *Last Century of a Sephardic Community: The Jews of Monastir, 1939–1943* (New York, 2003), 254.
17. *L'Indépendant*, Jan. 9, 1939.
18. *L'Indépendant*, July 25, 1939.
19. Anissimov, *Primo Levi*, 17.
20. Mikhail Beizer, *The Jews of St. Petersburg* (Philadelphia, 1989), 184. Beizer reports "more than 200 such reconversions" on page 184 and "at least a hundred" on page 185.
21. John Davis, *The Jews of San Nicandro* (New Haven, Conn., 2010).
22. Kirschenblatt-Gimblett, "Coming of Age," 45.
23. Chief Rabbi A. B. N. Davids of Rotterdam to Chief Rabbi A. S. Levisson of Leeuwarden, Dec. 16, 1938, Tresoar, Leeuwarden, 250/192.
24. Alma Mahler, *Gustav Mahler: Memories and Letters* (London, 1946), 89–90.

25. Felix Gilbert, *A European Past: Memoirs 1905–1945* (New York, 1988), 59–60.
26. Dora Amann memoir, LBINY ME 1431.
27. Bronsen, *Joseph Roth*, 599.
28. Dora Amann memoir, LBINY ME 1431.
29. Simone Pétrement, *La vie de Simone Weil*, vol. 2 (Paris, 1973), 187–88.
30. Susan Sontag, "Simone Weil," *New York Review of Books*, Feb. 1, 1963.
31. Quoted in Pope John Paul II, "Homily at the Beatification of Edith Stein," *Carmelite Studies* 4 (1987), 303.
32. Letter to Sister Adelgundis Jaegerschmid, OSB, Feb. 16, 1930, *The Collected Works of Edith Stein*, vol. 5, *Self-Portrait in Letters, 1916–1942* (Washington, D.C., 1993), 62.
33. Review by Gunther Windhager, *American Journal of Islamic Social Sciences* 19:3 (2002), 143.
34. Gerhard Langer memoir, LBINY ME 1527.
35. Harriet Pass Freidenreich, *Female, Jewish, and Educated: The Lives of Central European University Women* (Bloomington, Ind., 2002), 33.
36. Richard Koch memoir, LBINY ME 1512, 91.
37. James Strachey, ed., *The Standard Edition of the Complete Psychological Works of Sigmund Freud* (London, 1955), vol. 13, xv.
38. F. R. Bienenfeld, *The Religion of the Non-Religious Jews* (London, 1944), 9.
39. Ibid., 27.
40. Freidenreich *Female, Jewish and Educated*, 139.
41. Kopelev, *Education of a True Believer*, 101–13.
42. Hamerow, *Remembering a Vanished World*, 141.
43. Louis-Albert Revah, *Julien Benda: Un misanthrope juif dans la France de Maurras* (Paris, 1991)—though Revah perhaps pushes this interpretation too far.
44. Edward Timms, *Karl Kraus, Apocalyptic Satirist: Culture and Catastrophe in Habsburg Vienna* (New Haven, Conn., 1986), 238–39.
45. Edward Timms, *Karl Kraus, Apocalyptic Satirist: The Post-War Crisis and the Rise of the Swastika* (New Haven, Conn., 2005), 19–20.
46. Ritchie Robertson, "The Problem of 'Jewish Self-Hatred,'" in Herzl, Kraus, and Kafka," *Oxford German Studies* 16 (1986), 99.
47. Timms, *Karl Kraus, Apocalyptic Satirist: Culture and Catastrophe*, 237.
48. Harry Zohn, *Karl Kraus and the Critics* (Columbia, S.C., 1997), 22.
49. Timms, *Karl Kraus, Apocalyptic Satirist: The Post-War Crisis*, 154.
50. Letter to Arnold Zweig (dispatched as from Zurich but in fact written in Hindås, Sweden), Dec. 15, 1936, in Kurt Tucholsky, *Politische Briefe*, ed. Fritz J. Raddatz (Reinbek bei Hamburg, 1969), 117–23.
51. "Herr Wendriner steht unter der Diktatur," in Kurt Tucholsky, *Gesammelte Werke*, vol. 8, 1930 (Reinbek bei Hamburg, 1975), 237–40.
52. Harold L. Poor, *Kurt Tucholsky and the Ordeal of Germany, 1914–1935* (New York, 1968), 218–19.
53. Lawrence Baron, "Theodor Lessing: Between Jewish Self-Hatred and Zionism," *LBIYB* 26 (1981), 334.
54. Entries for March 16 and Feb. 19, 1935, in Kurt Tucholsky, *Die Q-Tagebücher 1934–35*, eds. Mary Gerold-Tucholsky and Gustav Huonker (Reinbek bei Hamburg, 1978), 186 and 142.
55. Letter to Arnold Zweig, Dec. 15, 1936, in Tucholsky, *Politische Briefe*, 117–23.
56. Michael Hepp, "Einführung," in Michael Hepp, ed., *Kurt Tucholsky und das Judentum* (Oldenburg, 1996), 10.
57. Marcel Reich-Ranicki, *The Author of Himself: The Life of Marcel Reich-Ranicki* (London, 2001), 67.
58. Hepp, "Einführung," 12.
59. Walter Grab, "Kurt Tucholsky und die Problematik des jüdischen Selbsthasses," in Hepp, ed., *Kurt Tucholsky*, 39, 44.

60. Shulamit Volkov, *Germans, Jews, and Antisemites: Trials in Emancipation* (Cambridge, 2006), 7.
61. Steven Games, *Pevsner—The Early Life: Germany and Art* (London, 2010), 187.
62. Werner Warmbrunn memoir, LBINY ME 1418.
63. Matthias Hambrock, *Die Etablierung der Aussenseiter: der Verband national-deutscher Juden 1921–1935* (Cologne, 2003), 190.
64. Carl Jeffrey Rheins, "German-Jewish Patriotism, 1918–1935: A Study of the Attitudes and Actions of the Reichsbund jüdischer Frontsoldaten, the Verband nationaldeutscher Juden, the Schwarzes Fahnlein, Jungenschaft, and the Deutscher Vortrupp, Gefolgschaft deutscher Juden" (Ph.D. diss., State University of New York at Stony Brook, 1978), 60.
65. Jonathan Wright and Peter Pulzer, "Gustav Stresemann and the *Verband nationaldeutscher Juden:* Right-Wing Jews in Weimar Politics," *LBIYB* 50 (2005), 211.
66. Rheins, "German-Jewish Patriotism," 183.
67. Louis-Albert Revah, *Berl, un juif de France* (Paris, 2003), 240.
68. Bernard Morlino, *Emmanuel Berl: Les tribulations d'un pacifiste* (Paris, 1990), 261 and 266.
69. Ibid., 284.
70. Ibid., 301.
71. Revah, *Berl*.
72. Irène Némirovsky, *Le Vin de solitude* (Paris, 2009), 234.
73. Miriam Price, review of *The Dogs and the Wolves*, *Times Literary Supplement*, Oct. 30, 2009; Myriam Anissimov, quoted in Yann Ploustagel, "Les secrets d'une vie," *Le Monde 2*, Sept. 1, 2007.
74. Frederic Raphael, "Stench of Carrion," *Times Literary Supplement*, April 30, 2010.
75. Jonathan Weiss, *Irène Némirovsky: Her Life and Works* (Stanford, Calif., 2007), 57.

10: THE LINGUISTIC MATRIX

1. Singer, *Shosha*, 1.
2. Aharon Appelfeld (a native of Czernowitz), "A city that was and is no longer," *Haaretz*, March 6, 2008.
3. Manger, "Idn un di daytshe kultur," 472.
4. Letter to E. F. Klein, Aug. 29, 1782, Moses Mendelssohn, *Gesammelte Schriften*, vol. 7 (Stuttgart, 1974), 279.
5. Theodor Herzl, *Gesammelte Zionistische Werke*, vol. 1 (Tel Aviv, 1934), 94.
6. Zosa Szajkowski, "The Struggle for Yiddish during World War I: The Attitude of German Jewry", *LBIYB* 9 (1964), 145.
7. Edith Stein, *Life in a Jewish Family* (Washington, D.C., 1986), 127.
8. Léon Lamouche, "Quelques mots sur le dialecte espagnol parlé par les Israélites de Salonique," *Mélanges Chabaneau Romanische Forschungen* 23 (Erlangen, 1907), 969–91 (1–23).
9. Parush, *Reading Jewish Women*, 62.
10. Irving Howe, *World of Our Fathers* (New York, 1976), 18–19.
11. Jacob Lestchinsky, "Di shprakhn bay yidn in umophengikn poyln," *YIVO-bleter* 22 (1943), 147–62.
12. Désiré Samuel van Zuiden (born 1881), quoted in Bart T. Wallet, " 'End of the jargon-scandal'—The decline and fall of Yiddish in the Netherlands (1796–1886)," *Jewish History* 20:3/4 (2006), 333.
13. Ghitta Sternberg, *Ştefăneşti: Portrait of a Romanian Shtetl* (Oxford, 1984), 251.
14. Gitter, *Story of My Life*, 19.
15. Stephen D. Corrsin, "Language Use in Cultural and Political Change in Pre-

1914 Warsaw: Poles, Jews, and Russification," *Slavonic and East European Review* 68:1 (1990), 86.

16. Chone Shmeruk, "Hebrew-Yiddish-Polish: The Trilingual Structure of Jewish Culture in Poland," in Gutman et al., eds., *Jews of Poland*, 289–311.

17. H. S. Kazdan, *Di geshikhte fun yidishn shulvezn in umophengikn poyln* (Mexico City, 1947), 343.

18. Sarah Schenirer, "Yidishkayt un yidish," *Beys Yankev* 8 (1931), 71–72, reprinted in Joshua A. Fishman, *Never Say Die! A Thousand Years of Yiddish in Jewish Life and Letters* (The Hague, 1981), 173–76.

19. Sabina Lewin, "Observations on the State," 68.

20. David E. Fishman, *The Rise of Modern Yiddish Culture* (Pittsburgh, 2005), 86.

21. Susanne Marten-Finnis, "The Jewish Press in Vilna: Traditions, Challenges, and Progress during the Inter-War Period," in Dmitrieva and Petersen, eds., *Jüdische Kultur(en) im Neuen Europa*, 140.

22. Kuznitz, "Origins of Yiddish Scholarship," 128.

23. Hamerow, *Remembering a Vanished World*, 187.

24. Meir Yellin, "Di letste pleiade yidishe shraybers in lite," DRCTAU T 57/6, 4.

25. Joshua A. Fishman, "The Sociology of Yiddish," in Fishman, ed., *Never Say Die!*, 19.

26. Abram et al., eds., *Der mishpet ibren kheyder*, 37.

27. Rachel Erlich, "Politics in the Standardization of Soviet Yiddish," *Soviet Jewish Affairs* 3:1 (1973), 71–79. See also Kuznitz, "Origins of Yiddish Scholarship," 171.

28. Ibid.

29. Gennady Estraikh, *Soviet Yiddish; Language Planning and Linguistic Development* (Oxford, 1999), 129; see also Rakhmiel Peltz, "The Dehebraization Controversy in Soviet Yiddish Language Planning: Standard or Symbol?" in Joshua A. Fishman, ed., *Readings in the Sociology of Jewish Languages*, vol. 1 (Leiden, 1985), 125–50.

30. Speech by Y. Liberberg at a national conference of Yiddish language planners in Kiev, May 1934, YA 1522/2/8.

31. Estraikh, *Soviet Yiddish*, 71.

32. Altshuler, *Soviet Jewry on the Eve of the Holocaust*, 90. All statistics derived from the 1939 Soviet census are drawn from this source.

33. Estraikh, *Soviet Yiddish*, 13.

34. Fishman, *Rise of Modern Yiddish Culture*, 85.

35. Mikhail Krutikov, *From Kabbalah to Class Struggle: Expressionism, Marxism, and Yiddish Literature in the Life and Work of Meir Wiener* (Stanford, Calif., 2011), 210.

36. Elissa Bemporad, "The Yiddish Experiment in Soviet Minsk," *East European Jewish Affairs* 37:1 (April 2007), 91–107.

37. See, e.g., Joan G. Roland, *Jews in British India: Identity in a Colonial Era* (Hanover, N.H., 1989).

38. Zachary M. Baker, "Yiddish in Form and Socialist in Content": The Observance of Sholem Aleichem's Eightieth Birthday in the Soviet Union," *YIVO Annual* 23 (Evanston, Ill., 1996), 209–31.

39. Ira Rosenswaike, "The Utilization of Census Mother Tongue Data in American Jewish Population Analysis," *JSS* 33:2/3 (1971), 141–59.

40. Arditty-Puller, "Poésie d'une Salonique Disparue."

41. Angel Pulido, *Le Peuple judéo-espagnol: Première base mondiale de l'Espagne* (Paris, 1923), 142.

42. Eliezer Papo, "Serbo-Croatian Influences on Bosnian Spoken Judeo-Spanish," *European Journal of Jewish Studies* 1:2 (2007), 343–63.

43. Sam Levy, "Grandeur et Décadence du 'Ladino,'" *Le Judaïsme Sépharadi* 23 (October 1934).

44. Haim Vidal Sephiha, " 'Christianisms' in Judeo-Spanish (Calque and Vernacular)," in Fishman, ed., *Readings*, 179–94.
45. Quoted in Levy, "Grandeur et Décadence."
46. Esther Benbassa and Aron Rodrigue, eds., *A Sephardi Life in Southeastern Europe: The Autobiography and Journal of Gabriel Arié, 1863–1939* (Seattle, 1998), 24.
47. Henri Guttel, "Ladino Literature in the 19th and 20th Centuries," *Encyclopaedia Judaica*, 2nd ed. (Detroit, 2007), vol. 12, 433–34.
48. Rivka Havassy, "New Texts to Popular Tunes: Sung-Poems in Judeo-Spanish by Sadik Gershón and Moshé Cazés (Sadik y Gazóz)," in Hilary Pomeroy and Michael Alpert, eds., *Proceedings of the Twelfth British Conference on Judeo-Spanish Studies, 24–26 June, 2001: Sephardic Language, Literature and History* (Leiden, 2004), 149–57.
49. C. M. Crews, *Recherches sur le judéo-espagnol dans les pays balkaniques* (Paris, 1935), 7–12.
50. Levy, "Grandeur et Décadence."
51. Devin E. Naar, ed., *With Their Own Words: Glimpses of Jewish Life in Thessaloniki Before the Holocaust* (catalogue of exhibition of materials from the community archives, Thessaloniki, 2006), 43.
52. David M. Bunis, ed., Moshé Cazés, *Voices from Jewish Salonika: Selections from the Judezmo Satirical Series* Tio Ezrá I Su Mujer Benuta *and* Tio Bohor I Su Majer Djamila (Jerusalem, 1999), 110 and 139.
53. Gitter, *Story of My Life*, 25.
54. Julia Krivoruchko, "The Hebrew/Aramaic Component in the Romaniote Dialect," *World Congress of Jewish Studies* 13 (2001).
55. Dalven, *Jews of Ioannina*, 23.
56. Ibid., 106.
57. Ibid., 108 ff.
58. Ibid., 86–90.
59. George Jochnowitz, "Religion and Taboo in Lason Akodesh (Judeo-Piedmontese)," *International Journal of the Sociology of Language* 30 (1981), 107–18.
60. Examples may be heard at http://www.giuntina.it/Audio_Podcast/I_sonetti_giudaico-romaneschi_di_Crescenzo_Del_Monte_2.html.
61. Speech by delegate from Czernowitz, *Second Jewish International Conference on the Suppression of the Traffic in Girls and Women, 22–24 June 1927, Official Report*, 15–20.

11: THE POWER OF THE WORD

1. Richard Grunberger, "Jews in Austrian Journalism," in Josef Fraenkel, ed., *The Jews of Austria: Essays on their Life, History and Destruction* (London, 1967), 87.
2. Stefan Zweig, *The World of Yesterday* (London, 1943), 85.
3. Roth, *What I Saw*, 212.
4. Quoted in Modris Eksteins, "The *Frankfurter Zeitung*: Mirror of Weimar Democracy," *Journal of Contemporary History* 6:4 (1971), 8.
5. Peter de Mendelssohn, "Als die Presse gefesselt war," in W. Joachim Freyburg and Hans Wallenberg, eds., *Hundert Jahre Ullstein* (Frankfurt am Main, 1977), 195.
6. Lion Feuchtwanger, *Paris Gazette* (New York, 1940), 29.
7. Hannah Arendt, et al., "Tentative List of Jewish Periodicals in Axis-Occupied Countries," *JSS*, 9:3 (1947), Supplement.
8. *Haynt*, Aug. 19 and 21, 1938.
9. Chaim Finkelstein, *'Haynt'—a tsaytung bay yidn: 1908–1939* (Tel Aviv, 1978).

10. *Baranovitsher kuryer,* May 1, 1936.
11. *Baranovitsher kuryer,* July 17, 1936.
12. M. Tsanin, "Der oyfgang un untergang fun der yidisher prese in poyln," *Kesher* 6 (1989), 115–16.
13. Abraham Brumberg, "On Reading the Bundist Press," *East European Jewish Affairs* 33:1 (2003), 115.
14. Nathan Cohen, "Shund and the Tabloids: Jewish Popular Reading in Inter-War Poland," *Polin* 16 (2003), 189–211.
15. Kadya Molodowsky, "Di Khvalye fun vidershtand," *Literarishe bleter* Nov. 17, 1933.
16. Eva Plach, "Feminism and Nationalism in the pages of *Ewa: Tygodnik*, 1928–1933," *Polin* 18 (2005), 241–62.
17. Ellen Kellman, "Feminism and Fiction: Khane Blankshteyn's Role in Inter-War Vilna," *Polin* 18 (2005), 221–39.
18. Article by Moyshe Shalit, *Literarishe bleter,* Jan. 31, 1930.
19. Rachel Erlich, "Politics in the Standardization of Soviet Yiddish," *Soviet Jewish Affairs* 3:1 (1973), 71–79.
20. *Literarishe bleter,* Jan. 11, 1929, and subsequent issues. See also issue dated Jan. 31, 1930.
21. Article by Nakhmen Mayzel, *Literarishe bleter,* Jan. 18, 1929.
22. Article by Yoshue Perle, *Literarishe bleter,* Jan. 1, 1938.
23. White, "Jewish Lives in the Polish Language," 117.
24. Anna Shternshis, *Soviet and Kosher: Jewish Popular Culture in the Soviet Union, 1923–1939* (Bloomington, Ind., 2006), 64–65.
25. Estraykh, *Soviet Yiddish,* 64.
26. Bemporad, "Red Star on the Jewish Street," 239.
27. Gennady Estraikh, "The Kharkiv Yiddish Literary World, 1920s–mid-1930s," *East European Jewish Affairs* 32:2 (2007), 79.
28. Ibid., 82.
29. Ibid., 83.
30. Anna Shternshis, "From the Eradication of Illiteracy to Workers' Correspondents: Yiddish-Language Mass Movements in the Soviet Union," *East European Jewish Affairs* 32:1 (2002), 136.
31. Wolf Wieviorka, "Der 'emes' iz ontshvigen gevoren," *Parizer haynt,* Nov. 1, 1938.
32. Molho, *Salonica and Istanbul,* 30.
33. Bunis, ed., Cazés, *Voices from Jewish Salonika,* 100–1 and 117.
34. Yehuda Eloni, "German Zionism and the Rise to Power of National Socialism," *Journal of Israeli History* 6:2 (1985), 250. See also Arnold Paucker, "Robert Weltsch: The Enigmatic Zionist: His Personality and His Position in Jewish Politics," *LBIYB* 54 (2009), 323–32.
35. *Jüdische Rundschau,* April 4, 1933.
36. Weltsch, *An der Wende,* 29–35.
37. Ibid., 293.
38. *Jüdische Rundschau,* July 2, 1935.

12: A PEOPLE OF MANY BOOKS

1. Stephen D. Corrsin, " 'The City of Illiterates'? Levels of Literacy among Poles and Jews in Warsaw, 1882–1914," *Polin* 12 (1999), 238.
2. Examples in YA 1471/153, 155, 160, and 173.
3. David Neuman, "Batei kneset she-ba-ir," *Davar,* Aug. 28, 1938, reprinted in Cohen, ed., *Sefer butchatch,* 90–91.
4. Y. Cohen, "Al kehilat butchatch," ibid., 95.
5. Gottesman, *Redefining the Yiddish Nation,* 78–79.
6. Hagit Cohen, "The USA-Eastern Europe Yiddish Book Trade and the Forma-

tion of an American Yiddish Cultural Center, 1890s–1930s," *Jews in Russia and Eastern Europe* 2–57 (2006), 67.

7. Report in YA 1400 M4/7/69.
8. Nathan Cohen, *Sefer, sofer ve-iton: merkaz ha-tarbut ha-yehudit be-varsha, 1918–1942* (Jerusalem, 2003), 168.
9. Samuel D. Kassow, "The Left Poalei Zion," in Gennady Estraikh and Mikhail Krutikov, eds., *Yiddish and the Left* (Oxford, 2001), 127.
10. *Vilner tog*, July 12, 16, 25, 26, 27, and 28, 1926.
11. *Vilner tog*, Aug. 15, 1926.
12. Weinreich letter to editor of *Vilner tog*, July 29, 1926.
13. "Radon," report by Economic-Statistical Section of C. K. B., Warsaw, circa 1935, YA 116 Poland 1/6/25.
14. Zalcman, *Histoire véridique*, 117.
15. Bemporad, "Red Star on the Jewish Street," 117–18.
16. Max A. Luria, "A Study of the Monastir Dialect of Judeo-Spanish Based on Oral Material Collected in Monastir, Yugoslavia" (Ph.D. diss., Columbia University, 1930), 7.
17. Bemporad, "Red Star on the Jewish Street," 267.
18. Shlomo Even-Shoshan, ed., *Minsk, ir va-em*, vol. 2 (Tel Aviv, 1985), 54.
19. Marcus Moseley, "Life, Literature: Autobiographies of Jewish Youth in Inter-war Poland," *JSS*, n.s. 7:3 (2001), 7.
20. Ibid., 9.
21. Ellen Kellman, "*Dos yidishe bukh alarmirt!* Towards the History of Yiddish Reading in Inter-War Poland," *Polin* 16 (2003), 213–41.
22. S. Niger, "New Trends in Post-War Yiddish Literature," *JSS* 1:3 (1939), 342.
23. Feyge Hofshteyn, " 'Zikhroynes vegn Dovidn" (typescript, Ramat Aviv, 1975), DRCTAU T-31/58.
24. Marina Bergelson-Raskin, "My Family, the Bergelsons," TAU DRI T-31/55, 10.
25. Chone Shmeruk, "Yiddish Literature in the USSR," in L. Kochan, ed., *The Jews in Soviet Russia since 1917* (London, 1970), 260; and Judel Mark, "Yiddish Literature in Soviet Russia," in Gregor Aronson et al., eds., *Russian Jewry 1917–1967* (New York, 1969), 238.
26. Rubenstein, *Tangled Loyalties*, 313.
27. Altshuler, *Soviet Jewry on the Eve of the Holocaust*, 160–61.
28. Régine Robin, "Les difficultés d'une identité juive soviétique," *Cahiers du monde russe et soviétique* 26:2 (1985), 252.
29. A. Finkelstein, "Di yidishe bikher-produktsye funem 'ukrmelukhenatsmindfarlag' farn tsvaytn finfyor (1933–1937)," *Sovetish (literarishe almanakh)* 9–10 (1939), 528.
30. *Ershter alveltlekher yidisher kultur-kongres, pariz, 17–21 sept. 1937: stenografisher barikht* (Paris, 1937), 265–68.
31. Bat-Ami Zucker, "American Jewish Communists and Jewish Culture in the 1930s," *Modern Judaism* 14:2 (1994), 180–81.
32. Ibid., 184.
33. *Literarishe bleter*, Aug. 4, 1933, 493–94.
34. Isaac Bashevis Singer, *A Young Man in Search of Love* (New York, 1978), 19–21.
35. "A shmus mit Itzik Manger," *Literarishe bleter*, Jan. 11, 1929.
36. Sol Liptzin, "Itzik Manger, 1901–1969," in Leichter, ed., *Anthology of Yiddish Folksongs*, vol. 7, xxxii.
37. "A shmus mit Itzik Manger," *Literarishe bleter*, Jan. 11, 1929.
38. Singer, *A Young Man in Search of Love*, 162–63.
39. Borukh Sinai Hillel [Brad Sabin Hill], "Der letste yidishe bukh fun farn khurbn poyln," *Afn shvel* 337–38 (2007), 36–39.
40. Report in YIVO 1400 M4/7/69.
41. David Mazower, "Sholem Asch: Images of a Life," in Nanette Stahl, ed., *Sholem Asch Reconsidered* (New Haven, Conn., 2004), 14.

42. Howe, *World of Our Fathers*, 449.
43. Singer, *A Young Man in Search of Love*, 10.
44. Howe, *World of Our Fathers*, 449.
45. Zalcman, *Histoire véridique*, 53–54.
46. Quoted in Alexander Wat, *My Century: The Odyssey of a Polish Intellectual* (New York, 2003), 58.
47. Asch letter to board of *Forverts*, undated [1939], in *Di tsukunft* (Fall 2007–Winter 2008), 36–41; Asch letter to his wife, Feb. 2, 1939, in M. Tsanin, ed., *Briv fun sholem asch* (Bat Yam, 1980), 107.
48. Anita Norich, "Sholem Asch and the Christian Question," in Stahl, ed., *Sholem Asch Reconsidered*, 251–65.
49. Max Brod, ed., *The Diaries of Franz Kafka* (Harmondsworth, 1972), 252.
50. Franz Kafka, *Letters to Milena*, ed. Willi Haas (New York, 1962), 213.
51. Nahum N. Glatzer, *The Loves of Franz Kafka* (New York, 1986), 60–61.
52. Ibid.
53. Shore, *Caviar and Ashes*, 138.
54. White, "Jewish Lives," 80.
55. Shore, *Caviar and Ashes*, 136.
56. S. L. Shneiderman, "Notes for an Autobiography," http://www.lib.umd.edu/SLSES/donors/autobio.html.
57. Thomas Venclova, *Aleksander Wat: Life and Art of an Iconoclast* (New Haven, Conn., 1996), 14–15.
58. Rubenstein, *Tangled Loyalties*, 128–29.
59. Ibid., 100.
60. Abraham Brumberg, *Journeys through Vanishing Worlds* (Washington, D.C., 2007), 197.
61. Diary entry, Feb. 7, 1938, Emil Dorian, *The Quality of Witness: A Romanian Diary 1937–1944* (Philadelphia, 1982), 20. Sebastian is referred to in Dorian's diary as "M.S."
62. Kuznitz, "Origins of Yiddish Scholarship," 192.
63. Kassow, "The Left Poalei Zion," 115.
64. [Alfred] Abraham Greenbaum, *Jewish Scholarship and Scholarly Institutions in Soviet Russia 1918–1953* (Jerusalem, 1978), 23.

13: MASQUES OF MODERNITY

1. Michael Ignatieff, "The Rise and Fall of Vienna's Jews," *New York Review of Books*, June 29, 1989.
2. Hannah Arendt, *The Jewish Writings*, ed. Jerome Kohn and Ron H. Feldman (New York, 2007), 322–23.
3. Michael Steinlauf, "Polish-Jewish Theater: The Case of Mark Arnshteyn: A Study of the Interplay among Yiddish, Polish and Polish-Language Jewish Culture in the Modern Period" (Ph.D. diss., Brandeis University, 1987), 259.
4. Howe, *World of Our Fathers*, 213, 471, and 494.
5. *Sunday Times* (London), Oct. 29, 1922.
6. Lisa Dianne Silverman, "The Transformation of Jewish Identity in Vienna" (Ph.D. diss., Yale University, 2004), 208.
7. Andrei Levinson, quoted in Vladislav Ivanov, "Habima and 'Biblical Theater,'" in Susan Tumarkin Goodman, ed., *Chagall and the Artists of the Russian Jewish Theater* (New Haven, Conn., 2008), 36.
8. Yitskhok Ber Turkow-Grudberg, *Varshe, dos vigele fun yidishn teater* (Warsaw, 1956), 25.
9. Obituary by Richard F. Shepard, *New York Times*, May 22, 1980.
10. *Folks-tsaytung*, Oct. 19, 1933, quoted in Brumberg, "On Reading the Bundist Press," 111.

11. Nakhmen Mayzel, "Tsvantsik yor yidish teater in poyln," *Fun noentn over* 1:2 (1937), 155.
12. Steinlauf, "Polish-Jewish Theater," 16 and 276 ff.
13. Mayzel, "Tsvantsik yor," 156.
14. Quoted in Benjamin Harshav, "Art and Theater," in Goodman, ed., *Chagall and the Artists of the Russian Jewish Theater*, 70.
15. Jeffrey Veidlinger, *The Moscow State Yiddish Theater: Jewish Culture on the Soviet Stage* (Bloomington, Ind., 2000), 159–60.
16. Seth L. Wolitz, "*Shulamis* and *Bar Kokhba*: Renewed Jewish Role Models in Goldfaden and Halkin," in Joel Berkowitz, ed., *Yiddish Theatre: New Approaches* (Oxford, 2003), 87–104.
17. Y. Nisinov, "Der teater fun sotsialistishn yidishn folks-shafn," *Sovetish (literarisher almanakh)* 9–10 (1939), 453.
18. Vitaly Shentalinsky, *The KGB's Literary Archive* (London, 1995), 22–71.
19. Veidlinger, *Moscow State Yiddish Theater*, 196.
20. Ibid., 3.
21. Hannah Arendt, "We Refugees" (1943), in Arendt, *Jewish Writings*, 274 and 297.
22. Richard Taylor and Ian Christie, eds., *Inside the Film Factory: New Approaches to Russian and Soviet Cinema* (London, 1991), 129.
23. Interview with Molly Picon, New York, 1977, quoted in Eric H. Goldman, "A World History of Yiddish Cinema" (Ph.D. diss., New York University, 1979), 22.
24. Natan Gross, *Toldot ha-kolnoa ha-yehudi be-polin, 1910–1950* (Jerusalem, 1990), 52–58.
25. Ibid., 77.
26. J. Hoberman, *Bridge of Light: Yiddish Film Between Two Worlds* (Hanover, N.H., 2010), 296.
27. Reich-Ranicki, *The Author of Himself*, 5.
28. Edith Liebenthal (née Friedler) memoir, LBINY 1506, 3.
29. Hetty Berg, "Jews on Stage and Stage Jews, 1890–1940" in Chaya Brasz and Yosef Kaplan, eds., *Dutch Jews as Perceived by Themselves and Others* (Leiden, 2001), 159–71.
30. Isaac Babel, *The Collected Stories of Isaac Babel* (London, 1998), 59.
31. Esther Schmidt, "From Reform to Retreat: The Establishment of Viennese Cantorial Associations and Professional Journals at the End of the Nineteenth Century," paper delivered at Warburg House, Hamburg, 2007.
32. Braunthal, *In Search of the Millennium*, 25.
33. Isaschar Fater, *Yidishe musik in poyln tsvishn beyde velt-milkhomes* (Tel Aviv, 1970), 24.
34. Gold, *Life of Jews*, 92.
35. Gottesman, *Redefining the Yiddish Nation*, 38.
36. Quoted in Abraham Bik, "Etapn fun khasidizm in varshe," in P. Katz et al., eds., *Pinkes varshe*, vol. 1 (Buenos Aires, 1955), cols. 185–86.
37. Gold, *Life of Jews*, 114.
38. Fater, *Yidishe musik in poyln*, 163.
39. Gottesman, *Redefining the Yiddish Nation*, 13.
40. Fater, *Yidishe musik in poyln*, 47.
41. Ibid., 19.
42. Gottesman, *Redefining the Yiddish Nation*, 152.
43. Fater, *Yidishe musik in poyln*, 99.
44. By M. Yanovski, YA 1522/4/32.
45. Beregovski, *Old Jewish Folk Music*, 23, 24, 28.
46. Walter Zev Feldman, "Remembrance of Things Past: Klezmer Musicians of Galicia, 1870–1940," *Polin* 16 (2003), 56.

47. Jeffrey Wollock, "Soviet Recordings of Jewish Instrumental Folk Music, 1937–1939," *ASRC Journal* 34:1 (2003), 14–32.
48. *Emes*, Aug. 22, 1937, quoted in Jeffrey Wollock, "The Soviet Klezmer Orchestra," *East European Jewish Affairs* 30:2 (2000), 22–23.
49. *Der shtern*, July 5, 1939, quoted ibid., 29–30.
50. Philippe Naucelle, "Ernest Bloch, Compositeur juif," *Affirmation*, March 31, 1939.
51. *New York Times*, April 29, 1917.
52. Alexander L. Ringer, *Arnold Schoenberg: The Composer as Jew* (Oxford, 1990), 26–27.
53. Schoenberg to Kandinsky, April 19, 1923, in Jelena Hahl-Koch, ed., *Arnold Schoenberg, Wassily Kandinsky: Letters, Pictures and Documents* (London, 1984), 76.
54. Kandinsky to Schoenberg, April 24, 1923, ibid., 77.
55. Letter to Anton Webern, August 4, 1933, http://81.223.24.109/letters/search_show_letter.php?ID_Number=2398.
56. Steven Beller, *Vienna and the Jews, 1867–1938: A Cultural History* (Cambridge, 1989), 229.
57. Quoted in Joseph Gutmann, "Is There a Jewish Art?" in Claire Moore, ed., *The Visual Dimension: Aspects of Jewish Art* (Boulder, Colo., 1993), 13.
58. Howe, *World of Our Fathers*, 584.
59. Quoted in Gutmann, "Is There a Jewish Art?" in Moore, ed., *The Visual Dimension*, 13.
60. *Samedi*, June 20, 1939.
61. Richard Dorment, "From Shtetl to Château," *New York Review of Books*, March 26, 2009.
62. Irina Antonova, foreword to *Chagall Discovered: From Russian and Private Collections* (Moscow, 1988), 9.
63. Wullschlager, *Chagall*, 31.
64. Aleksandra Shatskikh, *Vitebsk: The Life of Art* (New Haven, Conn., 2007), 28.
65. *Literarishe bleter*, Feb. 25, 1938.
66. Quoted in Matthew Affron, "Die Konzeption einer neuen jüdischen Identität: Marc Chagall, Jacques Lipchitz," in Stephanie Barron, *Exil: Flucht und Emigration europäischer Künstler* (Munich, 1997), 115.
67. Paula Salomon-Lindberg, *Mein "C'est la vie" Leben: Gespräch über ein langes Leben in einer bewegten Zeit* (Berlin, 1992), 91–92.
68. Herbert Freeden, *Jüdisches Theater in Nazideutschland* (Tübingen, 1964), 4.
69. Herbert Freeden, "A Jewish Theatre under the Swastika," *LBIYB* 1 (1956), 150.
70. Horst J. P. Bergmeier et al., comps., *Vorbei = Beyond Recall* (Bear Family Records, Hambergen, 2001), book plus eleven sound discs and one videodisc.
71. Sylvia Rogge-Gau, *Die doppelte Wurzel des Daseins: Julius Bab und der Jüdische Kulturbund Berlin* (Berlin, 1999), 73.

14: YOUTH

1. Rubin, "Nineteenth-Century Yiddish Folk Songs of Children," 230.
2. Aharon Vinkovetzky, Abba Kovner, and Sinai Leichter, eds., *Anthology of Yiddish Folksongs*, vol. 1 (Jerusalem, 1983), 7.
3. Ibid., vol. 2 (Jerusalem, 1984), 113–14.
4. Liebmann Hersch, "Principal Causes of Death," 56–77.
5. U. O. Schmelz, *Infant and Early Childhood Mortality among the Jews of the Diaspora* (Jerusalem, 1971), 46.
6. Liebmann Hers[c]h, "Delinquency among Jews," 528.
7. M. Schwarzmann, "L'Institut de recherches scientifiques pour la protection sanitaire des populations juives," *Revue "OSÉ,"* October 1938, 2, 7.

8. L. Finkelstein, "L'état de santé," 4.
9. President and Secretary, Allatini Orphanage to Community Council, Salonica, May 16, 1939, YA 207/87.
10. Martin Wolins, preface to Janusz Korczak, *Selected Works* (Washington, D.C., 1967), vii–viii.
11. Ibid., 87.
12. Ibid., 128.
13. For a comparative table, see Joshua Fishman, *Yiddish: Turning to Life* (Amsterdam, 1991), 402–3, which yields a percentage of 66 percent. Excluding university and *yeshiva* students, the percentage is at least 68 percent (some *yeshiva* enrollments are not given). Excluding both higher education and afternoon/evening schools, the proportion rises to 69 percent—but that includes in the Jewish column all the pupils in afternoon schools administered by the orthodox Khoyrev and Beth Jacob systems (the exact enrollment in these is not given but it was certainly a considerable percentage of those attending these schools). If these are excluded from the calculation, the proportion of Jewish students who received basic education in state schools rises well beyond 70 percent. These figures relate to 1934–35.
14. S. M. Berlant and Z. Rosenthal, Presidium, Tarbut, Czernowitz, to Joint Distribution Committee (New York), Oct. 10, 1937, JDCNY AR 33–44/905.
15. Schulman, *History of Jewish Education*, 93.
16. Bemporad, "Red Star on the Jewish Street," 190.
17. Ibid., 168.
18. Schulman, *History of Jewish Education*, 130 ff.
19. Greenbaum, *Jewish Scholarship*, 119 ff.
20. Schulman, *History of Jewish Education*, 159.
21. Ibid., 160.
22. *Oktyabir*, Sept. 27, 1939, quoted in Even-Shoshan, ed., *Minsk, ir va-em*, vol. 2, 45.
23. E.g., A. V. Yefimov, *Naye geshikhte, 1789–1870: Lernbukh farn 8ten klas fun der mitlshul* (Moscow, 1941).
24. Horst Hannum, ed., *Documents on Autonomy and Minority Rights* (Dordrecht, 1993), 686.
25. Heller, *On the Edge of Destruction*, 221.
26. Statistics in reports submitted to the American Jewish Joint Distribution Committee. The reports are not always mutually consistent. A useful comparative table is in JDCNY AR 33–44/826.
27. Lestchinsky, "Economic Aspects," 336.
28. Nathan Eck, "The Educational Institutions of Polish Jewry," *JSS* 9:1 (1947), 11.
29. Kazdan, *Di geshikhte fun yidishn shulvezn*, 208–11.
30. "Jewish Schools in Poland," January 1937, JDCNY AR 33–44/827.
31. Gonshor, "Kadye Molodowsky," 85–88.
32. Martin, *Jewish Life in Cracow*, 169.
33. "The Plight of Jewish Children in Ostrog," October 1937, JDCNY AR 33–44/822.
34. "Tsol yidishe shul-kinder in der shtot Vilne in lernyor 1929–30," YA 116 Poland 1/3/19.
35. Kazdan, *Di geshikhte fun yidishn shulvezn*, 519.
36. Otto Hutter message to the author, Nov. 4, 2008.
37. "Viennese memoir 1924–1938," in Moses Aberbach, *Jewish Education and History: Continuity, Crisis and Change* (Abingdon, 2009), 192.
38. Binyamin Shimron, "Das Chajesrealgymnasium in Wien, 1919–1938" (privately distributed typescript, Tel Aviv, 1989), 16–17.
39. Aberbach, *Jewish Education*, 190.

40. Otto Hutter message to the author, Nov. 4, 2008.
41. Sonia Wachstein memoir, LBINY ME 1068, 71.
42. Quoted in Shimron, "Das Chajesrealgymnasium," 36. (This and other disobliging comments on Kellner are omitted from the English version of Shimron's school history.)
43. Aberbach, *Jewish Education*, 185.
44. Wachstein memoir, LBINY ME 1068, 72.
45. Altshuler, *Soviet Jewry on the Eve of the Holocaust*, 118–27.
46. Raphael Mahler, "Jews in the Liberal Professions in Poland, 1920–39," *JSS* 6:4 (1944), 341.
47. Interview with Marian Małowist, *Polin* 13 (2000), 335.
48. International Conference on Jewish Social Work, London, July 1936, synopsis of reports, WL doc 1240/4, XVI/14.
49. Ibid.
50. Rabbi M. Rabinowicz to district officer, June 26, 1933, quoted in Regina Renz, "Small Towns in Inter-War Poland," *Polin* 17 (2004), 151.
51. Jeff Schatz, "Jews and the Communist Movement in Interwar Poland," *Studies in Contemporary Jewry* 20 (2004), 17.
52. Werner Warmbrunn memoir, LBINY ME 1418.
53. "Die Ziele des Blau-Weiß," November 1913, in Jehuda Reinharz, ed., *Dokumente zur Geschichte des deutschen Zionismus 1882–1933* (Tübingen, 1981), 115.
54. Elias to Martin Bandmann, June 14, 1920, quoted in Jörg Hackeschmidt, "The Torch Bearer: Norbert Elias as a Young Zionist," *LBIYB*, 49 (2004), 67.
55. Gerhard Schreiber memoir, LBINY ME 1416.
56. *Der moment*, Dec. 20, 1937.
57. Lyric by Nokhem Yud, trans. Abraham Brumberg, *Jewish Quarterly* 204 (Winter 2006–2007).
58. Director, State of New York Education Department Motion Picture Division to Medem Sanatarium Committee, March 2, 1937, YA 1474/4/37.
59. "Sefer ha-yevul shel bet sefer ha-ivri be-Jagielnica," DRCTAU 32/62.
60. Jeffrey Shandler, ed., *Awakening Lives: Autobiographies of Jewish Youth in Poland before the Holocaust* (New Haven, Conn., 2002).
61. Ibid., 217.
62. Ibid., 261–2.

15: UTOPIAS

1. Werner Angress, *Between Fear and Hope: Jewish Youth in the Third Reich* (New York, 1988), 46.
2. Ibid., 48.
3. Ibid., 57.
4. Gertrude van Tijn, "A Short History of the Agricultural and Manual Training Farm, Werkdorp Nieuwesluis," JDCNY AR 1933–44, folder 703.
5. Memoir by Anni Wolff, http://www.spinnenwerk.de/wolff/wolff-1.htm.
6. Gertrude van Tijn, "Werkdorp Nieuwesluis," *LBIYB* 14 (1969), 194.
7. Alfred A. Greenbaum, "Soviet Jewry during the Lenin-Stalin Period I," *Soviet Studies* 16:4 (1965), 413–14.
8. Miriam A-Sky, "Memoirs about a Jewish Province in the Ukraine," *Freeland* 12:2 (October–November 1959), 2–4.
9. Ibid.
10. Allan Laine Kagedan, *Soviet Zion: The Quest for a Russian Jewish Homeland* (New York, 1994), 103.
11. Ruth Rubin, *A Treasury of Jewish Folksong* (New York, 1950), 98–99 (translation amended).

12. I am grateful for this information to my colleague Sheila Fitzpatrick, who has examined the files of this paper for the late 1930s.

13. Gershon Shapiro, *Di yidishe kolonye friling: zikhroynes fun a forzitser fun a yidishn kolkhoz* (Tel Aviv, 1991), 142.

14. Ibid., 70–71.

15. Jonathan L. Dekel-Chen, *Farming the Red Land: Jewish Agricultural Colonization and Local Soviet Power, 1924–1941* (New Haven, Conn., 2005).

16. Robert Weinberg, *Stalin's Forgotten Zion: Birobidzhan and the Making of a Soviet Jewish Homeland* (Berkeley, 1998), 23.

17. Robert Weinberg, "Purge and Politics in the Periphery: Birobidzhan in 1937," *Slavic Review* 52:1 (1993), 15.

18. Ibid., 18.

19. Ibid., 19.

20. Antje Kuchenbecker, *Zionismus ohne Zion: Birobidžan: Idee und Geschichte eines Jüdischen Staates in Sowjet-Fernost* (Berlin, 2000), 184.

21. Nicole Taylor, "The mystery of Lord Marley," *Jewish Quarterly* 198 (Summer 2005).

22. M. Magid, "Valdhaym," *Forpost* 2:7 (1938), 158–85.

23. N. Barou, "Jews in the Soviet Union (Notes on pre-war economic position of Soviet Jewry)," *Left News*, London, August 1944, 2926.

24. Kuchenbecker, *Zionismus ohne Zion*, 141.

25. *Foreign Relations of the United States: Conferences at Malta and Yalta, 1945* (Washington, D.C., 1955), 924.

26. Jelinek, *Carpathian Diaspora*, 187.

27. Secretary, ORT Executive (Paris) to Sh. Reiss (Grenoble), Dec. 18, 1935 (copy), CAHJP ORT/165.

28. *Naylebn*, April 1937, 14–15.

29. Zalcman, *Histoire véridique*, 64.

30. Ibid., 70.

31. Ibid., 79.

32. Michel Astour, "Ten Years Ago: A Memorial Reminiscence of Dr I. N. Steinberg," *Freeland* 20:1 (January 1967), 5–8.

33. Notes of discussion on June 1, 1938, CAHJP ICA/Lon/693 (A).

34. Walter Fletcher to L. B. Prince, Jan. 7, 1939, CAHJP ICA/Lon/693 (B).

35. "Plough Settlement Association Limited," undated memorandum [1938], CAHJP ICA/Lon/693 (B).

36. JC, Jan. 20, 1939.

37. Gerald G. Frankel (Kenya) to L. B. Prince (London), July 23, 1939, CAHJP ICA/Lon/694 (A).

38. Under Secretary, Colonial Office to H. O. Lucas, March 25, 1939, CAHJP ICA/Lon/693 (B) and sim., May 25, 1939, ibid.

39. JC, April 28, 1939.

40. JC, Jan. 27, 1939.

41. Niall Fergusson, *The World's Banker: The History of the House of Rothschild* (London, 1998), 1003.

42. Statement in *Le Petit Parisien*, Jan. 16, 1937, quoted in Carla Tonini, "The Polish Plan for a Jewish Settlement in Madagascar," *Polin* 19 (2007), 471.

43. JC, May 12, 1939.

44. *Affirmation* (Paris), May 5, 1939.

16: IN THE CAGE, TRYING TO GET OUT

1. Wachstein memoir, LBINY ME 1068, 106.

2. Goeschel, *Suicide in Nazi Germany*, 100.

3. Wachstein memoir, LBINY ME 1068, 103.

4. Kellner to Werner Senator, June 30, 1938, quoted in Brian Amkraut, *Between Home and Homeland: Youth Aliya from Nazi Germany* (Tuscaloosa, Ala., 2006), 193; report by Dr. Leo Lauterbach to the Executive of the Zionist Organization on "The Situation of the Jews in Austria," April 29, 1938, extract in Yitzhak Arad et al., eds., *Documents on the Holocaust*, 8th ed. (Lincoln, Neb., 1999), 92.

5. A. J. Sherman, *Island Refuge: Britain and Refugees from the Third Reich 1933–1939*, 2nd ed. (Ilford, Essex, 1994), 134.

6. Dalia Ofer, *Escaping the Holocaust: Illegal Jewish Immigration to the Land of Israel, 1939–1944* (New York, 1990), 14.

7. Mark Wischnitzer, "Bericht über die Lage der Juden in der Tschechoslovakei," n.d. [late 1938] CAHJP HM2/9373.13 (copy of document in Osobyi archive, Moscow, 1325/1/74).

8. Hugo Jellinek (Brno) to Nadja Jellinek (Palestine), Aug. 12 (or Sept. 12), 1938, Jellinek correspondence.

9. Hugo to Nadja Jellinek, n.d. (August–September 1938), ibid.

10. Hugo to Nadja Jellinek, Aug. 21, 1938, ibid.

11. Hugo to Nadja Jellinek, Aug. 21, 1938, ibid.

12. Kurt Krakauer memoir, LBINY ME 1405.

13. Hugo to Nadja Jellinek, Oct. 14, 1938, Jellinek correspondence.

14. John Abels (Abeles) memoir, LBINY ME 1128, 45.

15. JC, Feb. 24, 1939.

16. Ascher, *Community under Siege*, 6 and 135–43.

17. V. Bazarov, "HIAS and HICEM in the system of Jewish relief organizations in Europe, 1933–41," *East European Jewish Affairs* 39:1 (2009), 72.

18. Diary entry, May 6, 1938, in Dorian, *Quality of Witness*, 30–31.

19. JC, April 29, 1938.

20. Jacob Lestchinsky, "A shtile khoydesh in poyln," *Parizer haynt*, Aug. 23, 1938.

21. *Proceedings of the Intergovernmental Committee, Evian, July 6th to 15th, 1938: Verbatim Record of the Plenary Meetings.*

22. Copy of communiqué enclosed with Sir H. Kennard (Warsaw) to Lord Halifax, March 31, 1938, BNA FO 371/21808.

23. Jerzy Tomaszewski, "The Civil Rights of Jews in Poland 1918–1939," *Polin* 8 (1994), 120.

24. Kennard (Warsaw) to Halifax, March 28, 1938, BNA FO 371/21808.

25. Reich-Ranicki, *The Author of Himself*, 107.

26. Kennard (Warsaw) to Foreign Office, Nov. 1, 1938, BNA FO 371/21808.

27. A. J. Drexel Biddle, Jr., to Secretary of State, Nov. 5, 1938, in John Mendelsohn and Donald S. Detwiler, eds., *The Holocaust: Selected Documents* (New York, 1982), vol. 3, 23–24.

28. Text in Sir G. Ogilvie-Forbes (Berlin) to Foreign Office, Oct. 31, 1938, BNA FO 371/21808.

29. Issue dated Oct. 29, 1938, quoted in Karol Grünberg, "The Atrocities Against the Jews in the Third Reich as Seen by the National-Democratic Press (1933–1939)," *Polin* 5 (1990), 110.

30. Jerzy Tomaszewski, "The Polish Right-Wing Press, the Expulsion of Polish Jews from Germany, and the Deportees in Zbąszyń," *Gal-Ed* 18 (2002), 89–100.

31. Harvey F. Fireside (Heinz Wallner) memoir, LBINY ME 1486, 57.

32. Goeschel, *Suicide in Nazi Germany*, 103.

33. Ibid.

34. Raymond Geist to George S. Messersmith, Oct. 28, 1938, quoted in Richard Breitman et al., eds., *Refugees and Rescue: The Diaries and Papers of James G. McDonald, 1935–1945* (Bloomington, Ind., 2009), 143–44.

35. Aide-mémoire (1939) by Robert H. Harlan (in possession of Lois S. Harlan).

36. *JC*, Jan. 6, 1939.
37. Norbert Elias, *Reflections on a Life* (Cambridge, 1994), 52.
38. Werner Warmbrunn memoir, LBINY ME 1418.
39. "The Fate of German Returning Emigrants" (report by Jewish Central Information Office, Amsterdam), March 31, 1936, YA 448 (Israel Cohen Papers), series 1, file 9.
40. Gertrude van Tijn memoir, LBINY ME 643, 6.
41. Gertrude van Tijn to American Jewish Joint Distribution Committee, Dec. 26, 1938, JDCNY AR 33–44/695.
42. *Yidishe bilder*, Dec. 9, 1938.
43. Report on Refugee Work in Holland in February 1939 (probably by Gertrude van Tijn), Amsterdam, March 7, 1939, JDCNY AR 33-44/189.
44. Richard Perls, for Jewish Institute for the Blind, Berlin, to Viscount Samuel, Dec. 6, 1938, WL doc 606.
45. Monika Sonke, "Die Israelitische Taubstummen-Anstalt in Berlin-Weissensee," in Vera Bendt and Nicola Galliner, *"Öffne deine Hand für die Stummen": Die Geschichte der Israelitischen Taubstummen-Anstalt Berlin-Weissensee, 1873 bis 1942* (Berlin, 1993), 61.
46. Hoffman and Schwarz, "Early but Opposed," 297–98.
47. Shapiro, *Between the Yeshiva World and Modern Orthodoxy*, 158.
48. Hoffman and Schwarz, "Early but Opposed," 267.
49. Hildesheimer, *Jüdische Selbstverwaltung*, 111; Leonard Baker, *Days of Sorrow and Pain: Leo Baeck and the Berlin Jews* (New York, 1978), 246.
50. Rolf Wiggershaus, *The Frankfurt School: Its History, Theories and Political Significance* (Cambridge, 1994), 128.
51. Kaplan, *The Jewish Feminist Movement*, 49.
52. Amkraut, *Between Home and Homeland*, 100–1.
53. Vicky Caron, *Uneasy Asylum: France and the Jewish Refugee Crisis, 1933–1942* (Stanford, Calif., 1999), 202.
54. Joint Distribution Committee, European Executive Council, February Report, March 17, 1939, JDCNY AR 33-44/189.
55. Gertrude van Tijn memoir, LBINY ME 643, 16.
56. "Report on the Position of the Refugees Work in Holland on April 30th 1939 by Gertrude van Tijn," May 9, 1939, WL doc 502.
57. Letter to Elise Steiner, March 1, 1939, WL doc 1146/29.
58. Letter to Elise Steiner, May 14, 1939, WL doc 1146/50.
59. Letter to Elise Steiner, April 5, 1939, WL doc 1146/38.
60. Meir Michaelis, *Mussolini and the Jews: German-Italian Relations and the Jewish Question in Italy, 1922–1945* (Oxford, 1978), 28.
61. Ibid., 33–34. Mussolini's article appeared in *Il Popolo d'Italia*, May 29, 1932.
62. Dan Vittorio Segre, *Memoirs of a Fortunate Jew: An Italian Story* (Bethesda, Md., 1987).
63. Michaelis, *Mussolini and the Jews*, 120 ff.
64. Iael Nidam-Orvietto, "The Impact of Anti-Jewish Legislation on Everyday Life and the Response of Italian Jews, 1938–1943," in Joshua D. Zimmerman, ed., *Jews in Italy under Fascist and Nazi Rule, 1922–1945* (Cambridge, 2005), 168.
65. Editorial of Sept. 8, 1938, quoted in Renzo De Felice, *The Jews in Fascist Italy: A History* (New York, 2001), 321.
66. Anissimov, *Primo Levi*, 53.
67. De Felice, *Jews in Fascist Italy*, 325.

17: CAMPING

1. Chronicle of the Jewish Community of Bamberg. 1930–1938 by Martin Morgenroth, in Karl H. Mistele, *The End of a Community: The Destruction of the Jews of Bamberg, Germany, 1938–1942* (Hoboken, N.J., 1995), 207.
2. Leni Yahil, "Jews in Concentration Camps prior to World War II," in Yisrael Gutman and Avital Saf, eds., *The Nazi Concentration Camps* (Jerusalem, 1984), 74–76.
3. Sonia Wachstein memoir, LBINY ME 1068, 100.
4. Felix Klein memoir, LBINY ME 1414; Sonia Wachstein memoir, LBINY ME 1068, 113.
5. Bruno Stern to Robert H. Harlan, Aug. 17, 1943 (possession of Lois S. Harlan).
6. Recollections of Harvey P. Newton (Hermann Neustadt), written in 1944, Gross Breesen Rundbrief, 28 (1994), http://grossbreesensilesia.com/.
7. Altshuler, *Soviet Jewry on the Eve of the Holocaust*, 26–27.
8. David R. Shearer, *Policing Stalin's Socialism: Repression and Social Order in the Soviet Union, 1924–1953* (New Haven, Conn., 2009), 317.
9. *Memoirs of Nikita Khrushchev*, vol. 2, *Reformer 1945–1964* (University Park, Pa., 2006), 174–75 and 196.
10. Mikhail Mitsel, "The final chapter: Agro-Joint workers—victims of the Great Terror in the USSR, 1937–40," *East European Jewish Affairs* 39:1 (2009), 91.
11. Ibid., 86.
12. Ibid., 87.
13. Shapiro, *Di yidishe kolonye friling*, 150.
14. Gerben Zaagsma, "The Local and the International—Jewish Communists in Paris Between the Wars," *Simon Dubnow Institute Yearbook* 8 (2009), 358.
15. Report to Gulag NKVD, 1939, on conditions in Karagandinskii Corrective Labor Camp, Archive Department of the Center for Legal Statistics and Information under the Procurator of the Karaganda Region, Karaganda, Kazakhstan, AOTsPSIpPKO sv. 10 uro, d. 79, ll. 85–95, copy at http://gulaghistory.org/items/show/766.
16. Zalcman, *Histoire véridique*, 188.
17. *Vilner tog*, Jan. 2, 1939.
18. Report by Harvey C. Perry and Julianna R. Perry on visit to Poland, July 20–27, 1939, reproduced in Henry Friedlander and Sybil Milton, eds., *Archives of the Holocaust*, vol. 2 (New York, 1990), 618.
19. *JC*, Jan. 6, 1939.
20. *JC*, Jan. 13, 1939.
21. *Correspondance Juive*, June 20, 1939.
22. Caron, *Uneasy Asylum*, 62.
23. *JC*, Feb. 24, 1939.
24. Anne Grynberg, *Les Camps de la honte: Les internés juifs des camps français 1939–1944* (Paris, 1999), 20–21.
25. Ibid., 57.
26. Moore, *Refugees from Nazi Germany*, 98–99.
27. Müller, *Anne Frank*, 86.
28. C. L. van den Heuvel and P. G. van den Heuvel-Vermaat, *Joodse Vluchtelingen en het Kamp in Hellevoetsluis* (Hellevoetsluis, 1995), 25.
29. *Rotterdamsch Nieuwsblad*, Jan. 3, 1939.
30. Prof. D. Cohen (Chairman, Jewish Refugees Committee, Amsterdam), circular letters, March 17 and 28, 1939, Bibl. Ros. Vereenigingen (Comité–G).
31. "Report on the Position of the Refugees Work in Holland on April 30th 1939 by Gertrude van Tijn," May 9, 1939, enclosure A, WL doc 502.

32. "Camps," memoranda by Jewish Refugees Committee, Amsterdam, May and June 1939, JDCNY AR 33–44/700.

33. Gino Huiskes and Reinhilde van der Kroef, comp., *Vluchtelingenkamp Wester-bork*, Westerbork Cahiers 7 (Assen, 1999), 25.

34. Weizmann testimony to Royal Commission on Palestine, Nov. 25, 1936, in Barnett Litvinoff, ed., *The Letters and Papers of Chaim Weizmann*, Series B: Papers, vol. 2 (New Brunswick, N.J., 1984), 102.

35. Diary entry, Jan. 12, 1939, in Dorian, *Quality of Witness*, 56–57.

36. *Der moment*, Nov. 24, 1938.

37. Tsentralrat fun di prof. klasen-fareynen in varshe, *Barikht fun der tetikeyt fun tsentral-rat un di ongeshlosene fareynen far di yorn 1937–1938* (Warsaw, April 1939), 24, YA 1400 MG 9 and 10/box 36/220.

38. "The Jewish Community of Prague," report to Joint Distribution Committee, Aug. 14, 1939, JDCNY AR 33–44/535.

39. Memorandum on Latvia by E. K. Schwartz, May 1, 1939, JDCNY AR 33–44/727.

40. Report dated July 26, 1939, by Martin Rosenblüth (London), CZA S7/902, copied in Frank Nicosia, ed., *Archives of the Holocaust*, vol. 3 (New York, 1990), 323.

41. Kurt Krakauer memoir, LBINY ME 1405.

42. Hilfsverein der Juden in Deutschland to Council for German Jewry, London, Feb. 3, 1939, WL doc 606.

43. Council for German Jewry, London, to Hilfsverein der Juden in Deutschland, Feb. 6, 1939, ibid.

44. Council for German Jewry, London, to Reichsvereinigung der Juden in Deutschland, Aug. 16, 1939, ibid.

45. Report on Germany and Austria, February 1939, submitted with Morris Troper (Paris) to AJDC (New York), March 17, 1939, JDCNY AR 33-44/189.

46. Morris Troper (Paris) to JDC (New York), March 17, 1939, JDCNY AR 33-44/189.

18: ON THE EVE

1. Article by Yoshue Perle, *Literarishe bleter*, Jan. 1, 1939.

2. Shandler, ed., *Awakening Lives*, 376.

3. Pickhan, "*Yidishkayt* and class consciousness," 258.

4. Shapiro, "Polish *Kehillah* Elections," 218.

5. "A ruf tsu der yidisher arbetndiker froy," election leaflet, Vilna, 1939, YA 1400/11/128.

6. "Birger veyler!" election leaflet, Vilna, May 1939, ibid.

7. M. Troper (Paris) to Joseph Hyman (New York), June 10, 1939, JDCNY AR 33-44/794.

8. "2 yor arbet un kamf" (report on Tsukunft, 1937–39), YA 1400 MG 9&10/40/269.

9. Howard (Chanoch) Rosenblum, "Promoting an International Conference to Solve the Jewish Problem: The New Zionist Organization's Alliance with Poland, 1938–1939," *Slavonic and East European Review* 69:3 (1991), 480.

10. Ibid., 489.

11. JC, March 3, 1939.

12. Nowogrodski, *Jewish Labor Bund in Poland*, 251.

13. L. Jaffe (Warsaw) to head office of Keren Hayesod, Jerusalem, March 10, 1939, CZA S5/544.

14. Laurence Weinbaum, "Jabotinsky and the Poles," *Polin* 5 (1990), 159.

15. J. Marcus, *Social and Political History of the Jews in Poland, 1918–1939* (Berlin, 1983), 410.

16. *Affirmation*, May 26, 1939.
17. Yaakov-Yosef Gerstein (in Yednitsy/Edineţi) to his children in Palestine, July 9, 1939, CAHJP INV/8494, 44.
18. See Morris Troper for JDC to Comite Voor Joodsche Vluchtelingen, Oct. 16, 1939, JDCNY AR 1933–44, folder 44.
19. Chaya Brasz, " 'Dodenschip' Dora," *Vrij Nederland*, May 1, 1993, 38–41.
20. Memoir of Gertrude van Tijn, LBINY ME 643, 17.
21. Sherman, *Island Refuge*, 253.
22. O. D. Kulka, "The '*Reichsvereinigung* of the Jews in Germany' (1938/9–1943)," in *Patterns of Jewish Leadership in Nazi Europe 1933–1945*, Proceedings of the Third Yad Vashem International Historical Conference, Jerusalem, 1979, 45–58.
23. Letter from Goldmann, n.d. [May 1939], quoted in Kurt Jacob Ball-Kaduri, *Vor der Katastrophe: Juden in Deutschland 1934–1939* (Tel Aviv, 1967), 252–53.
24. Hartwig Behr und Horst F. Rupp, *Vom Leben und Sterben: Juden in Creglingen* (Würzburg, 1999), 177.
25. Silvia Cohn to Hilde Cohn, June 27, 1939, quoted in Trude Maurer, "Jüdisches Bürgertum 1933–1939: Die Erfahrung der Verarmung," in Stefi Jersch-Wenzel et al., eds., *Juden und Armut in Mittel- und Ost-Europa* (Cologne, 2000), 389.
26. "Le déclin du judaïsme autrichien, *Revue "OSÉ,"* March 1940, 30.
27. Lorenz Mikoletzky, ed., *Archives of the Holocaust*, vol. 21 (New York, 1995), 1199.
28. Report by Wohnungsreferat, Israelitische Kultusgemeinde Wien, May 16, 1939, WL doc 1254/2.
29. Erwin Lichtenstein, *Die Juden der freien Stadt Danzig unter der Herrschaft des Nationalsozialismus* (Tübingen, 1973), 88–89; *Manchester Guardian Weekly*, Jan. 20, 1939.
30. Police-President to Jewish Community, Danzig, Jan. 21, 1939, reproduced in Sheila Schwartz, ed., *Danzig 1939: Treasures of a Destroyed Community* (Detroit, 1980), 19.
31. Greiser to Carl Burckhardt, Feb. 9, 1939, in Lichtenstein, *Die Juden*, 101.
32. "Bericht über den Auswanderungstransport von Danzig mit der 'Astir' von Irma Feibusch" (a passenger on the *Astir*), Lichtenstein, *Die Juden*, 226–31.
33. *L'Univers Israélite*, July 28, 1939.
34. Leyzer Ran, "Vilna: A fertel yorhundert yidisher teater," in Itzik Manger, Jonas Turkow, and Moyshe Perenson, eds., *Yidisher teater in eyrope tsvishn beyde velt-milkhomes* (New York, 1968), 233–34.
35. Bemporad, "Red Star on the Jewish Street," 240.
36. Even-Shoshan, ed., *Minsk, ir va-em*, vol. 2, 78.
37. Esther Benbassa and Aron Rodrigue, *The Jews of the Balkans: The Judeo-Spanish Community, 15th to 20th Centuries* (Oxford, 1995), 142.
38. *L'Indépendant*, Feb. 9, 1939.
39. "Kipur al Kal" (Yom Kippur in the Synagogue), *Acción*, 11:3106 (1939), reprinted in Bunis, ed., Cazés, *Voices from Jewish Salonika*, 390–92.
40. "Le estás bevyendo la sangre" (You're driving him crazy), *Mesajero* 4:1008 (1939), reprinted in Bunis, ed., Cazés, *Voices from Jewish Salonika*, 406–8.
41. Correspondence in YA 207/87.
42. President and Secretary, Asilo de Locos to Community Council, May 17, 1939, YA 207/87.
43. Report of the Refugees Committee, Amsterdam, August–October 1939, WL doc 502.
44. Hugo to Nadja Jellinek, n.d. [late March–May 1939], Jellinek correspondence.
45. Gisela Schlesinger (Vienna) to Anna Nadler (Sydney), June 21, 1939, ibid.

46. Max Weinreich, "A Tentative Scheme for the History of Yiddish," 5th International Congress of Linguists, Brussels, Aug. 28–Sept. 2, 1939, *Résumés des communications* (Bruges, 1939), 49–51.
47. Albert Resis, "The Fall of Litvinov: Harbinger of the German-Soviet Non-Aggression Pact," *Europe-Asia Studies* 52:1 (2000), 35.
48. *Ha-kongres ha-tsiyoni ha-21: Din ve-heshbon stenografi* (Jerusalem, 1939), 222–23. The phrase appears in Genesis 32:9 and 2 Kings 19:30–31.

19: EXISTENTIAL CRISIS

1. *New York Times*, March 26, 1933.
2. Jacob Lestchinsky, "Vu iz der oysgang?" *Naye Shtime*, July 1938, 8.
3. Jacob Lestchinsky, "Farshveygen oder bald entfern?" *Unzer lebn* (Białystok), July 21, 1939. The article probably also appeared in other Yiddish papers.
4. Arendt, *Origins of Totalitarianism*, esp. 454 ff.
5. Transcript of interview with Prinz, Oral History Archive, Institute of Contemporary Jewry, the Hebrew University of Jerusalem, printed in Herbert A. Strauss and Kurt R. Grossman, eds., *Gegenwart im Rückblick: Festgabe für die Jüdische Gemeinde zu Berlin 25 Jahre nach dem Neubeginn* (Heidelberg, 1970), 232. The original article appeared in the *Jüdische Rundschau*, April 17, 1935.
6. *Leder- un shikh-tsaytung*, May 1937, 4.
7. Benjamin and Barbara Harshav, *American Yiddish Poetry: A Bilingual Anthology* (Berkeley, 1986), 304–7.
8. Y. Rapoport, "Tsurik zum geto?" *Naye shtime*, July 1938, 12–13.
9. A[haron] Kremer, "Tsurik in geto?" *Parizer haynt*, July 12, 1938.
10. Karlip, "Between Martyrology and historiography," 257.
11. Ibid., 271 [translation amended].
12. The biblical reference is to Esther 3:13 (Jewish Publication Society of America translation).
13. *Haynt*, Aug. 25, 1939. For the background to this article, see Dubnow-Erlich, *Life and Work of S. M. Dubnow*, 233–36.
14. See above p. 13.
15. Zygmunt Bauman, "Exit Visas and Entry Tickets: Paradoxes of Jewish Assimilation," *Telos* 77 (1988), 51.

SOURCES

UNPUBLISHED SOURCES

American Jewish Joint Distribution Committee archive, New York
Bibliotheca Rosenthaliana, University of Amsterdam
British National Archives, Kew
Central Archives for the History of the Jewish People, Jerusalem
Central Zionist Archives, Jerusalem
Goldstein-Goren Diaspora Research Center archive, Tel Aviv University
Robert H. Harlan materials relating to Kristallnacht (in possession of Lois S. Harlan)
Archive of the International Institute of Social History, Amsterdam
Jellinek family correspondence (in possession of Paulette Jellinek)
Jewish Historical Museum, Amsterdam
Jewish Museum, Berlin
Leo Baeck Institute Archive, Center for Jewish History, New York
Netherlands Institute for War Documentation, Amsterdam
Tresoar, Leeuwarden
Wiener Library archive, London
Yad Vashem Archives, Jerusalem
YIVO Archive, Center for Jewish History, New York

DISSERTATIONS

Bemporad, Elissa. "Red Star on the Jewish Street: The Reshaping of Jewish Life in Soviet Minsk, 1917–1939." Ph.D. diss., Stanford University, 2006.

Goldman, Eric A. "A World History of the Yiddish Cinema." Ph.D. diss., New York University, 1979.

Gonshor, Anna Fishman. "Kadye Molodowsky in *Literarishe Bleter*, 1925–1935: Annotated Bibliography." M. A. thesis, McGill University, 1997.

Karlip, Joshua Michael. "The Center That Could Not Hold: *Afn Sheydveg* and the Crisis of Diaspora Nationalism." Ph.D. diss., Jewish Theological Seminary, 2006.

Kuznitz, Cecile. "The Origins of Yiddish Scholarship and the YIVO Institute for Jewish Research." Ph.D. diss., Stanford University, 2000.

Luria, Max A. "A Study of the Monastir Dialect of Judeo-Spanish Based on Oral Material Collected in Monastir, Yugoslavia." Ph.D. diss., Columbia University, 1930.

Rheins, Carl Jeffrey. "German-Jewish Patriotism, 1918–1935: A Study of the Attitudes and Actions of the Reichsbund jüdischer Frontsoldaten, the Verband nationaldeutscher Juden, the Schwarzes Fahnlein, Jungenschaft, and the Deutsche Vortrupp, Gefolgschaft deutscher Juden." Ph.D. diss., State University of New York at Stony Brook, 1978.

Silverman, Lisa Dianne. "The Transformation of Jewish Identity in Vienna, 1918–1938." Ph.D. diss., Yale University, 2004.

Sloin, Andrew. "Pale Fire: Jews in Revolutionary Belorussia, 1917–1929." Ph.D. diss., University of Chicago, 2009.

Steinlauf, Michael. "Polish-Jewish Theater: The Case of Mark Arnshteyn: A Study of the Interplay among Yiddish, Polish and Polish-Language Jewish Culture in the Modern Period." Ph.D. diss., Brandeis University, 1987.

Sternberg, Frances Glazer. " 'Cities of Boundless Possibilities': Two Shtetlekh in Poland: A Social History." Ph.D. diss., University of Missouri–Kansas City, 2000.

Tanny, Jarrod. "City of Rogues and Schnorrers: The Myth of Old Odessa in Russian and Jewish Culture." Ph.D. diss., University of California, Berkeley, 2009.

White, Angela. "Jewish Lives in the Polish Language: The Polish-Jewish Press, 1918–1939." Ph.D. diss., Indiana University, 2007.

Yalen, Deborah Hope. "Red *Kasrilevke*: Ethnographies of Economic Transformation in the Soviet Shtetl, 1917–1939." Ph.D. diss., University of California, Berkeley, 2007.

Zeindl, Eva. "Die Israelitische Kultusgemeinde Horn." Mag. phil. Diplomarbeit, University of Vienna, 2008.

WEBSITES AND DIGITAL PUBLICATIONS

Gross-Breesen Emigrant Training Farm, http://grossbreesensilesia.com/.

Gulag History, http://gulaghistory.org/.

Jewish Women's Archive, http://jwa.org/.

Wolf Lewkowicz letters, http://web.mit.edu/maz/wolf/.

Correspondence of Arnold Schönberg, http://www.schoenberg.at/index.php?option=com_content&view=article&id=365&Itemid=324&lang=en.

S. L. Shneiderman, "Notes for an Autobiography," http://www.lib.umd.edu/SLSES/donors/autobio.html.

PUBLISHED SOURCES

Newspapers and Periodicals

Acción (Salonica)

Affirmation (Paris)

AJR Information (London)

L'Ancien Combattant Juif (Paris)

Baranovitsher kuryer (Baranowicze)

Bikher-nayes (Warsaw)

Boschblaadjes (Amsterdam)

Byuleten funem institut far yidisher kultur bay der alukrainisher visnshaft-lekher akademye (Kiev)

Contemporary Jewish Record (New York)

Correspondance Juive (Geneva)

C.V. Zeitung (Berlin)

Dos emese vort (Vilna)

Folks-tsaytung (Libau)

Folks-tsaytung (later *Naye folks-tsaytung*, Warsaw)

Forpost (Birobidzhan)

Freeland (New York)

Ha'Ischa (Amsterdam)

Haynt (Warsaw)

L'Indépendant (Salonica)

In kamf (Warsaw)

Der Israelit (Frankfurt am Main)

Jewish Chronicle (London)

De Joodsche Middenstander (Amsterdam)

Le Judaïsme Sépharadi (later *Le Judaïsme Séphardi*, Paris)

Jüdischer Kulturbund Monatsblätter (Hamburg)

Jüdische Rundschau (Berlin)

Kinderfraynd (Warsaw)

Leder- un shikh-tsaytung (Warsaw)

Literarishe bleter (Warsaw)

Der moment (Warsaw)

Naye prese (Paris)

Naye shtime (Warsaw)

Dos naye vort (Warsaw)

Nieuw Israelitisch Weekblad (Amsterdam)

Paix et Droit (Paris)

Parizer haynt (Paris)

Le Progrès (Salonica)

Revue "OSÉ" (Paris)

Samedi (Paris)

Shulfraynd (Vilna)

Shul un lebn (Warsaw)

Sovetish (literarisher almanakh) (Moscow)

Sovetishe literatur (Kiev)

Der transport arbeter (Warsaw)

Tsaytshrift—literatur-forshung (Minsk)

L'Univers Israélite (Paris)

Unzer ekspres (Warsaw)

Unzer lebn (Białystok)

Vilner ekspres (Vilna)

Vilner tog (Vilna)

Yedies fun yidishn visnshaftlekhn institut (Vilna)

Yidishe bilder (Riga)

Yidishe shtime (Kovno)

Die Zukunft (Paris)

Literary Works Discussed in the Text

Agnon, S. Y. *Oreah natah lalun* (Tel Aviv, 1939; English ed., *A Guest for the Night*, New York, 1968).

An-Sky, S. *Der dybbuk* (Vilna, 1919).

Asch, Sholem. *Mottke ganef* (first published in Yiddish, 1916; English ed., *Mottke the Thief*, London, 1935).

Asch, Sholem. *Der man fun natseres* (published in English as *The Nazarene*, New York, 1939).

———. *Three Cities* (first published in Yiddish, 1929–31; English ed., New York, 1933).

Babel, Nathalie, ed. *The Complete Works of Isaac Babel* (New York, 2005).

Bettauer, Hugo. *Die Stadt ohne Juden, ein Roman von Übermorgen* (Vienna, 1922; English ed., New York, 1926).

Céline, Louis-Ferdinand. *Bagatelles pour un massacre* (Paris, 1937).

Der Nister, *Di mishpokhe mashber* (first vol. only, Moscow, 1939; second vol., New York, 1948; English ed., *The Family Mashber*, London, 1987).

Ehrenburg, Ilya. *The Stormy Life of Lasik Roitschwantz* (first Russian ed., Berlin, 1929; English ed., New York, 1960).

Feuchtwanger, Lion. *Paris Gazette* (New York, 1940).

Grossman, Vasily. "In the Town of Berdichev," in *The Road: Stories, Journalism, and Essays* (New York, 2010), 15–32.

Kisch, Egon Erwin, *Tales from Seven Ghettos* (London, 1948).

Kulbak, Moshe. *Di zelmenyaner* (Minsk, 1931–35).

Némirovsky, Irène. *David Golder* (Paris, 1929).

———. *Le Vin de solitude* (Paris, 1935).

Opatoshu, Joseph. *Roman fun a ferd ganif* (*Tale of a Horse Thief*, Vilna, 1928; first published, 1912).

Schulz, Bruno. *The Complete Fiction of Bruno Schulz* (New York, 1989).

Singer, Isaac Bashevis. *Shosha* (English ed., New York, 1978; first published in Yiddish, 1974).

Tucholsky, Kurt. "Herr Wendriner steht unter der Diktatur," in *Gesammelte Werke*, vol. 8, *1930* (Reinbek bei Hamburg, 1975).

Books and Articles

Aberbach, David. "Patriotism and Antisemitism: The Crisis of Polish-Jewish Identity between the Wars." *Polin* 22 (2010), 368–88.

Aberbach, Moshe. "Viennese Memoir 1924–1938." In David Aberbach, ed., *Jewish Education and History: Continuity, Crisis and Change* (Abingdon, 2009), 151–206.

Abram, Leyb, et al., eds. *Der mishpet ibren kheyder* (Vitebsk, 1922).

Abramowicz, Hirsz. *Profiles of a Lost World: Memoirs of East European Jewish Life before World War II* (Detroit, 1999).

Abravanel, Nicole. "Paris et le séphardisme ou l'affirmation sépharadiste à Paris dans les années trente." In W. Busse and Marie-Christine Varol-Bornes, eds., *Hommage à Haïm Vidal Sephiha* (Berne, 1996), 497–523.

Ackerman, Walter. " 'Nach Palästina durch Wirballen'—a Hebrew Gymnasium in Lithuania." *Studies in Jewish Education* 7 (Jerusalem, 1995), 38–53.

Alon, Gedalyahu. "The Lithuanian Yeshivas." In Judah Goldin, ed., *The Jewish Expression* (New Haven, Conn. 1976), 452–68.

Altbauer, Moshe. "Bulgarismi nel 'Giudeo-Spagnolo' degli Ebrei di Bulgaria." *Ricerche Slavistiche* 4 (1955–56), 72–75.

Altmann, Alexander. "The German Rabbi: 1910–1939." *LBIYB* 19 (1974), 31–49.

Altshuler, Mordechai. *Soviet Jewry on the Eve of the Holocaust: A Social and Demographic Profile* (Jerusalem, 1988).

Amishai-Maisels, Ziva. "Chagall's 'White Crucifixion.' *Art Institute of Chicago Museum Studies* 17:2 (1991), 138–53, 180–81.

Amkraut, Brian. *Between Home and Homeland: Youth Aliya from Nazi Germany* (Tuscaloosa, Ala., 2006).

Andermann, Martin. "My life in Germany before and after 30 January 1933." *LBIYB* 55 (2010), 315–28.

Angress, Werner. *Between Hope and Fear: Jewish Youth in the Third Reich* (New York, 1988).

Anissimov, Myriam. *Primo Levi: Tragedy of an Optimist* (New York, 1999).

Antonova, Irina, et al., comps. *Chagall Discovered: From Russian and Private Collections* (Moscow, 1988).

Apter-Gabriel, Ruth. *Chagall: Dreams and Drama: Early Russian Works and Murals for the Jewish Theatre* (Jerusalem, 1993).

Aptowitzer, Victor, et al., eds. *Abhandlungen zur Erinnerung an Hirsch Perez Chajes* (Vienna, 1933).

Arad, Yitzhak, et al., eds. *Documents on the Holocaust*, (8th ed. Lincoln, Neb., 1999).

Arbet un kamf: Barikht fun tsentraln profesioneln rat fun di yidishe klasn-faraynen in poyln (Warsaw, August 1939).

Arditti, Adolfo. "Some 'dirty words' in modern Salonika, Istanbul, and Jerusalem." *Jewish Language Review* 7 (1987), 209–20.

Arendt, Hannah. *The Jewish Writings* (New York, 2007).

———. *The Origins of Totalitarianism* (New York, 1994).

Aronson, Gregori, ed. *Vitebsk amol: geshikhte, zikhroynes, khurbn* (New York, 1956).

Aronson, Gregor[i], et al. *Russian Jewry 1917–1967* (New York, 1969).

Asaria, Zvi. *Die Juden in Köln von den Ältesten Zeiten bis zur Gegenwart* (Cologne, 1959).

Asch, Sholem. *Briv fun sholem asch.* Ed. M. Tsanin (Bat Yam, 1980).

Ascher, Abraham. *A Community under Siege: The Jews of Breslau under Nazism* (Stanford, Calif., 2007).

Aschheim, Steven E. *Beyond the Border: The German-Jewish Legacy Abroad* (Princeton, N.J., 2007).

Aylward, Michael. "Early Recordings of Jewish Music in Poland." *Polin* 16 (2003), 59–69.

Bacon, Gershon. "The Missing 52 Percent: Research on Jewish Women in Interwar Poland and Its Implications for Holocaust Studies." In Dalia Ofer and Lenore J. Weitzman, eds., *Women in the Holocaust* (New Haven, Conn., 1998), 55–67.

———. *The Politics of Tradition: Agudat Yisrael in Poland, 1916–1939* (Jerusalem, 1996).

Baker, Leonard. *Days of Sorrow and Pain: Leo Baeck and the Berlin Jews* (New York, 1978).

Baker, Zachary M. "'Yiddish in Form and Socialist in Content': The Observance of Sholem Aleichem's Eightieth Birthday in the Soviet Union." *YIVO Annual* 23 (1996), 209–31.

Ball-Kaduri, Kurt Jakob. *Vor der Katastrophe: Juden in Deutschland 1934–1939* (Tel Aviv, 1967).

Baratz, Léon. *La question juive en U.R.S.S. (Réponse à M. Georges Friedmann)* (Paris, 1938).

Barkai, Avraham. *From Boycott to Annihilation: The Economic Struggle of German Jews 1933–1945* (Hanover, N.H., 1989).

Barkai, Avraham, and Paul Mendes-Flohr. *German-Jewish History in Modern Times*, vol. 4, *Renewal and Destruction: 1918–1945* (New York, 1998).

Baron, Lawrence. "Theodor Lessing: Between Jewish Self-Hatred and Zionism." *LBIYB* 26 (1981), 323–40.

Bartoszewski, Władysław T., and Antony Polonsky, eds. *The Jews in Warsaw: A History* (Oxford, 1991).

Bartov, Omer. *Erased: Vanishing Traces of Jewish Galicia in Present-Day Ukraine* (Princeton, N.J., 2007).

Bassok, Ido. "Mapping Reading Culture in Interwar Poland—Secular Literature as a New Marker of Ethnic Belonging among Jewish Youth." *Jahrbuch des Simon-Dubnow-Instituts* 9 (2010), 15–36.

Bauer, Yehuda. *American Jewry and the Holocaust: The American Jewish Joint Distribution Committee, 1939–1945* (Detroit, 1981).

Bauman, Zygmunt. "Exit Visas and Entry Tickets: Paradoxes of Jewish Assimilation." *Telos* 77 (1988), 45–77.

Bazarov, V. "HIAS and HICEM in the System of Jewish Relief Organizations in Europe, 1933–41." *East European Jewish Affairs* 39:1 (2009), 69–78.

Behr, Hartwig, and Horst F. Rupp. *Vom Leben und Sterben: Juden in Creglingen* (Würzburg, 1999).

Beizer, Mikhail. *The Jews of St. Petersburg: Excursions through a Noble Past* (Philadelphia, 1989).

Beller, Steven. *Vienna and the Jews, 1867–1938: A Cultural History* (Cambridge, 1989).

Bemporad, Elissa. "Behavior Unbecoming a Communist: Religious Practice in Soviet Minsk." *JSS*, n.s., 14:2 (2008), 1–31.

———. "The Yiddish Experiment in Soviet Minsk." *East European Jewish Affairs* 37:1 (2007), 91–107.

Benain, A., and A. Kichelewski. "*Parizer Haynt* et *Naïe Presse*: Les itinéraires paradoxaux de deux quotidiens parisiens en langue yiddish." *Archives juives* 36:1 (2003), 52–69.

Benbassa, Esther, and Aron Rodrigue. *The Jews of the Balkans: The Judeo-Spanish Community, 15th to 20th Centuries* (Oxford, 1995).

———, eds. *A Sephardi Life in Southeastern Europe: The Autobiography and Journal of Gabriel Arié, 1863–1939* (Seattle, 1998).

Bendt, Vera, and Nicola Galliner. "*Öffne deine Hand für die Stummen*": Die Geschichte der Israelitischen Taubstummen-Anstalt Berlin-Weissensee, 1873 bis 1942* (Berlin, 1993).

Benveniste, Annie. *Le Bosphore à la Roquette: La communauté judéo-espagnole à Paris (1914–1940)* (Paris, 1989).

Benz, Wolfgang, and Barbara Distel, eds. *Der Ort des Terrors: Geschichte der nationalsozialistischen Konzentrationslager.* Vols. 2 and 3 (Munich, 2005 and 2006).

Beregovski, Moshe. *Old Jewish Folk Music: The Collections and Writings of Moshe Beregovski.* Ed. and trans. Mark Slobin (Philadelphia, 1982).

Berger, Joseph. *Shipwreck of a Generation* (London, 1971).

Berger, Shlomo. "East European Jews in Amsterdam: Historical and Literary Anecdotes." *East European Jewish Affairs* 33:2 (2003), 113–20.

Berghahn, Marion. *Continental Britons: German-Jewish Refugees from Nazi Germany* (New York, 2007).

Berkowitz, Joel, ed. *Yiddish Theatre: New Approaches* (Oxford, 2003).

Berkowitz, Michael. *The Crime of My Very Existence: Nazism and the Myth of Jewish Criminality* (Berkeley, Calif., 2007).

Bezalel, Yitzhak. "Bikoret mahutanit shel mister green: ben gurion al yehudei saloniki." *Pe'amim* 109 (2006), 149–53.

Beznosik, K., M. Erik, and Y. Rubin, eds. *Antireligyezer literarisher leyenbukh* (Moscow, 1930).

Bickel, Shlomo. *Dray brider zaynen mir geven* (New York, 1956).

———, ed. *Sefer kolomey* (New York, 1957).

Binder, S., et al. *Yidn in kaunas* (Kaunas, 1939).

Blakeney, Michael. "Proposals for a Jewish Colony in Australia: 1938–1948." *JSS* 46:3/4 (1984), 277–92.

Blatman, Daniel. "The Bund in Poland, 1935–1939." *Polin* 9 (1996), 58–82.

————. *For Our Freedom and Yours: The Jewish Labour Bund in Poland 1939–1949* (London, 2003).

————. "Women in the Jewish Labor Bund in Interwar Poland." In Dalia Ofer and Lenore J. Weitzman, eds., *Women in the Holocaust* (New Haven, Conn., 1998), 68–84.

Blau, Bruno. "The Jewish Population of Germany 1939–1945." *JSS* 12:2 (1950) 161–72.

————. "On the Frequency of Births in Jewish Marriages." *JSS* 15:3/4 (1953), 237–52.

Blecking, Diethelm. "Jews and Sports in Poland before the Second World War." *Studies in Contemporary Jewry* 23 (2008), 17–35.

Blom, J. C. H., et al., eds. *The History of the Jews in the Netherlands* (Oxford, 2002).

Boas, Jacob. "German Jewry's Search for Renewal in the Hitler Era as Reflected in the Major Jewish Newspapers (1933–1938)." *Journal of Modern History* 53:1 (On Demand Supplement, 1981), 1001–24.

————. "The Shrinking World of German Jewry." *LBIYB* 31 (1986), 241–66.

Bockelmann, Werner, et al., eds. *Dokumente zur Geschichte der Frankfurter Juden, 1933–1945* (Frankfurt am Main, 1963).

Bogdanski, Mayer. "Dos yidishe kultur-lebn in farmilkhomdikn pyeterkov." *Oksforder yidish* 1 (1990), 39–52.

Bohlman, Philip V. *Jewish Music and Modernity* (New York, 2008).

————, ed., *Jewish Musical Modernism, Old and New* (Chicago, 2008).

Brasz, Chaya. " 'Dodenschip' Dora." *Vrij Nederland*, May 1, 1993, 38–41.

Brasz, Chaya, and Yosef Kaplan, eds. *Dutch Jews as Perceived by Themselves and by Others: Proceedings of the Eighth International Symposium on the History of the Jews in the Netherlands* (Leiden, 2001).

Braunthal, Julius. *In Search of the Millennium* (London, 1945).

Brechtken, Magnus. *"Madagascar für die Juden": Antisemitische Idee und politische Praxis 1885–1945* (Munich, 1998).

Breitman, Richard, et al., eds. *Refugees and Rescue: The Diaries and Papers of James G. McDonald, 1935–1945* (Bloomington, Ind., 2009).

Bristow, E. J., *Prostitution and Prejudice: The Jewish Fight against White Slavery, 1870–1939* (Oxford, 1982).

Brodersen, Mome. *Walter Benjamin: A Biography*. Ed. Willi Haas (London, 1996).

Bronsen, David. *Joseph Roth: Eine Biographie* (Cologne, 1974).

Brumberg, Abraham. *Journeys through Vanishing Worlds* (Washington, D.C., 2007).

————. "On Reading the Bundist Press." *East European Jewish Affairs* 33:1 (2003), 100–17.

Brunot, Louis Gronow[s]ki-. *Le dernier grand soir: Un juif de Pologne* (Paris, 1980).

Brustein, William I. *Roots of Hate: Anti-Semitism in Europe Before the Holocaust* (Cambridge, 2003).

Brzoza, Czesław. "The Jewish Press in Kraków." *Polin* 7 (1992), 133–46.

Buch der Erinnerung: Juden in Dresden deportiert, ermordet, verschollen, 1933–1945 (Gesellschaft für Christlich-Jüdische Zusammenarbeit Dresden e.V., Dresden, 2006).

Buergenthal, Thomas. *Ein Glückskind* (Frankfurt am Main, 2007).

Bunim, Shmuel. "Sur les traces de quelques cafés juifs du Paris des années trente." *Les Cahiers du Judaïsme* 26 (2009), 46–51.

Bussgang, Julian J. "The Progressive Synagogue in Lwów." *Polin* 11 (1998), 127–53.

Byrnes, R. F. "Edouard Drumont and *La France Juive*." *JSS* 10:2 (1948), 165–84.

Cahan J. L., ed. *Yidisher folklor* (Vilna, 1938).

Cahnman, Werner J. "The Decline of the Munich Jewish Community, 1933–38." *JSS* 3:3 (1941) 285–300.

Cammy, Justin D. "Tsevorfene bleter: The Emergence of Yung Vilne." *Polin* 14 (2001), 170–91.

Cang, Joel. "The Opposition Parties in Poland and their Attitude towards the Jews and the Jewish Problem." *JSS* 1:2 (1939), 241–56.

Carlebach, Alexander. *Adass Yeshurun of Cologne: The Life and Death of a Kehilla* (Belfast, 1964).

Caron, Vicki. *Uneasy Asylum: France and the Jewish Refugee Crisis 1933–1942* (Stanford, Calif., 1999).

Cazés, Moshé. *Voices from Jewish Salonika: Selections from the Judezmo Satirical Series* Tio Ezrá I Su Mujer Benuta *and* Tio Bohor I Su Majer Djamila. Ed. David M. Bunis (Jerusalem, 1999).

Chagall, Marc. *My Life* (New York, 1994).

Chernow, Ron. *The Warburgs* (New York, 1993).

Chrust, Josef, and Yosef Frankel, eds. *Katovits: perihatah u-shekiatah shel ha-kehilah ha-yehudit: sefer zikaron* (Tel Aviv, 1996).

Cohen, Hagit. "The USA-Eastern Europe Yiddish Book Trade and the Formation of the American Yiddish Cultural Center, 1890s–1930s." *Jews in Russia and Eastern Europe* 57:2 (2006), 52–84.

Cohen, Israel. *Contemporary Jewry: A Survey of Social, Cultural, Economic and Political Conditions* (London, 1950).

———. *Vilna* (Philadelphia, 1943).

Cohen, Mark. *Last Century of a Sephardic Community: The Jews of Monastir, 1939–1943* (New York, 2003).

Cohen, Nathan. *Sefer, sofer ve-iton: merkaz ha-tarbut ha-yehudit be-varsha, 1918–1942* (Jerusalem, 2003).

———. "*Shund* and the Tabloids: Jewish Popular Reading in Inter-War Poland." *Polin* 16 (2003), 189–211.

Cohen, Raya. *Yehudim eropim ve-eropim yehudim: bein shte milhamot 'olam* (Tel Aviv, 2004).

Cohen, Y., ed. *Sefer butchatch* (Tel Aviv, 1955–56).

Constantopoulou, Photini, and Thanos Veremis, eds. *Documents on the History of the Greek Jews*, 2nd ed. (Athens, 1999).

Coppa, Frank J. "The Hidden Encyclical of Pius XI Against Racism and Anti-Semitism Uncovered—Once Again!" *Catholic Historical Review* 84:1 (1998), 63–72.

Corrsin, Stephen D. "Language Use in Cultural and Political Change in Pre-1914 Warsaw: Poles, Jews, and Russification." *Slavonic and East European Review* 68:1 (1990), 69–90.

———. " 'The City of Illiterates'? Levels of Literacy among Poles and Jews in Warsaw, 1882–1914." *Polin* 12 (1999), 221–41.

Crane, Richard Francis. "Surviving Maurras: Jacques Maritain's Jewish Question." *Patterns of Prejudice* 42:4 (2008), 385–411.

Crews, C. M. *Recherches sur le Judéo-espagnol dans les pays balkaniques* (Paris, 1935).

Crhova, Marie. "Jewish Politics in Central Europe: The Case of the Jewish Party in Interwar Czechoslovakia." *Jewish Studies at the Central European University*, vol. 2 (Budapest, 2002), 271–301.

Cultural Forum of the Jewish Community in Thessaloniki, 2nd ed., vol. 1 (Thessaloniki, 2005).

Dalven, Rae. *The Jews of Ioannina* (Philadelphia, 1990).

Davis, John. *The Jews of San Nicandro* (New Haven, Conn., 2010).

Dawidowicz, Lucy. "Max Weinreich: Scholarship of Yiddish." In *The Jewish Presence* (New York, 1977), 163–76.

Dekel-Chen, Jonathan. *Farming the Red Land: Jewish Agricultural Colonization and Local Soviet Power 1924–1941* (New Haven, Conn., 2005).

———. "A Reexamination of Jewish Agricultural Settlement in Soviet Crimea and Southern Ukraine, 1923–1941." *Shvut* 12:28 (2004–2005), 21–46.

DellaPergola, Sergio. "Arthur Ruppin Revisited: The Jews of Today, 1904–1994." In S. M. Cohen and G. Horenczyk, eds., *National Variations in Modern Jewish Identity: Implications for Jewish Education* (Albany, N.Y., 1999), 53–84.

———. "Changing Patterns of Jewish Demography in the Modern World." *Studia Rosenthaliana*, 23:2 (1989, special issue), 154–74.

Dmitrieva, Marina, and Heidemarie Petersen, eds. *Jüdische Kultur(en) im Neuen Europa: Wilna 1918–1939* (Wiesbaden, 2004).

Don, Yehuda. "The Economic Effect of Antisemitic Discrimination: Hungarian Anti-Jewish Legislation, 1938–1944." *JSS* 48:1 (1986), 63–82.

Don, Yehuda, and George Magos. "The Demographic Development of Hungarian Jewry." *JSS* 45:3/4 (1983), 189–216.

Doorselaer, Rudi van. "Jewish Immigration and Communism in Belgium, 1925–1939." In Dan Michman, ed., *Belgium and the Holocaust: Jews, Belgians, Germans* (Jerusalem, 1998), 63–82.

Dorian, Emil. *The Quality of Witness: A Romanian Diary 1937–1944*. Ed. Marguerite Dorian (Philadelphia, 1982).

Dubnow-Erlich, Sophie. *The Life and Work of S. M. Dubnow* (Bloomington, Ind., 1991).

Dubnova-Erlich (Dubnow-Erlich), Sophie. *Bread and Matzoth* (Tenafly, N.J., 2005).

Eck, Nathan. "The Educational Institutions of Polish Jewry." *JSS* 9:1 (1947), 3–32.

Ehmann, Annegret, et al. *Juden in Berlin 1671–1945: Ein Lesebuch* (Berlin, 1988).

Eksteins, Modris. "The *Frankfurter Zeitung*: Mirror of Weimar Democracy." *Journal of Contemporary History* 6:4 (1971), 3–28.

Elazar, Dahlia S. " 'Engines of Acculturation': The Last Political Generation of Jewish Women in Interwar East Europe." *Journal of Historical Sociology* 15:3 (2002), 366–94.

Elias, Norbert. *Reflections on a Life* (Cambridge, 1994).

Eloni, Yehuda. "German Zionism and the Rise to Power of National Socialism." *Journal of Israeli History* 6:2 (1985), 247–62.

Endelman, Todd M., ed. *Jewish Apostasy in the Modern World* (New York, 1987).

Engelman, Uriah Zevi. "Intermarriage among Jews in Germany, USSR, and Switzerland." *JSS* 2:2 (1940), 157–78.

Erlich, Rachel. "Politics and Linguistics in the Standardization of Soviet Yiddish." *Soviet Jewish Affairs* 3:1 (1973), 71–79.

Erlich, Victor. *Child of a Turbulent Century* (Evanston, Ill., 2006).

Ershter alveltlekher yidisher kultur-kongres, pariz, 17–21 sept. 1937: stenografisher barikht (Paris, 1937).

Estraikh, Gennady. *In Harness: Yiddish Writers' Romance with Communism* (Syracuse, N.Y., 2005).

———. "The Kharkiv Yiddish Literary World, 1920s–mid-1930s." *East European Jewish Affairs* 32:2 (2007), 70–88.

———. *Soviet Yiddish: Language Planning and Linguistic Development* (Oxford, 1999).

———. "Vilna on the Spree: Yiddish in Weimar Berlin." *Aschkenaz* 16:1 (2006) 103–27.

Estraikh, Gennady, and Mikhail Krutikov, eds. *Yiddish and the Left* (Oxford, 2001).

Even-Shoshan Shlomo, ed. *Minsk, ir va-em*, vol. 2 (Tel Aviv, 1985).

Fater, Isaschar. *Yidishe musik in poyln tsvishn beyde velt-milkhomes* (Tel Aviv, 1970).

———. *Yidishe musik un ire problemen* (Tel Aviv, 1985).

Feldman, Walter Zev. "Remembrance of Things Past: Klezmer Musicians of Galicia, 1870–1940." *Polin* 16 (2003), 29–57.

Felice, Renzo De. *The Jews in Fascist Italy: A History* (New York, 2001).

Fergusson, Niall. *High Financier: The Lives and Time of Siegmund Warburg* (London, 2010).

———. *The World's Banker: The History of the House of Rothschild* (London, 1998).

Filderman, Wilhelm. *Memoirs and Diaries*, vol. 1, *1900–1940*. Ed. J. Ancel (Tel Aviv, 2004).

Fink, Carole. *Defending the Rights of Others: The Great Powers, the Jews, and International Minority Protection, 1878–1938* (Cambridge, 2004).

Finkin, Jordan D. *A Rhetorical Conversation: Jewish Discourse in Modern Yiddish Literature* (University Park, Pa., 2010).

Fisher, Krysia, ed. *The Society for the Protection of Jewish Health: Fighting for a Healthy New Generation* (New York, 2005).

Fishman, David E. *The Rise of Modern Yiddish Culture* (Pittsburgh, 2005).

Fishman, Joshua A., ed. *Never Say Die! A Thousand Years of Yiddish in Jewish Life and Letters* (The Hague, 1981).

———, ed. *Readings in the Sociology of Jewish Languages*, vol. 1 (Leiden, 1985).

———, ed. *Studies on Polish Jewry 1919–1939* (New York, 1974).

———. *Yiddish: Turning to Life* (Amsterdam, 1991).

Fleming, K. E. *Greece: A Jewish History* (Princeton, N.J., 2008).

Flinker, David, et al., eds. *The Jewish Press That Was: Accounts, Evaluations and Memories of Jewish Papers in Pre-Holocaust Europe* (Tel Aviv, 1980).

Fraenkel, Josef, ed. *The Jews of Austria: Essays on Their Life, History and Destruction* (London, 1967).

Frankel, Jonathan, and Dan Diner, eds. *Studies in Contemporary Jewry*, vol. 20, *Dark Times, Dire Decisions: Jews and Communism* (Oxford, 2004).

Freeden, Herbert. "A Jewish Theatre under the Swasitika." *LBIYB* 1 (1956), 142–62.

———. *Jüdisches Theater in Nazideutschland* (Tübingen, 1964).

Freidenreich, Harriet Pass. *Female, Jewish, and Educated: The Lives of Central European University Women* (Bloomington, Ind., 2002).

———. *Jewish Politics in Vienna, 1918–1938* (Bloomington, Ind., 1991).

———. *The Jews of Yugoslavia: A Quest for Community* (Philadelphia, 1979).

Freyburg, W. Joachim, and Hans Wallenberg, eds. *Hundert Jahre Ullstein* (Frankfurt am Main, 1977).

Friedlander, Henry, and Sybil Milton, eds. *Archives of the Holocaust*. 22 vols. (New York, 1989–93).

Friedländer, Saul. *Nazi Germany and the Jews*, vol. 1 (New York, 1997).

Friedman, Jonathan C. *The Lion and the Star: Gentile-Jewish Relations in Three Hessian Communities 1919–1945* (Lexington, Ky., 1998).

Friedman, Philip. "Polish Jewish Historiography Between the Wars (1919–1939)." *JSS* 11:4 (1949), 373–408.

Friedman-Cohen, Carrie. "Rokhl Oyerbakh [Rachel Auerbach]: Rashe prakim le-heker hayeha ve-yetsirata." *Hulyot* 9 (2005), 297–304.

Friedmann, Georges. *De la sainte Russie à l'URSS* (Paris, 1938).

Friesel, Evyatar. *The Days and the Seasons: Memoirs* (Detroit, 1996).

Frishman, Judith, and Hetty Berg, eds. *Dutch Jewry in a Cultural Maelstrom 1880–1940* (Amsterdam, 2007).

Frojimovics, Kinga. "Who Were They? Characteristics of the Religious Streams Within Hungarian Jewry on the Eve of the Community's Extermination." *Yad Vashem Studies* 35:1 (2007), 143–77.

Fromm, Annette B. *We Are Few: Folklore and Ethnic Identity of the Jewish Community of Ioannina, Greece* (Lanham, Md., 2008).

Fuchs, Richard. "The 'Hochschule für die Wissenschaft des Judentums" in the Period of Nazi Rule." *LBIYB* 12 (1967), 3–31.

Games, Stephen. *Pevsner—The Early Life: Germany and Art* (London, 2010).

Gechtman, Roni. "Socialist Mass Politics Through Sport: The Bund's Morgnshtern in Poland, 1926–1939." *Journal of Sports History* 26:2 (1999), 326–52.

Gelber, N. M. "Jewish Life in Bulgaria." *JSS* 8:2 (1946), 103–26.

Gilbert, Felix. *A European Past: Memoirs 1905–1945* (New York, 1988).

Ginio, Eyal. " 'Learning the beautiful language of Homer': Judeo-Spanish speaking Jews and the Greek language and culture between the Wars." *Jewish History* 16:3 (2002), 235–62.

Gitelman, Zvi Y. *Jewish Nationality and Soviet Politics: The Jewish Sections of the CPSU, 1917–1930* (Princeton, 1972).

Gitter, Benno. *The Story of My Life* (London, 1999).

Glatzer, Nahum N. *The Loves of Franz Kafka* (New York, 1986).

Glicksman, William M. *A Kehillah in Poland During the Inter-War Years* (Philadelphia, 1969).

Glikson, S. *Der yidishe frizir-arbeter in varshe* (Warsaw, 1939).

Glück, Israel A. *Kindheit in Lackenbach: Jüdische Geschichte im Burgenland* (Constance, 1998).

Goeschel, Christian. *Suicide in Nazi Germany* (Oxford, 2009).

Golan, Reuven. "Aus der Erlebniswelt eines jüdischen Jugendlichen in Kiel Anfang der dreißiger Jahre." In Erich Hoffmann and Peter Wulf, eds., *'Wir Bauen das Reich': Aufstieg und erste Herrschaftsjahre des Nazionalsozialismus in Schleswig-Holstein* (Neumünster, 1983), 361–68.

Gold, Ben-Zion. *The Life of Jews in Poland before the Holocaust* (Lincoln, Neb., 2007).

Goodman, Susan Tumarkin, ed. *Chagall and the Artists of the Russian Jewish Theater* (New Haven, Conn., 2008).

Gottesman, Itzik Nakhmen. *Redefining the Yiddish Nation: The Jewish Folklorists of Poland* (Detroit, 2003).

Green, Nancy L., ed. *Jewish Workers in the Modern Diaspora* (Berkeley, Calif., 1998).

———. "The Girls' *Heder* and the Boys' *Heder* in Eastern Europe Before World War I." *East/West Education* 18:1 (1997), 55–62.

Greenbaum, Alfred [Avraham]. *Jewish Scholarship and Scholarly Institutions in Soviet Russia, 1918–1953* (Jerusalem, 1978).

———. *Rabanei brit ha-moatsot bein milhamot ha-olam* (Jerusalem, 1994).

———. "Soviet Jewry during the Lenin-Stalin Period I." *Soviet Studies* 16:4 (1965), 406–21.

———. "Soviet Jewry during the Lenin-Stalin Period II." *Soviet Studies* 17:1 (1965), 84–92.

Greenberg, Gershon. "Ontic Division and Religious Survival: Wartime Palestinian Orthodoxy and the Holocaust (Hurban)." *Modern Judaism* 14:1 (1994), 21–61.

Gross, Natan. "Mordechai Gebirtig: The Folk Song and the Cabaret Song." *Polin* 16 (2003), 107–17.

———. *Toldot ha-kolnoa ha-yehudi be-polin, 1910–1950* (Jerusalem, 1990).

Gruner, Wolf. "Armut und Verfolgung: Die Reichsvereinigung, die jüdische Bevölkerung und die antijüdische Politik im NS-Staat 1939–1945." In Stefi Jersch-Wenzel et al., eds., *Juden und Armut in Mittel- und Ost-Europa* (Cologne, 2000), 407–33.

Grynberg, Anne. *Les camps de la honte: Les internés juifs des camps français 1939–1944* (Paris, 1999).

Guterman, Alexander. "The Congregation of the Great Synagogue in Warsaw: Its Changing Social Composition and Ideological Affiliations." *Polin* 11 (1998), 112–26.

Gutman, Yisrael, et al., eds. *The Jews of Poland between Two World Wars* (Hanover, N.H., 1989).

Guttman, M. J. "Der zelbstmord bay yidn un zayne sibes." In *Shriftn far ekonomik un statistik*, vol. 1 (1928), 117–21.

Hackeschmidt, Jörg. "The Torch Bearer: Norbert Elias as a Young Zionist." *LBIYB* 49 (2004), 59–74.

Ha-kongres ha-tsiyoni ha-21: din ve-heshbon stenografi (Jerusalem, 1939).

Hadar, Gila. "Space and Time in Saloniki on the Eve of World War II, and the Expulsion and Destruction of Saloniki Jewry, 1939–1945." *Yalkut Moreshet* 4 (2006), 41–79.

Haffner, Sebastian. *Defying Hitler* (New York, 2002).

Hahl-Koch, Jelena, ed. *Arnold Schoenberg, Wassily Kandinsky: Letters, Pictures and Documents* (London, 1984).

Hamerow, Theodore S. *Remembering a Vanished World: A Jewish Childhood in Inter-War Poland* (New York, 2001).

Hametz, Maura. "Zionism, Emigration, and Antisemitism in Trieste: Central Europe's 'Gateway to Zion,' 1896–1943." *JSS*, n.s., 13:3 (2007) 103–34.

Harris, Tracy K. *Death of a Language: The History of Judeo-Spanish* (Newark, N.J., 1994).

Harshav, Benjamin. *The Meaning of Yiddish* (Stanford, Calif., 1990).

Häsler, Alfred A. *The Lifeboat Is Full: Switzerland and the Refugees 1933–1945* (New York, 1969).

Hasomir's Sangbog (Copenhagen, 1937).

Havassy, Rivka. "New Texts to Popular Tunes: Sung-Poems in Judeo-Spanish by Sadik Gershón and Moshé Cazés (Sadik y Gazóz)." In Hilary Pomeroy and Michael Alpert, eds., *Proceedings of the Twelfth British Conference on Judeo-Spanish Studies, 24–26 June, 2001: Sephardic Language, Literature and History* (Leiden, 2004), 149–57.

Heilman, Samuel C. "The Many Faces of Orthodoxy." Part 1. *Modern Judaism* 2:1 (1982), 23–51; Part 2, 2:2 (1982), 171–98.

Heller, Celia. *On the Edge of Destruction: Jews of Poland between the Two World Wars* (New York, 1977).

Hepp, Michael, ed. *Kurt Tucholsky und das Judentum* (Oldenburg, 1996).

Heřman, Jan. "The Development of Bohemian and Moravian Jewry, 1918–1938." *Papers in Jewish Demography 1969* (Jerusalem, 1973).

Hers[c]h, Liebmann. "Delinquency among Jews: A Comparative Study of Criminality among the Jewish and Non-Jewish Population of the Polish Republic." *Journal of Criminal Law and Criminology* 27:4 (1936), 515–38.

Hersch, Liebmann. "Complementary Data on Jewish Delinquency in Poland." *Journal of Criminal Law and Criminology* 27:6 (1937), 857–73.

———. *Farbrekherishkayt fun yidn un nit-yidn in poyln* (Vilna, 1937).

———. "The Principal Causes of Death Among Jews." *Medical Leaves* 4 ([1942]), 56–77.

Hetényi, Zsuzsa. *In a Maelstrom: The History of Russian-Jewish Prose (1860–1940)* (Budapest, 2008).

Heuvel, C. L. van den, and P. G. van den Heuvel-Vermaat. *Joodse Vluchtelingen en het Kamp in Hellevoetsluis* (Hellevoetsluis, 1995).

Hewitt, Nicholas. *The Life of Céline: A Critical Biography* (Oxford, 1999).

Hildesheimer, Esriel. *Jüdische Selbstverwaltung unter dem NS-Regime: Der Existenzkampf der Reichsvertretung und Reichsvereinigung der Juden in Deutschland* (Tübingen, 1994).

Hillel [Brad Sabin Hill], Borukh Sinai. "Der letste yidishe bukh fun farn khurbn poyln." *Afn shvel* 337–38 (2007), 36–39.

Hirsch, Francine. "The Soviet Union as a Work-in-Progress: Ethnographers and the Category Nationality in the 1926, 1937, and 1939 Censuses." *Slavic Review* 56:2 (1997), 251–78.

Hoberman, J. *Bridge of Light: Yiddish Film between Two Worlds* (Hanover, N.H., 2010).

Hoffman, Christhard, and Daniel R. Schwarz. "Early but Opposed—Supported but Late: Two Berlin Seminaries which Attempted to Move Abroad." *LBIYB* 36 (1991), 267–304.

Hofmeester, Karin. "Holland's Greatest Beggar: Fundraising and Public Relations at the Joodsche Invalide." *Studia Rosenthaliana* 33:1 (1999), 47–59.

Honigsman, Jacob. *Juden in Westukraine: Jüdisches Leben und Leiden in Ostgalizien, Wolhynien, der Bukowina und Transkarpatien, 1933–1945* (Constance, 2001).

Horkheimer, Max. "Die Juden und Europa." *Zeitschrift für Sozialforschung*, 8:1/2 (1939–40), 115–37.

Howe, Irving. *World of Our Fathers* (New York, 1976).

Hughes, H. Stuart. *Prisoners of Hope: The Silver Age of the Italian Jews 1924–1974* (Cambridge, Mass., 1983).

Huiskes, Gino, and Reinhilde van der Kroef, comps. *Vluchtelingenkamp Westerbork*, Westerbork Cahiers 7 (Assen, 1999).

Hundert, Gershon, ed. *The YIVO Encyclopedia of Jews in Eastern Europe.* 2 vols. (New Haven, Conn., 2008).

Hyman, Paula. *From Dreyfus to Vichy: The Remaking of French Jewry 1906–1939* (New York, 1979).

Israel, Jonathan, and Reinier Salverda, eds. *Dutch Jewry: Its History and Secular Culture, 1500–2000* (Leiden, 2002).

Ivanov, Alexander. "From Charity to Productive Labour: The World ORT Union and Jewish Agricultural Colonization in the Soviet Union, 1923–38." *East European Jewish Affairs* 37:1 (2007), 1–28.

———. "Facing East: The World ORT Union and the Jewish Refugee Problem in Europe, 1933–38." *East European Jewish Affairs* 39:3 (2009), 369–88.

Jacob, Max. *Lettres de Max Jacob à Edmond Jabès* (Pessac, 2003).

Jacobson, Dan. "A Memoir of Jabotinsky." *Commentary* 31:6 (June 1961).

Jay, Martin. *Adorno* (Cambridge, Mass., 1984).

———. *The Dialectical Imagination: A History of the Frankfurt School and the Institute of Social Research, 1923–1950* (London, 1973).

Jeffery, Keith. *The Secret History of MI6* (New York, 2010).

Jelinek, Yeshayahu. *The Carpathian Diaspora: The Jews of Subcarpathian Rus' and Munkachevo, 1848–1948* (New York, 2007).

———. "Jewish Youth in Carpatho Rus: Between Hope and Despair, 1920–1938." *Shvut* 7:23 (1998), 147–65.

Jochnowitz, George. "Formes méridionales dans les dialectes des Juifs d'Italie centrale." In *Actes du XIIIe Congrès International de Linguistique et Philologue Romanes, 1971*, vol. 2 (Québec, 1976), 527–42.

———. "Religion and Taboo in Lason Akodesh (Judeo-Piedmontese)." *International Journal of the Sociology of Language* 30 (1981), 107–18.

Johnpoll, Bernard K. *The Politics of Futility: The General Jewish Workers' Bund of Poland 1917–1943* (Ithaca, N.Y., 1967).

Jüdisches Alltagsleben im Bayerischen Viertel: Ein Dokumentation (Orte des Erinnerns), Bd. 2 (Kunstamt Schöneberg, Berlin, 1995).

Kafka, Franz. *The Diaries of Franz Kafka*. Ed. Max Brod (Harmondsworth, 1972).

———. *Letters to Milena*. Ed. Willi Haas (New York, 1962).

Kagedan, Allan Laine. *Soviet Zion: The Quest for a Russian Jewish Homeland* (New York, 1994).

Kahan, Arcadius. *Essays in Jewish Social and Economic History* (Chicago, 1986).

Kahn, Lothar. "Julien Benda and the Jews." *Judaism* 7:3 (1958), 248–55.

Kahn, Máximo José. "Salónica sefardita: El lenguaje." *Hora de España* 17 (May 1938), 25–41.

Kaminska, Ida. *My Life, My Theater* (New York, 1973).

Kaniel, Asaf. "Gender, Zionism, and Orthodoxy: The Women of the Mizrahi Movement in Poland, 1916–1939." *Polin* 22 (2010), 346–67.

———. "Hamizrahi ve-rabbanei polin, 1917–1939." *Gal-Ed* 20 (2006), 81–99.

———. "Orthodox Zionist Youth Movements in Interwar Poland." *Gal-Ed* 21 (2007), 77–99.

Kantorovitch, N. "Di tsiyonistishe arbeter-bavegung in poyln." In S. Federbush, ed., *Velt federatsie fun poylishe yidn, yorbukh*, vol. 1 (New York, 1964), 113–57.

Kaplan, Edward K., and Samuel H. Dresner. *Abraham Joshua Heschel: Prophetic Witness* (New Haven, Conn., 1998).

Kaplan, Eran. *The Jewish Radical Right: Revisionist Zionism and Its Ideological Legacy* (Madison, Wis., 2005).

Kaplan, Marion. *Between Dignity and Despair: Jewish Life in Nazi Germany* (Oxford, 1998).

———. *The Jewish Feminist Movement in Germany: The Campaigns of the Jüdischer Frauenbund, 1904–1938* (Westport, Conn., 1979).

Karlip, Joshua M. "Between Martyrology and Historiography: Elias Tcherikower and the Making of a Pogrom Historian." *East European Jewish Affairs* 38:3 (December 2008), 257–80.

Karpinovitch, Avraham. "Sipuro hamufla shel urke nachalnik." *Kesher* 18 (1975), 93–101.

Katz, Blumke. "Mayn lerer, max weinreich." *Oksforder yidish* 2 (1991), 241–54.

Katz, Jacob. "Was the Holocaust Predictable?" *Commentary*, May 1975.

Katz, P., et al., eds. *Pinkes varshe*, vol. 1 (Buenos Aires, 1955).

Katz, Steven T., ed. *The Shtetl: New Evaluations* (New York, 2007).

Katzburg, Nathaniel. *Hungary and the Jews 1920–1943* (Ramat Gan, 1981).

Kavanagh, Sarah. *ORT, The Second World War, and the Rehabilitation of Holocaust Survivors* (London, 2008).

Kazdan, H. S. *Di geshikhte fun yidishn shulvezn in umophengikn poyln* (Mexico City, 1947).

Kellenbach, Katharina von. "Denial and Defiance in the Work of Rabbi Regina Jonas." In Omer Bartov and Phyllis Mack, eds., *In God's Name: Genocide and Religion in the Twentieth Century* (New York, 2001), 243–58.

Kellman, Ellen. "*Dos yidishe bukh alarmirt!* Towards the History of Yiddish Reading in Inter-War Poland." *Polin* 16 (2003), 213–41.

———. "Feminism and Fiction: Khane Blankshteyn's Role in Inter-War Vilna." *Polin* 18 (2005), 21–39.

Kerem, Yitzchak. "The Greek-Jewish Theater in Judeo-Spanish (1880–1940)." *Journal of Modern Greek Studies* 14:1 (1996), 31–45.

Kertzer, David I. *The Popes Against the Jews: The Vatican's Role in the Rise of Modern Anti-Semitism* (New York, 2001).

Kichelewsky, Audrey. "Being a Jew and a Communist in 1930s France: Dilemmas Seen Through a Yiddish Daily Newspaper, the '*Naye Prese.*'" In A. Grabski, ed., *Żydzi a lewica: Zbiór studiów historycznych* (Warsaw, 2007), 85–118.

Kiel, Mark W. "The Ideology of the Folks-Partey." *Soviet Jewish Affairs* 5:2 (1975), 75–89.

Kieval, Hillel J. "Negotiating Czechoslovakia: The Challenges of Jewish Citizenship in a Multiethnic Nation State." In Richard I. Cohen et al., *Insiders and Outsiders: Dilemmas of East European Jewry* (Oxford, 2010), 103–19.

Kirschenblatt-Gimblett, Barbara. "Coming of Age in the Thirties: Max Weinreich, Edward Sapir, and Jewish Social Science." *YIVO Annual* 23 (1996), 1–104.

Klemperer, Victor. *I Shall Bear Witness* (London, 1998).

Kobrin, Rebecca. *Jewish Bialystok and Its Diaspora* (Bloomington, Ind., 2010).

Kochan, Lionel, ed. *The Jews in Soviet Russia since 1917* (London, 1970).

Koestler, Arthur. *Arrow in the Blue* (London, 1952).

———. *The Invisible Writing* (London, 1954).

Kopelev, Lev. *The Education of a True Believer* (New York, 1980).

Korczak, Janusz. *Selected Works* (Washington, D.C., 1967).

Kosmala, Beate. *Juden und Deutsche in polnischen Haus: Tomaszów Mazowiecki, 1914–1939* (Berlin, 2001).

Kovačec, August. "Les Sefardim en Yougoslavie et leur langue." *Studia Romanica et Anglica Zagrebiensia* 25/6 (1968), 161–77.

Krajzman, Maurice. *La Presse Juive en Belgique et aux Pays-Bas: Histoire et analyse quantitative de contenu.* 2nd rev. ed. (Brussels, 1975).

Krasney, Ariela. "The *Badkhn*: From Wedding Stage to Writing Desk." *Polin* 16 (2003), 7–28.

Kriegel, Annie, and Stéphane Courtois. *Eugen Fried: Le grand secret du PCF* (Paris, 1997).

Krivoruchko, Julia G. "The Hebrew/Aramaic Component in Romaniote Dialects." *World Congress of Jewish Studies* 13 (2001).

Krutikov, Mikhail. *From Kabbalah to Class Struggle: Expressionism, Marxism, and Yiddish Literature in the Life and Work of Meir Wiener* (Stanford, Calif., 2011).

———. "Imagining the Image: Interpretations of the Shtetl in Yiddish Literary Criticism," *Polin*, 17 (2004), 243–58.

———. "Marxist Intellectuals in Search of a Usable Past: Habsburg Mythology in the Memoirs of Béla Balázs and Meir Wiener," *Studia Rosenthaliana*, 41 (2009), 111–40.

Krzykalski, Kazimierz. "Martin Bubers Reise nach Polen am Vorabend des II. Weltkrieges (März–April 1939) im Spiegel der polnischsprachigen jüdischen Presse." *Judaica* 51 (1995), 67-82.

Kuchenbecker, Antje. *Zionismus ohne Zion: Birobidžan: Idee und Geschichte eines Jüdischen Staates in Sowjet-Fernost* (Berlin, 2000).

Kulka, O. D. "The 'Reichsvereinigung of the Jews in Germany' (1938/9–1943)." In *Patterns of Jewish Leadership in Nazi Europe 1933–1945*, Proceedings of the Third Yad Vashem International Historical Conference (Jerusalem, 1979), 45–58.

Laansma, S. *De Joodse gemeente te Apeldoorn en het Apeldoornsche Bosch* (Zutphen, 1979).

Lackmann, Thomas. *Das Glück der Mendelssohns: Geschichte einer deutsche Familie* (Berlin, 2007).

Lacouture, Jean. *Léon Blum* (Paris, 1977).

Lamouche, Léon. "Quelques mots sur le dialecte espagnol parlé par les Israélites de Salonique." *Mélanges Chabaneau Romanische Forschungen* 23 (Erlangen, 1907), 969–91 (1–23).

Landau, Philippe-E. "La presse des anciens combattants juifs face aux défis des années trente." *Archives juives* 36:1 (2003), 10–24.

Landau-Czajka, Anna. "The Image of the Jew in the Catholic Press during the Second Republic." *Polin* 8 (1994), 146–75.

Laqueur, Walter. "Three Witnesses: The Legacy of Viktor Klemperer, Willy Cohn, and Richard Koch." *Holocaust and Genocide Studies* 10:3 (1996), 252–66.

Laserson, Max M. "The Jewish Minorities in the Baltic Countries." *JSS* 3:3 (1941), 273–84.

Leder, Mary. *My Life in Stalinist Russia* (Bloomington, Ind., 2001).

Lehman, Shmuel, ed. *Ganovim-lider mit melodyes* (Warsaw, 1928).

Lensing, Leo A. "The *Neue Freie Presse* Neurosis: Freud, Karl Kraus, and the Newspaper as Daily Devotional." In Arnold D. Richards, ed., *The Jewish World of Sigmund Freud: Essays on Cultural Roots and the Problem of Religious Identity* (Jefferson, N.C., 2010), 51–65.

Lestchinsky, Jacob. "Aspects of the Sociology of Polish Jewry." *JSS* 28:4 (1966), 195–211.

———. "Di shprakhn bay yidn in umophengikn poyln." *YIVO-bleter* 22 (1943), 147–62.

———. "Economic Aspects of Jewish Community Organization in Independent Poland." *JSS* 9:4 (1947), 319–38.

———. "The Economic Struggle of the Jews in Independent Lithuania." *JSS* 8:4 (1946), 267–96.

———. "The Industrial and Social Structure of the Jewish Population of Interbellum Poland." *YIVO Annual of Social Science* 11 (New York, 1957), 243–69.

———. *Vohin geyen mir? Idishe vanderungen amol un haynt* (New York, 1944).

Łętocha, Barbara. "Chwila, ha-yomon ha-yehudi-polani ha-nafuts be-yoter." *Kesher* 20 (November 1996), 128–36.

Levin, Dov. *The Lesser of Two Evils: Eastern European Jewry Under Soviet Rule, 1939–1941* (Philadelphia, 1995).

Levy, Robert. *Ana Pauker: The Rise and Fall of a Jewish Communist* (Berkeley, Calif., 2001).

Lewin, Sabina. "Observations on the State as a Factor in the History of Jewish Private Elementary Schooling in the Second Polish Republic." *Gal-Ed* 18 (2002), 59–71.

Leydesdorff, Selma. "The Veil of History: The Integration of Jews Reconsidered." In Jonathan Israel and Reinier Salverda, eds., *Dutch Jewry: Its History and Secular Culture (1500–2000)* (Leiden, 2002), 225–38.

———. *We Lived with Dignity: The Jewish Proletariat of Amsterdam, 1900–1940* (Detroit, 1994).

Libinzon, Zalmen. "Vegn dem yidishn fakultet in moskve." *Oksforder yidish* 3 (1995), 753–70.

Lichtenstein, Erwin. *Die Juden der freien Stadt Danzig unter der Herrschaft des Nationalsozialismus* (Tübingen, 1973).

Lindberg, Paula Salomon. *Mein 'C'est la vie' Leben: Gespräch über ein langes Leben in einer bewegten Zeit* (Berlin, 1992).

Lipman, Mussia. "Itonut yehudit be-vilna ba-tsel arba'a mishtarim." *Kesher* 2 (1987), 51–60.

Lipschitz, Simone. *Die Amsterdamse Diamantbeurs* (Amsterdam, 1990).

Livingstone, Rodney. "Some Aspects of German-Jewish Names." *German Life and Letters* 58:2 (2005), 164–81.

London, Louise. *Whitehall and the Jews: British Immigration Policy, Jewish Refugees and the Holocaust, 1933–1948* (Cambridge, 2000).

Löwe, Armin. *Der Beitrag jüdischer Fachlaute und Laien zur Erziehung und Bildung hörgeschädigter Kinder in Europa und in Nordamerika* (Frankenthal, 1995).

Lowenthal, E. G. "The Ahlem Experiment." *LBIYB* 14 (1969), 165–79.

———. *Bewährung im Untergang: Ein Gedenkbuch* (Stuttgart, 1965).

Maggs, Peter B., ed. *The Mandelshtam and 'Der Nister' Files* (Armonk, N.Y., 1996).

Mahler, Raphael. "Jews in the Liberal Professions in Poland, 1920–39." *JSS*, 6:4 (1944), 291–350.

Malino, Frances, and Bernard Wasserstein, eds. *The Jews in Modern France* (Hanover, N.H., 1985).

Malinovich, Nadia. *French and Jewish: Culture and the Politics of Identity in Early Twentieth Century France* (Oxford, 2008).

Manger, Itzik, Jonas Turkow, and Moyshe Perenson, eds. *Yidisher teater in eyrope tsvishn beyde velt-milkhomes* (New York, 1968).

Marcus, J. *Social and Political History of the Jews in Poland, 1918–1939* (Berlin, 1983).

Marcus, Simon. *Ha-safah ha-sefaradit-yehudit bi-tseruf reshimat ha-pirsumim ve-ha-mehkarim 'al safah zo* (Jerusalem, 1965).

Maritain, Jacques. *A Christian Looks at the Jewish Question* (New York, 1939).

Marrus, Michael R. *The Unwanted: European Refugees in the Twentieth Century* (New York, 1985).

Marten-Finnis, Susanne, and Markus Winkler. "Location of Memory versus Space of Communication: Presses, Languages, and Education among Czernowitz Jews, 1918–1941." *Central Europe* 7:1 (2009), 30–55.

Martin, Sean. *Jewish Life in Cracow 1918–1939* (London, 2004).

Maurer, Trude. "Jüdisches Bürgertum 1933–1939: Die Erfahrung der Verarmung." In Stefi Jersch-Wenzel et al., eds., *Juden und Armut in Mittel- und Ost-Europa* (Cologne, 2000), 383–403.

Mayzel, Nakhmen. "Tsvantsik yor yidish teater in poyln." *Fun noentn over* 1:2 (1937), 154–67.

Mazower, Mark. *Salonica: City of Ghosts* (London, 2004).

Melzer, Emanuel. *No Way Out: The Politics of Polish Jewry 1935–1939* (Cincinnati, 1997).

Mendelsohn, Ezra. *The Jews of East Central Europe between the Wars* (Bloomington, Ind., 1983).

———. *Zionism in Poland: The Formative Years, 1915–1926* (New Haven, Conn., 1981).

Mendelsohn, John, and Donald S. Detwiler, eds. *The Holocaust: Selected Documents in Eighteen Volumes.* 18 vols. (New York, 1982).

Michaelis, Meir. *Mussolini and the Jews: German-Italian Relations and the Jewish Question in Italy 1922–1945* (Oxford, 1978).

Michman, Jozeph, ed. *Dutch Jewish History* (Jerusalem, 1984).

Miłosz, Czesław. *Native Realm: A Search for Self-Definition* (New York, 1968).

Milton, Sybil. "The Expulsion of Polish Jews from Germany, October 1938–July 1939: A Documentation." *LBIYB* 29 (1984), 169–99.

Minc, Pinkus. *The History of a False Illusion: Memoirs on the Communist Movement in Poland (1918–1939).* (Lewiston, N.Y., 2002).

Mistele, Karl H. *The End of a Community: The Destruction of the Jews of Bamberg, Germany, 1938–1942* (Hoboken, N.J., 1995).

Mitsel, Mikhail. "The Final Chapter: Agro-Joint Workers—Victims of the Great Terror in the USSR, 1937–40." *East European Jewish Affairs* 39:1 (2009), 79–99.

Molho, Michael, ed. *In Memoriam: Hommage aux Victimes Juives des Nazis en Grèce* (Thessaloniki, 1973).

Molho, Michael. *Usos y costumbres de los Sefardies de Salonica* (Madrid, 1950).

Molho, Rina. *Salonica and Istanbul: Social, Political and Cultural Aspects of Jewish Life,* Analecta Isisiana, 83 (Istanbul, 2005).

Moore, Bob. *Refugees from Nazi Germany in the Netherlands, 1933–1940* (Dordrecht, 1986).

Moore, Claire, ed. *The Visual Dimension: Aspects of Jewish Art* (Boulder, Colo., 1993).

Morlino, Bernard. *Emmanuel Berl: Les tribulations d'un pacifiste* (Paris, 1990).

Moseley, Marcus. "Life, Literature: Autobiographies of Jewish Youth in Interwar Poland." *JSS*, n.s., 7:3 (2001), 1–51.

Mosse, George L. *Confronting History: A Memoir* (Madison, Wis., 2000).

Mousli, Béatrice. *Max Jacob* (Paris, 2005).

Müller, Melissa. *Anne Frank: The Biography* (London, 2000).

Naar, Devin E., ed. *With Their Own Words: Glimpses of Jewish Life in Thessaloniki Before the Holocaust* (Thessaloniki, 2006).

Nadler, Allan L. "The War on Modernity of R. Hayyim Elazar Shapira of Munkacz." *Modern Judaism* 14:3 (1994), 233–64.

Nahum, Henri. *La Médecine française et les Juifs 1930–1945* (Paris, 2006).

Nicosia, Francis. *The Third Reich and the Palestine Question* (Austin, Texas, 1985).

Niger, S. "New Trends in Post-War Yiddish Literature." *JSS* 1:3 (1939), 337–58.

Nikžentaitis, Alvydas, et al., eds. *The Vanished World of Lithuanian Jews* (Amsterdam, 2004).

Nowogrodski, Emanuel. *The Jewish Labor Bund in Poland 1915–1939* (Rockville, Md., 2001).

Ofer, Dalia. *Escaping the Holocaust: Illegal Jewish Immigration to the Land of Israel, 1939–1944* (New York, 1990).

Oosterhof, Hanneke. *Het Apeldoornsche Bosch: Joodsche psychiatrische inrichting 1909–1943* (Heerlen, 1989).

Otte, Marline. *Jewish Identities in German Popular Entertainment, 1890–1933* (Cambridge, 2006).

Papo, Eliezer. "Serbo-Croatian Influences on Bosnian Spoken Judeo-Spanish." *European Journal of Jewish Studies*, 1:2 (2007), 343–63.

Parondo, Carlos Carrete, et al. *Los Judíos en la España contemporánea: Historia y visiones, 1898–1998* (Cuenca, 2000).

Parush, Iris. *Reading Jewish Women: Marginality and Modernization in Nineteenth-Century Eastern European Society* (Hanover, N.H., 2004).

Passelecq, Georges, and Bernard Suchecky. *L'Encyclique cachée de Pie XI: Une occasion manquée de l'Eglise face à l'antisémitisme* (Paris, 1995).

Patai, Raphael, *Apprentice in Budapest: Memories of a World That Is No More* (Salt Lake City, Utah, 1988).

———, ed. *Between Budapest and Jerusalem: The Patai Letters, 1933–1938* (Salt Lake City, Utah, 1992).

———. *Journeyman in Jerusalem: Memories and Letters, 1933–1947* (Salt Lake City, Utah, 1992).

Paucker, Arnold. "Robert Weltsch: The Enigmatic Zionist: His Personality and His Position in Jewish Politics." *LBIYB* 54 (2009), 323–32.

Pauker, Marcel. *Ein Lebenslauf: Jüdisches Schicksal in Rumänien 1896–1938*. Ed. William Totok and Erhard Roy Wiehn (Constance, 1999).

Perloff, Marjorie. *The Vienna Paradox: A Memoir* (New York, 2004).

Pétrement, Simone. *La vie de Simone Weil*, vol. 2 (Paris, 1973).

Philipponnat, Olivier, and Patrick Lienhardt. *La vie d'Irène Némirovsky* (Paris, 2007).

Pickhan, Gertrud. "*Yidishkayt* and Class Consciousness: The Bund and Its Minority Concept." *East European Jewish Affairs* 39:2 (2009), 249–63.

Pinkes fun yidishe druker in poyln (Warsaw, 1949).

Pinson, Koppel S. "Arkady Kremer, Vladimir Medem, and the Ideology of the Jewish Bund." *JSS* 7:3 (1945), 233–64.

Plach, Eva. "Feminism and Nationalism in the Pages of *Ewa: Tygodnik*, 1928–1933." *Polin* 18 (2005), 241–62.

———. "Introducing Miss Judea 1929: The Politics of Beauty, Race, and Zionism in Inter-War Poland." *Polin* 20 (2008), 368–91.

Plasseraud, Yves, and Henri Minczeles, eds. *Lituanie juive, 1918–1940: Message d'un monde englouti* (Paris, 1996).

Plaut, Joshua Eli. *Greek Jewry in the Twentieth Century, 1913–1983: Patterns of Jewish Survival in the Greek Provinces Before and After the Holocaust* (Cranbury, N.J., 1996).

Polak, Henri. *Het "wetenschappelijk" antisemitisme: Weerlegging en vertoog* (Amsterdam, 1933).

Polonsky, Antony. "The Bund in Polish Political Life, 1935–1939." In Ezra Mendelsohn, ed., *Essential Papers on Jews and the Left* (New York, 1997), 166–97.

———. *Politics in Independent Poland, 1921–1939: The Crisis of Constitutional Government* (Oxford, 1972).

Poor, Harold L. *Kurt Tucholsky and the Ordeal of Germany, 1914–1935* (New York, 1968).

Proceedings of the Intergovernmental Committee, Evian, July 6th to 15th, 1938. Verbatim Record of the Plenary Meetings.

Pulido, Angel. *Le Peuple judéo-espagnol: Première base mondiale de l'Espagne* (Paris, 1923).

Rakovsky, Puah. *My Life as a Radical Jewish Woman: Memoirs of a Zionist Feminist in Poland* (Bloomington, Ind., 2002).

Ran, Leyzer, ed. *Yerusholaim d'lite.* 3 vols. (New York, 1974).

Rauscher, Anton, ed. *Wider den Rassismus: Entwurf einer nicht erschienenen Enzyklika (1938): Texte aus dem Nachlass von Gustav Gundlach SJ* (Padeborn, 2001).

Ravitzky, Aviezer. "Munkács and Jerusalem." In S. Almog et al., eds., *Zionism and Religion* (Hanover, N.H., 1998).

Rayski, Adam. *Nos illusions perdues* (Paris, 1985).

Rawidowicz, Simon, ed. *Sefer Shimon Dubnov* (London, 1954).

Reich-Ranicki, Marcel. *The Author of Himself* (London, 2001).

Reinharz, Jehuda, ed. *Dokumente zur Geschichte des deutschen Zionismus 1882–1933* (Tübingen, 1981).

Reitter, Paul. *The Anti-Journalist: Karl Kraus and Jewish Self-Fashioning in Fin-de-Siècle Europe* (Chicago, 2008).

———. "Interwar Expressionism, Zionist Self-Help Writing, and the Other History of "Jewish Self-Hatred." *LBIYB* 55 (2010), 175–92.

Renz, Regina. "Small Towns in Inter-War Poland." *Polin* 17 (2004), 143–51.

Resis, Albert. "The Fall of Litvinov: Harbinger of the German-Soviet Non-Aggression Pact." *Europe-Asia Studies* 52:1 (2000), 33–56.

Revah, Louis-Albert. *Berl, juif de France* (Paris, 2003).

———. *Julien Benda: Un misanthrope juif dans la France de Maurras* (Paris, 1991).

Ringer, Arnold L. *Arnold Schoenberg: The Composer as Jew* (Oxford, 1990).

Ritterband, Paul, ed. *Modern Jewish Fertility* (Leiden, 1981).

Roberts, Joanne. "Romanian—Intellectual—Jew: Mihail Sebastian in Bucharest, 1935–1944." *Central Europe* 4:1 (2006), 25–42.

Robertson, Ritchie. "The Problem of 'Jewish Self-Hatred' in Herzl, Kraus, and Kafka." *Oxford German Studies* 16 (1986), 81–108.

Robin, Régine. "Les difficultés d'une identité juive soviétique." *Cahiers du monde russe et soviétique* 26:2 (1985), 243–54.

Rogge-Gau, Sylvia. *Die doppelte Wurzel des Daseins: Julius Bab und der Jüdische Kulturbund Berlin* (Berlin, 1999).

Rogozik, Janina Katarzyna. "Bernard Singer, The Forgotten 'Most Popular Jewish Reporter of the Inter-War Years in Poland.' " *Polin* 12 (1999), 179–97.

Ro'i, Yaacov, ed. *Jews and Jewish Life in Russia and the Soviet Union* (London, 1995).

Rosenbaum, E., and A. J. Sherman. *M. M. Warburg & Co., 1798–1938: Merchant Bankers of Hamburg* (London, 1979).

Rosenblum, Howard (Chanoch). "Promoting an International Conference to Solve the Jewish Problem: The New Zionist Organization's Alliance with Poland, 1938–1939." *Slavonic and East European Review* 69:3 (1991), 478–501.

Rosenthal, Erich. "Trends of the Jewish Population in Germany, 1910–39." *JSS* 6:3 (1944), 233–74.

Roth, Joseph. *The Wandering Jews* (New York, 2001).

———. *What I Saw: Reports from Berlin 1920–1933* (New York, 2003).

Rothenberg, Joshua. "The Przytyk Pogrom." *Soviet Jewish Affairs* 16:2 (1986) 29–46.

Rothmüller, Aron Marko. *The Music of the Jews: An Historical Appreciation* (London, 1953).

Rothschild, Joseph. "Ethnic Peripheries Versus Ethnic Cores: Jewish Political Strategies in Interwar Poland." *Political Science Quarterly* 96:4 (1981–82), 591–606.

Rothstein, Robert A. "How It Was Sung in Odessa: At the Intersection of Russian and Yiddish Folk Culture." *Slavic Review* 60:4 (2001), 781–801.

Rotman, Liviu, and Raphael Vago, eds. *The History of the Jews in Romania*, vol. 3, *Between the Two World Wars* (Tel Aviv, 2005).

Rozen, Minna. "Jews and Greeks Remember Their Past: The Political Career of Tzevi Koretz (1933–43)." *JSS*, n.s., 12:1 (2005), 111–66.

———. ed. *The Last Ottoman Century and Beyond: The Jews in Turkey and the Balkans, 1808–1945*. 2 vols. (Tel Aviv, 2002–2005).

Rubenstein, Joshua. *Tangled Loyalties: The Life and Times of Ilya Ehrenburg* (Tuscaloosa, Ala., 1999).

Rubin, Ruth. "Nineteenth-Century Yiddish Folksongs of Children in Eastern Europe." *Journal of American Folklore* 65:257 (1952), 227–54.

———. *Treasury of Jewish Folksong* (New York, 1950).

Ruppin, Arthur. *The Jewish Fate and Future* (London, 1940).

———. *The Jews in the Modern World* (London, 1935).

Sale, Giovanni. *Hitler, la Santa Sede e gli ebrei* (Milano, 2004).

Salomon, Alice. *Charakter ist Schicksal: Lebenserinnerungen* (Weinheim, 1983).

Saloniki: ir va-em be-yisrael (Jerusalem, 1967).

Sandrow, Nahma. *Vagabond Stars: A World History of Yiddish Theater* (Syracuse, N.Y., 1996).

Saporta y Beja, Enrique. "Le parler judéo-espagnol de Salonique." *Tesoro de los Judíos Sefardíes* 9 (1966), 82–89.

Scharf, Rafael F. *Poland, What Have I to Do With Thee . . . Essays Without Prejudice* (London, 1996).

Schatz, Jeff. "Jews and the Communist Movement in Interwar Poland." *Studies in Contemporary Jewry* 20 (2004), 13–37.

Schmelz, U. O. *Infant and Early Childhood Mortality among the Jews of the Diaspora* (Jerusalem, 1971).

Schulman, Elias. *A History of Jewish Education in the Soviet Union* (New York, 1971).

Schwartz, Sheila, ed. *Danzig 1939: Treasures of a Destroyed Community* (Detroit, 1980).

Schwarz-Kara, Itzig. *Juden in Podu Iloaiei: Zur Geschichte eines rumänischen Schtetls* (Constance, 1997).

Sebastian, Mihail. *Journal 1935–44* (London, 2001).

Second Jewish International Conference on the Suppression of the Traffic in Girls and Women, 22–24 June 1927, Official Report (London, 1927).

Segre, Dan Vittorio. *Memoirs of a Fortunate Jew: An Italian Story* (Bethesda, Md., 1987).

Seltzer, Robert M. "Coming Home: The Personal Basis of Simon Dubnow's Ideology." *AJS Review* 1 (1976), 283–301.

Sha'ari [Schaary], David. "The Jewish Community of Cernăuţi between the Wars." *Shvut* 7:23 (1998), 106–46.

——. *Yehudei bukovina bein shtei milhamot ha-olam* (Tel Aviv, 2004).

Shandler, Jeffrey, ed. *Awakening Lives* (New Haven, Conn., 2002).

Shapiro, Gershon. *Di yidishe kolonye friling: zikhroynes fun a forzitser fun a yidishn kolkhoz* (Tel Aviv, 1991).

Shapiro, Marc B. *Between the Yeshiva World and Modern Orthodoxy: The Life and Works of Rabbi Jehiel Jacob Weinberg, 1884–1966* (Oxford, 1999).

Shapiro, Robert Moses. "The Polish *Kehillah* Elections of 1936." *Polin* 8 (1994), 206–26.

Shatskikh, Aleksandra. *Vitebsk: The Life of Art* (New Haven, Conn., 2007).

Shearer, David R. *Policing Stalin's Socialism: Repression and Social Order in the Soviet Union, 1924–1953* (New Haven, Conn., 2009).

Shentalinsky, Vitaly. *The KGB's Literary Archive* (London, 1995).

Sherman, A. J. *Island Refuge: Britain and Refugees from the Third Reich 1933–1939*. 2nd rev. ed. (Ilford, Essex, 1994).

Sherman, Joseph, and Ritchie Robertson, eds. *The Yiddish Presence in European Literature: Inspiration and Interaction* (Oxford, 2005).

Shore, Marci. *Caviar and Ashes: A Warsaw Generation's Life and Death in Marxism, 1918–1968* (New Haven, Conn., 2006).

Shternshis, Anna. "From the Eradication of Illiteracy to Workers' Correspondents: Yiddish-Language Mass Movements in the Soviet Union." *East European Jewish Affairs* 32:1 (2002), 120–37.

——. *Soviet and Kosher: Jewish Popular Culture in the Soviet Union, 1923–1939* (Bloomington, Ind., 2006).

Sicher, Efraim. "The Trials of Isaak [Babel]." *Canadian Slavonic Papers* 36:1–2 (1994), 7–42.

Siegel, Ben. *The Controversial Sholem Asch* (Bowling Green, Ohio, 1976).

Silber, Michael K., ed. *Jews in the Hungarian Economy 1760–1945* (Jerusalem, 1992).

Simon, Walter B. "The Jewish Vote in Vienna." *JSS* 23:1 (1961), 38–48.

Sinclair, Clive. *The Brothers Singer* (London, 1983).

Singer, Isaac Bashevis. *A Young Man in Search of Love* (New York, 1978).

Skourtis, Ioannis. "The Zionists and Their Jewish Opponents in Thessaloniki between the Two World Wars." In I. K. Hassiotis, ed., *The Jewish Communities of Southeastern Europe from the Fifteenth Century to the End of World War II* (Thessaloniki, 1997), 517–25.

Slezkine, Yuri. *The Jewish Century* (Princeton, N.J., 2004).

Sorsby, Maurice. *Cancer and Race: A Study of the Incidence of Cancer among Jews* (London, 1931).

Soxberger, Thomas. "Sigmund Löw (Ziskind Lyev), a 'revolutionary proletarian' writer." *East European Jewish Affairs* 34:2 (2004), 151–70.

Stahl, Nanette, ed. *Sholem Asch Reconsidered* (New Haven, Conn., 2004).

Stahl, Rudoph. "Vocational Retraining of Jews in Nazi Germany." *JSS* 1:2 (1939), 169–94.

Stampfer, Shaul. "Hasidic Yeshivot in Inter-War Poland." *Polin* 11 (1998), 3–24.

Starr, Joshua. "Jewish Citizenship in Rumania (1878–1940)." *JSS* 3:1 (1941), 57–80.

Stein, Edith. *The Collected Works of Edith Stein*, vol. 5, *Self Portrait in Letters, 1916–1942* (Washington, D.C., 1993).

———. *Life in a Jewish Family* (Washington, D.C., 1986).

Steinlauf, Michael C. "Jewish Theatre in Poland." *Polin* 16 (2003), 71–91.

Sternberg, Ghitta. *Stefanesti: Portrait of a Romanian Shtetl* (Oxford, 1984).

Stille, Alexander. *Benevolence and Betrayal: Five Italian Jewish Families under Fascism* (London, 1992).

Strauss, Herbert A., and Kurt R. Grossmann, eds. *Gegenwart im Rückblick: Festgabe für die Jüdische Gemeinde zu Berlin 25 Jahre nach dem Neubeginn* (Heidelberg, 1970).

Szajkowski, Zosa. "The Struggle for Yiddish during World War I: The Attitude of German Jewry." *LBIYB* 9 (1964), 131–58.

Tanny, Jarrod. "*Kvetching* and Carousing under Communism: Old Odessa as the Soviet Union's Jewish City of Sin." *East European Jewish Affairs* 39:3 (2009), 315–46.

Tartakower, Arieh. "The Migrations of Polish Jews in Recent Times." In S. Federbush, ed., *American Federation of Polish Jews Yearbook*, vol. 1 (New York, 1964), English section, 5–46.

Theilhaber, Felix A. *Der Untergang der deutschen Juden: Eine volkswirtschaftliche Studie* (Munich, 1911).

Tijn, Gertrude van. "Werkdorp Nieuwesluis." *LBIYB* 14 (1969), 182–99.

Timms, Edward. *Karl Kraus, Apocalyptic Satirist: Culture and Catastrophe in Habsburg Vienna* (New Haven, Conn., 1986).

———. *Karl Kraus, Apocalyptic Satirist: The Post-War Crisis and the Rise of the Swastika* (New Haven, Conn., 2005).

Tomaszewski, Jerzy. "The Civil Rights of Jews in Poland 1918–1939." *Polin* 8 (1994), 115–27.

———. "Jabotinsky's Talks with Representatives of the Polish Government." *Polin*, 3 (1988), 276–93.

———. "Jews in Łódź in 1931 According to Statistics." *Polin* 6 (1991), 173–200.

———. "The Polish Right-Wing Press, the Expulsion of Polish Jews from Germany, and the Deportees in Zbąszyń." *Gal-Ed* 18 (2002), 89–100.

Tonini, Carla. *Operazione Madagascar: La questione ebraica in Polonia 1918–1968* (Bologna, 1999).

———. "The Polish Plan for a Jewish Settlement in Madagascar." *Polin* 19 (2007), 467–78.

Trebitsch, Michel. " 'De la situation faite à l'écrivain juif dans le monde moderne': Jean-Richard Bloch entre identité, littérature et engagement." *Archives Juives* 36:2 (2003), 43–67.

Tsanin, M. "Der oyfgang un untergang fun der yidisher prese in poyln." *Kesher* 6 (1989), 108–19.

Tucholsky, Kurt. *Die Q-Tagebücher 1934–5*. Ed. Mary Gerold-Tucholsky and Gustav Huonker (Reinbek bei Hamburg, 1978).

———. *Politische Briefe*. Ed. Fritz J. Raddatz (Reinbek bei Hamburg, 1969).

Turkow-Grudberg, Yitskhok Ber. *Varshe, dos vigele fun yidishn teater* (Warsaw, 1956).

Ullstein, Herman[n]. *The Rise and Fall of the House of Ullstein* (London, n.d. [1944]).

Ussoskin, Moshe. *Struggle for Survival: A History of Jewish Credit Co-operatives in Bessarabia, Old-Rumania, Bukovina and Transylvania* (Jerusalem, 1975).

Veidlinger, Jeffrey. *The Moscow State Yiddish Theater: Jewish Culture on the Soviet Stage* (Bloomington, Ind., 2000).

Veil, Simone. *Une vie* (Paris, 2007).

Venclova, Thomas. *Aleksander Wat: Life and Art of an Iconoclast* (New Haven, Conn., 1996).

Vinkovetzky, Aharon, Sinai Leichter, et al., eds. *Anthology of Yiddish Folksongs* (7 vols., Jerusalem, 1983–2004).

Vital, David. *A People Apart: A Political History of the Jews in Europe, 1789–1939* (New York, 2001).

Vitali, Christoph. *Marc Chagall: Die Russischen Jahre, 1906–1922* (Bonn, 1991).

Wachowska, Barbara. "The Jewish Electorate of Inter-War Łódź in the Light of the Local Government Elections (1919–1938)." *Polin* 6 (1991), 155–72.

Wagner, M. L. *Caracteres generales del judeo-español de Oriente* (Madrid, 1930).

Wallet, Bart T. " 'End of the jargon-scandal'—The decline and fall of Yiddish in the Netherlands (1796–1886)." *Jewish History* 20:3/4 (2006), 333–48.

Wasserstein, Bernard. *Britain and the Jews of Europe 1939–1945*. 2nd ed. (New York, 1999).

Wasserstein, Bernard, et al. *Hannah Arendt en de geschiedschrijving: Een controverse* (Nijmegen, 2010).

Wat, Aleksander. *My Century: The Odyssey of a Polish Intellectual* (Berkeley, Calif., 1988).

Weber, Eugen. *Action Française: Royalism and Reaction in Twentieth Century France* (Stanford, Calif., 1962).

———. *The Hollow Years: France in the 1930s* (New York, 1996).

Weil, Emmanuel. *Le Yidisch Alsacien-Lorrain* (Paris, 1920).

Weinbaum, Laurence. "Jabotinsky and the Poles." *Polin* 5 (1990), 156–72.

Weinberg, David. *A Community on Trial: The Jews of Paris in the 1930s* (Chicago, 1977).

Weinberg, Robert. "Jews into Peasants? Solving the Jewish Question in Birobidzhan." In Yaacov Ro'i, ed., *Jews and Jewish Life in Russia and the Soviet Union* (London, 1995).

———. "Purge and Politics in the Periphery: Birobidzhan in 1937." *Slavic Review* 52:1 (1993), 13–27.

———. *Stalin's Forgotten Zion: Birobidzhan and the Making of a Soviet Jewish Homeland* (Berkeley, Calif., 1998).

Weiser, Kalman. "The Yiddishist Ideology of Noah Prylucki." *Polin* 21 (2009), 363–400.

Weiss, Jonathan. *Irène Némirovsky: Her Life and Works* (Stanford, Calif., 2007).

Weissman, Deborah. "Bais Ya'akov as an Innovation in Jewish Women's Education: A Contribution to the Study of Education and Social Change." *Studies in Jewish Education* 7 (1995), 278–99.

Weizmann, Chaim. *The Letters and Papers of Chaim Weizmann.* Ed. Meyer Weisgal et al. 25 vols. (Oxford and New Brunswick, N.J., 1968–84).

———. *Trial and Error* (New York, 1966).

Weltsch, Robert. *An der Wende des modernen Judentums* (Tübingen, 1972).

Wiese, Leopold von. "Das Ghetto in Amsterdam." *Jüdische Wohlfartspflege und Sozialpolitik* 1:12 (December 1930), 445–49.

Wieviorka, Annette. "Les Juifs de Varsovie à la veille de la Seconde Guerre mondiale." In André Kaspi, ed., *Les Cahiers de la Shoah*, vol. 1 (Paris, 1994), 47–66.

Wiggershaus, Rolf. *The Frankfurt School: Its History, Theories and Political Significance* (Cambridge, 1994).

Wischnitzer, Mark. "Jewish Emigration from Germany 1933–1945." *JSS* 2:1 (1940), 23–44.

Wodziński, Marcin. "Languages of the Jewish communities in Polish Silesia (1922–1939)." *Jewish History* 16:2 (2002), 131–60.

Wójcik, Mirosław. "Like a Voice Crying in the Wilderness: The Correspondence of Wolf Lewkowicz." *Polin* 17 (2004), 299–323.

Wollock, Jeffrey. "The Soviet Klezmer Orchestra." *East European Jewish Affairs* 30:2 (2000), 1–36.

———. "Soviet Recordings of Jewish Instrumental Folk Music, 1937–1939." *ASRC Journal* 34:1 (2003), 14–32.

Worms, Fred S. *A Life in Three Cities: Frankfurt, London, and Jerusalem* (London, 1996).

Wright, Jonathan, and Peter Pulzer. "Gustav Stresemann and the *Verband nationaldeutscher Juden*: Right-Wing Jews in Weimar Politics." *LBIYB* 50 (2005), 199–211.

Wullschlager, Jackie. *Chagall: A Biography* (New York, 2008).

Yahil, Leni. "Jews in Concentration Camps prior to World War II." In Yisrael Gutman and Avital Saf, eds., *The Nazi Concentration Camps* (Jerusalem, 1984), 69–100.

Yavetz, Zvi. *Erinnerungen an Czernowitz: Wo Menschen und Bücher lebten* (Munich, 2007).

Yeshurun, Yefim, ed. *Vilne: a zamelbukh gevidmet der shtot vilne* (New York, 1935).

Yodfat, Aryeh. "Jewish Religious Education in the USSR (1928–1971)." *Journal of Jewish Education* 42:1 (1972), 31–37.

———. "The Soviet Struggle to Destroy Jewish Religious Education in the Early Years of the Regime, 1917–1927." *Journal of Jewish Education* 40:3 (1970), 33–41.

Yoyvel-heft gevidmet dem 5 yorikn yoyvel fun di pirkhey agudas yisroel in ontverpn (Antwerp, Adar 5696/March 1936).

Zaagsma, Gerben. "The Local and the International—Jewish Communists in Paris between the Wars." *Simon Dubnow Institute Yearbook* 8 (2009), 345–63.

Zalcman, Moshé. *Joseph Epstein alias Colonel Gilles* (Quimperlé, 1984).

———. *La véridique histoire de Moshé, ouvrier juif et communiste au temps de Staline* (Paris, 1977).

———. *Sur le chemin de ma vie: avant et après le goulag* (Quimperlé, 1992).

Zeltser, Arkadi. "Inter-war Ethnic Relations and Soviet Policy: The Case of Eastern Belorussia." *Yad Vashem Studies* 34 (2006), 87–124.

Zimmerman, Joshua D., ed. *Jews in Italy under Fascist and Nazi Rule, 1922–1945* (Cambridge, 2005).

Zlatkes, Gwido. "Urke Nachalnik: A Voice from the Underworld." *Polin* 16 (2003), 381–412.

Zohn, Harry. *Karl Kraus and the Critics* (Columbia, S.C., 1997).

ACKNOWLEDGMENTS

I wish to thank all the libraries and archives in which I have worked on this book: the University of Chicago Library; the Leopold Muller Memorial Library of the Oxford Centre for Hebrew and Jewish Studies; the Staatsbibliothek/Preussischer Kulturbesitz and the Jewish Museum in Berlin; the Israel National Library, the Central Zionist Archives, the Joint Distribution Committee Archive, and the Central Archives for the History of the Jewish People in Jerusalem; the Diaspora Research Institute of Tel Aviv University; the Bibliotheca Rosenthaliana of the University of Amsterdam, the Jewish Historical Museum, the Netherlands Institute of War Documentation, and the International Institute for Social History in Amsterdam; the Centre de documentation juive contemporaine and the German Historical Institute in Paris; YIVO, the Leo Baeck Institute, and the New York Public Library Dorot Jewish Division in New York; and the Wiener Library and German Historical Institute in London.

I have been fortunate in enjoying the help of a succession of outstanding research assistants: Leah Goldman, Harold Strecker, Sean Dunwoody, Sarah Panzer, Aidan Beatty, Yuliya Goldshteyn, Rachel Feinmark, and Tomasz Blusiewicz, all of the University of Chicago.

My publishers, Alice Mayhew of Simon & Schuster and Andrew Franklin of Profile Books, have shown the patience of saints.

Finally I wish to thank all those who have offered me documentation, advice, and information in the course of my work on this book, including David Aberbach, Hadassah Assouline, Haim Avni, Anat Banin, Gunnar Berg, Hans Blom, Rachel Boertjens, Philip Bohlman, Karin Brandmeyer, David Bunis, Henry Cohn, Steven Fassberg, Hanna Feingold, Eike Fess, Sheila Fitzpatrick, Cornell Fleischer, Leo Greenbaum, Shirley Haasnoot, Lois S. Harlan,

Martin Heuwinkel, Brad Sabin Hill, Otto Hutter, Radu Ioanid, Paul Jankowski, Paulette Jellinek, David S. Katz, Monica Keyzer, Julia Kolesnichenko, Julia Krivoruchko, Mikhail Krutikov, Cilly Kugelman, Simon Kuper, Cecile Kuznitz, Nicholas de Lange, Herman Langeveld, Annette Mevis, Fruma Mohrer, Lucy Nachmia, Antony Polonsky, Aubrey Pomerance, Berel Rodal, Norman Rose, Rochelle Rubinstein, Monika Saelemaekers, Emile Schrijver, Jan Schwarz, A. J. Sherman, Andrey Shlyakhter, Henry Srebrnik, Anthony Steinhoff, Jürgen Stenzel, Hermann Teifer, Carla Tonini, Wout Visser, David Wasserstein, Margaret Wasserstein, Paul Wexler, Hy Wolfe, and Jeffrey Wollock.

ILLUSTRATION CREDITS

Beeldbank WW2—Netherlands Institute for War Documentation: 35

Bet Hatfutsot, Tel Aviv, courtesy of Ala Perelman-Zuskin: 16

Belmont Music Publisher, Los Angeles / ARS, New York, VBK, Vienna; courtesy of Schoenberg Centre, Vienna: 17

Central Archives for the History of the Jewish People: 25, 26

Central Zionist Archives: 37

Christine Fischer-Defoy, courtesy of Jewish Museum, Berlin: 19

Ruth Gross, courtesy of Jewish Museum, Berlin: 36

Israel National Library: 3

Jewish Historical Museum, Amsterdam: 1

Jewish Museum of Thessaloniki: 5

Leo Baeck Institute: 2, 7, 10, 15

NIW Photo Archive, Amsterdam: 12, 13, 21

Georgii Petrusov: 22

S. S. Prawer: 9

Spaarnestad Photo Archive: 18, 32, 34

United States Holocaust Memorial Museum: 4, 6, 20, 23, 24, 27, 33

YIVO Institute for Jewish Research: 8, 14, 28, 29, 30, 31

INDEX

Aberbach, Moses, 327, 328, 437
abortion, 159, 173, 252
Abramovich, Rafael, 68
Abramowicz, Hirsz, 75, 109, 437
Abramovitsh, S. Y.: *see* Mendele
    Moykher Sforim
Abramsky, Yehezkel, 147, 151, 437
Acción, 260, 424
acculturation, xviii, xix, 151, 159, 164,
    198, 233, 434
Action Française (movement), 32
Action française (newspaper), 182
Adorno, Theodor W. (né
    Wiesengrund), 197–98, 381,
    437
Africa, 73, 357–59
Agnon, Shmuel Yosef (né Czaczkes),
    26, 265, 437
agriculture, 18, 74–75, 343, 357
    collectivization and, 38, 346–49,
        352, 356
    hachsharot and, 339–40, 342, 343,
        382
Agro-Joint, 343, 344, 349, 354–55,
    360, 395
Agudas Yisroel, 47, 76, 88, 127, 129,
    130, 250, 340
    education and, 139, 165, 267,
        322
    politics and, 55–56, 72, 77, 410,
        411
    in Vilna, 108, 110
agunot ("chained women"), 156–57,
    169
alcoholism, 15, 315
Aleksandrów dynasty, 129, 139
Alexandria, 124, 240
Alliance Israélite Universelle, 52, 117,
    120, 122, 236–37, 268, 326
Alsace, 3, 12, 80, 181, 225
Alter, Abraham Mordechai, 55, 437
Alter, Wiktor, 69, 70–71, 227, 437
Altmann, Alexander, 380, 437
Altshuler, Mordechai, 89, 272

Ambidjan (American Birobidzhan
    Committee), 352
American Jewish Joint Distribution
    Committee, *see* Joint, the
Amsterdam, 22, 24, 62, 68, 176–77,
    225, 239, 248, 375
    diamond industry in, 100–101, 167
    as New Jerusalem, 98–105
    refugees in, 378, 393, 425
Amsterdam Jewish Refugees'
    Committee, 341, 378, 393, 403,
    414–15
Ancel, Jean, 48
Andermann, Martin, 42, 437
Anders (né Stern), Günther, 198, 438
Anglo-American Commission, 360
Anglo-Jewish Association, 37
"Anna O," 159
An-sky, S. (Shloyme Zaynvl Rapoport),
    71, 109, 117, 227, 288
anti-Semitism, xvii–xix, 1, 19,
    28–50, 159, 160, 281, 335,
    425, 434–35
    arts and, 287, 296, 305
    Christians and, 29–33, 37
    conversion and, 199, 200, 204,
        205–6, 306
    crime and, 175, 176, 177, 182
    Jewish, 211–15
    Jewish response to, 46–50, 62
    in literature, 35, 219–20
    luftmenshn and, 171, 175
    name-changing and, 198
    phantom vessels and, 415–16
    press and, 198, 243, 244, 250
    sports and, 194, 195
    Zionism and, 45, 46, 57, 340
    see also concentration camps;
        internment camps; *specific*
        places
Antwerp, 88, 100, 127, 368, 415,
    416
Arabs, 74, 338, 339, 413, 422
Aragon, Louis, 66

ABOUT THE AUTHOR

Bernard Wasserstein is the Ulrich and Harriet Meyer Professor of Modern European Jewish History at the University of Chicago. He has taught at Brandeis and Glasgow universities and from 1996 to 2000 was president of the Oxford Centre for Hebrew and Jewish Studies. The recipient of a Guggenheim Award in 2008, he is this year (2011–12) a guest fellow at the Swedish Collegium for Advanced Studies. His previous books include *The Secret Lives of Trebitsch Lincoln*, which was awarded the Gold Dagger for Non-Fiction by the Crime Writers' Association, *Vanishing Diaspora: The Jews in Europe since 1945*, and *Barbarism and Civilization: A History of Europe in Our Time*.